IN THE NAME OF AMERICA

The conduct of the war in Vietnam
by the armed forces of the United States
as shown by published reports

Compared with the Laws of War
binding on the United States Government
and on its citizens

Director of Research
Seymour Melman

Research Associates
Melvyn Baron   Dodge Ely
Edward Connely

A study commissioned and published by
Clergy and Laymen Concerned About Vietnam
January, 1968

Distributed by E. P. Dutton & Co., Inc.
201 Park Ave. So., New York, N.Y. 10003

IN THE NAME OF AMERICA

First Printing, January, 1968
Second Printing, March, 1968

Distributed by E. P. Dutton & Co., Inc.
201 Park Ave. So., New York, N.Y. 10003

Produced by The Turnpike Press, Inc.
Annandale, Virginia 22003

TABLE OF CONTENTS

Perspective for Readers

ACKNOWLEDGMENTS

Fifteen months ago, as the Vietnamese war continued to widen, discussions in our Executive Committee meetings centered more and more around reports from reliable newspapers and journals which seemed to point to a breakdown of moral constraint by the United States and Allied military personnel in Vietnam.

By moral constraint, we did not mean an adherence to broad and general moral precepts. Norms of moral constraint are defined as rules established by international treaties which are ratified by the government of the United States and are therefore part of the supreme law of this land. These "norms" comprise "laws of war," and laws protecting civilians in times of war, and are binding upon all American citizens, civilian and military. It should be made clear that we had neither the expertise nor the climate (cessation of military conflict) for making a formal legal study.

It did seem appropriate, however, to compare the conduct of American operations in Vietnam with the laws of war. As persons who stand within the Judeo-Christian tradition, we felt an urgent obligation to see if our suspicions were borne out by reliably reported written accounts of behavior of American military personnel in Vietnam.

Seymour Melman, Professor of Industrial Engineering at Columbia University, had been conducting a continuing Program of Study on Military Power. He proposed the present inquiry to the Committee as being of importance for both scholarly and moral-political considerations. Our Committee commissioned this Study in October, 1966 and asked Prof. Melman to assume the position of Director of Research. Without him the project might never have been completed, and his judgment and care for the highest standards of scholarship have indebted the committee to him.

A "Commentary on the Erosion of Moral Constraint in Vietnam" appears at the beginning of the study. Our thanks are due to Dr. Robert McAfee Brown, Professor at Stanford University, to Rabbi Arthur Lelyveld, President of the American Jewish Congress, and to Father John Sheerin, Editor of *Catholic World*, who collaborated in writing the Commentary. Testimony to their careful and incisive work are the signatures of more than twenty-five distinguished church and synagogue leaders who have joined them in putting their names to the Commentary.

Richard A. Falk, Albert G. Milbank Professor of Universal Law & Practice at Princeton University, has contributed a thoughtful essay intended to assist the reader in understanding the significance of "laws of war." We are grateful to Mr. Falk for his advice and counsel during the final preparation of the study.

As Research Associates, Melvyn Baron, Edward Connelly and

Dodge Ely have been responsible, on a daily basis for more than a year, for the actual research and preparation of the main body of the study. We are also grateful for the assistance of Tim Coulter, Michael Golash, Paul Rockwell, Robert Sanders and David Stern. We are indebted to Henry Gibbs, Jr., Dr. Mervyn Jaspan, William Pepper and Dr. Bernhard Bihari for their help in assembling the material.

We are grateful to the librarians of the N.Y. Public Library, the Libraries of Columbia University, and the Library of Congress for their substantial cooperation in facilitating the review of newspapers, clipping files, periodicals and press dispatches. We wish to reserve a particular word of thanks for several persons who have contributed their able critical comment on various aspects of the documentation: Professor Tom Farer, International Law, Columbia University; Malcolm Browne, the New York *Times;* and Marcus Raskin, the Institute for Policy Studies.

For the long and arduous task of typing the study, we are indebted to Erna Gold, Donna Kruger, Carol Reck and Doris Willingham for their patience. Iris Rozencwajg and Ted Johnson made substantial contributions in the final editorial stages. David H. Scull, President of the Turnpike Press in Annandale, Virginia, has been of immeasurable assistance in the editorial work and careful administration of the final stages of production of the study.

Every effort has of course been made to select excerpts without affecting the context, to put each item into print accurately and with proper identification, and to secure all required reprint permissions. The research and editorial staff accepts full responsibility for any errors which may have crept in due to the very tight publication schedule. The publishers would appreciate being informed of any errors which should be corrected in a later edition.

Richard Fernandez
Executive Secretary
Clergy and Laymen Concerned
About Vietnam

December, 1967

CREDITS

Permission from the sources indicated, to reproduce previously copyrighted material appearing in this volume, is gratefully acknowledged with full credit.

U.S. NEWSPAPERS AND NEWS SERVICES

The New York Times: all articles © 1962/63/64/65/66/67 by *The New York Times* Company. Reprinted by permission.

United Press International: all articles Copyright by the United Press International. Reprinted by permission.

The Akron Beacon Journal: Copyright © 1967 by the *Akron Beacon Journal.* Reprinted by permission.

Buffalo Courier: Copyright 1965 by the *Buffalo Courier.* Reprinted by permission.

The Christian Science Monitor: Copyright by *The Christian Science Monitor.* Reprinted by permission.

The Denver Post: Copyright © by the *Denver Post.* Reprinted by permission.

The Evening Star (Washington): Copyright 1967 by *The Evening Star.* Reprinted by permission.

Honolulu Advertiser: Copyright 1966 by the *Honolulu Advertiser.* Reprinted by permission.

Los Angeles Times: Copyright 1967, *Los Angeles Times.* Reprinted with its permission.

The New York Post: Copyright © 1966 & 1967 by the *New York Post.* Reprinted by permission.

St. Louis Dispatch: Copyright 1966 by the *St. Louis Post Dispatch.* Reprinted by permission.

The Sun (Baltimore): Reprinted from *The Sun* by permission.

World Journal Tribune: Copyright 1966 by the *World Journal Tribune.* Reprinted by permission.

York Gazette: Copyright 1966 by the *York Gazette* Co. Reprinted by permission.

U.S. PERIODICALS

Air Force/Space Digest: Reprinted with permission from *Air Force/Space Digest,* official publication of the Air Force Association, 1750 Pennsylvania Ave., N.W. Washington, D.C.

Army: Copyright 1965 by the Association of the United States Army. Reprinted by permission.

Aviation Week and Space Technology: Copyright *Aviation Week and Space Technology.*

Chemical Week: Copyright by *Chemical Week.* Reprinted by permission.

The Christian Century: Copyright 1966 Christian Century Foundation. Reprinted by permission from the June 29, 1966, issue of *The Christian Century.*

PERSPECTIVE FOR READERS

COMMENTARY BY RELIGIOUS LEADERS ON THE EROSION OF MORAL CONSTRAINT IN VIETNAM

I. INTRODUCTION

The news dispatches that follow do not make pleasant reading. Their cumulative effect is overpowering, for they do not merely confirm what we all know, that the war in Vietnam is dirty and inhumane, but they also establish something few of us have known, that American conduct in Vietnam has been characterized by consistent violation of almost every international agreement relating to the rules of warfare. All war is hell: this has been used as an argument to justify any means to achieve victory as well as an argument for the condemnation of all war; but so long as men have fought they have sought to establish rules and to set limits beyond which, by common consent, decent men will not go. If there are such offenses as "crimes against humanity," as the United States tried to demonstrate after World War II, then American conduct in Vietnam is condemned by those very standards of conduct which we imposed on a defeated enemy in the Nuremburg Trials. When we measure American actions in Vietnam against the minimal standards of constraint established by the Hague Convention of 1907 and the Geneva Conventions of 1929 and 1949, our nation must be judged guilty of having broken almost every established agreement for standards of human decency in time of war.

The international laws controlling the conduct of wars are not statements of maximum ethical conduct, but only the bare minimum of moral obligations that nations and individuals must accept even in time of war. Any nation that cherishes the religious heritage America claims should set for itself particularly high standards of moral constraint, far beyond the minimum demanded by international law. And yet the awful truth is that on occasion after occasion we have failed in Vietnam to observe even these minimal standards of moral constraint. Our sense of moral shock at the discovery of this fact compels us to present this information to the hearts and consciences of all Americans.

There is a legal case to be made against our actions in Vietnam and it is, we believe, a devastating one. It is not within our competence or province to make such a case, and the documentation here presented does not purport to be a legal brief. We have, however,

1

included a legal opinion by Mr. Richard Falk, attorney and international law expert at the Woodrow Wilson School of Public and International Affairs (Center of International Studies) of Princeton University, to indicate the kinds of questions that can be raised about our actions in the light of international law. But we cannot wait for the time-consuming procedures of international tribunals; even if it could be established here and now that our actions fall within a technically legal framework of permissibility, we believe they fall squarely under the proscription of moral law. Our conclusion, after reading the attached pages, is that in instance after instance the United States has far exceeded the bounds of what is morally permissible in Vietnam.

The citizen who knows of wrongs committed in the name of his country, and remains silent, is thereby implicated in the perpetuation of those wrongs. In a free society, if some men are guilty, all men are responsible. And it is because we feel a sense of responsibility for actions committed in the name of our nation that we release this report.

II. RESPONSE TO ANTICIPATED OBJECTIONS

We foresee several kinds of objections to this report, and here respond briefly to them.

(1) Some critics will challenge the accuracy and authority of the documentation, on grounds that isolated press reports are unreliable, the reporters biased or the dispatches slanted.

In response, we repeat that while the document does not pretend to be a legal brief, it does claim to be responsible and fair. Many of the correspondents are reporters of international repute. They were on the scene, and they have been trained to observe with care and to report with accuracy. They have no vested interests to protect. Furthermore, the dispatches have been taken from a wide variety of sources: reporters for newspapers from all over the country and all over the world are cited, many wire services and mass media from the broadest possible spectrum of interests have been quoted. This diversity of documentation should help to forestall the charge of slanting or manipulating. Indeed, it is the cumulative impact of the dispatches, drawn from such a dazzling diversity of sources, that makes reading them such a heartache. The burden of proof is surely upon those who wish to discredit these dispatches, rather than upon those who are persuaded by them.

(2) Other critics, granting the accuracy of the dispatches, will raise a second objection: why document only American war crimes, when those of the Vietcong are as bad if not worse? This is a fair question. Our daily press keeps us informed of the brutalities and atrocities committed against South Vietnamese and Americans

by the enemy. But a number of things can be said in response to this objection.

a. The crimes and atrocities of the Viet Cong are already well-known and widely documented in the American and world press. No one is suggesting that terrible crimes have not been committed by the other side, or that their activities should be condoned; such facts can be assumed as having been reliably reported by our press and other communications media.

b. But it is not so readily believed that Americans, and those under American command (for whose actions the American command is responsible) have also engaged in violations of international law, many of which are immoral as well as illegal. Where wrongs have been permitted it is the duty of moral men to call attention to all such acts, regardless of who has actually committed them. In examining our conscience, however, we can only examine the American conscience, and it can be assumed that we might take steps to rectify certain types of American conduct.

c. There is something dangerous in the assumption that if the Viet Cong commit war crimes, this removes the stigma from *our* misconduct. It can never be allowed as a moral principle that because one side tortures prisoners, for example, the other side is entitled to do likewise. To accept such a principle would destroy any sense of moral discrimination between the combatants, and constitute an acknowledgement that we accept Viet Cong conduct as a proper criterion for our own military behavior.

d. The defensiveness with which the question is sometimes phrased suggests that the kind of evidence contained in these dispatches touches a raw nerve of guilt in the questioner. We do not like to admit that Americans are responsible for the kinds of actions here described and would rather avoid the implications of such knowledge by countering that the other side is just as bad or worse. But we must not resort to this easy evasion of moral questions. No matter what kind of condemnation may be heaped upon the Viet Cong, we must keep our own actions under constant moral scrutiny.

(3) Other critics will argue: our nation has shown a high degree of constraint in Vietnam. Americans have unleashed only a small portion of the power they possess. Why chastize the United States when it has shown remarkable moral sensitivity?

We acknowledge that our government *has* exhibited constraint on many levels. We have resisted the plea that we bomb Hanoi back into the stone age; we have not followed the formula that whenever we wish we could cover Vietnam with asphalt and still have the boys home by Christmas. We have not bombed the dikes in North Vietnam nor have we used atomic weapons against the Vietnamese, either North or South. Our tremendous military power is indeed held in check.

But this is only part of the story. At least two further comments are necessary.

a. We cannot justify our present limits of constraint by contrasting it with a theoretical maximum to which we have not proceeded. We cannot justify the deaths of 100,000 civilians, for example, simply by pointing out that it might well have been 200,000. We cannot justify napalm as a "civilized" means of killing civilians by pointing out that we do not drop it on every village in every air strike. We cannot justify the destruction of civilian villages in their entirety by pointing out that we have not destroyed large cities in their entirety.

b. That which is morally unthinkable today becomes an accepted commonplace tomorrow. How far we have gone since the first outbreak of American criticism of the bombing of Guernica! We now tolerate increasing use of gas warfare, which we once condemned. We now take for granted the forced evacuation of civilians and the destruction of their villages, which we once condemned. We now routinely defoliate crops, which we once condemned. At each new stage of the war we inch closer to the breakdown of any moral discriminations whatever. Our concept of what is allowed seems to expand like a rubber band. Thus it is crucially important that Americans be forced continually to ask what constitutes morally tolerable limits of action.

III. AREAS OF PARTICULAR CONCERN

It is not necessary to summarize the content of the news dispatches following this report; but we must call attention to certain kinds of actions described within them. American moral constraint seems to have eroded particularly in four areas.

(1) **The treatment of prisoners.** One of the most widely accepted rules of modern warfare is the insistence on humane treatment of prisoners. The Geneva Convention of 1949 is particularly clear on such matters. Murder of prisoners, cruel treatment, torture or the use of torture to secure information, "outrages upon personal dignity," the taking of hostages, are only a few of the things expressly forbidden.

While it is understandable, if deplorable, that in the heat of battle men sometimes overstep the bounds of restraint, there is no justification whatever, once the battle has subsided, for treating prisoners in ways contrary to accepted international agreements. And yet, as the dispatches document, the United States has scorned almost all of the provisions relating to treatment of prisoners. Torture, murder, brutal methods of interrogation, mutilation, strangling and extreme physical privation are shadows on our record in Vietnam.

Defenders of American policy try to justify this maltreatment by pointing out that although there have been isolated examples of abuse of prisoners by Americans, almost all of the brutal treatment of enemy prisoners is done by members of the South Vietnamese army. But such apologists fail to note that the Americans turn prisoners they capture over to the South Vietnamese, both for custody and for questioning. Americans thus become morally accountable for what happens to the prisoners, for they know from past performance that the methods of Vietnamese treatment of prisoners are brutal.

Thus we are morally responsible for what happens to prisoners we turn over to the South Vietnamese. But we are legally accountable as well, for the rules of international warfare make plain that those who have taken prisoners bear responsibility for the treatment given to them by those in whose custody the prisoners are placed. (Geneva Convention of 1949, Article 12.) Consequently, when we read that prisoners captured by our side have been suffocated or drowned or disfigured or tortured or electrocuted, Americans cannot escape the burden of moral or legal guilt. We stand responsible for what is done, both in the sight of international law and in the sight of the informed conscience.

(2) **The indiscriminate killing of civilians.** Brutal treatment of prisoners, premeditated and deliberate, is always shocking; but the killing of civilians is particularly shocking in Vietnam, both because of the inordinately high ratio of civilian casualties to military casualties and because our military policies appear designed to tolerate high percentages of civilian casualties.

The distinction between combatants and non-combatants, military and civilian personnel, is an ancient one. All the treaties and conventions on laws of warfare make clear that specific measures must be taken to minimize civilian casualties, and that particular precautions must be taken to avoid them whenever possible. But in almost all military operations in Vietnam it is clear in advance that civilians will be inevitable casualties. For example, one of our most "ordinary" military operations, pattern bombing from high altitudes, is completely indiscriminate; any persons within a given area, whether military or civilians, guerillas or children, young soldiers or aged civilians, are likely to be wounded or killed. Not only do bombs dropped from our B-52s fail to discriminate between military and civilian personnel, but the strafing of villages from low-flying planes is similarly impartial in failing to distinguish combatants from non-combatants. When sampans are bombed or strafed, the bombs and the bullets tear the flesh of civilians just as cruelly as the flesh of military. Our naval bombardment of coastal villages, often situated in areas where no battle is being waged, is similarly indiscriminate. Even when we concentrate on villages assumed to have a high percentage of Viet Cong leaders, or to be headquarters for Viet Cong activities, such information is sometimes inaccurate, and the dispatches indicate a high number of "mistakes," in which we have bombed, strafed or napalmed "friendly" villages, thus driving the civilian toll even higher.

When we make a "body count" of the enemy soldiers we have destroyed, the high number of bodies with no weapons upon them suggests that among those we identify as military personnel are many civilians. Occasionally we give civilians a choice by declaring an area to be a "free bomb zone," meaning that we consider anything or anyone remaining within it a military target. This gives civilians within the area two options: they can become refugees or die. There are no other options.

The use of gas is particularly indiscriminate, although some have claimed that we use gas for "humane" reasons, since it is kinder to "flush out" tunnels with gas than with bombs or flames. The gas that is not fatal to robust soldiers may be lethal to children, pregnant women, the sick and the aged in those tunnels. But when the individuals, military or civilian, come to the surface, the humaneness ends, for they then find themselves the object of "anti-personnel" weapons that are particularly ill-fitted to distinguish between combatant and non-combatant.

Individuals may be strafed from the air. They may be shot at with M-16 rifles whose bullets not only enter the human body but expand upon doing so, causing needless and excruciating pain far beyond that necessary to incapacitate the victim. They may have napalm or white phosphorus bombs dropped on them. Napalm, a jelly-like gasoline, clings to the skin and cannot be scraped off, burning and melting human flesh, while white phosphorus continues to burn even within the human body. Napalm sucks up all the oxygen in confined areas so that those who escape being burned to death will suffocate for lack of air. Fragmentation weapons are cannisters containing hundreds of pellets or pieces of sharp metal; when they explode the pellets lodge deep in the bodies of all within range. These can be timed to go off at intervals, so that long after an air raid civilians returning to their villages or fields may be cruelly wounded by the chunks of flying metal.

There are those who will reply that one of the characteristics of modern warfare is that it is no longer possible to distinguish between combatants and non-combatants. But if this principle of discrimination between combatants and non-combatants is discarded or conveniently overlooked, then we must recognize that we have indirectly adopted the principle that "anything goes," and that anyone who is not a member of our side is a legitimate target, whether woman or child, aged or infirm, the invalid in the hospital or the infant in the cradle. More and more this is happening in Vietnam, and the high incidence of civilian casualties, while officially deplored, continues to be justified on the ground that in this kind of a war such deaths are inevitable.

But Americans should be clear about what this means. If we are ready to condone an indefinite number of civilian deaths, then we must at least have the honesty to say so, and not hide any longer behind rhetoric about "liberating" a people we are in fact gradually destroying. The Second Vatican Council explicitly condemned "any act of war aimed indiscriminately at the destruction of entire cities or of extensive areas along with their population." As the dispatches show, this is an almost precise description of what we are doing in Vietnam.

(3) **Indiscriminate hardships on civilians.** In addition to killing an inordinate number of civilians in Vietnam, we have made life in their native country incredibly hard for those who manage to survive. Our military aim is to deprive the fish of the sea, the fish being the Viet Cong guerillas and the sea being the native population. The goal is to dry up the sea and thus eliminate all resources of food and communications that the guerillas might garner from the civilian population. But in the process of doing this we destroy many more civilians than guerillas. We also destroy the means of livelihood for more civilians than guerillas. We act in ways that do not sufficiently discriminate between the legitimate needs of a civilian population and the military necessities of guerilla warriors.

From the perspective of American affluence one of the least significant to us of these civilian hardships is the pillaging committed by South Vietnamese troops. Such pillaging is not only a violation of international laws of war, however, but the theft of small items such as chickens and pigs, and the theft of larger items such as buffalos, works an incredible hardship on the poor peasants. In the light of such acts, they have little reason to think of our troops as "liberators" and have every reason not only to be confused but to be resentful when their "liberators" enter a village, destroy every hut and then burn all the crops in the surrounding fields. Yet today this is a routine military action to ensure that the Viet Cong will not repossess the village or harvest the crops. In order to deprive the guerillas of food, we also defoliate crops and jungle from the air, spraying large areas with chemicals that not only ruin the present yield but may make new crops impossible for years to come. Unfortunately, the main casualties of this program are not the guerillas but children, pregnant women and old people.

One of the most flagrant violations of civilian rights is the forcible relocation of large units of people, in specific violation of Article 49 of the Civilians Convention of 1949, an article framed to avert repetition of the forcible relocations that took place in World War II. We give the civilians in Vietnam no choice but to abandon their homes and countryside. We take the "refugees" we have created to relocation centers, usually surrounded by barbed wire, where they are forced to live until such time as we determine a new location for them. The camps are invariably overcrowded and understaffed, sanitary conditions are appalling, inhabitants are underfed, the sick get minimal treatment. In the process of relocation, families are often broken up and orphaned children are left bewildered and uncared for. Indeed, one of the worst aspects of the refugee situation is the treatment of orphaned children; the closest living relative is declared responsible for the orphan, and in this way the Americans avoid responsibility for those whose parents we may have killed.

Frequently in the taking of villages mass arrests are made, and our troops attempt to induce, by terror tactics, confessions of Viet Cong support. We train and support "counter-terror" troops of South Vietnamese to frighten civilians into siding with us. Collective punishment becomes an established policy; an "example" is made of an entire village suspected of harboring Viet Cong—a particularly immoral and ruthless denial of human individuality.

(4) **Inadequacy of attempts to alleviate civilian hardships.** There are many in our armed forces who are genuinely dedicated to the alleviation of hardships our military presence has inflicted upon Vietnamese civilians. But the dispatches make clear that our overall policy in this matter is not even minimally adequate. As already mentioned, it is our deliberate policy to create "refugees" by forcibly removing civilians from their homes, and the centers to which we send them are far from adequate. Scarcely more than token gestures are made in the direction of treating refugees humanely.

The dispatches describe the incomparably fine medical and hospital treatment accorded to the American wounded. Such prompt attention to our war-injured deserves the highest praise. But the remarkable efficiency with which this is done suggests that it should be possible to give some kind of reasonably adequate treatment to wounded Vietnamese civilians as well. And yet the reports of the hospital conditions where Vietnamese are cared for are appalling. In the overcrowded and understaffed hospitals for the South Vietnamese few things are more heart-rending than the condition of women and children and the aged. It is our responsibility to provide good medical centers for all these war-injured, and our consistent failure to do so is in clear violation of Article 32 of the Civilians Convention.

Not only do we fail to furnish adequate hospital facilities for the South Vietnamese, but on a number of occasions we have deliberately destroyed existing hospitals of the enemy as well as caches of their medical supplies. Such acts are among the gravest breaches of international law and international trust. This lack of recognition that a hospital—any hospital—is a sanctuary in time of war, this willingness to inflict further terror on the defenseless wounded, should haunt the consciences of Americans.

IV. ITEMS INDIRECTLY RAISED BY THE DISPATCHES

There are three other matters that are only raised indirectly in the dispatches, which nevertheless have important moral implications.

(1) One of these is the cumulative nature of what we are doing in Vietnam. It is clear that if we were to "flatten Hanoi" there would be a tremendous moral outcry, not only in America but across the world, at this wanton destruction of civilians. And yet for several years we have been doing piecemeal what would not be tolerable if done in one concerted action. We do not "flatten Hanoi," but we do flatten hundreds upon hundreds of villages, day after day, week after week. We do not sink ships in Haiphong harbor (except by mistake), and yet in raid after raid we destroy sampans, many of which turn out to contain nothing but frightened civilians. Is it proper to kill tens of thousands of civilians, provided we space the killing over a tolerably long period? To destroy hundreds of civilian villages, just so long as we do not destroy them all at once?

(2) Public discussions of ways to end the war or begin negotiations tend to center on the necessity of our taking the initiative by ceasing the bombing of the north. That such action would represent an important first step toward gaining credibility for our desire to negotiate is widely accepted. But it tends to blunt the fact that while there is much hardship in the north because of our bombing, the major suffering and destruction are located not in the north but in the south. It is significant that the actions described in the dispatches are located almost exclusively in South Vietnam.

(3) Another disturbing matter raised by the dispatches centers on the racial dimension of the war. We need to ask ourselves whether it is likely that our nation, or our soldiers, would give moral consent to the things we are doing in Vietnam if they were being done against white people. The demeaning term "gooks," and the use of such language as "skunk hunting" to describe shooting at Vietnamese from low-flying planes, are only symbols of the problem. We were morally shocked when the Germans destroyed the entire village of Lidice in Czechoslovakia, and when a "scorched earth" policy became routine for the Nazi armies. And yet we are not shocked at the total destruction of South Vietnamese villages. Would we find ourselves passively consenting to such atrocities if they were being committed against the French or the Irish or the Danes? The destruction of a Vietnamese "hut" appears to us a minor

matter; would we feel the same way if it were the croft of a high-land Scot or the home of a Dutch banker?

The question must be asked, even if the answer is still buried deep within the American subconscious.

V. INTERNATIONAL IMPLICATIONS OF OUR ACTIVITY

What implications do these breaches of responsibility have for international relationships?

(1) America is the most powerful nation on earth. We should not wait until an international tribunal tells us whether we have been at fault. We should question ourselves now about our moral concern. When we honor international agreements we help to make their moral thrust more binding upon all nations. When we fail to honor international agreements, this induces other nations to follow our example and contributes to the breakdown of international trust. If America does not uphold international law, it can scarcely expect other nations to do so; and if no nations do so, international relations are reduced to the law of the jungle.

Our persistent violation of the rules of war can only serve to destroy what little remaining trust there may be in the word of the United States, and we see evidence each day in the press of the free world that trust in us has atrophied into cynicism.

(2) The gradual breakdown of our moral constraint must inevitably induce the enemy to feel a compulsion to commit similar acts of moral lawlessness. As the dispatches indicate, we have been experimenting in Vietnam with many kinds of gas warfare. In the past this has been one of the most universally abhorred forms of war; but we have now stepped over that dividing line by our use of vomiting gas, tear gas and paralyzing gas, and we have made almost inevitable the use of gas in retaliation upon our own forces. As this happens, we will feel impelled to use yet stronger counter measures and may find ourselves moving into bacteriological warfare. Each limit that we transgress, however slowly or tentatively, means that another frontier of moral constraint has disappeared irretrievably from the international scene. We, as the first nation to use the atomic bomb (and to use it on civilians), should be particularly sensitive to the international implications of our own rewriting of the laws of permissible warfare. Had gas been used against us first, there would have been violent outcries of shock in our nation. Yet our use of gas against the Vietnamese has been accepted as a matter of "military necessity." Thus does our international image as a nation to be trusted erode almost to the crumbling point.

(3) What does our conduct in this war suggest about our conduct

in future wars? Will not the gradual intensification of our moral numbness make us increasingly indifferent to violations of international law or morality in the future? If we can indiscriminately destroy villages in this war, what is to prevent us from indiscriminately destroying towns and cities in the future? If we can now destroy the crops of one nation, what is to prevent us in the future from destroying the crops of surrounding nations? If no limits are set, no limits will be honored, and the erosion of our moral discrimination will someday be complete.

VI. DOMESTIC IMPLICATIONS OF OUR ACTIVITY

Scarcely less important than their international implications are the effects of the erosion of constraint upon our own domestic health as a nation.

(1) What does a nation do to its soul when it trains its young men to engage in what becomes the indiscriminate slaughter of women, children, the aged and the defenseless, when it teaches its soldiers to destroy crops and thereby hasten the malnutrition of already feeble children? Who stands on such an Olympian height as to demand of our young men that as a matter of course and of "military necessity" they must be instructed to do such deeds as a part of their normal daily activity? What nation can so train its young without destroying its soul?

(2) What scars are left on the lives of those who are told that it is fitting and proper for them to do such things? Not only are they destroying innocent human lives, but by ordering our men to do such things we are destroying them. Soldiers who destroy civilian huts usually find the act repulsive; but they are told by their country that they become heroes by doing things all decent men abhor. Who in his late teens or early twenties can systematically destroy homes and crops, turn prisoners over to others for certain torture, kill children and yet escape morally unscathed? The hands that commit such deeds are hands that will forever have the blood of the innocent upon them.

(3) What does it mean for the future of our country that those who return to civilian life will be those who have adjusted themselves to all kinds of brutality, those who will have learned to shoot first and question afterward, those who will have found that force of arms determines what is right, those who will have concluded that he who has power has morality on his side and has it on his own terms?

(4) What does it do to us as a nation to discover that to support American presence in Vietnam seems to support the violation of almost every canon of international law or moral constraint? To

support our presence in Vietnam means to support a policy that fails to honor international agreements, that accepts brutalizing tendencies as an inevitable byproduct of that presence, that allows the rubric of "military necessity" to go bail for the national conscience, and justifies acts that both international law and common morality denounce. As American civilians find motivations to defend these actions, their own morality must inevitably break down.

If we do not take international law seriously when it works to our military disadvantage, how can we be surprised if members of minority groups do not take domestic law seriously when it works to their civilian disadvantage? We cannot morally condone one level of human activity in southeast Asia and then morally condemn the same level of human activity in North America. Ethics cannot be determined by geography, and breaking domestic law in Milwaukee can only be consistently condemned if breaking international law in Ben Suc is similarly condemned.

These are instances of the kind of erosion of domestic law we may expect at home if we continue to let international law erode abroad.

VII. THE POSSIBILITY OF CHANGE

Some may feel that criticism of American actions or policy during time of war is unpatriotic. On the contrary, one reason for pressing such issues as these dispatches highlight is to appeal from America ill-informed to America better-informed, to bring about changes in policies and actions that at present go beyond the bounds of legality or morality. There is indication that as Americans engage in this essentially patriotic function they can, in fact, be instruments in bringing about modifications of present policy.

No one, for example, who reads about the request of *Terre des Hommes* to the White House, to have war-injured Vietnamese children flown in American planes to other countries for medical treatment, can fail to be shocked by the callous response of our government that there was no space available for such acts of mercy, and that our government did not foresee having such space available in the future. That might have appeared to be the end of the matter; our government had committed itself to a policy of disregarding children who needed medical attention that could not be given in their native land.

And yet, because of continuing pressures on our government by groups of private citizens, and more recently by doctors of the Committee of Responsibility, the policy has been reversed; and in July 1967 our government, through William Bundy, Assistant Secretary of State for the Far East, indicated that the U.S. government would indeed provide free air transportation to this country for war-injured South Vietnamese children needing specialized medical treatment available only in the United States.

Thus the determined efforts of some citizens have brought about a reversal of an earlier policy, moving from a callous to a more humane position. If this can happen on such an issue as the treatment of children injured by indiscriminate use of napalm, there is no reason why it could not happen in other areas as well. Thus the full publication of such facts as these dispatches document can hopefully sensitize the American conscience to such a degree that other reversals of present policy can be effected.

VIII. CONCLUSION

As Americans, we are not happy or proud to learn what we have learned in reading these dispatches. They are cogent evidence that our country has failed to honor the minimal constraints that civilized people have agreed upon as necessary in the waging of war. We honor those within our armed forces who have tried to act within the limits of constraint established by international law. We sympathize with individuals who, in situations of stress, commit acts of which they are later ashamed, or who impetuously issue orders they later wish they could recall. But our armed forces are instructed in the rules of international warfare, and they know that they can be held personally accountable for infractions of them.

But we cannot locate the problem only in southeast Asia. Responsibility is channeled up through the echelons of military command and devolves also upon the civilians who control the military, our elected and appointed officials in Washington. Even there the responsibility does not end. It reaches out also to encompass every citizen who voted our policy-makers into office. It rests finally upon each one of us.

It is for this reason that we issue this report not only to the President and those in Washington who make the policy decisions, but also to every citizen. A responsible citizenry must be an informed citizenry. After reading these pages, no citizen will be able to plead ignorance of the relation between international law and human morality on the one hand and our conduct in Vietnam on the other. It will then be up to him—to us— to raise the kind of outcry that will necessitate a reexamination of our actions in Vietnam.

To this end, we call upon our policy-makers to deal responsibly with the material gathered in the following pages. There is a variety of ways in which they could respond, and there are various levels of response which citizens could seek from them:

    a. to the degree that the evidence in the dispatches is corroborated, specific violators of international law should be prosecuted according to established procedures;

b. orders should be given that the types of violations reported in these dispatches are under no circumstances to be committed in the future, and that strong measures will be taken immediately against future violators;

c. our overall military policy should be revised so that occasions for the violation of the minimal laws of wartime constraint are reduced to an absolute minimum;

d. if it is deemed impossible to fight a war in Vietnam without consistently violating both legal and moral constraints, this fact should candidly and honestly be admitted to the American public, with the corollary that our subsequent military actions in Vietnam are designed to do whatever is necessary to "win," even though this means holding morality and international law in contempt;

e. if such is to be our policy, there should be occasion for a new discussion (free from the slander that dissent is equivalent to disloyalty) of whether or not the United States is morally justified in continuing to fight a war in Vietnam that inevitably includes consistent violation on our part of even minimal legal and moral standards of civilized and humane behavior.

Different readers will stop at different points along such a scale of alternatives. Indeed, the signers of this commentary would not all agree on the alternatives to be followed. Where we do agree, however, is in the belief that it will not suffice for our policymakers, or the American people, to pass over this report in silence.

SIGNERS
OF THE COMMENTARY

Bishop Ralph T. Alton
Madison, Wisconsin

Dr. John C. Bennett,
President,
Union Theological Seminary

Dr. Robert McAfee Brown,
Professor,
Stanford University

Bishop William Crittenden
Diocese of Erie, Pennsylvania

Dr. Harvey G. Cox,
Professor,
Divinity School
Harvard University

Dr. Edwin T. Dahlberg,
Former President,
National Council of Churches

Dr. Truman Douglass,
Executive Vice President,
Board of Homeland Ministries of
The United Church of Christ

Father Robert Drinan,
Dean,
Boston College Law School

Dr. Joseph Fletcher,
Professor,
Episcopal Theological Seminary

Rabbi Roland Gittelsohn
Temple Israel
Boston, Massachusetts

Bishop Charles F. Golden
Nashville, Tennessee

Rev. Dana McLean Greeley,
President, Unitarian
Universalist Association

Rabbi Abraham Heschel,
Professor,
Jewish Theological Seminary

Bishop Fred Holloway
Charleston, West Virginia

Rabbi Wolfe Kelman,
Professor,
Jewish Theological Seminary

Dr. Martin Luther King, Jr.
President,
Southern Christian
Leadership Conference

Rabbi Arthur Lelyveld,
President,
American Jewish Congress

Rabbi Albert Lewis
Temple Isaiah
Los Angeles, California

Bishop John Wesley Lord
Washington, D.C.

Dr. Martin Marty,
Professor, Divinity School,
University of Chicago

Bishop Paul Moore, Jr.,
Suffragan Bishop of the Diocese
Washington, D.C.

Bishop J. Brooke Mosley, D.D.
Diocese of Delaware
Wilmington, Delaware

Dr. Robert V. Moss, Jr.,
President,
Lancaster Theological Seminary

Bishop C. Kilmer Myers
Diocese of California
San Francisco, California

Father John Sheerin,
Editor,
Catholic World

Dr. Eugene Smathers,
Moderator,
Presbyterian Church USA

Dr. Douglas V. Steere,
Chairman,
Friends World Committee
for Consultation,
Haverford, Pennsylvania

Bishop R. Marvin Stuart,
Denver, Colorado

Bishop Ralph Ward, Jr.,
Syracuse, New York

Institutions listed for identification only.

15

INTRODUCTION

This documentation on U.S. military behavior in Vietnam in relation to the laws of war was prompted by the following considerations.

1) Continuing studies on characteristics of military power suggested that one of the limits of military power was its competence to cope with guerrilla-type rebellions of a primarily civil war nature. In 1958 while studying the problems of *Inspection for Disarmament* (Columbia University Press, New York) I found that secret military operations (now called guerrilla warfare) are essentially a political development with a major military expression. We found in 1958 that guerrilla-type movements would succeed under the following conditions: (p. 27):

"A. A group of men exists which is prepared to carry out the clandestine production (of weapons) even at the cost of considerable personal sacrifice and risk. These men have strong allegiance to a guiding ideal.

"B. The central working group is backed by a substantial part of a population, including a government or quasi-government, which backs up the operating groups and shields them from the inspecting authorities.

"C. The operators of the clandestine production system learn how to simulate appearances that will seem to be ordinary and innocent in the eyes of the inspectors."

This theoretical formulation derived from the study of secret military operations, independently of Vietnam, indicated that military power has not been competent to suppress a political movement with these characteristics.

It seems that a pattern of disregard of the laws of war is imposed by the pressure to intervene in a guerrilla internal war where one side enjoys major popular support in the conduct of its operations.

Under such conditions the differentiation between, for example, civilian and military activity becomes extremely difficult. In a conventional national army the troops performing the work of supply are readily identified. In the guerrilla movement the men and women doing the work of supply are often part of and therefore indistinguishable from the ordinary civilian population. Therefore the tactics that are directed toward the suppression of a guerrilla-type force and its surrounding civilian base invite disregard of laws of war.

2) During recent years I perceived that many Americans had developed the concept that war is fought (must be fought) without constraint. Young people especially had no conception that rules of constraint of considerable scope had been internationally agreed upon and were part of the supreme law of our own country, as treaties ratified by the Senate and signed by the President.

On national responsibility for constraint in war: International society has recognized that war is not to be unrestrained. That is one basic meaning of the Geneva Conventions and of the "customary" laws of war. This point is made clear in the opening paragraphs of U.S. Army Field Manual 27-10 on the *Laws of Land Warfare*, selected excerpts from which appear in the section entitled "The Law."

However, the military methods used by U.S. forces in South Vietnam may make good military tactical sense where the primary strategic military objective is that of draining the human supporting sea in which the National Liberation Front guerrillas operate. Evidently the very attempt to pursue these military-political strategies invites significant violation of the minimal moral constraints that are embodied in the laws of war.

As the U.S. offers other and smaller nations a model of violation of laws of war it diminishes its own military security. For the trend of military technology is toward the cheapening of even the most destructive weapons: nuclear, biological. Since there are no competent defenses against multiple assaults by diverse potent weapons, the U.S. is confronted by an increasing array of smaller states wielding high-potency weapons. Under these conditions moral constraint is the final defense for all, and the erosion of moral constraint spells insecurity for all.

3) Fragmentary reports on U.S. military operations in Vietnam suggested some incidence of acts that appeared to be contrary to the laws of war. The question became: are these unusual, rare, individual acts, or have such acts become a regular mode of behavior—policy—hence the responsibility of senior officers of the United States Government?

It has been noted in many press dispatches that soldiers of the National Liberation Front and of the army of North Vietnam have committed acts that are atrocities. It is sometimes argued that such action by the military opponent justifies even more extreme behavior by the armed forces of the United States. Legally, it is evident that multiple violations of laws do not cancel each other out. There are no legal grounds for placing the U.S. above the law in its behavior in Vietnam. Morally, the United States has special obligations that are associated with being the richest and militarily the most powerful nation in the world. Rich people and rich nations have more options than poor ones. Politically, it is significant that in 1965 "President Johnson directed Secretary of State Dean Rusk . . . to inform the international committee of the Red Cross that the United States was abiding by the 'humanitarian principles' of the 1949 Geneva Convention and that it expected 'other parties' in the Vietnamese war to do the same" (*The New York Times*, 14th August 1965).

All these considerations indicated the importance of reviewing a reliable body of data on the performance of U.S. forces in Vietnam. I judge that the reports of many American newsmen given in great number are at least a starting point toward defining the actual state of affairs.

The materials collected in this documentation are drawn from diverse sources. The particular selection of materials for quotation and classification is the responsibility of the editors and researchers alone, and is not attributable to the managements, editors or writers of newspapers, magazines, books, or other media in which the cited materials originally appeared.

This documentation is not a legal document: it is not an indictment, or a lawyers' brief, or a judgment of a court of law. This documentation is a portrait of behavior in violation of minimal moral constraint, as defined by various laws of war. Treaty clauses from the Laws of War are cited here for their ordinary, colloquial meaning—without appeal to the sorts of qualifications and interpretations that may be contained in the scholarly literature on law, or in various court decisions.

Our purpose was to collect enough data to reveal patterns of conduct which transcend any individual act of war. The patterns are established mainly by chronological ordering, except in cases where a passage out of chronological sequence brings forth patterns of action more clearly.

The conduct of the war implies usages which are not unique to a single occurrence, or arbitrary. Individual acts thus are less important in themselves than in relation to each other, as they pattern out into modes of action. For example, the mistreatment of a prisoner of war is an illegal act in itself. If it is the abberant act of an individual soldier, one expects that the soldier will be disciplined by his superior. If he is not disciplined, his superior shares his guilt for that act. If the mistreatment is generalized in the war area, without the restraining force of law operating through channels of military justice, then it has become a sanctioned mode of behavior, sanctioned on a level higher than that of the officers and men in the field.

The same criterion can be applied to other acts in warfare. If a naval commander orders the shelling of a coastal area with the intention of killing enemy troops known to be there, the customary rule of military necessity demands that the officer in charge weigh the military gain to be achieved against suffering that may be caused to non-combatants incidental to the bombardment of the presumed target. The commander may fail in his judgment and cause unnecessary suffering for quite limited or even perfunctory military gains. If he continues to order similar acts of warfare, and there is no restraint exerted on him, these acts too become sanctioned by higher authority and that higher authority bears collateral or even paramount responsibility for the acts.

The recurring patterns of behavior are most crucial where evidence points to systematic actions unmistakably directed against the entire enemy population. For example: an officer orders the bombardment of a populated area at a considerable distance from any battle in progress, where neither enemy troops nor military works are of sufficient vulnerability to suffer a concrete military disadvantage from the bombardment. If the officer in the case acted on faulty information or poor judgment the acts committed under his command can be judged for lack of restraint without reference beyond these acts and their results. However, when a war action of a certain kind becomes habitual, it takes on the character of policy.

The very extensiveness of the documentation data is important in itself. For the evidence is so extensive as to be internally supporting, and in that sense self-verifying. Thus it would be unreasonable to assume that the patterned violation of the laws of war could occur as a result of chance alone. Neither is it reasonable to assume that reports of such events could have appeared in such profusion as a result of chance factors alone. Accordingly, it is reasonable to assume that only the operation of systematic policy factors could give rise to the regularity of behavior that is reported in the documentation.

When violation of the laws of war becomes government policy, this generates a crisis of integrity for American society, for the laws of war are, under the Constitution (Art. 6), part of "the supreme law of the land." A crisis of integrity is the result of contradiction between law and the behavior of officials or citizens sworn to uphold the law, between their obligations and their performance. The integrity of a society is challenged when its ideals and its behavior are opposed, when the values one is taught to live by are contradicted by demanded behavior; in the present case, when rule of law is contradicted by the orders of officials whose first obligation is to uphold the law. Citizens then confront the choice of obeying the law or obeying the orders of men who currently hold public office.

The following are some of the problems facing Americans who wish to conserve the rule of law as a basic feature of American society: What can be done to compel officials of the U.S. to obey the law; If the laws of war are not being enforced, is the citizen obliged to obey them (i.e., must *all* laws be obeyed); What action can a citizen take when the Department of Justice becomes a Department of *Selective* Justice; What should a citizen do who recognizes his responsibility under the laws of war, including the Nuremberg Principles, not to comply with orders (like the draft) to commit war crimes; When there is contradiction between an Act of Congress or an Executive Order and the laws of war, how can a citizen be protected against reprisal for having obeyed the laws of war; What legal steps are feasible to restrain the Executive Branch of the U.S. Government from committing war crimes, and from preparing to commit war crimes; What machinery of law can be brought to bear on these issues—lawsuits, petitions for restraining orders, actions by grand juries or Federal attornies; What should law-abiding citizens do when public officials, formal wielders of legal authority, use the machinery of law to enforce violation of law?

Seymour Melman
Columbia University

NOTE ON THE RESEARCH METHOD

The essential method of this research project required the review of news dispatches to major U.S. news media with the view of ascertaining whether U.S. actions in Vietnam have departed from norms of constraint established in treaty-binding articles of the conventional law of war and in the customary law of war, adhered to by the United States.

A preliminary selection of treaty clauses was made from the Hague Conventions of 1907 (mainly the Annex to the Fourth Hague Convention) and the Geneva Conventions of 1949. The conduct of the war in Vietnam would be tested in the light of norms of constraint established in these Conventions.

The research for this documentation was designed to focus on prime American news sources (newspapers, news services, and periodicals; in the final selection of material priority was given to eyewitness reports of American newsmen on the scene in Vietnam. A few books and a few non-U.S. newspapers and periodicals are cited also.*

Originals or photocopies of all selections given in the text are in our possession for reference. Since many articles contained material pertinent to more than one category of treaty clauses, appropriate passages were marked off and numbered. These passages, as well as a few complete dispatches, were eventually typed on cards, classified and reproduced in the text.

The researchers have sought to avoid selecting material out of context. To help maintain objectivity each article was read by at least two persons.

Much material originally read and tentatively categorized was

---

*NOTE: Various news entries in this documentation originated with a major news service whose longstanding policy does not permit attribution outside the pages of its client newspapers. Such dispatches are given here with citation of filing date and place only.

eventually omitted both for reasons of space and priority. Some categories disappeared altogether when the data at hand was judged insufficient. In no case was material omitted which would have revealed a significant break in a pattern of behavior which emerged from the materials in each part of the documentation.

The air war against North Vietnam was omitted from treatment here for several reasons. A number of responsible eyewitness reports on the results of bombing in North Vietnam have had considerable publicity in the U.S.—mainly the dispatches of Harrison Salisbury to *The New York Times*. There is some reason to believe from these reports that non-military targets and persons have been bombed and strafed in areas where the suffering inflicted is not merely incidental to the destruction of military targets. However, an effort to determine a pattern in this bombing of North Vietnam would require a large body of cumulative data on an almost day to day basis. To our knowledge no American reporters have been permitted to go along on bombing missions over North Vietnam. This fact can only partially be ascribed to the type of aircraft used in these missions. The accumulation of on-the-scene reports from North Vietnam in sufficient quantity to meet our standards would have led us to an overwhelming dependence on non-American news sources which we decided to avoid as a matter of principle.

Neither the conduct of the armies of the National Liberation Front or the Democratic Republic of Vietnam have been made the subject of this inquiry. As Americans we thought that the most appropriate task was the determination of our own military actions in the light of our own laws.

Only an undeterminable fraction of relevant events are recorded in this documentation during the period of major coverage (1965, 1966, Spring 1967). Many military operations proceed without the presence of reporters or observers. Journalists do not necessarily report all the data available to them. Newspapers do not print all dispatches received. The published sources used here reflect only a small part of journalistic activity in Vietnam, by American and foreign reporters.

As evidence that the situation has not materially changed since the major research was completed, several news dispatches with dates through December, 1967, have been added just before going to press.

In no instance did the researchers solicit reports on the conduct of the war in Vietnam. Every entry in the documentation originated with and was published by organizations and persons unrelated to the present researchers. Thus, the materials cited here originated independently of the present inquiry.

Melvyn Baron
Dodge Ely

INTERNATIONAL LAW AND
THE CONDUCT OF THE VIETNAM WAR

Richard A. Falk
Princeton University

The publication of this volume provides a notable opportunity. It contains the raw data created by the fury of American participation in the Vietnam War. This data has been organized into categories that conform to the basic divisions traditional to the international law of war. These fundamental rules of warfare have been incorporated over the centuries into a series of international treaties. The most significant of these treaties are the Hague Conventions of 1899 and 1907 and the four Geneva Conventions of 1949. Reading about the conduct of warfare in Vietnam creates an overwhelming presumption that the United States government and its military command are authorizing combat tactics that flagrantly and persistently violate the rules of war in a great variety of respects.[1]

In 1861 Sir Henry Maine wrote that "The grandest function of the Law of Nature was discharged in giving birth to modern International Law and to the modern Law of War." The natural law basis of international law emphasizes the extent to which its rules of conduct, especially those applicable to warfare, have arisen in response to the dictates of conscience. The importance of the moral dimension of international law is reinforced by the absence of any regular institutions through which to enforce rules of conduct against delinquent states. Therefore, it is entirely appropriate and in the spirit of international law to mobilize the community's sense of moral outrage that has been provoked by the United States war actions in Vietnam. A central objective of international law is to encourage action by individuals, by governments, and by the organized international community to protect a state that is the victim of wrongful uses of force. Among the actions on behalf of the victim are those that avail themselves of the rectifying procedures of a society "of laws, not men." Whenever significant groups of citizens in the United States protest that conduct of their Government is both illegal and immoral they deserve a hearing and an impartial answer. The allegation of illegality of war conduct in Vietnam should be studied by Congress and tested by the courts. This volume contains data that suggests the plausibility of these allegations of illegality. If the allegations are well-founded that the United States conduct of the war in Vietnam violates international law, then Congress and the courts are Constitutionally empowered and obliged to act to restrain further illegal action by the Executive Office.

The laws of war have been developed by governments over the years to establish certain minimum and reasonable constraints upon the absolute discretion of states to pursue belligerent objectives by any means at their disposal. These laws, therefore, express a moral consensus reached by senior statesmen—not by idealistic reformers—and their contents have been endorsed by governmental institutions throughout the world as serving the national interest of their various countries. These international treaties, in part, translate into legal form the underlying moral consensus and establish guidelines for what is and what is not permissible belligerent policy. The United States service field manuals, distributed for the guidance of military personnel, affirm the conculsion that "the conduct of armed hostilities is regulated by the law of land warfare." The indictment of Nazi war criminals at Nuremberg in 1945 charged the defendants, in addition to the crime of waging aggressive war and crimes against humanity, with specific violations of the laws of war. On December 11, 1946, the General Assembly of the United Nations in a unanimous Resolution affirmed "the principles of international law recognized by the Charter of the Nuremberg Tribunal and the judgment of the Tribunal." These Nuremberg Principles affirm the criminal responsibility of individuals for the commission of war crimes and, in the event of prosecution, the unavailability of the excuse of "superior orders," i.e., it is no excuse, although it may diminish the punishment, to establish that a particular violation of the laws of war was committed in the course of carrying out an order of a superior officer. The obligation, then, to comply with these laws of warfare takes precedence over the obligations of a citizen to obey his government.

In reading these materials, however, it is important to refrain from arriving at *legal* conclusions. These reports on battlefield operations are unverified newspaper accounts. Any particular report may be unreliable. Cross-examination is not made available to the United States Government, nor is a statement of explanation available. Despite the one-sided presentation of the facts, it is difficult to refrain from two sorts of conclusions relevant to a legal assessment of United States combat practices in Vietnam:

(1) The United States is relying upon a series of combat practices that are in clear violation of the obligations of the laws of war;

(2) These combat practices are so widespread in their occurrence as to suggest that their systematic commission is a direct result of decisions reached at the highest levels of civilian and military command.

Writing beneath the shadow of the bloody Thirty Years' War, Hugo Grotius, the great Dutch international lawyer, included this passage in the Prolegomena to his classic study *De Jure Belli ac Pacis (The Law of War and Peace)* in 1625:

Fully convinced, by the considerations which I have advanced, that there is a common law among nations, which is valid alike for war and in war, I have had many weighty reasons for undertaking to write upon this subject. Throughout the Christian world I observed a lack of restraint in relation to war, such as even barbarous races should be ashamed of; I observed that men rush to arms for slight causes, or no cause at all, and that when arms have once been taken up there is no longer any respect for law, divine or human; it is as if, in accordance with a general decree, frenzy had openly been let loose for the committing of all crimes.

There is a similar sense of "frenzy. . . let loose" that arises from reading through the material presented in this volume. The words of Grotius have a tragic timeliness more than three centuries after their composition. One cannot read of the war acts of the United States in Vietnam without feeling that an absence of tactical and moral restraint conditions our policies there, an absence that is at once neglectful of our moral and of our legal heritage, as well as totally contradicting that peculiar blend of idealism and pragmatism that has guided our participation in world affairs since the time of our own turbulent, revolutionary beginnings as an independent republic.

Let us be clear. The United States Government has pursued limited objectives by limited means, at least as of August 1967, in the sense of claiming to seek a negotiated settlement with North Vietnam and by not using all of the power at its disposal, a capability sufficient to obliterate North Vietnam, but not sufficient necessarily to prevent China and/or the Soviet Union from inflicting great destruction upon us or our allies in response. But these limits, to the uncertain extent that they *actually* exist—as distinct from enjoying a *rhetorical* existence in the rationales of the Administration—constitute a *strategic* framework of restraint within which the belligerence proceeds unmindful of the restraints relevant to the level of actual combat operations.

International society possesses very little in the way of governmental institutions. Law-making and law-enforcing are largely products of the activity and of the will of the principal sovereign states. Rules of international law are created typically in two ways —either by agreement among the states that are bound (treaty-made law) or by patterns of practice that harden into obligations through the sense that adherence is a matter of duty rather than discretion (custom-made law). In modern international law, additional rules of conduct may be created by the action of the political organs of the United Nations reflecting the will of the international community.

In relation to the subject matter of the law of war, the formal rules embodied in treaties have been largely declaratory of earlier patterns of practice that had already enjoyed the status of customary international law. To this extent, a state is bound by an international treaty governing the conduct of war whether or not it has formally become a party to it. The treaty is in part a very authoritative and self-consistent indication as to the contents of the underlying "unwritten law" that evolves out of the practices and beliefs of nations. This "unwritten law" expresses the fundamental and prevailing consensus that the conduct of war is subject to certain kinds of restraints.[2] In this respect, the great "law-making" treaties at The Hague and Geneva are to be understood more in the nature of "law-declaring" instruments that clarify patterns of pre-existing obligations. It is important to acknowledge, then, that the sense of moral outrage widely shared by peoples and government is itself relevant to the identification of rules of international law. Such shared attitudes identify the limits of acceptable behavior and possess or come to possess the quality of law. Therefore, the legal quality of war acts in Vietnam cannot be separated from the moral reaction to their commission. Attributing this moral agency to international law is especially necessary in view of the absence of legislative procedures available to bring a new law into being and administrative procedures to interpret existing law in light of changed circumstances.

International law also appears to have been violated by North Vietnam and by the National Liberation Front in a number of respects. The violations by the other side do not vindicate our own unless committed in specific reprisal. Our basic combat tactics appear unrelated to the degree to which the other side conforms or not to governing rules of international law. Besides, the violations on the other side are mainly those entailed by pursuing a guerrilla strategy against an opponent that enjoys a great superiority in military and material resources. If the war was allowed to reach an outcome on the basis of an internal play of Vietnamese, or even South Vietnamese forces, there is little doubt that North Vietnam and the National Liberation Front would have long since succeeded. It is the massive American military presence, including its great weapons superiority, that accentuates recourse to illegal practices by both sides. Such illegality is an almost inevitable consequence of guerrilla warfare on the scale taking place in Vietnam.

Does this argument imply that the laws of war are obsolete to the extent that they are applied to modern guerrilla warfare? On a formal level, the United States service manuals confirm the minimum application of the laws of war to civil strife, following the language of Article 3 of the Geneva Conventions of 1949. This minimum application emphasizes that non-combatants and prisoners "shall in all circumstances be treated humanely" and generally affirms the obligation of belligerents to avoid unnecessary suffering and destruction of property. Such laws may be frequently unrealistic from the perspective of military necessity in the circumstances of guerrilla combat, but it should be emphasized that the very purpose of the laws of war is to constrain the conduct of war within minimum standards of human decency and, thereby, reject any absolute conception of military necessity. If military necessity requires recourse to "indecent" behavior, then at the very least, it creates a great need to justify the commitment to such a military operation by those who urge or authorize it.

The basic justification for recourse to war is defensive necessity, that the nation-state under attack must organize itself for war to protect its autonomy and to uphold its right to exist. The security of the United States, the most powerful state in human history, is probably less endangered by the outcome of the struggle for control of Vietnam than is that of any other country in the world. The idea of defensive necessity is not very readily (or credibly) available to those who would explain or justify the American involvement in the Vietnam War. In the absence of defensive necessity, American political leaders are asking a great deal of their population when citizens are conscripted to fight in a remote country on behalf of a regime that itself scorns the values of decency and democratic liberty that the traditions of the United States affirm. Violation of the legal rules, then, is one way to assess or measure the overall quality and consequence of the United States involvement in Vietnam.

It is also claimed that the laws of war are futile because they are almost never enforced, except possibly by the victors against the vanquished after the fighting has ceased. Such a contention overlooks the critical fact that most of the impact of international law upon the behavior of states arises from the processes of self-enforcement. The laws of war are standards of guidance that are accepted as part of the framework within which belligerent objectives are pursued. The mutuality of the obligation is the main sanction—that is, the reciprocal expectation that self-enforcement will be duplicated by the other side and that violative conduct will, in contrast, generate reprisals and render it more difficult to bring the hostilities to an end through a process of communication (negotiations) and compromise (settlement). In general, governments have an interest, as well, in not encouraging their own soldiers to engage in acts that flaunt the contents of their conscience. The domestic spillovers of the erosion of conscience arising from the conduct of international warfare is one danger-fraught cost, the relevance of which to violence in the urban centers of the United States is increasingly apparent.

Finally, it remains to point out that the material in this volume does not touch upon the broad question of whether the overall participation of the United States in the Vietnam war violates international law. There is a very considerable body of scholarly opinion that supports the conclusion that bombing North Vietnam amounts to "aggression," and quite substantial scholarly opinion that the entire participation by the United States in Vietnam constitutes "illegal intervention" in a civil war. These issues relate to the permissibility of an involvement in the war itself, whereas this book is concerned with a moral questioning of the nature of this involvement to the extent that it entails a consistent and pervasive reliance upon tactics that appear to be war crimes. The legal rules are set forth not to encourage legal debate as much as to provide benchmarks for a searching moral reappraisal of the United States involvement in the Vietnam War. Underlying this form of presentation is a single question—how can we grow morally reconciled to the conduct of a war that departs so drastically and so pervasively from legal rules designed to place minimum constraints on warfare?

FOOTNOTES

1. In the next section of this book headed "The Law" will be found relevant articles from five of The Hague and Geneva conventions, the principles of international law known as the Nuremberg Principles, and excerpts from the U.S. Army Field Manual dealing with the Law of Land Warfare.

2. This idea was expressed in the Nuremberg Judgment in the following language: "The convention [the Hague Convention of 1907] expressly stated that it was an attempt 'to revise the general laws and customs of war' which it thus recognized to be then existing, but by 1939 these rules laid down in the convention were recognized by all civilized nations, and were regarded as declaratory of the laws and customs of war which are referred to in Article 6(b) of the Charter." These laws and customs to the extent "declaratory" are, therefore, binding on a particular state whether or not it is a formal party to a treaty covering the same subject matter.

THE LAW

INTERNATIONAL CONVENTIONS RELATING TO THE CONDUCT OF WAR — ARTICLES CITED IN THIS REPORT

Hague Convention No. IV, Annex
Regulations Respecting the Laws and Customs of War on Land
18 October 1907
(Short reference: Hague—Laws)

Article 4

Prisoners of war are in the power of the hostile Government, but not of the individuals or corps who capture them.

They must be humanely treated.

All their personal belongings, except arms, horses, and military papers, remain their property.

Article 22.

The right of belligerents to adopt means of injuring the enemy is not unlimited.

Article 23

In addition to the prohibitions provided by special Conventions, it is especially forbidden—

(a) To employ poison or poisoned weapons.

(b) To kill treacherously individuals belonging to the hostile nation or army.

(c) To kill or wound an enemy who, having laid down his arms, or having no longer means of defence, has surrendered at discretion.

(e) To employ arms, projectiles, or material calculated to cause unnecessary suffering.

(g) To destroy or seize the enemy's property, unless such destruction or seizure be imperatively demanded by the necessities of war.

Article 25.

The attack or bombardment, by whatever means, of towns, villages, dwellings, or buildings which are undefended is prohibited.

Article 26.

The officer in command of an attacking force must, before commencing a bombardment, except in cases of assault, do all in his power to warn the authorities.

Article 28.

The pillage of a town, even when taken by assault, is prohibited.

Article 46.

Family honour and rights, the lives of persons, and private property, as well as religious convictions and practice, must be respected.

Private property cannot be confiscated.

Hague—Laws, Cont.

Article 47.

Pillage is formally forbidden.

Article 50

No general penalty, pecuniary or otherwise, shall be inflicted upon the population on account of the acts of individuals for which they cannot be regarded as jointly and severally responsible.

Hague Convention No. IX
Concerning Bombardment by Naval Forces In Time of War
18 October 1907.
(Short reference: Hague—Naval)

. . . Chapter I—The Bombardment of Undefended Ports, Towns, Villages, Dwellings or Buildings

Article 1

The bombardment by naval forces of undefended ports, towns, villages, dwellings or buildings is forbidden.

A place cannot be bombarded solely because automatic submarine contact mines are anchored off the harbor.

Article 2

Military works, military or naval establishments, depots of arms or war material, workshops or plans which could be utilized for the hostile fleet or army, and the ships of war in the harbor, are not, however, included in this prohibition. The commander of a naval force may destroy them with artillery, after a summons followed by a reasonable time of waiting, if all other means are impossible, and when the local authorities have not themselves destroyed them within the time fixed.

He incurs no responsibility for any unavoidable damage which may be caused by a bombardment under such circumstances.

If for military reasons immediate action is necessary, and no delay can be allowed the enemy, it is understood that the prohibition to bombard the undefended town holds good, as in the case given in paragraph 1, and that the commander shall take all due measures in order that the town may suffer as little harm as possible.

Article 3

After due notice has been given, the bombardment of undefended ports, towns, villages, dwellings, or buildings may be commenced, if the local authorities, after a formal summons has been made to them, decline to comply with requisitions for provisions or supplies necessary for the immediate use of the naval force before the place in question.. .

Geneva Conventions
12 August 1949
Article 3.
Common to All Three Geneva Conventions

In the case of armed conflict not of an international character occurring in the territory of one of the High Contracting Parties, each Party to the conflict shall be bound to apply, as a minimum, the following provisions:

(1) Persons taking no active part in the hostilities, including members of armed forces who have laid down their arms and those placed *hors de combat* by sickness, wounds, detention, or any other cause, shall in all circumstances be treated humanely, without any adverse distinction founded on race, colour, religion or faith, sex, birth or wealth, or any other similar criteria.

To this end, the following acts are and shall remain prohibited at any time and in any place whatsoever with respect to the above-mentioned persons:

(a) violence to life and person, in particular murder of all kinds, mutilation, cruel treatment and torture;

(b) taking of hostages;

(c) outrages upon personal dignity, in particular humiliating and degrading treatment;

(d) the passing of sentences and the carrying out of executions without previous judgment pronounced by a regularly constituted court, affording all the judicial guarantees which are recognized as indispensable by civilized peoples.

(2) The wounded and sick shall be collected and cared for.

An impartial humanitarian body, such as the International Committee of the Red Cross, may offer its services to the Parties of the conflict.

The Parties to the conflict should further endeavor to bring into force, by means of special agreements, all or part of the other provisions of the present Convention.

The application of the preceding provisions shall not affect the legal status of the Parties to the conflict.

Geneva Convention
Relative to the Protection of Civilian Persons
in Time of War
12 August 1949

(Short reference: Geneva—Civilians)

Article 5.

Where in the territory of a Party to the conflict, the latter is satisfied than an individual protected person is definitely suspected of or engaged in activities hostile to the security of the State, such individual person shall not be entitled to claim such rights and privileges under the present Convention as would, if exercised in the favour of such individual person, be prejudicial to the security of such State.

Where in occupied territory an individual protected person is detained as a spy or saboteur, or as a person under definite suspicion of activity

Geneva—Civilians, Cont.

hostile to the security of the Occupying Power, such person, shall, in those cases where absolute military security so requires, be regarded as having forfeited rights of communication under the present Convention.

In each case, such persons shall nevertheless be treated with humanity, and in case of trial, shall not be deprived of the rights of fair and regular trial prescribed by the present Convention. They shall also be granted the full rights and privileges of a protected person under the present Convention at the earliest date consistent with the security of the State or Occupying Power, as the case may be.

Article 24.

The Parties to the conflict shall take the necessary measures to ensure that children under fifteen, who are orphaned or are separated from their families as a result of the war, are not left to their own resources, and that their maintenance, the exercise of their religion and their education are facilitated in all circumstances. Their education shall, as far as possible, be entrusted to persons of a similar cultural tradition.

The Parties to the conflict shall facilitate the reception of such children in a neutral country for the duration of the conflict with the consent of the Protecting Power, if any, and under due safeguards for the observance of the principles stated in the first paragraph.

They shall, furthermore, endeavour, to arrange for all children under twelve to be identified by the wearing of identity discs, or by some other means.

Article 27.

Protected persons are entitled, in all circumstances, to respect for their persons, their honour, their family rights, their religious convictions and practices, and their manners and customs. They shall at all times be humanely treated, and shall be protected especially against all acts of violence or threats thereof and against insults and public curiosity.

Women shall be especially protected against any attack on their honour, in particular against rape, enforced prostitution, or any form of indecent assault.

Without prejudice to the provisions relating to their state of health, age and sex, all protected persons shall be treated with the same consideration by the Party to the conflict in whose power they are, without any adverse distinction based, in particular, on race, religion or political opinion.

However, the Parties to the conflict may take such measures of control and security in regard to protected persons as may be necessary as a result of the war.

Article 29

The Party to the conflict in whose hands protected persons may be, is responsible for the treatment accorded to them by its agents, irrespective of any individual responsibility which may be incurred.

Article 31.

No physical or moral coercion shall be exercised against protected persons, in particular to obtain information from them or from third parties.

Geneva—Civilians, Cont.

Article 32.

The High Contracting Parties specifically agree that each of them is prohibited from taking any measure of such a character as to cause the physical suffering or extermination of protected persons in their hands. This prohibition applies not only to murder, torture, corporal punishment, mutilation and medical or scientific experiments not necessitated by the medical treatment of a protected person, but also to any other measures of brutality whether applied by civilian or military agents.

Article 33.

No protected persons may be punished for an offence he or she has not personally committed. Collective penalties and likewise all measures of intimidation or of terrorism are prohibited.

Pillage is prohibited.

Reprisals against protected persons and their property are prohibited.

Article 49.

Individual or mass forcible transfers, as well as deportations of protected persons from occupied territory to the territory of the Occupying Power or to that of any other country, occupied or not, are prohibited, regardless of their motive.

Nevertheless, the Occupying Power may undertake total or partial evacuation of a given area if the security of the population or imperative military reasons so demand. Such evacuations may not involve the displacement of protected persons outside the bounds of the occupied territory except when for material reasons it is impossible to avoid such displacement. Persons thus evacuated shall be transferred back to their homes as soon as hostilities in the area in question have ceased.

The Occupying Power undertaking such transfers or evacuations shall ensure, to the greatest practicable extent, that proper accommodation is provided to receive the protected persons, that the removals are effected in satisfactory conditions of hygiene, health, safety and nutrition, and that members of the same family are not separated.

The protecting Power shall be informed of any transfers and evacuations as soon as they have taken place.

The Occupying Power shall not detain protected persons in an area particularly exposed to the dangers of war unless the security of the population or imperative military reasons so demand.

The Occupying Power shall not deport or transfer parts of its own civilian population into the territory it occupies.

Article 50.

The Occupying Power shall, with the cooperation of the national and local authorities, facilitate the proper working of all institutions devoted to the care and education of children.

The Occupying Power shall take all necessary steps to facilitate the identification of children and the registration of their parentage. It may not, in any case, change their personal status, nor enlist them in formations or organizations subordinate to it.

Should the local institutions be inadequate for the purpose, the Occupy-

Geneva—Civilians, Cont.

ing Power shall make arrangements for the maintenance and education, if possible by persons of their own nationality, language and religion, of children who are orphaned or separated from their parents as a result of the war and who cannot be adequately cared for by a near relative or friend.

A special section of the Bureau set up in accordance with Article 136 shall be responsible for taking all necessary steps to identify children whose identity is in doubt. Particulars of their parents or other near relatives should always be recorded if available.

The Occupying Power shall not hinder the application of any preferential measures in regard to food, medical care and protection against the effects of war, which may have been adopted prior to the occupation in favour of children under fifteen years, expectant mothers, and mothers of children under seven years.

Article 53.

Any destruction by the Occupying Power of real or personal property belonging individually or collectively to private persons, or to the State, or to other public authorities, or to social or cooperative organizations, is prohibited, except where such destruction is rendered absolutely necessary by military operations.

Article 55.

To the fullest extent of the means available to it, the Occupying Power has the duty of ensuring the food and medical supplies of the populations; it should, in particular, bring in the necessary foodstuffs, medical stores and other articles if the resources of the occupied territory are inadequate.

The Occupying Power may not requisition foodstuffs, articles or medical supplies available in the occupied territory, except for use by the occupation forces and administration personnel, and then only if the requirements of the civilian population have been taken into account. Subject to the provisions of other international Conventions, the Occupying Power shall make arrangements to ensure that fair value is paid for any requisitioned goods.

The Protecting Power shall, at any time, be at liberty to verify the state of the food and medical supplies in occupied territories, except where temporary restrictions are made necessary by imperative military requirements.

Article 56.

To the fullest extent of the means available to it, the Occupying Power has the duty of ensuring and maintaining, with the cooperation of national and local authorities, the medical and hospital establishments and services, public health and hygiene in the occupied territory, with particular reference to the adoption and application of the prophylactic and preventive measures necessary to combat the spread of contagious diseases and epidemics. Medical personnel of all categories shall be allowed to carry out their duties.

If new hospitals are set up in occupied territory and if the competent organs of the occupied State are not operating there, the occupying authorities shall, if necessary, grant them the recognition provided for in Article 18. In similar circumstances, the occupying authorities shall also grant recognition to hospital personnel and transport vehicles under the provisions of Articles 20 and 21.

Geneva—Civilians, Cont.

In adopting measures of health and hygiene and in their implementation, the Occupying Power shall take into consideration the moral and ethical susceptibilities of the population of the occupied territory.

Article 59.

If the whole or part of the population of an occupied territory is inadequately supplied, the Occupying Power shall agree to relief schemes on behalf of the said population, and shall facilitate them by all the means at its disposal.

Such schemes, which may be undertaken either by States or by impartial humanitarian organizations such as the International Committee of the Red Cross, shall consist, in particular, of the provision of consignments of foodstuffs, medical supplies and clothing.

All the Contracting Parties shall permit the free passage of these consignments and shall guarantee their protection.

A Power granting free passage to consignments on their way to territory occupied by an adverse Party to the conflict shall, however, have the right to search the consignments, to regulate their passage according to prescribed times and routes, and to be reasonably satisfied through the Protecting Power that these consignments are to be used for the relief of the needy population and are not to be used for the benefit of the Occupying Power.

Article 147.

Grave breaches to which the preceding Article relates shall be those involving any of the following acts, if committed against persons or property protected by the present Convention: wilful killing, torture or inhuman treatment, including biological experiments, wilfully causing great suffering or serious injury to body or health, unlawful deportation or transfer or unlawful confinement of a protected person, compelling a protected person to serve in the forces of a hostile Power, or willfully depriving a protected person of the rights of fair and regular trial prescribed in the present Convention, taking of hostages and extensive destruction and appropriation of property, not justified by military necessity and carried out unlawfully and wantonly.

Articles 146 and 148 of this convention are identical to Articles 129 and 131, respectively, of the "Prisoners of War" Convention as well as to Articles 49 and 51 of the Convention on the "Wounded and Sick."

Geneva Convention Relative to the Treatment of Prisoners of War
12 August 1949
(Short reference: Geneva—Prisoners of War)

Article 4.

A. Prisoners of war, in the sense of the present Convention, are persons belonging to one of the following categories, who have fallen into the power of the enemy:

(1) Members of the armed forces of a Party to the conflict, as well as members of militias or volunteer corps forming part of such armed forces.

(2) Members of other militias and members of other volunteer corps, including those of organized resistance movements, belonging to a Party

Geneva—Prisoners of War, Cont.

to the conflict and operating in or outside their own territory, even if this territory is occupied, provided that such militias or volunteer corps, including such organized resistance movements, fulfill the following conditions:

(a) that of being commanded by a person responsible for his subordinates;

(b) that of having a fixed distinctive sign recognizable at a distance;

(c) that of carrying arms openly;

(d) that of conducting their operations in accordance with the laws and customs of war.

(3) Members of regular armed forces who profess allegiance to a government or an authority not recognized by the Detaining Power.

(4) Persons who accompany the armed forces without actually being members thereof, such as civilian members of military aircraft crews, war correspondents, supply contractors, members of labour units or of services responsible for the welfare of the armed forces, provided that they have received authorization from the armed forces which they accompany, who shall provide them for that purpose with an identity card similar to the annexed model.

(5) Members of crews, including masters, pilots and apprentices, of the merchant marine and the crews of civil aircraft of the Parties to the conflict, who do not benefit by more favourable treatment under any other provisions of international law.

(6) Inhabitants of a non-occupied territory, who on the approach of the enemy spontaneously take up arms to resist the invading forces, without having had time to form themselves into regular armed units provided they carry arms openly and respect the laws and customs of war.

B. The following shall likewise be treated as prisoners of war under the present Convention:

(1) Persons belonging, or having belonged, to the armed forces of the occupied country, if the occupying Power considers it necessary by reason of such allegiance to intern them, even though it has originally liberated them while hostilities were going on outside the territory it occupies, in particular where such persons have made an unsuccessful attempt to rejoin the armed forces to which they belong and which are engaged in combat, or where they fail to comply with a summons made to them with a view to internment.

(2) The persons belonging to one of the categories enumerated in the present Article, who have been received by neutral or non-belligerent Powers on their territory and whom these Powers are required to intern under international law, without prejudice to any more favourable treatment which these Powers may choose to give and with the exception of Articles 8, 10 15, 30, fifth paragraph 58-67, 92, 126 and, where diplomatic relations exist between the Parties to the conflict and the neutral or non-belligerent Power concerned, those Articles concerning the Protecting Power. Where such diplomatic relations exist the Parties to a conflict on whom these persons depend shall be allowed to perform towards them the functions of a Protecting Power as provided in the present Convention, without prejudice to the functions which these Parties normally exercise in conformity with diplomatic and consular usage and treaties.

Geneva—Prisoners of War, Cont.

C. This Article shall in no way affect the status of medical personnel and chaplains as provided for in Article 33 of the present Convention.

Article 5.

The present Convention shall apply to the persons referred to in Article 4 from the time they fall into the power of the enemy and until their final release and repatriation.

Should any doubt arise as to whether persons, having committed a belligerent act and having fallen into the hands of the enemy, belong to any of the categories enumerated in Article 4, such persons shall enjoy the protection of the present Convention until such time as their status has been determined by a competent tribunal.

Article 7.

Prisoners of war may in no circumstances renounce in part or in entirety the rights secured to them by the present Convention, and by the special agreements referred to in the foregoing Article, if such there be.

Article 12.

Prisoners of war are in the hands of the enemy Power, but not of the individuals or military units who have captured them. Irrespective of the individual responsibilities that may exist, the Detaining Power is responsible for the treatment given them.

Prisoners of war may only be transferred by the Detaining Power to a Power which is a party to the Convention and after the Detaining Power has satisfied itself of the willingness and ability of such transferee Power to apply the Convention. When prisoners of war are transferred under such circumstances, responsibility for the application of the Convention rests on the Power accepting them while they are in its custody.

Nevertheless, if that Power fails to carry out the provisions of the Convention in any important respect, the Power by whom the prisoners of war were transferred shall, upon being notified by the Protecting Power, take effective measures to correct the situation or shall request the return of the prisoners of war. Such requests must be complied with.

Article 13.

Prisoners of war must at all times be humanely treated. Any unlawful act or omission by the Detaining Power causing death or seriously endangering the health of a prisoner of war in its custody is prohibited, and will be regarded as a serious breach of the present Convention. In particular, no prisoner of war may be subjected to physical mutilation or to medical or scientific experiments of any kind which are not justified by the medical, dental or hospital treatment of the prisoner concerned and carried out in his interest.

Likewise, prisoners of war must at all times be protected, particularly against acts of violence or intimidation and against insults and public curiosity.

Measures of reprisal against prisoners of war are prohibited.

Article 14.

Prisoners of war are entitled in all circumstances to respect for their persons and their honour.

Geneva—Prisoners of War, Cont.

Women shall be treated with all regard due to their sex and shall in all cases benefit by treatment as favourable as that granted to men.

Prisoners of war shall retain the full civil capacity which they enjoyed at the time of their capture. The Detaining Power may not restrict the exercise, either within or without its own territory, of the rights such capacity confers except in so far as the captivity requires.

Article 16.

Taking into consideration the provisions of the present Convention relating to rank and sex, and subject to any privileged treatment which may be accorded to them by reason of their state of health, age or professional qualifications, all prisoners of war shall be treated alike by the Detaining Powers, without any adverse distinction based on race, nationality, religious belief or political opinions, or any other distinction founded on similar criteria.

Article 17.

Every prisoner of war, when questioned on the subject, is bound to give only his surname, first names and rank, date of birth, and army, regimental, personal or serial number, or failing this, equivalent information.

If he wilfully infringes this rule, he may render himself liable to a restriction of the privileges accorded to his rank or status.

Each Party to a conflict is required to furnish the persons under its jurisdiction who are liable to become prisoners of war, with an identity card, showing the owner's surname, first names, rank, army, regimental, personal or serial number or equivalent information, and date of birth. The identity card may, furthermore, bear the signature or the fingerprints, or both, of the owner, and may bear, as well, any other information the Party to the conflict may wish to add concerning persons belonging to its armed forces. As far as possible the card shall measure 6.5 x 10 cm. and shall be issued in duplicate. The identity card shall be shown by the prisoner of war upon demand, but may in no case be taken away from him.

No physical or mental torture, nor any other form of coercion, may be inflicted on prisoners of war to secure from them information of any kind whatever. Prisoners of war who refuse to answer may not be threatened, insulted, or exposed to unpleasant or disadvantageous treatment of any kind.

Prisoners of war who, owing to their physical or mental condition, are unable to state their identity, shall be handed over to the medical service. The identity of such prisoners shall be established by all possible means, subject to the provisions of the preceding paragraph.

The questioning of prisoners of war shall be carried out in a language which they understand.

Article 20.

The evacuation of prisoners of war shall always be effected humanely and in conditions similar to those for the forces of the Detaining Power in their changes of station.

The Detaining Power shall supply prisoners of war who are being evacuated with sufficient food and potable water and with the necessary clothing

Geneva—Prisoners of War, Cont.

and medical attention. The Detaining Power shall take all suitable precautions to ensure their safety during evacuation, and shall establish as soon as possible a list of the prisoners of war who are evacuated.

If prisoners of war must, during evacuation, pass through transit camps, their stay in such camps shall be as brief as possible.

Article 22.

Prisoners of war may be interned only in premises located on land and affording every guarantee of hygiene and healthfulness. Except in particular cases which are justified by the interest of the prisoners themselves, they shall not be interned in penitentiaries.

Prisoners of war interned in unhealthy areas, or where the climate is injurious for them, shall be removed as soon as possible to a more favourable climate.

The Detaining Power shall assemble prisoners of war in camps or camp compounds according to their nationality, language, and customs, provided that such prisoners shall not be separated from prisoners of war belonging to the armed forces with which they were serving at the time of their capture, except with their consent.

Article 82.

A prisoner of war shall be subject to the laws, regulations and orders in force in the armed forces of the Detaining Power; the Detaining Power shall be justified in taking judicial or disciplinary measures in respect of any offence committed by a prisoner of war against such laws, regulations or orders. However, no proceedings or punishments contrary to the provisions of this Chapter shall be allowed.

If any law, regulation or order of the Detaining Power shall declare acts committed by a prisoner of war to be punishable, whereas the same acts would not be punishable if committed by a member of the forces of the Detaining Power, such acts shall entail disciplinary punishments only.

Article 129.

The High Contracting Parties undertake to enact any legislation necessary to provide effective penal sanctions for persons committing, or ordering to be committed, any of the grave breaches of the present Convention defined in the following Article.

Each High Contracting Party shall be under the obligation to search for persons alleged to have committed, or to have ordered to be committed, such grave breaches, and shall bring such persons, regardless of their nationality, before its own courts. It may also, if it prefers, and in accordance with the provisions of its own legislation, hand such persons over for trial to another High Contracting Party concerned, provided such High Contracting Party has made out a *prima facie* case.

Each High Contracting Party shall take measures necessary for the suppression of all acts contrary to the provisions of the present Convention other than the grave breaches defined in the following Article.

In all circumstances, the accused persons shall benefit by safeguards of proper trial and defense, which shall not be less favourable than those provided by Article 105 and those following of the present Convention.

Geneva—Prisoners of War, Cont.

Article 130.

Grave breaches to which the preceding Article relates shall be those involving any of the following acts, if committed against persons or property protected by the Convention: wilful killing, torture or inhuman treatment, including biological experiments, wilfully causing great suffering or serious injury to body or health, compelling a prisoner of war to serve in the forces of the hostile Power, or wilfully depriving a prisoner of war of the rights of fair and regular trial prescribed in this Convention.

Article 131.

No high Contracting Party shall be allowed to absolve itself or any other High Contracting Party of any liability incurred by itself or by another High Contracting Party in respect of breaches referred to in the preceding Article.

Geneva Convention
for the Amelioration of the Condition
of the Wounded and Sick in Armed Forces in the Field
12 August 1949
(Short reference: Geneva—Wounded)

Article 14.

Subject to the provisions of Article 12, the wounded and sick of a belligerent who fall into enemy hands shall be prisoners of war, and the provisions of international law concerning prisoners of war shall apply to them.

Article 15.

At all times, and particularly after an engagement, Parties to the conflict shall, without delay, take all possible measures to search for and collect the wounded and sick, to protect them against pillage and ill-treatment, to ensure their adequate care, and to search for the dead and prevent their being despoiled.

Whenever circumstances permit, an armistice or a suspension of fire shall be arranged, or local arrangements made, to permit the removal, exchange and transport of the wounded left on the battlefield.

Likewise, local arrangements may be concluded between Parties to the conflict for the removal or exchange of wounded and sick from a besieged or encircled area, and for the passage of medical and religious personnel and equipment on their way to that area.

Article 17.

Parties to the conflict shall ensure that burial or cremation of the dead, carried out individually as far as circumstances permit, is preceded by a careful examination, if possible by a medical examination, of the bodies, with a view to confirming death, establishing identity and enabling a report to be made. One half of the double identity disc, or the identity disc itself if it is a single disc, should remain on the body.

Bodies shall not be cremated except for imperative reasons of hygiene or for motives based on the religion of the deceased. In case of cremation, the circumstances and reasons for cremation shall be stated in detail in the death certificate or on the authenticated list of the dead.

Geneva—Wounded, Cont.

They shall further ensure that the dead are honourably interred, if possible according to the rites of the religion to which they belonged, that their graves are respected, grouped if possible according to the nationality of the deceased, property maintained and marked so that they may always be found. For this purpose, they shall organize at the commencement of hostilities an Official Graves Registration Service, to allow subsequent exhumations and to ensure the identification of bodies, whatever the site of the graves, and the possible transportation to the home country. These provisions shall likewise apply to the ashes, which shall be kept by the Graves Registration Service until proper disposal thereof in accordance with the wishes of the home country.

Article 19.

Fixed establishments and mobile medical units of the Medical Service may in no circumstances be attacked, but shall at all times be respected and protected by the Parties to the conflict. Should they fall into the hands of the adverse Party, their personnel shall be free to pursue their duties, as long as the capturing Power has not itself ensured the necessary care of the wounded and sick found in such establishments and units.

The responsible authorities shall ensure that the said medical establishments and units are, as far as possible, situated in such a manner that attacks against military objectives cannot imperil their safety.

Article 21.

The protection to which establishments and mobile medical units of the Medical Service are entitled shall not cease unless they are used to commit, outside their humanitarian duties, acts harmful to the enemy. Protection may, however, cease only after a due warning has been given, naming, in all appropriate cases, a reasonable time limit, and after such warning has remained unheeded.

Article 22.

The following conditions shall not be considered as depriving a medical unit or establishment of the protection guaranteed by Article 19:

(1) That the personnel of the unit or establishment are armed, and that they use the arms in their own defense, or in that of the wounded and sick in their charge.

(2) That in the absence of armed orderlies, the unit or establishment is protected by a picket or by sentries or by an escort.

(3) That small arms and ammunition taken from the wounded and sick and not yet handed to the proper service, are found in the unit or establishment.

(4) That personnel and material of the veterinary service are found in the unit or establishment, without forming an integral part thereof.

(5) That the humanitarian activities of medical units and establishments or of their personnel extend to the care of civilian wounded or sick.

Geneva—Wounded, Cont.

Article 33.

The material of mobile medical units of the armed forces which fall into the hands of the enemy, shall be reserved for the care of wounded and sick.

The buildings material and stores of fixed medical establishments of the armed forces shall remain subject to the laws of war, but may not be diverted from their purpose as long as they are required for the care of wounded and sick. Nevertheless, the commanders of forces in the field may make use of them, in case of urgent military necessity, provided that they make previous arrangements for the welfare of the wounded and sick who are nursed in them.

The material and stores defined in the present Article shall not be intentionally destroyed.

Article 50

Grave breaches to which the preceding Article relates shall be those involving any of the following acts, if committed against persons or property protected by the Convention: wilful killing, torture or inhuman treatment, including biological experiments, wilfully causing great suffering or serious injury to body or health, and extensive destruction and appropriation of property, not justified by military necessity and carried out unlawfully and wantonly.

Articles 49 and 51 of this Convention are identical to Articles 129 and 131, respectively, of the "Prisoners of War" Convention, as well as to Articles 146 and 148 of the "Civilians" Convention.

At the beginning of each chapter will be found citations to the articles from the Hague and Geneva Conventions which are especially relevant to the subject matter of that chapter.

THE "NUREMBERG PRINCIPLES" OF INTERNATIONAL LAW

On December 11, 1946 the General Assembly of the United Nations unanimously affirmed "the principles of international law recognized by the Charter of the Nuremberg Tribunal and the judgment of the Tribunal." Subsequently, the General Assembly entrusted the formulation of the Nuremberg principles to the International Law Commission, an organ of the United Nations composed of experts in international law representing all the legal systems in the world and expected to promote the progressive development and codification of international law. It should be appreciated that the United States (together with France, Britain, and the Soviet Union) took a leading role in the drafting of the Nuremberg Charter and in the prosecution of the German leaders that led to the Nuremberg judgment. We present below the text of the Nuremberg principles, Nos. I through V and No. VI(b) bearing most directly on the individual responsibility that arises from the commission of war crimes. The approval of these principles by the General Assembly and their formulation by the International Law Commission, together with the participation of the United States Government in this process, makes these principles highly authoritative guides as to the character of the relevant legal obligations of citizens and leaders.

1. Principles of International Law Recognized in the Charter of the Nuremberg Tribunal and in the Judgment of the Tribunal

As formulated by the International Law Commission, June-July 1950.

Principle I

Any person who commits an act which constitutes a crime under international law is responsible therefor and liable to punishment.

Principle II

The fact that internal law does not impose a penalty for an act which constitutes a crime under international law does not relieve the person who committed the act from responsibility under international law.

Principle III

The fact that a person who committed an act which constitutes a crime under international law acted as Head of State or responsible government official does not relieve him from responsibility under international law.

Principle IV

The fact that a person acted pursuant to order of his Government or of a superior does not relieve him from responsibility under international law, provided a moral choice was in fact possible to him.

Principle V

Any person charged with a crime under international law has the right to a fair trial on the facts and law.

Principle VI

The crimes hereinafter set out are punishable as crimes under international law:

a. Crimes against peace:

(i) Planning, preparation, initiation or waging of a war of aggression or a war in violation of international treaties, agreements or assurances;

(ii) Participation in a common plan or conspiracy for the accomplishment of any of the acts mentioned under (i).

b. War crimes:

Violations of the laws or customs of war which include, but are not limited to, murder, ill-treatment or deportation to slave-labour or for any other purpose of civilian population of or in occupied territory, murder or ill-treatment of prisoners of war or persons on the seas, killing of hostages, plunder of public or private property, wanton destruction of cities, towns, or villages, or devastation not justified by military necessity.

c. Crimes against humanity:

Murder, extermination, enslavement, deportation and other inhuman acts done against any civilian population, or persecutions on political, racial or religious grounds, when such acts are done or such persecutions are carried on in execution of or in connexion with any crime against peace or any war crime.

Principle VII

Complicity in the commission of a crime against peace, a war crime, or a crime against humanity as set forth in Principle VI is a crime under international law.

THE U.S. GOVERNMENT AND
THE LAW OF LAND WARFARE

Reproduced on the following pages are the Table of Contents and a few excerpts from applicable sections of THE LAW OF LAND WARFARE, U.S. Dept. of the Army Field Manual No. 27-10, U.S. Government Printing Office, dated 18 July 1956, reprinted in 1963. Due to limited sales this Manual is no longer available through the G.P.O. The International Affairs Division of the Office of the Judge Advocate General, Dept. of the Army, is responsible for the promulgation and distribution of the Manual.

TABLE OF CONTENTS

SELECTED EXCERPTS
CHAPTER 1
BASIC RULES AND PRINCIPLES

Section I. GENERAL

1. Purpose and Scope

The purpose of this Manual is to provide authoritative guidance to military personnel on the customary and treaty law applicable to the conduct of warfare on land and to relationships between belligerents and neutral States. Although certain of the legal principles set forth herein have application to warfare at sea and in the air as well as to hostilities on land, this Manual otherwise concerns itself with the rules peculiar to naval and aerial warfare only to the extent that such rules have some direct bearing on the activities of land forces.

This Manual is an official publication of the United States Army. However, those provisions of the Manual which are neither statutes nor the text of treaties to which the United States is a party should not be considered binding upon courts and tribunals applying the law of war. However, such provisions are of evidentiary value insofar as they bear upon questions of custom and practice.

2. Purposes of the Law of War

The conduct of armed hostilities on land is regulated by the law of land warfare which is both written and unwritten. It is inspired by the desire to diminish the evils of war by:

a. Protecting both combatants and noncombatants from unnecessary suffering;

b. Safeguarding certain fundamental human rights of persons who fall into the hands of the enemy, particularly prisoners of war, the wounded and sick, and civilians; and

c. Facilitating the restoration of peace.

3. Basic Principles

a. Prohibitory Effect. The law of war places limits on the exercise of a belligerent's power in the interests mentioned in paragraph 2 and requires that belligerents refrain from employing any kind or degree of violence which is not actually necessary for military purposes and that they conduct hostilities with regard for the principles of humanity and chivalry.

The prohibitory effect of the law of war is not minimized by "military necessity" which has been defined as that principle which justifies those measures not forbidden by international law which are indispensable for securing the complete submission of the enemy as soon as possible. Military necessity has been generally rejected as a defense for acts forbidden by the customary and conventional laws of war inasmuch as the latter have been developed and framed with consideration for the concept of military necessity.

b. Binding on States and Individuals. The law of war is binding not only upon States as such but also upon individuals and, in particular, the members of their armed forces.

4. Sources

The law of war is derived from two principal sources:

a. Lawmaking Treaties (or Conventions), such as the Hague and Geneva Conventions.

b. Custom. Although some of the law of war has not been incorporated in any treaty or convention to which the United States is a party, this body of unwritten or customary law is firmly established by the custom of nations and well defined by recognized authorities on international law.

Lawmaking treaties may be compared with legislative enactments in the national law of the United States and the customary law of war with the unwritten Anglo-American common law.

5. Lawmaking Treaties

a. Treaties to Which the United States Is a Party. The United States is a party to the following conventions pertinent to warfare on land:

(1) **Hague Convention No. III of 18 October 1907, Relative to the Opening of Hostilities** (*36 Stat.*[1] *2259, Treaty Series 538*), **cited herein as** *H. III.*

(2) **Hague Convention No. IV of 18 October 1907, Respecting the Laws and Customs of War on Land** (*36 Stat. 2277; Treaty Series 539*), **cited herein as** *H. IV,* **and the Annex thereto, embodying the Regulations Respecting the Laws and Customs of War on Land (***36 Stat. 2295; Treaty Series 539*), **cited herein as** *HR.*

(3) **Hague Convention No. V of 18 October 1907, Respecting the Rights and Duties of Neutral Powers and Persons in Case of War on Land** (*36 Stat. 2310; Treaty Series 540*), **cited herein as** *H. V.*

---

[1] *United States Statutes at Large.*

(4) **Hague Convention No. IX of 18 October 1907, Concerning Bombardment by Naval Forces in Time of War** (*36 Stat. 2351; Treaty Series 542*), **cited herein as *H. IX.***

(5) **Hague Convention No. X of 18 October 1907, for the Adaptation to Maritime Warfare of the Principles of the Geneva Convention** (*36 Stat. 2371; Treaty Series No. 543*), **cited herein as *H. X.***

(6) **Geneva Convention Relative to the Treatment of Prisoners of War of 27 July 1929** *(47 Stat. 2021; Treaty Series 846*), **cited herein as *GPW 1929.***

(7) **Geneva Convention for the Amelioration of the Condition of the Wounded and Sick of Armies in the Field of 27 July 1929** (*47 Stat. 2074; Treaty Series 847*), **cited herein as *GWS 1929.***

(8) **Treaty on the Protection of Artistic and Scientific Institions and Historic Monuments of 15 April 1935** (*49 Stat. 3267; Treaty Series 899*), **cited herein as the *Roerich Pact*. Only the United States and a number of the American Republics are parties to this treaty.**

(9) **Geneva Convention for the Amelioration of the Condition of the Wounded and Sick in Armed Forces in the Field of 12 August 1949** (*T. I. A. S.*[a] *3362*), **cited herein as GWS.**

(10) **Geneva Convention for the Amelioration of the Condition of Wounded, Sick and Shipwrecked Members of Armed Forces at Sea of 12 August 1949** (*T. I. A. S. 3363*), **cited herein as *GWS* Sea.**

(11) **Geneva Convention Relative to the Treatment of Prisoners of War of 12 August 1949** (*T. I. A. S. 3364*), **cited herein as *GPW.***

(12) **Geneva Convention Relative to the Protection of Civilian Persons in Time of War of 12 August 1949** (*T. I. A. S. 3365*), **cited herein as *GC.***

* * * *

6. Custom

Evidence of the customary law of war, arising from the general consent of States, may be found in judicial decisions, the writings of jurists, diplomatic correspondence, and other documentary material concerning the practice of States. Even though individual States may not be parties to or otherwise strictly bound by *H. IV* and *GPW 1929*, the former convention and the general principles of the latter have been held to be declaratory of the customary law of war, to which all States are subject.

The Preamble to the *HR* specifically provides:

Until a more complete code of the laws of war has been issued, the High Contracting Parties deem it expedient to declare that, in cases not included in the Regulations adopted by them, the inhabitants and the belligerents remain under the protection and the rule of the principles of the law of nations, as they result from the usages established among civilized peoples, from the laws of humanity, and the dictates of the public conscience.

Similarly, a common article of the Geneva Conventions of 1949 (*GWS, art. 63; GWS Sea, art. 62; GPW, art. 142; GC, art. 158*) provides that the denunciation of (withdrawal from) any of the Geneva Conventions of 1949, * * * **shall in no way impair the obligations which the Parties to the conflict shall remain bound to fulfil by virtue of the principles of the law of nations, as they result from the usages established among civilized peoples, from the laws of humanity and the dictates of the public conscience.**

7. Force of the Law of War

* * * *

b. Force of Treaties Under the Constitution. Under the Constitution of the United States, treaties constitute part of the "supreme Law of the Land" (art. VI, clause 2). In consequence, treaties relating to the law of war have a force equal to that of laws enacted by the Congress. Their provisions must be observed by both military and civilian personnel with the same strict regard for both the letter and spirit of the law which is required with respect to the Constitution and statutes enacted in pursuance thereof.

c. Force of Customary Law. The unwritten or customary law of war is binding upon all nations. It will be strictly observed by United States forces, subject only to such exceptions as shall have been directed by competent authority by way of legitimate reprisals for illegal conduct of the enemy (see par. 497). The customary law of war is part of the law of the United States and, insofar as it is not inconsistent with any treaty to which this country is a party or with a controlling executive or legislative act, is binding upon the United States, citizens of the United States, and other persons serving this country.

8. Situations to Which Law of War Applicable

a. Types of Hostilities. War may be defined as a legal condition of armed hostility between States. While it is usually accompanied by the commission of acts of violence, a state of war may exist prior to or subsequent to the use of force. The outbreak of war is usually accompanied by a declaration of war (see par. 20).

Instances of armed conflict without declaration of war may include, but are not necessarily limited to, the exercise of armed force pursuant to a recommendation, decision, or call by the United Nations, in the exercise of the inherent right of individual or collective self-defense against armed attack, or in the performance of enforcement measures through a regional arrangement, or otherwise, in conformity with appropriate provisions of the United Nations Charter.

b. Customary Law. The customary law of war applies to all cases of declared war or any other armed conflict which may arise between the United States and other nations, even if the state of war is not recognized by one of them. The customary law is also applicable to all cases of occupation of foreign territory by the exercise of armed force, even if the occupation meets with no armed resistance.

c. Treaties. Treaties governing land warfare are applicable to various forms of war and armed conflict as provided by their terms. The Hague Conventions apply to "war." Common Article 2 of the Geneva Conventions of 1949 states:

In addition to the provisions which shall be implemented in peacetime, the present Convention shall apply to all cases of declared war or of any other armed conflict which may arise between two or more of the High Contracting Parties, even if the state of war is not recognized by one of them.

The Convention shall also apply to all cases of partial or total occupation of the territory of a High Contracting Party, even if the said occupation meets with no armed resistance.

Although one of the Powers in conflict may not be a party to the present Convention, the Powers who are parties thereto shall remain bound by it in their mutual relations. They shall furthermore be bound by the Convention in relation to the said Power, if the latter accepts and applies the provisions thereof. (*GWS, GWS Sea, GPW, GC, art. 2.*)

* * * *

9. Applicability of Law of Land Warfare in Absence of a Declaration of War

As the customary law of war applies to cases of international armed conflict and to the forcible occupation of enemy territory generally as well as to declared war in its strict sense, a declaration of war is not an essential condition of the application of this body of law. Similarly, treaties relating to "war" may become operative notwithstanding the absence of a formal declaration of war.

10. When Law of Land Warfare Ceases To Be Applicable

The law of land warfare generally ceases to be applicable upon:

a. The termination of a war by agreement, normally in the form of a treaty of peace; or

b. The termination of a war by unilateral declaration of one of the parties, provided the other party does not continue hostilities or otherwise decline to recognize the act of its enemy; or

c. The complete subjugation of an enemy State and its allies, if prior to *a* or *b;* or

d. The termination of a declared war or armed conflict by simple cessation of hostilities.

However, certain designated provisions of the Geneva Conventions of 1949 (see *GC, art. 6;* par 249 herein) continue to be operative, notwithstanding the termination of any antecedent hostilities, during the continuance of a military occupation. Insofar as the unwritten law of war and the Hague Regulations extend certain fundamental safeguards to the persons and property of the populations of occupied territory, their protection continues until the termination of any occupation having its origin in the military supremacy of the occupant, notwithstanding the fact the Geneva Convention relative to the Protection of Civilian Persons may have ceased to be applicable.

11. Civil War

a. Customary Law. The customary law of war becomes applicable to civil war upon recognition of the rebels as belligerents.

b. Geneva Conventions of 1949.

In the case of armed conflict not of an international character occurring in the territory of one of the High Contracting Parties, each Party to the conflict shall be bound to apply, as a minimum, the following provisions:

> **(1) Persons taking no active part in the hostilities, including members of armed forces who have laid down their arms and those placed *hors de combat* by sickness, wounds, detention, or any other cause, shall in all circumstances be treated humanely, without any adverse distinction**

founded on race, colour, religion or faith, sex, birth or wealth, or any other similar criteria.

To this end, the following acts are and shall remain prohibited at any time and in any place whatsoever with respect to the above-mentioned persons:

(a) violence to life and person, in particular murder of all kinds, mutilation, cruel treatment and torture;

(b) taking of hostages;

(c) outrages upon personal dignity, in particular, humiliating and degrading treatment;

(d) the passing of sentences and the carrying out of executions without previous judgment pronounced by a regularly constituted court, affording all the judicial guarantees which are recognized as indispensable by civilized peoples.

(2) The wounded and sick shall be collected and cared for.

An impartial humanitarian body, such as the International Committee of the Red Cross, may offer its services to the Parties to the conflict.

The Parties to the conflict should further endeavour to bring into force, by means of special agreements, all or part of the other provisions of the present Convention.

* * * *

Section II. CRIMES UNDER INTERNATIONAL LAW

498. Crimes Under International Law

Any person, whether a member of the armed forces or a civilian, who commits an act which constitutes a crime under international law is responsible therefor and liable to punishment. Such offenses in connection with war comprise:

a. Crimes against peace.

b. Crimes against humanity.

c. War crimes.

Although this manual recognizes the criminal responsibility of individuals for those offenses which may comprise any of the foregoing types of crimes, members of the armed forces will normally be concerned only with those offenses constituting "war crimes."

499. War Crimes

The term "war crime" is the technical expression for a violation of the law of war by any person or persons, military or civilian. Every violation of the law of war is a war crime.

500. Conspiracy, Incitement, Attempts, and Complicity

Conspiracy, direct incitement, and attempts to commit, as well as complicity in the commission of, crimes against peace, crimes against humanity, and war crimes are punishable.

501. Responsibility for Acts of Subordinates

In some cases, military commanders may be responsible for war crimes committed by subordinate members of the armed forces, or other persons subject to their control. Thus, for instance, when troops commit massacres and atrocities against the civilian population of occupied territory or against prisoners of war, the responsibility may rest not only with the actual perpetrators but also with the commander. Such a responsibility arises directly when the acts in question have been committed in pursuance of an order of the commander concerned. The commander is also responsible if he has actual knowledge, or should have knowledge, through reports received by him or through other means, that troops or other persons subject to his control are about to commit or have committed a war crime and he fails to take the necessary and reasonable steps to insure compliance with the law of war or to punish violators thereof.

* * * *

CHAPTER I
PRISONERS OF WAR AND
THE WOUNDED IN THE FIELD

The following Articles from International Conventions relevant to this chapter are quoted in full:

Geneva Conventions
12 August 1949
Article 3.
Common to All Three Geneva Conventions

In the case of armed conflict not of an international character occurring in the territory of one of the High Contracting Parties, each Party to the conflict shall be bound to apply, as a minimum, the following provisions:

(1) Persons taking no active part in the hostilities, including members of armed forces who have laid down their arms and those placed *hors de combat* by sickness, wounds, detention, or any other cause, shall in all circumstances be treated humanely, without any adverse distinction founded on race, colour, religion or faith, sex, birth or wealth, or any other similar criteria.

To this end, the following acts are and shall remain prohibited at any time and in any place whatsoever with respect to the above-mentioned persons:

(a) violence to life and person, in particular murder of all kinds, mutilation, cruel treatment and torture;

(b) taking of hostages;

(c) outrages upon personal dignity, in particular humiliating and degrading treatment;

(d) the passing of sentences and the carrying out of executions without previous judgment pronounced by a regularly constituted court, affording all the judicial guarantees which are recognized as indispensable by civilized peoples.

(2) The wounded and sick shall be collected and cared for.

An impartial humanitarian body, such as the International Committee of the Red Cross, may offer its services to the Parties of the conflict.

The Parties to the conflict should further endeavor to bring into force, by means of special agreements, all or part of the other provisions of the present Convention.

The application of the preceding provisions shall not affect the legal status of the Parties to the conflict.

Geneva Convention Relative to the Treatment of Prisoners of War
12 August 1949
(Short reference: Geneva—Prisoners of War)

Article 12.

Prisoners of war are in the hands of the enemy Power, but not of the individuals or military units who have captured them. Irrespective of the individual responsibilities that may exist, the Detaining Power is responsible for the treatment given them.

Prisoners of war may only be transferred by the Detaining Power to a Power which is a party to the Convention and after the Detaining Power has satisfied itself of the willingness and ability of such transferee Power to apply the Convention. When prisoners of war are transferred under such circumstances, responsibility for the application of the Convention rests on the Power accepting them while they are in its custody.

Nevertheless, if that Power fails to carry out the provisions of the Convention in any important respect, the Power by whom the prisoners of war were transferred shall, upon being notified by the Protecting Power, take effective measures to correct the situation or shall request the return of the prisoners of war. Such requests must be complied with.

Article 13.

Prisoners of war must at all times be humanely treated. Any unlawful act or omission by the Detaining Power causing death or seriously endangering the health of a prisoner of war in its custody is prohibited, and will be regarded as a serious breach of the present Convention. In particular, no prisoner of war may be subjected to physical mutilation or to medical or scientific experiments of any kind which are not justified by the medical, dental or hospital treatment of the prisoner concerned and carried out in his interest.

Likewise, prisoners of war must at all times be protected, particularly against acts of violence or intimidation and against insults and public curiosity.

Measures of reprisal against prisoners of war are prohibited.

Article 17.

Every prisoner of war, when questioned on the subject, is bound to give only his surname, first names and rank, date of birth, and army, regimental, personal or serial number, or failing this, equivalent information.

If he wilfully infringes this rule, he may render himself liable to a restriction of the privileges accorded to his rank or status.

No physical or mental torture, nor any other form of coercion, may be inflicted on prisoners of war to secure from them information of any kind whatever. Prisoners of war who refuse to answer may not be threatened, insulted, or exposed to unpleasant or disadvantageous treatment of any kind.

Prisoners of war who, owing to their physical or mental condition, are unable to state their identity, shall be handed over to the medical service. The identity of such prisoners shall be established by all possible means, subject to the provisions of the preceding paragraph.

The questioning of prisoners of war shall be carried out in a language which they understand.

Article 130.

Grave breaches to which the preceding Article relates shall be those involving any of the following acts, if committed against persons or property protected by the Convention: wilful killing, torture or inhuman treatment, including biological experiments, wilfully causing great suffering or serious injury to body or health, compelling a prisoner of war to serve in the forces of the hostile Power, or wilfully depriving a prisoner of war of the rights of fair and regular trial prescribed in this Convention.

Geneva Convention
for the Amelioration of the Condition
of the Wounded and Sick in Armed Forces in the Field
12 August 1949

(Short reference: Geneva—Wounded)

Article 15.

At all times, and particularly after an engagement, Parties to the conflict shall, without delay, take all possible measures to search for and collect the wounded and sick, to protect them against pillage and ill-treatment, to ensure their adequate care, and to search for the dead and prevent their being despoiled.

Whenever circumstances permit, an armistice or a suspension of fire shall be arranged, or local arrangements made, to permit the removal, exchange and transport of the wounded left on the battlefield.

Likewise, local arrangements may be concluded between Parties to the conflict for the removal or exchange of wounded and sick from a besieged or encircled area, and for the passage of medical and religious personnel and equipment on their way to that area.

Article 17.

Parties to the conflict shall ensure that burial or cremation of the dead, carried out individually as far as circumstances permit, is preceded by a careful examination, if possible by a medical examination, of the bodies, with a view to confirming death, establishing identity and enabling a report to be made. One half of the double identity disc, or the identity disc itself if it is a single disc, should remain on the body.

Bodies shall not be cremated except for imperative reasons of hygiene or for motives based on the religion of the deceased. In case of cremation, the circumstances and reasons for cremation shall be stated in detail in the death certificate or on the authenticated list of the dead.

They shall further ensure that the dead are honourably interred, if possible according to the rites of the religion to which they belonged, that their graves are respected, grouped if possible according to the nationality of the deceased, property maintained and marked so that they may always be found. For this purpose, they shall organize at the commencement of hostilities an Official Graves Registration Service, to allow subsequent exhumations and to ensure the identification of bodies, whatever the site of the graves, and the possible transportation to the home country. These provisions shall likewise apply to the ashes, which shall be kept by the Graves Registration Service until proper disposal thereof in accordance with the wishes of the home country.

Article 50

Grave breaches to which the preceding Article relates shall be those involving any of the following acts, if committed against persons or property protected by the Convention: wilful killing, torture or inhuman treatment, including biological experiments, wilfully causing great suffering or serious injury to body or health, and extensive destruction and appropriation of property, not justified by military necessity and carried out unlawfully and wantonly.

Hague Convention No. IV, Annex
Regulations Respecting the Laws and Customs of War on Land
18 October 1907   (Short reference: Hague—Laws)

Article 4

Prisoners of war are in the power of the hostile Government, but not of the individuals or corps who capture them.

They must be humanely treated.

All their personal belongings, except arms, horses, and military papers, remain their property.

Article 23

In addition to the prohibitions provided by special Conventions, it is especially forbidden—

(c) To kill or wound an enemy who, having laid down his arms, or having no longer means of defence, has surrendered at discretion.

See also (pages 29-42) the following additional Articles relevant to this chapter: Geneva—Prisoners of War: 4, 5, 7, 14, 16, 20, 22, 82, 129, 131; Geneva—Wounded: 14.

PROTECTION OF THE WOUNDED

The Making of a Quagmire, David Halberstam, 1964, p 119 *

...It is true that the Vietcong were better at hating than our Vietnamese, though at times Government troops could be very cruel. Once, south of Bac Lieu, Vietnamese Marines had fought a particularly bitter battle but had captured a number of Vietcong prisoners. According to a Vietnamese friend of mine who was there, the enemy were very cocky and started shouting anti-American slogans and Vietnamese curses at their captors. The Marines, who had lost an officer that day and were in no mood to be called lackeys of the Americans, simply lined up the seventeen guerrillas and shot them down in cold blood. "They had to believe their own propaganda," my friend said.

14 Jun 64   New York Times Magazine **
              Neil Sheehan: "When the Rains Come to Vietnam"

...Frequently the wounded drown in the filth because they are unable to pull themselves to the surface again after being hit and falling forward.

---

* Where a book is quoted in this report, the title is underlined, and the author, year of publication, and page where the selection begins are given. The publisher is listed in the full citation to be found among the credits, p. vii et seq.

** Where a newspaper story or magazine article is quoted in this report, the date the story was filed is given, and the place of filing if stated. The name of the periodical and date of publication are given; also the name of the writer if stated and the story title if any. Permissions to reprint will be found on p. vii et seq.

Later, their bodies are pulled out and stacked in neat rows along the narrow dikes, like broken toy soldiers, until their comrades load the corpses into the helicopters for evacuation.

...Any black-clad Vietcong dead abandoned by the guerrillas, who usually carry off their casualties, are left where they have fallen for the peasants to bury. In a few hours, the broiling tropical sun, which reappears between downpours, bloats and ripens the bodies until the smell of death cloys the air like a sickening perfume.

The New Face of War, Malcolm W. Browne, 1965, p. 58

...Viet Cong military prowess has impressed many Americans in Viet Nam, and some helicopter men frankly respect their enemy.

I returned from an operation once in a Huey that also was carrying a wounded Viet Cong prisoner, his arms bound behind him, and a Vietnamese Army Lieutenant. The lieutenant was on a seat between the two American door gunners, and the prisoner was on the floor in front of the officer. As the helicopter took off, the prisoner groaned slightly, and the officer gave him a sharp kick. One of the American gunners lost his temper and did something that could have (but did not) get him court-martialed.

Yanking the Vietnamese officer roughly by the shoulder, the gunner yelled, "Knock it off, you. The Viet Cong are better soldiers than you'll ever be, and this man deserves at least the proper treatment of a prisoner of war."

18 Jun 65   Time
             DONGXOAI, June 18

...Laughing Larry Luong fights the Viet Cong because he is a professional soldier, and also because the Communists killed his peasant father by dragging him across a thorny durian patch, then burying him up to his neck for several days before decapitating him. Larry customarily shoots Viet Cong prisoners, giggling the while, not because he is cruel, but because he knows that if he hands them over to local authorities, they would only be released to rejoin the Communists.

19 Nov 65   New York Times, Neil Sheehan
             SAIGON, South Vietnam, Nov 18

...Reports from the Iadrang valley said that the ambush against the Airmobile battalion was sprung in the afternoon while the Americans were marching toward a new position from a small clearing about a mile and a half to the south west.

...As soon as the ambush was sprung, the battalion radioed for air support. United States Air Force, Navy and Marine jets and propeller-driven fighter bombers swooped into the valley.

Planes dipped to treetop level and raked the Communist attackers with bombs, 20-mm. cannon fire and flaming napalm. A few of the bombs were believed to have landed among American troops in the confusion.

...Throughout the night, aircraft and artillery pulverized the area around the perimeter with bombs, high-explosive shells and napalm fire bombs as other planes dropped flares to illuminate the scene.

...Sprawled among the wounded and dead Americans were the khaki-clad bodies of North Vietnamese soldiers, Chinese-made and Soviet-made rifles lying beside them.

Witnesses said that some of the Americans had been so enraged by the sight that they shot a few wounded North Vietnamese out of hand.

22 Nov 65   (See Note Page 20)
                PLEIKU, VIET NAM, Nov 22

   ...The fighting brought out other qualities in some. One soldier shot
every wounded enemy soldier who moved as his decimated unit policed up a
battlefield. He had heard that two days earlier three American prisoners
had been found bound hand and foot and shot through the head. He said he
was exacting revenge.
   There was another reason to shoot the enemy wounded lying scattered
among the trees. One blew himself up with a grenade as a squad approached
him, nearly taking them with him. Another tried to pull a pin from a grenade as a medic was taking his pulse, but he lacked the strength to remove
it and fell back in a faint. He was shot.

29 Nov 65   Newsweek

   ...Some of the American wounded, caught by the enemy, had apparently
been given the coup de grace with a bullet in the head. "They were not
interested in taking prisoners," said McTigue grimly. But neither were
some of the Americans. In one place, the GIs came upon three wounded
North Vietnamese. One lay huddled under a tree, a smile on his face.
"You won't smile anymore," snapped one of the soldiers, pumping bullets
into his body. The other two met the same fate.

The New Face of War, Malcolm W. Browne, 1965, p. 4-7.

   ...The other two landing craft were going ashore about one mile farther
up the river. The idea of this exercise, it was explained to me, was to
seize two sets of hamlets running back from the river front, trapping the reported Viet Cong battalion in the wide expanse of rice fields in between.
   ...I was standing on a high path running parallel to the river near a
machine-gun position, looking out over the field where our Viet Cong
battalion was supposed to be trapped. The green rice was nearly waist high,
and there might easily be a battalion concealed in this field for all anyone
know.
   Suddenly, a man leapt up about fifty yards away and began to run. This
was it!
   Every machine gun, Tommy gun, rifle and pistol in our sector poured
fire at that man, and I was amazed at how long he continued to run. But
finally he went down, silently, without a scream.
   Our little army continued to pour intense fire into the field and several
huts until it occurred to someone that no one was shooting back, and it
might be safe to move forward a little.
   Some of the troops began to move into the huts, shooting as they went.
   ...We found him on his back in the mud, four bullet holes stitched
across the top of his naked chest. He was wearing only black shorts. He
was alive and conscious, moving his legs and arms, his head lolling back
and forth. There was blood on his lips.
   The Dan Ve squad, all young peasant boys, looked down at the man and
laughed, perhaps in embarrassment. Laughter in Viet Nam does not always
signify amusement.
   Perhaps as an act of mercy, perhaps as sheer cruelty, one of the men
picked up a heavy stake lying in the mud and rammed one end of (sic) it into
the ground next to the wounded man's throat. Then he forced the stake down
over the throat, trying to throttle the man. The man continued to move.
Someone stamped on the free end of the stake to break the wounded man's
neck, but the stake broke instead. Then another man tried stamping on the
man's throat, but somehow the spark of life still was too strong. Finally,
the whole group laughed, and walked back to the path.
   The firing had stopped altogether, and several old peasant men were
talking to the officers of our party. Two of the old men had a pole and a
large fish net.

The peasants--I think they were hamlet elders--walked out to the wounded man, rolled him into the fish net, and with the net slung between them on the pole, carried him back to the path. As they laid him out on the ground, two women, both dressed in baggy black trousers and blouses, ran up from one of the huts. One of them put a hand to her mouth as she saw the wounded man, whom she recognized as her husband.

She dashed back to her hut and returned in a moment carrying a bucket, which she filled with black water from the rice field. Sitting down with her husband's head cradled in her lap, she poured paddy water over his wounds to clean off the clotting blood. Occasionally she would stroke his forehead, muttering something.

He died about ten minutes later. The woman remained seated, one hand over her husband's eyes. Slowly, she looked around at the troops, and then she spotted me. Her eyes fixed on me in an expression that still haunts me sometimes. She was not weeping, and her face showed neither grief nor fury; it was unfathomably blank.

I moved away some distance to where the operation commander was jabbering into a field telephone. When his conversation ended, I handed him a 500-piastre note (worth about $5.00), asking him to give it to the widow as some small compensation.

"Monsieur Browne, please do not be sentimental. That man undoubtedly was a Viet Cong agent, since these hamlets have been Viet Cong strongholds for years. This is war. However, I will give her the money, if you like."

Dec 65   Ramparts
               Bernard Fall: "This isn't Munich, It's Spain"

...In this war, there is no respect for the wounded. The Communist prisoner in the photograph had been shot in the back. He was bleeding when I found him lying on the floor in a Vietnamese Army Command Post. A journalist from a New York paper came in and asked to photograph him. The South Vietnamese officer in the room raised the wounded man matter-of-factly and propped him against a table leg for the photographer. The prisoner grimaced in pain.

I told an American officer who was with the unit that the man was wounded and should get some attention. His answer: "Yes, I know he needs help, but there isn't anything I can do about it. He's in Vietnamese hands. That is why I walked away, don't you see?" I saw. I also walked away and said nothing.

5 Feb 67   (See Note Page 20)
               SAIGON, Feb 5

...There have been news reports and pictures of rough treatment of prisoners taken by South Vietnamese military units in the field. There also have been substantiated accounts of on-the-spot executions of prisoners. Torture of prisoners in the field has not been uncommon.

While American authorities concede this is true, they maintain that it has happened in the first stages when prisoners are seized. When prisoners reach higher unit headquarters levels, this sort of treatment is ruled out, they say.

MUTILATION OF THE DEAD

27 Jun 65   New York Times Magazine
              Jack Langguth, "Ambush"
              SAIGON

...Burying the dead weighs heavily with the Vietnamese. Vietcong soldiers withdraw from their battles with the dead across their backs or piled into ox-carts. Their thoroughness has often made Vietcong casualties all but impossible to estimate. Both the Government and the Communist leaders know the importance of proper burials to the morale of the survivors.

13 Dec 65   New York Times (See Note Page 20)
            BENCAT, SOUTH VIETNAM, Dec 12

Hatchets used like tomahawks replace bayonets in the hands of some
G.I.s today in a hand-to-hand jungle fight.

A hatchet squad of Bravo Company, First Battalion, 502nd Regiment,
101st Airborne Division, routed a Vietcong unit after a savage encounter
that resembled Indian fighting on the early American frontier.

Moving down a trail in the tangled jungle of Zone D, 35 miles north of
Saigon, an area long a Communist stronghold, Bravo Company encountered
a Vietcong unit.

Sgt. Frederick Lopez, from Santa Barbara, Cal., dropped to his knees
and opened fire. The Vietcong ran off the trail into thick jungle. A half-
dozen G.I.s, some with faces blackened, unslung hatchets and slipped into
the underbrush in pursuit.

A grenade bounced onto the trail, wounding four Americans as it exploded. Helicopters picked them up later.

In the hand-to-hand fight, one of the Vietcong was killed. The Americans said he was the one who had thrown the grenade.

The fighting men had bought the hatchets themselves, paying about $1
each for them. In a jungle war, the soldiers say, bayonets are unwieldy.

Bravo Company is commanded by Capt. Thomas Taylor, son of the
former United States Ambassador to South Vietnam, Maxwell D. Taylor.

May 66   True
            Malcolm Browne, "We're Turning into Animals"

...The jungle changes men. Tempers run thin and men learn to hate
as they have never hated before in their lives. Take Lt. Col. Henry
Emerson for example. Emerson is commander of the 2nd Battalion, 502nd
Airborne. He offered a case of Scotch to the first one of his men to kill a
Viet Cong with a hatchet, and every GI was trying for the booze, enlisted
men and officers alike. There were Pfcs from the back country of West
Virginia who strapped hatchets to their belts and there was even Capt.
Thomas Taylor, commander of Bravo Company and the son of the former
Army Chief of Staff and U.S. Ambassador to Viet Nam, Gen. Maxwell D.
Taylor. They all packed hatchets and it was called the "Hatchet Battalion."

Special "hatchet teams" — commandos with blackened faces and nerves
of ice — would often run small patrols deep in enemy territory, sometimes
encountering swarms of VC and then having to fight their way out against
impossible odds.

One day the column crunched along and a jungle bird warbled a little
way off. There was a flicker of movement, and suddenly it was there on
the trail — an ugly black grenade with a wisp of smoke shooting from its
wooden handle. It was there for only a split second. Chinese-type potato-
masher grenades have short fuses. When it went off, four Americans were
hurt, one of them screaming in agony.

The crash of the explosion left GIs stunned, momentarily, but then
some began firing and others charged into the thick of the jungle, intent on
getting the Viet Cong who had thrown the grenade. He got only a few hundred feet away before a GI found him, wounded, and won himself a case of
Scotch with four or five swift strokes of his hatchet.

The GI came out, his face an expressionless mask. He held up the
severed head by the hair. Some of his buddies took turns hefting the grisly
trophy. Then it was paraded around the clearing where the four wounded GIs
had been taken.

They buried the thing in the jungle, but one sweating trooper who saw
the beheading almost threw up. "Thank God, I have only 49 days left in
this sink-hole," he screamed. "We're turning into animals!"

Beheading the enemy in Viet Nam is normal, only now Americans were
doing it, and in this case to a wounded foe. "I hope there is no misunder-

standing about this," the CO remarked. "That VC threw a grenade at my men and he was killed in battle."

But some newsmen had seen it all and there were quiet repercussions. This wasn't the chivalrous kind of combat Americans are supposed to favor. The Scotch offer was discontinued and fears that publicity about the incident would cause a stink led to dropping the "Hatchet Battalion" label.

1 Aug 65   New York Herald Tribune
              SAIGON

A Vietnamese counter-insurgency team borne by a United States helicopter yesterday swooped on a Viet Cong strategy session — held in a cemetery tomb — and killed an important Communist leader, U.S. sources disclosed.

...The body of the Viet Cong leader was carried into the town square at Vinh Long as a warning to other guerrillas in the area.

16 Oct 65   (See Note Page 20)

...Versace seemed convinced that the majority of the Vietcong followers were misled by false ideals.

...He did not believe in carrying a weapon on operations except for a hidden pistol. He wanted to show the oppressed people in Camau that he came to them with the Vietnamese troops to tell them about the better life he offered.

...Two days later, we flew into a Special Forces Outpost, a heavily fortified camp along a canal — triangular with bunkers and barbed wire. There were 400 rough-tough Vietnamese militiamen and 12 American Special Forces men.

Versace went there to talk to prisoners. One of the prisoners was hanged on a tree near the camp as an example to the Viet Cong and hostile people living opposite the camp and along the canal.

14 Nov 65   The Sun (Baltimore) (See Note Page 20)
              BAU BANG, VIET NAM, Nov 13

If war looked at its face in the mirror the morning after, this is what it would have seen along a highway north of Saigon today:

The burnt out ruins of a pastel-painted village still smoking.

Viet Cong bodies sprawled by the side of the road in attitudes of chaotic repose — legs and arms stiffened in grotesque statuary — with the flies buzzing about in the humid tropical air.

Maj. Gen. Jonathan Seaman, Commander of the U.S. 1st Infantry Division, handing out purple hearts to American wounded, arrayed on canvas stretchers on the shaded patio of a rubber plantation.

Anxious Vietnamese farmers in coolie hats awaiting permission from an American Colonel to go into the woods and butcher a water buffalo killed in the Highway 13 battle Friday between U.S. infantrymen and the Viet Cong.

...Killing 10 Communists for every American lost, the big red one claimed 146 Viet Cong dead and laid a number of them out by the side of the road to prove it.

"It's good propaganda for V.C. in the area to see them sprawled out here," said an American captain, "And it lets the rest of our boys know that we've been in a fight."

As always in Viet Nam, in battle or lull, the incredibly over-loaded suburban busses rolled by. Sullen faces stared out of the grimy windows at the sprawled bodies.

...Just beyond the dismantled village, a bulldozer droned back and forth, digging a grave 12 feet deep for a tangle of bodies, inseparable and unidentifiable, all the victims of the artillery barrage.

"We were lucky," said a Colonel from the division. "As far as we can tell, no women or children were killed in the attack on the village. We hated to flatten that village, because we're going to be here a long time and we have to get along with these people and pacify them some day, but that's where the mortar and recoilless rifle was coming from."

4 Aug 66   (See Note Page 20)
               SAIGON, Aug 4

Thousands of unmarked graves, some containing the bodies of as many as 30 Viet Cong, dot the battlefields of South Viet Nam.

The crude graves, soon overgrown and hidden by jungle growth, are mute testimony to the Viet Nam War.

A Viet Cong soldier goes into battle knowing that the best burial he can expect will be a hurried dumping into a shallow hole. This he will get if his own comrades find him.

The dead Viet Cong found by government troops may be dumped into a river and eventually carried out to sea, bulldozed into a common grave with others killed around him, or left in a jungle clearing as a crude warning to other Viet Cong who might pass that way.

A skull whitened in the tropical rain is a common sight. Enemy bodies sometimes come down the Saigon River from the battle-scarred Hobo Woods and the Iron Triangle.

The Vietnamese government takes the view that the Viet Cong are bandits and don't deserve even a minimal funeral ceremony. The government makes no attempt to identify enemy dead, other than searching the bodies for documents.

Australian troops operating out of Vung Tau attempted to have dead Viet Cong buried in a cemetery at the province capital. The province chief refused.

In contrast, only a few American bodies have been lost on the battlefield. Dead Americans, Australians and New Zealanders are flown home. South Korean dead are cremated and their ashes sent home.

The dead of the South Vietnamese Forces are buried with full military honors when their bodies are recovered. Most Vietnamese dead are recovered because the Viet Cong rarely hold a battlefield for more than a few hours.

The Viet Cong can sometimes be kind to the dead. Bodies of American crewmen from downed aircraft and helicopters have been found in neat graves, their personal belongings buried with them.

But some bodies are mutilated.

Most Vietnamese have a superstitious fear about the fate of their bodies. Ancestor worship, an important part of their polyglot religious beliefs, requires that a body be ceremonially buried.

5 Nov 66   (See Note Page 20)
               SAIGON

...In other developments:

U.S. military officials reported that Communists are not clearing their dead from the battlefields as they once did. "It's a matter of pressure on them," said one U.S. general. "They still try to get the bodies away, but because of pressure and pursuit by our troops, it is getting tougher and tougher for them to bring it off."

Removing the dead is one of the main principles of guerrilla warfare, since it denies the enemy accurate knowledge of his success. Also, Vietnamese custom dictates proper care for the dead, and this is usually accomplished when at all possible.

9 Nov 66   New York Times

...As Colonel Whitted spoke, American troops were loading 16 Vietcong bodies on helicopters.

"We're giving the bodies back to Victor Charles," the colonel said. "We'll dump the bodies in the next clearing and the V.C. can bury them if they want to."

8 Mar 67   New York Post (See Note Page 20)
             DA NANG, Mar 8

The U.S. Marine Corps today released the record of a trial in which a young Leatherneck said he shot a Vietnamese civilian and then cut off his ear because he thought "it was a common thing to do after a kill."

The testimony was from Pfc. Ronald C. Piatkowski, 18, of Trenton, New Jersey, who was convicted of attempted murder and sentenced to 10 years in prison and a dishonorable discharge.

He was accused of helping to murder a Vietnamese civilian, Nguyen Qua, and mutilating the body by cutting off the left ear.

Piatkowski told the general court-martial during his trial Jan. 15-16 that he was one of 10 Marines who left their base camp at Chu Lai last Sept. 22 on a combat reconnaissance patrol through two nearby villages.

...Piatkowski said he heard shots and turned and saw a Vietnamese man.

Piatkowski said he saw his squad leader shooting at the man "and I seen the whole first team open fire."

He testified the man ran and fell behind some bushes. Piatkowski walked over.

"Here the man was lying behind this heavy brush, face up," he said.

"His eyes were fluttering and his jaw moved. I called my squad leader and said that the man was moving.

"I asked what I should do. He replied back 'What do you think you should do? Shoot him.' Then I...I shot the man. From there I asked my squad leader if I could cut off the man's ear. I did so and they helped me drag the man over to the bushes."

The defense attorney asked Piatkowski why he shot the man.

"Sir, I really don't know why," he said. "I really don't know why I shot at the man. I figured he was dead when he was lying there. The squad leader told me to shoot him. I just fired."

When asked by his lawyer why he cut off the man's ear, Piatkowski replied from the stand:

"Sir, I heard about it... I had heard stories about this when I was back in the States, when I was in Boot Camp and I.T.R. (Infantry Training Regiment) and counter guerrilla warfare school. Men that had been in Vietnam on the line, they talked about these places and I talked to them after classes to find out what Vietnam was really like and I heard stories about them doing this, and things like this. I thought actually, it was a common thing to do after a kill."

12 Jun 67   Nation
             Desmond Smith, "There Must Have Been Easier Wars"

..."Don't film," said the young lieutenant, with a smile.

...The lieutenant had been referring to the scene before us: A trooper was spraying insect repellent on a human ear. There was no blood. It was quite small and brown and hairless.

"No, sir," I said, "we won't film that."

But I was curious to know more about this ear fetish. I had often heard that though it was forbidden, the practice of clipping ears was widespread. A PIO back at An Khe had told us that the going rate for a VC ear among souvenir hunters was $30. But that was just talk; this was the real thing. So I walked out of the coconut grove and across the paddy dike. There I saw my first atrocity. His head slumped against the bank, a look of agony frozen beneath the shock of black hair. Both ears had been severed at the root so all that remained were two bloody circles about the size of 50¢ pieces. Someone had thrown a Pepsi-Cola can on the bank of the paddy, and the red, white, and blue container had come to rest on the boy's shoulder. He didn't look to have been more than 15. An impulse made me throw the can away. I remember thinking that this was the first time I'd ever seen the face of the enemy, and it was just a kid. Winning hearts and minds? I almost threw up at the thought.

THE RESPONSIBILITY OF THE UNITED STATES

21 Jul 66   St. Louis Post-Dispatch
WASHINGTON, July 20

Sen. Stephen M. Young, D-Ohio, said today the South Vietnamese are executing many prisoners of war turned over to them by American fighting forces. Young said that "in the name of humanity and decency" (the United States) should stop transferring Viet Cong prisoners to South Vietnamese units...

"Probably more of these prisoners are executed than are permitted to survive," he told the Senate.

At the same time, Young said, the conscience of the world would find it revolting if North Viet Nam tried and executed American airmen held prisoner there...

20 Jul 66   Congressional Record — Senate, July 20, 1966, 15638

MR. YOUNG of Ohio. Mr. President, the United States is signatory to the Geneva Convention requiring humane treatment of prisoners of war. It has been our policy and practice throughout all of our involvement in the miserable civil war raging in Vietnam to surrender and turn over to officers of the ARVN forces all Viet Cong prisoners of war we have taken. Our officers in the field in South Vietnam and our officials in Washington, in the name of humanity and decency, should rescind this policy and practice. It is well known that not only are these prisoners of war taken by Americans in combat mistreated following the time they are turned over to South Vietnamese authorities, but also the facts are, and they are well known, that many of these prisoners of war are executed. Probably more of these prisoners of war are executed than are permitted to survive. How can we Americans evade responsibility for the mistreatment of these war prisoners? The Geneva Convention, which had the all-out support of our Government, when the provisions were written relative to humane treatment of prisoners of war and agreeing to those provisions, makes us responsible.

The Convention terms this a contingent responsibility. Article 12 of the Convention provides that the transfer of prisoners of war may be made to allies with a contingent responsibility that such allies — in this particular, the South Vietnamese — do not mistreat the prisoners of war.

...An argument has been made by some that were the United States to declare war against the Government of North Vietnam, then we would be obligated to treat humanely all prisoners of war taken by us. I assert that even without a formal declaration of war, the demands of humanity and the provisions of the Convention apply to us and should be respected by civilian officials of the U.S. Government and our military officers in the field in Vietnam. This regardless of whether or not there is a declaration of war by us against the Government of North Vietnam.

It is urgent, it seems to me, that we reverse our policy regarding treatment of prisoners of war in Vietnam and accept our responsibility to treat all war prisoners we take with decency and humanity.

25 Jul 66   New York Post, Peter Hamill

The fact is that American soldiers — who are now doing almost all of the fighting — are violating the Geneva Convention relative to the Treatment of

Prisoners of War every day. It is a violation for soldiers of one army to turn over prisoners of war to soldiers of another army. And that is precisely what we do.

Every correspondent in Vietnam knows this, and has seen it for himself. An American unit will move into a village, or an area, and round up every male. A South Vietnamese liaison officer will then interrogate each man, and if he believes the man is a Viet Cong guerrilla, or even a sympathizer, the man will be taken off to a detainment camp. After detailed interrogation, he is usually executed.

That is why there are no huge POW camps springing up in the American West, as they did during the Second World War, and why, in South Viet Nam, officials only smile at your naivete when you ask to visit an internment camp.

28 Jul 65   New York Times, Lloyd Garrison
                WASHINGTON, July 27

The Administration is taking steps toward insuring that both sides in the Vietnam conflict abide by the principles of the Geneva Convention in treating prisoners of war.

Informed sources said today that the Administration's concern arose in part from widespread publicity given to the torture of Vietcong captives by South Vietnamese troops.

The State Department disclosed that it was conducting discussions with the South Vietnamese Government in an effort to curb what is reported to be the frequent use of torture by South Vietnamese troops to extract information.

In recent months numerous news photographs of such excesses have appeared in the United States and abroad.

The State Department confirmed also that Secretary of State Dean Rusk talked two weeks ago with Samuel A. Gonard of Switzerland the head of the International Committee of the Red Cross, about moves to improve the treatment of prisoners by both South Vietnamese authorities and the Vietcong.

5 Aug 66   (See Note Page 20)
                SAIGON, Aug 5

The prisoner of war is the odd man out in the Viet Nam War.

In North and South Viet Nam there are about 25,000 of them, by unofficial estimate. Untold numbers have vanished. About 23,000 are held by the South. The Communists hold a few thousand at least, including more than 100 Americans.

The Geneva Convention providing for the humane treatment of war prisoners gets scant attention either North or South. The United States is trying to influence both its friends and its foes to stick to the rules. U. S. concern increased when the Communist Regime paraded American pilots through Hanoi and threatened to try them as war criminals.

The United States has lost more than 300 planes over the north, some with two men aboard and one with at least eight. Although many airmen were rescued by helicopters, far more are listed as missing in action.

Through July 21, official U. S. figures list 212 Americans missing in North and South Viet Nam. Another 62 are "confirmed captured" in the North and South. Five have died in prison. Thirty two once listed as missing have returned, at least four having escaped from Red prison camps.

Hanoi Radio periodically carries broadcasts purportedly made by some of the captives. Some letters occasionally come out to families. Such communications are long on propaganda and short on news. The International Red Cross has not been permitted to inspect any North Vietnamese camps.

In South Viet Nam the Communist forces hold at least another 28 Americans whose plight is even more mysterious. The actual number must be higher.

The men who have been captured in ground fighting are held in crude camps in Viet Cong-controlled jungle areas.

A few have escaped and a few released. Stories mentioning them have been written by Communist correspondents who claim to have visited Viet Cong units in the South.

The Viet Cong admitted executing three Americans last September. Hanoi Radio said the prisoners, all soldiers captured in the South, were killed in reprisal for death sentences meted out by the South Vietnamese government to captured Communist agents...

U. S. fighting men in Viet Nam accept that a prisoner's best chance to live is to fall into the hands of a disciplined hard-core Viet Cong unit. The local guerrilla forces almost never take prisoners. Even with a hard-core unit a prisoner's chances are rated poor even though the Reds scatter surrender leaflets promising good treatment.

As badly as the Americans may fare, they are probably far better off than the Vietnamese captured by either side.

By the very nature of their hit-and-run tactics the Viet Cong have taken relatively few South Vietnamese prisoners. They hold a few hundred in their jungle camps but any reasonable estimate is impossible.

The shooting of prisoners is common. American and South Vietnamese units frequently come across dead men who have been found and shot by retreating Viet Cong units.

The record of the South Vietnamese is little better. Commanders openly consider Viet Cong prisoners traitors and frequently have them shot. American military advisers serving with South Vietnamese units report such executions.

Even so, the South Vietnamese hold an estimated 23,000 men nominally classified as war prisoners — although the number probably includes some political detainees and some who were rounded up in military sweeps.

Most of these are held in the Chi Hoa camp in Saigon, the Tam Hiep camp in Binh Duong province and a relatively new "model prison" at Bien Hoa. There are also camps in each of four military corps areas and another on a prison island.

The U. S. Commander in Viet Nam, Gen. William C. Westmoreland, has pressed the South Vietnamese to improve the camps. Westmoreland has also tried, with mixed success, to put an end to the practice of shooting prisoners on the field.

The United States has always agreed to turn over to South Viet Nam all prisoners captured by American forces. They are generally questioned for battlefield intelligence and passed along to the South Vietnamese in a few days.

A Division Commander was recently asked where such prisoners were taken.

"A hole in the ground, I'm afraid," he replied.

However, the Vietnamese have insisted that the United States continue to turn over all prisoners.

The only prisoners known to be held by the United States are 19 North Vietnamese seamen pulled from the sea after their torpedo boats were sunk in the Tonkin Gulf, outside South Vietnamese waters. It is generally accepted that the United States is holding these men in hopes of swapping them for Americans held by the North.

The U. S. Navy also takes captives along the coast when sampans and supply craft are stopped. Sometimes these seizures take place outside South Vietnamese territorial waters, but so far, a Navy spokesman says, such captives are turned over to the Saigon government.

Nov 66 Argosy
     Milt Machlin, "Big Battle Coming"

(The editors of Argosy have declined permission to give the verbatim text of a selection from the above cited article. The following describes the contribution of that selection.)

(The author witnesses a transfer of prisoners from American soldiers to ARVN. He states that he personally never witnessed mistreatment of prisoners by Americans but suggests that it is otherwise with prisoners held by ARVN. He reports having heard from some sources that the majority of prisoners are killed by ARVN, particularly the wounded ones. It is implied that wounded prisoners are killed because the shortage of hospital beds makes caring for them impractical. The author refers to rules which forbid the transfer of prisoners, but states that the war is an irregular one, and compliance with such rules has been avoided so far.)

INTERROGATION

12 Jun 64   Life

...But, searching thoroughly, they flushed 43 guerrillas hiding in dugouts, dragged them out and set about learning where their weapons were hidden.

The Vietnamese commander whipped the captives with a bamboo cane and booted them as they lay trussed on the ground. The women and children watched the torture of their husbands and fathers with steady faces. The guerrillas were jackknifed into positions of agony. They were held under the river's surface and tortured with water that was forced into their noses. Rags were put over their faces and then water was poured over the rags to give the impression of drowning. Photographer Okamura protested: this seemed needless and cruel. A soldier replied, "but this is my duty." But the prisoners would not talk.

The New Face of War, Malcolm W. Browne, 1965, pp. 116, 117

...But some of the forms of torture employed are more sinister, in that they maim or disfigure. Most of these are used in the field by Vietnamese troops on Viet Cong prisoners or suspects, and the object is to extract tactical intelligence.

They can involve beating and cutting, or worse. Many a news correspondent or U. S. Army military advisor has seen the hands whacked off prisoners with machetes. Prisoners are sometimes castrated or blinded.

In more than one case a Viet Cong suspect has been towed after interrogation behind an armored personnel carrier across the rice fields. This always results in death in one of its most painful forms.

Vietnamese troops also take their share of enemy heads.

Americans have learned to be suspicious of Vietnamese claims of victory over the Viet Cong, and are usually satisfied with the validity of these claims only when they see visual evidence, such as bodies.

One day, an American battalion advisor was seated in his headquarters shack in the Mekong Delta when a grinning Vietnamese officer walked in and said, "Big victory. We killed seventeen Viet Cong today." The American smiled doubtfully, and said, "Where are they?"

"Oh, out there near the road, about five kilometers from here."

"But, Nhut, you know we have to have evidence before we can report that on the American side."

Nhut scratched his head and walked out. The American thought the matter was ended. But an hour later, Nhut returned and asked the American to step outside. Outside, a truck had parked, surrounded by grinning Vietnamese rangers. In the truck were seventeen bloody heads, stacked like melons.

But by and large, things like this in the field appear to be more acts of revenge and hatred than merely adjuncts of intelligence interrogation. Many soldiers enjoy beating up Viet Cong prisoners. The subjects of interrogation so often die under questioning that intelligence seems to be a secondary matter.

In 1963, the American advisory command began experimenting with small field lie detectors for use by Vietnamese troops on Viet Cong suspects.

The innovation drew wide international publicity, most of it unfavorable. Leading American publications attacked the little lie detectors as nothing more than toys, which in the hands of unskilled operators could result in nothing but injustice. The criticism was probably valid.

But seasoned field men here regarded the criticism as wholly irrelevant.

"Stuff like that gives me a pretty good idea of how little Americans know about the war we're fighting here," a U. S. Army Special Forces officer told me.

"Sure, those lie detectors would be no good in a U. S. court of law, but this ain't a U. S. court of law, it's Viet Nam. I figure it this way. These little lie detectors must give the defendant a clean bill at least some of the time. As it is, when the Rangers or Airborne get their hooks into some guy, he doesn't stand even a chance. The lie detector would give him some chance. And it might cut down the unpleasant preliminaries to the executions."

The New Face of War, Malcolm W. Browne, 1965, pp. 161, 162

...The two figures suddenly stopped and threw up their arms in sur-render. The lieutenant commanding our vehicle ordered the gunner to cease fire as we closed on our captives. The troops leapt out to grab them.

Our two guerrilla prisoners turned out to be brothers, eight and nine years old. One had fallen or been hit by something, and his hand was broken, a spear of bone protruding through the muddy skin. Both boys looked at us incuriously, and neither face registered any trace of emotion. One boy had a coil of electric mine-detonating wire over his shoulder, and the other had two grenades slung from a rope around his waist. The boys were roughly stripped of their gear.

...The lieutenant in charge of our platoon walked up to the boys and asked them where the Viet Cong had gone. No answer.

"Well, then, where have they hidden their weapons and supplies?"

No answer. One of the boys spat into the mud in front of him.

"You'll answer my questions, or you'll be sorry," the lieutenant said. No answer. The officer pulled out his .45 automatic and pointed it in the face of the older boy.

"Where did they go?" The boy did not answer, but gazed straight into the officer's eyes.

Furious, the officer fired three quick shots into the ground in front of the boy's feet. The boy did not flinch or answer.

...After twenty minutes of combing fruitlessly through the hamlet, the troops climbed up on their vehicles, and the boys and the old man were shoved through the back hatch of one of the M113s.

None of the new passengers had ever ridden in one of these machines, and none knew that you must hold on to nylon straps hanging from the ceiling or there is danger of being badly hurt. Pieces of machinery and loose oilcans fly around the interior of the vehicle every time it hits a bump. So our three captives were pretty badly scraped and banged up as we moved on to the next hamlet, and soldiers laughed when the bedraggled trio was hauled out again. The boy's broken hand had been hurt some more, and was now bleeding pro-fusely, but his face was still emotionless.

This hamlet, too, was deserted. But from one of the huts, a soldier let out a whoop. He had found a huge, silk Viet Cong flag. Another soldier, pok-ing a stick in muddy holes he passed, also hit it lucky. One of the holes contained a young man with a rifle, who popped up like a jack-in-the-box when the stick gouged his shoulder. Here was an authentic prisoner, and four or five soldiers took turns beating him up until he was bloody and unconscious. They shot him later, but not until the American advisors were safely out of the way.

1 Jul 65   (See Note Page 20)
             SAIGON, July 1

A wounded Communist from North Viet Nam was under interrogation to-night as a member of the Viet Cong task force that killed one American, destroyed three planes and damaged three others in a hit-and-run attack on the Da Nang Air Base. The damage is estimated at $5 million.

A U.S. Spokesman said the prisoner was identified as Do Xuan Hien, 29, of the North Vietnamese province of Thanh Hoa. He was quoted as saying he infiltrated into South Viet Nam in April with the 3rd battalion of the 18th regiment of North Viet Nam's 325th Division.

The spokesman said the prisoner reported he was attached to a special unit for the attack on the air base, launched at 1:30 A.M. from a graveyard outside the perimeter wire. He was picked up by a search patrol.

7 Jul 65   New York Times, Jack Langguth
             SAIGON, July 6

Harsh and brutal measures have increased on both sides as the intensity of the war in South Vietnam has risen.

...On the other hand, Americans have urged for years that Communist prisoners, and particularly deserters from the Vietcong, be treated better by the Government. This was based on the expectation that word of good treatment would circulate among the people and spur defections.

The Vietnamese officials at prison camps have only occasionally shown themselves impressed by the American argument.

During the Phubon battle last week, at least five Communist prisoners were shot because the capturing Government troops felt they could not guard them properly.

At another place a day later a Western newsman watched while a Government guard stepped forward without warning and beat a 15-year-old youth accused of aiding the Viet Cong.

With a greater United States participation in the war, brutality has begun to occur among the American troops as well.

One American helcopter crewman returned to his base in the central highlands last week without a fierce young prisoner entrusted to him. He told friends that he had become infuriated by the youth and had pushed him out of the helicopter at about 1,000 feet.

When a superior warned him that he would be court-martialed, the crewman changed his story. He said that the prisoner had attacked him and had fallen accidentally.

26 Jul 65   The Sun (Baltimore) (See Note Page 20)
              TAM LOC, July 25

...Shortly before the shooting incident, Staff Sgt. John S. Fitts of San Diego, Cal., noticed two camouflaged foxholes, and two Viet Cong were captured. One had a rifle.

Militia troops accompanying the Marines took over the prisoners and began beating and kicking them, demanding to know where their fellow guerrillas and arms caches were.

After several beatings, one of the Viet Cong broke down and showed the troops where four American-made shotguns had been hidden in the sand. Some of the Marines appeared shaken by the brutality.

The Marines also rounded up 13 Viet Cong suspects, tying four of them together with a rope.

A small child, apparently the son of a suspect, followed the Marines for several miles to the landing zone where helicopters picked up the troops and their prisoners.

The boy pressed his hands together in the traditional form for Buddhist prayer when the suspects were led away to the helicopters. He refused candy offered by several Marines.

If the father is determined not to be a Viet Cong, he probably will be reunited shortly with his son.

27 Aug 65   (See Note Page 20)
              SAIGON, Aug 27

Women are caught up in the war in Viet Nam — some as active combatants, others as spies or saboteurs, and others as innocent bystanders. Both the Vietnamese army and the Viet Cong deal harshly with hostile women they catch. Some are executed, others tortured in an effort to extract information.

...The U. S. Army's 173rd Airborne Brigade reported that women in a 200-member Viet Cong force threw grenades at them in an operation 25 miles north of Saigon.

These combat women when caught cannot expect gentle treatment at the hands of the Vietnamese army.

A Vietnamese regiment sweeping a mangrove swamp on the South China Sea flushed two women, one armed with a Russian rifle.

A soldier held his knife at the breast of one woman. Other soldiers wrestled the second woman to the ground.

At knifepoint, the women refused to say how they came by the rifle and documents found on them. They said they were just civilians. They were bound, blindfolded and taken away as prisoners.

...Last month a laundress tried to smuggle powerful explosives in her girdle into a U. S. helicopter base at Soc Trang. Vietnamese security police caught her, questioned her, then took her out into a nearby rice field and shot her.

31 Aug 65   (See Note Page 20)
              AP LA GHI, Aug 31

...On the way back through the swamps, the 3rd Battalion of the 13th regiment encountered a woman with a black scarf hiding in the bushes. The troops searched her roughly and found documents purportedly dealing with Viet Cong military plans.

Nearby a second woman was found cowering. She was armed with a Russian rifle. She was wrestled to the ground while a soldier held a knife on the other woman.

At knife point, the women refused to say how they came by the rifle and the documents and maintained they were civilians, not Viet Cong. They were bound, blindfolded and taken as prisoners to the waiting boats.

5 Sep 65   New York Times, James Reston
             SAIGON, Sep 2

...The whole problem of encouraging Vietcong deserters and questioning them for intelligence information, and housing them, is also serious. Not even a coward would lightly leave the Communist ranks to take refuge in the pig pens the South Vietnamese have provided for them.

This has been left primarily to the Vietnamese themselves and they are treating their prisoners with that degree of brutality that only a civil war seems to produce. Their attitude toward defectors is illustrated by what they do to their own men.

Lately, they have been tattooing on the chests of their men "Satcong"— Kill Vietcong. This is supposed to boost their morale and at the same time discourage them from defecting to the other side.

12 Mar 66   (See Note Page 20)
              SAIGON, March 12

...Ky's government issued a statement emphasizing that captured Viet Cong are not considered prisoners of war, but rather rebel Communist prisoners who must be helped "to have a chance to return to the right cause."

An open arms policy outlined last December was reiterated, apparently
for its value in propaganda and psychological warfare. Spokesmen said the
government has been treating prisoners well all along.

The policy is that the prisoners' faith must be respected, without regard to race or nationality. The instructions also state:

"Interrogation must be based on a humane policy, and torture must be
strictly avoided."

Vietnamese interrogators in the field have been observed on occasion
striking Viet Cong suspects when they felt they were lying or withholding
information on enemy troop movements.

18 April 66   Honolulu Advertiser, Steve Northrup
               (from Congressional Record — Appendix, April 27, 1966, A2286
               QUI NHON, VIETNAM —

...Next the Koreans rounded up a dozen or so male suspects and a quantity of Vietcong military gear. The only problem was they couldn't find out
which of the suspects owned the gear.

So they grabbed one man out of the group, hustled him over to a trench
that looked suspiciously like a grave, and blindfolded him.

A ROK soldier fired one shot directly over the prisoner's head. For a
second the prisoner thought he was dead, then he began quivering.

The blindfold was jerked off and quick as a flash the prisoner ran over
to the group and picked out one man — the owner of the military gear. He
quickly told all he knew of the guerrilla operation.

3 July 66   St. Louis Post-Dispatch, Richard Dudman
             (from Congressional Record — Senate, July 12, 1966, 14533)
             WASHINGTON, July 2 —

...Some observers are impressed by reports of prisoner interrogation
indicating that captured North Viet Namese now believe that their side faces
defeat. Others concede that enemy morale may be sagging, but await what
they consider a clearer indication, in the form of mass defection of Communist forces in squad or platoon strength.

22 July 66   Christian Science Monitor, Earl W. Foell
              UNITED NATIONS, N. Y.

American forces in Vietnam have been quietly instructed to cease turning
Viet Cong captives over to South Vietnamese troops.

...By keeping Viet Cong prisoners from falling prey to possible South
Vietnamese torture, Washington has sought to telegraph a practical show of
good faith to Hanoi — and to international middlemen involved in moves to
save the fliers.

...This also strongly implies what many reputable reporters have
given eyewitness accounts of: South Vietnamese torture and execution of
Viet Cong and North Vietnamese prisoners.

Neither of these violations is permitted by the 1949 Geneva convention. South Vietnam became a party to the treaty in 1954. Washington
ratified it in 1956. North Vietnam, in 1957.

25 July 66   New York Post, Pete Hamill

We were on a knoll outside of Bong Son, in South Viet Nam, watching
the fighting in the mountains across the valley. Three sleek fighter planes
rushed across the valley floor, coming from the sea, and then veered up
and over the mountains, as their cargo of napalm skidded across the jungle
in a brilliant orange ball. A long trail of blue smoke was snaking down the
valley when we saw the three soldiers come up with the two Vietnamese.

"Prisoners," a major said, standing outside a tent in the headquarters
battalion where the First Cavalry was running Operation Masher. "I'm
glad I'm not them."

The Vietnamese had their hands tied behind their backs, and wore short pants and black shirts. Their feet were bare. One of them was about 18, the other in his 30s.

"Sit down," one of the young soldiers said. He motioned ominously with his M-16, and the two prisoners sat down. The younger one looked hard and resigned; the older seemed about to cry. I asked the major what would happen to them.

"Oh, we'll turn them over to the ARVN (the South Vietnamese Army)," he said. "They'll interrogate them for a couple of hours, and then decide whether they are VC."

"What happens then?"

"If they're lucky," he said, training his binoculars on the foothills, "they'll just be shot."

After a while, a squat ARVN captain showed up and the two Vietnamese were put into a Jeep and taken away. In their eyes you could see the look of men who had just been informed of the manner of their deaths.

I have been thinking about those two men during the terrible furor over the fate of American pilots who have been captured during the bombing in the North. If those pilots are tried and executed, Hanoi will be guilty of stupidity along with murder. But before we go off self-righteously to turn the North into a desert, we had better be sure we are morally pure.

25 Jul 66   (See Note Page 20)
             CAM LO, VIET NAM, July 25

"Take prisoners — we need all the information we can get."

These are the orders going out to U.S. Marine commanders seeking a North Vietnamese Army division along the Northern rim of South Viet Nam in Operation Hastings.

In the 11 days of the pursuit the Marines have killed 698 Communists — a figure arrived at by body count. But they have taken only a dozen prisoners.

...The apparent determination of the North Vietnamese soldiers to fight rather than surrender, even when escape is impossible, has perplexed Marine intelligence officers.

...A company of the 4th Marines encountered a band of North Vietnamese regulars in holes and called for a Vietnamese interpreter to appeal to them to surrender. The North Vietnamese, instead of giving up, shot at the interpreter.

The Marines then overran them, killing 20. Most of the dead North Vietnamese were heavily bandaged from earlier wounds and had been left behind with a few rifles and hand grenades.

6 Oct 66   New York Times, Charles Mohr
            ANMY, South Vietnam, Oct. 5

...The foot soldiers of the Seventh Regiment took a number of prisoners in the village. One was a sleekly muscled young man, one of the few young men ever found by allied troops in villages.

As he was being led to a helicopter, a South Vietnamese national policeman and an interpreter assigned to the Americans slapped and kicked him to extract information. No American officers were present, and the enlisted men seemed confused and unsure about whether to interfere.

The interpreter kicked the prisoner in the groin, and the policeman punched him in the face and stomach.

"Viet Cong," said the policeman.

"Everything is V.C. according to him," said a boyish-looking American with distaste. "That's the Vietnamese National Guard for you."

9 Oct 66   The Sun (Baltimore) (See Note Page 20)
             PHU CAT, VIETNAM, Oct 8

...Vietnamese and American intelligence men question the prisoners to determine just what they are. Communist regulars are sent to what is called a re-orientation camp at Pleiku in the central highlands. Noncombatants, even though they may be Communist sympathizers, are sent home, under the eyes of the Vietnamese National Police.

...The combined count of prisoners is in excess of 600 known Communist troops and 1,400 suspects. Intelligence officers say about 25 per cent of the suspects are turning out to be guerrillas, as compared to the usual 5 or 10 per cent for such suspects.

25 Dec 66   World Journal Tribune, William Tuohy
             BINH CHANH, Dec 24

The prisoner was about 25 years old, 5 feet high, with wide-set eyes, a shock of black hair, and was wearing mud-spattered black pajamas.

His face was bruised, he was scared, but very brave. He was a member of the Viet Cong who had been captured earlier in the day by troops of the 4th Battalion, 9th Regiment, U. S. 25th Division — just half a dozen miles south of Saigon.

Now, he was undergoing questioning.

His interrogators were three Vietnamese military security men assigned to the battalion and a handful of United States counter intelligence agents.

They were after two types of information: tactical combat details about the prisoner's unit that would allow the battalion to mount a quick reaction strike, and more general information about the prisoner's life and role in the Viet Cong.

"Good intelligence is the name of the game in this war," said Bruce Baum, 22, a Counter Intelligence Corps agent.

The prisoner was taken to one tent, while the U. S. intelligence agents remained in another tent. The prisoner was being questioned by the Vietnamese interrogators, and their methods are not always those prescribed in U. S. police manuals.

"This fellow was one of a group of 20 from the 5th Battalion of the 165A Regiment, which operates in this area," Baum said.

"He was picked off in a near-perfect ambush, and we'd like to know where the rest of his outfit is. We want to get his name, the number of his unit, its strength, location, weapons, escape route, as much as we can.

"If we can get enough information in a hurry, we can go after them and hit them. If not, any information we get is valuable."

A Vietnamese interrogator entered the tent to report that the prisoner was adamant. He was giving several names and it looked as if he could not be easily cracked, certainly not in time to take any immediate tactical advantage.

"About half the prisoners we get spill everything," said Baum.

"But the political cadre almost never talk. The easiest ones to crack, of course, are the young Vietnamese boys drafted by the Viet Cong.

"We find that it is much better to let the Vietnamese security men do the questioning. If we try to use them simply as interpreters, about half the effectiveness of the interrogation is lost."

The Vietnamese occasionally slap the prisoner around, but U. S. intelligence agents insist that this is more by way of warning than out-and-out third degree. The point is debatable.

"A slap in the face is intended to startle the prisoner," said one U. S. agent. "It is designed to show him that lies will not be accepted. This also breaks down his composure and makes him more willing to talk."

This is known as "the Oriental way" of handling prisoners.

The Vietnamese interrogators again appeared at the door of the U. S. intelligence tent to report that the prisoner was still giving several names and telling obvious lies, such as variously stating the size of his unit.

"This fellow is obviously a main force soldier and very tough," said Baum. "He'd rather be beaten than talk. He is very skillful. If we don't get anything out of him here, we send him back to division."

As the questioning continued in the other tent, the U. S. agent spoke of the "black list." This is a masterfile of 8,000 names of Viet Cong and Viet Cong suspects in the tactical operating area of the 25th Division.

The black list is designed to be an over-all locater of Viet Cong types. However, systematic listing of such suspects is only now getting under way, and the list admittedly contains many glaring errors.

Eventually, intelligence agents hope to get a fairly accurate listing of the Viet Cong in the area — which has always had a high percentage of sympathizers.

In the intelligence war being waged in the delta, the U. S. and Vietnamese agents hope to be able to pay a call at every door that is thought to house VC sympathizers.

Psychologically speaking, the agents explained, the overt call by policemen on known or suspected Viet Cong families tends to have a disruptive effect on their morale, and eventually increases the government's control in an area. It further demonstrates that the government is indeed aware of who is sympathetic to the Viet Cong.

All this takes time, and the U. S. Intelligence effort is hardly off the ground because U. S. troops are only now moving into these crowded delta areas and learning something about them.

It is an axiom of guerrilla warfare that, as a government military presence is maintained and felt in the countryside, friendly intelligence increases at a geometric rate. With the arrival of U. S. troops in force in the key area just south of Saigon, U. S. intelligence experts hope that proffered information about the Viet Cong will increase markedly.

In the next tent, the captured prisoner was still uncooperative.

The Vietnamese interrogators menacingly cocked a carbine as if to shoot the prisoner. He remained unyielding.

Then, a vicious-looking police dog was brought in. However, the shepherd was a pointer-type scout dog rather than a watchdog, and he was not cooperative. He wagged his tail and lay down on the floor.

The prisoner was not intimidated.

Finally, after another round of tough questioning by the Vietnamese, the prisoner said:

"Take me out and shoot me."

"Well, we're not going to get anything from him," said a U. S. agent in resignation. "Let's send him back to division."

14 Jan 67   World Journal Tribune, Mike Miller
             BEN SUC, SOUTH VIETNAM, Jan 14

...A revolutionary development force of the Big Red One 1st Infantry Division has been in this village for five days, and the Viet Cong still are coming out of their holes.

...Ben Suc is a lesson in what it takes to root the Viet Cong out of a village stronghold. The Americans must stay long enough to find all the guerrillas and security troops must remain to see that other Viet Cong don't come back.

"We usually stay in a village only a couple of days, then pull out," said Sgt. Duffer. "These Viet Cong only took a couple of days' rations into their tunnels. Now we are beginning to starve them out."

Two guerrillas came up last night, begging for food. They were fed after leading their captors to a hidden weapons cache.

23 Mar 67   (See Note Page 20)

PLEI DJERENG, VIETNAM, March 23

In the tangled underbrush it was impossible to see more than a dozen yards ahead.

Suddenly an automatic rifle snapped two quick bursts. Two North Vietnamese soldiers — alone and apparently lost — dropped dead in their tracks only 30 feet from a U.S. column.

The American company cheered the lieutenant who had cut them down. Capt. Richard E. Ator of Tacoma, Washington, the company commander, was less pleased.

"I wish we hadn't killed them," he said. "He should have aimed at their legs to wound them. Then we could have questioned them. We want information badly. In one month our battalion has taken only one prisoner, despite daily fights with the NVA (North Vietnamese Army)."

The incident points up an outstanding feature of the war in the Central Vietnamese Highlands along the Cambodian border: The need for intelligence about what the North Vietnamese are up to.

Victor Charlie, Kuno Knoebl. 1967, p. 113

...I witnessed the interrogation of a captured Viet-Cong soldier. The youngster, perhaps twenty, was squatting in front of an American military policeman and two Vietnamese. His feet were shod in "VC sandals," their soles cut from auto tires. His black shirt was torn and he was bleeding slightly from a small wound on his upper arm.

He had been dragged out of a bunker after he fired at approaching American soldiers. His bruised lips showed that he had not been treated gently. His arms were tied behind his back. One Vietnamese, acting as interpreter, questioned him. It soon became clear that the boy knew nothing. He may have been just an ordinary soldier, but now the war was over for him and all he feared — rightly, as it turned out — was that he would not survive the next few hours.

He readily named his commander, the number of his unit, its arms and strength. He told where he had come from, who he was, and what his comrades' names were. The vietnamese began to question him about the Communist organization within the NLF. I don't believe the boy understood the question or that the word "Communism" had much meaning for him. His answers became uncertain, and a soldier began beating him with the butt of a rifle until he fainted. When he revived, he was asked again: Who are the officials of the People's Revolutionary Party? What is the structure of the village committees? What does he know about Marxism? With every question the rifle butt smashed into his back with a dull thud. The man tried hard to understand the questions, but he obviously could not. Just once — when he heard the name of Ho Chi Minh — did his face light up in recognition, and he began to talk. He knew the name of the man who had driven out the white colonial masters, but knew nothing about Communism and Communist organization. He was executed on the grounds that he had refused to supply information.

...The interrogation of prisoners is usually rough in war, but in Viet-Nam it is often a matter of overwhelming cruelty. One method used to make a prisoner talk is to tie slip-knotted cords around his throat and feet, so that if he moves, the noose around his throat slowly tightens. Then he is laid in a rice paddy, where the water is no deeper than eight inches. The prisoner can keep from drowning by raising his head; but the noose around his throat draws tighter at every movement of his head. Within fifteen or twenty minutes he has strangled himself. Another method is to hang a captive by the feet over a rain barrel and slowly submerge him in it. He is not kept under long enough to drown at first; the process is repeated until the man talks or dies. In the delta, South Vietnamese soldiers use U.S. armored personnel carriers as instruments of torture. A Viet-Cong is tied to the vehicle by a rope and slowly dragged through the rice paddies. A victim may survive being pulled through one or two of the water-covered fields, but he is dead by the third.

27 Jan 67   The Washington Post, Jesse W. Lewis, Jr.
             HONNOC MOUNTAINS, SOUTH VIETNAM, Jan 26

"We need another prisoner real bad right now," said Lt. Col. William H. (Wild Bill) Miller, as automatic rifle fire and grenade explosions rang out 150 feet above the helicopter landing pad at Landing Zone 19, about half the size of a basketball court.

"This mountain has been a haven for the North Vietnamese for years and I'd sure like to know what we've found."

· But in the fighting so far in the natural caverns of this mountain complex in Binhdinh Province, 240 miles north of Saigon, the soldiers of this 25th Division battalion have been able to capture but one prisoner.

Everybody else they've encountered while inching their way through the tunnels they've shot and killed, sometimes with .45-caliber automatics as close as a few yards away.

...The operation began Jan. 19 when reports indicated that main units of the 18th Regiment of the Peoples Army of North Vietnam (PAVN) were in the area.

...Another important find was 10 million piastres (about $925,00) (sic) in unissued promissory notes. These notes are used, intelligence officers said, to pay farmers for rice and other foodstuffs and would be redeemable when the South was "liberated."

The one man U.S. troops were able to capture was ill with malaria and told them he was being treated in the subterranean hospital that was uncovered during the search.

...The reason Miller wanted another prisoner now is to find out how much the PAVN unit knew about the Americans and to find out more about PAVN.

But because of the type of fighting, it was impossible to take prisoners "especially after what happened to the captain," said one soldier.

12 May 67   New York Times
             WASHINGTON, May 11

The United States has recently renewed its effort to win North Vietnam's agreement to an exchange of prisoners of war but so far Hanoi has shown no interest, United States officials said tonight.

In July the United States captured 19 North Vietnamese sailors in the Gulf of Tonkin when their torpedo boats attacked American naval vessels. The sailors have been retained in custody. American officials hoped to use them in prisoner exchanges with North Vietnam.

...The 19 sailors are the only North Vietnamese prisoners held by the United States. All North Vietnamese soldiers captured in South Vietnam are turned over to Saigon authorities. Hanoi holds about 190 American prisoners. About 200 Americans are missing in North Vietnam and may have been captured.

30 Sep 65   New York Times, Neil Sheehan
             SAIGON

...In mid-August, Secretary of State Dean Rusk informed the International Committee of the Red Cross in Geneva that the United States was implementing the Geneva Convention in Vietnam, and that it had plans to help South Vietnam create adequate facilities and procedures for handling of prisoners. Secretary Rusk's message was in reply to an earlier letter from the Red Cross requesting the United States to honor the convention here.

At the same time, Tran Van Do, the Vietnamese Foreign Minister, asserted in response to a similar appeal that South Vietnam was already observing the convention, and that Vietcong prisoners "have always been receiving the most humanitarian treatment."

Neither of these statements, however, has altered the actual fashion in which prisoners are handled.

...The United States is in the unhappy position of asking humane treatment for American prisoners of Communists while it has declined to guarantee similar treatment to Vietcong taken prisoners by American ground combat units.

Such prisoners, after a preliminary interrogation, are handed over to the Vietnamese authorities by whom of course they can be and frequently are subjected to brutality.

TORTURE AND MURDER

13/13 Vietnam: Search and Destroy, Gordon Baxter, 1967, pp. 85, 87

(The copyright owners of 13/13 Vietnam: Search and Destroy have declined permission to publish textual material in this documentation. The following describes the essential contribution made by a selection from this book.)

(The author tells of the interrogation of some old farmers and the selection of those who appear politically suspect for further interrogation.

He reveals that sometimes prisoners are mistreated, both threatened and beaten. He describes instances which he witnessed and refers to photos in the text. Justification for such action on the part of GI's is offered.

The author states that the Oriental is confused by the behavior of Americans when he sees, on the one hand, the beating of a prisoner and, on the other hand, the giving of cigarettes and bandages to the same prisoner. This is due, says the author, to a failure on the Oriental's part to fully appreciate the capacity of Americans for both brutality and fellow-feeling.

It is noted that prisoners are better cared for in rear areas away from battle.)

1 Jul 66   New York Times, R. W. Apple, Jr.
             SAIGON, SOUTH VIETMAN, June 30

United States officials are quietly putting into effect an important change in their handling of prisoners of war.

Vietcong and North Vietnamese fighters captured on the battlefield will no longer be turned over to the South Vietnamese Army immediately after the fighting has died down. Instead, they will be sent to American divisional headquarters and kept in American hands until they can be transferred to new Vietnamese prisoner-of-war compounds.

At the moment, the new system applies only to captives taken in the III Army Corps area, the Saigon region. It contains the prisoner-of-war camp at Bienhoa, the only one that has been completed. But as others are opened within the next two or three months at Danang and Pleiku, the change will take effect in other areas.

The system has been adopted to enable the United States to meet its responsibility under Article 12 of the Geneva Convention of 1949 governing the treatment of prisoners of war. The article requires a country turning prisoners over to another country to guarantee their well being.

26 Jan 67   Chicago Daily News, Raymond R. Coffey
              SAIGON

...The three Viet Cong returned to their families Monday represented in several respects a new approach to the prisoner question, an approach it is hoped will produce some reciprocity.

The United States turns its enemy prisoners over to the Vietnamese and all enemy prisoners are officially in Vietnamese custody.

...It also was made clear that the three Viet Cong were being freed in "direct response" to the recent release of two American construction workers, Thomas R. Scales and Robert Monahan, and a Filipino woman by the Viet Cong.

The New Face of War, Malcolm W. Browne, 1965, pp. 114, 115, 116

...Torture has been an adjunct to interrogation for many years in South Viet Nam, and there are no prospects that this pattern will change in the foreseeable future.

To the average American, all forms of torture are revolting. But given the situation in Viet Nam, distinctions must be made between degrees of torture.

The Vietnamese police probably use the mildest forms in interrogating political (or Viet Cong) prisoners.

There is a small, American field generator used extensively in Viet Nam for powering pack radios. The device is mounted on a tripod and is operated by hand cranks on both sides, turned by one man. The generator produces a high enough voltage to produce a severe but not fatal shock.

The "ding-a-ling" method of interrogation involves connection of electrodes from this generator to the temples of the subject, or other parts of the body. In the case of women prisoners, the electrodes often are attached to the nipples. The results are terrifying and painful, but subjects are not permanently damaged. This technique is often applied at provincial interrogation centers by police, and in the field by soldiers.

Another method involves the near drowning of the subject. In late 1963, a young Vietnamese woman working as a secretary at the British Embassy in Saigon was arrested on grounds that she had provided shelter for a Buddhist monk wanted by Diem's police. She described her experience this way:

"I waited in a room with some other prisoners, who were led off one at a time for interrogation. Finally my turn came. I was taken to a bare office where there were two desks and a bench. The man interrogating me was seated at one of the desks.

"He asked me if I knew anything about the monk. Actually, I did, but of course I denied it. Then two other large men came into the room. They ripped off my dress and forced me to lie down on the bench, tying me tightly to it with pieces of rope. Next to the bench was a bucket of filthy water. Some of this was poured over my face and I choked and vomited. Then a big cloth was placed over my face — tightly — and the water was poured on it. I couldn't breathe. Just as I was about to lose consciousness, the cloth was taken off. Then one of the men beat me on the soles of the feet with a heavy club. I screamed terribly from the pain. The other began beating my stomach with his fist. The cloth was put over my face again, and this time I passed out. When I came to, I was ordered to dress and clean up the room. They told me I would be questioned again tomorrow."

It happened that this woman was not questioned again, because the following day, Diem was overthrown in a bloody coup.

But the wet-cloth interrogation technique is still used. It has at least the merit that it is not fatal and leaves no physically harmful effects.

...Presumably, the "mild" forms of torture sometimes leave psychological effects, however. At this writing, nearly a dozen former political Buddhist prinsoners are patients at the Cong Hoa Hospital, Viet Nam's main military hospital. All are highly disturbed mental patients. They were released from Diem's prisons nearly one year ago.

25 Apr 65   New York Herald Tribune, Beverly Deepe
            SAIGON, Apr 25

The atrocities are not committed only by the Communist forces. Vietnamese government troops, while seldom torturing non-suspect civilians, are known to torture Viet Cong prisoners and suspects. One Vietnamese army captain explained that government troops try to get intelligence information from Viet Cong prisoners in the heat of battle.

American advisers and intelligence officers have urged the Vietnamese forces to be more lenient with Viet Cong prisoners and to keep them alive for additional intelligence.

In one known case, two Viet Cong prisoners were interrogated on an airplane flying toward Saigon. The first refused to answer questions and was thrown out of the airplane at 3,000 feet. The second immediately answered all the questions. But he, too, was thrown out.

...One of the most infamous methods of torture used by the govenment forces is partial electrocution — or "frying," as one U.S. advisor called it.

This correspondent was present on one occasion when the torture was employed. Two wires were attached to the thumbs of a Viet Cong prisoner. At the other end of the strings was a field generator, cranked by a Vietnamese private. The mechanism produced an electrical current that burned and shocked the prisoner.

Vietnamese officers report that sometimes the wires are attached to the male genital organs, or to the breasts of a Viet Cong woman prisoner.

The water torture, also used by government forces, is painful but seldom fatal. One person forces the prisoner to gulp water, while another applies pressure on his stomach. This forces the water out and creates a feeling similar to drowning.

...Other techniques, usually designed to force onlooking prisoners to talk, involve cutting off the fingers, ears, fingernails or sexual organs of another prisoner. Sometimes a string of ears decorates the wall of a government military installation. One American installation has a Viet Cong ear preserved in alchohol.

21 Jun 65   New York Times
              SAIGON, SOUTH VIETNAM, June 20

...Brutality by Government troops in handling Vietcong prisoners and an inadequate program for the care of defectors has discouraged the flight of many to areas administered by Saigon.

The findings of the survey are based on interviews by professional interrogators of Vietcong prisoners and defectors. The detailed interviews were carried out in such places as Government camps for defectors, and in jails and cages where Vietcong captives are held.

30 Sep 65   New York Times, Neil Sheehan
              SAIGON

...Vietnamese Army police and paramilitary organizations such as the national guard and the militia frequently shoot Vietcong captives out of hand, beat or brutally torture them or otherwise mistreat them.

Many Vietcong are also non-uniformed partisans, in other words armed civilians or terrorists and agitators who have traditionally been treated with severity by uniformed armies and established governments in wartime.

The favorite methods of torture used by Government troops are to slowly beat a captive, drag him behind a moving vehicle, apply electrodes to sensitive parts of his body or block his mouth while water spiced with hot pepper is poured down his nostrils.

21 Jul 66   Congressional Record — House, 15924, Mr. Ottinger

(Mr. Ottinger (at the request of Mrs. Thomas) was granted permission to extend his remarks at this point in the Record and to include extraneous matter.)

...Two weeks ago, the North Vietnamese Government marched American airmen through the streets of Hanoi. This in itself was a violation of the rules of war and an offense against common decency.

11 Aug 66   UPI, New York Times
             DANANG, SOUTH VIETNAM, August 10

Government officials today displayed in a movie theater a dozen prisoners they said were Vietcong who had infiltrated the Buddhist uprising in Danang earlier this year.

The prisoners, 10 men and two women, made "repentance" speeches. No translations were made for foreign newsmen.

Government officials told the journalists they would be permitted to question the prisoners for five minutes following the public part of the meeting, but as soon as the meeting was over the prisoners were led away.

Phan Minh Cong, Danang's police chief, said the prisoners were Vietcong political cadres who had been sent to Danang "to stir up trouble during the civil unrest in April."

Arizona Republic, Robert J. Sarti
(from Congressional Record — Senate, August 16, 1966, 18687) Sen.
Morse did not supply date of article

A young decorated veteran of the Vietnam fighting is on his way back to the war zone today, but he's bound never to shoulder a rifle again — at least not in Southeast Asia.

For poetry-writing, philosophy-reading, Spec. 4 Paul Edwin Fritz of Tempe, a former John Birch Society member and two-time volunteer for duty in Vietnam, is now dead set against U.S. policies there and he's willing to go to jail in support of his convictions.

...Fritz says he has seen and participated in attacks which have destroyed a peasant village on the scantiest evidence of Viet sympathizers there. He also claims direct knowledge of the use of torture by both sides.

9 Oct 65   New Republic, Benard B. Fall
            "Vietnam Blitz"

...Another aspect of the progressive irrelevance of the human aspects of the Vietnam war is the universally callous attitude taken by almost everybody toward the crass and constant violations of the rules of war that have been taking place. The long-suffering (and far too long silent) International Red Cross finally addressed an appeal in July 1965 to both sides, exhorting them to live up to the Red Cross and Geneva agreements; and it was hardly an accident that Secretary of State Dean Rusk chose August 12, 1965, the sixteenth anniversary of the Geneva Convention on War Victims, to reaffirm America's adherence to the treaty, which was fully ratified by the United States Senate. Both North and South Vietnam also have ratified it.

As personal questions to both American and Vietnamese unit commanders have shown (and I made a point of touching on the subject with most of them), there is only the vaguest idea among them as to what exactly is covered by the 1949 Convention; in the few cases where the terms "rules of war" meant anything at all, the officer concerned very often confused the rules of land warfare of The Hague with the Geneva Convention on Prisoners of War of 1929, the 1949 Convention, the Red Cross Convention, and the American Code of the Fighting Man. Several officers would argue that the VC were all "traitors" and thus could be shot out of hand, in yet another misinterpretation of the laws covering treason. But in that case, following the logic of the State Department's assertion that the North Vietnamese were "foreign aggressors," North Vietnamese regulars caught inside South Vietnam would have to be treated as regular POW's, as were American pilots until now if shot down over North Vietnam. Needless to say, no such distinction was made between North Vietnamese regulars and VC regulars, nor between both of them and the VC guerrillas: they are all being treated under the same appalling conditions. The attitude of "this isn't our war; it's a Vietnamese war" could hold as long as US combat troops were not operating on their own and taking prisoners all by themselves. Now, this is no longer possible and the Viet Cong are in the position of virtually bulldozing the United States into accepting responsibility for what happens to prisoners; they can shoot in reprisal American POW's whom they hold whenever America's Vietnamese ally executes VC prisoners, as just happened in Danang. Two American Servicemen had to pay with their lives for that gratuitous gesture. The September 29 announcement by Hanoi that henceforth American pilots caught in the North will be treated as "war criminals" is a direct consequence of Washington's lack of foresight on the POW problem.

...On September 11, 1965, the Saigon Daily News, a newspaper published entirely for the English-speaking Western community of Vietnam, showed on its front page a large photograph of American servicemen standing with drawn weapons over a heap of what the caption describes as "dead VC" — all lying face down on the ground, and with their hands tied behind their backs. If, contrary to the caption, the dead were not Viet Cong, but, instead, helpless villagers shot by the Communists, I'd be only too happy if some of my friends in Saigon corrected the record, or if the Pentagon would issue a detailed denial of the event and a believable explanation of what actually happened.

25 Jul 62   New York Times, Homer Bigart

...American advisers have seen Vietcong prisoners summarily shot. They have encountered the charred bodies of women and children in villages destroyed by napalm bombs.

25 Mar 65   (See Note Page 20)
             SAIGON, VIETNAM, March 25

...Most controversial of all is the practice of torturing prisoners, generally with electric shocks or smothering with wet towels. Murder and torture have been standard accessories to Viet Cong tactics for years. Prisoners often are killed outright or tortured to death. Troops on both sides are fond of beheading their enemies to get grisly trophies.

It is a war in which no quarter is given on either side.

America, deeply involved as it is in the Vietnamese conflict, has inevitably become involved in the "dirtier" sides of the war. U.S. advisors generally are somewhere around when prisoners are taken, and often witness ugly things.

4 Jun 65   (See Note Page 20)
            SAIGON, June 4

...As the fighting grows hotter it becomes more brutal. Neither side is taking many prisoners any more. Soldiers caught off side now are generally shot on the spot or tortured to death.

So far, the odds seem about even.

14 Aug 65   (See Note Page 20)
DANANG, VIETNAM, Aug 14

A sharp-eyed marine corporal, automatic rifle at the ready, spotted a blur of black in the banana trees and bushes near the Vietnamese hut.

Reflexes conditioned by long years of training snapped into action and the American leatherneck emptied his M-14 rifle into the fleeing Vietnamese. The man stumbled, spun around and fell, riddled with bullets. When the advancing marines approached the body, they found no weapon and no identification on the corpse. The man was dressed in the black pajamas worn universally by Vietnamese peasants and the VC guerrillas.

Had the marine killed a VC or a harmless civilian? Not even the Vietnamese troops accompanying the marines could say for sure.

Because the man had been shot in a VC controlled village that had fired on the marines, the official report of the action carried the man as a confirmed VC kill.

A major feature of the Viet Nam war is that the VC guerrillas dress like peasants and when superior government or American forces charge into their positions weapons are quickly buried or wrapped in plastic and thrown into rice paddies. The Viet Cong then either try to sneak out of the village or run for an underground tunnel whose mouth is camouflaged and usually escapes detection.

When government troops come, the villagers immediately take refuge in an air raid shelter, a standard feature of the rural Vietnamese home. Those who continue to move or attempt to flee are regarded, usually with reason, as Viet Cong.

Tragically, sometimes they are only frightened civilians trying to reach safety or possible loved ones at their home.

It is virtually impossible and extremely dangerous for troops to attempt to give chase to fleeing persons inside a village. Most are without roads. The Western grid pattern of a town layout is unknown in the countryside. Soldiers laden with packs, weapons and other combat gear would have to smash through fences, often made of bamboo. The villagers know the quickest routes.

. . . Dealing with prisoners is no easy task either. Normally only a few men of military age are found during an operational sweep. If they have papers, they may be forged. If they do not, the identity cards may have been seized and destroyed by the Viet Cong.

Some Vietnamese commanders, operating on instinct, shoot prisoners summarily if they feel they are Viet Cong. Because government control has been ineffective or non-existent over most of the countryside for some time, no files, military finger prints, photos and the like are available to police.

Some commanders feel their suspects would probably only be released if turned over to district officials who would have no evidence on which to act. American advisers disapprove of such executions. But they say, with the difficulty of identifying VC from the rest of the population that many communists escape because there is no way to pinpoint them from the sea of faces in the chaos of the war.

What is difficult for the Vietnamese soldiers is virtually impossible for American soldiers. Rare is the GI who can speak even a few words of Vietnamese. So Americans must depend on Vietnamese troops to point the finger at the enemy and guide them through the villages in pursuit of the Viet Cong. There are not enough Vietnamese troops for this, and too few of those available speak enough English.

Thus American soldiers and marines are faced with fighting an enemy that refuses to come into the open and normally wears no uniform. Thus mistakes and civilian casualties are inevitable in the strange war that Americans from privates to generals are still trying to come to grips with.

13 Sep 65   Newsweek

...To their credit, U.S. authorities in South Vietnam have repeatedly pressed the South Vietnamese Government to improve its treatment of prisoners. But so far such pressure has had scant effect and individual Americans in South Vietnam are often made accomplices to their allies' brutality. U.S. helicopter pilots have reportedly found themselves obliged to stand by while Viet Cong prisoners were thrown out of their planes by South Vietnamese troops. And on one operation witnessed by a U.S. photographer, a U.S. enlisted man and an Australian officer made no protest when a Vietnamese officer shot a suspected guerrilla out of hand.

28 Nov 65   New York Times Magazine
              William Tuohy, "A Big 'Dirty Little War' "

...But if the Vietcong cruelly employs terror, South Vietnamese troops have behaved brutally, too. Anyone who has spent much time with Government units in the field has seen the heads of prisoners held under water and bayonet blades pressed against their throats. Photographs of such incidents were common until the Government decided the publicity was not improving Saigon's public relations. In more extreme cases, victims have had bamboo slivers run under their fingernails or wires from a field telephone connected to arms, nipples, or testicles. Another rumored technique is known as "the long step." The idea is to take several prisoners up in a helicopter and toss one out in order to loosen the tongues of the others.

Some Vietcong suspects do not survive long enough for the third degree. Earlier this year, in an operation along the central coast, a Government detachment failed to flush V.C. troops suspected of lurking in the area. However, several villagers were rounded up and one man was brought before the company commander. The Vietnamese officer briefly questioned the suspect, then turned to his adviser, an Australian warrant officer, and said, "I think I shoot this man. Okay?"

"Go ahead," said the adviser.

The officer fired a carbine round point-blank, striking the villager below the chest. The man slumped and died. The patrol moved on. Later, a correspondent asked the adviser, who had seemed a decent enough fellow, why he had given his approval. The Australian cited the British experience in putting down the Malayan insurgency and said, "These people could have moved to a Government area. In this war they are either on our side or they are not. There is no in-between."

...American advisers find it hard to dissuade the Vietnamese from using force on prisoners. Says one U.S. specialist. "The Vietnamese do their questioning out of our sight because they know we feel guilty about their methods. They say, "You people are a bunch of softies. This is a rough war and this is the way to get information — the only way." So the Vietnamese major says to the American adviser, 'I suggest you take a walk and don't come back for half an hour. We're going to do this anyway, so it is better if you aren't here."

"I myself don't believe in the effectiveness of torture, but it is very difficult to tell a Vietnamese paratrooper whose buddies have just been wiped out to go easy on a prisoner and make sure he gets back for questioning."

"There are better ways of getting information from prisoners than torture," says another American paramilitary expert. "Sure, you can start cutting off fingers and the guy will talk. But you never know whether the information is accurate."

22 May 66   (See Note Page 20)

... — The military government appeared to have the upper hand at Da Nang. Its forces seized one small pagoda. Holed-up rebels and government marines exchanged gunfire unofficially estimated to have killed 22 persons and wounded 200. The government units, under orders to shoot only in response to rebel fire, surrounded the rebel complex with a cordon of tanks and machine gun nests.

— A Vietnamese marine officer executed a rebel army private captured during heavy fighting around the central market place. In the presence of newsmen, he shot the captive in the chest with a pistol. A Marine said the man had thrown three grenades at government forces.

17 Jun 66   Commonweal, Gordon C. Zahn
The Crime of Silence — Are We Accomplices in Mass Murder in Vietnam?
(from Congressional Record — Senate, June 29, 1966, p. 14017)

...There are war criminals in our midst, and what is far worse, we know of them and their deeds — and close our eyes to them.

For example, some of these criminals were shown on Chicago television not too long ago in a film documentary prepared by the Canadian Broadcasting System. One memorable sequence concerned an act that, to say the least, was a clear violation of the Geneva conventions. A Vietcong captive was stretched out on the ground with one of his captors kneeling on his groin while another poured hatfuls of water down the victim's nostrils. When the unfortunate captive finally died — still "on camera," mind you — his body was unceremoniously kicked aside into a ditch. It is hard to decide which was worse: the disgusting deed itself or the picture of the others who stood around (Americans included, needless to say) looking quite pleased, even entertained, by the gruesome proceedings.

21 Nov 66   (See Note Page 20)
SAIGON, Nov 21

...The Vietnamese war is an unconventional conflict and the prisoner problem is confused because terrorists are not covered by the Geneva Convention.

Only regular, uniformed troops are officially covered by the Convention. Terrorists, saboteurs or spies are tried as criminals and are not privileged to be treated as prisoners of war.

The Saigon government has custody of most North Vietnamese captured in fighting, including those seized by U.S. units.

Brig. Gen. H.L. Moore, Jr., of the U.S. Army's Provost Marshal's office, says South Vietnam holds 572 North Vietnamese prisoners turned over by the Americans. These and other captives are held in camps at Pleiku, Da Nang, Dalat and Bien Hoa.

U.S. experts oversee their treatment. Moore described the camps as operating with "strict accountability, fair treatment... orderliness and sanitation are commendable."

This wasn't always so. The shooting of prisoners was common a year ago. Some Vietnamese field commanders still consider Viet Cong prisoners as traitors and frequently have them shot, sources report.

South Viet Nam holds more than 20,000 persons loosely classified as war prisoners. However, this number includes some political detainees and many who were rounded up in military sweeps and not yet screened.

The only North Vietnamese known to be held by the United States are 19 seamen pulled from the Gulf of Tonkin, outside South Vietnamese waters, when their torpedo boats were sunk.

The U.S. Navy sometimes takes captives near the coast when they stop suspected communist supply craft and sampans. These are turned over to the Saigon government.

One thousand or more suspects may be seized on a U.S. sweep through several villages. Most are released in the first screening. Others are winnowed at battalion and division command level processing.

Moore says a few Vietnamese "surrendered" several times once they discovered they could get an airplane ride to an interrogation center and a free meal or two.

17 Apr 67   CDN, New York Post
               SAIGON, April 17

Following is from a dictionary of Vietnamese slang that newcomers to the Saigon scene may find helpful:

... Co di mo tom — To let go or feed for lobster. Translated this means to kill prisoners. Derived from the time-honored Vietnamese custom of killing prisoners, putting them in a bag and tossing them into the river.

PRISON CAMPS

7 Jun 65   New York Times
               SAIGON, June 6

Surveys taken among Vietcong prisoners and defectors have outlined a high morale and confidence that the Communist forces will win their battle in South Vietnam.

American officials, describing the interviews also suggest that the Government of South Vietnam could draw more defectors by ending brutal practices at its military prison camps.

25 Dec 66   New York Times, Jonathan Randal
               SAIGON, SOUTH VIETNAM, Dec 24

In a war otherwise belabored with statistics, none of the belligerents in the Vietnam conflict are keen about revealing the number of prisoners they hold.

In past wars, belligerents have tended to keep exact numbers secret as a hedge against peace negotiations or prisoner exchanges. But in Vietnam, the reasons for reticence vary from lack of adequate accounting on the South Vietnamese and American side to doctrinal subbornness in Hanoi.

... American sources admit that until this year no meaningful prisoner records were kept by the South Vietnamese Government, which is responsible for Vietcong and North Vietnamese troops captured by any allied soldier on its territory.

... Because of these worrying signs and because of Hanoi's very real threat to try downed American pilots, the United States has stepped up its pressure on the Saigon regime to provide adequate prisoner of war camps for Vietcong and North Vietnamese prisoners.

Once again, official sources are reluctant to provide detailed statistics, but it is believed nearly 2,000 enemy soldiers are held by the South Vietnamese authorities.

Beginning in July, the Saigon Government opened three prisoner of war camps in each of the three northernmost corps areas. A final camp is under construction in the fourth corps in the Mekong River Delta center of Mytho.

The South Vietnamese Army is also screening civilian jails across the country where prisoners of war as well as Vietcong sympathizers and common criminals had been imprisoned until the formal camps were built ...

28 Jul 65   New York Times
              Lloyd Garrison
              WASHINGTON, July 27

...Vietcong prisoners are divided by the South Vietnamese into two categories: "hard-core" Communists and those considered susceptible to "rehabilitation". The latter are placed in special camps. Some are eventually returned to civilian life, usually in zones considered safe from Vietcong penetration. A few are taken into the South Vietnamese Army.

1 Jul 66   New York Times, R. W. Apple, Jr.
              SAIGON, SOUTH VIETNAM, June 30

...In the opinion of most international lawyers, the United States, if it had wished to take a narrowly legalistic position, could have avoided applying the provisions of the convention here.

Article 4 provides a series of definitions of prisoners of war. The Vietcong, and to a degree that is not so clear the North Vietnamese regulars, fall outside of these definitions because they do not wear distinctive insignia, follow the "laws and customs of war" or belong to a country recognized by their adversaries.

Nevertheless, Secretary of State Dean Rusk, in a letter to the International Committee of the Red Cross on Aug. 10, 1965, made clear that the United States intended to apply the convention in Vietnam. The South Vietnamese Government took a similar position.

The American command here adopted last month a definition that goes far beyond the convention. It promises prisoner of war status of "any captive member of the North Vietnamese armed forces or main force Vietcong, whether captured in combat or not," and to certain others.

...Government officials, once openly hostile to the convention, now grudgingly accept the American position. Much remains to be done, however, to persuade the average South Vietnamese soldier to stop using torture.

...North Vietnamese captives have begun to flow into the camp at Bienhoa, but so far the Government continues to treat most Vietcong captives as traitors rather than prisoners of war, confining them in civil jails. About 18,000 Vietcong or suspects are now held by the Government.

"It is asking a lot of a soldier to treat a rebel from his own village as a prisoner of war under international law," a Government official sympathetic to the American position said. "But within six to eight months, I think we will have the problems overcome."

Paradoxically, the South Vietnamese release guerrillas held in civil jails at the rate of several thousand a month after "rehabilitation." Prisoners of war would be detained until the war ends.

1 Jul 66   New York Times, R. W. Apple, Jr.
              SAIGON, SOUTH VIETNAM, June 30

...Since January 1, the United States has captured 3,384 enemy soldiers, according to figures issued in Washington.

25 Jan 67   Los Angeles Times, William Tuohy
              SAIGON

Of the thousands of enemy suspects captured by allied forces in Vietnam, only about 2,500 are actually being held as prisoners of war, U.S. military sources revealed Tuesday.

A military spokesman made the figure public, he said, in order to draw attention to the vast difference between enemy suspects detained and those finally classified as prisoners of war.

In 1966, more than 10,000 enemy suspects were captured, but only a fraction were ultimately classified as Viet Cong or North Vietnamese soldiers.

...All prisoners captured by American forces are eventually turned over to the Vietnamese government, which currently operates three POW camps in Da Nang, Pleiku, and Bien Hoa. Two other camps are under construction at Can Tho and Bien Hoa.

The Vietnamese government, American military sources said, in describing what happens to those captured, can take "considerable pride" in the treatment of POWs.

The Americans transfer their prisoners to the Vietnamese under Article XII of the Geneva Convention on the treatment of those captured in wartime.

In August, 1965 the South Vietnamese government officially declared the existence of an "armed conflict" in the nation, thereby recognizing that the Geneva conventions applied in Vietnam.

Before that, the Vietnamese government described the war as a rebellion, which, legally, does not have the same status under the 1949 convention.

One reason that the United States government is taking pains to see that the conventions are respected is the existence of scores of U.S. prisoners in Viet Cong and North Vietnamese hands.

The United States still holds 19 North Vietnamese sailors taken off patrol boats in the Gulf of Tonkin. These men have not been handed over to the South Vietnamese because of the special nature of their capture.

...U.S. Military sources said that a screening process has been set up in U.S. brigade and division headquarters to handle captured suspects.

The screening tries to sort out those captured into categories: innocent civilians, returnees, "civil defendants," which includes saboteurs and terrorists who are prosecuted by Vietnamese civil authorities, and finally prisoners of war, either Viet Cong or North Vietnamese.

POWs are defined as those captured bearing arms in the field, and they receive the full protection of the Geneva Convention, U.S. sources said.

U.S. officers admit the difficulty of distinguishing between war prisoners and civil defendants. A special tribunal consisting of three or more officers including a lawyer, tries to differentiate these doubtful cases.

Currently, U.S. advisers are assigned to the POW camps to make sure proper treatment is applied. According to U.S. military sources, the camps have been set up in model fashion, and families of Viet Cong are allowed to visit the prisoners.

13 Apr 67   New York Times (See Note Page 20)
              BIENHOA, SOUTH VIETNAM, April 12

— Only 3,200 prisoners — roughly 4 per cent of the thousands captured by South Vietnamese forces and their allies — have been sent to prisoner of war camps, United States and Vietnamese military officers said today.

The bulk, they said, are detained, questioned and released. Some others, classified as criminals and political prisoners, are turned over to the civilian police.

Authorities permitted newsmen today to visit the prisoner of war camp here, one of four in the country. "We hope that by showing good treatment, the enemy will do likewise," said Col. Nguyen Ca. who administers the prison system.

There are 913 prisoners at the 30-acre Bienhoa camp, about 20 miles north of Saigon. About 300 infiltrated from North Vietnam and the others are Vietcong guerrillas, including 18 women.

The Bienhoa camp is a sundrenched dusty plain. Behind the double. barbed-wire walls are rows of corrugated tin sheds, each holding 50 prisoners. Sentries patrol the fence constantly.

By Vietnamese rural standards, the camp was clean.

Jul 66   International Review of the Red Cross, P. 362

Handing over of a list of prisoners. — The Government of the Republic of Vietnam in Saigon has handed over to the International Committee of the Red Cross a further list of prisoners who had fought for the NLF (Vietcong). This list comprises 41 new names which brings the total number of prisoners' names notified to the ICRC by the South Vietnamese authorities to over 200.

Nov 66   International Review of the Red Cross, p. 597, 598

Prisoners. — The Red Cross of the Republic of Vietnam has also participated in the visits carried out by ICRC delegates to Vietnam prisoners held by the Government. Members of its Central Committee accompany the International Committee representatives, for whom they act as interpreters. Vietnamese first-aiders assist in relief distributions. Delegates of the Vietnam Red Cross and of the ICRC have been authorized to go again to the island of Con-Son (Poulo-Condore) where they were able to visit prisoners of war and interview a number of them.

In addition, the ICRC Central Tracing Agency has received further lists of prisoners' names, thus bringing the total of notified prisoners of war by the Government of the Republic of Vietnam to 516. The number of North Vietnamese prisoners held by the American forces, and of which the list has been communicated to Geneva and transmitted to Hanoi, is 19.

CHAPTER II
CIVILIANS, SUSPECTS
AND COMBATANTS

The following Articles from International Conventions relevant to this chapter are quoted in full:

Geneva Convention
Relative to the Protection of Civilian Persons
in Time of War
12 August 1949
(Short reference: Geneva—Civilians)

Article 27.

Protected persons are entitled, in all circumstances, to respect for their persons, their honour, their family rights, their religious convictions and practices, and their manners and customs. They shall at all times be humanely treated, and shall be protected especially against all acts of violence or threats thereof and against insults and public curiosity.

Women shall be especially protected against any attack on their honour, in particular against rape, enforced prostitution, or any form of indecent assault.

Without prejudice to the provisions relating to their state of health, age and sex, all protected persons shall be treated with the same consideration by the Party to the conflict in whose power they are, without any adverse distinction based, in particular, on race, religion or political opinion.

However, the Parties to the conflict may take such measures of control and security in regard to protected persons as may be necessary as a result of the war.

Article 29

The Party to the conflict in whose hands protected persons may be, is responsible for the treatment accorded to them by its agents, irrespective of any individual responsibility which may be incurred.

Article 31.

No physical or moral coercion shall be exercised against protected persons, in particular to obtain information from them or from third parties.

Article 32.

The High Contracting Parties specifically agree that each of them is prohibited from taking any measure of such a character as to cause the physical suffering or extermination of protected persons in their hands. This prohibition applies not only to murder, torture, corporal punishment, mutilation and medical or scientific experiments not necessitated by the medical treatment of a protected person, but also to any other measures of brutality whether applied by civilian or military agents.

Article 33.

No protected persons may be punished for an offence he or she has not personally committed. Collective penalties and likewise all measures of intimidation or of terrorism are prohibited.

Pillage is prohibited.

Reprisals against protected persons and their property are prohibited.

Article 147.

Grave breaches to which the preceding Article relates shall be those involving any of the following acts, if committed against persons or property protected by the present Convention: wilful killing, torture or inhuman treatment, including biological experiments, wilfully causing great suffering or serious injury to body or health, unlawful deportation or transfer or unlawful confinement of a protected person, compelling a protected person to serve in the forces of a hostile Power, or willfully depriving a protected person of the rights of fair and regular trial prescribed in the present Convention, taking of hostages and extensive destruction and appropriation of property, not justified by military necessity and carried out unlawfully and wantonly.

See also (pages 29-42) the following additional Articles relevant to this chapter: Geneva—Civilians: 3, 5, 146, 148.

COUNTER-TERROR

21 Oct 65   The Sun (Baltimore) (See Note Page 20)
                   WASHINGTON, Oct 20

Sen. Young (D-Ohio) says he has learned the Central Intelligence Agency hired persons to disguise as Viet Cong and discredit Communists in Viet Nam by committing atrocities.

The CIA and Rep. Gallagher, (D-N. Y.), said it is not so.

Young, who recently returned from Viet Nam, at first told newsmen a CIA man informed him the CIA hired South Vietnamese who dressed as Viet Cong, then committed such acts as killing men and raping women.

Tonight, however, the Senator denied saying the information came from a CIA man, but said he got it from an American military officer whom he did not name.

Nevertheless, Young said, "I confirmed through the CIA today that it employed some South Vietnamese nationals to pose as Viet Cong — and I take a dim view of that."

Gallagher said "It may well be that he (Young) spoke to a Viet Cong disguised as a CIA man."

Gallagher said Young's statement "is appalling, and it reflects a carelessness with facts."

Gallagher is a member of the House Foreign Affairs Committee and said that like Young, he was briefed when he was in Saigon about four months ago.

"It is obvious," Gallagher said in a statement, "that he (Young) misunderstood the essence of the briefing or failed to distinguish between the terms of identification of the opposing forces in Viet Nam... no one could possibly conceive such an exercise as Sen. Young describes.

21 Oct 65   New York Herald Tribune, Tom Lambert
             WASHINGTON

The CIA and the State Department went into an uproar yesterday when a news service reported Sen. Stephen Young as saying that he had been told the intelligence agency had committed atrocities in Viet Nam to discredit the Communist Viet Cong guerrillas.

...Their reactions stemmed from an Associated Press dispatch quoting Sen. Young as saying that a CIA agent in Viet Nam told him the CIA had committed atrocities there to underscore the Viet Cong guerrillas reputation for cruelty.

Asked about the report, Sen. Young modified it considerably.

He told the Herald Tribune that "a man who claimed to be working for the CIA" in Viet Nam alleged that the intelligence agency had hired some South Vietnamese to masquerade as Viet Cong, adding:

"It was alleged to me that several of these executed two village leaders and raped some women."

In an elaboration of the remarks attributed earlier to him, the Senator indicated at one point he believed a group of the purported masqueraders had committed the alleged atrocities.

But he added "I still don't know, I don't believe such an incident occurred, but I could see how it could have occurred."

"CIA has employed some South Vietnamese and they have been instructed to claim they are Viet Cong and to work accordingly," the Senator said, "but of course no one could tell me any American instructed anyone to perpetrate outrages."

...Although he later diluted considerably the import of the remarks attributed to him Sen. Young was steadfast in his opposition to CIA's employment of South Vietnamese to pose as Viet Cong guerrillas.

22 Jan 65   New York Times, Jack Langguth
             DANANG, Jan 22

An American Special Forces soldier in South Vietnam usually has three hired Chinese bodyguards to protect him.

These are the Nungs, a mercenary band of professional soldiers who serve with Special Forces teams along the Laotian border.

At each post there are about a dozen Americans; three dozen Nungs, and a few hundred Vietnamese irregular guard troops.

...When American troops arrived three years ago they began picking up the bill for the Nungs' services. As a result, the Chinese soldiers came directly under United States control. An American captain who advises the Vietnamese directly commands his Nung unit.

The Nungs are paid 1,000 piasters (about $8) a month more than Vietnamese soldiers of the same rank. The disparity causes continuing friction.

The Nungs, who are huskier and more ruthless soldiers make no secret of their contempt for the Vietnamese. "The Nungs are bloodthirsty," said Jock Hague of Melbourne, an Australian warrant officer.

...The Nungs, who keep their camp spotlessly clean, are provided with rations considerably better than those of the Vietnamese troops. Besides paying them promptly each month, the Americans keep the Nungs supplied with beef, chicken and pork.

3 Mar 65   (See Note Page 20)
            KHE SAHN, Mar 3

... Because the Special Forces recruit their own mercenary forces
in the area in which they operate, each camp gets some Viet Cong guerrillas. The official figure here is about a third.

The Communists are weeded out and shot as fast as possible but
because of the high turnover in Special Forces, more keep appearing.

15 Mar 65   (See Note Page 20)
             SAIGON, VIETNAM, March 15

... None of the defenders inside Kannak (except for nine American
Special Forces men) was a regular soldier. The defenders, all "Civil
Irregular Defense Group" volunteers, were non-Vietnamese mountain
tribesmen (called Montagnards), commanded, paid, equipped, trained
and uniformed by Americans.

... The U.S. Special Forces commander, cigar-puffing Col. John
Spears, was grimly pleased as he marched around the piles of enemy
bodies the following day. The idea has not always been so successful.
The Special Forces operation has become one of the most controversial
aspects of America's military aid to Viet Nam. In the course of training
and arming approximately 10,000 Cambodians, tribesmen, Chinese and
Vietnamese, the United States has run into some acute diplomatic and
military problems.

Traditional bitterness between Vietnamese Lowlanders and Viet Nam's
racial minority groups is the worst of these problems.

When American Special Forces men, actually the fighting arm of the
Central Intelligence Agency, moved out into the hills three years ago,
there was suspicion in Saigon that the Americans would start siding with
the tribesmen against Vietnamese.

26 Mar 65   (See Note Page 20)
             TOKYO, Friday, March 26

Tribesmen of Chinese ancestry were involved in two operations against
Viet Cong forces in recent weeks and killed 11 terrorists, according to a
U.S. Marine publication distributed today.

Torii Teller, a weekly magazine issued by the U.S. Marine Air Station
in Iwakuni, Japan, identified them as the Nungs, a minority tribal group of
about 7,000 who originally inhabited regions bordering Yunnan province in
China and North Viet Nam.

Many Nungs have migrated South and joined U.S. Special Forces as
paid soldiers.

Torii Teller supplemented its article with two pictures.

The magazine quoted Capt. Steven V. Sosa, Senior Army Special
Forces Advisor to a Chinese unit at Da Nang, as describing them as "one
of the toughest fighting units in the Republic Forces."

"They have been soldiers for centuries and nearly all stationed at
Da Nang are combat veterans. U.S. Army Special Forces and U.S.
Marine Advisors that accompany the Nungs on patrol rate them as top
notch," the magazine quoted Sosa as saying.

The magazine said the Nungs were involved in two operations in the
March 8-22 period against Viet Cong forces in jungled terrain near the
Laotain border. It said they killed 11 Viet Cong soldiers.

Torii Teller said the Nungs are used "primarily for long-range patrols,
infiltration and counter-reaction engagements."

One picture showed a Nung, rifle in hand, moments after alighting
from an aircraft. The other picture showed two Nungs rushing for cover
in a shrub area near the Viet Nam-Laos border as a helicopter hovered
overhead.

7 Nov 65   New York Herald Tribune, David Wise
            WASHINGTON

...The tall, tough ethnic Chinese, who have been fighting as mercenaries in Viet Nam for years, have earned the respect of U.S. Special Forces
troops, who regard the Nungs as dependable and fierce warriors.

...The roughly 1,200 Nungs fighting in separate Nung units are organized
into groups of companies in three different corps areas. There are more
than half a dozen Nung companies in South Vietnam.

...On Oct. 19 two of these Nung companies, wearing red, white and blue
scarves, were airlifted by helicopter into the Ho Bo woods, 35 miles west of
Saigon, to clean out a Viet Cong hideout after it had been pounded from the
air by B-52 bombers.

...The South Vietnamese broke up the Nung units and integrated them
into the army. But after U.S. Special Forces moved into South Viet Nam a
few years ago, the Nungs found they could get higher pay by enlisting as civilian irregulars with the men with the green berets. They went from camp to
camp joining the Special Forces units that offered the highest pay.

U.S. Special Forces C teams in the field used the Nungs as defenders
of the "inner perimeter" of Special Forces camps.

...By last June, however, with the pace of the fighting picking up all
over South Viet Nam, the Army decided it needed a "reaction force" that
could speedily come to the rescue of Special Forces camps under attack.

The Nungs were reorganized and their number increased into their
present company strength. The Nung companies are known as a Mike
Force, which is shorthand for Multipurpose Reaction Force. They have
the threefold function of reinforcing beseiged camps, reinforcing threatened camps, and performing reconnaissance duties, i.e., looking for the
enemy.

Technically, U.S. officials said, the Nungs are not in the South Vietnamese Army but are civilians. They receive 30 per cent more pay than regular
South Vietnamese Army soldiers.

...The Defense Department denies reports that the Nungs have trussed
up prisoners by running wires through their hands and cheeks and securing
the wires with sticks. But they are officially described as tough characters.

...There has been little written or said about the Nungs up to now, but
Pentagon officials insist this is not because there is anything secret or
mysterious about their role in Viet Nam.

29 Sep 65   New York Herald Tribune, Jimmy Breslin
             DA NANG, VIET NAM

...At 12:00 o'clock, a helicopter came in and the shirtless Marine in
the tent said it was going to Da Nang. The ship was in an area on the side
of the air strip. A young red-headed machine gunner sat in the doorway,
chewing on a chocolate cracker from a C-ration tin. He kicked a small spool
of wire out of the doorway and made room.

"We just rode Nuongs, you can tell that by the wire here," he said.

"Why?" he was asked. Nuongs are Chinese mercenaries from Formosa.
A battalion of them are in Viet Nam, collecting good salaries for fighting
for the Saigon government. One of them works as a guard at the United
States embassy in Saigon.

"They always want the wire for the prisoners," the kid said. "Don't you
know that? They get a VC and make him hold his hands against his cheeks.
Then they take this wire and run it right through the one hand and right
through his cheek and into his mouth. Then they pull the wire out through
the other cheek and stick it through the other hand. They knot both ends
around sticks. You never seen them with prisoners like that? Oh, you
ought to see how quiet them gooks sit in a helicopter when we got them
wrapped up like that."

20 Aug 66   (See Note Page 20)
         MY THO, VIET NAM, Aug 20

...Government forces are beset by jealousies and rivalries. There are numerous armed groups, starting from the national police, the oldest institution of law in the delta, ranging through the regular army, the popular and regional forces known as roughs and puffs, the Special Forces strike force battalions, the counter-terrorist groups and so on.

Pay differences create animosity. A counter-terrorist team soldier makes 4,500 piasters (about $40) a month, a popular force soldier makes 1,500 piasters ($12).

5 Aug 66   The Sun (Baltimore) (See Note Page 20)
         MOC HOA, VIET NAM, Aug 4

The South Vietnamese government is showing that terror can be a two-way street. Through "Skull and Crossbones" commandos it is carrying the work, with fire and retribution, to the Viet Cong and the areas where they operate.

The commandos, created this year, now number 2,500, by the best available estimates. Most provinces have several 12-man teams. They are under the command of province chiefs, and can be used in any way they wish, including kidnaping and assassination.

The Kien Tuong province chief used a 60-man group of commandos on a conventional operation in the plain of reeds due west of Saigon.

The night before the operation a noncommissioned officer connected with it said: "If the Viet Cong think they know what destruction is, let them see what we can do. Come with us."

The commandos made two helicopter assaults, hitting villages on the Cambodian border.

Can Den village was separated from Cambodia by a 20-foot canal. It consisted of houses well spaced out to thwart air attacks.

A captured Viet Cong dentist had told interrogators the locations of a medical school and a weapons factory in the area. These were quickly located by the commandos, who found a huge, hot charcoal stove for melting metal to make hand grenades.

The area is regarded as completely Viet Cong. Most of the villagers were seen running off into Cambodia. Two girls were caught near the weapons factory. They were obviously involved in the weapons business.

The leader of the commandos decided to execute them, "as an example to all those who help the Viet Cong."

His plans were thwarted by the commander of a Regional Force Unit also in the village, who claimed that he had captured the girls first and that they were not to be killed.

The girls were eventually put into a helicopter and flown to the province capital for questioning.

The regional forces captain was not happy. "The commandos should operate alone, not with us," he commented. "The things they do are not what we do. They are unconventional. Better they do it alone."

The commandos argue they have no choice but to be tough. "Someone has to do the dirty work" is one explanation.

The dirty work in the area attacked included the intimidation of some women. The women, found hiding with their children in a village, were threatened with rifles, and closely questioned about the whereabouts of their husbands and the other village men.

The torch was put to every house.

The scorched-earth policy was carried out to include every fowl and animal they found.

Encountering a herd of 40 water buffalo, the commandos pumped several grenades into them to slow them down. Then the leader took two men with him and killed or maimed the lot in 15 minutes.

A buffalo represents about one year's income for a Vietnamese farmer.

A woman tried to pull a bundle of clothing from a burning house. A commando took it from her and threw it back into the flames. "These people must remember that supporting the Viet Cong can do them no good." a commando said.

"One must tell the story. We must spread terror. By spreading terror we hope to counter terror," one of the commandos explained.

Government figures show that the Viet Cong, in its program of terrorizing those who serve the Saigon regime, have killed or kidnapped 2,800 officials since January 1964. In May alone, the government says, 115 officials were assassinated and 115 abducted ...

As in other units of the South Vietnamese forces, Americans often serve in an advisory capacity. The South Vietnamese call the signals.

The commandos are a varied lot, including army veterans, mercenaries and adventurers. The experiment is new, but the idea is old — an eye for an eye, a tooth for a tooth.

1 Mar 67   The West Australian (Perth, Australia)

Even on the fringe of the Vietnam war its consequences were horrifying, Dr. M.A. Jaspan, head of the W.A. University's centre for Asian studies, said yesterday.

He has just returned with Mrs. Jaspan from a ten-week field trip to Cambodia to study the Cham tribe, near the South Vietnamese border.

Dr. and Mrs. Jaspan said that American aircraft intermittently raided Cambodian peasant villages near the border, making 59 to 60 attacks a year.

They had seen pregnant women and children hideously disfigured by third-degree burns from napalm.

In mid-January about 15 American helicopters flew across the border into neutral Cambodia, descended on a village, shot people for unknown reasons, including some children — accidentally — and also livestock, and took hostages to South Vietnam.

The attack was being investigated by the International Control Commision.

Dr. Jaspan said the village assualted was Bathu, in Svay Rieng province. Nearby villages had also been attacked.

Further attacks had been made on frontier villages near Mimot, in Kompong-cham province.

The Cambodian government was urging villagers not to leave the near-border areas, partly because widespread panic could result, and partly because South Vietnamese would take over abondoned Cambodian territory.

The American policy of spraying destructive chemicals on South Vietnamese farms and forests was creating a refugee problem for Cambodia.

The chemicals often killed livestock and killed or maimed children.

Nothing grew on the destroyed land for several years. Many farmers would never again be able to work a farm.

They either drifted to the outskirts of Saigon or headed for Cambodia, to live in houseboat villages on the Mekong and get labouring work.

Even in the Cambodian capital, 70 miles from the border, the explosions from heavy bombs dropped by B52s in Vietnam shook windows.

Those bombs were released at 16,000 to 25,000 ft, and their destruction in peasant-village country was wholly indiscriminate.

Dr. Jaspan spoke of dead livestock, defoliated farms and raped women.

"There is a great deal of refined torture by both sides," he said.

The Viet Cong, not the allied forces, were winning the hearts and minds of the South Vietnamese, he said.

All the military might in the world could not bring that war to an end. The more destruction the Americans created, the more Vietnamese turned against them.

For example, South Korean troops — the worst of them all — would pacify an area by rounding up unarmed villagers and shooting in cold blood anyone who informers said had had anything to do with the Viet Cong.

"It is pacification by brutality," he said. "They do not gain the sympathy of the population."

9 Jan 67   The Evening Star (Washington), Peter Arnett
            RACH KIEN, VIETNAM

Here in Rach Kien, center of the richest rice district in Vietnam, U.S. troops are learning first-hand the dilemmas of the Mekong Delta.

They must fight a war and pacify the countryside at the same time. And more and more peasant farmhouses are being destroyed.

The orders to a battalion of the U.S. 25th Division are specific:

Shoot only when shot at, use artillery fire extremely sparingly, avoid destroying crops and especially homes.

... The battalion flew in a few days before Christmas. There was no place to bivouac other than in the houses within the village. The countryside is so lush that every inch of ground is planted in rice.

So the Americans moved into about half the village, occupying 30 houses. Some had been abondoned, others still held families.

... The commander of the American unit, Lt. Col. Charles A. Gillis, of Colorado Springs, Colo., paid immediate indemnity for two thatched homes knocked down by the blast from landing helicopters. One home owner received 4,000 piasters, another 1,000.

The scheme to retake and pacify Rach Kien was formulated without conferring with provincial officials. Therefore the town is not included in the 1967 pacification budget for Long An province.

"All the talk and negotiations in the world are useless if we don't have the money to pay for these homes, and we need it in a hurry," one U.S. officer commented.

Lack of funds is also holding up schemes to rebuild the school, now occupied by U.S. soldiers as a supply depot and mess hall, and also to clean up the large dispensary, which the Viet Cong used as a rest center.

The Americans have built up the homes they occupy into sandbagged fortifications, with machine guns poking out of doorways and windows.

Col. Gillis says he realizes the danger to the town now that U.S. troops have taken half of it over. "If the Viet Cong attack through that part of town which we don't occupy then I know I might have no choice but to smash the homes to pieces with mortars and heavy weapons fire," Gillis said.

The Americans have destroyed some of the peasant farmhouses that sit in islands of greenery amidst paddy rice grown shoulder high. The Americans have been hit by mortars almost every night. It appears that only the Viet Cong guerrillas and their families have remained in many nearby homes, and they snipe at every American who passes by.

... The Americans got an unfortunate choice of Vietnamese soldiery to assist them. The province chief sent a platoon of his provincial reconnaissance unit to Rach Kien. These soldiers were formerly called "CT" (counter terrorist) teams, specializing in murder, mayhem and infiltration of enemy lines.

They are reputedly tough fighters, but in Rach Kien they tended to try to take over the village.

Col. Gillis is on the alert to solve the problems. He and his officers hope that they can cut down the sniper fire and drive the Viet Cong out of the area before they have to reduce the whole countryside to ashes.

16 Jan 67   Der Spiegel
            "Red Ants"

In the mud of the only street of Rach Kien four heads lay bleeding. Wild men with long hair and heavy weapons had shortly before hewed them off (the necks of) four Vietnamese and had brought them as trophies into the little village in the Mekong Delta.

The four decapitated men were reputedly Vietcong terrorists, the wild men "Counter-terrorists" of the South Vietnamese Government.

For years now they have been combing — a death's head on their camouflage uniforms — the canals, ricefields and villages of the Mekong Delta for communist partisans.

But just like the 40,000 Saigon soldiers stationed in the Delta who under their General Dang Van Quang would rather hunt lucrative private business rather than the rebels, they have run aground in their attempt to purge the river delta of red guerrillas.

On the contrary: The more heads they hewed off, the more civilians they shot, all the larger became the numbers of Viet Cong adherents.

... The country population is well-disposed toward the partisans anyway. Once (the population) was pillaged by the big landowners in Saigon. Today, after an agrarian reform of the Vietcong, (the population) has faith that the guerrillas are the best defense against the return of the landlords.

18 Jan 67   (See Note Page 20)
            RACH KIEN, VIETNAM, Jan 18

She was a slim, pretty farm girl and her eyes were frozen in fear. Her hands were bound behind her.

A knife flashed forward and stopped short of her chest.

A Vietnamese soldier swished the blade from side to side and then pointed it steadily at her as he snarled questions. She stuttered answers in a hoarse whisper.

Other Vietnamese soldiers called remarks punctuated by jeers and laughter.

A squad of 12 American infantrymen had brought in the girl because she lacked identification credentials. They shuffled around, not knowing what to do, not understanding a word of what was said. An interpreter stood by passively, seemingly confused.

The Americans were from a company of the 2nd Battalion, 14th Infantry, 25th Infantry Division on a two-day operation just south of their base camp at Rach Kien, on the northern fringe of the Mekong Delta.

The battalion's mission was to experiment and find ways of beating the Viet Cong in the delta.

High-up American military and political strategists were keeping the outfit under close scrutiny. What the 2nd Battalion learned would be applied as American forces pushed farther south.

The mission was a touchy one combining military tactics with civic action programs aimed at winning the people.

The troops were under strict orders — from the high U.S. command in Vietnam — to do everything possible to avoid hurting civilians, to avoid alienating them.

The GI's were not to shoot first and were to make sparing use of artillery and air support.

The men were told repeatedly that success in the Mekong Delta hinged on winning the civilians to the Government side. The delta is the nation's richest and most densely populated area. The Viet Cong have become deeply rooted into the countryside and among the people.

The rice paddies were thick with mud, sometimes chest-deep. Snipers picked away at the 2nd battalion from countless patches of trees that dotted the paddies. To reach the treeline meant crossing swampy open flatlands.

A company of Vietnamese troops was assigned to help the battalion in this terrain. They were known as PRUS (Provincial Reconnaissance Units) and they lived alongside the Americans, ate with them, and were considered an integral part of the program to find techniques for defeating the Communists and winning the people in the delta.

The PRU outfit may be an unusual one to be working on such a sensitive mission. Not long ago the outfit was known as a CT (Counter Terrorist) Unit. It was specially trained to give Viet Cong terrorists their own medicine — assassination, destruction and terror.

On their camouflaged shirtfronts the PRUS wear an emblem with a skull and crossbones. Their ranks include ex-criminals and ex-Viet Cong (on whose chests the Government has tattooed "Sat Cong," (Kill Cong) to prevent them from returning to their former comrades).

An element of this company of PRUS met the farm girl as the GIs led her toward their encampment.

After several minutes or haranguing by the knife-wielding interrogator, the Americans took the girl with them.

She trembled the rest of the afternoon. She toyed with the cans of C-ration food given her and seemed near tears much of the time.

Next morning she was picked up by an American helicopter and she was flown to Rach Kien for questioning by intelligence specialists.

She was released within minutes when it was established she didn't have an identification card because she was under 16 and thus not required to have one.

On patrol that day the PRUS made contact with the enemy and heavy fighting resulted. They moved in aggressively and claimed to have killed 13 of the enemy while loosing none of their own.

They returned to Rach Kien at dusk.

The village, which once had more than 3,000 people, had dwindled over the past year to a little more than 350 as life became more precarious for civilians and the Viet Cong exerted increasing control. Some villagers fled to the cities, others joined the Viet Cong.

The presence of the American battalion had brought some life back to the market place, beside a bridge crossing a canal.

The returning PRUS chose this bridge as the spot to place trophies of their victorious afternoon — the heads of four of the enemy.

The American battalion commander, Lt. Col. Charles Gillis, of Colorado Springs, Colo., a dedicated and hard-working officer, describes the job facing his men at Rach Kien as one of the roughest imaginable.

23 Jan 67   New York Times, Tom Buckley
             NHATRANG, SOUTH VIETNAM, Jan 22

...Furthermore, the Special Forces is continuing to add to its bag of tricks. Independent guerrilla bands composed of Special Forces officers and lowland Vietnamese or montagnard irregulars are now operating in jungles and mountains throughout the country.

These units of up to 200 men operate from their own secret bases and are able to remain in the field indefinitely, being supplied with food and ammunition in an ingenious but still classified manner.

Beyond that there are the operations that give meaning to the term unconventional warfare. These are the unpublicized raids and reconnaissance patrols by mixed teams of Special Forces, Marines and Thai or Montagnard guerillas into North Vietnam, the so-called counterterrorist activities that include the assassination of Vietcong village chiefs as well as spy-thriller types of operations.

The heart of the Special Forces operations in Vietnam remains its "A" teams. These are the units of two officers and nine enlisted men, all highly trained specialists in communications, medicine, intelligence, weapons, fortifications and demolition, who have established between 75 and 100 outposts in hostile territory.

Those camps, which are under the nominal command of Vietnamese Special Forces officers, are manned by 300 to 500 mercenaries — the civilian irregular defense groups.

18 Feb 67   The Washington Post, Chalmers M. Roberts
               SAIGON, Feb 18

...One form of psychological pressure on the guerrilla which the Americans do not advertise is the specially trained Provincial Reconnaissance Units which have been tested in the paddylands south of Saigon.

The PRU work on the theory of giving back what the Viet Cong deals out — assassination and butchery. Accordingly, a Viet Cong unit on occasion will find the desemboweled remains of its fellows along a well-trod canal bank path, an effective message to guerrillas and to non-committed Vietnamese that two can play the same bloody game.

20 May 67   Christian Science Monitor (See Note Page 20)
               NHATRANG, VIETNAM

...The Special Forces' effort now is vastly bigger than in the initial, clandestine days of 1961-62 when men posing as butterfly collectors and geologists planned and built camps on the central Vietnamese plateau and manned them with montagnards from the region's primitive tribes.

The number of camps is secret, but it is believed to total more than 70, each staffed by a 12-man Special Forces "A" team, but commanded by a Vietnamese captain.

BODY COUNT

25 Jul 62   New York Times, Homer Bigart

...Moreover, one rarely sees a uniformed Vietcong guerrilla; generally the Communist rebels are indistinguishable from peasants. Thus, many of the "enemy" dead reported by the South Vietnam Government were ordinary peasants shot down because they had fled from villages as the troops entered. Some may have been Vietcong sympathizers, but others were running away because they did not want to be rounded up for military conscription or forced labor.

23 Nov 64   'Christian Science Monitor, John Hughes
               BEN TRANH, VIETNAM

...Sometimes the soldiers shoot first and ask questions afterwards. Sometimes government troops claim Viet Cong dead when some observers suspect that uninvolved civilians are among the total.

Artillery and air power, not available to the Viet Cong, are used extensively by government forces, especially to soften up areas thought to be hostile before the infantry move in.

Among some observers there is little doubt that innocent civilians bear the brunt of some of those barrages and strikes rather than the Viet Cong.

Indeed there are instances where the Viet Cong are known to have drawn government fire onto civilians in order to stir resentment against the government.

6 Jun 65   New York Times, Jack Langguth
               SAIGON, SOUTH VIETNAM, Sunday, June 6

...Vietcong casualty figures have always been difficult to pinpoint. As the Communists withdrew from Quangngai last Monday, United States jet bombers pounded the hills into which they were headed.

Many Vietnamese — one estimate was as high as 500 — were killed by the strikes. The American contention is that they were Vietcong soldiers. But three out of four patients seeking treatment in a Vietnamese hospital afterward for burns from napalm, or jellied gasoline, were village women.

8 Jul 66   St. Louis Post-Dispatch, Richard Dudman
            WASHINGTON, July 8

...South Korean forces in Viet Nam, now numbering about 20,000 and expected to rise soon to 40,000, are considered first class troops in aggressiveness, discipline and general fighting ability.

"They go through an area and kill everything in sight," said an American officer recently.

Some American officials believe, however, that their high "kill ratio" — running up to 20 enemies killed for every Korean killed — must mean that many noncombatant men, women and children are counted among the enemy dead.

The trend is evident that the war is being taken over by the American forces and to some extent, by the South Korean forces, which are financed by the United States.

17 Mar 66   (See Note Page 20)
             WASHINGTON, March 16

Six civilians died for every Vietcong killed in some recent search-and-destroy missions in South Vietnam, Representative Clement J. Zablocki, Democrat of Wisconsin, said today.

Mr. Zablocki, who visited Vietnam last month, said an overall ratio of two civilians for one Vietcong apparently is the result of the war so far.

Oct 66   David McLanahan, "Notes on a Summer in Vietnam"

...The government of South Vietnam and the United States are going to continue to have a difficult time with the peasants. They occupy most of the habitable territory away from the coast. They aren't much affected by the government now and the Vietcong can more or less control any contact they do have. The hamlets are really indefensible being too spread out and close to impenetrable terrain for any realistic amount of troops to protect. These unfortunate people absorb most of the horror of the war. When they are living they are classified as poor peasants under the domination of the Vietcong, and when they die they are classified as Vietcong for impressive casualty ratios (which usually run eight or ten Vietcong to one "friendly").

The Vietcong can't be militarily defeated — especially by relying on superior firepower. From what I have seen most of the everyday action consists of air strikes alone on "Vietcong" villages or air strikes in conjunction with "sweeps," where the troops move through an area gathering Vietcong suspects and draft dodgers and fighting when meeting resistance. If they meet resistance from a village — which may mean as little as a single shot or nothing at all — the village is usually destroyed along with anyone who happens to get in the way. The common pattern is that the men of the village hide in nearby jungles or mountains until the sweep is over. If the soldiers stay nearby the men are likely to join the Vietcong, if not the men go back to the villages. If the villages are destroyed the men join the Vietcong and the women and children go to refugee camps.

I had a close look at this situation when I visited a Special Forces camp which is located deep in territory controlled by the Vietcong. We flew over miles and miles of what had been hamlets but which now only had a few structures standing. There wasn't anyone in the rice fields. We learned later that the Marines had started a sweep in this area but had met such heavy resistance and had taken so many casualties that they had to pull back. Instead they destroyed the hamlets by air.

Oct 66   David McLanahan, "Notes on a Summer in Vietnam"

...People in Vietcong-controlled villages should not be subjected to air strikes and sweeps. They have no control over their destiny. Do the American people require women and children-inflated casualty ratios? The Pentagon recently made a show of giving money to families of persons killed when some "friendly" villages were mistakenly bombed. What hypocrisy! These are the same people the Pentagon is proud of killing when they happen to live in an area a few miles away which it can't isolate from the Vietcong.

31 Aug 65   (See Note Page 20)
              AP LA GHI, Aug 31

...Curfew in the river is 6 P.M. After sunset, nothing is supposed to move. From the bridge, a junior officer called out on a megaphone ordering the sampan to approach for inspection. The five occupants jumped into the water and swam for shore. As they began climbing the bank, machine guns mowed them down.

...Three miles farther upstream another sampan was picked up by a roving spotlight. Again the megaphone on the bridge ordered the occupants to heave to. The men in the sampan struggled in the stiff current but quickly lost headway.

Capt. Phong, the Vietnamese skipper, faced a decision: Was the sampan the forward observer for a Viet Cong mortar squad or was her crew one of hapless fishermen too uneducated to understand the complicated curfew regulations.

30 Jun 66   Christian Science Monitor
              Takashi Oka, The Vietnam War
              (from the Congressional Record, Senate, June 30, 1966, p. 14148)

...If the village is in a Communist area or, as in most cases, in the middle, the peasant is continually in the path of operations, conducted by both sides. I have been with government forces on such operations. Most villages we entered were deserted; anyone found, especially ablebodied men, was immediately grilled.

The villagers are the potential enemy, as far as the soldiers are concerned, and if I were a soldier, inching my way forward along slippery paths with obstacles and traps barring my way, and mines, grenades, and ambushes an ever-present threat, I might feel the same way.

The Making of a Quagmire, David Halberstam, 1964, p. 85

...Now, as we skimmed across the paddies, our gunner suddenly opened up with a burst, and a farmer fell down. Later the pilot asked him what he had seen, and the young man, who was very inexperienced, claimed that he had seen the farmer go for a gun. But the pilot and I had been watching too, and we were sure that the farmer had done nothing, that the youngster was nervous. The pilot reprimanded the soldier, but of course that did not save the farmer somewhere back in the paddies.

25 Jul 65   The Sun (Baltimore) (See Note Page 20)
              TAM LOC, July 25

U.S. Marines and government troops launched a major assault today to avenge a recent Viet Cong attack in the defense area around Chu Lai beachhead. But the Viet Cong eluded the troops, and the marines' only victim was an old man who had run at their approach.

...The old man, clad in the black pajamas favored by the peasants and Viet Cong alike, jumped up as the Marines advanced through a group of pine trees. He started moving away and when a warning shot was fired, he broke into a dead run. An automatic rifle and other weapons cut him down.

Nearby his wife wailed out her grief. Her husband had broken one of the cardinal rules of the Viet Nam war — don't run when government troops approach.

4 Aug 65   The Evening Star (Washington) (See Note Page 20)
            DA NANG, VIET NAM, Aug 4

...This week marines teamed with South Vietnamese troops to over-run the Viet Cong-dominated village of Chan Son, 10 miles south of Da Nang. Among 25 persons they killed were a woman and four children.

Two of the children died at the hands of a young marine who tossed a grenade into a village air raid shelter and shouted:

"Whoosh, I'm a killer today. I got me two Viet Cong."

That was before the children's bodies were found.

Maj. Gen. Lewis W. Walt, commander of the 25,300 U.S. Marines in Viet Nam, deplored the five deaths.

22 Aug 66   (See Note Page 20)
             BINH TUY PROVINCE, VIET NAM, Aug 22

The daily operational reports from combat companies included this item:

"Located small Viet Cong campsite. Also 12 chickens."

The chickens were practically all there was to show for a major U.S. land, sea and air operation.

...Intelligence said perhaps two regiments of guerrillas, almost 5,000 men would be caught in the pincers.

The area, only about 50 miles east of Saigon, had been in Viet Cong hands for almost 18 months — since Communist guerrillas smashed into a coastal village and drove out the South Vietnamese army garrison.

"Anything that moves on that beach is enemy. Those are the instructions I have given my troops," said lean, greying Marine Col. Richard Brenneman of Wooster, Ohio.

Oct 66   David McLanahan, "Notes on a Summer in Vietnam"

...The average American soldier is in a difficult dehumanizing situation. Everything is alien except the solidarity of the immediate group. I never heard an enlisted man speak of "Charlie" in terms of something human. Survival often depends on primitive instincts. A medical corpsman told me of seeing soldiers use big rocks to crush the heads of boys found carrying hand grenades. I had a chilling experience one afternoon while site-seeing (sic) with some Vietnamese friends. We came across two young soldiers 18 or 19 years old. One had a large barreled gun. I asked what it was and he said "An M-?" (grenade launcher) and with seeming pride that he had killed two persons with it thirty minutes ago. His friend shoved his rifle forward and said, "Yea, and I got one with this too." A few minutes later I learned what had happened — earlier in the morning a Marine had been shot through the head by a sniper. The two soldiers were on a patrol looking for the sniper. They put a grenade and some shots into a hut killing two old women and a girl. This disturbed the neighbors greatly. A Marine jeep came around and we were told to clear out of the area as they were "expecting a riot." I doubt these soldiers would brag about this kind of killing with clear heads but it shows how war can at least temporarily affect young minds.

Victor Charlie, Kuno Knoebl, 1967, p. 172

..."We are soldiers, our job is to seek out and destroy the enemy. Whatever else happens is none of our business," Colonel Moore of the 1st Air Cavalry Division said in Bong Son. Soon, the specific nature of the country and the war will be completely ignored. The guerrillas are looked upon and fought as soldiers of an enemy army, the population in Viet-Cong-occupied territory is considered "hostile" and treated accordingly.

8 Jan 67   New York Times, Tom Buckley
            THANHPHONG, SOUTH VIETNAM, Jan 7

American troops moved unopposed today through a corner of the strategic Mekong River Delta, where they were committed for the first time yesterday.

...The landing, scheduled for Wednesday, was delayed for two days by rough seas. Officials then held up the announcement until today to give the South Vietnamese marine brigade a chance to join the operation.

...Three Vietnamese were killed in the assault. One was a sniper, reports said. The others proved to be a young man and woman who were fired on as they walked through the underbrush near an outpost of American marines.

The area of the assault, in the Thanhphu district of Kienhoa Province, is about 55 miles south of Saigon. It is an area of scattered hamlets, rice fields, jungle and mangrove swamp lying between two mouths of the Mekong. It is said to have been an undisputed fiefdom of the Viet Cong for nearly 20 years.

13/13 Vietnam: Search and Destroy, Gordon Baxter, 1967, p. 66

(The copyright owners of 13/13 Vietnam: Search and Destroy have declined permission to publish textual material in this documentation. The following describes the essential contribution made by a selection from this book.)

(The author reveals that all persons running out of huts during search and destroy operations are under suspicion. There is a photo in the text of an old man on the ground who was shot to death as he ran from his hut. The old man was left where he fell because he was unarmed. Enemy action prevents the GI's from taking the time to check his identity.)

17 Aug 66   Herald Statesman (See Note Page 20)
            SAIGON, SOUTH VIETNAM

...Civilians are often reluctant to leave their villages. Instead, they build bomb shelters near their huts.

In some cases, civilians killed in military operations are simply listed as Viet Cong.

26 Nov 66   (See Note Page 20)
            SAIGON, Nov 26

...The validity of Saigon and Washington announcements of the enemy dead has been questioned by both U.S. officers and correspondents in the field. In some cases in the past the counts have unquestionably been inaccurate and frequently they appear inflated.

...In many instances, estimates of spotter plane pilots on the results of air strikes and artillery bombardment were thrown into the "confirmed body count" figure.

Some pilots have privately said they were making only rough estimates and were unable to tell in many cases whether the bodies were civilian or military. They also could not be sure whether they were in fact dead or live Viet Cong who were caught in the open and playing dead.

4 Mar 65   The Evening Star (Washington) (See Note Page 20)
            QUI NHON, VIET NAM, March 3

...U.S. advisers say much of the trouble in Binh Dinh is the reluctance of the 22nd Division, which administers the province militarily, to take a firm stand.

Some of the Communist victories are not even reported in Saigon. The Viet Cong overran two outposts at Gia Huu Feb. 7, killing or capturing every man except seven and dragging off an artillery piece. No government relief forces were sent.

As the situation grows worse in Binh Dinh, air strikes are flown over populated areas.

A U.S. pilot back from a raid said: "I killed 40 Viet Cong today. That's the number they told me were in the village, anyway, and I leveled it."

Victor Charlie, Kuno Knoebl, 1967, p. 209

...The official casualty ration is 1:3. That is, for every allied soldier killed or wounded in battle, three guerrillas are put out of action. Yet, it is almost impossible to determine the exact number of Viet-Cong casualties. The rebels seldom leave their dead and wounded on the field; in most instances, it is they who decide when to break off the fight, disengage, and withdraw. The Americans, like the South Vietnamese, must depend on estimates. They support their claims by presenting the number of weapons captured. But the quantity of captured weapons hardly serves as an absolute basis for determining casualties. It is even more difficult to establish guerrilla losses after bombing strikes and artillery barrages than after a field battle; no one can state with any degree of accuracy after several villages have been bombed that "80 or 100 or 150 Viet-Cong were killed." The pilots I have talked to concede that it is seldom possible to fix the number of guerrillas killed.

During these attacks many civilians, not just rebel soldiers, are hit. I have heard private but authoritative estimates that more than 30 per cent of those officially reported to be Viet-Cong dead are really noncombatants, old men, women, and children. Officials in Saigon told me that a 30 per cent margin of error must be considered when figuring the number of casualties.

14 Mar 66   Newsweek
              Arnaud de Borchgrave, "The War in Vietnam: Then and
              Now — the Difference."

...Inhibitions: Thus, twelve years later, domestic political considerations still play a major inhibiting role in the prosecution of the war against the Communists. Leaflets have to be dropped on villages before artillery can fire into VC-held areas. And the guerrillas, in turn, know that artillery barrages, which usually follow helicopter reconnaissance flights, mean the Americans are probably softening up a landing zone. The element of surprise is all too often sacrificed to keep down casualties amount Vietnamese civilians and U.S. troops.

...On this visit, as twelve years ago, I witnessed massive conventional operations that yielded little besides inflated KIA (killed in action) figures — many of them civilians. When U.S. troops capture only 18 weapons for 314 dead, as was the case in one recent Marine sweep, you know instinctively that bonafide noncombatants are among the KIA announced at the daily briefing in Saigon. And last month, during the U.S.'s massive Operation White Wing, Special Forces officers — who were admittedly prejudiced against conventional tactics — estimated that we were killing or wounding ten civilians for every VC.

20 Nov 64   New York Times, Peter Grose
              THUDAUMOT, SOUTH VIETNAM, Nov. 19

More than 7,000 Vietnamese troops concentrated in a forest area of about 40 square miles near here today in the largest Government-initiated operation of the Vietnamese war.

...Later there were unconfirmed reports that 42 persons were killed in the initial air strikes that preceded the troop landings. Officers could not determine from these reports whether the victims were Vietcong troops or civilians living in the district. There were no weapons found with the bodies, according to the reports.

5 Jun 65   New York Times, Jack Langguth
             SAIGON, SOUTH VIETNAM, June 4

... Final figures from the Quangngai battle which ended on Monday, showed 392 Government soldiers either killed or missing, the Vietcong captured 446 rifles and carbines and 90 larger weapons, including three .30-caliber machine guns, five 60-mm. mortars and two 57-mm. recoilless rifles.

Although Saigon maintains that 560 Communist soldiers were killed in the action, only 20 Vietcong weapons were captured.

21 Aug 65   New York Times, Charles Mohr
             SAIGON, SOUTH VIETNAM, Aug 20

... The battle near Chulai, in which United States marines trapped and killed a "confirmed" total of 563 Vietcong guerrillas in a two-day battle, was "pretty well terminated," ...

... Officers at the scene said the confirmed count did not include estimates of enemy dead made by observation planes and pilots during bombardments by fighter-bombers, artillery and guns of Seventh Fleet warships. These are estimated to have accounted for considerably more Vietcong casualties.

... "Scores" of enemy weapons, including 81-mm. weapons and 57-mm. recoilless rifles were reported captured. A spokesman said that marines were checking the area today looking for Vietcong still holding out in isolated tunnels and caves.

3 Sep 65   New York Times, Neil Sheehan
             SAIGON, SOUTH VIETNAM, Sept 2

A force of several South Vietnamese army battalions killed 22 Vietcong guerrillas today in an engagement in Quangngai Province 320 miles northeast of Saigon, an American military spokesman announced.

... Five insurgents and 11 weapons were captured and 46 suspects rounded up. Government troops suffered light casualties.

... In another operation in Quangngai, 25 miles south of the Chulai airfield, six National Guard companies reinforced by three reconnaissance platoons killed three guerrillas and captured 15 suspects.

20 Oct 65   New York Times, Neil Sheehan
             SAIGON, SOUTH VIETNAM, Oct 19

... Units of the United States' First Infantry Division seized 115 Vietcong suspects today during an operation near the so-called Iron Triangle, a Communist jungle base near Bencat, about 25 miles north of the capital.

A spokesman said five of the suspects were later identified as guerrillas. One was killed while trying to escape, and a weapon was also seized.

12 Aug 66   New York Times,
             SAIGON, SOUTH VIETNAM, Aug 11

... In other developments, United States marines remained in contact with a force of several thousand Vietcong in the rice paddies west of Tamky on the coast.

... Since the operation began last Saturday the marines have been credited with killing 257 and capturing 42 and seizing 31 weapons.

9 Oct 66   New York Times (See Note Page 20)
             PHUCAT, VIETNAM, Oct 8

The United States First Cavalry Division (Airmobile) almost has more prisoners than it can handle.

Capt. Ralph Stevens, 28 years old, of Wolfeboro, N.H., in charge of the division's prison compound at Phucat, said:

"I've got 389 live bodies on hand right now. Some are Vietcong, some are North Vietnamese and some are just civilians."

South Vietnamese and United States intelligence officers question the prisoners to determine just what they are.

Soldiers are sent to what is called a reorientation camp at Pleiku, in the Central Highlands. Noncombatants, even though they may be Communist sympathizers, are sent home, under the eyes of the South Vietnamese National Police.

...The count of prisoners shows more than 600 known enemy soldiers and 1,400 suspects. This is called the largest prisoner count of the war. Intelligence officers say about 25 per cent of the suspects are turning out to be guerrillas, against the usual 5 or 10 per cent.

23 Nov 64   Christian Science Monitor, John Hughes
            BEN TRANH, VIET NAM

...In reply, the government of South Vietnam is fielding an army trained for conventional warfare. In its frustration, it, too, resorts to violent measures. A Viet Cong suspect, who may have vital intelligence, is given the water torture until he talks. Or until he doesn't. The water torture means keeping his head under the water of a rice paddy for as long as he can take without expiring.

Or a prisoner is invited to provide his captors with military information — while being persuaded with a knife.

Prisoners are rare on both sides. Living off the country, and seeking to move about it as unhindered as possible, the Viet Cong consider prisoners an encumbrance. Thus few who fall into their hands survive.

10 Jul 66   (See Note Page 20)
            SAIGON, July 10

...Older prisoners fervently dedicated to the Communist cause are a rarer species. One reason for this is that many hardcore Viet Cong commit suicide rather than surrender.

Still others, to the chagrin of U.S. troops, are killed by the Vietnamese after they are captured. Many Americans oppose the shooting of prisoners in the field for humanitarian reasons and also because it's not a sound practice from the viewpoint of intelligence.

In fact, U.S. and Vietnamese officers are engaged in a running battle over the handling of prisoners. Many of the Americans believe the Vietnamese have overlooked the value of trying to gain intelligence from prisoners.

Theoretically, the most important prisoners who end up in government hands go to stockades in the Vietnamese army's four corps areas. Some are sent to national prison camps to serve sentences for insurgency against the government.

Undoubtedly, many are tried and executed.

But no clear-cut pattern has generally emerged in either the processing or treatment of prisoners. As in so many other respects, the Vietnamese war seems to be in a category of its own.

Victor Charlie, Kuno Knoebl, 1967, p. 110

...The next morning a booming voice sounded again over the village. This time it did not come from the sky but from the nearby jungle: "Peasants," it thundered, "countrymen, your village is surrounded. Do not resist or we will shoot back. Do not resist."

The village was abandoned. The villagers had tied down their four water buffaloes in the bed of a small stream. The women and children had fled into the village bunker. The men had vanished into the jungle. They knew the habit the government troops and Americans had of seizing every man between fifteen and sixty-five in a Viet-Cong area and treating him as a guerrilla. Even if he actually was a government supporter, he would be put in a prison camp and questioned. And you did not get out of a camp so quickly — if you got out of it at all — without injury to body and soul ...

14 Oct 65   St. Louis Post-Dispatch
              SAIGON, SOUTH VIETNAM, Oct 14

...Between 12,000 and 14,000 U.S. and Vietnamese troops took part in the offensive that began last Sunday. These included 8,000 of the First Cavalry.

Thirty-four Viet Cong were reported killed and 100 suspects were captured.

7 May 66   New York Times
              SAIGON, Saturday, May 7

...Yesterday morning another battalion of Airmobile troops, moving eastward from the mountain ridge, ran into more enemy soldiers and fought them until late afternoon.

The spokesman said some of the enemy found dead during the fighting wore khaki and forest green uniforms and others black pajamas.

Some of the 31 prisoners captured said they had been instructed to pretend they were Vietnamese farmers, the spokesman said.

"That's why we took so many Vietcong suspects — 389 of them," said an officer. "We went around to all the fields and picked up all the people working the edges of the fields. Probably a high percentage of the people we picked up will turn out to be Vietcong who were playing farmer. We know they all carry black pajamas in their packs."

31 Oct 66   New York Times
              SAIGON, VIETNAM, Oct 30

...To the southeast of Saigon, 1,200 Australians encircled a village of 6,000 Vietnamese and were searching for Vietcong guerillas. By late tonight they had reported taking three prisoners.

3 Mar 67   New York Times
              SAIGON, SOUTH VIETNAM, March 21

...In an operation that the First Cavalry Division (Airmobile) has been conducting in Binhdinh Province, an enemy platoon was ambushed, with 10 killed. A total of 392 guerrillas have been reported killed and 2,699 suspects held for investigation since the operation began, on Feb. 12.

22 Apr 67   New York Post (See Note Page 20)
              SAIGON, April 22

...At the same time it was announced that units of the U.S. 1st Air Cavalry Division had closed out Operation Lejeune, their first in the 1st Corps region. The Air Cavalry reported killing 155 enemy and detaining 756 suspects during the 16-day operation.

5 Jun 65   UPI, New York Times
              SAIGON, June 4

...A Marine spokesman said 19 guerrillas had been killed and 11 wounded by 1,000 marines in a series of ground battles. One guerrilla and 43 suspected guerrillas were taken prisoner.

13 Sep 65   New York Times, R. W. Apple, Jr.
              SAIGON, SOUTH VIETNAM, Sept 12

...At Quangtri, north of Hue near the border of North Vietnam, other South Vietnamese troops engaged a band of guerrillas in a small-arms skirmish. Two guerrillas were killed, 19 were captured and 38 persons were detained as suspected guerrillas.

10 Dec 65   (See Note Page 20)
              SAIGON, Dec 10

...Marine and Air Force planes kept up support of the U.S.-Vietnamese drive, flying 206 sorties over the rice paddies since early Thursday night. They pounded 25 buildings, bunkers and gun emplacements with rockets, bombs, and 20mm cannon fire, spokesmen reported.

...From the battle scene between Chu Lai and Da Nang, Associated Press correspondent George Esper reported that the Marines had killed 26 Viet Cong, including two women, shortly after they joined the scrap yesterday. One Viet Cong was captured and 40 suspects detained.

Pilots said as many as 125 communists may have been killed in the air strikes.

3 Jan 66   (See Note Page 20)
              SAIGON, VIET NAM, Monday, Jan 3

U.S. airborne troops, in a push to drive the Viet Cong toward the Cambodian border, have killed 201 guerillas and captured 69, a U.S. military spokesman said today. He added that 444 Communist suspects were detained.

12 Mar 66   Chicago Tribune Press Service, Chesly Manly
              (from Congressional Record — Appendix — April 6, 1966, A2003)
              QUI NHON, VIETNAM, March 12

...In 4 months the Koreans have killed 1,155 Vietcong by body count (the estimated total is 1,273), captured 466, and detained 2,085 suspects, of whom 20 percent turn out after investigation to be Vietcong. Korean casualties in the same period were 74 killed, 234 wounded, and 1 missing.

12 Oct 66   New York Times
              SAIGON, SOUTH VIETNAM, Oct 11

...The airmobile soldiers also captured eight enemy soldiers today, bringing to 503 the number of prisoners taken since the operation began. Never before have the airmobile soldier captured more of the enemy than they have killed.

11 Nov 66   New York Times
              SAIGON, SOUTH VIETNAM, Nov 10

...Thirty miles southeast of Saigon, Australian infantrymen combed fishing villages of Longson Island for Vietcong. They announced they had killed one guerrilla, captured six and were interrogating 542 suspects.

TREATMENT OF SUSPECTS

20 Dec 66   (See Note Page 20)
              BUNG DIA, VIET NAM, Dec 20

...Then the helicopters started coming in and the troops piled aboard. Within minutes they were put down in this mostly Viet Cong village about 10 miles south of their base camp.

Their job was to throw a cordon around the village of about 2,000 persons while Vietnamese soldiers and their American advisers moved through hunting out the Viet Cong or their sympathizers.

The infantry men of the 1st Division, the "Big Red One," carried out their part of the operation swiftly.

One of the parts was played by the battalion commanded by Lt. Col. Rufus C. Lazzell, 37, of Springfield, Va. There was some minor sniper fire, but no major resistance, as the battalion moved into position. Its job was to trap people who tried to flee after helicopters bearing loudspeakers hovered over the area, telling the people to stay in their homes...

...The way it turned out they picked up about 40 people who were trying to flee, either from the village itself or from the nearby jungle. They were taken to a checkpoint for interrogation. At least half of them had the appearance of hard type Viet Cong guerrillas.

Among them was a 14-year-old girl, seized when she tried to run and then was found to have a false identity card.

Darkness fell, and the American Infantry men pulled back to their perimeter to again take out the now not so shiny cards and to think again about things like Christmas, which was only five days away.

14 Mar 67   World Journal Tribune, Jim G. Lucas
            VINH MY, SOUTH VIET NAM, March 14

Capt. Ngo Huu Phuoc, commanding the 2nd Battalion, 32nd Vietnamese Regiment, had called a village meeting.

"You, Pham, stand up," he ordered, and the village barber rose, sheepish and reluctant. His townsmen tittered in anticipation.

"You, Minh, and you, Quang, on your feet," Phuoc said. Eventually 67 of Vinh My's 4,000 citizens heard their names called and were forced to stand.

"I know you are Viet Cong," Phuoc said. "It is not important how I know. You, Pham, the barber, are a Viet Cong tax collector. You, Minh, the seamstress, your son is a Viet Cong squad leader; your house is a message drop. You, Quang, who run the village coffee shop, you are a courier and an informer.

"I do not intend to kill you, as I should. I do not intend to lock you up. That is what the Viet Cong said I would do, and I will not oblige them. But if there is a single incident in Vinh My, if one mine explodes among us, I will shoot Pham first. If there is another, I will shoot Minh and Quang. If I must, I will shoot you all."

Since then, there has not been a single incident in this delta village.

25 Mar 67   Saturday Evening Post
            Steward Alsop, "Vietnam: The President's Next Big Decision"

(The editors of Saturday Evening Post have declined permission to give the verbatim text of a selection from the above cited article. The following describes the contribution of that selection.)

(The County Fair technique used by U.S. Marines in pacification is described: the surrounding of the village, the herding of the population together, the weeding out of suspected guerrillas, the shooting of persons attempting to escape, the entertainment and feeding of the villagers as the suspected guerrillas are whisked off to interrogation points.

The author points to the difficulty of handling a population organized internally by a guerrilla movement. He imagines such an operation by a foreign army against an American town and suggests that the normal reaction by both Vietnamese and Americans is bound to be negative.)

3 Apr 67   The Nation, Edward Lamb
           SAIGON, April 3

The United States Army, First Division, has a giant military base at Lai Khe, some hundred miles north of Saigon. It was from this heavily armed position that the Big Red Division cleared and flattened the Iron Triangle. And when I was there it was the scene of operations described as County Fairs — a Madison Avenue approach to the conversion of the Vietcong in several hostile neighboring villages.

Just 8 miles north, we moved in with the American troops as they staged the spectacle for the hamlet of Am Loi. It is a typical town of some 500 inhabitants who had lived under the VC for many years. U.S. and South Vietnamese troops surrounded the village at four in the morning — a cordon of mortars, tanks and more than a battalion of heavily armed troops. The town having been effectively sealed, a company of Americans and a sizable number of South Vietnamese, including defectors and informers from the village, surprised the sleeping villagers. I tagged along as the troops searched every hut and interviewed every villager.

Seventy-seven suspected members of the Vietcong were herded into a quickly roped-off compound, to be held there in the broiling sun for some eight hours. They were joined by six or seven "guerrillas" captured on the outskirts of the hamlet. There were some eight draft dodgers but no one from North Vietnam. The hard core from Hanoi usually stay out of town both day and night. During the entire time of the "County Fair" operation, the old men of the hamlet were confined to their huts, ostensibly to guard their belongings from the South Vietnamese soldiers, who are pretty much hated by the villagers.

Tents were erected. Food, including beans and hot dogs, as well as balloons and candy, were distributed. Another tent housed doctors and dentists, who accepted volunteer but very scared patients. All the time, a jazz band played.

The American soldiers who went into town remained quietly on the outskirts. The captured men were questioned in a darkened room. Each suspect came in and faced his accuser, hiding behind a black-face mask. U.S. Maj. Robert Sweitzer said that at least 10 per cent of the men would admit their membership at the outset, another 10 per cent would "come clean" when hauled away to the military base camp. The balance would be returned to their homes in the hamlet.

After several hours the fair ended, since it was necessary to get away from the village well before dark. The prisoners were marched down the road to the waiting helicopters. We passed dead Vietcong. Our soldiers leave the dead where they find them. Land mines were all over the place, and Major Sweitzer ordered the draft dodgers to precede us. At least a dozen bamboo booby traps were unearthed. Several dozen 5-gallon cans of concentrated sugar were captured in the village and destroyed. Sixty bags of rice were hauled away.

The alleged VC's were torn away from their tearful families. Rations were packed and loaded aboard military transports. The carnival was over. Some political indoctrination had been attempted and the troops were safely out of the hamlet.

I talked to dozens of Americans about this hit-and-run tactic. Many believe it may be a good promotional stunt, but not of much permanent social significance. For good or ill, the County Fair technique is hitting about a dozen villages in South Vietnam every week.

13 Aug 65   (See Note Page 20)

...Rusk, in an Aug. 10 letter to Samuel Gonard, President of the International Committee of the Red Cross, Geneva, said:

"The U.S. Government has always abided by the humanitarian principles enunciated in the Geneva conventions and will continue to do so.

"In regard to the hostilities in Viet Nam, the U.S. Government is applying the provisions of the Geneva conventions and we expect the other parties to the conflict to do likewise ...

"Those involved in aggression against the Republic of Viet Nam rely heavily on disguise and disregard generally accepted principles of warfare.

...From the outset it has therefore been difficult to develop programs and procedures to resolve fully all the problems arising in the application of the provisions of the conventions."

Rusk said Washington is developing plans to help the Saigon regime improve care for a growing number of Viet Cong captives, and further instruction on the Geneva rules is being given to U.S. and Vietnamese and South Vietnamese soldiers.

23 Mar 65   St. Louis Post-Dispatch, Richard Dudman
             (from Congressional Record, Senate, April 1, 1965, p. 6554)
             SAIGON, March 23

Vietnamese marines were taking few prisoners this month in northern Binh Dinh Province. American advisers saw them shooting a dozen suspects a day on the spot in an area heavily infested with Vietcong.

An American captain had this to say about the Vietnamese captain of their battalion:

"They caught a girl about 19 year old in a Vietcong village. She was suspected of being a Vietcong herself. My counterpart beat her up and kicked her in the stomach."

26 May 65   (See Note Page 20)
             WITH THE 2ND MARINE BATTALION, VIET NAM, May 26

...The brutality of a war that often mixes guerrillas with civilians still throws some of the Marines off guard, even the old professionals.

Thomas, who saw service in Korea, said Vietnamese troops accompanying the Marines on one patrol started to push a girl into a bunker thought to contain a Viet Cong. The girl was from the Viet Cong village and government troops under these circumstances normally push villagers into suspected Viet Cong hiding places first in case the Communists start shooting.

"Forcing that girl into the bunker really got to me, I'll tell you." Thomas said.

Before she was all the way in, however, someone decided a smoke grenade would do just as well.

24 Jul 65   New York Herald Tribune
             SAIGON, July 24

...U.S. sources disclosed Vietnamese security police seized a 34-year-old laundress at the base Wednesday as she was attempting to smuggle in a powerful explosive concealed in her girdle. Witnesses said that, after an hour's questioning, she was escorted to a rice field at the end of the air strip and shot to death by the security police.

Americans did not seem upset by the justice dispensed by the Vietnamese.

"This is a rough area around here," one American said. "The Viet Cong are everywhere. This is how the Vietnamese security people handle them when they are caught."

28 Nov 65   New York Times Magazine
             William Tuohy, "A Big 'Dirty Little War' "

...To the aching frustration of U.S. commanders trained in more conventional tactics, this is a war in which countless hours are spent vainly tracking an elusive quarry through almost impenetrable jungle, muddy rice fields and blazing sand dunes. Friend is often indistinguishable from foe. Napalm and fragmentation bombs sometimes fall on defenseless peasants; artillery shells are fired at random into the paddy fields. An appalling number of victims are women, children and old men; some are participants but most are noncombatants.

...On some occasions the tactics of U.S. troops have been sadly inept for the situation. Thus, in a remote hamlet in the central highlands, a burly, red-faced captain entered with a patrol of paratroopers and ordered the villagers rounded up. "Ask these people where the Vietcong went," the captain told a nervous Vietnamese interpreter. An old man who might have been the village elder began speaking rapidly. "Sit down and shut up, loudmouth," bellowed the captain — in English.

Then the captain ordered a soldier, "Take him 100 yards down the road. Maybe if they think we're going to blow his head off, they'll talk."

The villagers did not talk; the women and children wailed and sobbed. Embarrassed, the paratroopers began loading two dozen peasants aboard a truck to take them to the district town. The soldiers were as gentle as possible and courteous, but the villagers continued to cry. For all they knew they were being packed off to exile, imprisonment or execution. A lieutenant wondered about the efficacy of such tactics, but asked plaintively, "Well, if they're not V. C. sympathizers, what are they doing way out here? Why don't they live in the city?"

5 Sep 66   The Sun (Baltimore) (See Note Page 20)
            AN BIEN, VIET NAM, Sept 4

It was a very small hamlet, only three huts and a handful of people scattered along a canal. But at this moment it portrayed the war's extremes of terror and tenderness.

...A short distance away and out of their sight, another mother, this one in her 70s, watched tearfully as soldiers kicked and beat two men who by all evidence were Viet Cong guerrillas.

...Thirty feet away, a 28-year old man and another man about 30 came out of another bunker.

Soldiers searched them and found Viet Cong propanganda papers assailing the "American Imperialists and Ky's lackeys."

The men had no identification cards. They claimed they were farmers.

An officer and two enlisted men glared at them. "If you don't tell us where the Viet Cong and your weapons are you'll be sorry," said one soldier. "We'll beat you, drown you in the mud and slit your bellies. Then we'll finish you with bullets."

The prisoners' arms were tied and they trembled.

"Don't beat us," said one, "we are only farmers." He began to weep.

"You'd better start talking," said the officer.

The men only shuddered.

Riflebutts smacked into them and knees smashed into their bellies. One man was dunked and held under muddy water. The other was held by his hair and kicked.

The groaning men sprawled on the ground. One said "Last night ... many Viet Cong ... I saw many Viet Cong. No weapons. I didn't see any weapons. They passed through here, I don't know where they went."

The officer growled, "Tie them to that tree. If they don't talk better than that, we'll see. If there's a helicopter we'll take them to headquarters. If not, we'll handle them here."

Dec 65   Ramparts, Bernard Fall, "This isn't Munich, It's Spain"

...This is a photograph of a South Vietnamese prisoner cage. I took the picture inside a camp where Americans were present. No attempt was made to hide the cage, an iron frame covered completely with barbed wire. About four feet high, it is used for bringing prisoners to "reason." I was not told what kind of prisoners are put in the cage, but no matter who they are, this is a pretty violent process. The prisoner cannot stand up or sit down — if he moves out of a crouch he falls against the sharp barbed wire; there is so much wire that his body is punctured all over. This makes Christ's Crown of Thorns look like a child's toy.

25 Dec 66   World Journal Tribune, William Tuohy
            BINH CHANH, Dec 24

...As the questioning continued in the other tent, the U.S. agent spoke of the "black list." This is a masterfile of 8,000 names of Viet Cong and Viet Cong suspects in the tactical operating area of the 25th Division.

The black list is designed to be an over-all locater of Viet Cong types. However, systematic listing of such suspects is only now getting under way, and the list admittedly contains many glaring errors.

Eventually, intelligence agents hope to get a fairly accurate listing of the Viet Cong in the area — which has always had a high percentage of sympathizers.

In the intelligence war being waged in the delta, the U.S. and Vietnamese agents hope to be able to pay a call at every door that is thought to house VC sympathizers.

Psychologically speaking, the agents explained, the overt call by policemen on known or suspected Viet Cong families tends to have a disruptive effect on their morale, and eventually increases the government's control in an area. It further demonstrates that the government is indeed aware of who is sympathetic to the Viet Cong.

Victor Charlie, Kuno Knoebl, 1967, p. 159

... The villagers were terrified. Suddenly, an old man began wailing. He stumbled from one soldier to the next, then squatted on the ground and covered his face with trembling hands. "What's wrong?" I asked the sergeant leading the patrol.

"He's the village elder. He's afraid. He thinks we're going to kill him because he let the Charlies into the village."

"Will you?"

"Why should we? If we do, we'll just be helping the Communists," the sergeant replied.

The American began the questioning. Nobody had seen or heard anything. The old man didn't say another word, but sat there sobbing and shaking with fear. There was nothing to be gotten out of the two men either. They, too, were afraid; every time an armed soldier came near they drew back — but said nothing.

"We'll have to question the old man," the sergeant said. Two montagnards pulled the village elder to his feet. But he refused to stand up, and the moment they let go, he slumped to the ground again. The American made a sign to two soldiers who grabbed the man and stood him against the wall of a wooden hut. A third released the safety catch on his carbine and pointed the barrel at the old man's chest.

"All right, now talk," the sergeant said. The old man began speaking slowly, while his eyes kept seeking the face of one of the men who had been armed with crossbows. This Jarai was about thirty, toothless, with long hair tied in a knot. The sergeant noticed that the old man kept looking at this man for help. He ordered that the man be arrested and the village elder freed.

Victor Charlie, Kuno Knoebl, 1967, p. 214

... The next village had already been hit badly. More than half the huts were burned down and the rice fields were pock-marked with bomb craters. The villagers assembled as the Americans marched in. They sat silently in front of their ruined huts. Women held crying children in their arms. When a young American tried to comfort a child, it began screaming while the mother stared in terror at the foreign white giant.

Two young peasants came from behind the huts, followed by their families. They were all dragging sacks and boxes, apparently everything they owned. One man waved a small colored leaflet, a safe-conduct pass dropped by allied planes over guerrilla areas. The bound Vietnamese told the interpreter that he and his friend, together with their families, wanted to go with the Americans: They feared the Viet Cong and had to flee.

After some discussion helicopters were called in. They flew both families and a few other peasants, who had been arrested, out of the valley. I saw the families later in the main camp. Both men were behind barbed wire in a prisoner camp for Viet-Cong insurgents. The women and children squatted apathetically in a small grass-covered area also ringed by barbed wire. American military police stood guard.

"Why are these people under arrest?" I asked one of the guards.
"They are VC suspects."
"What will happen to them?"
"They will be questioned and then turned over to the Vietnamese authorities. They know what to do with Communists."

25 Mar 67   Saturday Evening Post, Richard Armstrong "Believe me, he can kill you"

..."What cut it for me was one day when the Air Police were trying to trace some pilfered supplies. They found a Vietnamese carpenter goofing off in his sack. They woke him up, and he took one look at these burly characters and started running. They yelled 'halt,' which he didn't understand, and then this A.P. shot him in the back. It was cold-blooded murder. I'm going skiing for a few weeks at Lake Tahoe and try to forget this place ever happened."

12 Jun 67   Nation, Desmond Smith, "There must have been Easier Wars"

...During Mass, patrols were out, and my thoughts were interrupted by Captain Bernstein who had given orders that a bunch of women walking along the tree line were to be brought in...."Search their baskets."
The GIs opened up the baskets. In one of them was a tiny child who immediately began bawling his head off.
"Get Sergeant Han!"
Han, the Vietnamese irregular who traveled with the company, came running. For the next couple of hours, the Captain interrogated each of the women. How many guerrillas does she have in her village? How long has she been a member of the Liberation Front? Every person that lives in this valley has worked willingly, or under compulsion, for the VC; what does she do for the VC? Where was her husband? All their husbands, the women said, had gone to live on Route 1, away from the bombing and the Americans. None of them were members of the liberation Front. Now Bernstein was sure the women were lying, that they were certain to be wives of local VC. He told the Sergeant to separate the women from one another and, holding the I.D. card of the first woman, he radioed her name to base. "X-Ray, Uniform, Alpha, November...break...Hotel, Alpha, November, Hotel, break... 37 years old...village Tan Qhon."
After a ten-minute wait, the answer came back: the woman's husband was positively identified as a member of the Second VC Regiment. "A hard-hat," said Bernstein, laconically, Hard-hat is GI slang for hard-core regular guerrillas. I asked what would happen to her.
"I'm going to call in a chopper, and send her back to LZ English," Bernstein said. "She's VC, and she's got information. We'll get it out of her somehow."
Now the woman, and her little bundle of child, were separated from the main group by Sergeant Han and led to the edge of the clearing. In an hour or so she would be taken away. Meanwhile she would sit in the punishing sun with a tag on her — "VCS": VC suspect.

26 Jan 67   San Francisco Chronicle

Enemy Casualties: McNamara said Viet Cong field reports show for the entire year of 1966: 55,000 killed in action, 10,000 captured and 13,000 military defectors. This comes to a total of 78,000. Adding the Pentagon's estimate of the 1966 net gain in enemy strength, 48,000 to that total, McNamara said the enemy must have recruited a total of 103,000 new men in 1966 from South and North Vietnam.
Although he said the captured and defection figures are "the most certain", a U.S. military spokesman in Saigon said Tuesday that only 2500 of the 10,000 enemy suspects captured in 1966 were kept as military prisoners.

CHAPTER III
USE OF GAS

The following Article from an International Convention relevant to this chapter is quoted in full:

Hague Convention No. IV, Annex
Regulations Respecting the Laws and Customs of War on Land
18 October 1907
(Short reference: Hague—Laws)

Article 23

In addition to the prohibitions provided by special Conventions, it is especially forbidden—

(a) To employ poison or poisoned weapons.

(b) To kill treacherously individuals belonging to the hostile nation or army.

(e) To employ arms, projectiles, or material calculated to cause unnecessary suffering.

See also (pages 29-42) the following additional Articles relevant to this chapter: Geneva—Civilians: 5, 27, 29, 31, 32, 33.

23 Mar 65   New York Times, Max Frankel
             WASHINGTON, Mar 22

The United States disclosed today that it was giving the South Vietnamese some temporarily disabling "types of tear gas" for combat use against the Vietcong.

...Officials, obviously sensitive to the propaganda problems posed by the disclosure, insisted that the use of "nauseous gases" was "not contrary to international law and practice."

The United States is not a party to any valid international agreement outlawing the use of gas, but it has shared a general abhorrence of "inhuman" forms of warfare. A spokesman said the State Department did not consider the gases used in Vietnam to be the kind barred from warfare by law or consensus.

...However, the Administration did not reveal the chemical characteristics of the gases used in Vietnam. One spokesman said they were not the simple forms of tear gas that produce only eye, skin and respiratory irritations, but rather tear gases mixed with nauseating agents.

According to reference works, vomiting gas in undiluted forms can produce, in progressive order, irritation of the eyes and mucous membranes, viscous discharge from the nose, sneezing, coughing, severe headache, acute pains and tightness of the chest, nausea and vomiting. Reports from Vietnam said one of the gases used there had caused extreme nausea and another had acted as a cathartic.

22 Mar 65   (See Note Page 20)
                SAIGON, VIET NAM, Mar 22

...The Pentagon said gas supplied by the United States is released from dispensers operated by Vietnamese helicopter personnel.
...The exact nature of the chemicals is secret, but they are believed to be mixtures including tear gas — perhaps chloracetophenone or brombenzylcyanide. One type is reported to cause nausea and another loosens the bowels.
...The informants said fighter-bombers as well as helicopters have been equipped to dispense the gases over Vietnamese battlefields. Some gases are loosed in powdered form, others in grenades.
..."It is a humane way of clearing out an enemy area where women and children are being held," an Officer said.

24 Mar 65   The Times (London)
                SAIGON, March 23

...The spokesman added that the use of gas had not been brought about by the experience of Saigon demonstrations but by an incident in central Vietnam where, again, members of the Vietcong had been known to be among the villagers. They had, he said, been trying new tactical techniques.
This last phrase is known to indicate that there is a much better and highly humane reason for using a gas which, though it would strengthen the American case, is deemed not capable of being disclosed for intelligence reasons. A hint is seen in yesterday's reference to the use of gas concerning hostages — but it appears that this tactic has not been particularly successful either.
...Observers who have watched the war intensifying in savagery on the part of both the Vietcong and the Government forces cannot but find something ironic in the outcry caused by what is probably the least harmful weapon used here so far. The Americans have emphasized repeatedly that to meet an all-out subversive war which gives no quarter any weapon deemed suitable will be used. These have already been officially admitted to include napalm and white phosphorus incendiary bombs and the "lazy dog" fragmentation bomb. Terrible they may be but, say the observers, it is really time it was realized that a terrible war is being waged here.

23 Mar 65   (See Note Page 20)
                WASHINGTON, Mar 23

The White House said today President Johnson was not consulted before riot control gases were used in South Viet Nam. The decision was pictured as a routine one handled by area commanders.
George E. Reedy, White House Press Secretary, said it was not the kind of thing Johnson would have to approve in advance any more than he would decide on whether to use .32 caliber small arms ammunition.

24 Mar 65   (See Note Page 20)
            WASHINGTON, Mar 24

Secretary of State Dean Rusk denied today that the United States is waging gas warfare in Viet Nam, and said non-killing tear and nausea gases will continue to be used as needed in saving innocent lives.

...Rusk said that riot-control agents are not banned by the 1925 Geneva Convention prohibition on what he termed military gases. The tear and nausea gases, sent to South Vietnamese forces in 1962, are available commercially and have been used repeatedly by police in other countries around the world, as well as in the United States, he said.

29 Mar 65   (See Note Page 20)
            SAIGON, VIET NAM, Mar 29

...One Captain objected, however, to claims that gas was humane on civilians. He said: "What the hell, by pumping gas down there we can knock out groundfire, so that lets us get closer on the ground and from the air to kill all the more of the enemy.

"If women and children are down there at the time, it will be no better for them than it is now."

U. S. advisers concerned with pacification efforts in some provinces fear that use of gas will mean a propaganda boost for the Viet Cong.

"Personally, I don't think that the benefits from gas will outweigh its defects," one pacification adviser said. "Once the word gets around this province that we are using gas, then the pressure will be on from the population."

2 Apr 65   Time

...Hardly anybody noticed the word "nonlethal." Compared with napalm bombs that incinerate whole villages, or white phosphorous shells that burn a man to the bone, the temporarily disabling gases used in Viet Nam seem more humane than horrible.

4 Apr 65   New York Herald Tribune
            SAIGON

..."We were in Tay Ninh Province — Viet Cong country. So overnight we dug foxholes in case of a Viet Cong mortar attack.

"During the night we talked. The tank commander explained why he wanted to use gas. The idea was to encircle the Viet Cong fortifications, make the guerrillas stand and fight, and then use the non-lethal gas to take over their positions.

"The Viet Cong troops live in an eight-mile-long network of trenches, tunnels and foxholes. There are hundreds of women and children living with the hard-core unit.

"The Viet Cong there are invulnerable to helicopter rockets, to machine guns. The big bombs, even 1,000-pound bombs, knock them out only with a direct hit. Those trenches are 10 feet deep.

"They've built air-raid shelters so hard that the tanks can't crack them by running over them. Every family has its own shelter. Every time the bombs come the Viet Cong simply go underground."

4 Apr 65   (See Note Page 20)
             AP BINH THANH, VIET NAM, April 4

The Viet Cong has started supplying its troops with primitive — but apparently effective — gas masks. A dozen of the masks were found hidden in a Communist regimental headquarters overrun by government troops in a cane field region about 15 miles west of Saigon yesterday.

U. S. authorities disclosed two weeks ago that nonlethal gas is being used "in certain tactical situations" in Viet Nam. The Viet Cong gas masks are primitive affairs. They are constructed from large plastic bags commercially available in Vietnamese cities.

...The gas mask is presumably pulled over the head and tied at the neck when a gas attack comes. A Vietnamese soldier experimented by placing one on his head while his comrades blew smoke in his face. He said he could not smell the smoke.

A woman in AP Binh Thanh village near the headquarters was asked about the gas masks.

"The Viet Cong used them to protect themselves against the spray from the planes," she said.

She presumably meant the defoliation aircraft that have flown over the cane field region, clearing jungle along canals and highways with chemicals.

May 65   Army
             Jack Raymond, "Gas As a Weapon"

...Secretary McNamara described the three types of nonlethal gas used in Vietnam as follows:

DM (Diphenylaminochloroarsine), a pepper-like irritant, which causes irritation of the eyes, mucous discharge from the nose, sneezing, coughing, headache, tightness in the chest and nausea and vomiting. On the average, DM incapacitates for periods of from one half to two hours.

CM (Chloroacetophenome), a tearing agent which is also an irritant to the upper respiratory passages and may cause irritations to the skin. It is a common form of tear gas. On the average it incapacitates for approximately three minutes.

CS (O-chlorobenzalmalononitrile), a more recently developed lacrimatory agent which causes pains in the chest, choking and violent coughing, nausea and vomiting. On the average it incapacitates for from five to ten minutes.

There are many other types of non-lethal gases. Their effects depend upon the mixtures of the chemicals. They are not "casualty-producing" under field conditions, although obviously they can be harmful to children and to the aged and ailing.

...The use of gas is dependent upon meteorological conditions. If the wind is blowing the wrong way, or if it is blowing too fast in any direction, or if it is raining or snowing, the combat use of gas may be impeded. A shift in the wind may endanger friendly troops (and civilians). If the dosage is merely irritating, the enemy lives through it and fights again.

20 Jan 67   Science, "Chemical and Biological Warfare (II):
             The Weapons and the Policies"

...The three remaining agents are sometimes placed together in the "riot control" category, although one — DM — is a vomiting agent. It causes sneezing and coughing, nausea, vomiting, severe headache, and acute pain and tightness in the chest; symptoms may last up to 3 hours. Another agent, CS, is one of the more recently developed agents of the general tear-gas type. It causes extreme burning and tearing of the eyes, difficulty in breathing, tightness of the chest, stinging of the skin, running nose, dizziness, and — in heavy concentrations — nausea and vomiting. The third, CN, has effects generally like those of CS, but it also causes burning, itching, and, occasionally, blisters. Effects of these two agents last for a few minutes.

The agent DM alone "is not approved for use in ... any (riot control) operation where deaths are not acceptable." However, the field manual reports that it may be used combined in munitions with CN and in "military or paramilitary operations, in counterinsurgency operations, or in limited or general war ... where possible deaths are acceptable." Chemical agents CN and CS may be used to flush "unmasked enemy troops from concealed or protected positions, to reduce their ability to maneuver or use their weapons, and to facilitate their capture or their neutralization by other weapons." They are also regarded as useful "in the conduct of raids and ambushes against guerrilla forces and in defense against insurgent or guerrilla attacks and ambushes." All three, DM, CS, and CN, have been authorized for use — and used in many of these ways — in Vietnam.

8 Oct 65   New York Herald Tribune
            SAIGON

American soldiers used tear gas against the Viet Cong yesterday as thousands of U. S. paratroopers launched a major offensive in Zone D, long a Communist stronghold, a U. S. military spokesman said.

...Although there was no official announcement of the reason for using tear gas, informed sources said the authorization was given because it was felt that employing it would be more humane than resorting to grenades to flush out the guerrillas hiding among the civilians.

8 Oct 65   (See Note Page 20)
            SAIGON, VIET NAM, Oct 8

Thousands of U. S. paratroopers invaded a Viet Cong jungle stronghold today and used tear gas against the guerrillas, a U. S. military spokesman reported.

...There were no details on the gas attack, part of a major operation launched by elements of the 173rd Airborne Brigade against the "Iron Triangle." This is an area roughly four miles wide and seven miles long that Communist guerrillas have ruled for years.

...The paratroopers, moving in by road convoy and giant helicopters, also were equipped with "Mighty Mite" blower machines that can force tear gas or smoke into underground shelters. A spokesman said none of the machines had been used so far.

2 Jan 66   (See Note Page 20)
            BAO TRAI, VIET NAM, Jan 2

American forces, moved into position by a vast convoy of men and equipment, are headed toward their southernmost penetration of South Viet Nam. The densely-populated land around Bao Trai, 20 miles west of Saigon, is rich with sugar cane and rice. Pursuing the entrenched Viet Cong here means new tactics. The terrain is not jungled, but flat, open and swampy. U. S. soldiers must battle both the enemy — and the swamps.

They met an early challenge from the terrain today when American helicopters sprayed a powerful, nonlethal tear gas on pockets of the Viet Cong with little apparent effect. The guerrillas remained entrenched and kept the Americans pinned down in the swamps.

...The initial layers of gas were put down by helicopters. Then U.S. paratroopers from the 2nd Battalion of the 173rd Airborne Brigade, fired gas grenades from their rifles. The Viet Cong, holed up in thickets of wild sugar cane and bamboo, seemed generally unaffected by the gas. Some were seen to move off, according to Staff Sergeant Richard Banks from Pensacola, Florida.

...The gas was identified as CN type. It was the first time American troops have been known to use it on such a large scale. Its use was officially authorized by Gen. William C. Westmoreland, Commander of U.S. Forces in Viet Nam, last October. Banks said only three or four men in his squad had been issued gas grenades. "The idea was to use them in (sic) special occasions when he had the chance of flushing the Viet Cong out into the open. Then we would give him a chance to surrender."

4 Jan 66   New York Times
            SAIGON, SOUTH VIETNAM, Jan 3

Shells from United States artillery fell among American paratroopers operating west of Saigon this morning, killing or wounding a number of them.

The mishap occurred as the American troops, members of the 173d Airborne Brigade, continued their sweep through Haunghia province in the northernmost section of the Mekong Delta ricelands.

...Later tonight, the spokesman confirmed reports from the scene that the 173d had sprayed tear gas from helicopters yesterday in an attempt to drive Vietcong soldiers out of jungle hiding places from which they were raking the Americans with sniper fire.

The spokesman emphasized that this was not the first time that gas had been employed in such a manner. In fact, United States troops have used it a number of times in various ways since Gen. William C. Westmoreland, the United States Commander in Vietnam, authorized its use in October.

Field commanders reported that the gas attack had not been notably successful, but some sources in Saigon speculated that the capture of an unusually large number of Vietcong suspects by the 173d — more than 500 at last count — might have resulted from the effects of the gas.

5 Jan 66   Wall Street Journal, William Beecher
            WASHINGTON

(The editors of Wall Street Journal have declined permission to give the verbatim text of a selection from the above cited article. The following describes the contribution of that selection.)

(Three objections to the use of gas warfare are noted by some officials:
  1) Favorable enemy propaganda from such use.
  2) Danger to U.S. troops if bombs and artillery are not used to soften up a village prior to assault, since the enemy may have primitive protective masks reasonably effective against gas attack.
  3) Problem of caring for large numbers of sick enemy troops who might be captured as a result of a gas attack.)

6 Jan 66   Le Monde
            (translated from the French)
            SAIGON, 5 Jan

American specialists in Chemical warfare are presently studying new methods of utilization for tear gases which unit commanders are authorized to use in certain situations against the Vietcong, notably when the rebels mix with the local population in order to hinder troop activity.

The most recent method consists in dropping chain grenades from a low-flying airplane in order to achieve saturation of an area as large as a football field by means of an irritating gas made of fine particles which was developed by British chemists.

The cylindrical grenades can be launched by hand or by rifle. An explosive charge then disperses the powder over a large area and vaporizes it.

Inhalation of the gas produces a violent irritation of the mucous membranes causing a great deal of salivation. The victims experience a burning sensation in the lungs and at humid areas of the skin. But above all, the gas "for its major effect sustains an insurmountable desire to run away", an American officer revealed.

Grenades of this type were used during the last week-end in Operation Marauder in the north of the Mekong Delta, and many of the Vietcong were dislodged from their holes in this manner.

Specialists are also studying the use of a powerful air-pump, the Mighty Mite, which launches a stream of gas at a speed of nearly 300 kilometers an hour which then penetrates the grottos and tunnels. In this way, South Korean troops successfully brought forth around thirty people who were dug in in a tunnel near Tuy-Hoa.

10 Jan 66   (See Note Page 20)
           SAIGON, Jan 10

...About 8,000 men, most of them from the U. S. 1st Infantry Division and the 173rd Airborne Brigade, were in the third day of Operation Crimp against the Iron Triangle. The triangle of 15 square miles of jungle has been a stronghold of the Viet Cong for years. The Allied force reached the Saigon River boundary of the triangle, but did not cross into the triangle itself.

...The U. S. troops continued their methodical work of scorching the area and demolishing caves and tunnels.

...As the assault helicopters set down, the soldiers saw buildings afire from air strikes. Up in flames went a field of unharvested rice. The troops pushed across an abandoned rubber plantation.

...The Americans and Australians were harassed by snipers as they set fire to the few houses and rice storage buildings that had escaped the air blows. In some houses they found food cooking in fireplaces. Bicycles were abandoned. Pigs and chickens scurried among the troops. When a woman was spotted coming out of a tunnel, riot control gas grenades were hurled in. Out rushed 300 women, children and old men.

10 Jan 66   (See Note Page 20)
           THUNG LAP, Jan 10

...The helicopters continued on over the bomb-torn jungles on the northern bank of the river. The Communist sharpshooters there that had plagued pilots for years were quiet, apparently silenced by the many B-52 strikes of recent months.

...All day snipers were heard but not seen. The few civilians that had survived in what the Communists call a "liberated zone" seemed to have disappeared mysteriously.

Food was cooking in fireplaces. Bicycles lay across paths. Pigs and chickens ran about among the troops.

Then a woman was spotted rising out of a tunnel. A soldier dashed toward her and she vanished. Several other soldiers reported that civilians popped in and out of tunnels, and children's footprints led toward them.

Vietnamese interpreters shouted, "Come out. We won't shoot you." There was no response. Riot-control gas was put into the tunnels with grenades and mighty-mite pumps to flush out the civilians. Then people began to respond. By the end of the day, some 300 women, children and old men stood trembling in their wet and muddy clothing. They waited for evacuation to a government-controlled district capital.

"I really feel sorry for the women and kids," said one GI. "I hope someday they'll understand what we are trying to do here."

Victor Charlie, Kuno Knoebl, 1967, pp. 256, 257

...However, the success of the Staley Plan demanded that the peasants abandon their villages. The depopulated settlements were burned down, and the crops destroyed to deprive the guerrillas of hiding places and food.

...Both unoccupied and occupied areas were poisoned. Rice fields, plantations, and jungles were sprayed with chemicals to destroy plant life — a measure that has done the United States tremendous harm throughout the nonwhite world. The chemicals were not injurious to man and beast in most cases — but this is hard to explain to a peasant who sees his meager crop wither after it has been poisoned.

Nonlethal gases — such as tear gas — were also used. I have seen unconscious women and children dragged out of tunnels and bunkers into which tear gas bombs had been thrown. The effect on the peasants was frightful. Several times peasants who had been brought under control this way tried to flee, screaming. They believed that the troops wanted to gas them to death.

13 Jan 66   The Sun (Baltimore), Peter Arnett
               TRUNG LAP, VIET NAM, Jan 12

It was a long, bloody mile we walked today. At times it was an inferno. Riot gas drifted through the trees, burning where it touched a man's sweating skin. The wounded writhed on the ground, looking grotesque in their black gas masks.

...One of Dailey's scout platoons far ahead had been pinned down for three hours by Viet Cong troops firing machine guns from a concrete bunker reinforced with steel. The platoon had taken some casualties and Dailey was hurrying to relieve them.

Armed helicopters came swooping down to assist the beleaguered platoon. A hoarse shout came over the radio: "Stop firing, stop firing. You're too close."

Helicopters carrying gas came in to assist. They plastered the Viet Cong bunker with scores of tear gas grenades. As the pungent fumes drifted back up the trail, Dailey yelled, "Gas masks on everyone."

The tight, rubber masks are terrible to wear in the heat of Viet Nam. Breathing is difficult and sweat builds up inside.

Pfc. Travis Jones, Chicago, said, "I saw a movie called "The Hill" that depicted the ultimate punishment for a man — running up and down a sand hill in a gas mask. Well, let me tell you something, man, that film was right."

It was while the rifle company was stumbling forward in the masks that the next mine exploded, booming from the edge of a house being burned and felling two sergeants.

One of them tried to tear his mask from his face as he lay on the ground. The medics had to restrain him.

13 Jan 66   Reuters, New York Times
               SAIGON, Jan 12

Non-toxic gas and smoke being used against Vietcong guerrillas in tunnels northwest of Saigon have killed one Australian soldier and sent six others to hospitals, officials said today. Cpl. Robert Bowtell, 21, of Sydney died of asphyxiation although he was wearing a gas mask.

124

5 Jan 66   Wall Street Journal, William Beecher
            WASHINGTON

(The editors of Wall Street Journal have declined permission to give the verbatim text of a selection from the above cited article. The following describes the contribution of that selection.)

(There are three situations in Viet Nam where gases stronger than mere tear gas (what the military calls riot-control agents) could be used.
1) Against enemy troops in caves or underground fortifications.
2) Against troops concentrated on the ground.
3) Against troops mixed with the population in a village.

In the third situation the typical response of the military has been an almost total destruction of the village through bombardment with napalm and fragmentation weapons followed by the use of artillery.

When the troops enter the village using small arms the first situation obtains. Both enemy soldiers and non-combatants are hiding in shelters and bunkers underground and it is customary for U.S. or South Vietnamese soldiers to drop grenades into these places to protect themselves. Professional officers regret the kinds of action which lead to the death or injury of non-combatants. They note that this has been true in all wars. In Viet Nam, when time allows, leaflets are dropped to warn non-combatants to leave the area before it is struck.)

22 Feb 66   New York Times
             WASHINGTON, Feb 21

Defense Department officials explained today that the new tactic of a helicopter-borne tear gas attack was designed to flush Vietcong troops out of bunkers and tunnels before the attack by B-52 bombers.

One of the past limitations of B-52 "saturation bombing" attacks was that little or no damage was done to the Vietcong troops unless a direct hit was made on a tunnel or bunker in which they were hiding. The purpose of the gas attack was to force the Vietcong troops to the surface, where they would be vulnerable to the fragmentation effects of the bomb bursts.

23 Feb 66   New York Times
             SAIGON, Feb 22

...In Bindinh Province, near the area where the United States First Cavalry Division (Airmobile) has been fighting since Jan 25, a Vietnamese Marine battalion suffered light casualties in a clash in which the Vietcong were said to have lost 50 men, including a guerrilla company commander.

The marines also took 11 Vietcong prisoners and captured a light machine gun and other weapons.

This morning, the First Cavalry troops, fighting what they believed to be a battalion of hard-core Vietcong guarding a regimental headquarters, swept cautiously through a triangle of thick jungle after the zone had been battered by artillery and B-52 bombers.

Before the bombers struck the area, 12 miles southwest of Bongson, hundreds of tear-gas grenades were dropped from helicopters. The first soldiers to enter the zone wore gas masks. Similar tactics were used in the area yesterday, apparently to flush the Vietcong from fortified positions so that the bombs could have maximum effects.

28 Mar 66   Christian Science Monitor, John Hughes
             HONG KONG

As far as gas is concerned, experts are again adamant that the gas used is non-poisonous.

They say the gas used is chlorobenzolmalonitrile which they say is a normal "riot control agent" like that used by British forces in Cyprus. However, some experts say the gas can be concentrated with more potent effect.

Gas is used for two purposes in Vietnam, first to flush out Viet Cong and civilians hiding in bunkers, and second to fill tunnel systems and make them inaccessible to the Viet Cong.

Recently American and Australian forces have been discovering tunnel systems too complex and long to be destroyed by high explosives. Thus they have been pumping them full of gas. Normally the effect should last for 12 months, they say, but in Vietnam, a moist climate, it could wear off in four months.

10 May 66   New York Times
                WASHINGTON, May 9

United States planes dropped 7,200 pounds of tear gas-producing powder on a Vietcong headquarters northwest of Saigon yesterday, Defense Department sources said today.

Army transport planes spread the gas in powdered form over an area about 70 miles north-west of the South Vietnamese capital and near the Cambodian border, the sources said.

United States troops moved into the area with gas masks.

The department spokesman said earlier reports that nausea gas had been used were wrong.

Nausea gas, it was explained, results in prolonged sickness and vomiting. Tear gas, on the other hand, is mainly a choking agent that constricts mucous membranes and tear ducts. Tear gas diffuses more quickly.

The spokesman described the use of the tear gas as "tactical," as authorized by the military command in Vietnam...

A North Vietnamese broadcast after tear gas was used in September said "U. S. Marines impudently used toxic gas, killing or seriously affecting many civilians." United States spokesmen, however, said the material was "just old-fashioned tear gas that affects the eyes and makes people cry."

At that time defense spokesmen said the policy concerning the use of tear gas or other non-lethal gas was set by Gen. William C. Westmoreland, commander of the United States forces, and not by the Pentagon.

The chemical used in Vietnam is said to be CS1, designed as a riot-control agent. Its technical name is O-chlorobenzalmalononitril.

22 Jan 67   Los Angeles Times (See Note Page 20)
                HO BO WOODS, SOUTH VIET NAM

U.S. troops began pumping nauseating gas Saturday into a huge tunnel complex that may have been headquarters for the Viet Cong's 4th Military Region.

American infantrymen probing the blackened underground labyrinth had exchanged shots with fleeing guerrillas Thursday and Friday. They were called out Saturday, and a blower pump was brought in to force nauseous gas through the maze of passages.

"This stuff will bring out anyone still in the tunnel," said Capt. James E. Leonard of Van Wert, Ohio, who is in the 1st Infantry Division's chemical section.

Men of "A" Company, 5th Infantry Mechanized, 25th Infantry Division had explored nearly 1,000 yards of tunnel when they were called out. The complex is located in the Ho Bo Woods about 25 miles northwest of Saigon.

The men, all volunteers known as "tunnel rats," had found 18 graves, 26 rifles and pistols, French and American maps, analyses of American op-

erations in the area, and detailed plans of past Viet Cong attacks including
the Dec. 4 suicide assault on Saigon's Tan Son Nhut Air Base. Maps and
diagrams pinpointed American billets in Saigon gave weight to the belief that
the tunnel had served as headquarters for planning terror attacks in the
city...

11 May 66   New York Times
             SAIGON, May 10

United States troops who swept through a densely jungled section near
the Cambodian border after a large-scale tear gas attack last week found no
evidence of enemy soldiers or installations, a United States spokesman said
tonight.

He said men of the First Infantry Division, protected by gas masks,
searched the area about 70 miles northwest of Saigon hours after three helicopters had dropped 7,200 pounds of a tear gas-producing powder. The drop
was one of the largest of the war.

For the first time the powder was dropped in 80-pound drums fitted with
explosive charges designed to detonate 25 seconds after leaving the aircraft.
With the helicopters flying at 3,000 feet, the drums were supposed to burst
open just after they crashed through the treetops.

Maj. William G. Dismore, division chemical officer, said that the drop
was an experiment and that even though no enemy soldiers had been killed
or captured, he considered it a success.

26 Mar 66   Chemical Week

...Gas Attack: Vietcong troops concentrating near underground command
centers are flushed out with riot-control gases that are blown into passageways. Decisions on when to use the gases are made by field commanders,
officials say.

Common tear gas, called CN, vomit-inducing CS, and the peppery irritant labeled DM, are forced into tunnels by portable blowers. Gas grenades
are dropped into tunnels to clear them of VC. After prisoners, hostages,
records and useful material have been removed, colored-smoke bombs are
used to locate all exits.

Then the tunnels are closed. Since some multilevel tunnel networks
cover half a square mile, thorough dynamiting would be prohibitively expensive. Instead, the tunnels are filled with boobytraps and gas before the exits
are sealed with explosives. Irritating agents in crystalline form are also
scattered through the tunnels. The crystals sublimate, releasing gas slowly
in the sealed tunnels, and making them uninhabitable for months.

It does the returning Vietcong little good to unseal the tunnels. They
must dig new headquarters, while living in the open, vulnerable to air attack,
or move into homes of villagers.

Rand Corp. interrogators, paid by the Defense Dept., report that villagers now blame the presence of VC for American air raids. Relations between civilians and the guerrillas are suffering commensurately.

And captured VC tell of growing discontent among their forces. Instead
of living between skirmishes in the comparative comfort and safety of the
tunneled havens, the weary jungle fighters have to spend more and more time
digging new lairs.

VC prisoners also report eating cold rations, to keep new locations secret from U.S. reconnaissance planes using infrared equipment to find VC
cooking fires.

Some Problems: Gases are used less uniformly in combat above ground.
Effectiveness varies with wind, speed and direction, humidity and distribution of VC forces.

Since the gases are released from helicopters and blown downward by
the rotors, missions are flown at low levels. This exposes pilots to close-
range ground fire. Field troops dislike working with gas; heat and humidity

in Vietnam make the gases irritating to exposed skin, and close-fitting gas masks are uncomfortable.

Communist propaganda against the gases have backfired. Saigon officials report that VC units have panicked when U.S. crop-dusters fly over. The herbicides are being mistaken for antipersonnel chemicals.

U.S. field commanders have pressed the joint chiefs of staff to permit use of more exotic gases in Vietnam. Chemical warfare specialists argue that the new incapacitating gases — which stun, confuse or induce hallucinations — deserve to be tested in combat.

Although the proposition comes close to violating the Geneva conventions, officials have found the idea appealing. A plan for escalating the use of gas may have been part of American startegy prior to the public outcry last year against the commercial riot-control agents. Had these chemicals been accepted in the conflict, other gases could have been introduced for limited experimental use.

Recent developments could strengthen pressures to use the new gases. Aerial reconnaissance reports indicate an increasing use of Vietnamese villagers as shields. VC vehicles, food stores, munitions and medicines have been spotted in unconcealed areas inside villages. Pilots must choose between letting the supplies move on to battle zones or jeopardizing civilian support by strafing the villages.

Some commanders argue privately it would be more humane to stun an entire village, enter under minimum gunfire, and separate the VC from civilian residents.

14 Jul 66   Christian Science Monitor, John Dillin
               QUAN LOI, VIETNAM

...In an interview here, Maj. Gen. William E. Depuy, commander of the "Big Red One," discussed the recent encounters...

...During the interview, General Depuy conceded that the Americans had used gas in their latest encounter. He said it was a non-lethal type. The gas is a form of powder, so fine that it floats in the air. It was dropped in big barrels from helicopters.

The Viet Cong were apparently expecting its use. The men in the black pajamas all had homemade gas masks of plastic and gauze.

"Had the enemy been in there we could pretty well have knocked out his will to fight before we went in there," he said. "The whole purpose for using riot-control agents is to reduce casualties."

Major Dismore said the division would probably use the gas again in the same way when it felt it faced a sizable troop concentration.

After the initial dense clouds are formed by the exploding canisters, crystals fall on the foliage and remain active for up to a week, Major Dismore said. When agitated, as by a soldier's foot, they give off gas.

After the drop last Thursday, the initial cloud rolled across the country, forcing the men in a headquarters four miles away to pull on their masks.

Oct 66   Argosy
            Milt Machlin, "Front Line Report: Vietnam"

(The editors of Argosy have declined permission to give the verbatim text of a selection from the above cited article. The following describes the contribution of that selection.)

(The author describes his experience in the field. As he sits down to relax near the unit's interrogation tent, an explosion occurs and shortly thereafter he feels the effect of CS gas pouring from a tunnel being cleared not far away. He describes the extremely hot pain affecting all his exposed skin, his attempt to run away, and the blisters which later appeared on his arms because he had failed to wash them sufficiently.)

20 Nov 66   World Journal Tribune (See Note Page 20)
             SAIGON, Nov 19

...A typical Viet Cong village of thatched huts in the jungle will have connecting tunnels with entrances concealed under cooking fires, well shafts or river banks. Ventilation holes are hidden by bushes.

...The "tunnel rats" seeded the floors with gas crystals that vaporize when disturbed, and blew up some of the main shafts. Engineers calculated it would take more than five tons of explosives to destroy the whole network.

10 Apr 65   Chemical Week, "'Benevolent' Weapon"

The present furor over the use of nonlethal gas in Vietnam put a new spotlight on the growing importance of chemicals in modern warfare. Government expenditures for the development of chemical and biological agents has grown by $175 million — to $275 million — in the last five years. Hottest area of research is that of psychochemical agents — e.g., compounds that induce temporary, partial disabilities (blindness, deafness, paralysis amnesia).

5 Jan 66   Wall Street Journal, William Beecher

(The editors of Wall Street Journal have declined permission to give the verbatim text of a selection from the above cited article. The following describes the contribution of that selection.)

(There are differences of opinion within the Pentagon on the use of gas in Vietnam. At least one official has been told that he should not admit that debate on the use of gas is going on.)

10 Apr 65   Chemical Week, " 'Benevolent' Weapon"

...One recently developed agent is BZ, a derivation of lysergic acid. Its effects haven't been fully disclosed, but it's classified as a psychochemical compound. Better known is CNS, a powerful tear gas that causes intense eye irritation, vomiting, colic and diarrhea. Its effects can last several weeks.

Another standard incapacitating agent is the gas known as B7. Quickly dispersed by an exploding artillery shell or rocket, the chemical immobilizes enemy soldiers by causing headache, giddiness and even hallucinations. Its chemical nature remains secret.

5 Jan 66   Wall Street Journal, William Beecher

(The editors of Wall Street Journal have declined permission to give the verbatim text of a selection from the above cited article. The following describes the contribution of that selection.)

(CNS is described as a gas proposed for use in Vietnam. A mild dose may cause diarrhea, colic and nausea. These may last for weeks. CNS can be disseminated by bombs, mortar shells and grenades as well as spray tanks. An attacking force would find it useful since it dissipates quickly in fresh air.)

5 Jan 66   Wall Street Journal, William Beecher

(The editors of Wall Street Journal have declined permission to give the verbatim text of a selection from the above cited article. The following describes the contribution of that selection.)

(Large quantities of the psychochemical BZ have been stored by the Army. Heat from burning grenades and bombs vaporizes the powdered BZ whose tiny particles are then carried by the mildest breezes. A low concentration of BZ can cause incapacitation for up to 10 days. Characteristic effects include loss of muscular coordination, headaches, disorientation and hallucinations. No permanent injury is envisaged by experts.)

20 Jan 67   Science, "Chemical and Biological Warfare (II):
             The Weapons and the Policies"

   ...The incapacitant now standardized for use is known as BZ. It has
both physical and mental effects, but its precise nature is not clear; un-
classified information is notably less ample than for other chemical agents.
The Army technical manual (TM 3-215) lists the following effects: interference with ordinary activity; dry, flushed skin; tachycardia; urinary reten-
tion; constipation; slowing of physical and mental activity; headache; giddiness;
disorientation; hallucinations; drowsiness; maniacal behavior (sometimes); and
increase in body temperature. The weapons-employment manual warns that
there are "critical limitations to the use of BZ" but cites the usefulness of
incapacitants against intermingled enemy and friendly military units and
against mixed populations of friendly, enemy, and civilian personnel.

20 Jan 67   Science, "Chemical and Biological Warfare (II):
             The Weapons and the Policies"

   ...Biological munitions are produced at Pine Bluff Arsenal, a 15,000-
acre installation outside Pine Bluff, Arkansas, which employs about 1400
people. Pine Bluff also produces toxic-chemical munitions and riot-control
munitions. Its job runs from manufacturing the agents to filling and assembling weapons. Research and development on chemical weapons, and some
production and assembly of them, take place in a number of subunits of the
Edgewood Arsenal, in Maryland. Various chemical munitions, reportedly
including nerve gas, "incapacitants," and anticrop weapons, are produced
at Rocky Mountain Arsenal in Denver. The U.S. also operates a major manufacturing plant — at an estimated annual cost of $3.5 million — in Newport,
Indiana, where Sarin, a lethal nerve gas, is produced and loaded into rockets,
land mines, and artillery shells. The plant is managed under contract by
the Food Machinery Corporation, has 300 employees, and is reported to have
been operating 24 hours daily since 1960.

12 May 67   New York Post (See Note Page 20)
             SKILLMAN, NEW JERSEY

   The Army is quietly teaching its Chemical Corps officers how to use a
powerful mind-altering psychedelic drug called Agent BZ as a possible
combat weapon.
   A copy of a lesson plan outlines effects resulting from the mysterious
chemical, ranging from giddiness to hallucinations.
   "Research to throw light upon mental illness has brought as a byproduct the discovery of synthesis of a growing list of substances capable
of producing 'model psychosis,' " the lesson plan explains.
   "These brief controllable drug-induced disturbances in mental function are often profoundly disorganizing and, while they last, would without
doubt be severely crippling to a military group in which they might occur."
   The lesson plan discusses the use of marijuana, mescaline, LSD, or
lysergic acid diethylamide, and Agent BZ as possible weapons.
   Marijuana and mescaline are ruled out by the lesson plan as useful military weapons because they require such large doses.
   LSD is listed as having "great promise," but it is BZ which is described
as "our standard incapacitating agent."
   A Pentagon spokesman described BZ as a "delayed acting temporarily
incapacitating agent producing incapacitating physical and mental effects."
   Two researchers at the New Jersey Neuro-Psychiatric Institute here,
one of the nation's foremost centers for treatment and research in mental
disturbances, said they were reasonably certain what BZ is.
   The researchers, who declined to be identified, agreed after seeing the
symptoms listed in the Army document that the substance probably is related
to belladonna, a plant extract which is one of the oldest drugs used in war.

CHAPTER IV
DESTROYING HUTS AND VILLAGES

The following Articles from International Conventions relevant to this chapter are quoted in full:

Hague Convention No. IV, Annex
Regulations Respecting the Laws and Customs of War on Land
18 October 1907
(Short reference: Hague—Laws)

Article 22.

The right of belligerents to adopt means of injuring the enemy is not unlimited.

Article 23

In addition to the prohibitions provided by special Conventions, it is especially forbidden—

(g) To destroy or seize the enemy's property, unless such destruction or seizure be imperatively demanded by the necessities of war.

Article 46.

Family honour and rights, the lives of persons, and private property, as well as religious convictions and practice, must be respected.

Private property cannot be confiscated.

Article 50

No general penalty, pecuniary or otherwise, shall be inflicted upon the population on account of the acts of individuals for which they cannot be regarded as jointly and severally responsible.

Geneva Convention
Relative to the Protection of Civilian Persons
in Time of War
12 August 1949
(Short reference: Geneva—Civilians)

Article 53.

Any destruction by the Occupying Power of real or personal property belonging individually or collectively to private persons, or to the State, or to other public authorities, or to social or cooperative organizations, is prohibited, except where such destruction is rendered absolutely necessary by military operations.

See also (pages 29-42) the following additional Articles relevant to this chapter: Geneva—Civilians: 29, 31, 32, 33, 146, 147, 148.

Vietnam Diary, Richard Tregaskis, 1963, p. 63

Friday, October 19 ... One of the American advisers, Lt. Edwin C. Brooks (of Dubuque, Iowa), was on his first action this time, and he happened to be next to the one Vietnamese Ranger who was hit.

"When we got there," the sturdy, crew-cut Brooks said, "three or four VC's began firing. One of the Vietnamese troopers was hit in the head. The next round landed right at the feet of an American sergeant who was with us, named Black (Glenell C. Black of Orlando, Fla.)

"The Vietnamese company commander brought fire to bear after the man was hit. Then they burned out a couple of known VC houses."

17 Apr 65   (See Note Page 20)
               SAIGON, VIETNAM, April 17

...Since Friday, ground troops have been searching the tangled jungle north of the Black Virgin Mountain trying to assess the damage caused by 1,000 tons of bombs dropped by 230 U.S. warplanes.

The ground troops still have to discover evidence that the jungled region was what intelligence reports said it was, a major Viet Cong head-quarters region, U.S. sources said. No Viet Cong bodies have been found and only a handful of weapons have been picked up.

Planes from all four U.S. services, the Marines, Navy, Air Force and Army, participated. A U.S. spokesman made it clear to newsmen on briefings the day of the raid that they expected major results.

Ground troops are expected to continue scouring the region which is described as being blotchy jungle and thick. Many buildings were not hurt by the saturation bombing apparently because of the heavy jungle cover. These are being burned by the ground troops.

15 Jun 65   New York Times, Jack Langguth
               PHUOCVINH, SOUTH VIETNAM, June 14

More than 1,000 South Vietnamese airborne troops were moved into an area north of Dongxoai today while United States paratroopers here waited for their first full-scale clash with the Vietcong.

...The American battalion is ready to move out by helicopter to take part in the battle if the Vietcong engage Government forces. If there is no action, the Americans expect to set out from their defensive positions in the next day or two, raid and burn a Vietcong village and then withdraw to their regular base at Vungtau.

6 Jul 65   (See Note Page 20)
               SAIGON

...Fresh human footprints in the paddyfields and dozens of empty thatched houses showed a wholesale withdrawal before the combined operation of Americans, Vietnamese and Australians, their second of the war. This time they concentrated on a section 30 miles northeast of Saigon.

More than 1,000 paratroopers of the U.S. Army's 173rd Airborne Brigade made up the biggest national contingent of the task force, as was the case in the first combined operation last week. All were lifted in by helicopters with orders to search out and destroy the Viet Cong and their homes, supplies and installations.

This followed up a bombardment of the jungle Monday with 500 tons of bombs by about 25 Guam-based B52 jets of the U.S. Strategic Air Command.

...The helicopters drew some ineffective shots in flight.

A sniper fired on a U.S. platoon that was destroying three confiscated fish traps. He hit nobody and got away after the Americans shot back.

9 Jul 65   New York Times, Jack Langguth
            SAIGON, SOUTH VIETNAM, Friday, July 9

...With the return of American paratroops from Zone D, an hour-by-hour report of their activities was presented yesterday.

9:55 A.M.: A unit of the American airborne force encountered 150 Vietcong guerrillas dug into a well-fortified jungle village. The area was crisscrossed with tunnels through which the Communists escaped, dragging off their dead and wounded.

The Americans said the troops wore black uniforms and blue scarves. They estimated that there were 50 Vietcong casualties.

Besides destroying the village, the paratroops captured one 50-caliber machine gun.

11 Jul 65   New York Times (See Note Page 20)
             ANHOA, SOUTH VIETNAM, July 10

The United States marines based across the bay used to call this island "Little Hawaii" because of its rolling surf and happy people. In one day Anhoa became a little hell.

When the marines landed here yesterday they found the South Vietnamese coastal patrol headquarters overrun by Vietcong guerrillas. At the headquarters itself, 16 South Vietnamese sailors had been killed, as had two United States Navy advisers, both shot in the head. Nearby the Vietcong had slain six members of the local militia.

As the day wore on 3 marines died in Vietcong fire and 13 were wounded. The guerrillas lost 6 killed and 51 taken prisoners.

The heaviest toll, according to United States sources, was about 100 civilians caught in the cross fire.

Anhoa lies just across the bay from the United States Marine installations at Chulai.

...In addition to the Vietnamese Navy installation, Anhoa has about 1,500 civilian inhabitants.

Alpha Company, 120 marines, moved west across the island, with its first objective the village of Xuarmy. The Vietcong had dug themselves in beside every house.

Other marines were taking the town of Longthanh, which had also been occupied by the Vietcong.

Another Marine company was moving across Anhoa from the east, and the whole Marine force linked up by evening.

Just before nightfall the marines were ordered to burn Anhoa and Xuarmy to prevent the Vietcong from reoccupying them.

3 Aug 65   New York Times (See Note Page 20)
            CHANSON, SOUTH VIETNAM, Aug. 2

A loudspeaker warning to clear out went unheeded and United States Marines and Vietnamese troops found a woman and two children among 25 persons they killed in an assault that overran this Vietcong-dominated village today.

The woman died of a wound in the side, perhaps from one of the 1,000 artillery shells poured into the area, 10 miles south of the Danang air base. A wailing child beside her had an arm injury.

A grenade hurled by a marine under sniper fire blasted two children to death in an air-raid shelter. One or two other civilians were also believed to be among the 25 persons killed during the fight.

Hunting the Vietcong at close quarters, a marine shouted: "Kill them! I don't want anyone moving."

Survivors said they had feared to leave the village because of the possibility that they might be hit by planes' fire or artillery.

The marines burned huts they believed were the sites of sniper fire. A sergeant said orders called for this.

9 Aug 65   (See Note Page 20)
             BIEN HOA, VIETNAM, Aug. 9

...It was shortly after 6 A.M. Saturday, Aug. 7.

The mission: To clear a 35-mile jungle area east and southeast of Bien Hoa in search of Viet Cong guerrillas, to destroy any huts and bunkers the enemy might use as a staging and rest area for small units, or for storage of rice and ammunition.

In the operation, which ended today, the battalion destroyed 18 huts, 13 bunkers and two bridges. No Viet Cong guerrillas were sighted, but this was expected.

...At the outset the company encountered about 15 Vietnamese — men, women and children — coming out of the woods. All were searched and questioned by Tran Quoc Bao, a 22-year-old South Vietnamese army sergeant assigned as an interpreter.

Some of the Vietnamese were riding carts pulled by water buffalo. They told Bao they were woodcutters from Hoi An, a nearby village. Bao told Taylor he did not believe they were Viet Cong. They were released, told to go home and not return.

No civilians were supposed to be in the area in the first place. Since it had been declared a free strike zone and ordered cleared.

Shortly after release of the woodcutters a 60 mm mortar shell exploded about 130 yards away from company A's right flank. After several checks, Taylor determined it was enemy fire. No one was hurt.

Much deeper in the jungle, the troops picked up a 16-year-old boy carrying a dead rabbit and an anteater. He told Bao he was a trapper from Bien Hoa. Taylor wasn't satisfied with his story so the boy was removed by helicopter for questioning by intelligence agents.

"Since the Viet Cong have no radios here, they use kids to carry messages and as spotters for troop movements," Taylor explained.

...Company A destroyed several huts and bunkers after searching them. The troops blew them up with grenades and dynamite.

One of the bunkers proved to be specially tough. Two grenades tossed at it failed to do the job. Finally Sgt. William McMullen of Leadville, Colo., head of a demolition team, walked up to the entrance and tossed a grenade inside to the rear. That did it.

12 Aug 65   The Times (London)
             SAIGON, August 11

Members of the 1st Battalion, the Royal Australian Regiment killed four Vietcong and destroyed five enemy villages in a five-day operation north of Saigon, the Australian Army Force headquarters reported today. About seven tons of rice, 100 lbs of salt, a large quantity of peanuts, and weapons and clothing were destroyed. Australian casualties were reported to be "very light."

3 Oct 65   (See Note Page 20)
             SAIGON, VIETNAM, Oct. 3

...A battalion of Marines swarmed ashore in amphibious vehicles and
helicopters from two U.S. 7th Fleet attack transports and a helicopter
carrier.

The Marines came under attack from a Viet Cong junk base, but the
Viet Cong guns were pounded by U.S. aircraft.

The heaviest opposition came soon after the landing, but the Marines
secured two beachheads, then drove inland where they knocked out Viet Cong
bunkers and fortifications, the spokesman said.

...The Marines repulsed the attack and suffered light losses, the
spokesman said, but they were believed the heaviest casualties inflicted on
the unit since it began patrolling the area five miles south of the big Da Nang
Marine base 10 days ago. Viet Cong losses were not known.

"The Viet Cong came out like rats from holes," one Marine said.

The Marines held off the Viet Cong until reinforcements arrived. The
clash took place in dense brush near a complex of seven villages honeycombed
with guerrilla fortifications.

...Military spokesmen in Saigon reported these other developments:

U.S. Army 1st Cavalry troopers moved into a Viet Cong stronghold
without opposition near An Khe, 260 miles northeast of Saigon. They destroyed 42 structures and seized 2,200 pounds of rice and wheat in the search
and clear operation.

10 Jan 66   (See Note Page 20)
              TRUNG LAP, VIET NAM, Jan. 10

...Civilians poured through Allied lines. Spriggs' company had 312
refugees Sunday -- 163 children, 66 moths (sic), 65 old women, 14 old men
and 4 young men. He had almost as many on Monday. Thousands of other
civilians came into the ranks of other Allied forces after heavy raids by
B-52 bombers and artillery barrages. Apparently few civilians were injured
in spite of intense prebombardment.

Spriggs found one woman, seven months pregnant, with stomach wounds
and her left leg torn with shrapnel. "She started having labor pains and we
managed to get a helicopter in to help her. I heard later she and the baby
were all right," Spriggs said.

The women, children and old men came quietly. But not their husbands.
"Everyone in this place is a Viet Cong, they are 100 percent," an interpreter told a U.S. officer. "Every man who can carry a rifle is out there
shooting at us, or hiding from us."

The fact that the Viet Cong got away can be attributed to two reasons.
The Allies attempt to push quickly through to the river to trap the Viet Cong
on one hand, and then burn down every house and destroy every tunnel on
the other.

15 Sep 66   (See Note Page 20)

...Advices (sic) from Bong Son said one company came under heavy
automatic weapons fire after nightfall from the vicinity of a hostile village,
Lien Hoi Two.

Various huts both there and in a companion hamlet, Lien Hoi One, had
been burned during a sweep aimed at enemy forces believed to total two
regiments. Controversy accompanied the flames.

Some newsmen said they saw soldiers using matches to set huts in Lien
Hoi One afire Wednesday after they were shot at from the village. The
divisional command denied this. It issued a two-page statement saying the
fires were probably started by preliminary air strikes and artillery shells
and the wind fanned the flames.

Though American soldiers are restricted in such cases, South Vietnamese troops are not. Lt. Col. Robert H. Siegrist, a cavalry battalion

commander, said a government platoon working with his men set fire to 13 of Lien Hoi Two's 60 or 70 houses Thursday after a raid yielded six enemy rifles, some ammunition and Viet Cong literature.

"This is standard procedure for the Vietnamese when they believe the buildings are used by the Viet Cong," Siegrist said.

16 Sep 66   (See Note Page 20)
              SAIGON, Sept 16

The U.S. Military Command acknowledged today that American troops burned down a Vietnamese village which it described as a hostile, fortified complex.

An announcement by the official U.S. spokesman contradicted a statement yesterday from the U.S. 1st Air Cavalry Division which said razing of the village was caused by air strikes and artillery fire.

News correspondents who were at the village, Lien Hoa (sic), said they had seen some cavalry soldiers set fire to thatched roof houses with matches.

The incident occurred during a multibrigade operation of the 1st Air Cavalry in the central coastal area. The village was about 43 miles northwest of coastal Qui Nhon.

The U.S. Headquarters spokesman said that after the village was razed Wednesday cavalrymen seized 70 Viet Cong suspects and that after questioning, 62 of these were turned over to South Vietnamese troops as prisoners.

The spokesman described the village as a fortified complex of two hamlets known as Lien Hoa One and Two which he said was "definitely hostile."

He said two U.S. helicopters and a F100 Supersabre were shot down in this area the day before the burning. He said 1st Cavalry ground troops received "considerable fire" from bunkers in the village complex.

The spokesman said that villagers had been forewarned by loudspeakers that U.S. air and artillery strikes would be made against the village.

The spokesman said the villagers and a Viet Cong force had left the locality by the time cavalrymen entered the area. He said there were no reports of any civilian casualties.

The spokesman said the cavalrymen rounded up the 70 suspects when they entered the village complex.

He said the village was burned to deny further use of the area by the enemy and because it was a threat to the 1st Cavalry troops.

18 Sep 66   The Sunday Star (Washington) (See Note Page 20)
              THE CROW'S FOOT, VIET NAM

When and why does an American troop commander in Viet Nam order the burning of an enemy village?

"Not today, for any reason," said bespectacled, unshaven Capt. Nelson Newcombe as he noticed wisps of thin white smoke spiralling over a cluster of brown thatched huts that made up the hamlet of An Huu.

He barked into his radio: "Who the hell's burning down those houses? There'll be no burnings today, that's an order."

The 2nd platoon of Newcombe's company had moved across a soggy, mile-wide paddyfield earlier in the day Thursday to search for Viet Cong and enemy weapons. Shot at in the operation, they had put the torch to some of the meager dwellings.

Newcombe again insisted over the radio that they stop. He had enough of burning villages.

Just the previous day in a lightning raid on the nearby Linh Hoi One hamlet, his men put the torch to a few houses still left standing after a long air bombardment and artillery barrage.

...The argument against destroying villages is that this will destroy the hope of ever getting cooperation from the people. This argument often has been dropped, however, when U.S. troops have operated in incorrigibly hostile areas.

Such an area was the Crow's Foot. U.S. planes dropped millions of leaflets on the hamlets, warning residents that homes would be destroyed if the Viet Cong hid there.

...''We have to do something about these villages. We know they are used by the enemy. But how far can you go?''

When the rapid-fire assault began, Newcombe's troops burst through Linh Hoi One without seeing a soul. Believing the local population had fled along with the enemy troops, they began burning down the few houses that remained standing.

At this point, scores of women, children and old men poured from deep hideouts under the homes. They appeared more angry than upset as they watched their flimsy dwellings go up in smoke.

Newcombe figured that by burning down the houses, the enemy would be pre-occupied rebuilding them in the next few months and spend less time fighting the war. And the torch also would serve as a reminder that punishment was always near for those who forcibly opposed the government...

And some ask: is it morally right to punish women and children by burning homes for sin committed by their husbands, sons and brothers?

Newcombe figures that sometimes you have to.

17 Sep 66   New York Times (See Note Page 20)
             SAIGON, Sept 16

The United States military command acknowledged today that American troops had burned down a South Vietnamese village that it described as a hostile, fortified complex.

An announcement by the official United States spokesman contradicted a statement yesterday from the United States First Cavalry Division (air mobile) that said that the village had been razed by air strikes and artillery fire.

News correspondents who had been at the village, Lienhoa, said they had seen some First Cavalry soldiers set fire to thatched-roof houses with matches.

...The spokesman described the village as a fortified complex of two hamlets, known as Lienhoa One and Two, and which he described as ''definitely hostile.''

...The spokesman said that villagers had been forewarned by loud-speakers that air and artillery strikes would be made against the village.

...He said the village had been burned to deny further use of the area to the enemy, and because it was a threat to the First Cavalry troops.

...The incident occurred during an operation involving several brigades in the central coastal area. The village was about 43 miles northwest of coastal Quinhon, the capital of Bindinh Province.

The United States headquarters spokesman said that after the village was razed Wednesday, air mobile soldiers seized 70 Vietcong suspects and that, after questioning, 62 of these were turned over to South Vietnamese troops as prisoners.

...The spokesman said the soldiers had rounded up the 70 suspects when they entered the village complex.

28 Sep 66   Herald Statesman (See Note Page 20)
             LINH HOI, VIET NAM

This is the way life goes in a village caught in the vortex of war. Artillery shells burst among the flimsy thatched huts of Linh Hoi. Napalm seared through coconut trees and corn.

Far below the splintering shrapnel, in a deep earth bunker, the sounds of a newborn baby's first cries briefly drowned out the holocaust overhead.

The aged village midwives ceremonially dug a hole for the placenta, nodding to each other wisely. This baby would live long. Wasn't a child's life span measured by the depth that his placenta is buried? And they already were 30 feet below ground.

The hours moved on. In normal times, the good spirits might well take note and coax the newborn child to manhood through the barriers of disease and malnutrtiion that kill half the peasant Vietnamese before puberty.

But these were not normal times. War had become part of the disease of Viet Nam. Within 34 hours, the sleeping baby awakened and choked on smoke seeping down in the bunker. The midwives, the neighbors, and the visitors who had crowded into the bunker when the artillery and aircraft first came over, swarmed out into the bright light above.

Men of the U.S. 1st Cavalry Division (Airmobile) had swept through the village once without locating a soul. Now they were systematically burning the houses to the ground. They were amazed as hundreds of women, children and old men poured from the ground.

The mother and her baby stayed below.

Much later that day, Lt. Jasper Campesi of Chicago, leading his platoon around the edge of Linh Hoi, saw the pair. The mother, probably 18 years old, was "kinda holding herself in," said Campesi.

An old man, a conical straw hat perched on his head, was tenderly clutching the naked baby. Its tiny fists were clenched instinctively over its eyes to close out the light.

Campesi beckoned to one of his men. They put the young mother in a string hammock and tied it under a long bamboo pole. They placed the baby on her stomach, threw a mat over the pole to shut out the sun, and moved off across the paddy-fields to where the helicopters were coming. It was a crude but effective ambulance.

By the time Campesi arrived, the helicopters had stopped coming in. There were just too many people to evacuate, and there was no question that they were all Viet Cong sympathizers. So why move them? Linh Hoi was in one of the tiny valleys streaking into the foothills along the central Vietnamese coast. Leave the people where they were: that was the decision.

"But we can't leave her," said Campesi, looking down at the mother lying on the dry paddyfield dike. "Her belly looks split open. She needs medical attention."

Another officer commented, "Are you kidding? These people are tough, they don't need our help. I bet she could get up right now and walk back to her village."

The troops started taking sides, but the argument was resolved simply enough. The radio failed, and they couldn't get more helicopters anyway.

The mother was pulling at Campesi's trouser leg. The fear had left her eyes. There seemed to be arrogance there now, sharpened by what looked like scorn at the bickering and indecision of the troops. She pointed back at her smoldering village, and patted the bamboo pole beside her.

"Take me back" she was saying. The little old man had picked up the pink-skinned baby and was walking away. Campesi and another soldier hoisted the pole, with the mother slung underneath, to their shoulders.

The fate of the baby was now in the hands of the spirits.

Just a few hundred yards away, a young man was dying punctured by shell fragments and bullets probably in the battle earlier that day. A member of the local Viet Cong militia force, now he was home with his family to die.

His wife wept uncontrollably on the earth floor beside his crude bed. Two young children were in her arms, another child at her knee. The man's mother wailed at the American troops and pointed to the sky.

"Take my son and make him well," she was saying, but it was all too late. Carried out to the open paddyfield, the young man died.

The Americans offered to bury him. The wife and mother declined.

They told an interpreter "Just let us take him across the river to bury him at the pagoda. He was born here, he has died here. So let us have him."

Oct 66   Argosy
              Milt Machlin, "Front Line Report Vietnam"

(The editors of Argosy have declined permission to give the verbatim text of a selection from the above cited article. The following describes the contribution of that selection.)

(The author, in a dialogue, shows the conflict which arises when reporters attempt to cover a military action up close but are restrained from doing so by military authorities.

The U.S. Marines are burning a village in the distance. The reporters attempt in vain to get closer to take pictures. The author says that he is thwarted by the military for what seems to be other than security reasons. He also says that the military attempt to conceal this kind of action. The Marines were attacked from the village, one Marine was killed and, according to the author, since the burning of the village was justified, the story should be told.)

16 Sep 65   New York Times, Charles Mohr
              CAMNE, SOUTH VIETNAM, Sept 15

...In early August, a Marine battalion burned perhaps 500 houses in the embarrassing presence of a television camera crew.

...Around them is some evidence that the war is hard for the Vietnamese, too. Although Defense Department spokesmen had criticised the Columbia Broadcasting System for saying that 150 were burned in Camne, marines and Vietnamese officials insist that the correct figure was 500.

2 Jan 67   Newsweek
              "War of Ambush"

...Operating from the town of Binh Chanh, the commander of the 4/9th, Lt. Col. Robert A. Hyatt, keeps his men going around the clock to keep the Viet Cong off balance. By day, they comb the countryside to ferret out the enemy; by night, patrols slip out along the narrow dikes to set up ambushes.

...In the morning, it was time for the patrols to move out and check the dozens of farm huts in the neighborhood. The fields were empty — oddly so, since the rice was ripe and ready for harvest. Then some sniper rounds popped in the distance as a patrol slithered along a dike and came to a house. Inside, they found two old men and a younger man. They also found 40 pounds of salt and 2,000 pounds of rice. "That's too much for them to have for themselves," declared the Vietnamese interpreter, Sgt. Nguyen Huu Ngoc, and the young man was taken along for questioning.

...The captured VC, who identified himself as a runner for 165A Viet Cong Regiment, had been found cowering in the mud mortar shelter in a thatch-roofed peasant house. There, the GI's also found a cache of U.S. ammunition and 4,500 pounds of rice and, while the woman who owned the place howled in protest, they soaked the house with kerosene and burned it down, but not until the woman had removed her prize possession — a grandfather clock.

The object here was to spread the word around the neighborhood that anyone harboring VC would be punished. The Americans also hope that their tactics may encourage local wives and mothers to try talking their sons and husbands into leaving the Viet Cong. By sternness tempered with justice, the Americans aim to isolate the VC from the local population. It is too early to tell if these tactics will work. But after a few days of U.S. operations at Hung Long, the people were far politer if not noticeably friendlier. Perhaps more to the point was the fact that the day after the U.S. ambush of the Viet Cong, an additional 70 farmers — the highest number yet since the Americans arrived — came out from Binh Chanh and went to work harvesting the rice.

22 Jan 67   Cleveland Plain Dealer, John Bixler

...."What I didn't like was when we burned the village down. The women and kids were crying and begging you not to burn them down. A lot of them stay inside and you have to drag them out.

"Ma, that's not good to see. I look back at what was once a village and the people crying, but as the sergeant told me, that's war. I guess he was right. It was a VC (Viet Cong) Village and we had to do it".

This is an excerpt from a letter from a U.S. fighting man in Vietnam, Sgt. Dennis Pena, to his parents, Mr. and Mrs. Benny Pena, 1601 Clark Avenue, S.W.

9 Mar 67   New York Times, R. W. Apple, Jr.
             AT THE CAMBODIAN BORDER, SOUTH VIETNAM, March 8

...What was once a virgin jungle has been scarred by American fire-power in Operation Junction City.

This afternoon, one could see from a helicopter dozens of towering geysers of white smoke, the results of bomb runs by American jet fighter-bombers from Saigon.

The area looked deserted. The border hamlet Logo was bulldozed by the Third Brigade last week. It had proved too convenient a base for Viet-cong snipers.

Victor Charlie, Kuno Knoebl, 1967, p. 211

...We had landed on the flat top of a hill. The troops went down through tall elephant grass to An Lao Valley. Presumably, the guerrillas driven from the coast had taken shelter here. The mission of these troops was to comb the valley and "pacify" it; the guerrillas were to be driven farther west.

...The next morning the U.S. troops reached the first village. It was abandoned. The GI's knocked on the floors of the huts looking for hidden tunnels and trenches, but there was nothing. Then I saw smoke rising from one of the huts. I thought some peasants were there, but inside were two young American soldiers. They had started the fire, then they moved to the next hut and burned it down too; in half an hour, the village was burning. I asked one of the soldiers why he had started the fire. He laughed and said, "The Charlies will know we've been here."

A few days later this incident became the subject of controversy at a press conference in Camp DOG. A Swedish colleague, who had also seen the houses put to the torch, asked whether there was an explicit order to burn peasant huts. "No, there is no such order," came the answer. "But we didn't know the houses were burned down." I said that I had personally seen the village set on fire. The colonel in charge of the press conference said he believed me, but he doubted that the village was harmless. "Perhaps the soldiers found weapons or a Viet-Cong flag; perhaps the Americans had been shot at from the huts," he said.

"No, they weren't," the Swedist correspondent answered. "The houses were empty, and there were no weapons or flags or anything else in them to show that guerrillas had been there." However, a few American correspondents made the point that the burned huts weren't important; after all, this was war, and such incidents always happened.

The colonel still doubted that we had the facts straight. After the Swede offered to develop the photos he took to show what had happened, the Colonel finally admitted, "Yes, it can happen." I was confused by the officer's attitude, but was more disturbed by that of the American correspondents, who apparently viewed our questions as a betrayal of America's just cause. We were unable to make them understand that to burn down one hut arbitrarily could nullify years of political and psychological work and an investment of tens of thousands of dollars.

Victor Charlie, Kuno Knoebl, 1967, p. 111

...Meanwhile, the camouflaged guerrillas crouched in their foxholes waiting for the first enemy. Hours passed. Then the first American soldiers appeared.

...Suddenly, four shots rang out. A GI dropped his gun, grabbed his right upper arm, then dropped to the ground. Other Americans returned the fire. A machine-gun fusillade swept the dense foliage, followed by silence. Four soldiers lay hugging the ground in the manioc field just outside the village, hid behind the trunks of coconut trees. Every time one of the men in the manioc field tried to rise, a shot whistled across the level ground.

The American officers had not expected resistance. They called by radio for artillery support. Ten minutes later shells roared over the Americans and exploded among the huts. In another ten minutes they had destroyed the village. Flames, smoke, and ashes filled the air.

The Americans advanced again, and this time they met no resistance. The snipers had fled. Distraught women and children crept out of their foxholes and looked at the soldiers with hate. Their ruined dwellings smoldered all around them. A Vietnamese interpreter questioned an old peasant and learned how the Viet-Cong had evacuated the village, leaving the two guerrillas behind to "warn" them when the Americans arrived.

"They do this very often," Colonel Moore said to me later. "They shoot at us because they know we will return the fire. They provoke us into destroying the villages. After we leave, they return and tell the peasants: 'See, this happened because we weren't here. Only we can defend you from the imperialists.'"

Two days later, with U.S. troops ten miles to the south, the Viet Cong returned to the village and built new fortifications for the next attack, knowing that next time the peasants would be fighting alongside them.

18 Aug 67   The New York Times
             CULADUNG ISLAND, SOUTH VIETNAM, Aug 16

"The Vietcong are really shook when we go into their backyard and hit them," the blond, blue-eyed Navy officer said. "Well, we hit them today and they'll know they're no longer safe in the areas they control."

Lieut. Frederick E. Trani, 27 years old, of Hyde Park, N.Y., leaned back against the landing craft, his face still tense from the raid he had led on this Communist-controlled island in the mouth of the Bassac River, deep in the Delta.

Lieutenant Trani is the leader of a platoon of Seals, the little-publicized group of Navy frogmen trained in the Art of infiltration and guerrilla attacks, which they have been conducting quitely for eight months in the Mekong Delta. The name Seals is taken from the words sea, air and land.

This morning, the Seals launched their largest and one of their most daring raids. Twenty men of the Seal team and six South Vietnamese raiders swept onto this island where, for five hours, they dynamited bunkers, burned houses and stores of rice, blew up sampans and killed three Vietcong who had failed to run as had all the others.

...The Seal decided to go it alone with a daylight attack backed by Veitnamese river assault group boats and United States Navy "Seawolves," armed helicopters.

At 8 A.M., after the frustrating maneuvering in the sampans through a sleepless night, the attack force assembled at the southern entrance of the canal.

..."There are some buildings and sampans coming up on your left," crackled a radio message from the helicopters."

The command boat, immediately behind the landing craft opened fire with machine gun and heavy mortars as it drew abreast of the thatch roofed huts. Buildings and trees snapped and flew apart under the assualt.

For one hour the boats moved slowly up the canal, the mortars and machine guns spitting occasionally at the woodline on the shores. This island had long been declared a Vietcong stronghold and a free-fire zone, which means anything on the island is an approved target.

...Heavy smoke was visible as the Seals found targets, working a half mile inland. There they found a hamlet, with a huge stock of rice, an obvious resupply center.

"We burned every house in that hamlet," said Lieut. (jg) William Bishop, 26 years old, of Chicago. "Those VC are going to remember we aren't afraid t come to them."

Five hours later, as a torrential rain pelted down, they returned to the landing craft. One of the Vietnamese Seals had been wounded in the leg by his own grenade fragment, the only casualty in the group.

"We destroyed 14 tons of rice, burned 53 houses, destroyed 14 bunkers and six sampans," said Lieutenant Trani.

He added that the Vietcong apparently were frightened away. "That's the onl bad part — we only got three of them."

CHAPTER V
SCORCHED EARTH

The same Convention Articles relevant to Chapter IV (p. 131) are also applicable to this chapter. Hague—Laws: 22, 23(g), 46, 50; Geneva—Civilians: 29, 31, 32, 33, 53, 146, 147, 148.

23 May 65   New York Herald Tribune
            SAIGON

...Near the big coastal city of Hue, U.S. Marines moved out on Friday from their defensive positions around Phu Bai air base and swept through Viet Cong-dominated villages eight miles to the west. The Marines set crops on fire and burned or dynamited huts in a scorched-earth operation.

6 Jan 66   The Evening Star (Washington) (See Note Page 20)
            SAIGON, Jan 6

To break the back of the Viet Cong, U.S. and allied forces are adopting a program of destroying houses and crops in areas which feed and shield the Communist forces.

For years, Americans refused to participate in "scorched earth" efforts, leaving them to the Vietnamese. Now Americans are directly involved. They are trying to protect innocent people.

The broad-based program includes the establishment of free-bombing zones in Viet Cong regions, killing rice crops in enemy areas, and burning other crops and homes.

The rich, intensely cultivated flat lands south of the Vaico Oriental River west of Saigon are prime "scorched earth" targets, U.S. paratroopers from the 173rd Airborne Brigade began operating there last weekend. They laid their base camp among the blackened frames of burned houses. Within two miles of the paratroopers' camp not a house was left standing. Constant pounding by artillery and planes had reduced every building to rubble.

The paratroopers' mission was to move out farther, round up all the people they could find, evacuate them north of the river to resettlement camps, and burn and destroy everything eatable and livable.

Patrols waded in neck-deep canals slicing through the canefields, crept stealthily down high dikes, and pushed through thick brush.

Every house they encountered they burned to the ground. Most were of thatch, but some were large with heavy wooden frames and neat gardens.

Every cooking utensil was smashed, every banana tree severed, every mattress slashed. On the first day, the men of C Company found more than 60 Vietnamese women and children weeping as they lay in trenches around their devastated homes. These were sent in helicopters to Bao Trai district, north of the river, and resettled.

Their menfolk stayed hidden in the canefields and the canals, sniping at the searching paratroopers and mining the trails. The province chief had told the Americans that every man south of the river was a Viet Cong.

"They must be either shootin' or diggin' all the time," said one paratrooper as he picked his way from one covered bunker to the next. These bunkers, some built years ago, others fresh, were in strategic positions around every home and canal...

The American paratroopers are remaining in the area, enlarging the "scorched earth" zone. They know that the Viet Cong will rebuild the razed homes when they leave, make new earthenware pots and breed new chickens.

Capt. Henry Tucker from Columbus, Miss., said: "Maybe if we can keep them busy rebuilding their houses and replanting the crops, then they'll have no time for shooting."

10 Jan 66   (See Note Page 20)
            TRUNG LAP, Jan 10

A lone American spotter plane circled over a maze of camouflaged tunnels and Viet Cong fortifications just south of the Saigon River. Only the pilot and a few American officers knew the mission: to collect intelligence for the biggest and most ambitious U.S. operations of the war in Viet Nam.

An American combat force of some 8,000 paratroopers, infantrymen and artillerymen was to converge the next morning on this bomb-scarred, triangular-shaped Communist stronghold of 15 square miles.

...As the assault helicopters set down, the soldiers saw that every surrounding building was on fire from air strikes that had just ended. A field of unharvested rice blazed; the draft of the many rotor blades fanned the flames 50 feet high.

...The battalion swept yesterday through what once had been a garden spot of Viet Nam. Two generations of Communist guerrillas had fortified the area. Decades of bombing and scorched earth warfare by French, Vietnamese and now Americans had obliterated the paradise. The few houses and rice storage shelters that had escaped burning or blasting by air strikes were set on fire by the advancing Americans. They hacked down banana trees, leaving a flaming wake.

6 Mar 66   St. Louis Post-Dispatch, (See Note Page 20)
            SAIGON, March 5

Bright flames spread quickly through the thatched roof. The American soldier threw his torch onto a part of the building not yet in flames and backed off from the intense heat.

Sections of the roof began falling to the dirt floor of the deserted farmhouse and a shower of sparks splashed across the family altar.

Buddhist religious scrolls smoldered and then burst into flames. The glass covering photographs of honored ancestors cracked and broke in the heat. Then the pictures themselves disappeared.

It was a Viet Cong house, they said. As part of the war it was destroyed together with neighboring homes. Whatever the sentiments of the villagers, the Viet Cong had used their hamlet to stage ambushes and attacks on government troops.

A daily estimate is made of Viet Cong killed and captured. Statistics are kept on the number of American and allied troops killed, wounded, or missing in action. No one can guess with precision the number of Vietnamese civilians slain or wounded or the number of homes destroyed since the war began in earnest some five years ago.

Guesses run well over 100,000 civilian dead. The number of civilian war refugees in this country of 13 million far exceeds the dead.

Probably no modern war can compare to this in terms of proportional civilian misery. The Vietnamese peasant is caught in the middle of forces which, for the most part, he cannot understand. Oddly enough, all the fighting basically is for his allegiance.

...Both sides are cold-blooded about the realities of Viet Nam. The Communists, who started it, adhere to the dictum that the people are the water that the insurgent fish swim in. No one has come up yet with a way to destroy the fish without tearing up the river as well.

Civilians, many of whom wish simply that the war would go away at whatever political cost, are caught in an insoluble dilemma when the war surges around their hamlets.

The fighting mostly takes place in the so-called contested areas where neither side holds absolute sway. Or in fringe areas controlled by the Viet Cong or government but without the majority of the population being committed one way or the other.

A common sequence of events begins with a strong Viet Cong force moving into the general area.

...Shortly after dawn a battalion or more arrives by helicopter outside the village, following an artillery barrage and an aerial bombardment to soften possible resistance.

If the Viet Cong stay in the village, they probably will order the villagers under pain of death to remain to be caught up in the fighting. If the Viet Cong are gone and the civilians try to flee the coming operation they may be shot and blasted by artillery as they try to run away.

...A farmer in a field off the flank of American troops sweeping through an enemy village waved hopefully. One cynical American shot at the man and two others joined in. As some of their comrades began chiding the trio, the man in the field dropped his hat, grabbed a carbine from bushes and blasted away at the Americans before trying, unsuccessfully, to flee to safety.

Villages, often haphazardly, have been labeled enemy or pro-government when in reality they are neither and both. A handful of snipers from a village, a Viet Cong squad possibly from a different area, can result in tragedy for the inhabitants. Air strikes, mortars and artillery are called in to silence the snipers. The poor but somehow neat huts of the Vietnamese peasants are blasted or burned.

"I wish to God there were some other way we could do this," a Marine officer once said. "I can't send my men against dug-in positions without support. It would be murder."

...In areas of military operation whole villages have been destroyed, water buffalo killed, rice scattered and destroyed, animal fodder burned.

The aim is to deny the Viet Cong any sanctuary. The ultimate plan is to pacify Viet Cong areas and, as the British did in Malaya, deny hope, food, information and life itself to the insurgents. It also calls for relocating those willing to back the government side.

...Those in the middle pay a terrible price.

Some of it is hard to understand in western terms. Near Cu Chi, where the U.S. 25th Division is setting up its Viet Nam home, thousands of Vietnamese have been relocated from villages laid out in a crazy-quilt pattern off highway 1 into a relatively easy to defend grid system along the road.

Bulldozers are smashing down the old villages, clearing away clumps of brush and bamboo thickets and blowing tunnels to take the pressure off the highway and Cu Chi. The area has been under Viet Cong domination for nearly two decades.

In the process, the villagers had to leave the land of their ancestors, family grave plots. Land to a Vietnamese is sacred in the way a stock certificate could never be. The Buddhist religion revolves around the honoring of ancestors.

The heaviest devastation probably has been wrought by the Vietnamese and American Air Forces. Most of this cannot be gauged because Vietnamese and allied troops are unable to penetrate many areas dominated by the Viet Cong.

Normally more than 300 sorties are flown daily against various targets in South Viet Nam. Most of the bombs, napalm and cannon fire are directed against what are described as Viet Cong concentrations. This usually means a village.

...At any given hour of the day, hundreds of fires can be seen from burning villages in this country.

21 Apr 66   Honolulu Advertiser
             Bob Jones, "Area Denial" 25th's Aim
             (from Congressional Record, House, May 17, 1966, p. A2659)
             CU CHI, VIETNAM

Signs began popping up around the Hau Nghia province countryside, erected by the Vietcong who face an increasingly difficult existence:

"National Liberation Front Country. Keep out. Anyone advancing beyond this point will be killed."

Maj. Gen. Fred C. Weyand, commander of the 25th Infantry Division, immediately ordered the signs torn down and new ones put up in their place: "25th Division territory. Viet Cong will be killed."

In a series of operations named for their Hawaii links (Honolulu, Faro Leaf, Kahuku, Makaha, Kahala, Kaneohe and Kaena), Weyand's troops for nearly three months have been chasing the Viet Cong from the treacherous Ho Bo Woods north of the province to the Oriental (Vaico) River in the south.

The number of VC killed by body count (468) was not spectacular, even considering the additional 971 "possible" kills the Tropic Lightning troops of the 2nd Brigade logged.

But as Weyand explained: "One of our primary missions here is area denial. We make sure the Viet Cong can't use the territory."

...Except for isolated incidents wherein the VC set up nighttime road blockades or tax travelers on Highway 1, the division has pretty much denied this traditional rice-and-peanut supply province to large units of Viet Cong.

"We belong here," said a division major. "We intend to live and stay here and rid the province of the Communist influence that's been here for 20 years. We intend to do it by aggressive military action and agressive civic action."

...Northeast of the 50-mile wide, 50 mile deep province is the famous Iron Triangle, a patch of heavy forestation that even the crack U.S. airborne troops haven't been able to deny to the VC.

To the north is Tay Ninh province and War Zone C, reputed to be the VC command center for the whole country.

...The province is a main travel route from easterly War Zone D and the Cambodian border for VC supply and replacement units. Since it produces a wealthy 960 tons of pineapple and other fruit and 1,050 tons of protein-rich peanuts every year, it is a natural supply area for the VC.

It is one of the few provinces north of Saigon with a surplus of rice, cattle, pigs and poultry, also badly needed by underfed VC armies.

16 July 66   Saturday Evening Post
             Harold Martin, "My Son in Vietnam"

...Signs of Charley were few. There were ricks of wood here and there, cut for the charcoal "factories" — primitive clay ovens in deep pits under thatched roofs — and in an open field we came on an oven at work. The orders are that anything in the area that might be useful to a guerrilla must

be destroyed — crops, wild game, hooches, even ovens — for charcoal is
an ingredient of gunpowder.

29 Jan 67   New York Times (Section 4)

...Thus, virtually all of the week's activity was forced by the aggressive patroling of American units in connection with large-scale search-and-
destroy operations.

In Operation Thayer II in Binh Dinh Province, two brigades of the First
Cavalry airmobile division and a brigade of the 25th infantry division combed
through the hamlets in an effort to root out the Viet Cong infrastructure and
give the Government's revolutionary development program a chance to get
started. A total of 1,417 enemy dead are claimed since the operation began
on Oct. 25.

Operation Cedar Falls, whose objective was to deny a sanctuary to the
Viet Cong by laying it waste, was brought to a close last Thursday. It took
place in the so-called Iron Triangle area of rubber plantations, scrub jungle,
and paddy fields, totaling about 60 square miles, about 30 miles northwest
of Saigon.

Whole villages were bulldozed and burned, and more than 6,000 persons —
all but a handful, women, children, and old men — were transferred to temporary camps under the threat of bombing. Wide swathes, like firebreaks,
were slashed through the plantations as a means of observing future Viet
Cong movements and scores of helicopter landing pads were cut so that troops
can be brought in quickly.

Miles of tunnels, laboriously dug by the guerrillas over a period of as
much as 20 years were explored and then blown up. They yielded truckloads
of documents that are now being sifted by intelligence experts and are expected
to have a bearing on future American operations. Also seized was 3,709 tons
of rice, more than enough to feed 10,000 men for a year, and 9,000 pounds
of salt. Enemy dead were put at 720.

To some observers, it seems that between defoliation, which continues
quietly, and the new scorched earth tactics of Cedar Falls, American strategy is part of the way toward a solution to the problem of denying the guerrillas the cover of the countryside by destroying it.

18 Feb 67   The Washington Post, Chalmers M. Roberts
             SAIGON, Feb. 18

...The Viet Cong have been dug in for years. As Gen. William Westmoreland has obtained more manpower, he has been able to go after their
redoubts, those training, rest and supply areas built up so arduously for
20 years or more.

American situation maps formerly showed vast belts of red labeled "war
zones," the Viet Cong lairs. With improved intelligence, these zones have
been broken down into 85 specific areas pockmarking Vietnam. Here are
caches of food, arms, medicine, and clothing together with medical facilities and classroom and training areas.

To get these vitals of the Viet Cong, both as supply and havens for the
main force and guerrillas, is what Westmoreland intends to do in 1967.

The recent Operation Cedar Falls was a beginning, and it uncovered
thousands of feet of laboriously constructed tunnels, massive supplies, and
caches of critical rice. These zones turn out to be rather compact, around
a mile square.

As one general who participated in Cedar Falls put it, "We finally woke
up to using bulldozers, and there will be a lot more of that."

24 Feb 67   (See Note Page 20)
             WASHINGTON, Feb. 24

...The first major operation of the base-smashing campaign was Operation Cedar Falls, the 30,000-man sweep of the so-called Iron Triangle. It

left 720 Viet Cong dead, 516 captured and 7,000 Vietnamese evacuated in the creation of a zone which now can be bombed at will.

Sources say hundreds and perhaps thousands of persons may also be removed from the larger but more sparsely populated Tay Ninh area of war Zone C, where the current operation is under way.

25 Feb 67   Christian Science Monitor

...United States forces have launched the first parachute jump and the greatest ground-air offensive of the war. Some 45,000 troops have begun a 250-square mile encirclement of the Viet Cong national headquarters and main base in War Zone C near the Cambodian border.

This drive continues Gen. William C. Westmoreland's 1967 strategy of destroying the half dozen or so major base areas of the Viet Cong operations of this sort are an extension of "search and destroy" — United States troops make no attempt to hold the territory in question — but the results are less temporary than this might imply.

The bases have taken the Communists years to build up — 20 years, in some cases. In the tunnel complexes are vital caches of rice, arms, medicine, and clothing, as well as important intelligence documents.

Once these major staging and supply bases are blasted and bulldozed, the Viet Cong, even if they reoccupy their former strongholds, cannot quickly rebuild and resupply them.

Operation Cedar Falls, carried out some six weeks ago in the Iron Triangle, was the first of these base-area assaults. The present operation, Junction City, is the second. Given the sparser population of Zone C's Tay Ninh Province in comparison with the "Iron Triangle," there should be fewer civilians removed from their homes in the present campaign.

13 Mar 67   (See Note Page 20)
NORTHERN PLAIN OF REEDS, VIETNAM, March 13

The 25th Division's Wolfhounds trudged through the vast swamplands 30 miles west of Saigon, destroying homes, food, gardens, livestock and even pets — everything that could be of use to the Communists.

...The operation was launched last Wednesday but was not announced until today for security reasons. It covered more than 100 square miles in the northern end of the Plain of Reeds, an area of swamp and marsh long dominated by the Viet Cong and a major route for Communist units moving between the Mekong Delta and Cambodia into Communist War Zones C and D.

Scores of civilians who had slipped back into the area after an earlier operation to evacuate them were taken to Government controlled areas. Hundreds of fires dotted the countryside as U.S. infantrymen destroyed homes, farm wagons and even piles of rice straw.

...Col. Marvin Fuller, Commander of the 25th's Second Brigade, said anyone living in his operational area was presumed to be Viet Cong. He said the systematic slaughter of water buffalo, ducks, chickens and pigs was to deny fresh meat to enemy battalions.

Some of the GIs caught ducks and carried them back to their base camp for cooking.

Hundreds of tons of rice have been destroyed or removed. The list of seized Communist equipment included one phonograph and 75 records.

14 Mar 67   (See Note Page 20)
SAIGON, Tuesday, March 14

Headquarters reported Monday that U.S. troops were scouring 100 square miles of swamplands along Cambodia's border in a new operation to deprive the Viet Cong of a stronghold threatening Saigon. Anything useful to the Communists -- homes, livestock, gardens, even dogs — was being destroyed.

...The operation, involving U.S. 25th Division Wolfhounds, began last Wednesday under the code name Waialua, after a town in Hawaii, former base of the division. The location is the northern Plain of Reeds, an area that starts 30 miles west of Saigon.

Col. Marvin Fuller, commander of a brigade in the operation, said anyone living in the operational area is presumed to be Viet Cong. Inhabitants were being evacuated to Government-controlled areas. Fuller said water buffalo, ducks, chickens and pigs were being slaughtered to deny fresh meat to enemy battalions. Dogs were killed because in a pinch the Viet Cong slaughtered them for food.

The new operation, along with Operation Junction City to the north, appeared to be part of the stepped up pressure on the Communists in both Vietnams by U.S. military forces.

...After the announcement in Saigon of scorched earth Operation Waialua, a broadcast dispatch from Hanoi reported the Viet Cong accused the United States of carrying out a policy of "burn all, destroy all, kill all" in South Vietnam.

...Associated Press correspondent John T. Wheeler reported from a command post of Operation Waialua in the Plain of Reeds that fires dotted the countryside as U.S. infantrymen set the torch to homes, farm wagons and piles of rice straw. Hundreds of tons of rice have been destroyed or removed. Some GIs snatched up ducks for their own meals.

The area is mostly swampland and marsh, only sparsely settled.

24 Mar 67   (See Note Page 20)
GIONGH DINH, VIETNAM

The Vietnamese woman ignored the crying baby in her arms. She stared in hatred as the American infantrymen with shotguns blasted away at chickens and ducks. Others shot a water buffalo and the family dog.

While her husband, father and young son were led away, the torch was put to the hut that still contained the family belongings. The flames consumed everything — including the shrine to the family ancestors.

"Man, she'd cut you to pieces for a dime," one GI said.

"No, she'd pay 100 piasters an inch just to slit your throat," another said.

The American troops were acting under orders: destroy everything of any use to the Viet Cong along the main Communist infiltration route from the delta and Cambodia into War Zones C and D. Leave the Viet Cong nothing to eat, no shelter. Remove all civilians who could give the enemy a helping hand.

The area had been so thoroughly dominated by Communists for so long that pacification, "winning the hearts and minds of the people," was considered out of the question by higher headquarters.

The GIs didn't have much stomach for the job, but orders were orders. The job was done in an area involving more than 100 square miles.

"God, my wife would faint if she could see what I'm doing now," an infantryman said. "Killing Ole Charlie (Viet Cong) is one thing, but killing puppies and baby ducks and stuff like that — it's something else, man."

The GIs left the farm site and waded back into the swamp waters of the plain of reeds, swatting mosquitoes, eyeing the tree lines for enemy and praying for enough luck to get some alive.

Four miles from the smoldering farm house were more sullen, hate-filled eyes. They belonged to the bearded, sunburned members of another 25th Division unit clustered around the riddled body of a Viet Cong.

The pajama-clad guerrilla had emerged from a hidden tunnel, his hands raised in surrender. As the American infantrymen closed in, the Vietnamese suddenly whipped a grenade from his waistband and pitched it into the center of his would-be captors. An explosion, a burst of rifle fire, then silence.

And hate.

"Dirty, stinking war; dirty stinking Communist..." an officer muttered.

A rifleman threw the riddled body into a canal.

Above the scene helicopter rotor blades clawed at the sky, racing death with four badly wounded American riflemen. For the fifth victim of the blast, the race was over. A muddy poncho was his shroud.

..."Unless tactics are drastically modified when U.S. troops really get to work in the delta, the civilian casualty and refugee problem will take on fantastic proportions," predicts a senior U.S. official.

American commanders have begun calling in air strikes and artillery barrages against lone snipers hidden in tree lines in an attempt to cut U.S. casualties.

Half Vietnam's 15 millions are clustered in the Mekong Delta region south of Saigon. The tactics used by the 2nd Brigade of the 25th Division in stripping the countryside south of the Vaico Oriental (Cap O) River probably must be modified in the delta.

The 25th's tactics correspond closely to those used by the British to rout Communist insurgents in Malaya.

The British reasoned that the guerrilla had to be separated from the peasants on whom he counted for food, information and recruits. Where control was not possible, everything of use to the terrorists was destroyed.

...In previous operations, several hundred civilian refugees were evacuated and the area was declared open for unlimited pounding by artillery and air.

But some diehards slipped back in, risking their lives and the lives of their families for their cause.

The 25th's search and destroy operation turned up hundreds of tons of rice which was destroyed. Fuller's infantrymen ripped up vines, hacked down banana trees, killed all animals, destroyed farm implements, wagons and houses and even burned piles of rice straw in the fields. The Communists often hide weapons, ammunition and food under such piles.

Brutal as the war has become, American GIs have lost none of their basic warmth toward civilians once they are separated from the battle zone.

At the brigade's forward headquarters a score of women and children, a few accidentally wounded by American fire, waited for helicopters to lift them to government-controlled areas.

Almost immediately infantry men began gathering up combat rations to feed them. Then one GI showed up with candy. Many of the youngsters eyed the candy suspiciously and a few demanded that the GIs eat a handful of the sweets first.

This out of the way, the kids fell to with gusto and flashed smiles at the GIs. A grandmother turned on a near toothless grin as she alternately nursed her shrapnel wound on one arm and munched as best she could on the hard candy.

27 Mar 67   Akron Beacon Journal
              Editorial and Letter to Editor
              EDITORIAL: AMERICANS AT WAR

More compelling, more graphic, than any editorial we have written about the war in Vietnam is the letter printed on this page today.

Here are the reactions of an Akron district boy — he could be that lad from across the street — who willingly donned the uniform to serve his country.

He is sickened and conscience-stricken at the murderous devastation he is ordered to commit.

Here is a father who is torn between loyalty to his country and frustrated anger that his son should be plunged into such a mess.

And the 16-year-old sister who just can't believe that her big brother could be killing defenseless people.

This is the way the United States is "protecting" the rest of the world? Read the letter — and weep.

LETTER: WE BURNED EVERY HUT!

To the Editor:

Here are portions of a letter I have just received from my son, who is now stationed in Vietnam.

My son enlisted in the Army, asked to be sent to Vietnam and backed the government's strong policy toward the war in Vietnam — at least he did when he left his country last November. I believe what he has to say will be of interest to you and to your readers:

Dear Mom and Dad:

Today we went on a mission and I am not very proud of myself, my friends or my country. We burned every hut in sight!

It was a small rural network of villages and the people were incredibly poor. My unit burned and plundered their meager possessions. Let me try to explain the situation to you.

The huts here are thatched palm leaves. Each one has a dried mud bunker inside. These bunkers are to protect the families. Kind of like air raid shelters.

My unit commanders, however, chose to think that these bunkers are offensive. So every hut we find that has a bunker, we are ordered to burn to the ground.

When the 10 helicopters landed this morning, in the midst of these huts, and six men jumped out of each "chopper," we were firing the moment we hit the ground. We fired into all the huts we could. Then we got "on line" and swept the area.

It is then that we burn these huts and take all men old enough to carry a weapon and the "choppers" come and get them (they take them to a collection point a few miles away for interrogation). The families don't understand this. The Viet Cong fill their minds with tales that the GIs kill all their men.

So, everyone is crying, begging and praying that we don't separate them and take their husbands and fathers, sons and grandfathers. The women wail and moan.

Then they watch in terror as we burn their homes, personal possessions and food. Yes, we burn all rice and shoot all livestock.

Some of the guys are so careless! Today a buddy of mine called "La Dai" ("Come here") into a hut and an old man came out of the bomb shelter. My buddy told the old man to get away from the hut and since we have to move quickly on a sweep, just threw a hand grenade into the shelter.

As he pulled the pin the old man got excited and started jabbering and running toward my buddy and the hut. A GI, not understanding, stopped the old man with a football tackle just as my buddy threw the grenade into the shelter. (There is a four-second delay on a hand grenade.)

After he threw it, and was running for cover, (during this four-second delay) we all heard a <u>baby</u> crying from inside the shelter!

There was nothing we could do...

After the explosion we found the mother, two children (ages about 6 and 12, boy and girl) and an almost newborn baby. That is what the old man was trying to tell us!

The shelter was small and narrow. They were all huddled together. The three of us dragged out the bodies onto the floor of the hut.

IT WAS HORRIBLE!!!

The children's fragile bodies were torn apart, literally mutilated. We looked at each other and burned the hut.

The old man was just whimpering in disbelief outside the burning hut. We walked away and left him there.

My last look was: an old, old man in ragged, torn, dirty clothes on his knees outside the burning hut, praying to Buddha. His white hair was blowing in the wind and tears were rolling down...

We kept on walking, then the three of us separated. There was a hut at a distance and my squad leader told me to go over and destroy it. An oldish man came out of the hut.

I checked and made sure no one was in it, then got out my matches. The man came up to me then, and bowed with his hands in a praying motion over and over.

He looked so sad! He didn't say anything, just kept bowing, begging me not to burn his home.

We were both there, alone, and he was about your age, Dad. With a heavy heart, I hesitatingly put the match to the straw and started to walk away.

Dad, it was so hard for me to turn and look at him in the eyes, but I did. I wish I could have cried, but I just can't anymore.

I threw down my rifle and ran into the now blazing hut and took out everything I could save — food, clothes, etc.

Afterward he took my hand, still saying nothing and bowed down touching the back of my hand to his forehead.

Machine gun fire is coming into our village (Base Camp). We are being attacked, NOW as I am writing. I must go.

Next day: Everything's OK. It was just harassing fire. I was up for the better part of the night, though.

Well, Dad, you wanted to know what it's like here. Does this give you an idea?

Excuse the poor writing but I was pretty emotional, I guess, even a little shook.

YOUR SON . . .

4 Apr 67   Christian Science Monitor (See Note Page 20)
            SAIGON

...One technique is to move into a Viet Cong area, remove all the people to resettlement villages, and burn and destroy what remains.

But at least one-third of Vietnam's 15 million population would have to be resettled for this policy to succeed. And the Saigon government has trouble coping with the million refugees that have come in during the past two years.

Nevertheless, this "scorched earth" technique is the main one being used in the Vietnam war now. American military operations are longer in duration because the supply program has been fairly well solved.

CHAPTER VI
PILLAGE

The following Articles from International Conventions relevant to this chapter are quoted in full:

Hague Convention No. IV, Annex
Regulations Respecting the Laws and Customs of War on Land
18 October 1907
(Short reference: Hague—Laws)

Article 28.
The pillage of a town, even when taken by assault, is prohibited.

Article 47.
Pillage is formally forbidden.

Geneva Convention
Relative to the Protection of Civilian Persons
in Time of War
12 August 1949
(Short reference: Geneva—Civilians)
Article 33.

No protected persons may be punished for an offence he or she has not personally committed. Collective penalties and likewise all measures of intimidation or of terrorism are prohibited.

Pillage is prohibited.

Reprisals against protected persons and their property are prohibited.

27 Jan 66   The Evening Star (Washington), Richard Critchfield
(from Congressional Record, Senate, Feb 17, 1966, 3225)
TAN AN, SOUTH VIETNAM

...Thus, beginning with Diem's fall, government was made incidental to waging the war.

On the Provincial level, meanwhile, the army, jealous of its powers, exempted Vietnamese soldiers from the civilian penal code, even in crimes involving civilians.

Since the army lacked the judicial apparatus and military police to control its troops, the net effect was to turn loose in the countryside 550,000 young soldiers who had little reason to fear being arrested or prosecuted for crimes such as rape or petty theft.

The Vietcong leaders, meanwhile, were concentrating on getting their men to "eat, live and work" with the peasants. The Vietcong helped the peasants till their ricefields and sweep their houses, while through terrorism, they were eroding law and order in government-controlled areas.

The Making of a Quagmire, David Halberstam, 1964, pp 93-94

...After crossing the main canal and joining up with another battalion which had been covering the far side, we sat down and took a break. Trooper after trooper came by with a live chicken strapped to his pack. The American officer attached to this unit followed, and we looked accusingly at him. He caught our glances and said defensively, "What the hell can you do? They go all day and they don't get anything in the way of chow, and they put up with all this" — he gestured around him — "I can't tell them no. They've got little enough pleasure as it is." He was right, of course, but our officers were wondering what the reaction was in the village from which the chickens had been stolen, as well as the effect on the morale of the troops in our battalion who had been denied chickens.

The New Face of War, Malcolm W. Browne, 1965, pp. 150, 151, 153

...An American propaganda expert summed up the essential difference between red and white propaganda in Viet Nam this way:

..."For the last group, centered mostly in the larger towns, our main approach is bringing people up to date on what has happened since the end of the Ngo Dinh Diem regime. For one thing people are no longer forced to give their labor and time, building the hated strategic hamlets. We point out all the benefits being offered by the new revolutionary regime, and describe its aspirations for peace, prosperity and democracy.

...In other cases, civic action teams have been sent to innumerable hamlets on the heels of regular military units to find the hamlets robbed blind. Vietnamese soldiers are not issued food on operations but are expected to pay for the food they confiscate. They rarely do pay, especially when they are in areas considered Viet Cong territory, but help themselves to all the chickens, ducks, eggs and rice they can carry away. This makes things tough for the propagandists.

7 May 65   Time, "South Viet Nam"

...Since 1962, the coastal waters of South Viet Nam have been patrolled by "the Black Pajama Navy" — a force of 500 junks and 4,000 conscripts who resemble freebooters more than freedom fighters. Clad in black cotton bell-bottoms, draped with carbines and bandoleers, each of them wearing a tattoo that reads SAT CONG ("Kill Communists")on their chests, the "junkmen" look like tough customers. They have girls in every port, they dine on grilled octopus stewed in rotten fish sauce, they swipe fish from passing customers, and they claim to have searched 200,000 boats last year. But of the 830,000 persons aboard, only 1,850 were arrested, a mere 21 confirmed as Viet Cong infiltrators.

Such statistics have long led U. S. authorities in Saigon to pooh-pooh the idea of offshore routes as a major supply source for the Viet Cong. But when a 300-ton, steel hulled freighter out of North Viet Nam's port of Haiphong was sunk by air bombardment last February in Vungro Bay (Time, March 5), U. S. Navy advisers began reassessing things. The Vungro ship carried 100 tons of Viet Cong cargo, ranging from medical supplies to heavy artillery, and nobody knew how many other ships had made it in to the coast. With continued air interdiction of North Viet Nam's overland supply routes to the south, the Communists just might be shifting a considerable portion to sea — where there is vast opportunity for concealment.

5 Aug 65   The Evening Star (Washington) (See Note Page 20)
            DA NANG, VIET NAM, Aug 4

...In another incident, an officer asked permission to burn several huts as a punitive measure in a village the Viet Cong had used for concealment. He suggested, however, this might cause trouble with the rural pacification officer whose job it is to attempt to win over the villagers to the government side.

"Sure, I'm for pacification — five days out of the week," a senior officer said, and gave him permission to burn.

As it turned out, the marines didn't burn those particular huts, since they did not go back into the village. But many others have been burned. Some are set off with white phosphorous rockets, others with cigarette lighters, matches, grenades and flame throwers.

...Elsewhere, Leathernecks have killed water buffalo, chopped down banana trees and taken chickens and ducks for food.

All this strikes at villagers whose struggle to exist already is precarious.

Some marines explain that the water buffalo sometimes charge, wounding Leathernecks.

...Army officers concede that problems between the marines and civil population are probably due to the fact the marines were the first combat men assigned to Viet Nam and the first to mix with villagers.

The marines have carried out attempts in the pacification field. Villages occupied by the marines enjoy American medical treatment. Marines hand out rations and candy.

The breakdown in applying the theory of "winning the hearts and minds of the people" usually comes when marines charge a village that their commanders have labeled as Viet Cong.

The troops feel that all those they run across are enemies dedicated to their destruction. If they receive sniper fire as they charge across rice paddies toward the village, they consider the whole village an enemy strongpoint. Many react accordingly, especially when comrades are wounded or killed in the assault.

18 Sept 65   New York Times, Neil Sheehan
              BANMETHUOT, SOUTH VIETNAM

Undisciplined South Vietnamese troops have been terrorizing the civilian population here in Central Highlands and are creating considerable animosity toward the Government.

Troops have been looting the villages of mountain tribesmen, stealing from bars, stores and restaurants in towns, brawling in the streets, and breaking into homes and robbing inhabitants at gun point.

In a number of cases civilians who resisted have been beaten up and in at least one instance in late July, in Cheoreo north of here, a jewelry shopkeeper and two members of his family were murdered when a soldier tossed a grenade into the shop.

...Vietnamese military commanders, however, apparently either do not care or are unable to discipline their men. Incidents which began about three months ago have continued and civilians are virtually at the mercy of soldiers.

The worst rash of trouble in the Banmethuot area occurred during a 12 day period from late August into early September while about 7,000 Vietnamese Marine and Ranger paratroopers and regular infantrymen were clearing Highway 21 between here and Ninhdoa on the coast so that supply and food convoys could be brought into Banmethuot.

In at least four villages along the highway outside of town inhabited by
Rhade tribesmen, troops looted water buffaloes, chickens, household utensils, and any other articles which struck their fancy. Many other villages
further out along the highway are also believed to have been looted.

As far as is (sic) known, none of the Vietnamese troops involved in any
of the incidents have been apprehended or punished.

18 Oct 65   New York Times, Neil Sheehan
                   BANMETHUOT, SOUTH VIETNAM

...Instead of fleecing tourists from Saigon, as in the old days, the
Vietnamese townspeople are instead being fleeced by their own marines and
paratroopers, who sally in from the fields for periodic rampages.

The troops have taken to supplementing their salaries by stealing from
stores, helping themselves to beer and food in restaurants and bars and
then refusing to pay or simply breaking into houses and robbing the occupants at gunpoint.

21 Mar 66   (See Note Page 20)
                   AN KHE, Mar 21

The order to American troops operating in Viet Cong-controlled territory is to deny the enemy local livestock, fruit and vegetables. Veteran
troopers deny it to the enemy by eating it.

There are 12 basic C rations and as American soldiers have 12 months
to serve here it takes them only a matter of days to grow bored with the
regulation fare.

Some of them try for a variation by mixing such things as ham and lima
beans with beef and potatoes. The more venturesome spice their diet with
local chickens and pigs, coconuts and bananas and onions and peanuts.

Thus the American soldier has proven his ingenuity as he has in all
his wars.

Wary at first of eating available local food, the GI has now become an
expert at discerning the edibility of Vietnamese fruit and vegetables. And
homeless pigs and chickens have been known to launch suicide charges upon
American positions — and wound up in the cook pot.

4 Sept 66   New York Times Magazine
                   Frances Fitzgerald, "Life and Death of a Vietnamese Village"

...Nguyen Thanh Hung, a village "notable" and the only French-
speaker in the village, wears the parody of a crafty smile as he says, "I
cannot speak about politics. Here it is very far from the Government and
silence is golden, golden. I could not live here safely if I spoke." He looks
around right and left, out of the corners of his eyes, searching for suddenly
bilingual informers. "I cannot speak about the soldiers even — even when
they steal chickens and other things from the people." His whisper changes
to a louder-than-normal voice. "All I want is enough to eat and peace from
the artillery to sleep in."

"I do not like any soldiers — except when they bring medicine," says
one old woman, her head swathed in a bandage. "But it really makes no
difference. They have no time for us. They are too busy with their fighting."

10 Nov 66   New York Times, Jonathan Randal
                   DAUTIENG, SOUTH VIETNAM, Nov 8

...Another battalion of the division came under heavy enemy attack at
dawn and the Rangers were ordered to its assistance.

As they left they tried to persuade a 500-pound black-and-white pig
they had found near the hospital to follow them on a leash. But the pig
proved recalcitrant and was shot so that it would not provide food for the
Vietcong, who almost certainly returned soon after the Rangers left.

28 Nov 66   New York Times, R. W. Apple, Jr.
               VANLAO, SOUTH VIETNAM, Nov 27

...The unit involved was the Second Squadron of the Ninth South Vietnamese Armored Cavalry Regiment. Its mission was to search out and
destroy Vietcong guerrillas lurking in the clumps of trees that divide the
flooded rice paddies near this hamlet in the Mekong River delta 110 miles
southeast of Saigon.
    ...In the space of 90 minutes the squadron's 120 soldiers took hatfuls
of eggs, a dozen chickens, several ducks, at least a hundred pounds of rice,
enough fish to fill five sacks, three wicker chairs, a substantial quantity of
firewood and a stalk of bananas.
    ...In any event, their behavior seemed far removed from the standard
set by the Saigon high command and its American advisers, who are attempting to convert much of the South Vietnamese Army into a pacification
force — a force capable, in the jargon of Vietnam, of "winning the minds
and hearts of the people". Certainly the affection of the people of Vanlao
for the central Government was not enhanced.
    The behavior of the troops today was not exceptional. Vietnamese
soldiers fighting on the side of the French against the Vietminh in 1952
did the same thing, according to correspondents who accompanied them,
and the pattern has not changed.
    ...Then came the search for provisions, the high point of the day.
Almost everyone piled off the personnel carriers and joined in the pilferage.
When they returned with a duck or chicken, the soldiers looked at the Americans, giggled with embarrassment and said, "Vietcong chicken".

19 May 67   New York Times, R. W. Apple, Jr.
               MOCHOA, SOUTH VIETNAM, May 18

In this secluded corner of South Vietnam, many people consider the
Vietcong a secondary enemy.
    According to officials here, the peasants fear most the uniformed
soldiers of the Civilian Irregular Defense groups — trained and paid by the
United States — who regularly rape, beat, and rob the villagers they are
supposed to protect.
    Incidents involving irregulars occur every week.
    Members of the Special Forces — United States Army guerrilla-
warfare experts who wear the green beret — serve as advisers to the irregulars here in Kientuong Province, as in other parts of South Vietnam.
    ...The irregulars sometimes fight well, the officials said, but when
they pass through hamlets scattered along the fringes of the marshy wasteland known as the Plain of Reeds, they become vandals.
    ...On one recent occasion, a national policeman in Mochoa arrested
an irregular trooper in the marketplace. Within a few hours, friends of
the irregular had returned to batter the policeman. Another policeman was
killed by a rifleman in broad daylight on the main street two weeks earlier.
    As a result of such incidents, the police tend to ignore the crimes of
the irregulars. When a 40-year-old woman in a rural hamlet was raped,
then murdered along with her daughter, the culprits retreated to the haven
of a Special Forces camp, and the police soon gave up their pursuit.
    In February, a band of irregulars set up positions along a waterway
known as Canal 12, stopping every sampan that came along. They stole
some of the goods on the boats and levied taxes on the boatmen.

17 Sep 65   (See Note Page 20)
               BEN CAT, SOUTH VIET NAM, Sept 17

The windows are broken and the walls are pockmarked with bullets,
but the Roman Catholic church still stands in what once was the strategic
hamlet of Long Cau.

No one lives in the hamlet about 2-1/2 miles north of Ben Cat. The huts have been overgrown by the jungle. There are still people living in the brush along the trails around the village. They were driven there after the Viet Cong seized control of the area two years ago.

...One U. S. enlisted man was injured seriously when gored by a charging water buffalo. Several buffalo were shot.

22 Jun 66   New York Times
SAIGON, SOUTH VIETNAM, June 21

The United States Air Force turned its attention yesterday to a column of 10 water buffalos sighted along a road just north of the Mugia Pass on the Laotian-North Vietnamese border.

The spokesman said the buffalos were heavily laden with what was suspected to be enemy ammunition. The animals died under fire from F-105 Thunderchief jets. The spokesman said "there were no secondary explosions."

United States Marine pilots also strafed a column of 11 pack elephants in the mountains 35 miles southwest of Danang in South Vietnam yesterday. Five of the animals were killed, and five others seen to fall. Again there were no secondary explosions.

14 Mar 66   Christian Science Monitor, David K. Willis
WASHINGTON

...From universities and private citizens has come an outcry of moral indignation. In reply, Pentagon officials defensively but doggedly say:

In war, food is just as much a weapon as rifles. Standard procedure for American and South Vietnamese troops is to hold back as much food as possible from the Viet Cong.

If American troops find caches of rice hidden in sacks by Viet Cong outposts, they destroy them.

If troops invade a Viet Cong area and find the water buffalo that all Vietnamese depend upon, they round up as many as they can — the rest they kill.

Similarly, if it is felt that the Viet Cong need to be driven from an outpost, one way of making them move is spraying their crops with the crabgrass killer.

That, according to officials, is that. Unfortunate, unhappy, and to be avoided if possible, "But war is war," they say.

CHAPTER VII
USE OF ARTILLERY

The following Articles from International Conventions relevant to this chapter are quoted in full:

Hague Convention No. IV, Annex
Regulations Respecting the Laws and Customs of War on Land
18 October 1907
(Short reference: Hague—Laws)

Article 25.
The attack or bombardment, by whatever means, of towns, villages, dwellings, or buildings which are undefended is prohibited.

Article 26.
The officer in command of an attacking force must, before commencing a bombardment, except in cases of assault, do all in his power to warn the authorities.

See also (pages 29-42) the following additional Articles relevant to this chapter: Hague—Laws: 22, 23(g), 46, 50; Geneva—Civilians: 53, 146, 147, 148.

5 Jun 65   New York Herald Tribune
            SAIGON

United States Marine artillerymen killed 80 Communist Viet Cong guerrillas and wounded 60 others in a 75-minute bombardment Saturday near the Chu Lai Air Base, an American military spokesman said yesterday.

The barrage was the most successful operation, in terms of enemy casualties, the Marines have conducted since they landed in South Vietnam three months ago.

The action outside Chu Lai, 53 miles south of the main Marine base at Da Nang, began after a government district chief reported a battalion of Viet Cong near the village of Binh Son, nine miles southwest of the airstrip.

The Marines opened up with eight-inch self-propelled howitzers, saturating the area at long range. The first round was 50 yards short, the U.S. spokesman said, but the others fell in the midst of the Viet Cong.

South Vietnamese troops moved in after the bombardment, taking prisoner the 60 wounded Viet Cong and counting the bodies of the 80 dead.

4 Aug 65   New York Times, Charles Mohr
                BAOTRAI, SOUTH VIETNAM, Aug. 3

In recent days in Haunghia Province there have been popular demonstrations against both Vietcong terror and artillery fire by forces of the South Vietnamese government.
...The Vietnamese peasant can no longer make a safe choice in Haunghia easily.
If he chooses to be openly pro-Vietcong and moves to areas of absolute Vietcong control west of the Vaico River, he faces the danger of bombing during the rare government operations there. If he stays in the central part of the province, he is open to both Vietcong terror and occasional artillery bursts by government forces.
...The residents of Duclap staged a genuine demonstration of protest against the Vietcong road-mining squad — and genuine pro-Government demonstrations in Vietnam are rare.
However, an even larger demonstration, involving about 400 women, was also staged recently against the use of undirected artillery fire in central Haunghia.

28 Nov 65   New York Times, Charles Mohr
                SAIGON, SOUTH VIETNAM, Nov. 27

...Officials who have studied the problem believe such emphasis should continue because of the danger that increasingly destructive warfare will entirely uproot the already fragile structure of society and of local government.
These officials find that the population resents "undirected, harassing and interdictory" artillery fire even more than air strikes because the shells seem to come from nowhere with no warning. The officials say there is evidence that a good many churches, homes and public buildings have been destroyed in rural areas.

Jun 66   Air Force
                J. S. Butz, Jr., "Taking the Night Away from the Viet Cong"

...In place of offensive infantry actions, we are now conducting several air and artillery operations at night. An important one is harassing and interdiction (H & I) fire by artillery and mortars. This goes on in heavy volume all night, around US perimeters and is one reason why ammunition consumption is so high. Normally the targets are roads and trails which are located and zeroed-in on during the day. The purpose of this blind firing is to harass any VC moving near the US positions. H & I fire is considered to be a key defensive tactic because the VC probe or reconnoiter nearly every position every night.

20 Sept 66   New York Times
                SAIGON, SOUTH VIETNAM, Sept. 19

Six American soldiers were killed and 23 were wounded in three combat accidents early today and yesterday, a United States military spokesman said tonight.
In two of the accidents artillery shells fell short of their marks, killing a total of three soldiers of the 196th Light Infantry Brigade and wounding 19. In the third incident, a stray bomb killed three marines and wounded four.

22 Sep 66   (See Note Page 20)
             CU CHI, VIET NAM, Sept 22

...Col. Daniel B. Williams of Boonville, N.C., veteran artillery commander of the 25th Infantry Division, demands that each gun fire with pinpoint accuracy to avoid civilian and friendly troop casualties.

..."We're fighting three different types of artillery war in Viet Nam," says Williams.

"Here we attack a Viet Cong base area like the Ho Bo woods or the Boloi woods, where we are in contact with regular forces. This requires accurate and timely artillery fire. This leans toward the conventional type of war. We find, fix, and destroy.

"In an area in which you are in a pacification role, breaking up the local-force communist guerrilla structure requires a selective application of artillery. Some of the areas may be partially pacified.

"Thirdly, I use a delicate application of artillery fire for the guerrilla fighting. This calls for me to move my artillery battery around fast, re-organize fast, but give a far less volume of fire."

Nov 66   Argosy
             Milt Machlin, "Big Battle Coming"

(The editors of Argosy have declined permission to give the verbatim text of a selection from the above cited article. The following describes the con-tribution of that selection.)

(There is sustained day and night firing of heavy artillery to protect the American base area the author is visiting. The kill radius of the shells from these weapons is specified, including the 8-inch howitzer and the new 175 mm. M-103 cannon. The M-103 shell is destructive over an area 100 yards in radius, and has a range of 17 miles.

The author is given the opportunity to fire a shell into a suspected enemy area and he is later told that his shell destroyed a suspected enemy building.)

30 Nov 66   (See Note Page 20)
             SAIGON, Nov. 30

...But to U.S. military planners, the lush Delta is the ugliest part of Viet Nam, a place to be avoided unless there is no other choice.

There is no other choice now. The beautiful Delta might well be where the ugliest chapter of the Viet Nam war is written for the United States.

The problem in the Mekong Delta is that there are too many people, an estimated 7 million clustered along the myriad estuaries of the Mekong River that break out like veins across the countryside.

...The fantastic firepower of American artillery pieces and fighter-bombers that has meant the difference between defeat and victory in many battles to the North could wreak havoc among the Delta's crowded civilian population.

...American troops from the 25th Division, who have been based at Ben Luc in the northern edge of the Delta virtually as guinea pigs, already have felt the frustrations of the Delta.

The normal rules of engagement governing Americans in Viet Nam is to bring artillery fire to bear whenever fired upon, thereby cutting down casualties. But a U.S. platoon out of Ben Luc had to rout snipers from a village by themselves because of the possibility of high civilian casualties if the heavy runs were called in. Consequently, several Americans were wounded.

Will large American forces in the same position in the future be able or willing to exercise the same restraint?

5 Feb 67   The Sun (Baltimore) (See Note Page 20)
             SAIGON, Feb. 5

...United States B-52 bombers staged two raids before dawn today on
a suspected enemy headquarters 94 miles east northeast of Saigon.

...The United States command, in delayed reports, told of the deaths
of 22 Vietnamese villagers near Da Nang in two incidents attributed to mistaken United States air strikes and artillery shellings.

The bodies of fourteen civilians were brought in Tuesday to United States
marines. Eight villagers were killed and eighteen wounded Wednesday in a
guerrilla-infested area 12 miles southwest of Da Nang that has been hit
heavily by United States marine artillery.

3 Mar 67   UPI, Bryce Miller
             SAIGON

...The threat of an across-the-border offensive by North Vietnam —
which already has two divisions just South of the DMZ — came as U.S.
military authorities disclosed six Vietnamese had been killed and 26
wounded in the Mekong Delta in the accidental shelling of two more
friendly villages by U.S. artillery.

5 Mar 67   New York Times
             SAIGON, SOUTH VIETNAM, Mar. 4

...The military command also reported four accidents involving United
States forces in which 18 persons were killed and 45 were wounded. All but
8 wounded among the casualties were South Vietnamese civilians.

...The following accidents were reported today:

An artillery attack on five sampans 50 miles northeast of Saigon that
was requested by an aerial observer and approved by South Vietnamese
military officers, killed one person and injured two. The casualties were
later determined to be "friendly" civilians.

The explosion of an artillery shell 30 yards from where it left the gun
of the Fourth Infantry Division in the Central Highlands wounded eight
American soldiers.

Eleven shells from a 105-mm. gun in Trungluong, a village in the
Mekong delta, killed five South Vietnamese, wounded 24 others and destroyed
24 houses. The accident occurred Wednesday. The spokesman could not
explain why it had not been reported earlier.

An American spokesman suggested that an increase in artillery
accidents was not unlikely in face of the intensified war effort announced
by General William C. Westmoreland, the United States commander in
Vietnam. The possibility for error in artillery fire, he said, increases in
proportion to the rate at which the guns are fired.

4 Apr 67   Christian Science Monitor (See Note Page 20)
             SAIGON

...The 1965 actions, and battles early in 1966, were based on the
avowed necessity to "kill Cong." The United States mission became one of
knocking out main-force enemy battalions and regiments, leaving the Vietnamese to clean up local guerrillas. But lessons from the bitter Ia Drang
battle of November, 1965, hit home. The high number of American
casualties suffered there showed that maximum firepower would be required
in future actions.

By late 1966 more than 1,000,000 artillery shells were fired monthly.

United States war planes and Navy ships added their firepower.

...United States infantry commanders as a matter of course called in
air strikes and artillery whenever the enemy was encountered, even
snipers.

The firepower of Allied forces, more than anything else, has changed the war's nature, according to military authorities.

...As more American troops arrive, a need for even more is seen.

10 Jan 67   The Sun (Baltimore), Robert A. Erlandson
                  SAIGON, Jan. 9

One of the most brutal incidents of the war unfolded here today with the report that besieged South Vietnamese Rangers killed ten children and wounded sixteen more last night when Viet Cong used them as a human shield to attack the Ranger post.

Angry American sources immediately condemned the Reds, saying: "The civilian casualties are most regrettable. They are directly attributable to the callous use by the Viet Cong of civilians in military operations."

...United States Navy river patrol boats raced to the scene and evacuated the survivors, including nine wounded adults, to a hospital at My Tho. Officials were unable to procure additional details of the injuries or learn from which village the hostages were abducted.

The reports were that the Viet Cong advanced on the Ranger post about 10:45 last night blasting it with mortars and automatic weapons fire.

At 11 P.M., the report said, the fire curtain lifted and the Reds closed in, driving the civilians before them.

The Rangers warned them to stop, or they would shoot, the officials said. The Communists kept coming and opened up again with mortars and small arms, whereupon the Rangers returned fire, mowing down the frightened youngsters.

10 Jan 67   New York Times, Jonathan Randal
                  SAIGON, SOUTH VIETNAM, Jan. 9

...In a relatively rare use of human-shield tactics, two Vietcong companies spearheaded an attack on a South Vietnamese Ranger position late last night by shoving a group of Vietnamese civilians into a hail of fire by Government troops.

The Ranger company warned the Vietcong against advancing behind the civilian hostages, but the guerrillas renewed their attack. In the ensuing fight, 10 Vietnamese children were killed and 16 children and 9 adults were wounded.

12 Jan 67   New York Times, Tom Buckley
                  MYTHO, SOUTH VIETNAM, Jan. 10

A spokesman for the American mission in Saigon reported Monday that 10 children had been killed and 25 adults and children wounded when forced by the Vietcong to serve as human shields during an attack Sunday night on a South Vietnamese Ranger outpost.

"The civilian casualties are deplorable," the spokesman said. "They are directly attributable to the callous use by the Vietcong of civilians in military operation."

Tuesday in the provincial hospital here, some survivors of the attack said the casualties had been caused not by the Vietcong but by a midnight bombardment of their village by South Vietnamese artillery.

Col. John E. Lance, the senior American adviser to the South Vietnamese infantry division that was involved, acknowledged that the division's first report had been incorrect and that the villagers had been killed and wounded under bombardment. But he added: "There was an exchange of fire — artillery and Vietcong mortars. It was never established which metal hit the village."

A Vietnamese soldier who had come from his post in a nearby village to visit an uncle wounded in the attack said, however, that he was certain that it had been the artillery shells that had done the damage.

"I saw the gun flashes," he said. "What I think happened is that the Rangers saw lights in the village. They thought they were going to be attacked again and called in artillery."

14 Jan 67   Denver Post (See Note Page 20)

Vietnamese civilian casualties inflicted early this week during fighting in the Mekong Delta resulted from Government artillery fire, it was learned today.

An earlier official account had said the civilians were killed when the Viet Cong used them as human shields and Government troops had fired into them while protecting themselves from a Viet Cong attack.

Ten children were killed and 25 other persons were wounded in the incident. Conflicts and contradictions in the original account now have aroused controversy.

The first disclosure was made Monday by a U.S. spokesman who said the Viet Cong had used the civilians as a human shield while attempting to move toward a Vietnamese government ranger position. The spokesman said the Viet Cong had massed the civilians in front of them and attacked. The rangers saw the civilians, he said, and called to the Viet Cong to pull back or they would be fired on.

"But the Viet Cong kept moving forward, firing at the ranger positions from behind the civilians. The rangers had no choice but to return the fire, killing 10 children and wounding 25 other persons," the spokesman said. "These civilian casualties are very regrettable and are directly attributable to the callous use of civilians by the Viet Cong in military operations."

A U.S. government official said today the original account came first from the Vietnamese military reports and was confirmed by the U.S. military. Later when questions were raised, he said, the U.S. military investigated again and found that the casualties had been caused by Vietnamese Government artillery.

He still maintained, however, that the latest U.S. reports showed that the Viet Cong had used the civilians as a shield.

Sources who investigated the incident in Kien Hoa province about 40 miles south of Saigon said they found nothing to show that the Viet Cong had actually herded civilians in front of them as a shield. They said all the casualties occurred in a hamlet of the village of Chau Hung when buildings, including a Buddhist temple, were hit by artillery.

...The civilians who were wounded during the night were taken to a hospital at the delta town of My Tho. There, they said that artillery shells had fallen in the village, damaging buildings and killing and wounding people in them.

CHAPTER VIII
COASTAL BOMBARDMENT

The following Articles from International Conventions relevant to this chapter are quoted in full:

Hague Convention No. IX
Concerning Bombardment by Naval Forces In Time of War
18 October 1907.
(Short reference: Hague—Naval)

... Chapter I—The Bombardment of Undefended Ports, Towns, Villages, Dwellings or Buildings

Article 1

The bombardment by naval forces of undefended ports, towns, villages, dwellings or buildings is forbidden.

A place cannot be bombarded solely because automatic submarine contact mines are anchored off the harbor.

Article 2

Military works, military or naval establishments, depots of arms or war material, workshops or plans which could be utilized for the hostile fleet or army, and the ships of war in the harbor, are not, however, included in this prohibition. The commander of a naval force may destroy them with artillery, after a summons followed by a reasonable time of waiting, if all other means are impossible, and when the local authorities have not themselves destroyed them within the time fixed.

He incurs no responsibility for any unavoidable damage which may be caused by a bombardment under such circumstances.

If for military reasons immediate action is necessary, and no delay can be allowed the enemy, it is understood that the prohibition to bombard the undefended town holds good, as in the case given in paragraph 1, and that the commander shall take all due measures in order that the town may suffer as little harm as possible.

Article 3

After due notice has been given, the bombardment of undefended ports, towns, villages, dwellings, or buildings may be commenced, if the local authorities, after a formal summons has been made to them, decline to comply with requisitions for provisions or supplies necessary for the immediate use of the naval force before the place in question...

Hague Convention No. IV, Annex
Regulations Respecting the Laws and Customs of War on Land
18 October 1907
(Short reference: Hague—Laws)

Article 22.

The right of belligerents to adopt means of injuring the enemy is not unlimited.

See also (pages 29-42) the following additional Articles relevant to this chapter: Geneva—Civilians: 146, 147, 148.

---

4 Oct 65   (See Note Page 20)
            SAIGON, Oct 4

...At sea, the carrier Midway launched more than 70 sorties against suspected Viet Cong concentrations along the coast. Its pilots claimed to have destroyed 90 buildings, damaged 40 more, sunk three sampans and set off one large secondary explosion, probably of munitions or fuel.

No planes were lost, a spokesman said.

The cruiser Galveston fired 300 rounds of five-inch shells at a Viet Cong installation Sunday and destroyed 40 buildings, a spokesman said.

He reported destroyers blasted gun emplacements, a Viet Cong shelter, trenches and structures and an assembly area.

The U.S. Air Force said its planes flew 150 sorties during the 24-hour period ending today, dropped 228 tons of bombs, destroyed 216 buildings and damaged 126 others.

The Vietnamese Air Force flew 93 combat sorties.

15 Oct 65   (See Note Page 20)
            SAIGON, VIET NAM, Oct. 15

...In air activity, nine U.S. carrier-based planes struck bridges in North Viet Nam 125 miles south of Hanoi. A U.S. destroyer bombarded suspected Viet Cong coastal installations in northern coastal provinces of South Viet Nam and destroyed or damaged 27 buildings, a U.S. spokesman said.

30 Nov 65   New York Times, Neil Sheehan
            DUCHAI, SOUTH VIETNAM, Nov 29

Duchai is on the central Vietnamese coast, north of Saigon. Last May its complex of five prosperous fishing hamlets, set among fruit groves and palm trees behind a spacious beach, was occupied by Viet Cong guerrillas.

In mid-August, United States and Vietnamese military officials decided the Communists were using Duchai as a base for the operations in the area and that it should be destroyed.

For the next two months, until the Viet Cong finally withdrew in mid-October and Duchai was reoccupied by Government troops, it was periodically and ferociously shelled by Seventh Fleet destroyers and bombed by Vietnamese and American planes.

Vietnamese Government officials are certain that at least 184 civilians died during Duchai's two months of agony, but they concede that because of a lack of records and because confusion is still great, no one really knows how many civilians were killed. Some reasonable estimates run as high as 600.

Many more civilians would have been killed if a majority of the inhabitants had not abandoned their homes in terror and fled to nearby Government-controlled areas.

When an American visits Duchai these days, villagers seem to find a peculiar relief in telling him horror stories of how many of the 15,000 former inhabitants were killed by bombs and shells.

"There," said a fisherman pointing to a bomb crater beside a ruined house, "a woman and her six children were killed in a bomb shelter when it got a direct hit."

Duchai's solid brick and stucco houses, the product of generations of hard-earned savings by its fishermen, were reduced to rubble or blasted into skeletons.

Five-inch naval shells tore gaping holes in walls, and bombs of 750 to 1,000 pounds plunged through roofs, shattering interiors and scattering red rooftiles over the landscape.

Palm trees in a grove at the end of one hamlet were neatly decapitated by naval guns. Here and there napalm blackened the ruins.

At least 10 other hamlets in this heavily populated province of about 700,000 persons approximately 325 miles north of Saigon have been destroyed as thoroughly as the five in Duchai.

At least 25 other hamlets have been heavily damaged and countless others of an estimated 450 hamlets in Quangngai Province have been pockmarked by the war.

A visitor driving through the countryside southeast of Quangngai town, the provincial capital, sees evidence of fighting everywhere — walls pocked by machine-gun bullets or ripped open by artillery shells and roofs partially blasted by bombs.

Since last spring, Quangngai Province has been the scene of some of the heaviest (sic) and most sustained fighting between Government troops and Viet Cong guerrillas.

Each month 600 to 1,000 civilians wounded by bombs, shells, bullets, and napalm are brought to the provincial hospital in Quangngai town, the only civilian hospital in the province.

Officials say that about 30 per cent of these cases require major surgery. A recent visitor to the hospital found several children lying on cots, their bodies horribly burned by napalm.

Officials believe a majority of the civilian war wounded never get to the hospital because of a lack of transportation or because they live in areas still controlled by the Viet Cong.

Quangngai's energetic province chief, Dr. Bui Hoanh, has since late August been trying to regain full control from the Viet Cong of a belt of villages on both sides of strategic Highway 1, where about 350,000 persons or half the province's population live. The other 350,000 are still incontestably in Communist hands.

About 1,300 pacification workers have been recruited and given rudimentary training in public health, education, propaganda, police work, administration and reconstruction.

As the regular army clears the Viet Cong from a village, teams of pacification workers supported by militiamen move in and attempt to organize the population, rebuild the village and set up a local government.

In August, the province had almost 100,000 refugees on its hands. But since early September 49,000 of them have been resettled in their villages as military operations have pushed the guerrillas back. Of the original 15,000 inhabitants of Duchai, 12,000 returned in late October.

Dr. Hoanh is being assisted by James A. May, a 41-year-old American representative of the Agency for International Development in the province, and two other Americans and a Filipino on his staff. They provide advice on a host of problems as well as building materials, cooking oil, wheat, blankets, clothing and tools for refugees and villagers who have returned to their wrecked homes.

A six-man United States Army civic action team headed by Capt. Edward W. Arrington, 34, of McDail, West Virginia, which arrived in late September, has also been helping on a temporary basis.

The team's doctor, a preventive medicine sergeant and an interpreter have been moving around the villages, treating the sick and attempting to teach the villagers rudimentary sanitation. An engineer sergeant has been busy drawing plans for the Vietnamese to rebuild schoolhouses, dispensaries and roads and bridges.

In Duchai rubble is being cleared away and temporary tin-roofed shelters are being constructed for the homeless. Captain Arrington's engineer sergeant has taught the villagers how to manufacture crude concrete bricks to rebuild their homes.

Yet for all the efforts, the magnitude of the task far outstrips the time or energies of these men. It will take months to rebuild Duchai while every week other villages are being destroyed.

27 May 65   (See Note Page 20)
                WASHINGTON, May 27

The first naval gunfire attacks on Viet Cong targets ashore raised the possibility today that the U.S. Navy might augment the air strikes against North Viet Nam by bombarding ports and shipping.

However, the 7th Fleet destroyer attacks announced both here and in Saigon were part of the anti-infiltration patrol effort in South Viet Nam over the past week.

Defense Department authorities avoided directly answering whether any basic policy would prevent destroyers and cruisers of the fleet from laying down shellfire on North Viet Nam ports or coastal areas. It is from these ports that some supplies and re-enforcements for the Viet Cong move out.

Officials here would say only that such action could be carried out when and if needed and ordered.

The Saigon and Washington announcements today disclosed that four destroyers conducted six bombardments of three Viet Cong areas along the South Vietnamese coast, firing a total of 370 rounds, during a six-day period ending yesterday.

This was the first time since the end of the Korean war that U.S. Navy guns had been used against an enemy shore target.

28 May 65   New York Times, Jacques Nevard
               SAIGON, SOUTH VIETNAM, May 27

Warships of the United States Navy have been turning their guns against Vietcong troop concentrations and other coastal targets in South Vietnam an official American spokesman announced today.

In six operations from May 20 to yesterday, four destroyers of the United States Seventh Fleet pounded targets in the central area of South Vietnam with more than 370 rounds from their five-inch guns.

...There were few details today of the naval operations. In the only action specifically mentioned, the destroyer Somers was credited with having thwarted a Vietcong attack against Hailong district Headquarters in Binnthuan Province on May 21 by killing 12 of the Communist troops and wounding 20.

...The destroyers have also fired at targets in Binhdinh and Phuyen Provinces, spokesmen said.

24 Jul 65   New York Times
             SAIGON, SOUTH VIETNAM, July 23

Destroyers from the Seventh Fleet began this week to assume a more direct role in the Vietnam war with daily offshore shellings of suspected Vietcong coastal bases.

In two actions reported today, the Seventh Fleet destroyers Stoddard and Ingersoll fired a total of 420 rounds at the central Vietnam coast.

The Stoddard fired Tuesday and Wednesday nights against Vietcong concentrations near Danang. American Marine ground spotters called the firing "very effective harassment and interdiction fire on each target."

The Ingersoll fired 3- and 5- inch ammunition yesterday on what was described as a "Vietcong province headquarters" 125 miles south of Danang.

Spotters said 25 houses and five large stucco buildings had been destroyed. They estimated that seven Vietcong soldiers were killed in the attack and 15 wounded.

In neither case was return fire reported.

6 Aug 65   (See Note Page 20)
             SAIGON, VIET NAM, Aug 6

...Three months ago U.S. destroyers and cruisers opened fire for the first time on suspected Viet Cong targets in support of the ground war. Since then Navy guns have boomed on nearly 130 missions.

The Navy has gradually increased its number of vessels on patrol along the coast, searching for Communist infiltration of men, arms and equipment by sea.

..."The Navy's part in the war will increase in proportion to that of the other services," says Rear Admiral Norvell G. Ward of Annapolis, Md.

...Ward says the Navy's shore bombardment missions have proven both cheaper and more accurate than strikes against enemy positions from the air. Most of the missions so far have been confined to the northern part of the country, some of them in support of U.S. Marine action.

9 Aug 65   (See Note Page 20)

..."We made great use of naval gunfire," the briefing officer said. Walt reported the Galveston's guns wiped out two Viet Cong companies trying to flee a village. Two companies might mean 200 men. The General said he counted 17 Viet Cong bodies, all in uniform, in one rice paddy.

A Marine Lieutenant who investigated a hole in the ground found a head-high tunnel 100 yards long that was packed with 152 civilians, one dead Viet Cong and a wounded guerrilla.

The tunnel also yielded a store of ammunition and other supplies that were equipped with demolition charges.

10 Aug 65   Los Angeles Times (See Note Page 20)
             SAIGON

...Three destroyers of the U.S. 7th Fleet used their guns over the weekend to pound suspected areas along the South China seacoast from near Da Nang to a point 60 miles southeast of Saigon.

29 Aug 65   New York Times, James Reston
             SAIGON

...In the Mekong Delta in the south, the Navy also reported that the destroyer U.S.S. De-Haven fired over 355 rounds of 5-inch ammunition at Vietcong assembly areas on shore. "Spotters estimated very good effect on the targets," the communique said. "Six buildings were destroyed with very good shrapnel effect over a very large area."

The only difficulty with this is that the Viet cong do not usually have isolated training and supply centers apart from the South Vietnamese, but operate among the people where the shrapnel has "very good effect" on Communists and non-Communists alike.

4 Sep 65   St. Louis Post-Dispatch (See Note Page 20)
                  SAIGON, SOUTH VIET NAM, Sept 4

The Seventh Fleet Destroyer Keyes opened up yesterday on a Viet Cong assembly area in Quang Ngai province, about 300 miles north of Saigon. Spotters said the ship's fire destroyed or damaged 66 structures.

15 Oct 65   Times

...For weeks U.S. planes have bombed the Viet Cong concentrations, guns from the Seventh Fleet have pounded the coast east of Route 1, and government troops punched away — with casualties running into the hundreds for the Communists.

5 Nov 65   (See Note Page 20)
                  SAIGON, VIET NAM, Nov. 5

...Gunners of the U.S. 7th Fleet shelled Viet Cong holdings near the coast of the South China Sea. Aerial spotters said there was extensive damage to entrenchments and buildings.

26 Nov 65   (See Note Page 20)
                  SAIGON, VIET NAM, Nov 26

...The U.S. Destroyer Orleik went into action as floating artillery off the coast of the 1st Corps Area, which stretches south about 200 miles from the North Vietnamese frontier. It fired 700 shells at 19 Viet Cong targets, including assembly points and gun emplacements.

8 Jan 66   (See Note Page 20)
                  SAIGON, VIETNAM, Jan 8

...Gunners of four 7th Fleet destroyers were in action on the South China Sea coast. Observers say they had wrecked 30 buildings and sank three boats of the Viet Cong...

22 Feb 66   (See Note Page 20)
                  SAIGON, VIETNAM, Tuesday, Feb 22

...About 25 miles to the north, the U.S. 7th fleet destroyer Orleck, operating in consort with the cavalrymen and the Allied marines, poured 309 rounds from her twin-mounted five-inch guns into potential havens for enemy troops fleeing from the cavalrymen and marines.

Officials in Saigon said the Orleck's guns fired on more than 100 buildings along the coast and destroyed half of them.

The marines continued to press a Communist force of about 900 to 1,000 men in the Phuoc Valley at the northern end of the coastal hunting ground.

1 Apr 66   (See Note Page 20)
                  SAIGON, April 1

...The destroyer Robison (CQ) shelled a Viet Cong camp in the Saigon river delta in support of the U.S. Marines' Operation Jackstay and spotters said 30 structures were destroyed.

A collection of 175 Viet Cong huts eight miles northeast of Quang Ngai City was reported left wrecked or burning from a 32-shell bombardment by the destroyer Richard B. Anderson. Four sampans were sunk.

16 Aug 66   New York Times, R. W. Apple, Jr.
          ABOARD U.S.S. ST. PAUL, OFF SOUTH VIETNAM, Aug 14

Through the windows of the captain's air-conditioned sitting room, you can see the coastal plain and the gentle hills farther inland as they slide by. They look verdant and peaceful in the afternoon sun.

..."We're in our own private cocoon out here," a young marine said today. "You never see any enemy planes. You never see any enemy ships. You never see any enemy anything, and sometimes you wonder whether there really is an enemy."

...The massive guns in the St. Paul's three turrets can fire a 260-pound projectile 15 miles, so she is usually assigned targets well back from the coast.

...Since arriving off Vietnam on June 5, the St. Paul has fired, by day and by night, more than 4,400 rounds in support of United States and South Vietnamese ground troops.

17 Aug 66   New York Times, R. W. Apple, Jr.
          ABOARD THE CRUISER ST. PAUL, OFF SOUTH VIETNAM,
          Aug 15

This 17,350-ton cruiser, the last ship in the Pacific with a full complement of heavy guns, has almost as much firepower as a regiment of Army or Marine artillery.

...Last night, the ship fired 156 8-inch rounds (they cost $251 each) at 13 targets in southern Quangnam Province near Tamky. This was "harassing and interdiction fire" in support of the marines conducting an operation in the vicinity.

Harassing and interdiction fire is used on "possible enemy targets." The targets are places where allied troops think the enemy might be, based on past sightings, topography, intelligence and hunch.

In this case the targets were trail junctions and fords in a rectangle 4 miles long and 2 miles wide.

3 Oct 66   New York Times, Neil Sheehan
          WASHINGTON, Oct 2

...The ship is also normally immune to attack by ground forces and troops do not have to be tied up protecting her. The enemy does not possess a navy capable of seriously endangering either the warships or the resupply ships.

...The high velocity and flat trajectory, on the other hand, give the naval shell greater penetrating power than conventional artillery rounds and this has proven useful against enemy bunkers and other fortifications in South Vietnam.

...In May, 1965, Seventh Fleet ships fired 350 shells in support of American and South Vietnamese forces. Now more than 30,000 rounds a month are being expended.

23 Dec 66   UPI, St. Louis Post Dispatch
          SAIGON, Dec. 22

...Meanwhile, U.S. ships fired more than 650 shells at Communist positions along the northern coast of South Vietnam. The bombardment was carried out by four 7th Fleet destroyers and a heavy guided missile cruiser.

9 Jan 67   New York Times, Tom Buckley
          SAIGON, SOUTH VIETNAM, Jan. 8

American marines continued their sweep of the Thanhphong district in the Mekong Delta today, but again failed to find any of the Vietcong forces or the arsenals and fortifications that had been said to abound there.

...The heavy cruiser Canberra continued to bombard the district with eight-inch shells and Air Force B-57 bombers were reported to have destroyed "28 enemy structures." Details on these buildings were not made available.

Two of the three local Vietnamese reported killed in the operation thus far were officially described today as "two VC (Vietcong) who had been sniping at marine positions." When the bodies were seen yesterday, they appeared to be those of an unarmed young man and woman.

24 Jan 67   UPI, Los Angeles Times
             SAIGON

American artillery shells killed 10 South Vietnamese civilians and wounded 19 others in two accidental barrages last Saturday, the U.S. Command reported today. Both incidents were under investigation.

...While the marine barrage was under way, guns of the U.S. destroyer Norris poured artillery fire into the hamlet of Dong Ruy about 11 miles south of Da Nang, killing four civilians and wounding nine. The barrage was blamed on a "target plotting error."

The Navy guns were to have been aimed on a heavily bunkered Communist position 6,000 yards west of the hamlet.

18 Feb 67   The Washington Post
             SAIGON, Feb 17

...A little farther south along the coast, 2,000 U.S. Marines encountered little opposition in the third day of Operation Deckhouse VI, around the port of Sahuynh, which intelligence reports say has been used by the Viet Cong as a supply funnel.

The U.S. Command reported killing 48 Viet Cong in pre-assult bombardment Wednesday, but also hit civilians in the villages along the shore.

A total of 29 civilians were wounded at Sahuynh, and six others reportedly killed. The wounded were flown aboard the helicopter carrier Iwo Jima for treatment after villagers had brought them to the beach, their wounds wrapped in blood-soaked rags and blankets.

18 Apr 67   Christian Science Monitor, John Dillin
             SAIGON

...The guerrilla has a special importance in First Corps. Over 90 percent of the population lives clustered along the sea on a narrow, fertile, coastal plain. There they fish, grow rice, and carry on trade.

Rolling down to this coastal plain are the purple-tinted mountains of the Annam Cordillera, which at this point stands deep in some of the world's most dense jungles.

Large Viet Cong and North Vietnamese units are unable to operate openly or well on the open plain where the people are.

Thus it is the Viet Cong guerrilla, living among the people themselves, who extends the hand of Communist power.

United States marines, operating in small units of 8 to 14 men, have been devoting over 50 percent of their energy to this antiguerrilla warfare.

15 Jul 67   The New Yorker
             Jonathan Schell, "The Village of Ben Suc"

...The United States Army's Psychological Warfare Office has many hundreds of different leaflets, designed for subtly different situations. On one side of Leaflet No. APO-6227, for instance, a cartoon drawing represents the long trajectory of a large shell from a ship at sea to an inland village, where a human figure has been blown into the air and a grass-roofed house is bursting into pieces under the impact of the explosion. On the other side is a message in Vietnamese, reading, "Artillery from our ships will soon hit your village. You must look for cover immediately. From now on, chase the Vietcong away from your village, so the government won't have to shell your area again."

CHAPTER IX
AERIAL BOMBARDMENT
IN SOUTH VIETNAM

The following Articles from International Conventions relevant to this chapter are quoted in full:

Hague Convention No. IV, Annex
Regulations Respecting the Laws and Customs of War on Land
18 October 1907
(Short reference: Hague—Laws)

Article 23

In addition to the prohibitions provided by special Conventions, it is especially forbidden—

(a) To employ poison or poisoned weapons.

(b) To kill treacherously individuals belonging to the hostile nation or army.

(c) To kill or wound an enemy who, having laid down his arms, or having no longer means of defence, has surrendered at discretion.

(e) To employ arms, projectiles, or material calculated to cause unnecessary suffering.

(g) To destroy or seize the enemy's property, unless such destruction or seizure be imperatively demanded by the necessities of war.

Article 25.

The attack or bombardment, by whatever means, of towns, villages, dwellings, or buildings which are undefended is prohibited.

Article 26.

The officer in command of an attacking force must, before commencing a bombardment, except in cases of assault, do all in his power to warn the authorities.

See also (pages 29-42) the following additional Articles relevant to this chapter: Hague—Laws: 22, 46, 50; Geneva—Civilians: 3, 29, 31, 32, 33, 53, 146, 147, 148.

BOMBING – GENERAL

Introduction

19 Sept 65   New York Times Magazine
              Jack Langguth, "The War in Vietnam"

...I would say the war in South Vietnam changed irrevocably on
Feb. 19, 1965.
...on Feb. 19, America began using its immense air power in a
less-heralded way. U.S. jet pilots started to bomb South Vietnam.
...Secretary of State Dean Rusk often says that American policy in
Vietnam seems to him very simple. But what the United States is now
doing would make more sense, in a way, if one were to imagine South
Vietnam as a hostile country.

Imagine, then, all of its 15 million citizens implacably opposed to the
Americans. The only exception is an armed band of mercenaries, about
550,000 men, who fight on the American side. In this enemy land, the
Americans have made a successful coastal landing and have established
beachheads. They have overturned the elected leader of the country and
taken Saigon as greedily as the Germans took Paris.

The rest of the country, however, remains unsubdued. And so,
American pilots fan out over the country each day on hundreds of missions.
They bomb huts, afterward described as "structures," and they kill Viet-
namese, afterward described as "Communists."

In the meantime, the American Government prepares to send tens of
thousands more soldiers to storm the enemy territory. When the bombs
have blasted the people into submission and the infantrymen control the
country, the United States will be prepared to repair the damage it has
done.

Skin specialists, with devices perfected since Hiroshima, will treat
the napalm victims. Industrialists and bankers, with blueprints tested in
Tokyo and Bonn, will rebuild the economy. The huts at last will be turned
into structures.

The war may have lasted five years. The recovery could take another
15. By 1985, South Vietnam could be a new Asian showplace for the Western
way of life. Who has suffered but the half million or so natives who lost their
lives? Must one not break eggs to make an omelette?

This interpretation of American actions in Vietnam is exaggerated
nonsense, of course. The United States came here to help the Vietnamese.
American technicians have brought improved farming methods, medicine
and schools, rice and blankets. Gallant American soldiers came to help the
Vietnamese Army resist the murderous Vietcong. The people of Vietnam
may not understand the role of the U.S. or bow in gratitude for the gifts and
good works. But they are not hostile.

Then why are we bombing them every day?

I think the reason is simple: simple desperation. To trace the events
of the past 14 months may help to show how that desperation, feeding upon
American reverses, has grown into a full-fledged policy that would be
difficult now to reverse.

...When order of a sort had been restored to Saigon, I made a trip to
the Mekong Delta, where I was greeted by an officer with one of the helicopter
units. He was a jovial man, almost ready to return to the U.S. after a year
in Vietnam.

When he had talked with gathering gloom about problems in his province,
I asked the question that usually ended a discussion.

"What's the answer?" I asked.

"Terror," he said pleasantly. "The Vietcong have terrorized the
peasants to get their cooperation, or at least to stop their opposition. We
must terrorize the villagers even more, so they see that their real self-
interest lies with us. We've got to start bombing and strafing the villages

174

that aren't friendly to the Government. Of course, we won't do it. That's not our way of doing things and the people at home would not stand for it. But terror is what it takes."

"Thank God," I thought, "you are leaving the country."

At that time, about 16,500 American soldiers were in South Vietnam, ranging from 23-year-old West Point graduates to 45-year-old master sergeants.

... The new war is an American Marine setting fire to a hut because it looks like a Vietcong headquarters. It is American paratroopers abusing a village chief because they don't have interpreters to explain his importance. More than anything else, it is the bombing.

... At Songbe, Dongxoai, Bagia this spring, jets helped to turn the tide of major battles. What they are doing in the hundreds of other raids, when no ground troops are directing their fire or profiting from their bombs, is a different matter.

During his last trip to Vietnam, Secretary McNamara told reporters he had been disturbed by stories that American pilots were killing civilians in their raids over the South. He said he had asked many pilots during his five-day tour of Vietnam, and none of them said they were killing civilians. At any rate, killing civilians was not American policy.

Pilots, the ones the Secretary missed, know they are hitting civilian villages. Some of them fret over it and brood. Others don't care. There is an elaborate system to relieve their consciences — checks and instructions, approval by the Vietnamese provincial chief — all aimed at permitting only the bombing of the Vietcong. Yet the pilots know the difference between the system and its result.

In their most widely quoted phrase, Communist military tacticians have described their troops as living among the population "as fish live in the water." In trying to poison those fish, an opposing army must always risk polluting the water.

More selective than bombing is the sending of ground troops through the countryside to rout the Vietcong. But that requires a greater force than the South Vietnamese or than the United States now wishes to send.

... The majority of Vietnamese will probably be neither hostile nor friendly. They will hate the war, and they will pour into refugee centers to avoid it. They will be numb from pain and loss and hopelessness.

If the U.S. is prepared to use its planes to kill two or three for every Vietcong, the Communists may be defeated.

I ask myself these questions as I leave Vietnam: If one nation begins an ugly and inhuman war, does national honor require resisting even more brutally? But, then, why shouldn't America pursue a war on its terms, rather than follow rules that can only lead to failure?

15 Jun 65   The Evening Star (Washington) (See Note Page 20)
           DA NANG, SOUTH VIET NAM

Our flight of four jet fighter-bombers circled the Viet Cong village like silver birds in lining up for the attack. A smoke bomb dropped by a liaison plane marked the target, a cluster of huts in the jungle near Route 19 about 260 miles northeast of Saigon.

... The altimeter unwound like a clock gone mad and the plane plummeted at 450 miles an hour. It lurched slightly as two 500-pound cannisters of napalm were dropped.

A moment later a corner of the village was a roaring hell of burning jellied gasoline.

Intelligence had reported that Viet Cong troops used this and several other hamlets in the area in recent bloody ambushes along the vital east-west road.

How many guerrillas and civilians died in the village may not be known for days.

...The forward air controller, who was running the strike from an L19 spotter plane, radioed corrections to the jets in a dry, emotionless voice:

"Mary 71, this is Yucca. Let's put the last load of nape (napalm) about three yards to the east. Then start with the bombs."

Capt. Ralph Havens of Falls Church, Va., dropped his pair of cannisters. As he pulled up, the inferno caused by two tons of napalm had consumed an area three times the size of a football field.

...No sound of explosions penetrated the cockpit. The jet's own noise and the static and stream of words coming over the earphones blocked it out. The pilots call this cockpit isolation and some say it helps them keep from really comprehending what their bombs do.

On the ground, huts burned furiously. The forward air controller, who was flying slow enough to count, said eight huts were destroyed. Neither he nor the jet pilots saw anyone on the ground.

No doubt the villagers and the Viet Cong had taken refuge in foxholes and bunkers when the jets appeared. These afford some safety from bombs but not from napalm.

Burning for more than 20 minutes, the napalm sucks up air from underground bunkers, consuming the oxygen and causing death by suffocation.

Mar 66   Air Force/Space Digest
              Gen. Hunter Harris, Jr., USAF, "PACAF: Growing Task in a
              Critical Area"

...The Forward Air Controller operates in two environments. In the classic sense, he is on the ground with the Army ground commander, providing advice on the use of air and calling in air strikes from his ground position. His other environment is airborne in an O-1 type aircraft. Either by communicating with the ground or using known intelligence, or seeing new targets, he identifies and marks targets to be struck by the fighter-bombers.

The importance of this function in this war takes on peculiar significance. Practically all targets that can be struck by air must be identified and marked by a Forward Air Controller prior to the strike. This requirement is an outgrowth of the peculiar nature of the war in Vietnam, the difficulty in identifying friend from foe, good guy from bad guy, in an environment where all people look and dress alike, and where there is no battle line. Before an air attack can be authorized against any area other than direct combat between ground forces in contact, approval of the local province chief is required prior to the strike. This approval develops from another unique control system, frequently time-consuming and difficult. To cope with this, we have provided air liaison officers to each of the province chiefs, with a direct communications capability to the Direct Air Support Center and the Tactical Air Control Center. In essence, each of the province chiefs has, or soon will have, his own forward air control party.

Effectiveness of air as well as ground operations in this kind of war is most difficult to measure. It does not encompass just the destruction of airfields, dams, railroads, bridges, manufacturing resources, or only those things that we have, in the past, considered essential to the maintenance of a modern military force. Over the past twenty years, the Viet Cong (VC) have developed and mastered the art of camouflage and guerrilla warfare. The VC weapons are modern and effective. Since the enemy in South Vietnam is a guerrilla, living for the most part off the land, with an unsophisticated arsenal and using primarily his feet or sampans as modes of transportation, he is far less visible and vulnerable to classic targeting procedures. The measure, therefore, of whether air operations are effective against the Viet Cong must be reduced to its impact upon the things which the Viet Cong prizes and how it affects his ability to employ his forces in the manner which he prefers. Targets, therefore, consist of

the Viet Cong himself, his hidden supply and living areas, and his waterways
transportation system — the sampan.

It has been just over a year since we began the program of jet strikes
on both sides of the demilitarized zone.

The total air effort this year has resulted in significant impact on the
VC. Exactly how many VC have been killed by air is a difficult figure to
determine. US and VNAF are believed to have killed by air strikes more
than 20,000 Viet Cong during 1965, but exact confirmed figures are not
available.

Our air has destroyed or damaged some 125,000 structures and some
3,800 sampans. Reflecting the buildup in air activity is the fact that
seventy-five percent of this was accomplished in the last six months.

Mar 66   The Airman
              Hap Harris, "Sabremen over An Khe"
              (from Congressional Record, House, May 10, 1966 p. 9792)

...The briefing began. Our target for the F-100 mission: a Vietcong-
infested area about 40 miles from Pleiku and some 227 land miles northeast
of Tan Son Nhut Airbase.

Altitude of the target was 2,000 feet. It was located in a valley, alongside a river. Mountains nearby rose 1,500 feet above the valley floor. It
would be tricky. We were to "work" the valley floor with bombs and
20-millimeter cannon fire.
   ...   FIVE CENTURIES AND BOMBS

Our fighters whipped through the edges of more thunderstorms and
began a gradual descent through a hole in the undercast. A radio channel
change was made to get on the FAC's radio frequency.

"Baron 25, this is Light 81. How do you read?"

Baron 25 replied, "Reading you fine 81 flight, go ahead." Captain
Derrick answered, "Roger, Baron 25, 81 is a flight of five centuries with
antipersonnel-antimateriel bombs and rockets. We are approaching the
rendezvous point on an 070 degree radial."

Baron 25 came back with, "Understand 81. Do you have the river, the
one that comes in from the coast, in sight? There is some smoke from a
previous strike about 2 miles south of the river, inland about 15 miles."
Captain Derrick responded, "Roger, Baron 25. We have the river and
the smoke from the other strike in sight. What is your position?" The
FAC answered, "Baron 25 is just north of the river and northeast of the
burning area. I'll put a marking smoke rocket on your target which is on
the north side of the river. Rolling in to mark now."

From our seats in the sky we watched the smoke rocket streak
earthward from the tiny single-engine plane and explode. A dense cloud
of white smoke rose through the foliage over the Vietcong buildings. Captain
Derrick called, "Tally ho, 25. We have you and the mark."

"81 flight. Acknowledge that you have the FAC and the target in sight."
"Two, three, four, five," replied four different voices on the radio,
acknowledging.

"Baron 25, this is 81. Are there any friendlies in the area?" "81 from
25, negative on the friendlies. I'd like you to take out as many structures
as possible located in those trees within 200 meters east and west of my
smoke mark."

...The Vietcong assembly area near us was ablaze from the bombs and
20-millimeter cannon fire of our planes. Red flames soared above the green
palms and lush grasses. We were going in — closer to the ground. I glanced
at the speed indicator. I thought it read 300 knots.

...The foliage seemed a blur. Rice fields went by like telephone poles
on a fast railroad run. Billowing smoke rose hundreds of feet in the air.
Our cannons stuttered — for seconds that seemed like minutes. The slugs
were hitting their mark. Huts burst into flame. Smoke enveloped us. The
Vietcong entrenched position was dying.

...Twice more in G-pulling swoops we dived to the deck. Palm tops seemed to reach for us, small hut roofs loomed large as airplane hangars, pounding cannons, tongues of fire were everywhere in the Vietcong assembly area. Then we were up, up in the blue where the beauty of the clouds and the mountains slowed my pounding pulse.

...Baron 25 called in the bomb damage assessment to Captain Derrick, "81, you have 18 structures destroyed and 11 damaged. Good shooting."

14 Feb 66   Aviation Week
               C. M. Plattner, "Marine Control of Air Tested in Combat"
               DA NANG, VIETNAM

...This Aviation Week & Space Technology pilot recently rode along on a typical divert mission in the rear seat of an F-4B with pilots of Marine Fighter Attack Sqdn. 115 (VMFA-115) stationed at Da Nang.

The pre-briefed target was about 45 mi. west of Da Nang and approximately 5 mi. from the Laotian border in rugged mountainous terrain. The target was a suspected Viet Cong camp in a wooded area of about 4,000 ft. elevation.

...Each of the four F-4Bs was loaded with 8 Mk. 81 250-lb. bombs and a 600-gal. centerline tank, besides Raytheon Sparrow air-to-air missiles which always are carried.

...This was a typical ordnance load, although pilots would prefer 2.75-in. rockets and fragmentation bombs as a rule rather than general-purpose bombs. Most of the worthwhile targets are straw huts or targets in the open, one officer explained, and "frag" bombs and 2.75s are ideal for these targets. The 5-in. Zuni rocket, designed to penetrate armor and concrete, is not particularly useful here, he added.

With a few exceptions, the Marine Corps has not been using white phosphorous bombs, napalm or CBU (cluster bomb unit), all of which are feared anti-personnel weapons. These weapons, however, are widely used by the U.S. and South Vietnamese Air Forces elsewhere in Vietnam.

After takeoff and rendezvous, the flight leader checked in with the Air Force direct air support center near Da Nang and was given new coordinates for rendezvous with the Bird Dog, or air controller, in an O-1, and assigned a new target.

...The target was a Viet Cong storage area in a small patch of woods surrounded by rice paddies and fields about 30 mi. due south of Da Nang.

...As the F-4s came into the target area, the forward air controller said several Viet Cong had just been seen entering the wooded area and fired a smoke rocket to mark the location of the structures which were not visible to the F-4 pilots.

Initial runs were made with reference to a clock-code position and distance from the smoke. Subsequently, the aiming point was described in reference to the last bombs dropped in terse comments such as "a little long," "good hit abeam," or "about 50 ft. short."

Eight runs were made and one bomb dropped in each run in a standard racetrack pattern with roll-in from about 8,000 ft. on medium-angle runs with pullouts at about 1,500-2,000 ft. above the ground. Four direct hits were scored on the hidden structures as the forward air controller very capably used the bombing accuracy of the F-4 pilots to best advantage. One secondary explosion was seen and two other structures were damaged by very close hits.

1967   Aviation Week, Marketing Directory Issue
               George Alexander, "Sensors Developed in Simulated War Area"
               EGLIN AFB, FLA.

Villages, trucks, sampans loaded with rice or mortars, simulated surface-to-air missile (SAM) sites, live troops, an underground bunker and other typical Vietnamese ground targets have been sprinkled about a special 4 x 8-mi. test complex here for USAF's Project Underbrush.

The project, which began last Feb. 1, supports both operational testing and development of a wide variety of airborne image-forming sensors and systems. Basically directed toward reconnaissance, the effort has three major objectives:

Training of photo interpreters and testing of new interpretative techniques and devices.

Development of "change-detection" sensors which can discover additions, losses or alterations in a given target scene from an earlier pass above the same locale.

Accurate, unbiased evaluation of either production-line or development sensors and systems.

The value of Underbrush in satisfying these objectives, according to Buford B. Toole, chief of the special activities branch here in the Air Proving Ground Center's plans and requirements office, is the realism of the test complex. Only the huts in the three different villages are permanently sited, he said; all the other targets are moved about frequently and their mix varied.

... Three separate villages. One, the simplest target on the complex, is built on open, marshy land very similar to rice-growing regions of Southeast Asia. A sensor must work successfully against this village before progressing to the more difficult hamlets. The second village is in another part of the complex which is drier and has more foliage; the structures are generally located under a single level of foliage.

Trees are thick and closely grouped around the third village and this target area is considered to be "two-canopy" type foliage, the most difficult for sensors of the three. All of the huts and structures in the three villages have been built to simulate typical Southeast Asian habitations. Lashings tie the structures together and no nails are used.

... Underground bunkers. At present, only one such tunnel exists and it simulates a typical Viet Cong or North Vietnamese weapon repair bunker. A variable heat source is usually located at the bottom of the bunker to simulate the activity taking place there. Toole said additional bunkers and tunnels probably will be dug for future tests.

Sampans and river traffic. There are three sampans, each of different construction, which are moved about a small creek running through the test complex. Men, guns or rice can be the cargo of the sampans, and the vessels may be found navigating the stream, pulled up on a bank near one of the villages, or hiding under dense undergrowth.

Men and animals. Troops stationed here are frequently positioned on the complex to simulate both peaceful villagers and/or hostile soldiers. Horses also are used. Mannequins are most frequently used to simulate troops.

Free Bomb Zones

4 Jun 65   (See Note Page 20)
            SAIGON, June 4

... In the north, strikes have been limited to military installations, roads and waterways well south of Hanoi. There seems no immediate prospect of bombing North Viet Nam's cities or civilian industries.

But in the south, huge sectors of the nation have been declared "free bombing zones," in which anything that moves is a legitimate target. Tens of thousands of tons of bombs, rockets, napalm and cannon fire are poured into these vast areas each week. If only by the laws of chance, bloodshed is believed to be heavy in these raids.

25 Jun 65   (See Note Page 20)
            THUONG LANG, VIET NAM, June 25

Filling the air with war whoops, a company of American paratroopers charged into a bamboo thicket near Thuong Lang and found themselves in the middle of what apparently was a Viet Cong staging area.

The Communists had pulled out, but veterans of many patrols into Viet Cong country said the complex of thatched huts, bunkers, and trenches was one of the best concealed they had ever seen. Officers said they believed it had been used as a staging area for one or possibly two companies of Viet Cong troops.

...The paratroopers moved in shortly after dawn, after air strikes had hit the northern banks of the Dong Nai with heavy blows of bombs and napalm.

...The paratroopers stormed toward the tree line, their automatic weapons and grenade launchers spreading a deadly sheet of fire in front of them. Hurdling paddy dikes, some of the big Americans sank in the soft earth and went sprawling.

Inside the tree line they first found an abandoned hut with signs that breakfast had been broke up. Rice and fish were still cooking in pots, but there were no people. The paratroopers destroyed the hut. Two other companies joined Charley Company, and they began a sweep operation through the brush.

There were complaints that intelligence maps were outdated because no one had been in the area except the Viet Cong for 18 months. The unfamiliar terrain made the going tough.

As Charley Company started for one of its objectives, the troopers began giving the Indian war whoops of the old Wild West. They charged through the heavy bamboo and found the staging area. They set fire to the huts, but the flames spread quickly to the surrounding bamboo, and the Americans had to pull out.

Before moving on, however, they found a rice cache hidden in an anthill. They destroyed it and shot up and grenaded the entrances to an underground bunker.

Intermittent sniper fire continued as Charley Company moved on to a clearing. There, an automatic weapon opened up, and the lead man was hit by fragments in the hand and leg.

...A medical evacuation helicopter was called in and tried to land near the wounded man. The enemy opened upon the chopper, and the crew man was hit. The chopper circled and landed behind some brush about 2000 yards away.

...Now they found a huge ant hill with rice hidden inside. The rice was packed in new bags bearing imprints to show it was a gift from the United States. The paratroopers slashed open the bags with axes and machetes and destroyed the rice.

Some of the area the paratroopers moved through was once rich rice land. Most of it has not been worked for months. Tough sawtooth grass has overgrown the paddies. One theory was that the farmers had moved out because the Viet Cong had taken over such strong control. Another was that they had left because the region had been declared a free bomb zone, with anything in it a target for attacking planes. Bomb craters pocked wide areas of the abandoned rice lands.

At the end of the day, the paratroop battalion had picked up 30 persons suspected of being Viet Cong. They had destroyed an estimated 3-1/2 tons of rice. One American had been wounded and one was missing.

Dec 65   Ramparts
              Bernard Fall, "This Isn't Munich, It's Spain"

...It was a good thing for some Vietnamese peasants that we could find our secondary target and could get rid of our recalcitrant bomb, because if that target had been rained out or clouded over, we would have jettisoned out bombs in what is known as a "free bomb" zone. Now in a free bomb area you are authorized to drop your ordnance anywhere. Any target, any structure, any movement at all. The free bomb zones in South Vietnam change constantly, so it is difficult to give any accurate acreage for them. But, for example, the free bomb zone around Zone D adds up to something like 300 square miles. Anyone living in these areas is presumed to be the enemy. Or, at least, presumed to be "hostile" and therefore destroyable.

4 Jan 67   Vancouver Sun, Carl T. Rowan
             MANILA

...What worries me more is that, in applying our air power, our incredible firepower, a lot of innocent, helpless civilians are being killed every day in South Vietnam!

Nobody ever lost a war for killing the people, civilian or military, of an enemy territory. But the question is, has anyone won a war while killing the civilians of a friendly territory?

It is unintentional, perhaps a horrible inevitability of war; but the fact is that American firepower is killing many civilians, destroying the property and crops of the very people our GIs have gone to Vietnam to defend.

Indiscriminate Usage

Oct 65   New Republic
             Bernard B. Fall, "Vietnam Blitz"

...Indeed, as many an informed observer in Saigon will conceed, what changed the character of the Vietnam war was not the decision to bomb North Vietnam; not the decision to use American ground troops in South Vietnam; but the decision to wage unlimited aerial warfare inside the country at the price of literally pounding the place to bits.

There are hundreds of perfectly well-substantiated stories to the effect that this merciless bombing hurt thousands of innocent bystanders and that one of the reasons why few weapons are found in many cases is that the heaps of dead in the battle zone include many local villagers who didn't get away in time. And every observer in Vietnam meets several American officers who will curse loudly every time they hear a jet overhead, because it again means an invisible objective hit blindly-for an F-105 travels far too fast to see what he hits and must be guided on his target by a "FAC" - a Forward Air Controller in a spotter plane. The same goes for the incredible wastage of artillery ammunition. "In my area," said an American provincial adviser to me, "we shot a half-million dollars' worth of howitzer ammunition last month on unobserved targets. Yet the whole provincial budget for information-and intelligence-gathering is $300."

...Here again, operations research comes to our rescue. Thus far, interrogations seem to show that there is no positively hostile association between the devastation wrought upon the countryside, and the United States or the Saigon government. In the words of one of the experts, the aerial attacks on the villages "of course cause unhappiness, no doubt on the part of the villagers, (but) do not cause them automatically to become VC's. In fact we have never met one who has become a VC as a result of this." But perhaps the answer should have read: "...who has been willing to admit that he has become a VC as a result of this."

17 Jan 66   Nation
             Raymond R. Coffey, "The People Beneath The War"

...The one great weapon we have that the enemy still lacks is air power. But air power, the way it is being used in this war, is not always an asset. There have been many calls for an end to the bombing of North Vietnam, but it appeared to some in Vietnam that a more urgent problem was restricting the "in-country" bombing of South Vietnam.

Our pilots have done a magnificent job of providing close air support for troops engaged with the enemy on the ground. And no one argues with the use of air power in those situations. However, there are also hundreds of air strikes every day against villages and other targets "suspected" of harboring the Viet Cong in cases where there is no ground engagement. Thus one day just outside Saigon six Viet Cong were reported seen among a string of thatch huts lining a canal. Hours later, long after the enemy had left, I rode along with a forward air controller in a light Cessna who directed a flight of eight Skyraider dive bombers in an attack on the target... Four huts were destroyed, four were damaged and huge black craters were torn in the surrounding rice paddies. Should it take eight airplanes and thousands of pounds of bombs to knock out eight flimsy huts? And what evidence was there really that the huts and rice paddies were owned by the Viet Cong?

On another day, a paratroop unit approaching a small village drew half a dozen rounds of small-arms sniper fire. The unit halted and called in an air and artillery strike that levelled the village. It seemed an extraordinary response to a few rounds of sniper fire, and one not likely to "win the hearts and minds" of any innocent civilians in the village.

Many of the Vietnamese jamming the refugee camps all over the country make clear that they came into the government areas not out of any particular fondness for the government and not to escape the Viet Cong, but to get out from under our bombs. Top military authorities in Saigon say great care and discrimination is exercised in selecting targets. But some of the top counterinsurgency experts in the U.S. mission, and some of the advisers working out in the countryside, still believe the "in-country" bombings in some cases are hurting our cause among the uncommitted people.

The Making of a Quagmire, 1964, p. 86

...The land spreads out flat and open, but the villages are usually built about thirty yards inside treelines. These are the Asian equivalent of Normandy hedgerows; they offer excellent protection, and camouflage is one of the military arts that the Vietcong practice to perfection. When they arrive in a hamlet for the night, they will immediately prepare perfect defensive positions along the treeline. ("You can never tell our Air Force that," one Vietnamese colonel said. "The Air Force always wants to bomb the hamlet. You tell them, 'Bomb the treeline, the VC are always in the treeline,' and they pay no attention at all. The French were the same way; they always bombed the hamlet too.")

26 Aug 65   New York Times, James Reston
             SAIGON, Aug. 25

...The American bombing in North Vietnam may be an issue in the United States. But the bombing and artillery fire here in South Vietnam are even more remarkable, certainly more casual and therefore, probably more dangerous.

For example, there was a rumor of a Vietcong unit of some 50 men in the area the other morning when I was in Baotrai. Back of the dusty main street where the Americans are startling the population by building sidewalks, there was a South Vietnamese Ranger battalion, equipped with 105-mm. and 155-mm. artillery guns, which were firing away in the general direction of where the Vietcong were supposed to be.

...While he spoke, fighter-bombers were attacking an area about a mile out of town, and life was going on in the street as if nothing more alarming than a fire truck were coming around the corner.

Nobody took cover. Actually there was no cover to take.

...None of this gets into the communiques. It happens sporadically here and there all over the country every day — unreported bombings and unobserved shellings of unchecked enemies in uncertain locations — and what the cost of all this is in human death and suffering and resentment against America or the Vietcong, nobody knows.

5 Sep 65   New York Times, James Reston
            SAIGON, Sept 2

...There is therefore a quite natural and growing sense of determination to deal realistically with these threats, but on the side, particularly among the South Vietnamese, there is also a marked tendency to use airpower and

artillery fire indiscriminately, even to deal with unverified reports that Vietcong troops are in the neighborhood.

Punishing the enemy is essential but punishing the civil population with
blind shooting and bombing is obviously unnecessary and even stupid. Theoretically, American officers are supposed to have a veto on air strikes requested by the South Vietnamese, but this is hard to administer and the veto
power does not always serve its purpose.

6 Jul 66   St. Louis Post-Dispatch, Richard Dudman
             WASHINGTON, July 6

...As the war intensifies, United States forces rely increasingly on
bombs and artillery. Commanders concede that targets sometimes are
selected on inaccurate or outdated intelligence, so that whatever Viet Cong
were present have fled. Much of the artillery fire is "harassing and interdiction" fire aimed merely at likely places of enemy travel and concentration with the results unobserved. Much of the bombing and shelling is simply
at the request of Viet Namese commanders, with no independent check on the
validity of the targets.

A pattern is emerging in which bombs and shells pound the countryside,
civilians are encouraged and helped to move to the cities as refugees, and
anybody left in an area is assumed to be hostile. When all resistance has
been smashed, the idea is that the people will be transplanted back and helped,
through revolutionary development, along the road to pacification.

16 Aug 66   New York Times, Charles Mohr
             SAIGON, SOUTH VIETNAM, Aug. 15

...Many military men, particularly some advisers in the provinces, are
among the most vehement opponents of the present policy.

...They contend that there is something basically wrong with a system
by which paid Vietnamese informers can trigger air raids on villages and in
which the United States acts primarily as a mechanical arm for the Vietnamese
authorities.

"No agent ever calls an airstrike on his own village — it's always somebody else's," said one American caustically.

Nov 66   Flying
            Frank Harvey, "The Air War in Vietnam"

(The editors of Flying have declined permission to give the verbatim
text of a selection from the above cited article. The following describes
the contribution of that selection.)

(The roles of the Forward Air Controller are outlined. The FAC can
divert pre-planned air strikes to a target of his choosing. Since he knows
the topography of his area quite well, any suspicious change on the ground
may lead him to call in an air or artillery strike. He has life and death power
over the inhabitants of the villagers in his reconnaissance area.

The author goes along with a FAC on a mission in the Mekong Delta near
Contho. The FAC orders long-range artillery against a single hut. Later he
calls in an air strike on a string of huts in a tree line along a canal. They
watch the village huts explode as the F-100's unload 20 mm shells into them.

The FAC must be careful not to call in an air strike by mistake, thereby
killing many innocent people.

The author tells of a FAC he met who was relieved of duty because he
declared himself party to killing civilians as a result of calling in long-range
artillery.

The FAC tells about being ordered to call in artillery fire on a village
where three guerillas were reported. After complaining that he saw only
civilians in the village, he gave coordinates which landed the shells in a
rice paddy and killed no one.)

3 Dec 66   New York Post Magazine
             Barry Cunningham, "Viet Nam Notebook"

...A Jesuit missionary tells me his small Mekong Delta parish has been diminished by 20 women and children recently as result of an accidental U.S. airstrike. He refused to fly the flag of the National Liberation Front from his church steeple. As a penalty guerrillas herded children and womenfolk into church sanctuary, assuring them of no harm. Then they ran to government province chief and "informed" on the hamlet. Information was relayed to Americans that the French-built church was VC hideout. Computerized map co-ordinates were then relayed to F-100 warplanes, already aloft. Napalm arrived ten minutes later.

3 Dec 66   New York Post Magazine
             Barry Cunningham, "Viet Nam Notebook"

...Out at Bien Hoa air base, I encounter a Forward Air Controller (FAC). The former jet pilot has been assigned to a single-prop Cessna spotter plane, searching for Viet Cong hideaways in War Zone D. Target spotted, he leads in the napalm-splashing Air Force Supersabres and Thunderjets.
     But I'm astonished that he only arrived on the job in Viet Nam two weeks ago, and has been bringing in dozens of air strikes per day.
     "How do you locate the correct targets out there anyway?" I ask him.
     "It's tricky," he confesses modestly. "But I'm learning — mostly by trial and error."

15 Dec 66   The Reporter
             Denis Warner, "The Small, Hard War In The Delta"

...Some of the dangers in this situation already have shown up in prisoner defector, and refugee interrogations. A year ago I reported that the villagers blamed the Vietcong and not the Americans or the Vietnamese government for bombing and artillery attacks on villages occupied by guerrillas. Today their thinking has changed somewhat. When the bombing or shelling is preceded by adequate advance warning, the villagers still tend to blame the Vietcong — if there are large concentrations of them. If there is no warning and few Vietcong around, the villagers blame the Americans or the government." It is not so much that the villagers have changed but that there seems to be too much bombing and shelling with too little justification," said one official.
     One difficulty — which, fortunately, will be reduced progressively as the American forces assume more and more of the main-force role — is the attitude of province and district chiefs toward bombing and artillery fire. Instead of standing in the way of air and artillery attacks on villagers suspected of harboring the Vietcong, they too often take the preventive approach. The effect is to swell the number of refugees but not the ranks of those who are sympathetic to the government.
     Nor do most refugees receive the kind of treatment that might be calculated to win them over. Too often they cluster and fester around the cities and towns or give up and go back to take their risk with the Vietcong in the war. In Quang Nam Province, for example, there are 168,000 refugees, of whom all but eighty thousand are "scattered," the bureaucratic term for "totally neglected." During the past two years only twenty-one thousand have been resettled. The rest will be "carried over" until next year or will just drift back to where home used to be.

Collective Punishment

28 Dec 64   New York Herald Tribune, Stanley Karnow
             SAIGON

...North of Saigon not long ago, for instance, a Viet Cong battalion surrounded five hamlets, dug in and settled down to wait. Soon government troops arrived. But unable to dislodge the entrenched Viet Cong unit, their commanders called for aircraft.

Piloted by Americans, B-26's roared in to drop napalm bombs, which scarcely harmed the Viet Cong but killed some 50 peasants. And that may well have been the object of the Viet Cong exercise. Within a week, their clandestine radio was sanctimoniously denouncing "this monstrous crime of the U.S. imperialist aggressors and the Saigon puppet authorities."

18 Mar 65   Reuters, New York Times
             DANANG, Thursday, March 18

South Vietnamese planes bombed a nearby village yesterday, killing about 45 villagers, including 37 school children, military sources said today.

Vietnamese propeller-driven Skyraider fighter-bombers attacked the village after an observation plane had been shot at.

A Vietcong flag was flying over the village, Manquang, about 375 miles northeast of Saigon. Manquang is regarded as a Vietcong-controlled village although it is only five miles from the United States airfield here.

Villagers carrying coffins marched to Danang after the raid but were turned back by Vietnamese troops.

12 May 65   (See Note Page 20)
             SONG BE, May 12

The yellow Catholic church was rent with bomb holes and wreckage. Only the altar was undamaged.

As three Vietnamese soldiers tried to play the smashed organ, a recent gift from American well-wishers, Father Dominique Roanh lamented, "I know that all this damage had to be done but we are such a poor parish here. How can we ever repair it?"

At the nearby Song Be Public Hospital, the superintendent was showing visitors bomb holes in the grounds and Viet Cong bunker positions.

Deeper in the town, smoke curled from the wreckage of vendors stalls. The large brick market itself was sieved with holes.

In many places in the town of 15,000 people, bodies were being carried to makeshift hearses. Both the public and military hospitals were full.

"It's not very often you get the chance to pull in an air strike on both a church and a hospital in the same morning," said Capt. John Lynch, from Norfolk, Virginia, with regret in his voice.

Lynch was the Air Force ground observer who directed American B57 jets on bomb attacks on the church, the hospital and the marketplace.

The jets were called in to hit the three locations because Viet Cong troops who tried to overrun three military installations in the town yesterday had pulled back to the church, hospital and market.

A Catholic Ranger Battalion Commander, Capt. Le Hau Nghia, had volunteered to try and drive the Viet Cong from their dug-in heavy weapons positions beside the church. He led a charge but was killed. Fifty of his men were casualties.

Father Dominique, who studied at Chicago and Rhode Island and also spend four years in Canada, said the Viet Cong were not actually in the church itself but were all around it. Most of them were barechested and wore only shorts.

Similar groups had dug in around the hospital and the market place. Because of the shortage of troops the B57's were given the job of knocking out all three places.

Father Dominique was hiding in his house nearby when the bombers first came over. He saw the Viet Cong gunners manning 50 caliber machine guns shooting vigorously at the aircraft.

His first worry he said was for the choir boys and alter servers hiding in the church. None was hurt...

... Lynch said, "I felt bad for a while, but when I saw those 50 calibers opening up it resolved any doubts I had. We just had to stop the Viet Cong that way."

The Viet Cong appeared to deliberately move into the civilian areas of the city, looting beer and foodstuffs from the market place and taking over front porches and backyards of houses.

However only infrequently did they forcefully enter a house.

There is still no total on the civilian casualties. It could be as high as 80, which is nearly as high as the military casualties.

Government troops entering the city found civilians lying wounded on the roadsides or in their homes.

30 Sep 65   Christian Science Monitor, Takashi Oka
             SAIGON

Earlier this year, Communist guerrillas occupied a village on the mountainous road from Saigon to Delat. They harangued the population, then left.

The next day, American planes bombed the village and its Roman Catholic church. The Communists, who had been hiding in the jungle, came back and told the villagers, "Now you see what the Americans do to you."

This is the kind of incident, repeated in many parts of South Vietnam, that has caused a high-level study here of the use of tactical air power and firepower — in its broadest dimension.

... The spokesman said that during the past six months the percentage of bombing errors had gone down. But the number of incidents had increased because of the greater use of air and firepower.

On Sept. 16 and 17, for instance, American planes bombed first the northern part of the international bridge across the demilitarized zone between North and South Vietnam and then the southern part, killing several South Vietnamese policemen and their families.

Much broader than the question of bombing errors, however, is the whole issue of whether or not villages with civilian inhabitants should be targets of air or artillery attack.

Guerrilla war is a war without fronts. Bombing mountain or jungle fastnesses where the Viet Cong have their lairs is one thing.

But frequently the Viet Cong take up fortified positions within villages.

Should such villages enjoy immunity from air attack or bombardment?

Military officers tend to look at the problem from their own requirements as fighting men. Civilians emphasize the priority of psychological and political factors.

No one, military or civilian, ignores how complex are the factors that must be braided into a solution.

If an order went out that there was to be no bombing of villages, under any circumstances, how great a handicap would this mean for the Saigon and American forces?

At Binh Gia last December such an order did go out, and the village of refugees, which was occupied for several days by the Communists, suffered very little damage. But Binh Gia is generally considered to have been a defeat for the government forces.

Currently, the bombing of villages by American planes continues. But American military headquarters have repeatedly emphasized the need to reduce non-combatant casualties.

21 Nov 65   New York Times
             Editorial, "Bombing South Vietnam"

The increasing prospect of a long bitter struggle in South Vietnam — as revealed in the grim ground warfare of the Iadrang Valley — raises serious questions about an aspect of American strategy that has had too little public discussion. These questions arise out of the mounting ferocity of American air warfare in South Vietnam and the heavy damage it inflicts on South Vietnamese villages and the people who live in them. More sorties are now being flown by United States planes than in the Korean war, and the nature of guerrilla war makes it impossible to avoid killing innocent civilians as well as Vietcong.

...By September about 5 percent of South Vietnam's rural population had fled into the cities and refugee camps. In that month General Westmoreland, The American military commander in Vietnam, issued an order for restraint. He warned that "unnecessary force" would embitter the South Vietnamese peasantry and make victory more difficult.

Statistics cannot adequately describe the increasing intensity of American air attacks and the damage they are doing to the South Vietnamese countryside, but they do give some indication. The number of strike sorties rose month by month from about 1,000 in January, before American air units were engaged, to about 7,500 in July. In the past month alone, there have been about 12,000 strike sorties — more than in all 1964 — and about 11,000 buildings were destroyed or damaged.

It is one thing to use air power in close support of ground forces when significant Vietcong units have been engaged. It is quite another to wipe out villages remote from any specific combat area on the strength of reports — often ill-founded — that the Vietcong have been sheltered there...In Vietnam itself more is involved that the deaths, the carnage and the alienation of peasant loyalty. The bombs that destroy South Vietnam's villages are smashing the social structure of the countryside.

26 Dec 65   New York Times, Hanson W. Baldwin
             SAIGON, SOUTH VIETNAM

...United States soldiers and marines have been heavily dependent upon this fire support, as they were in World War II and Korea. The tonnage of bombs and napalm dropped, of rockets used and numbers of rounds of field artillery projectiles fired in a normal day's operations in Vietnam is staggering. Much of it, many think, is wasted.

Some consider the American soldier too dependent on this heavy fire support. They maintain that heavy strikes are called to eliminate a single sniper or to take one bunker, and that many tons of ammunition are wasted on "making splinters in the jungle."

The explanation given is that assault by bombs and rockets instead of by infantry may save American lives and result in increased Vietcong casualties. It is admitted that this may also cause increased though unintentional Vietnamese civilian casualties.

11 Aug 66   New York Times, Eric Pace
             CANTHO, SOUTH VIETNAM, Thursday, Aug 11

United States Air Force jets killed 24 persons, including at least eight civilians and possibly some Vietcong, in an air strike Tuesday on two Vietcong-controlled hamlets eight miles west of this southern provincial capital, American officers said today.

The number of wounded was put at 84.

The officers reported that a South Vietnamese captain on the province chief's staff had requested the raid after "highly reliable" intelligence had indicated that a Vietcong company was in the area of the hamlets, which form part of the village of Truongthanh, 80 miles southeast of Saigon.

...Two F-100 Supersabre jets carried out the strike, dropping napalm and what were described as "antipersonnel devices," presumably cluster bomb units. They also fired 20-mm. cannon shells that burst on impact.

...Colonel Wallace said that inquiries after the incident showed that wet Vietcong platoons had been in the hamlet, and that they had held the peasants there at gunpoint to prevent them from fleeing when they saw an American spotter plane flying overhead. Such spotter plane flights normally preceded air or artillery attacks.

Allied officers knew that the village was inhabited, Colonel Wallace said in an interview in his office here, but "there was no reason to suspect that there was undue hazard" to the populace when the mission was carried out.

...He said the bombs were accurately placed in the area designated by the South Vietnamese captain, Le Xuan, adding that if the Vietnamese officers "say go, we almost always go."

...South Vietnamese authorities sent ambulances to pick up the wounded and bring them to the provincial hospital here, where they were treated by teams of Vietnamese and American doctors and nurses.

Colonel Wallace said the Vietcong units, which withdrew from the hamlets after the raid, had apparently taken additional dead and wounded with them. Four of the wounded at the hospital are suspected to be Vietcong.

...Several villagers said they had been trying to escape by sampan to seek shelter near a nearby Government outpost when they were hit by ordnance from the planes. Vietnamese peasants frequently gather near Government outposts or churches during allied air strikes, on the assumption that they will not be bombed there.

Colonel Wallace said the inhabitants of the raided hamlets "were undoubtedly Vietcong sympathizers" and that if they had felt loyalty toward the Government, they could have moved out of the area earlier.

"This was not a cavalier decision to go out and 'zap' some village," he observed. "It was our best professional estimate of the situation, the intention was good and the nature of the target was appropriate for an air strike."

...At the hospital, peasants who were caring for wounded relatives said that the Vietcong visited their hamlet often at night, but they said they had no knowledge of any Vietcong unit in the area at the time of the strike.

16 Aug 66   New York Times, Charles Mohr
             SAIGON, SOUTH VIETNAM, Aug 15

In the view of American military and civilian observers, President Johnson asked the wrong questions when he inquired about the circumstances of the death and injury of more than 100 civilians in an air attack on a Mekong Delta hamlet last week. The questions he asked were: Were the Vietcong in the hamlets? Were the villagers forced by the Vietcong to remain in the village? Did the Vietcong shoot at the spotter plane?

The answers the President received to all three questions was, "Yes."

However, Vietnamese interpreters for Western newsmen and the Vietnamese doctor in the hospital where the injured were taken were unable to find a single victim who would say there were Vietcong in the hamlets.

"That's not the point," said one deeply disturbed American official. "The President asked the wrong questions."

The attack occurred eight miles west of Cantho, the headquarters for the IV Corps of the South Vietnamese Army.

The official South Vietnamese account of what happened is this:

A Vietnamese captain, serving as intelligence officer of Phongdinh Province, received "reliable" intelligence that two platoons — perhaps 60 men — of Vietcong had moved into two hamlets. His request for an air strike was approved successively by his province chief, a division commander and the corps headquarters.

In parallel action, the request was endorsed by American advisers and scheduled by Air Force officers in Saigon.

The interrogation of victims and relatives of victims indicated that the Vietcong had been in the hamlets, that they had fired at the Forward Air Control despite the pleas of the hamlets' residents not to do so, and that they had used their weapons to try to prevent the people from fleeing to safety.

Critics of the policy regarding air strikes and military force in inhabited areas in general had several points to make about the incident.

"The emphasis on whether the F.A.C. received ground fire was irrelevant," said one. "The air strike was already approved and scheduled and that hamlet was going to be bombed whether there was any ground fire or not."

An official military spokesman confirmed this when he said in a press briefing that when the Forward Air Control pilot first received fire he flew out of the area "so as not to tip them off as to what was coming."

Critics of the present policy think the President should have asked questions along the following lines:

Was the South Vietnamese Government able to offer the residents of the hamlets security from Vietcong incursion in an area only eight miles from a corps headquarters and about 1,000 yards from a militia outpost?

Did the villagers, therefore, have any means of resisting Vietcong visits to the area and could they be blamed or justly punished for the presence of Vietcong?

Are the military advantages expected to be gained from striking about 60 enemy soldiers important enough to offset the political and humanitarian liabilities of bombing hamlets?

Are existing orders exhorting United States forces to take special precautions to avoid inflicing civilian casualties being effectively observed?

Critics insist the answer to all of these questions is "No."

28 Aug 66   New York Times, Richard Eder
WASHINGTON, Aug 27

Gen. William G. Westmoreland, commander of United States forces in South Vietnam has been urged by the Administration to take all possible action to reduce civilian casualties in air raids.

...After some consideration Washington has decided to issue no directives putting specific restrictions on the use of air sorties in the South.

Some officials had suggested that air raids that did not involve support for tactical ground action might be barred. Bombing villages because they were dominated by the Vietcong or because fire might have been directed from them against passing United States planes caused heavy casualties and was of insignificant military value, the officials said.

17 Aug 66   Herald Statesman (See Note Page 20)
SAIGON, SOUTH VIETNAM

There are no sanctuaries in South Vietnam for unarmed civilians.

Almost daily, guerrilla warfare takes its toll of civilian lives. Civilians are not even safe in the streets of Saigon.

There are no statistics on civilian deaths, but they run into the thousands. More are likely to die.

Incidents last week, including the bombing of a Mekong River Delta village, charged U.S. Air Force jets with the death of 26 villagers and injury to another 124, emphasize the plight of the innocent civilians caught between the Viet Cong and allied forces.

There have been other such bombings in which civilians were killed, unnoticed or unknown to the public. As one Vietnamese officer put it: "It happens all the time."

...The killing of civilians results from the way the war is conducted, the selection of weapons.

Allied forces sometimes appear to be less selective in the selection of weapons than the Viet Cong. The allies have airpower and artillery, while the Viet Cong have none.

Whereas the Viet Cong might select for assassination one or two key leaders of a government-controlled village, South Vietnamese troops might call an air strike on a village to cut down a Viet Cong platoon or two — 30 to 60 men.

The bombing Aug. 9 of the Delta village is an example.

The attack was ordered against the village of Truong Thanh by Lt. Col. Le Cong Thuong, chief of Phuong Dinh Province. It had been reported that 50 Viet Cong were in and around the village.

Col. Thuong called for an air strike. His request was relayed to American forces and sent to divisional Vietnamese and corps military levels for approvals, a procedure which must be followed. It was okayed.

The air strike posed the questions: Why so much firepower? Why didn't a company of South Vietnamese ground troops — perhaps 150 men — surround the 50 Viet Cong?

Whenever American troops plan a search and clear operation in a village, they call on the civilians to come out to a collection point where they will be protected. This is done by a helicopter flying at low level with a loudspeaker.

When American troops take heavy fire from a Viet Cong village, they often have no choice but to reply with artillery or air strikes.

Civilians are often reluctant to leave their villages. Instead, they build bomb shelters near their huts.

In some cases, civilians killed in military operations are simply listed as Viet Cong.

Vietnam in the Mud, James Pickerell, 1966, p. 85

...As a unit of American troops approaches a village, the Viet Cong often provoke their fire by shooting a few rounds into their midst, and of course any casualties that result from the American fire are almost always innocent villagers. Although the villagers may be aware of the Viet Cong provocation, this does nothing to lessen their resentment of the Americans, particularly as they have been subjected to an endless lecture on American atrocities. Despite the rising number of Viet Cong who are killed by the increased American firepower, it must be remembered that more and more of the people are being killed as well.

A New Kind of War, Martha Gellhorn, 1966, p. 19

...Miss Phuong was corpulent, muscular but well padded; the only peasant of that shape I saw in Vietnam. She was a spinster, probably aged 35, though she looked older; at 35 peasant women are apt to have seven children.

...From 1960 to 1964, she looked after sick and wounded Vietcong in various parts of her province. Then she resigned. Her reasons were fascinating; the Vietcong would not let her become a member of the Party because they said she was petit bourgeois.

...She retired to her parents' hamlet; there was no fighting in her area.

Early this year, without warning, the hamlet was bombed, with regular bombs and phosphorus; everything burned, the orchards were destroyed and 20 people were killed or wounded. About 20 Vietcong cadres were in the hamlet, but as they had no property or families to look after, they could run to safety. After this first bombing, our planes came over to broadcast the "Open Arms" propaganda, and some Vietcong guerrillas shot at the planes. From then on she could not count the number of bombings, and artillery fired on them every night. They brought their wounded here, to the provincial hospital in My Tho. People lived in camouflaged shacks in the rice paddies as their one hope of survival.

Were they free to move to Government-held hamlets? Oh yes, she said, but only those went who had relatives there, or family in the Vietnam Government army, or a profession or money; about half of the people had now resettled in Government territory. The poorest peasants stayed behind, they did not believe they could find work anywhere else, they said they were farmers, it was all they knew how to do, and whether they lived or died they would stay on their land.

Life was terrible in the hamlets: the Vietcong collected heavy taxes, 30 per cent of whatever you had, money or rice; both sides drafted the boys; the people could not grow vegetables for fear of bombing, and could keep only a few chickens and a pig; they were hungry and always afraid; the Vietcong cadres were getting mean and superior; if the guerrillas came and shot at aircraft you were sure to be badly bombed at once.

But the poorest of them clung to this fearsome hopeless life in their own hamlets, which must prove that word spreads through Vietnam by grapevine, and the peasants have heard of the wretched conditions of refugees.

Vietnam in the Mud, James Pickerell, 1966, p. 63

...In most operations air power is used to "soften up" an area prior to putting troops on the ground, in raids on "free strike zones" where it has been decided that everyone living in the zones is a Viet Cong sympathizer, or on areas from which aircraft have received ground fire.

Though "softening up" an area is considered a necessary tactic wherever troops are to be moved in, without doubt there are more innocent villagers hurt or killed in the raids than Viet Cong. If American planes raid a treeline, under which the Vietnamese villages are built, the chances are that any Viet Cong would have been in their fox holes during the bombing. The VC have fox holes dug and waiting in almost every village in Vietnam, and it is necessary for a bomber to score a direct hit on one of the holes to kill a man inside. If anyone is hurt in one of these "softening up" attacks it will surely be a villager.

23 Jan 67   Aviation Week
             Cecil Brownlow, "Sustained Viet Buildup Urged to 1972"
             SAIGON

...Despite this, the over-all morale of pilots flying over both North and South Vietnam appears to remain high. But they have their complaints. The pilots flying in the south seldom have the opportunity of observing any tangible results of the action because, more often than not, they are bombing through dense foliage. When they observe results, they are likely to be foot bridges or thatch huts, targets that many regard as less than worthwhile, although they often are significant.

Some pilots also chafe at the rigorous flying safety program that has been instituted by Gen. Momyer. This stipulates that standard bomb runs should be terminated at 1,500 feet, an altitude that lies outside the range of most small-arms fire from the ground. Seventh Air Force officials contend that those who complain of this do not understand the intent of the program.

"There's not a target in South Vietnam that is worth a single aircraft or pilot," one official recently told Aviation Week & Space Technology. "Our point is that, if you are hitting a regular, pre-planned target you should stand off a bit. The time to throw caution to the winds is when you're going in in support of friendly troops who need your help. Then you really press your attack."

General Data

Henderson Gleaner-Journal, Henderson, Kentucky; J. A. Dear (from Congressional Record - Appendix, April 21, 1965, A 1910-11 Article entered in Record by Senator Cooper; date of publication not given.)
SAIGON, VIETNAM

...For all that, we have problems too, and some of them of our own making. The most serious is that which results from our decision to embrace a strategy of terror.

That's what bombing is. It doesn't discriminate between soldiers and/or women and children. Especially, I have in mind American air strikes in South Vietnam. We are killing innocents almost every day. (Twenty-three structures and five water buffalo were destroyed, etc.)

Morality aside, can you think of a worse way to win the hearts and minds of people in a political war? Neither can I.

15 Apr 65   New York Times, Seymour Topping
             SAIGON, SOUTH VIETNAM, April 14

...United States and South Vietnamese air commanders seem to take all possible precautions to insure the protection of civilian populations.

The responsibility for calling in air strikes often rests with forward air controllers who know the country well and who mark target areas with flares or rockets.

Official statistics on the air strikes against the Viet Cong show more than 1,000 persons killed monthly since last November. Prior to that, the figure was 200 to 300 monthly.

United States officials say the dead are all adult males. Independent observers believe there are some civilians among the dead.

30 Aug 66   New York Times, Eric Pace
             CANTHO, SOUTH VIETNAM, Aug. 28

A leading member of South Vietnam's junta declared today that the Vietcong were indirectly responsible for "a good majority" of the civilian casualties caused by allied planes and bombs.

..."They do it to create destruction and a kind of discontent among the populace," the general said in an interview at this provincial capital in the Mekong River delta. "These casualties are the accidents of war; one cannot avoid them."

...The statement came after an American military spokesman said casualties inflicted against civilians and allied military personnel since June had reached "epic proportions."

...By American count, at least 143 civilians and allied military personnel have been killed by allied air and artillery strikes since July 1.

General Chieu predicted, however, that the civilian casualty rate would decrease because more and more peasants would flee the parts of the countryside where Vietcong were likely to be.

...Authoritative sources said that several refugees were among the 63 people killed Aug. 9 in a United States air raid on two hamlets near Cantho.

...The general asserted, however, that most allied artillery and air attacks were based on good military intelligence, and did not involve errors by military authorities.

15 Jun 65   (See Note Page 20)
             SAIGON, June 15

Warplanes hit Communist targets on both sides of the 17th parallel today and the U.S. Air Force permitted correspondents for the first time to ride jets on bombing missions within South Viet Nam.

F100 Super Sabres sprayed napalm fire bombs, high explosives and 20MM cannon shells into Viet Cong-held hamlets. The daylight attacks on guerrilla holdings followed up 230 such strikes in the 24-hour period ended at 6 A.M.

Vietnam in the Mud, James Pickerell, 1966, p. 81

...The peasants generally live in groups of homes the Americans call hamlets. In a hamlet there are usually about a hundred families, with a population of five hundred to a thousand people, most of them being children. The typical hamlet is a single line of houses along the bank of a river or a canal, and nearly every home will front on the water, with a wide separation between the different houses. A hamlet may be only a hundred yards wide yet half a mile long. Other hamlets, built away from streams, may be circular in shape and contain a large number of rice paddies within the hamlet boundaries. The total perimeter around such a hamlet may be three to four thousand yards and if it is government controlled it will be fenced with a few interwoven strands of barbed wire.

12 Nov 66   New York Times, Hanson W. Baldwin

...Two objectives must be accomplished in this effort. That part of the population that is neutral or anti-Communist must be protected from reprisals; and that part that actively supports the Vietcong must be screened and identified and then isolated or converted.

In other words the "fish," as Mao Tse-tung calls the guerrillas, must be left high and dry, without the "sea" of a sympathetic civilian population to swim in.

12 Jun 67   Nation
           Desmond Smith, "There Must Have Been Easier Wars"

...So the war goes on. Like a buzzard, the olive-green helicopter banked and wheeled over the burned-out village.

...The village was a dust heap. The sienna-colored huts had been flattened by repeated air strikes. Trails of fresh blood splashed a crazy path among the broken coconut palms.

A top sergeant is busy emptying his back pack to make room for a mother-of-pearl Buddhist altar looted from the ruins. A baby carriage is lying in a heap of spent mortar cases. The earthworks of one of the village bunkers are littered with C-ration cans, spent ammunition, discarded copies of Stars and Stripes ("HO REJECTS JOHNSON PEACE OVERTURE"). A bulldozer heaves aside the one remaining wall of someone's home. On it is scrawled in English, "G.I., PLEASE DON'T BURN MY HOME!" "VC propaganda," mutters a GI. Another First Cav trooper is giving out black playing cards. On one side is a death's-head skull with paratrooper wings. Beneath this is the legend "Death From Above." The idea, I am told, is psywar at the company level. When Charlie returns to find his family dead, he is expected to get the message. The cards are stuck in dead mouths.

"What's the bulldozer doing here?" I asked.

"The captain is looking for rice and weapons — they've got to be buried somewhere!"

"What about the villagers?"

"Screw the villagers. Everyone here was VC."

Air Strikes

22 Feb 64   New Republic
           Bernard Fall, "How Much Time Do We Have In Vietnam?"

...More recently the Viet-Cong became so bold as to hold a cluster of villages in broad daylight. To dislodge the Viet-Cong, our side pounded the villages to pieces with medium field artillery and napalm, causing the encircled population hugh casualties. The Viet-Cong escaped.

12 Jun 64   Life

...A unit of Vietnamese soldiers, sent to take a Vietcong-controlled village near the Cambodian border, landed by helicopter. The village had been bombarded from the air and the soldiers met no resistance. They found no men except old men helping the women put out the fires.

18 Jun 65   (See Note Page 20)
           OVER D ZONE, VIET NAM, Jun 18

A few plumes of smoke rose over the vast green jungle 25 miles north of Saigon today, but otherwise there were no signs visible from the air of the huge bombardment by U.S. Air Force B52s a few hours earlier.

The jungle apparently had swallowed up the bombs.

There seemed little doubt that there were casualties on the ground, however, and many of them undoubtedly were civilians. Several sticks of bombs struck near the edge of open patches in the jungle, within a few hundred feet of cultivated rice lands and clusters of huts.

There seemed to be no damage to the huts. But there were no people or animals visible on the ground.

After the armada of eight-engine bombers had flown past, small B57 twin-jet fighter bombers swept in on runs over the same zone, pouring more bombs, rockets, napalm (fire-bombs) and cannon shells into the foliage and clearings and along streams.

The crash of bombs from the B57s shook planes flying past at 2,000 feet. Cannon shells twinkled in bright sparks on the jungle roof, and napalm canisters sent fireballs billowing up through the greenery briefly.

But the smoke from each blast dispersed quickly, leaving scarcely a trace.

Trees in the area are 100 or more feet tall. In the jungle the canopy is continuous, making impossible a thorough survey from the air of the raid's results.

Dateline: Viet Nam, 1966
Jim Lucas

(The copyright owners of Dateline Vietnam have declined permission to publish textual material in this documentation. The following describes the essential contribution made by a selection from this book.)

On July 22, 1965 the author sees a bombing mission from one of the Skyraiders in the raid. The target was supposed to have been the hamlet of Ap Phuoc Lo, but it was changed to another hamlet. The pattern of delivery is described: first 500 pound fragmentation bombs; then napalm; then strafing runs. The hamlet is declared 75 per cent destroyed.

On two occasions the author notes remarks by Lt. General Moore, Commander of the 2nd Air Division, which suggest that the character of the air war over the South had changed since March. Decisions had been made which permitted an expansion of air activity of the kind just witnessed.

29 Jul 65   (See Note Page 20)

...The big air and ground operation was aimed at clearing out a portion of Phuoc Tuy Province, in which the Viet Cong recently cut the strategic highway between Saigon and the military base at Vung Tau, on the coast. But it appeared the U.S. force had failed to find any important enemy units.

During air attacks in the vicinity Tuesday, U.S. Air Force Skyraiders bombed a village 1,700 yards from a convoy of U.S. troops and destroyed a Buddhist monastery. Four monks were badly wounded and about 20 others were slightly hurt.

1 Aug 65   New York Times, Jack Langguth
              SAIGON, SOUTH VIETNAM, July 31

...While ground action in Phuoctuy has proved frustrating to the American forces, the rate of United States air strikes elsewhere in South Vietnam has continued to increase.

More than a dozen hamlets and villages were hit yesterday. They were identified by the American command as either controlled by the Viet Cong or suspected of being Viet Cong bases.

29 Aug 65   New York Times, James Reston
              SAIGON, Aug 28

...The people in the South Vietnam hamlets now know that if they dig tunnels for the Vietcong and give them food and refuge, they are likely to be shelled or bombed, and this has undoubtedly complicated the enemy's problem, but it has raised a new problem on our side. For it has caused great suffering and destruction among the civilian population.

17 Sep 65   (See Note Page 20)
                 CAN THO, VIET NAM, Sept 17

The tactics of war are changing in parts of the lush, sweltering Mekong Delta — long a happy hunting ground for communist guerrillas.

...Long, tiring walks in search of elusive Viet Cong in the scorching heat are becoming rare. Nowadays the emphasis is on intelligence and caution. Troops are not committed to battle unless enemy strength is known.

In the past two weeks, U.S. planes have begun scorched-earth raids on Communist-held sections of the Delta. From the sky, one sees miles of cratered canals, bombed-out villages and streaks of black-brown napalm stains across the rich green fields and rice paddies.

Warned of an impending air strike, the villagers try to move out, and the Viet Cong try to stop them. Government psychological warfare teams seek to convince the villagers that the Viet Cong no longer can protect them.

Civilians often are killed and wounded unavoidably because the guerrillas seek sanctuaries in village fortifications. U.S. helicopters, in the face of enemy fire, are making unprecedented night mercy missions in flying the wounded to government hospitals. Government agents slip across Viet Cong borders where none dared venture before — and they gather valuable information from the wounded in the hospitals.

11 Sep 65   (See Note Page 20)

In the Mekong Delta, U.S. planes hit slightly west of targets they pounded yesterday, 150 miles south of Saigon, in an effort to destroy a Viet Cong Regimental Headquarters and trap as many as 2,000 guerrillas.

U.S. spokesmen described enemy losses as heavy. They said the planes hit again and again at canals used by the guerrillas and also destroyed several villages. The inhabitants of the area had been warned for weeks of the coming aerial assault, the spokesmen said.

Heavy rains and 30-mile-an-hour winds stalled a South Vietnamese ground effort to move in against the guerrilla regiment after the air strikes began yesterday.

24 Nov 65   New York Herald Tribune, Beverly Deepe
                 SAIGON

...In contrast to the aristocratic role Saigon's upper class women fill, is the plight of a young woman who recently lived in a war-infested province of the Mekong Delta. Nguyen Thi Bay, 19, who recently fled to Saigon, where she receives 1,000 piastres ($10) a month plus room and board as a maid, told this story:

"Last April, several jets circled over our house about five times and then bombed and strafed it. My parents were working in the rice field and I was paddling my sampan coming from a relative's house when I saw the flames pouring out of our house. I ran toward the house to try to salvage some of our belongings, but instead I found my elder brother near the family bomb shelter with blood gushing from his head and my younger 12-year-old brother with his face full of blood.

..."In our villages, the peasants built two kinds of shelters. One kind is inside the house right under the bed. When we hear any artillery, mortars or groundfire we just roll out of bed into the trench. The second kind is usually in the yard or garden and is used when aerial bombing and strafing starts. Even our family dog knew exactly which hole to run into. When there was mortar or artillery shelling, he ran into the shelter under the bed. But if there was bombing from airplanes he would lead the family to the big trench in the garden. He could even tell the difference between a cargo plane and a fighter; he didn't even run out of the house when a cargo plane passed over.

"Some of the families in our village have pretty plush bomb shelters. Some have put their money together to build a community shelter deep in the ground with concrete walls and floor so they can sleep there during the night-time."

The girl said that because more and more men were leaving for the battle-field the jobs of building the shelters and planting and harvesting the rice were being performed by women.

20 Jan 66   St. Louis Post-Dispatch (See Note Page 20)
             THRUNG LAP, Jan 20

...Noon was the time set for the allied truce to begin.

Peasants carrying baskets were pouring out of the distant treelines and paddy-fields toward Trung Lap, seemingly undisturbed by the roar of the artillery and the bombing.

"Where do they come from?" one American asked in perplexity as he gazed at the long lines of women and children. "We've been bombing and sweeping those places for days."

10 Aug 66   New York Times, Charles Mohr
             SAIGON, SOUTH VIETNAM, Aug 9

...Neither increased bombing of the North nor stepped-up American "spoiling attacks" on guerrilla bases in the South has appeared to reduce the enemy's ability to build up his forces in response to American increases.

14 Feb 66   Newsweek

...Guns Ablaze: "The next day, snipers hiding in a village managed to pin down the first platoon of 'B' Company, Second Battalion of the Seventh Cavalry Regiment. Calling in air strikes, the Americans charged into the village with guns ablaze. All they found were women — some of them nurs-ing their babies — and terrified children. 'You correspondents seem to feel sorry for the women,' remarked one soldier. 'But we've been fired at by women many times.' And in fact, one of the women was found with three rounds of ammunition taped under each of her breasts. 'Some uplift,' a GI cracked wryly."

15 Feb 66   New York Times, Neil Sheehan
             GIAHUU, South Vietnam, Feb 14

A massive allied offensive in this area has dramatized one of the major problems of the war — the high price the South Vietnamese peasants are being forced to pay for the death of a few hundred enemy troops and the capture of a few score weapons.

United States and South Vietnamese military spokesmen assert that the three-week-old offensive, aimed at crushing four enemy regiments operating here in Binhdinh Province and the adjacent northern Province of Quangngai, has resulted so far in the killing of 986 Vietcong guerrillas and North Viet-namese regulars and the seizing of 161 weapons.

Some high-ranking American military officials privately expressed doubt over the accuracy of the casualty figures, but it is believed that a few hundred enemy soldiers have been killed.

The Saigon military communiques have failed to mention what is apparent to a visitor to the battlefield — the appalling destruction wrought in Giahuu and about 15 other peasant hamlets on the central coast by artillery, barrages and aerial bombardments.

Giahuu and two adjacent hamlets along Highway 1 about 310 miles north of Saigon are a frightening example of this destruction.

South Vietnamese officials estimate that, within the three hamlets, about a thousand mud-and-thatch or brick-and-tile peasant homes have been blasted apart by bombs and shells or incinerated by napalm. Bomb craters, some as large as 10 feet deep and 20 feet across, pockmark the hamlets and the surrounding rice paddies and hillsides.

This region is noted for its coconut-tree groves, whose coconuts and coconut oil have provided a living for many of the peasants. Now hundreds of coconut trees in Giahuu alone have been snapped in half by high-velocity naval shells from the guns of Seventh Fleet warships.

Although most of the old men, women and children appear to have escaped death or injury by hiding in underground bomb shelters or fleeing to the hills and rice fields civilian casualties have still been considerable.

Only two civilians are known to have died in Giahuu, but in the village of Tamquan, two and a half miles south of here, at least a hundred civilians are estimated to have been killed during the fighting late last month.

United States and South Vietnamese military authorities have evacuated 90 seriously wounded civilians from hamlets in the area to the provincial hospital in Quinhon and have treated hundreds of others with light wounds.

Most of the wounds were inflicted by shell and bomb fragments or bullets.

One distraught woman appeared at a field medical station holding a child whose legs had been horribly burned by napalm. The child is not expected to live.

Thousands of refugees — some officials estimate as many as 5,000 — have also flocked to Highway 1 along which many of the South Vietnamese and American troops are concentrated, or to the Government-held district town of Bongson, 15 miles south of here, searching for safety from bombs and shells and seeking emergency provisions of wheat and cooking oil. These have been supplied by the United States aid mission to sustain them until they can return to their wrecked homes and attempt to rebuild.

No one here, however, really knows how many homes or coconut groves have been wrecked or how many civilians have been killed, injured or displaced throughout this region. The area has been under enemy control for more than a year now.

Government administration is virtually nonexistent. The primitive communications are either in disrepair or have been destroyed by the enemy.

South Vietnamese and American military and civilian officials have neither the time nor the inclination to make an accurate assessment of the damage.

Most of the destruction and the killing and wounding of civilians were, perhaps inevitable under the circumstances. The Vietcong and the North Vietnamese fought from an elaborate system of fortified bunkers and trenches built around and within the hamlets.

Headlong assaults across the open rice paddies would have inflicted prohibitive casualties on the advancing South Vietnamese and American troops, so the Communists had to be forced to abandon the hamlets by shellfire and air strikes.

Yet some American officials here asked privately whether this might not in the end prove to be a pointless, if bloody exercise.

The troops will not remain once the operation ends in a few weeks, and local South Vietnamese officials concede that they cannot hope to maintain control over these hamlets once the troops are gone.

High-ranking American military officials say they cannot afford to commit the limited number of American fighting units to long-range pacification projects because of growing Vietcong strength and the increasing infiltration of North Vietnamese regulars into the South.

These officials say the best they can do is to attempt to find and maul hard-core Communists units in an effort to relieve some of the pressure on the islands of Government control that remain in the enemy-dominated countryside.

...Thus, when the South Vietnamese paratroopers and the men of the United States First Cavalry Division (Airmobile) depart for some other battlefield in Vietnam, the Vietcong guerrillas and their North Vietnamese allies are expected to return to those hamlets.

...United States and South Vietnamese aircraft have been dropping leaflets telling the people that the Vietcong are responsible for the destruction because they built their trenches and bunkers within the hamlets.

Government loudspeaker trucks have repeated this message. Government officials are distributing other leaflets praising the Saigon regime and neatly printed brochures complete with photographs of enemy bomb atrocities in the capital.

Such propaganda, in the opinion of some experienced observers, is of questionable influence in these circumstances unless followed up by long-range indoctrination and concrete deeds to win the peasants' support.

...Except for emergency rations of wheat and cooking oil and a few hundred bolts of cloth and sewing kits along with rudimentary medical treatment, these peasants have also experienced little from the United States and the Saigon Government except bombs and bullets.

...An American visitor asked an old woman in the crowd through an interpreter what had happened to her.

"The planes destroyed my house, and the big guns cut down my coconut trees," she said.

Her mouth, stained reddish brown with the betel nut she chews, twisted as she spoke, and her voice rose into the wail Vietnamese peasant women use when they are describing personal sorrow.

"How many coconut trees did you have?" she was asked.

"Fifty," she replied, "and now 47 of them are gone."

"How will you earn your living now?"

"I don't know," she said.

6 May 66   (See Note Page 20)
             THAM SON, VIET NAM, May 6

A unit of the U.S. 1st Air Cavalry Division battled a Communist battalion today in a chattering exchange of machine-gun fire.

...After the cavalrymen became bogged down in their struggle with the enemy, air strikes were called in.

"I hate to do it," Worth said, "because there are probably civilians in there. But what are you going to do?"

Other soldiers weren't so worried about this.

"Give 'em hell," they shouted as rockets crashed into enemy bunkers.

"That is real fine," said one soldier as a dive bomber dropped a napalm bomb that sent huts and palm trees blazing. A follow-up bomber dropped earth-shaking 500-pounders that spread the flames.

The bombs sent up huge spouts of smoke and dust that obscured the vision on both sides.

...As the cavalry men fought around the cluster of huts, the Vietnamese occupants, mainly old men and children, began crawling out of holes. They wept and screamed and begged the Americans to stop shooting.

GIs shared their rations with the children and tried to reassure the older villagers, but they didn't stop shooting and neither did the Viet Cong.

Toward dusk the firing slacked off to only sporadic shooting, most of it American.

About this time, Pfc. Julius Hudson of Mobile, Ala., said: "I guess this was pretty tough. I was doing what everyone else was doing. I was doing my job."

As night fell, the American soldiers dug in and waited for daybreak to resume their chase.

30 Apr 66   (See Note Page 20)
             DUC BON, SOUTH VIET NAM, April 30

The bloodied and tattered family stumbled from the jungle. The father came first gripping the hand of a small boy; then came the mother carrying a baby. Their eyes were glazed.

Twelve hours earlier an American force of the 173rd Airborne Brigade had received intelligence that a large element — perhaps even a battalion — of hard core Viet Cong troops was camped near the village of Duc Bon.

The 173rd force was at Song Be, about 60 miles north of Saigon and about 15 miles east of the Cambodian border. Duc Bon was eight minutes away by helicopter.

The 2nd Battalion of the 173rd was readied for a morning assault. The paratroopers were eager to go because the intelligence said the Viet Cong force was an outfit they had tangled with before.

Shortly after dawn, artillery and jet planes blistered the suspected enemy area with shells, bombs and napalm. The helicopter assault was led by C Company and as the first wave hit the landing zone the thunderous sounds of rifles, machine guns and grenades split the air.

"They're here, they're here," said Capt. Tom Faley, 26, Harrisburg, Pa., commander of C Company.

But they weren't. After several minutes of intense firing it became quiet. Paratroopers moved into the jungle. A rifle was found here, the remains of a half-eaten breakfast there. But the enemy force apparently had been no more than a dozen men, and they had fled.

Then from the thicket the family appeared.

Two soldiers of C Company guided them. They had been discovered cowering under a tree toppled in the bombardment.

Fragments of bombs had caught the family as it scurried through the jungle. The father was bleeding in a dozen places from his back, sides and legs. The mother's hair was sticky with blood and her clothes had been shredded. Both children had bleeding scratches on their arms and legs.

They trembled at the sight of the American paratroopers. Viet Cong agitators had told them the Americans would beat them, kill them, and cut out the livers of the children.

A medic hurried to them and worked quickly to patch up the frightened family as best he could. A Vietnamese interpreter was called.

"The man says he's a farmer," he reported, "and he probably is in the daytime...at night I'm sure he's a VC guerrilla."

After further questioning it was decided the family should go back to command headquarters at Song Be.

All four shuddered when the whirling blades of the helicopter churned grass and dust as it landed to take them away. Inside the machine they clung desperately to each other as the helicopter took off. In eight minutes they had traveled further than ever before in their lives.

At the Song Be airstrip the family was separated. The mother and children, crying now, looked back bewildered as they were taken to a jeep. The father was taken to an American field hospital. Doctors dug out the many pieces of steel embedded in his body. While he was still on the operating table, a Vietnamese intelligence man leaned over him, relaying information to an American intelligence officer beside him.

"Name, Le Van Minh; age 35, occupation farmer, he says," the interpreter reported, the wife was 28; the children 4 and 1.

He leaned closer.

"What Viet Cong squad are you in?" he asked.

The man replied he wasn't in any Viet Cong squad. He said the Viet Cong has made him work for them from time to time in the last few years, carrying rice, building fortifications. But the Viet Cong had taken away his gun, he said.

"When did you see the Viet Cong last?"

About 2 o'clock this morning, the man answered, about 30 or 40 had come to his village and then left, heading south. These same men had come often to the village. They all wore the same kind of clothes and carried rifles.

Interrogation finished the bandaged man was taken to the provincial hospital at Song Be. Vietnamese military and national police authorities would take over from there.

The U.S. intelligence team went to the compound where civilian refugees are kept, to question the wife, and check if she and the man told the same story. Only officials were allowed in the compound.

The wife and two little boys probably will go eventually to a resettlement camp for refugees to try to start a new life in a strange place.

If things go well, the father may join them there some day.

22 Sep 66   World Journal Tribune (See Note Page 20)

Correspondent Bob Poos was with the Marines who took the heavily fortified village of Gia Binh from the North Vietnamese. Here is his eyewitness account.

GIA BINH, VIET NAM, Sept 22

...Landagre was with C Company of the 1st Battalion, 26th Marine Regiment. C Company and two others had been trying for five days to shoot their way into the heavily fortified village of Gia Binh, just south of the demilitarized zone that separates the two Viet Nams.

The Marines were stopped by heavy automatic weapons fire yesterday morning short of the North Vietnamese fortifications. They resumed the attack in midafternoon after the enemy positions had been pounded by 2,000-ton bombs (sic), 8-inch naval shells, and heavy artillery.

...All three companies — Charlie, Bravo, and Delta — gained their objective just before dark yesterday.

The village of scattered huts and a few masonry buildings sprawled over an area of 3,000 square yards. Air and artillery attacks had shattered many of the structures.

...After the barrage ended, Marines attending to their dead and wounded heard the frantic voices of Vietnamese women and children apparently trying to escape the battleground between the two forces.

12 Dec 66   (See Note Page 20)
              BEN LUC, Dec 12

Three sniper bullets whined through the rice that was ripening in the sun. Men of the U.S. Infantry Squad fell to their knees, the platoon Commander cursing quietly.

The snipers obviously were holed up in a village hidden in coconut groves and banana trees 800 yards across the shimmering paddy fields. Anywhere else in Vietnam the Americans could call in artillery, and maybe an air strike, to chase the snipers away.

But this was the Mekong Delta, a new kind of war for the U.S. troops in Vietnam. They had to take the village the hard way.

...Elsewhere in Vietnam, standard operating procedure is to pour in artillery and air strikes on snipers. In the Delta, however, the test units have been ordered not to do this. Too many innocent people live in the villages. To bring heavy fire down upon them might kill scores.

22 Nov 66   Herald Statesman, (See Note Page 20)
              MEKONG DELTA, SOUTH VIET NAM

Humming "When the Saints Go Marchin' In," the blue-helmeted pilot pointed his blunt-nosed F100F Super Sabre jet toward a patch of trees fringing a brown canal.

Maj. Swart Nelson of Phoenix, Ariz., was approaching the climax of his 230th combat mission in a relaxed mood.

A voice rasped in his radio earphones. Nelson stopped humming.

"Your target is a bunch of hooches (thatched shelters) along that finger of water, 55 meters (yards) short of the smoke," said the forward air controller flying a small prop plane several thousand feet below the oncoming wedge of three Super Sabres. "We think it is a VC base camp."

The spotter had fired a rocket to mark the target. White smoke spiraled up from a huddle of dun-colored shacks crowding a small stream.

"Here we go," Nelson called over the intercom to the hitch-hiking newsman in the seat behind him.

He shoved the stick forward, and the F100 dived.

Two hours earlier the three pilots had met in the ready room of the 531st Tactical Fighter Squadron at Bien Hoa air base, some 150 miles to the north northeast.

...The trip to target was a pleasant half hour, with the sun shining warm through the transparent canopy of Ramrod 3, Nelson's two-seater.

The sunlight glinted from endless rice paddies and swampland slipping past beneath the speeding warplanes. From that altitude, the country was a panorama of many shades of green.

"This is a nice little war," mused the 44-year-old Nelson. "Down here, we don't get any air opposition.

"We may run into some ground fire, but we'll be all right unless there's a lucky hit on a vital place."

Just then, the target area came into view — and the mood changed abruptly.

The Super Sabres drove home their attack in a pinwheel pattern.

The flight leader went in first, zooming low over the village and clobbering it with fiery napalm.

The second jet followed in a long, looping arc which brought him on target from a different quarter.

As he pulled out and clawed for the sky, Nelson began his run.

Down...down...down. The speed built up to 500 miles an hour. With the speed and the steep descent came sharply increasing forces of gravity.

The green trees and the bamboo huts grew bigger and bigger. The gravity forces mounted to five times normal.

Suddenly, there was a thump from the underside of the plane. One of Nelson's 500-pound bombs was away, slanting toward the huts.

Nelson pulled back on the stick and the jet screamed toward the clouds.

The weight fell away from the reporter's back and shoulders. Now it seemed as though he was being pulled from below.

The horizon flashed by, dizzily, and the snout of Ramrod 3 bored into the blue sky and white cloud.

Looking back over one shoulder, the newsman could see billows of dirty gray smoke and columns of flame rising from the huts.

Twice more, the jets raked the village.

Then they swung northward, as though headed for home, and buried themselves in a looming cloud bank.

But on the other side of the cloud, the F100s turned back and tore in on the village from a new direction.

This time, the 20mm cannon under the fuselage coughed dryly, sending streams of blue shells into the smoking target.

After four strafing runs, the flight leader radioed: "Let's go home."

25 Mar 67   Saturday Evening Post
            Richard Armstrong, "Believe me, he can kill you"

..."The main thing for a F.A.C. pilot," said Kerr, "is aggressiveness."
..."Just north of Quinhnon one day I noticed some fresh dirt in a stream bed about a click from a village. Three days later, an intelligence report said there were 300 V.C. in the village, and I directed a strike. After the first four planes hit the village and did not draw any ground fire, I told the next four to hit the stream bed. When the Vietnamese troops moved in after the strike, they collected 101 bodies and a pile of weapons in the stream bed. This was the exit of a V.C. tunnel from the village — their escape route — and we had caught them.

3 Apr 67   The Nation
             Karl H. Purnell
             SAIGON, April 3

The reconnaissance plane skimmed across the village at treetop level.
Standing knee deep in the rice fields, the farmers looked up from their work,
tipping their white conical hats forward and reflecting angry surprise at the
small silver plane roaring by just above them. Then a shot sounded from
behind the plane, a loud crack easily heard through the wind rushing by the open
windows of the plane. Pressing the small intercom button, I called to the
pilot. "Somebody's shooting at us."

He too had heard the shot and was pulling back on the stick, sending the
single-engine plane into a steep climb.

"You see where that came from?" he asked.

"No idea." It was indeed impossible to tell where the sniper was
located. He might have fired from one of the small, thatched huts in the
village or he might have been concealed in one of the many tree lines which had
flashed by as we buzzed the area.

"I sure don't like getting shot at." the pilot muttered. Then, almost as an
afterthought, "I'm wondering whether to call an air strike on that village."

...Until the shot was fired, it had been a routine mission. We had flown
down the coast, looking for enemy troop movements or suspicious construc-
tions that might signal a new Vietcong bunker or trench system. Many of the
villages had recently been burned out by the troops operating in the area. The
huts were little more than black skeletons of bamboo sticks protruding lifelessly
into the sky; the trees and shrubbery were scorched brown and gray. Endless
parallel tracks, interlaced among the fields and into the villages, showed where
tanks and armored personnel carriers had smashed and ploughed their way
through the area.

The green rice stalks, ready for harvesting, rippled in the breeze like a
field of rich Iowa wheat. However, the fields were not being harvested. The
peasants had scattered for the mountains or to the teeming refugee camps miles
to the north. The area had been designated a "fire free zone" where anything
that moved was fair game for troops, artillery and airplanes.

But the village below had somehow been spared. Either it was not "hard-
core VC" or the enemy had decided not to fight from the nearby trenches and
bunkers, so the troops had not bothered to destroy it. The fields were being
worked and the people were moving back and forth along the paths to the long
rows of huts. As we swept overhead, I had noticed that whole families were
busy shelling and drying rice in front of the small mud and thatch houses.

...The plane circled two more times and then the pilot's voice sounded
over the intercom.

"You know, I'm going to teach those folks a lesson. I'm calling for an air
strike."

Having made the decision, he began calling for his radio operator,
stationed back at the air base and ready to relay information to the central
control headquarters.

"This is Green Marker to Alpha."

A young, tense voice acknowledged the message.

"This is Alpha, go ahead Green Marker, over."

"This is Green Marker. I am calling air strike in a village down here
where someone just shot at me. It was probably a .30 or .50 caliber weapon.
Here are the coordinates of the village."

The pilot read off the exact location of the area below. Then there were
a few moments of silence as the operator cleared the strike through higher
channels.

"I sure don't like hitting villages, but they gotta learn to quit shooting
at us," the pilot said over the intercom.

Then the radio operator came back on. The strike had been cleared
through American and Vietnamese authorities. A call for jet bombers had
been placed.

"Probably take fifteen to twenty minutes before we can get the planes," the operator said.

Below, the villagers were unaware of the fate being organized for them. The jets would surprise them. They would appear on the horizon, dark and slim against the blue sky. There would be a primary pass for observation. Before the roar of the engines had settled across the village, the planes would do a climbing turn. Then they would level out and swoop in a neat arc toward the village. As they reached the bottom of the dive, two bright silver cylinders would drop from the planes' wings and drift toward the village. There would be a flash of brilliant orange and red fire, then a billow of smoke. Seconds later, the low "whrump" of the explosion would echo through the air. Then, as the planes straightened for a second pass, the rubble of the huts would still be smoking.

When it was over, only twisted trees and smoldering sticks would mark the spot where the village had stood. I had been through villages where this had happened. It was easy to imagine what it would be like in those huts below after the air strike.

After the wounded had been sorted out and placed in litters for the long hike to either a Vietcong camp or an American base, the dead would be prepared for burial. They would be placed in rough coffins and the women would wail and cry, clawing at the coffins and spreading tears across the white, unpainted boards.

The radio crackled again. It was a small stroke of luck for the village.

"Sir," said Alpha, "there don't seem to be any planes available right now. However, there is an ARVN artillery battery within range."

The pilot checked the map and located the Vietnamese artillery unit which was located at the base of a small mountain only 3 miles away.

"I guess we'll go ahead with that. Not the same as an air strike," he muttered over the intercom.

The pilot told the operator that he would call the artillery. Then, switching the frequency of the radio, he called the American adviser to the battery. The plane moved slightly to the north to avoid the incoming shells as the artillery unit lined up its direction of fire.

Suddenly, the artillery officer half whispered over the radio, "On the way, over."

The first round was short of the village. A spout of water leaped skyward as the shell exploded in a rice field. By now, the villagers realized what was happening. They had disappeared from the paths and the fields. The village was as deserted as the burned-out hamlets we had seen earlier in the afternoon. What was a bustling village only twenty minutes before was now an empty series of brown huts and green fields.

The pilot radioed corrections and a few minutes later the artillery officer said again: "On the way, over."

The second time, four shells landed simultaneously as the entire battery fired from the mountain base. Two rounds scored directly. A flash of fire and cloud of smoke rose up from the spot where a hut had stood. The other two shells burst in a nearby field.

In the next ten minutes, the artillery unit poured thirty-five rounds of the high explosive 105mm. shells into the village. Many of the shells exploded in nearby fields and only three or four huts were destroyed.

Finally the pilot called over the radio. "Okay, that will do it."

On the intercom, he muttered, "This ARVN artillery isn't worth a damn. With an air strike I could have put bombs within 20 feet of any spot in the village."

When the artillery had finished, the pilot circled once more over the village. Then in a final dive to 1,000 feet, he released two small rockets attached to the plane's wings.

The small plane shuddered from the shock as the rockets were fired, then climbed steeply.

"Hey, I got a haystack; no, two of them." Sure enough, each rocket had hit a stack of dry, brown grass and both were burning brightly a few yards from a hut.

As he started back toward the airfield, the sun was beginning to settle across the distant mountain. The pilot called his radio operator. "How about running over to the mess hall and tell them to hold up something to eat. We'll be back in about fifteen minutes."

"I sure am hungry," he added over the intercom.

Reasons for Policy

5 Mar 67   New York Times, Tom Buckley
              SAIGON, SOUTH VIETNAM, March 4

...In fact, casualty figures are widely thought to have a great deal to do with the tactics that are most frequently employed by commanders here. It has been doctrine in the United States armed forces to use fire-power instead of manpower in Vietnam. The wish to save American lives is based not only on humanitarian grounds, it is suggested, but also on domestic political considerations, since no one can be quite certain as to what the public response would be to several weeks of battle deaths in, say, the 500 range.

This unanswered question, there is some reason to believe, may in part be responsible for the inclination of the high command to continue trying to cope with a guerrilla enemy in largely conventional ways. For example, there are few major operations that do not begin without an aerial and artillery bombardment of the area that is to be attacked by ground troops.

          UPI, Milwaukee Journal, Michael Malloy
          (from Congressional Record - Senate, February 16, 1966,
              p. 3,000; Article entered by Senator Proxmire without date)

The contrast between the suffering farmers and the booming cities is partly intentional. Although officials do not like to talk about it publicly, American strategy is presently intended to force the peasants to take sides or suffer the consequences.

"They can come to the Government or they can go join the Vietcong, but they can't remain neutral and indifferent," a high ranking American spokesman explained.

The Province of Long An, for instance, has 585 hamlets. American aid goes only to the 76 hamlets which are considered pacified and the rest of the countryside is written off as enemy territory. Police confiscate rice, salt, sugar, and medicine bound for these villages.

This kind of economic warfare is intended to keep food and supplies away from the Vietcong. But it also means that life is going from bad to worse for at least half of the population of South Vietnam.

The benefits of American aid go first to the city people, who have always been pro-government, and second to the secure villages, which have never been pro-Vietcong. The peasants in the insecure areas are untouched by the battle for their hearts and minds.

Victor Charlie, Kuno Knoebl, 1967, p. 85

...Once I was present when a village north of Bong Song was bombarded for two days with napalm and demolition bombs; not a house was left standing — yet the Viet-Cong continued to fight back.

27 Jan 66   The Evening Star (Washington), Richard Critchfield
             TAN AN, SOUTH VIETNAM

...Two months after Diem's overthrow, an American-Vietnamese
fact-finding team was sent to Long An Province.
...After interviewing 1,500 peasant families, the team concluded
the war against the Vietcong "cannot ever be won" unless Saigon carried
out drastic reforms at the village level.
Its conclusions were:
Land must be distributed. The local militia must be paid regularly.
The use of artillery and bombs against villages must be limited.
Forced labor had to be stopped. Army extortion and food thefts must
be prevented.
Corruption and bribery must be eliminated among local officials. District
and provincial forces must send reinforcements when they were sought by
village outposts under attack.
These conclusions were pretty basic, yet today most of the troubles
remain largely unremedied.
Local militia are a little better paid and housed, but still not adequately.
Forced labor has been eliminated in most of the country. The introduction
of more armed helicopters, flareships, high-speed jets and more artillery
has reduced the need for ground reinforcements.
But there has been no serious land reform. Bombing and shelling of
villages has multiplied tenfold or twelvefold. Army extortion and food thefts
are as common as ever and corruption is still endemic.

Nov 66   Flying
             Frank Harvey, "The Air War in Vietnam"

(The editors of Flying have declined permission to give the verbatim text
of a selection from the above cited article. The following describes the contribution of that selection.)
(The author here considers the lucky young pilot who enters combat for
the first time in the flat Delta land, is directed to his target by a FAC, and
has little to fear from ground fire. The pilot learns what it is like to napalm
a village with human beings in it. He also gets accustomed to strafing runs
over villages where the villagers are cut down by his guns.
The author witnesses a strafing pass over a village by two jets while no
one is shooting at them from below.)

HUT COUNT

Introduction

25 Feb 65   New York Times, Jack Langguth
             SAIGON, SOUTH VIETNAM, Feb. 24

The United States Embassy disclosed today that American jet aircraft
were sent on air strikes against the Vietcong in South Vietnam during the
last week.
The bombing raids, including one today in Binhdinh Province, where
there is a heavy guerrilla concentration, mark the first use of jet bombers
in the war in the south.
...In the past the bombing raids on which American pilots have flown,
in propeller-driven A-1H Skyraider fighter-bombers, have been officially
described as "training flights."
To conform with the United States' position that its troops here are
military advisers and not combatants, the American mission had maintained
that a Vietnamese trainee accompanied the United States pilot on all flights
in the two-seat Skyraiders.

...Military spokesmen attribute the use of the jets to a change in Vietcong tactics. In the past, they said, there have seldom been assemblies of guerrillas in areas far enough from villages to make bombing possible.

Starting with a battle in the Anlao Valley early last December, the Communists have stepped up their attempt to divide South Vietnam at the southern boundary of Binhdinh Province.

The result would be the separation of the central Vietnamese provinces of Quangtri, Thuathien and Quangnam, the relatively secure provinces that include the cities of Hue and Danang, from Saigon and the southern part of the country.

...Although officials in Saigon would not comment on the probable size of the Vietcong force in Binhdinh Province, American officers on the scene estimated that the Communists had eight full-strength battalions, or about 4,000 men.

...One example of the severity of the problem in Binhdinh has been the experience in the Phumy district. Of the 115 hamlets controlled by the Government in September, only 10 have not been absorbed by the Communists.

26 Feb 65   New York Times, Jack Langguth
                SAIGON, Feb. 25

...Twelve B-57's struck at a Vietcong concentration in Phuoctuy Province, 30 miles from Saigon. It was the fifth day of American jet raids in the province.

...(As American jets dropped fragmentation bombs on guerrillas northeast of Saigon, American military authorities disclosed that the United States jets pounded the Vietcong in three areas of South Vietnam Wednesday, according to a Reuters dispatch from Saigon.)

3 May 65   New York Times, Jack Langguth
                SAIGON, SOUTH VIETNAM, May 2

United States Navy planes from the Seventh Fleet are now participating in strikes against the Vietcong, a United States military spokesman said today.

...In morning and afternoon raids, the eight planes dropped about 50 tons of bombs over a heavily forested area.

Forward air controllers, the pilots flying light observation aircraft over the target zone, reported about 35 structures destroyed. In the wooded terrain, a structure can range from a tin-roofed barrack to a small thatched hut for the storage of rice.

5 Dec 67   New York Post
                WASHINGTON

The U.S. has now dropped more bombs on North and South Vietnam than it dropped on Europe during World War II.

Top Air Force leaders said they found this total "stupifying" but attributed it to the unique nature of the bombing in the Vietnam war.

They said the B-52s, which carry 30 tons of bombs each pushed the total up as they bombed large areas of the countryside instead of precision like fighter bombers.

Unlike World War II when an armada of bombers could level a city, sometimes touching off a firestorm, Air Force leaders said the Vietnam bombing calls for picking away at the same targets over and over in populated areas.

...As of Nov. 15, the U.S. Air Force and Navy had dropped 1,630,500 tons of bombs on North and South Vietnam since July, 1965. This total comes out to:

    About 100 pounds of explosive for every person living in North and South Vietnam.

Over 12 tons of bombs for every square mile of territory in both countries.

Double the tonnage of bombs U.S. dropped furing the Korean War.

Triple the tonnage dropped by American planes in the Pacific Theater during World War II.

The U.S. dropped 635,000 tons of bombs during the Korean War and 502,781 tons in the Pacific Theater during World War II, according to Pentagon figures.

Slightly more than half — about 53 per cent — of the Vietnam War total landed in North Vietnam and the rest in South Vietnam.

Creation of Statistics

Vietnam Diary, Richard Tregaskis, 1963, pp. 342, 343

...This morning, I arranged a flight with a T-28 mission to napalm, rocket, and strafe some VC positions.

...The napalming mission was a neck-snapper. Before the flight began, Col. King introduced me to the two VNAF pilots, Lts. Si and Tham. Both were thoroughly eager-beaver types. Americanized, influenced by the aggressive example of senior adviser Lt. Col. Max King. And they flung their little T-28's around with a vengeance.

I rode with Lt. Si. Col. King was to have flown a third bird in our formation, but his T-28 washed out at the last minute with a mechanical malfunction. A jovial, blue-eyed tall son of the corn who was a B-17 and fighter pilot in World War II, King normally flies the T-28 missions "just about every other day." He told me that he makes the missions with his boys mainly for the sake of morale. "I want the pilots in this outfit to have a high morale, and everything that it takes to make a high morale. I want them to have uniform devices, like scarves and jungle hats, and star patches with tigers in them, everything they need to make them feel they mustn't let the outfit down. And it's the same with having American advisers around. They try harder if the American adviser is along."

...We took off at 10:07, sizzling in the clear heat of the canopy while trapped by the usual mountain of gear, and headed north over what appeared to be scattered farms beyond Pleiku. Abruptly we climbed over a steep green ridge, more than 5,000 feet high. Then we were diving in a breathless pass toward high-ribbed mountains covered with almost solid jungle.

We made nine neck-snapping passes into two separate collections of huts designated as VC villages. It was, as Col. King had said, a solidly VC area: "An interdiction target; No friendlies."

We whirled at maximum speed around the green-ribbed mountains for a good 15 minutes, while the guns stuttered or the rockets arced — two passes during which there was no sound, only the sharp pull-ups, and behind us, the boiling orange flames of napalm devouring the groups of houses.

...We saw no signs of antiaircraft on all these passes, and the raid was a success: Si and Tham filled out the report of 20 structures burned in enemy territory.

3 Mar 65   Buffalo Courier-Express, Lucian C. Warren
            (from Congressional Record — Appendix, Mar 9, 1965, A1053)
            BIEN HOA AIRBASE, SOUTH VIETNAM

"It was," said Air Force Capt. Charles C. Vasiliadi of Huntington, Long Island, upon return to 34th Tactical Group headquarters, "a very fine job. Twenty-nine hooches and there's plenty of those Viet Cong dead over there now."

Even in my benumbed state after going along on a Sky Raider (A1E) fighter-bomber mission and my amazement at finding myself all in one piece, I managed to ask, "What's a hooch?"

The captain explained that it wasn't whisky cellars that were being destroyed at the Viet Cong village 55 miles southwest of Saigon, but native huts of the Communists.

I can personally testify that all of the huts I saw riddled by bombs, napalm, and cannon fire, were indeed in the process of destruction, but I will confess that I didn't find time to count them, even though the chase plane in which I was permitted to ride, made five passes over the area, two at 20 feet off the ground.

...Because this is a civil war, the South Vietnamese insist that on any bombing raids each Sky Raider have one of their countrymen along on each plane.

...For a half hour, Captain Vasiliandi briefed three other American pilots upon their mission of interdiction, or wiping out of an enemy village. Soon after they equipped me with a parachute, Mae West life preserver, and even a .38 caliber revolver just in case.

...At 2 p.m., a small air controller plane joined the group. Its responsibility is to lead the way to the target and mark it.

At 2:15 p.m., the air controller laid down two smoke grenades on the ground, perhaps 1,000 feet apart, indicating the direction of the bomb run.

...The ground rose up swiftly as our plane streaked toward the Viet Cong village. Before it leveled and our plane pulled sharply up, I could see that the first batch of 500 pound general purpose bombs, two with VT fuses that made them burst with shrapnel just above the ground, had done their deadly work and thick, dark smoke was billowing upward.

The dive-bombing was repeated until some 9,000 pounds of bombs, including seven 500-pound general purpose ones, four 270-pound fragmentation ones, four 125-pound fragmentary clusters, and six 20-pound fragmentation bombs, had been dropped.

Then the planes headed back to the base with no casualties and not the slightest nick on any of the Sky Raiders.

...For those who think that we are not winning and cannot win this war, there is a great object lesson in the way our mission was pulled off. The estimates of the killed enemy were not available, but it is reasonable to assume that more than 100 of the Viet Cong were killed in their hooches and foxholes, while not a single casualty was inflicted on our side.

Dec 65   Ramparts
              Bernard Fall, "This Isn't Munich, It's Spain"

...Our "Skyraider" was loaded with 750-pound napalm bombs and 500-pound napalm bombs, plus our four 20-millimeter cannon. Our wing plane carried 7,500 pounds of high explosive anti-personnel bombs, plus our four cannon. We were the lead plane going in. My pilot was Major John C. Carson. The picture shows our wingman flying next to us.

We were airborne for one and one half hours before we reached our primary target. But as we came over the target the monsoon came down with quite incredible force and completely obscured the ground. Then a decision was made, in accordance with established procedures, to switch over to the alternate target which was described as a "Communist rest center" in the Camau Peninsula. A rest center may of course be anything, any group of huts, or it may be just a normal village in which Viet Cong troops have put down stake for, perhaps, 48 hours.

As we flew over the target it looked to me very much as any normal village would look: on the edge of a river, sampans and fish nets in the water. It was a peaceful scene. Major Carson put our plane into a steep dive. I could see the napalm bombs dropping from the wings. The big bombs, first. As we peeled back from our dive I took the picture you see here — an incredibly bright flash of fire as napalm exploded at the tree level. The first pass had a one-two effect. The napalm was expected to force the people — fearing the heat and the burning — out into the open. Then the second plane was to move in with heavy fragmentation bombs to hit whatever — or whomever — had rushed out into the open. So our wing-man followed us in and dropped his heavy explosives. Mushroom-like clouds drifted into the air. We made a second pass and dropped our remaining 500-pound napalm bombs. Our wingman followed. Then we went in a third time and raked over the village with our cannon. We came down low, flying very fast, and I could see some of the villagers trying to head away from the burning shore in their sampans. The village was burning fiercely. I will never forget the sight of the fishing nets in flame, covered with burning jellied gasoline. Behind me I could hear — even through my padded flying helmet — the roar of our plane's 20-millimeter cannon as we flew away.

Behind us flew a small, very dainty-looking aircraft, an OF-1, other-wise referred to as a "bird dog." It is a spotter plane — used to find tar-gets for the bombers and to determine whether the targets have been hit and — as the word goes in Vietnam — award you your "score". The "score" is usually worked out in numbers of structures hit and numbers of people seen dead on the ground. This information is reported to Air Intelligence, and eventually becomes part of the composite "score" for the week (the number of sorties flown plus what is called the "structure count" and the "body count.") These are the terms by which success is measured in the new Vietnam war.

There were probably between 1,000 and 1,500 people living in the fish-ing village we attacked. It is difficult to estimate how many were killed. It is equally difficult to judge if there actually were any Viet Cong in the village, and if so, if any were killed.

...During our attack probably ten to fifteen houses were hit. There is at least one family per house, and Vietnamese families average from six to eight persons. In each of these houses there must have been people maimed or killed — no one knows how many. I read an official report later which described the village as a Communist rest center, and said it had been successfully destroyed.

Indiscriminate Usage

5 Sep 65   New York Times, Charles Mohr
            SAIGON, Sept 4

In Kien Hoa Province south of Saigon, on Aug. 16, United States air-craft accidentally bombed a Buddhist pagoda and a Catholic church.

The Buddhists could not have been surprised, although two of them were terribly burned by napalm, because it was the third time their pa-goda had been bombed in 1965. A temple of the Cao Dai religious sect in the same area has been bombed twice this year.

In another delta province there is a woman who has both arms burned off by napalm and her eyelids so badly burned that she cannot close them. When it is time for her to sleep her family puts a blanket over her head.

The woman had two of her children killed in the air strike which maimed her last April and she saw five other children die. She was quite dispassionate when she told an American "more children were killed be-cause the children do not have so much experience and do not know how to lie down behind the paddy dikes."

...Although the daily air raids against North Vietnam have received most of the public attention, the ever increasing ferocity of aerial bombard-ment in South Vietnam may have a much greater ultimate effect on the out-come of the guerrila war here. Few Americans appreciate what their na-tion is doing in Viet Nam with air power.

The statistics give some meager measure of the effort.

The U.S. Air Force says that during August it destroyed 5,349 "struc-tures" or buildings and damaged 2,400 others. Thousands of more huts and buildings were knocked out by naval and marine air attacks. Although the exact figure is classified, the Air Force, Navy, Marines and South Vietnamese Air Force is now flying more than 11,000 sorties a month in contrast to about 2,000 in January.

The Air Force has not publicly released the figure, but it believes it has accounted for more than 15,000 "confirmed" kills since the first of the year.

"We are flying more sorties in this country that we did in Korea," an Air Force combat officer said.

But the statistics do not reflect the policy dilemma and the growing, although still muted, controversy over "in country air strikes."

...There is no criticism of traditional "close air support" — air strikes staged to assist ground troops who are engaged in combat with the enemy. In this role, fighter-bombers have done magnificent work and earned the fervent admiration of the ground troops. They have also saved many American and Vietnamese lives from an armed, determined enemy.

The real question involves the growing use of air to harass and interdict suspected Vietcong troop concentrations, buildings and transport. This amounts to strategic bombing with fighters against targets which are strategic only in the relative terms of a guerrilla war (somewhat like the Russians bombing Johnson City, Tex.).

But this is strategic bombing in a friendly, allied country. Since the Vietcong doctrine is to insinuate themselves among the population and the population is largely powerless to prevent their presence, no one here seriously doubts that significant numbers of innocent civilians are dying every day in South Vietnam.

...It used to be an accepted principle that a guerrilla war cannot be won without winning "the hearts and minds of the people," although some American officials will now bluntly say that "this is no longer relevant." To many American soldiers and officials here the principle still stands and they are agonizingly worried that while the U.S. is disrupting the Vietcong it may also be digging its political grave in Vietnam with 750-pound bombs.

Already more than 5 per cent of the population has fled into refugee camps. Although it is popular among Washington officials to say that the refugees are fleeing from Vietcong terrorism, some officials on the scene are quite willing to concede or even to volunteer that the majority are fleeing from the insecurity of the countryside and that air strikes are the largest single cause of that insecurity.

One army officer with considerable experience cringes when he reads the communiques listing dozens of "Vietcong sampans" sunk by bombs. He asks: "Don't they know the sampan is the bicycle of the Delta? You cannot just go around sinking sampans in this country."

No weapon is intrinsically bad in war (napalm is one of the very best), so a sophisticated understanding of the problem depends on some knowledge of the process called "target selection."

Distressingly, the whole air strike process follows a circular path which begins and ends with "agent reports" or the words of pro-Government Vietnamese intelligence agents operating in areas either controlled by or disputed by the Vietcong.

The agents report the presence of, say, a Vietcong platoon in an area. Hours or a day later the Vietnamese province chief may approve an air strike — a period which does not include the time it took the agent to walk or to bicycle to a Government headquarters. Some Americans believe that most agents are unreliable and most field advisers think that many often are.

The air strike itself is directed and controlled by forward air controllers called "FAC's," flying low in single-engine Cessna airplanes, and they are unquestionably very skillful in marking targets and telling pilots where to drop their bombs.

They are not infallible, however. The Catholic church stuck in Kien Hoa last month was not only outside the strike zone but had been specifically pointed out to the FAC, sources said.

When the strike is over the forward air controllers can do a good job of reporting on buildings destroyed or burning, but it is much more difficult for them to count bodies, especially those of real guerrillas holed up in shelters. Thus final strike evaluation depends in great measure on a report by the same "agent" who helped to originate the strike in the first place.

Aerial photography and classified electronic machines also play a role in target selection. Moreover, scores of "free strike zones" have been declared around South Vietnam. One Air Force officer estimates they cover about 5 per cent of the nation's area. In these zones, which are longtime Vietcong strongholds or enemy-infested wilderness, pilots can bomb at will and often use them to drop unexpended ordnance with which they do not want to land.

...Responsible sources said this week that no single command question is receiving so much concentrated attention at U.S. Headquarters here as the question of how to apply American power effectively but selectively.

...Col. John Groom, deputy, of the Tactical Air Control Center which controls air strikes, said, "The question is — how do we know that man on the ground is a Vietcong? It all depends on working with really good intelligence and we are doing our best. We do not make any preplanned strikes without the approval of the Vietnamese province chief."

Groom's humane thoughtfulness is apparent to a questioner. But another Air Force officer says, "Yes, we get the province chief's approval to get in and hit targets."

One officer will say, "It is not only wrong but silly to kill civilians or to hit any target which does not have military value, and that certainly does not apply to a civilian hamlet."

But another field-grade officer will say, "The Vietcong are not hard to find. The problem is that they hole up in these people-targets. I think we are going to have to give up our inhibitions about hitting people-type targets. The people will have to learn that if they are going to cohabit with the Vietcong they will get bombed."

...A civilian observer recently flew in an O-1 observation plane to watch two air strikes from a close-up grandstand seat. One left an apparently empty patch of jungle smoking from napalm. "There is no way to know whether we accomplished anything except through agent reports." said a pilot

The other strike involved four Navy planes which slammed a typical elongated delta hamlet with its houses strung out along a canal near Phuong Hiep in the Mekong rice bowl. Rockets flashed as they struck in a path hundreds of yards long and the deadly surf of napalm splashed through the village. There were also big, general purpose bombs.

"I wonder if any civilians were killed?" a pilot was asked. "Who the hell knows?" was the answer.

Vietnam in the Mud, James Pickerell, 1966, pp. 61, 62

...The daring bombing and strafing missions the Air Force undertake in Vietnam are heralded as vital contributions to the war, but it can be argued that eighty percent of such missions are doing more harm than good. The enemy targets that are available in South Vietnam are nothing like the factories, supply dumps, railroads, and bridges that our bombers so effectively destroyed in World War II and Korea. Viet Cong supplies are widely disbursed in small quantities and their storage areas are almost always impossible to spot from the air. The Viet Cong "factories" of which one hears consist simply of small handoperated lathes used for manufacturing crude weapons, or a couple of sewing machines for making uniforms, and are located inside thatched huts that look like any other peasant huts from the air. As to any roads, railroads or bridges, they are more valuable to us than to the VC and we try to keep them intact as long as possible.

The only real targets are people, but even the slowest bombers are too fast and too inaccurate ever to be sure of hitting the enemy and missing the friendly. There have been a few instances where large groups of Viet Cong have congregated in an area away from the villagers and decided to fight, and in such cases, if government troops are not too close to the target, bombing strikes can be effective, but such targets seldom present themselves and even then air power is no foolproof means to victory.

Vietnam in the Mud, James Pickerell, 1966, p. 59

...Whenever an American newspaper reports that government forces have destroyed a Viet Cong base area, one should know that this means they have destroyed a few thatched huts and several dirt bunkers, which can be rebuilt in a couple of days. If the VC lose one of their bases, they haven't really lost much, as their equipment is made up almost entirely of things they can carry with them when they move, and if the VC must retreat in haste they still can cache a thousand rifles in fifty small holes and be pretty sure most of them will not be discovered before they return.

Aviation Week & Space Technology
(from Congressional Record — Appendix, October 5, 1966, A5132)
Mr. Utt did not supply the date of article

(The following letter was written to the Editor of Aviation Week & Space Technology by an Air Force fighter-bomber pilot currently flying McDonnell F-4Cs in Vietnam. We present it to our readers as the unexpurgated views of a pilot on the firing line...)

...Third, we come to the matter of targeting, the effective use of the available power. When an article reads "structures destroyed" the definition means a straw-thatched hut. "Boat" means anything from a 12-foot one man dugout to slightly larger sampans. "Bridge" means a bamboo footbridge or a pair or logs felled across a stream. "Pack animal" means a water buffalo, cow, or even a pig or goat. Let's face the facts. The VC are not anywhere strong enough to occupy any permanent dwellings, let alone operate any warships in the rivers. Any such would have been bombed long ago.

To be sure, these targets must be hit to keep "Charlie" on the run, but at such cost?

Victor Charlie, Kuno Knoebl, 1967, pp. 271, 272

...The ability to move about freely in their own regions — plus the support of the population, which provides them with lodging and food — were among the sources of guerrilla strength in the first years of the war. But this advantage was lost as the war expanded. The peasants living in no-man's land often refused to take in and feed large guerrilla units because they feared reprisals and bombing attacks. Although American bombings in South Viet-Nam are not as effective as many believe — about three-quarters of all bombs crash somewhere in the jungle without even sending up a smoke cloud — such attacks are powerful psychologically.

The civil population suffers far more from the bombs than the guerrillas do, for the Viet-Cong is trained and accustomed to living a spartan and dangerous existence. The Viet-Cong can retreat to hideouts in the dense rain forests, but the peasants cannot escape the planes; their villages are easy targets and many American pilots prefer to unload their bombs on visible objectives than drop them somewhere in the jungle.

By mid-1966, more than 100,000 houses or huts had been destroyed from the air; by the end of 1966, the number will probably have reached 200,000. In other words, about one-fifth of all South Vietnamese housing will have been razed. Seventy per cent of the destruction is in the "liberated zones" of the NLF.

16 Aug 67   Providence Evening Bulletin (See Note Page 20)
              SAIGON

...U.S. planes flew 340 tactical sorties yesterday over South Vietnam.
Pilots reported they set off two secondary explosions and 11 fires, and destroyed or damaged numerous bunkers and other fortifications.

The Statistics

13 Jun 65   New York Times (See Note Page 20)
              SAIGON, June 12

Fifteen United States Air Force F-100 jets dropped 45 tanks of fiery
napalm and poured 750-pound bombs into a reported Vietcong concentration
14 miles west of Quangtri, a provincial capital 20 miles south of the border
with North Vietnam.

Senior officers of the I Corps feared that the Vietcong were preparing
a major followup to their successful operation in another part of the corps
area two weeks ago.

The pilots reported that they had set fire to an ammunition storage
area, destroying 21 structures and damaging 13 others.

Six other F-100's hammered a suspected Vietcong area with napalm
and bombs near the United States Marine Corps' outer defense perimeter
along the Chulai beachhead, 53 miles south of Danang.

Intelligence reports indicated that one bunker and six structures had
been destroyed and that one concrete building and 14 other structures had
been damaged.

9 Aug 65   New York Times, Jack Langguth
              SAIGON, SOUTH VIETNAM, Aug 8

United States bombers raked South Vietnam this weekend, destroying
hundreds of buildings and killing dozens of Vietnamese believed to have been
Vietcong. The war was being fought chiefly by the United States Air Force
and Navy pilots who were flying more than 250 missions each day within
South Vietnam.

Three of the biggest strikes were in the Mekong Delta, where the flat
paddy fields permit more precise bombing and more accurate estimates of
results than have been possible in the Central Highlands.

...An Air Force observation plane pilot estimated that a strike by four
F-100 jets near the IV Corps area capital of Cantho in the Mekong Delta had
killed at least 40 Vietcong.

The head of the mission, Capt. Ed K. Case of Safford, Ariz., noted
that his planes had caught the Communist force in the open.

"They started running for a grove of banana trees," he said. "We
dropped our ordnance right in the grove."

The jets also destroyed eight huts and sank a flat-bottomed fishing
boat that pilots said was filled with Vietcong. In a second strike near
Cantho, another four F-100's reported having killed at least 10 Vietcong
soldiers while bombing Communist automatic-weapons positions.

...Pilots from the Seventh Fleet also struck near Cantho, killing an
estimated 50 Vietcong soldiers and destroying 25 buildings. The target
of four A-1 Skyraiders was described as a "V.C. concentration" 25 miles
southwest of Cantho in Chuongthien Province.

15 Aug 65   (See Note Page 20)
              SAIGON, VIET NAM, Sunday, Aug 15

...Briefing officers said U.S. and Vietnamese planes, which have been
striking against the Viet Cong daily for several weeks, flew 193 combat
sorties in the 24-hour period that ended at 6 A.M. The pilots estimated
they destroyed 530 guerrilla structures. They said they believed they killed
a large number of Viet Cong, but no figure had been confirmed.

26 Aug 65   New York Times, Neil Sheehan
             SAIGON, SOUTH VIETNAM, Aug 25

...In South Vietnam, the military spokesman reported, American and
South Vietnamese air force pilots flew 181 sorties against Vietcong targets.

Officials estimated that the missions had destroyed or severly damaged
more than 200 buildings said to be occupied or used by the Vietcong and
sunk or damaged a number of sampans.

27 Aug 65   New York Times, Neil Sheehan
             SAIGON, SOUTH VIETNAM, Aug 26

...The air action in the south however continued to be heavy. United
States and Vietnamese Air Force pilots and Navy pilots from Seventh Fleet
carriers flew 262 combat sorties against suspected Vietcong troop concentrations and buildings said to be used or occupied by guerrillas.

Two hundred buildings were destroyed and 125 damaged along with
several sampans sunk or damaged. American pilots alone dropped 175 tons
of bombs.

30 Aug 65   New York Times, Charles Mohr
             SAIGON, South Vietnam, Aug 30

...Marine pilots operating in the northern part of South Vietnam said
Saturday they estimated they had killed 20 Viet Cong guerrillas, destroyed
136 buildings, and damaged 68 others.

Navy planes launched from the carrier Coral Sea flew more than 100
sorties against targets in South Vietnam and estimated that 18 Viet Cong
had been killed, 91 structures destroyed, 60 damaged, and six sampans sunk.

The United States Air Force of late has not reported estimates of
enemy killed, saying such figures awaited further study by Air Force intelligence experts. But as usual it launched a large number of air strikes —
90 in South Vietnam. In addition, the Vietnamese Air Force launched 70 air
strikes.

A military communique said 150 "Viet Cong buildings" were destroyed,
131 damaged, and ten sampans destroyed.

Capt. David F. Pine, 30 years old, of Phoenix, Ariz., took part in a
strike that destroyed 10 sampans and eight buildings on the coast of the
Mekong Delta, 50 miles south of Cantho.

He was quoted as having said: "We hit the enemy at the mouth of a
river flowing into the South China Sea, and we got those sampans dead
center. The forward air controller also gave us a tin-roofed building that
they had been trying to get for a long time, and we laid our ordnance right
on it. We won't have to worry about that building any more."

2 Sep 65   St. Louis Post-Dispatch (See Note Page 20)
             SAIGON, SOUTH VIETNAM, Sept 2

...Other U.S. and Vietnamese planes continued heavy air strikes
against suspected Viet Cong positions in South Viet Nam.

Reporters were told that U.S. planes flew more sorties in South Viet
Nam in August than in any single previous month of the war. The spokesman said pilots made 3,767 sorties, an average of 121 a day, compared
with 3,531 in July. Nearly 8,000 structures were reported damaged or
destroyed in the August raids.

There was no estimate on the number of Viet Cong killed in the strikes.

In the 24-hour period ended this morning, U.S. and Vietnamese pilots
made 120 sorties and reported destroying or damaging 540 enemy structures.

4 Sep 65   New York Times, Charles Mohr
              SAIGON, SOUTH VIETNAM, Sept 3

Air bombardment of rural South Vietnam reached a record pace yesterday as United States and South Vietnamese planes flew 532 missions
against a wide variety of targets.

...Instead, 265 missions were launched in the south from the carriers
Independence, Oriskany and Coral Sea. United States and South Vietnamese
Air Force planes flew 170 missions and United States Marine aircraft 97.
A mission, or sortie, is defined as a single combat flight by a single plane.

Hundreds of buildings and other targets in areas considered Vietcong-
controlled were destroyed or damaged, the spokesman reported.

At the same time, responsible sources reported acute military concern
about the possible political liabilities of civilian deaths in air strikes within
South Vietnam. They said that no command problem was receiving more
attention at American military headquarters than how to apply military
power selectively.

5 Sep 65   New York Times (See Note Page 20)
              QUINHON, SOUTH VIETNAM, Sept 5

...Air strikes against suspected Vietcong areas and installations
in South Vietnam continued at a heavy pace by Air Force, Navy, Marine,
and Vietnamese planes. More than 260 "structures" were destroyed and
145 damaged.

Such structures can be anything from a thatch hut to a plaster-
walled village house to a small Vietcong arms plant. Sometimes they are
even official buildings erected by the South Vietnamese Government but
abandoned because of Vietcong control of the area.

7 Sep 65   New York Times, Neil Sheehan
              SAIGON, SOUTH VIETNAM, Sept 6

...In air action in South Vietnam, United States and Vietnamese aircraft flew more than 300 combat sorties, striking at suspected guerrilla
concentrations with bombs, rockets and 20-mm. cannon shells.

A total of 585 structures, the vast majority of them thatched huts,
were destroyed or damaged. A bridge was destroyed and 17 sampans
were sunk or damaged.

10 Sep 65   New York Times, Charles Mohr
              SAIGON, SOUTH VIETNAM, Sep 9

...Intensive bombing of suspected Viet Cong areas within South
Vietnam continued yesterday with American and Vietnamese Air Force
planes flying more than 100 combat sorties for the fourth day in a row.
In one attack near Tuyhoa in central Vietnam, four American F-100
jets destroyed a total of 80 buildings in what was described as a Viet Cong
supply area but, evidently, was also a Vietnamese hamlet.

31 Oct 65   New York Times, Charles Mohr
              SAIGON SOUTH VIETNAM, Oct 30

...In the Air War, United States and South Vietnamese Air Force
pilots flew 285 bombing missions yesterday and early this morning in
rural South Vietnam, almost 100 more than what was considered a heavy
day six weeks ago. More than 300 buildings were destroyed and 170
others damaged.

12 Nov 65   New York Times, R. W. Apple, Jr.
              SAIGON, SOUTH VIETNAM, Nov 11

...About 550 United States fighter-bombers now operate over South
Vietnam. They are stationed either at Air Force or Marine Corps

bases or on the United States Navy aircraft carrier that manuevers in the South China Sea east of Saigon.

...According to informants at Air Force headquarters here, 1,200 to 1,300 strike aircraft are scheduled to be here by late February or March. The additional planes are to come from stations all over the United States.

...The goal of the Air Force is to be able to provide close air support to American ground commanders anywhere in South Vietnam within 15 minutes of their first request.

22 Nov 65   New York Times, Hanson W. Baldwin
            BIENHOA, SOUTH VIETNAM, Nov 21

...Last January, United States Air Force men, flying with Vietnamese co-pilots, flew 764 combat missions, or sorties; the Vietnamese Air Force flew 1,629.

In October, the sorties had risen to 4,297 for the United States Air Force, 3,021 for the Vietnamese Air Force.

The United States Navy flew many additional sorties.

...Whether this intensive and increasing use of air power is incurring some psychological liabilities among some noncombatants — and this is a debatable question here — it is certain that the in-country use of air power was a major factor in preventing a Vietcong victory last spring and early summer.

Dec 65   Air Force/Space Digest
            Kenneth Sams, "The Air War in Vietnam"

...Song Be was in the southern half of South Vietnam, on the fringe of Zone D, and this was not where the enemy was expected to make his major thrust. The big push was expected in the vast II Corps area of central Vietnam. On May 29, it looked as if this push had begun, on a fifteen-mile stretch of road between the coastal city of Quang Ngai and Ba Gia, a government outpost. Taking advantage of low cloud cover and heavy rains, battalion-size elements of an estimated nine-battalion enemy force, including reported units of the 325th Division, chewed up a government battalion committed piecemeal to an action which began with the ambush of a platoon on a road-clearing operation. In the next few days, heavy fighting raged in the area of the key coastal city of Quang Ngai with a heavy commitment of US air power. Between May 29 and June 4, when the enemy broke off the attack, 661 sorties were flown and some 750 tons of bombs and incendijel dropped on enemy positions. The air action took place despite a low overcast and it continued during the hours of darkness using the light of some 3,000 flares dropped by C-123 and C-47 aircraft. In these strikes, 1,430 structures were reported destroyed and 423 damaged. Airpower laid waste the area in which the enemy fought and an estimated 826 enemy troops were killed, mostly by air.

Dec 65   Air Force/Space Digest
            Kenneth Sams, "The Air War in Vietnam"

...Air activity in September set a new record. VNAF and USAF flew some 6,500 sorties, compared to 2,500 in February when the jets were first released for combat in Vietnam. Navy and Marine aircraft flew an additional 5,000 sorties against the VC. Air strikes in September killed some 1,500 Viet Cong (confirmed by body count) and destroyed nearly 10,000 structures.

...It is practically impossible in the Vietnam environment to get an accurate count on results. Many air strikes are not followed up by ground attack and the enemy always tries to remove his dead and wounded. However, based on conservative estimates, charts show a sharp upward trend in enemy killed by air and structures destroyed by air. In January, there were some 1,000 killed by air, rising to 2,800 in March, and some 3,300 in June. In July, more than 4,000 enemy troops were estimated to have died from air attacks. The number of enemy structures destroyed rose from some 2,000 in January to nearly 9,000 in March, the first full month of jet operations. In July, it climbed to over 10,000 and continued at that number in August and September.

7 Dec 65   (See Note Page 20)
                SAIGON, Dec 7

...The pace of the air attacks on North Viet Nam dropped off with Air Force and Navy planes unloading 31 tons of bombs in 11 missions. But U.S. and Vietnamese aircraft flew 406 strikes against suspected Viet Cong targets in the South and dropped 330 (sic) tons of bombs. They smashed jungle village buildings and sank 14 sampans on the Viet Cong's river and canal supply routes, spokesman said.

Feb 66   Air Force, "The Air War"

...The year-end tally, prepared last month at headquarters of the 2d Air Division in Saigon, shows that during 1965 pilots flew almost 50,000 sorties. Of these, 10,570 were tactical strikes over North Vietnam and 37,940 over South Vietnam, in support of US and Vietnamese army forces. On top of this, more than 1,000 B52 sorties were launched from Guam.
Here are other vital statistics from the 1965 record:
USAF tactical pilots dropped 80,290 tons of bombs. The B-52 tonnage has not been disclosed.
VNAF pilots flew more than 23,700 tactical strikes, most of them in South Vietnam. They used 26,600 tons of bombs.
...In the South, all strikes were directed by the USAF Tactical Air Control Center (TACC) at Tan Son Nhut Air Base, near Saigon. TACC directed all pilots of USAF, the Navy, Marines, and VNAF.
Air Force Forward Air Controllers (FAC), flying 0-1 spotter planes, logged 10,330 missions in 1965. They also flew most of the 22,200 USAF visual reconnaissance flights.
USAF and VNAF strike pilots, hitting targets marked by the FAC, destroyed 80,330 Viet Cong buildings and damaged 44,390. They sank 2,756 sampans. It is estimated they killed more than 20,000 Viet Cong troops in the year.

5 Jan 66   (See Note Page 20)
                SAIGON, VIET NAM, Jan 5

...U.S. Army, Navy and Air Force fighter-bombers pressed the air war in the South while staying away from North Viet Nam on the 13th day of a suspension of bombing as part of the worldwide American drive to induce Hanoi to enter negotiations. Aerial spotters reported Navy planes, in 136 sorties, destroyed an automatic weapons site, a motorized sampan, 119 structures, mostly huts, and some fortifications.

24 Jan 66   New York Times, Neil Sheehan
                SAIGON, Monday, Jan 24

...The pilots reported destroying 55 structures, most of them of the peasant type of bamboo and thatch huts, suspected of housing guerrillas, and damaging 29 other structures.

27 Jan 66   New York Times, Neil Sheehan
                SAIGON, Jan 26

The air war in South Vietnam continued at a brutal pace today. American and Vietnamese fighter-bombers lashed at suspected Vietcong troop concentrations and bases throughout the country with tons of high explosives and napalm.

American pilots estimated that they had destroyed 340 structures, most of them peasants' sapling-and-thatch huts, and had damaged 250 others.

Mar 66   Air Force, "Skoshi Tiger"

Since October 1965, twenty-two pilots of the US Air Force have been flying a squadron of twelve Northrop F-5A lightweight tactical fighters on a variety of missions in South Vietnam in an unprecedented combat evaluation of a new jet aircraft.

The F-5 combat trials were authorized in July 1965 by the Secretary of Defense at the request of the Air Force.

... The evaluation — called "Operation Skoshi Tiger" — was divided into three phases — "in-country" operations at Bien Hoa Air Base, "out-country" missions under simulated forward operating conditions at Da Nang, and a maximum-effort operation back at Bien Hoa.

... During phase one, the 4503d flew 1,600 sorties, delivered 3,000,000 pounds of ordnance, and destroyed or damaged more than 3,000 targets, including buildings, sampans, bunkers, vehicles, antiaircraft installations, and docks.

... The phase-two "out-country" operations from Da Nang occurred during the period when the US refrained from air attacks on North Vietnam, but 4503d crews flew missions against other Viet Cong targets.

13 Jun 66   (See Note Page 20)
             SAIGON, June 13

... Over South Viet Nam, American pilots flew 347 sorties Saturday in support of ground troops, and reported killing a possible 32 Viet Cong, sinking or damaging 15 sampans and destroying numerous fortifications and buildings. Vietnamese pilots Saturday flew 86 sorties in similar strikes.

9 Aug 66   New York Times
            SAIGON, SOUTH VIETNAM, Tuesday, Aug 9

... Yesterday, Air Force and Marine planes flew 406 sorties in South Vietnam. A sortie is a single flight by a single plane.

The planes were credited by military spokesmen with having destroyed or damaged 473 "enemy structures," 12 bunkers, 8 sampans and 7 "tunnel trenches, foxholes and fortified positions."

According to some American advisers to Vietnamese military units, "enemy structures" sometimes includes civilian houses. Once destroyed, they are listed as "enemy structures."

21 Aug 66   New York Times (See Note Page 20)
             SAIGON, Sunday, Aug 21

... In South Vietnam, American pilots flew 433 sorties and reported destruction of 655 huts and 52 sampans. South Vietnamese pilots flew 293 sorties, the spokesman said.

5 Sep 66   (See Note Page 20)

... In other air action in the south, a U.S. spokesman reported U.S. pilots flew 445 sorties — single combat missions by single planes — and claimed destruction or damage of 460 enemy huts, buildings, bunkers and trenches. South Vietnamese pilots at the same time flew 44 sorties.

20 Sep 66   New York Times
             SAIGON, South Vietnam, Sept 19

...The spokesman said that in 10 strikes in the demilitarized zone, pilots reported having destroyed 26 other military structures and started numerous fires.

Sep 66   Air Force, "The Pacific Air Forces"

...The Forward Air Controllers (FAC's), flying the 0-1 and operating with ground forces, have become the USAF trademark for the Vietnam conflict. Working with US Army, Vietnamese troops, and the province chiefs, he locates the target with a smoke marker and calls for strike aircraft.
...Since January, USAF sorties in the South have supported Operations White Wing, Harrison, Lincoln, Garfield, Hattiesburg, and Jim Bowie. In Operation Silver City, during March, 470 tactical strikes were flown. Combined with Navy, Marine, and VNAF air operations, these sorties destroyed or damaged nearly 23,000 enemy structures and over 800 VC sampans. Over 1,700 Viet Cong were reported killed by air during that single month.
In the past twelve months there was a marked rise in the number of air strikes in the South. Over 50,000 sorties were flown from July 1965 through June 1966.
By the end of June, the combined number of strikes flown against the Communists in both the North and South were averaging a thousand per month more than during Korea.
...The Strategic Air Command's B-52's were also a major factor in successful combat air operations in Vietnam during this period. They began flying missions in June 1965 and had flown more than 2,000 by July 1966, dropping a total up to that time of more than 70,000 tons of bombs.

12 Oct 66   The Sun (Baltimore) (See Note Page 20)
             SAIGON, Wednesday, Oct 12

...In South Viet Nam, U.S. pilots flew 386 sorties — individual flights — and claimed they destroyed or damaged more than 475 enemy sampans, bunkers, fortified positions and huts.

Aug 66   Air Force "Skoshi Tiger — Evaluating the F-5 in Combat"

...Approved, upon Air Force request, by Secretary of Defense McNamara in July 1965, the F-5 combat trial was conducted from October 1965 to March of this year. After the evaluation, the aircraft were assigned to the newly activated 10th Fighter Commando Squadron at Bien Hoa Air Base near Saigon. Since then, the unit has been flying daily interdiction and close-support missions, while waiting for the additional F-5's and pilots which began arriving last month. Seventh Air Force reported on June 1 that the eleven fighters in the squadron had flown more than 3,500 strike sorties in both North and South Vietnam.
...A variety of ordnance was carried by the F-5's, the more typical being 500- and 750-pound general-purpose and high-explosive bombs, incendijel, 2.75-inch rockets, and bomblets, plus armor-piercing incendiary and high-explosive rounds for the two nose-mounted 20-mm cannon. Loads ranged between 2,300 and 3,050 pounds.
...The F-5's were assigned to strikes against fortified gun positions, bridges, roads, vehicles, sampans, buildings, and troop concentrations. By June 1, Seventh Air Force had credited the F-5's with more than 450 enemy killed, eleven bridges destroyed, ninety-one secondary explosions, 170 sampans destroyed, and destruction or damage of numerous enemy-occupied buildings and fortifications ....

7 Oct 66   (See Note Page 20)
              SAIGON, Friday, Oct 7

...The U.S. command plans heavy reliance on artillery and air strikes to stem an expected offensive from North Viet Nam across the old demilitarized zone when a shift in monsoon winds brings seasonal rains and fog later this month to that region where North and South Viet Nam collide.

...Artillerymen have fired nearly a million shells in this sector over the last two months. Two thousand air strikes have pounded the Communist positions in the campaign that saw marines Wednesday capture Hill 484 the final objective on a four-mile ridge they had been clearing of North Vietnamese for 15 days.

14 Nov 66   The Sun (Baltimore), (See Note Page 20)
              SAIGON, Monday, Nov 14

...Air Force pilots reported hitting nine structures in a raid on bunkers and a storage area in the buffer zone between North and South Viet Nam. Others fliers reported destroying six enemy structures just north of the demilitarized zone near coastal route 1-A.

5 Dec 66   The Nation
              Desmond Smith, "Saigon: Drowning in Dollars"

..."I'm telling you it's the Godforsaken truth," said Harry, that morning in Saigon, as we ate breakfast in his room at the Caravelle. "We are quite cold-bloodedly razing every VC village in South Vietnam. Operation Wipe Out. They've got about 12,000 hamlets to go and the only hold right now is the terrific napalm shortage."

"Stop it, will you," I said. "This is a war isn't it? People get killed in a war don't they? But that's a good deal different from what you are saying."

"Come with me to Long An in the morning — it's fifteen minutes by chopper — and I'll show you the scorched bodies we left behind on Friday."

"I'm not interested. What's the point?"

"I want you to see what's really going on. Bring the cameras. This isn't a bloody war, it's genocide. The trouble with people like you is that you hate facts. I want you to smell the goddamned facts."

"Look, I don't believe Rusk when he calls the VC murderers, and I don't believe you when you want to prove to me that the U.S. Army is nothing more than Murder, Inc."

"But what I'm telling you is the truth. They've got even bigger plans, including the fire bombing of all of Zone D."

"When was the last time you wrote this story for your paper?"

"You must be kidding! I can't file this kind of story. For one thing, they'd never run it. For another, I'd be called home — back to the financial pages."

9 Jan 67   New York Times, Tom Buckley
              SAIGON, SOUTH VIETNAM, Jan 8

...In the South, a total of 408 sorties were reported to have destroyed or damaged "219 enemy structures, 109 bunkers and 27 sampans."

29 Jan 67   The Sun (Baltimore) (See Note Page 20)
              SAIGON, Jan 28

...Pilots of United States fighter-bombers said they killed 60 enemy soldiers and destroyed or damaged 188 Viet Cong bunkers, huts and fortified huts in 512 sorties. This is not far from the record of 549 such single combat flights set January 13.

9 Jan 67   Aviation Week
              Cecil Brownlow, "Air power Gives U.S. Edge in Vietnam War"
              SAIGON

...In March, 1965, as an example, the Air Force flew approximately 3,000 sorties in the south, dropping 5,200 tons of ordnance. In March, 1966, the figures stood at 15,000 sorties and 16,384 tons, respectively. USAF's highest sortie rate was attained in July when 17,777 were flown in the south with the expenditure of 20,000 tons of ordnance.

7 Feb 67   Toronto Star, Don Oberdorfer
              WASHINGTON

...According to the Defense Department, 225,000 tons were expended in North and South Viet Nam from Feb. 7, 1965, to the end of that year.

Last year, the Pentagon says, 512,000 more tons were delivered by air.

To this, about 70,000 tons can be added for the first five weeks of 1967, at current expenditure rates.

...The United States dropped 641,000 tons on Germany during World War II.

The United States delivered 650,000 tons on Japan and all other targets in the Pacific theater during World War II.

MISTAKES

5 Mar 65   (See Note Page 20)
              WASHINGTON, March 5

A big problem in the mixed-up, no-front Viet Nam war is bombing the enemy without killing friendly forces or civilians.

This was brought to the fore by an incident Monday, and U.S. airmen who flew missions in World War II and Korea wonder that more instances of accidental attack have not occurred in Viet Nam. There are mistakes even on well defined battlefields.

Three U.S. Air Force B57 bombers dropped four 500-pound bombs on a place marked erroneously by a forward air controller on March 1 — and four South Vietnamese soldiers were killed and 15 wounded.

The spot marked was more than a mile from the area in which Viet Cong were believed to be located. An Air Force spokesman in Saigon said the error was made because there were no definitive landmarks in the flat, featureless terrain of the delta region south of Saigon.

An Air Force officer here who has served in Viet Nam shook his head at the contrast there with fighting the comparatively formalized wars of World War II and Korea. In Viet Nam there are no battle fronts, no bomb lines to define target areas, the countryside is a carpet of trees with few roads for guidance, and both the "friendlies" and the "enemies" look alike.

29 Jul 65   The Evening Star (Washington) (See Note Page 20)
              LONG HUONG, SOUTH VIET NAM, July 29

...Two U.S. Skyraider fighter-bombers streaked over the long column of American troops clearing strategic route 15.

The planes, their machine guns firing, unleashed their bombs and rockets into the foothills of mountains believed to be a Viet Cong stronghold.

After the strikes, scouts at the head of the column moved in. Their senses quickened as they saw some figures approaching. The Americans held their fire until they could make out the yellow and brown robes of Buddhist monks and nuns.

Drawing closer, the troops could see some of the robes were smeared with blood. Six persons were being carried in slings. The group made the Buddhist sign of greeting, and the American troops moved forward to help.

The monks and nuns had been in a pagoda that had been hit mistakenly in the air strike. They were in an area through which the Viet Cong moved freely and had become victims of the confusion that often surrounds the war in Viet Nam.

...One woman said the group was gathered in the pagoda and tried to get into prepared shelters, but four were wounded seriously and about 20 slightly. She said there were a number of casualties at the village.

...All the casualties were treated and loaded aboard helicopters to be evacuated to the coastal port of Vung Tau.

The Americans dug in and no contact was reported with the Viet Cong during the night. A massive helicopter lift brought in more troops today after a heavy bombardment and air strikes.

31 Oct 65   New York Times
             SAIGON, SOUTH VIETNAM, Sunday, Oct. 31

Two United States planes bombed a friendly Vietnamese village yesterday, killing at least 48 civilians and wounding 55 more, a military spokesman said today.

According to the account given by the United States spokesman, the A-1E Skyraider fighter-bombers struck the village of Deduc with the approval of the Binhdinh Province chief and of a South Vietnamese military intelligence officer in that area.

However, it was not clear whether American or Vietnamese officers had originally selected the target and planned a raid on the village, which is not far from the major coastal town of Quinhon, 280 miles northeast of Saigon.

...The attack on Deduc was the worst such incident ever publicly confirmed in South Vietnam. However, there have been rumors of even larger civilian casualties in other mistaken air raids, including another one in Binhdinh Province several weeks ago.

...An Air Force forward air controller, flying in a small slow plane, had been patrolling the Deduc area for an hour. He allegedly questioned the target because it was near to the Government town of Bongson.

The forward air controller called an air liaison officer, who checked again with the South Vietnamese officials, and the target was again approved, the spokesman said. The bombing was then carried out.

...Spokesmen here could not say whether ground fire was received — or had been believed to be received — from the village. Nor was it known if the bombing of Deduc was ordered as part of the first Air Cavalry's infantry operation.

...A military committee on air firepower recently reported that only about one such mistake is reported for every 7,000 sorties (a sortie is a single combat flight by a single plane.) But members of the committee also said they did not delude themselves that more, unreported mistakes were not made.

31 Oct 65   (See Note Page 20)
             SAIGON, VIET NAM, Oct. 31

...Forty-eight civilians were killed and 55 were wounded in the strike in which the planes dropped 260-pound fragmentation and phosphorous bombs, which cause deep, excruciating burns. Many of the victims were believed to be women and children.

Both U. S. Embassy and military officials cleared all American personnel of any responsibility. The attack took place Saturday on De Duc, about 40 miles northwest of the U. S. desembarkation port of Qui Nhon.

1 Nov 65   New York Times, Charles Mohr
            SAIGON, SOUTH VIETNAM, Oct. 31

...A Vietnamese officer transposed the first two numerals of a grid coordinate, or map-reading code, thus directing two United States fighter-bombers to the village of Deduc rather than to a Viet Cong guerrilla concentration six miles farther west, the spokesman said.

The planes, A-1E propeller-driven Skyraiders, killed 48 South Vietnamese civilians and wounded 55 with 260-pound fragmentation bombs and white-phosphorous fire bombs.

...Deduc, the bombed village, is near the South China Sea, a little more than 300 miles northeast of Saigon.

...Yesterday, according to the information made available here, a Vietnamese infantry unit drew fire from an area with the map-coordinate location BR 788984 and called for air support.

...Military regulations require that all American air strikes in South Vietnam be directed by a "forward air controller," flying in a single-engine plane much like the pleasure craft that crowd American airports.

The air controller marks the target with smoke rockets or smoke grenades and tells the bomber pilots how to hit the assigned target accurately.

In this case, the controller had already been over the Deduc area and was familiar with it. He questioned the order to bomb because Deduc was close to an important government town, Bongson, and did not appear hostile.

His radioed request for clarification was passed by an American air liaison officer to South Vietnam's 22nd Division. According to a United States spokesman, this officer reaffirmed the map coordinates and again asked for the strike.

The bombing was then carried out. According to a traveler from the area, the pilots were surprised that the villagers did not run or take cover when they approached, as is usually the case in a pro-Viet Cong village.

...Although the latest error was apparently South Vietnamese, according to spokesmen, such mistakes have also been made by Americans. Several weeks ago, for example, American armed helicopters fired bullets and rockets at a friendly village near Kontum becuase of a map-reading error.

In addition, a number of officials suggest that from time to time villages are struck intentionally but in the erroneous belief that they are sheltering Viet Cong troops.

7 Nov 65   New York Times (Section 4)

...The air operation in South Vietnam alone is enormous. During October, pilots of the U.S. Air Force, Navy and Marine Corps and the Vietnamese Air Force flew nearly 10,000 sorties. Giant B-52's, flying from Guam, bombed areas which Government troops never have been able to penetrate. In addition, other planes struck daily at military and supply targets in North Vietnam.

The main problem with the bombing is that it inevitably results in civilian casualties in villages where the guerrillas hide. Sometimes the casualties are accidental; in one of the worst accidents, 48 South Vietnamese civilians were killed last week in the bombing of a village mistakenly believed to be controlled by Vietcong.

9 Nov 65   New York Times
            SAIGON, SOUTH VIETNAM, Nov. 8

For the second time in 10 days, American planes bombed a friendly South Vietnamese village by mistake yesterday.

A flight of United States Marine Corps A-4 Skyhawk, fighter-bombers, presumably based at the Chulai airfield, dropped eight 500-pound bombs on the village of Locthuongheit, 20 miles north of Quangngai, in the coastal region of central Vietnam.

One woman was killed and ten other civilians were wounded, an American military spokesman said today.

...The spokesman said that the strike had been directed by radar and that no forward air controller was in the area at the time.

Newsmen had been told repeatedly that no tactical strikes are made in South Vietnam unless an air controller is hovering over the target in a light plane, but a senior Air Force officer said tonight that some raids using radar were regularly carried out on a "blind" basis.

As in the bombing of a friendly village on Oct. 30, yesterday's error was reported to have been caused by a mistake in geographical plotting. An investigation is under way to determine whether Americans or South Vietnamese made the mistake.

...In addition to technical errors, faulty intelligence from South Vietnamese agents has resulted in a number of raids on friendly villages.

14 Nov 65   New York Times
SAIGON, SOUTH VIETNAM, Nov. 13

An investigation was begun today into the bombing of the South Vietnamese side of the demilitarized zone between North and South Vietnam for the third time in eight weeks.

It was not clear how the error occurred. It sent jet planes, apparently American, on an attack earlier today against the village of Xuanhoa. One civilian was killed and another wounded in the raid.

...An official American statement tonight said that the jets in today's attack were "presumed" to have been American. It said a board had been set up to investigate.

Vietnamese sources said a "number" of civilians and Vietnamese policemen had been hurt and heavy damage had been done. These sources said the police were threatening to desert because of the repeated bombings.

16 Nov 65   New York Times, Charles Mohr
SAIGON, SOUTH VIETNAM, Nov. 15

...Meanwhile, an investigation of the accidental bombing Saturday in the demilitarized zone between North and South Vietnam disclosed that the attack was carried out by three United States Navy jet planes as a "result of a navigational error," a military spokesman said today.

The spokesman said no disciplinary action would be taken against the pilots because there had been no violation of military discipline.

2 Jul 66   (See Note Page 20)
SAIGON, Jul. 2

Eight Vietnamese civilians — seven of them children — were killed and 52 persons wounded yesterday when a U. S. plane accidentally bombed a village, an Air Force investigation shows.

Nineteen of those wounded were reported in serious condition. U. S. Army helicopters sped to the village near Bien Hoa air base, about 15 miles north of Saigon, and evacuated those most seriously wounded to American military hospitals, a U. S. spokesman said today.

The spokesman gave this account:

The accident took place when three U. S. F100 Supersabre jet fighter-bombers jettisoned unused explosives while returning from a mission south of Saigon.

Two of the planes jettisoned their cannisters of antipersonnel bombs successfully over a deserted section of the Dong Hai River, about one mile northeast of the village.

But one cannister from the third plane dropped into the village market place and exploded in a two-room private elementary school containing a teacher and 50 pupils.

One pilot later reported he had noticed that one of the cannisters he was jettisoning apparently stuck for a second before it fell.

The U. S. military spokesman's account came after an earlier report said that all three planes accidentally bombed the village.

7 Jul 66   St. Louis Post-Dispatch, Richard Dudman
             WASHINGTON, July 7

...The other place where statistics are lacking is in civilian casualties resulting from bombing and artillery attacks by American and Viet Namese government forces.

"We don't keep them. Maybe the other side does," said a briefing officer when questioned about civilian casualties in an intensive American bombing and shelling attack in a heavily populated area in Quang Ngai province. The officer had just given precise figures on enemy troops whose bodies had been counted in a subsequent ground sweep.

...Westmoreland warned that "the use of unnecessary force leading to noncombatant casualties in areas temporarily controlled by the Viet Cong will embitter the population, drive them into the arms of the Viet Cong, and make the long-range goal of pacification more difficult."

The directive also said: "With due regard to security and success of the mission, whenever possible the people will be warned of impending air-strikes or operations by leaflets and broadcasts."

But an Army information officer in Saigon says that warnings allowed the Viet Cong to escape and are now given only infrequently.

"We require a report from some Viet Namese official in the area — a province chief or a district chief — that the people in the target zone are all unfriendly," he said. "We give a warning only when we're after something other than personnel, like an enemy ammunition factory, when we don't care whether the people get out or not."

Maj. Gen. James Humphreys, assistant director for health at the American aid mission in Viet Nam, says there are times when there are a great many more civilian casualties than military casualties in this war. He says, however, that sometimes the civilian casualties are less.

22 Aug 66   Newsweek, "A Matter of Probability"

...In one such incident, three U.S. jets flying near the 17th parallel mistook the U.S. Coast Guard cutter Point Welcome for an enemy trawler. Swooping down to strafe the vessel, the planes killed two of its crewmen and wounded four more as well as a British free-lance photographer who was aboard. But the Point Welcome's misfortunes paled alongside those of the Mekong Delta village of Truong Thanh.

Truong Thanh's troubles began when the Vietnamese province chief heard that a company of Viet Cong was sheltering in the village — which has long been guerrilla-dominated. Rather than risk a bloody ground battle, the province chief called for a U.S. air strike. His request was approved by both U.S. and Vietnamese authorities, and early one evening an American spotter plane flew over Truong Thanh to mark the target with a smoke bomb. Moments later, two F-100 Super Sabres flashed in, spitting 20-mm. cannon fire and showering the village with napalm and bombs. By the time the Super Sabres made their last pass, sixteen Truong Thanh residents, including six children, were dead and 124 lay wounded.

...Whoever was telling the truth, there remained a large question about the basic premises underlying the Truong Thanh raid. Many old Vietnam hands argue that there can never be any justification for such action against essentially civilian targets in a war which, by universal agreement, will ultimately be won by the side that enjoys the most popular support. Most military men, however, disagree with that thesis. Asked if it were true that under present U.S. military ground rules in Vietnam incidents such as occurred at Truong Thanh were apt to happen again, the U.S. provincial adviser replied: "Honestly, there is that probability."

27 Aug 66   New York Times, R. W. Apple Jr.
             SAIGON, SOUTH VIETNAM, Aug. 26

The commander of the United States First Infantry Division took pains today to absolve the Seventh Air Force of any blame in the accidental dropping of napalm on his troops.

...General Dupuy, a brisk, wiry soldier with a reputation for candor and articulateness, said at a press briefing in Saigon:

"I want to make it clear that the First Division called in the air strikes close because this was close combat. This is a rough business. When you're only off by 50 meters and the planes are going 150 or 200 miles an hour, these things are going to happen."

28 Sep 66   The Evening Star (Washington)
             HON BA, VIETNAM

Survivors of the tiny Montagnard village of Hon Ba, many of them stunned, some weeping, poked around today in the ruins of their homes — left in smoking ruins by a mistaken air strike.

U.S. Marine jets, after a different target, unloaded their 500-pound bombs on the village yesterday. The bombs left 35 dead, 16 wounded and leveled 120 homes, about three-fourths of the village.

The thatched huts caught fire and many that were not leveled by the bombs burned. A brisk wind spread the blaze.

...A young man sat amongst the ashes of his home and wept deep sobs that shook his body.

An American adviser from the nearby outpost commented: "Looks like he's lost everything: his house, his wife, his kids."

At the edge of another flattened hut a young woman nursed a baby. Other children played around the smoking ruins.

...U.S. Marine helicopters dropped off loads of rice, wheat, clothing, cooking utensils — and brightly painted coffins for the victims.

...An investigation is being conducted into how the Marine planes plastered the little place just seven miles southwest of Quang Ngai City.

The Montagnards at Hon Ba, many of them refugees, were known to have been loyal to the government.

30 Sep 66   (See Note Page 20)
             WASHINGTON, Sept. 30

...The latest incident came Tuesday when officials said two Marine pilots apparently overshot their targets and bombed a hamlet in northern South Viet Nam, killing 35 persons and injuring at least 17.

Officials said funds for the solatiums have been appropriated as part of the Defense Department budget since 1959. But before then, one officer said, "The officers and men got together and passed the hat to aid families they thought needy."

Officials stress, however, that the payments in no way constitute an admission of fault on the part of the United States for the incidents. Nor do they preclude claims by the injured relatives of the victims.

One general said the question of solatiums "really isn't important. We have a large-scale multibillion dollar claim program in South Viet Nam that accomplishes more than anything we pay in solatiums."

30 Sep 66   (See Note Page 20)
             WASHINGTON, Sept. 30

...Defense Department statistics indicated 11 misdirected U.S. attacks in South Viet Nam since July 1 have caused the deaths of at least 166 Vietnamese civilians and injuries to 252 others.

...A breakdown showed that airplanes have been responsible for eight of the misdirected assaults, artillery for two of them and helicopters for one.

28 Oct 66   New York Times
             SAIGON, SOUTH VIETNAM, Oct. 27

...Ground action has remained generally light over the last 24 hours, but a patrol of United States First Infantry Division soldiers killed eight South Vietnamese civilians and wounded seven when they mistook them for Vietcong early this morning.

A United States military spokesman said the infantrymen detected the civilians about eight miles north of Saigon at 4:15 A.M. walking "without lights or noise." The Americans, and a South Vietnamese National Police-man with them, concluded that "they must be V.C. (Vietcong)," the spokesman said. He said the civilians appeared to have been violating a dawn-to-dusk curfew.

...Earlier a similar patrol 10 miles east of Saigon killed three Vietcong and destroyed a sampan.

1 Dec 66   New York Times, Jonathan Randal
             SAIGON, SOUTH VIETNAM, Nov. 30

American artillery killed 3 South Vietnamese civilians and wounded 14 others today in an accidental shelling of a village 20 miles northwest of Saigon.

...First reports indicated the incident resulted from an error in firing data, and the spokesman said an investigation had started.

The spokesman said that "disciplinary action will be taken." In the past in similar incidents announcement of disciplinary action has been made only after the investigation established negligence.

Accidents involving the deaths of civilians generally have been written off as part of the nature of warfare.

3 Mar 67   UPI, Robert Kaylor
             LANG VEI, VIETNAM

...Grim-faced American ordnance experts probed meticulously through the ruins of wood and bamboo houses searching for a clue to the identity of the two planes that wiped out 70 percent of the village and left an estimated 100 dead and more than 200 others wounded.

The attack on the friendly village of 2,000 persons — apparently by either American or South Vietnamese planes — was the most tragic such incident of the War.

American Special Forces Capt. John J. Duffy of San Diego, Calif., stood in his hilltop camp Thursday and watched the two dark, delta-wing jets as they swept toward the peaceful village below.

It was getting dark and the planes' dark color made it impossible to see any markings but Duffy and the other Special Forces soldiers who watched knew they were friendly. U.S. jets often flew over Lang Vei from Laos, which is less than two miles away.

As Duffy watched, the dead plane wiggled its wing in the pilot's gesture of recognition.

Then it opened up with 20mm cannon.

Duffy said he thought they were firing at the camp and he ordered his men into bunkers. During the next 25 minutes, he and his men huddled in the bunkers as the planes made two more passes.

On the second one, the jets dropped what seemed to be 500-pound bombs. Two landed within the camp perimeter and a Vietnamese trooper who was trying to fire a flare to end the attack was killed.

Four CIDG (Civilian Irregular Defense Group) troops were also killed.

Most of the ordnance, including the deadly anti-personnel CBUs (Cluster Bomb Units), fell in the village.

Duffy said no American air strikes were planned and no air was "on call" within 10 kilometers of the village.

An Air Force explosive expert on the scene Saturday said fragments of the bombs found in the village were "definitely CBUs." He would not go further toward positively identifying the ordnance.

When Duffy and his men headed for their bunkers during the attack, many of the Bru tribesmen, one of the many Montagnard tribes in South Vietnam, were running for theirs. They got caught in the open by the cannon and bombs.

Duffy and his men could see the flaming village and they ran to help. The bomb bits had delayed fuses and they were still exploding.

"Bodies were all over the place," he said. "It was difficult to get in because of the intense heat.

"Many of the people were in bunkers and when the village started burning they suffocated," he said.

Duffy said the people would not come out of the bunkers.

"We had to physically drag them out."

4 Mar 67   World Journal Tribune (See Note Page 20)
             LANG VEI, VIET NAM

Some sifted the ashes that had been their homes. Others gathered around American servicemen who were distributing food and clothes. And some hid fearfully in the jungle.

This was Lang Vei this afternoon, less than 48 hours after two as yet unidentified jets screamed overhead dropping bombs, launching rockets and firing cannons that villagers say killed at least 100 Vietnamese civilians and wounded 175 more.

...Army Capt. John J. Duffy of San Diego pointed to mounds of fresh dirt covering graves and showed where earthen bomb shelters caved in on those who cowered inside.

...U.S. officials are unable yet to say whose aircraft bombed the village just before dark Thursday.

Duffy said many of the village's 2,500 residents fled their burning homes. Some still are hiding in the jungle that blankets the mountain around Lang Vei, 12 miles south of the demilitarized zone separating North and South Viet Nam.

..."There is no animosity toward us." Duffy noted as he wandered through the remains of the village returning waves right and left from the villagers. "They know we didn't call in the air strike. Their assumption is that they were Viet Cong aircraft."

4 Mar 67   (See Note Page 20)
             SAIGON, Mar. 4

...Photographs made at Lang Vei following the attack showed few large bomb craters. But massive devastation of shacks, trees and underbrush indicates that anti-personnel weapons of the type used by the United States in North and South Vietnam and Laos were involved. The U.S. weapons leave almost total devastation over an area the size of three football fields for each cluster used.

12 Apr 67   World Journal Tribune (See Note Page 20)
              SAIGON, April 12

The U.S. Air Force has reprimanded three of its pilots, docked their pay and temporarily grounded them for the worst bombing mistake of the Viet Nam war.

...The board of inquiry said the bombing mistake was "inadvertent and the result of navigation errors." It ordered the disciplinary measures against the flight leader and the two co-pilots who were responsible for navigation. The other pilot was cleared.

...This was the first report of disciplinary action taken against U.S. personnel responsible for a bombing mistake in the Viet Nam war. About a dozen such incidents have been reported, with about 500 casualties.

The bombed village was packed with refugees who had fled from Communist-controlled areas. The strike was aimed at a U.S. special forces camp overlooking Lang Vei in the mistaken belief it was a Communist fortification.

Both the two-seater F4C Phantoms dropped anti-personnel cluster bombs which missed the camp and fell into the nearby village.

24 Oct 67   Providence Evening Bulletin (See Note Page 20)
              SAIGON

...In a delayed report, the U.S. Command disclosed that U.S. gunship helicopters killed 17 vietnamese civilians by mistake and wounded 23 more in the Mekong Delta last Thursday.

The helicopters attacked a treeline along a canal from where they reported receiving gunfire. A spokesman said the gunships fired at the request of a South Vietnamese regimental commander who said his troops were receiving enemy fire. The spokesman said the incident occurred at dusk and the helicopters were unaware of two small hamlets in the area.

10 Aug 67   New York Post (See Note Page 20)
              SAIGON

Forty Vietnamese civilians were killed and 36 wounded by a U.S. Army helicopted returning enemy ground fire in the Mekong Delta, the U.S. Command announced today.

...The command said the civilians were killed nine days ago when a helicopter gun crew, supporting a militia outpost that was being overrun about 70 miles south of Saigon, "received permission to return enemy fire being received from a large group."

Field reports said the civilians were in a crowd of peasants returning from the rice fields and that a Viet Cong force mingled with them as it withdrew after overrunning a government outpost.

The command's announcement said "a report was received stating that a number of civilians were in the group from which the fire had originated. Forty Vietnamese civilians were killed and 36 wounded."

The command added that enemy casualties were unknown and an investigation was being made.

HELICOPTERS

2 Feb 65   New York Times (See Note Page 20)
              WASHINGTON, Feb 1

The tactics taught to Communist guerrillas in South Vietnam to shoot down United States planes are being countered successfully by saturation rocket and machine-gun firing plus a bit of deception, military experts said today.

...American experts said a prime method of breaking up Red guerrilla groupings is to send in armed helicopters and planes to fire salvos of rockets and machine-gun bullets around areas picked for landings by helicopters carrying South Vietnamese assault troops.

...One tactic is to send out a single machine in advance, and if it is fired on it can radio for armed helicopters and fighter-bombers and send word to divert troop-carrying helicopters away from the danger zone.

Another method is to send out small formations of troop-carrying, armed helicopters to draw ground fire. The decoy formation then summons aircraft with heavy fire-power to blast at the positions of the Vietcong who have exposed themselves.

28 Jun 65   New York Times, Jack Raymond
             BIENHOA, SOUTH VIETNAM, June 25

United States Air Force and Army pilots at the air base here have
teamed up in a three-plane battle tactic that, with the characteristic
ebullience of military professions, they call "hunter-killer operations."

The tactic, directed against Vietcong forces hidden in jungles, involves
these steps:

An Army helicopter scours the countryside in search of hide-outs. An
Army or Air Force light observation plane hovers behind and above to
act as "forward air controller." Lingering out of sight are Air Force
fighter planes, either jets or propeller-driven Sky-raiders.

As the helicopter nears guerrilla territory, it draws ground fire,
usually from machine guns near Vietcong bases. The helicopter drops a
flare and swoops out of harm's way. The forward air controller in his
observation plane drops sulphur and smoke bombs into the vicinity of the
ground fire.

At the same time, the forward air controller, in radio contact with the
helicopter and the waiting "killer planes," orders the lurking fighters to
attack.

The fighter-bombers swoop into the target zone and bomb and strafe
the base.

"We also call it 'skunk hunting,'" said Capt. John S. Lynch an Air
Force officer from Norfolk, Va.

...He added: "Day in and day out, whenever the weather permits —
and sometimes even when the weather is foul — we go skunk hunting. 'We
are going on a skunk hunt,' the squadron commander will say, and everyone answers, 'Roger.'"

The Vietcong forces have developed effective camouflage techniques
in the thick jungle. After one "hunter-killer" raid, South Vietnamese
ground troops scouring the area found what was virtually a four-lane highway. It could not be seen from the air because of the trees.

To insure that the raids will hit their intended victims, the Army and
Air Force pilots rely on South Vietnamese province chiefs to designate
regions presumably inhabited by Vietcong guerrillas. In these regions,
military officials are declared free to carry out bombing-and-strafing
operations without specific civilian approval.

Then the South Vietnamese military commander in each of the army's
four corps areas, with the assistance of United States advisers, may call
for air attacks against presumed Vietcong supply depots or military strong-
points.

Army HU-1B helicopters, known as "Hueys," first skim over the trees,
patrolling fog-filled valleys and daring the guerrillas to betray themselves.

"We are on 24-hour alert for these operations," said Capt. Charles C.
Vasiliadis of Huntington, L.I. He and a fellow fighter pilot, Capt. Don R.
Hood of Salt Lake City, were resting in an air-conditioned trailer at the
Bienhoa base after a morning action.

"We have to react quickly," he added. "We were told today that there
was a large body of Vietcong, probably remnants of forces that fought at
Dongxoai. So we went out with the helicopters in the lead and the forward
fire controller in his light plane and launched a search-and-attack operation.

"It was a pretty thick carpet of jungle they led us to. The overcast
was 1,700 feet, and not much room for maneuver. We got the signal to go
in, saw smoke trails left by helicopter smoke shells and, let me tell you, I
know there are Vietcong in there, because we drew plenty of ground fire."

23 Apr 65   Time

...Warrant Office Christopher G. Hunt, 21, of San Jose, Calif., an
Army helicopter pilot, currently operates out of Saigon airport, flying
either a UH-1B "Huey," which staggers into the air carrying 6,000

rounds of machinegun ammunition and 14 rockets, or a "Hawg," a version of the Huey, which packs 48 rockets.

...Hunt's biggest moment came two weeks ago, when he led a "skunk hunt" for a suspected Viet Cong supply depot about 60 miles northwest of Saigon. "We were lucky," says Hunt. "One of our guys just happened to come in at a proper angle, and he caught a glimpse of something under the trees. He drew fire, so we all went to have a look." It was quite a look: the area was alive with Viet Cong. Hunt and his outfit marked the targets with smoke rockets and called in Vietnamese and American planes, which destroyed 21 Viet Cong trucks, five large ammunition dumps, 43 Communist-occupied houses, and an estimated 2,000 tons of rice — "enough to feed 25,000 guerrillas for a year."

Jun 65   Air Force
              Jerry Greene "Air Power's Buildup in Vietnam"

...They have invented a dandy new game out here recently called "Hunter-Killer." A helicopter or an observation aircraft will drift along at low level to draw fire from enemy positions. This is the best known way of "finding" such emplacements. When "found", the snooper marks the spot, yells for help, and gets out as best and as fast as he can, while a swarm of loitering Skyraiders dives for the target.

15 Aug 65   New York Times (See Note Page 20)
              WASHINGTON, Aug 14

...General Westmoreland's order is specific on the latter point:

"(A) Discriminate use of artillery and weapons capable of mass casualties. Firing on targets in populated areas should be restricted whenever possible to close support missions and to clearly identifiable targets.

"(B) Reconnaissance by fire should be resorted to only when other means of reconnaissance are not possible and when it is essential to safe movement." ("Reconnaissance by fire" is firing into an area to flush out hidden enemy.")

The general told his commanders that they should "frequently impress upon your troops the need for prudence and good judgement in the employment of firepower."

Victor Charlie, Juno Knoebl, 1967, p. 210

...Meanwhile the 1st Air Cavalry mopped up an area stretching thirteen miles north from Bong Son. In the north, the Marine Corps began Operation Double Eagle on the coast. I flew back to the combat zone with five heavily armed GI's. Our helicopter squadron flew high at first, about 300 feet, but when we neared the target, the planes descended to a few yards above the tree tops. The advantage of this tactic is clear: The Viet-Cong hear the copters, yet they cannot see them until they are just overhead.

We flew over rice fields filled with black-clad peasants wearing cone-shaped hats. They did not acknowledge our presence but just stood there.

Before, the guerrillas had urged the peasants to flee as soon as a plane or helicopter appeared. The peasants had run, and the air gunners, believing they were fleeing guerrillas, shot at them. Hundreds had been killed in the first years of the war, especially in the delta, because of such misunderstanding. But the Viet-Cong had learned from these incidents and told the peasants what to do. They now stand still when a plane approaches; their best defense is no defense.

We flew in a wide arc over the paddies. Suddenly a machine gun in one of the helicopters near us began to hammer away. Our gunners immediately opened fire too. Then I saw two men below trying to reach the protecting embankments dividing the fields. We were about ten yards above them. They sank to their knees in the slime and could scarcely move; desparately they paddled the water with their hands trying to advance faster. They took a few more steps and fell; one tried to get up, collapsed, and sank into the mud.

The two dark specks lay below us in the gray water. Peasants who had made a thoughtless motion? Guerrillas who had tried recklessly to stop the approaching armada in its flight? Local partisans who had lost their nerve? I did not know. Two nameless dead. The peasants in the fields had continued working undisturbed. The war had worn them down to the point where they no longer showed fear or concern.

3 Dec 66   New York Post Magazine
             Barry Cunningham, "Viet Nam Notebook"

...''One Shot Charley'' gambit calls for guerrillas to lay low outside hamlet tree line and aim pot-shots at passing "Huey" helicopter gunships. Door gunners assume that the fire came from the innocent village. Under "rule of engagement," they unlimber 60 mm machine-guns, plus protruding rocket launchers, guaranteed to level the village.

Condolence award to relatives of civilian victims is 4,000 piastres, or $34.

16 Jan 67   New York Times (See Note Page 20)
             ST. LOUIS

The New Huey Cobra, helicopter to be used in Vietnam has fangs as deadly as its namesake.

The Emerson Electric Company of St. Louis developed the weapons system, which it says will give the 200-mile-an-hour Cobra "explosive fire-power".

The system can fire 400 grenades a minute and up to 4,000 machine-gun rounds per minute at the same time.

19 Apr 67   New York Times
             SAIGON, SOUTH VIETNAM, April 18

Gunners aboard United States Army helicopters killed 50 of the enemy yesterday, an American military spokesman reported.

The helicopter crews also sank 20 sampans, destroyed 34 enemy fortifications and damaged 11 others.

...The Hueys known as gunships carry combinations of rapid-fire machine guns, rockets, and automatic grenade launchers. The gunships are sent out to seek and kill the enemy. They also have the task of spraying landing zones before troops are put down.

Perhaps the most renowned gunships are those in the Ninth Cavalry Squadron of the First Cavalry Division (Airmobiles). Their pilots swing through the enemy-infested Anlao Valley northwest of Quinhon, asking to be shot at, in an operation they call "reconnaissance by fire."

If no one shoots at them, they spray a suspicious mountainside or thicket. When there is a response, the gunships handle the situation or, if necessary, call for help, which is seldom more than 10 minutes away by helicopter.

In other helicopter action yesterday, airmobile division craft armed solely with 2.75-inch rockets smashed 21 enemy fortifications and damaged 11 more.

13 Jun 67   New York Post, Barry Cunningham

...Israel's battle-hardened Defense Minister stressed the differences between the two wars over the weekend by noting how the Mideast combatants had used helicopters solely for arms shipment and casualty evacuation.

While serving the same purpose in Vietnam, Pentagon sources agree, U.S. choppers find their military usefulness chiefly as decoys: to draw fire from hostile villages.

SAMPANS

The New Face of War, Malcolm W. Browne, 1965, pp. 165, 166

... Accidental civilian casualties are much more often caused by the government side than the Viet Cong, because of artillery and air strikes. The usual justification given for this is that if civilians persist in living in Viet Cong zones they have to be prepared to take the consequences. But the consequences can be ghastly.

In the last week of September, 1964, an intelligence report reached a province headquarters in the Mekong Delta that thirty sampans loaded with Viet Cong troops were moving down a nearby canal. Within minutes, the sector commander was on the radio telephone to Saigon, talking to a mustachioed young Air Force officer in the operations room at the Tactical Operations Center. With commendable speed and efficiency, the young officer issued a scramble alert, and within three minutes, a flight of A1H single-seaters was roaring down the runway.

... The fighters found the thirty sampans with no difficulty, and the whole run was duck soup. Within fifteen minutes, every sampan had been blown to matchwood.

It wasn't for several days that the sector chief found out who had been in the sampans.

A trigger-happy field intelligence agent had seen and correctly counted the sampans, but his guess as to what was in them was not correct. They were all civilians, most of them women and children. Twenty-seven were killed and thirty seriously injured. The Air Force announced blandly that it would take steps to avoid a recurrence of such accidents.

But similar announcements have been made after many of the hundreds or thousands of such incidents in the past, and basically nothing changes. The Air Force sometimes saturates areas with bombs weighing up to 500 pounds. Some of them go off immediately, but the others are timed to explode many hours later, presumably after the Viet Cong has come back. Or peasants, who simply think it is safe to return to work. This kind of thing, regardless of whatever tactical advantage it may have, is to my mind little short of slaughter. It is not difficult to conceive of a farmer or his wife joining the National Liberation Front merely as an act of revenge after one of these accidental massacres.

17 Oct 65   New York Times, R. W. Apple, Jr.
             SAIGON, SOUTH VIETNAM, Oct 16

... In other air actions, American and South Vietnamese pilots flew 36 missions over North Vietnam and 324 over South Vietnam. River shipping was a prime target in the South, and 26 sampans were reported sunk.

13 Jan 66   New York Times
             SAIGON, Jan 12

Official South Vietnamese sources said today that American helicopters sank in error a South Vietnamese boat containing civilian passengers about 35 miles northwest of Saigon Saturday.

An official American spokesman said there had been "no basis" for believing that the vessel, evidently a passenger sampan operating on the Saigon River in Binhduong Province, was not a Vietcong boat.

The American spokesman said that the boat had disregarded a 24-hour curfew on river traffic in the area. He said that despite repeated warning

shots across its bow, the vessel "continued on its course and gave no
visual indication of being friendly."

The spokesman said the ship was sunk because it was considered to be
in "enemy hands."

The official South Vietnamese sources said that civilians, not Vietcong
guerrillas, were on the vessel....

14 Jan 66   (See Note Page 20)
            DA NANG, SOUTH VIET NAM, Friday, Jan 14

U.S. Marine jets mistakenly hit four small boats filled with civilians
and government militiamen yesterday and killed or wounded 25 persons, a
Marine spokesman reported today.

The American jets were ordered to bomb and strafe the boat by a
forward air controller who believed the vessels to be carrying armed Viet
Cong near a Marine operation 20 miles southwest of Da Nang. The Marine
spokesman said the sinking was under investigation and declined to give
the nationality or service of the forward air controller. Normally Marines
use their own forward air controllers in such cases.

14 Jan 66   (See Note Page 20)
            SAIGON, VIET NAM, Friday, Jan 14

...Radio Hanoi claimed U.S. planes, protecting the flank of the operation, sank a civilian boat in the Saigon River Jan. 8 inflicting 200 casualties,
but a U.S. Army spokesman denied this. The officer said the boat was a
large sampan without markings, ignored a warning from an armed helicopter
to head for shore, and was sunk. He added: "It was an enemy craft."

Jun 66   Navy
            H. R. Kaplan "The Coast Guard in Vietnam"
            (from Congressional Record — Appendix, July 20, 1966, A3830)

...The patrol function carried out by the Squadron has the intriguing
title, "Operation Market Time". It's a curiously peaceful name for so
dangerous a mission. No one knows exactly how it received its name, but
one theory is that it was derived from the thousands of commercial junks
plying these waters daily. In this part of the world, where refrigeration
facilities are virtually nonexistent, the junks serve as floating markets.
These marine markets have sometimes provided the Viet Cong with oppor-
tunities for smuggling men and supplies into battle zones.

...All that changed on August 23, 1965, While patrolling the northern
end of Phu Quoc island, Markey spotted a junk headed for Cambodian
waters. There was something about her that put Markey on his guard. He
ordered pursuit of the craft, overtaking it. The three men on board were
taken prisoner and turned over to Vietnamese naval authorities. Later
they confessed that they were members of the Viet Cong.

Two days later, on August 25, the cutters Point Mast, Point Comfort,
and Point Clear and a Navy destroyer escort shelled a Viet Cong staging
area not far from the Vietnamese Navy Junk Base at An Thoi. Using their
81-millimeter mortars, firing high explosive rounds, they saturated the
target area.

12 Aug 66   New York Times
            SAIGON, SOUTH VIETNAM, Aug 11

American planes raked a United States Coast Guard cutter with
machine-gun and rocket fire this morning, killing two coastguardsmen
and wounding five other persons aboard the vessel.

...A United States military spokesman said the attack had been
made by two Air Force supersonic Phantom fighter-bombers and a B-57
Canberra bomber.

...The spokesman was unable to explain why the Point Welcome had been unable to identify herself as a friendly ship. The cutter and the planes carried radios capable of using the same frequencies, he said, and there were prearranged light signals for identification.

Although there is some resemblance between the silhouettes of Coast Guard cutters and enemy trawlers, naval officers said, it would be difficult to confuse them in a close inspection.

22 Aug 66   New York Times, R. W. Apple, Jr.
              SAIGON, SOUTH VIETNAM, Aug 21

Gen. William C. Westmoreland, the American commander in Vietnam, has issued an order restricting the conditions under which United States warplanes are permitted to open fire on small vessels.

The sternly worded order is designed to "prevent the recurrence" of incidents such as the one Aug. 11 in which three Air Force planes strafed a United States Coast Guard cutter, killing two crew members and wounding five other people aboard the vessel.

In the future, United States pilots will be permitted to attack only when the coastal surveillance center in the area has identified a ship as hostile or the ship has identified itself by opening fire or taking other offensive action, such as beginning a torpedo run.

...Before the new order, the rules of engagement covering encounters between planes and small boats were extremely vague. In the opinion of most observers, that was the principal cause of the accidental attack on the cutter.

Other incidents of poor coordination between American ships and other United States units have since come to light. Last month, for example, a destroyer was informed by a spotter on the beach that it could open fire on all boats more than 2,000 yards offshore. Only the skepticism of the warship's skipper prevented the sinking of dozens of harmless fishing junks.

18 Oct 66   New York Times
              SAIGON, SOUTH VIETNAM, Oct 17

South Vietnamese Government troops, supported by United States helicopters and river patrol boats, attacked 150 to 200 Vietcong sampans in a Mekong delta canal about 50 miles southwest of Saigon yesterday.

Conflicting reports put enemy deaths at 25 to 147 and indicated that 68 to 121 of the sampans had been sunk. Allied casualties were reported as light, or not serious enough to impair the operation of the allied force.

The higher casualty figures on the Vietcong came from the South Vietnamese. But Americans reported the greater number of sampans sunk.

The Americans estimated that 51 Vietcong died in addition to the 25 they reported, but they said the other bodies could not be found for confirmation.

28 Dec 66   New York Post (See Note Page 20)
              SAIGON, Dec 28

Thousands of South Vietnamese troops fanned out across canal-laced rice fields deep in the Mekong Delta today and reported killing 89 Viet Cong in two days.

...U.S. headquarters said American Gunship helicopters destroyed 174 Viet Cong sampans in the last two days.

30 Dec 66   New York Times (See Note Page 20)
              SAIGON, SOUTH VIETNAM, Dec 29

...Copter gunners, trying to cut down the movements of Vietcong supplies on waterways south of Saigon, said they had destroyed 22 more sampans.

4 Mar 67   World Journal Tribune (See Note Page 20)
              SAIGON, March 4

The U.S. Command disclosed today that six Vietnamese civilians were killed and 26 wounded in accidental shellings by American artillery of a village and a group of river sampans.

... The first occurred Wednesday in Dinh Tuong Province when a U.S. artillery unit accidentally sent 11 howitzer shells into Trung Luong Village 30 miles southwest of Saigon, killing five civilians, wounding 24 and destroying 24 houses, the announcement said. No explanation was given for the delay in the report.

The second took place yesterday in Xuan Loc Province about 45 miles east-northeast of Saigon when an air observer requested and received clearance by the South Vietnamese Army to call in artillery fire on a group of five sampans. One person was killed, two wounded and one sampan destroyed, the announcement said. The persons later were determined to be "friendly."

5 Mar 67   (See Note Page 20)
              SAIGON, Mar 5

... Five sampans were spotted by a U. S. aerial observer on a stream 75 miles northeast of Saigon Friday and, after asking and receiving clearance from the South Vietnamese army, he called in artillery fire. One sampan of the flotilla was destroyed, one person was killed and two were wounded. The persons were later found to have been friendly.

5 Mar 67   World Journal Tribune
              SAIGON, Mar 4

... In the Mekong Delta, south of Saigon, 11 high explosive shells from U. S. Army artillery landed in a friendly village, killing five civilians and wounding 24. An air strike against sampans, approved by Vietnamese authorities, killed one person and wounded two others who later turned out not to be Communists.

31 Jan 66   Aviation Week
              C.M.Plattner, "Limited-War Concepts Weighed in Battle"
              SAIGON

Vietnam is evolving into a major proving ground for limited-war concepts and equipment. Some are proving their worth, but others are being discarded as they break down under the trials of war.

... Three key points stand out in the effort thus far:

*Number of difficult problems, such as adequate detection capability, remain to be solved.

... Problems encountered thus far in the war include:

*Target acquisition. No satisfactory means are now available by which forward air controllers (FAC) can acquire targets at night from spotter aircraft... Viet Cong troops and supplies move largely at night along waterways and roads — or trails — and airborne forward air controllers who closely monitor daytime activities on visual reconnaissance flights have no way of detecting enemy movements at night.

... The problem of interdicting supply routes extending from Cambodia into South Vietnam has been partially solved with two experimental projects, one run by the Air Force, the other by the Army. Both are aimed primarily at cutting down the flow of supplies at night on the Occidental and Vaico Oriental Rivers west of Saigon. The two projects are:

*Army's Lightning Bug Program. This is conducted with Army/Grumman OV-1B Mohawk reconnaissance aircraft and armed Bell UH-1Bs to intercept and destroy Viet Cong supplies and troops moving on waterways where curfews have been established between sunset and sunrise. The Mohawks, equipped with real-time readout capability for their sidelooking airborne radars (SLAR), are used to spot sampans moving down rivers, and armed UH-1Bs are called in to destroy the sampans.

   ...*USAF's Snipe Hunt. This program is similar to Lightning Bug in its goal, and Army Mohawks are used to detect targets. Rather than armed helicopters, however, USAF aircraft are used to knock out the sampans. Vigorous programs coordinated with the province chief are conducted in advance to preclude friendly sampan movements during curfew hours. Fairchild C-123 flare aircraft are called in to provide illumination for the strikes. Douglas AC-47 and A-1 attack aircraft, as well as North American F-100s, are used.

   Air Force officers believe that machine guns are among the most effective weapons for this type of mission and have used the AC-47 extensively in this project.

28 Jan 67   Milwaukee Journal
              SAIGON, VIETNAM

   ...Helicopter pilots reported destroying 33 sampans and killing 44 Vietcong Friday night and Saturday morning while flying the "firefly missions" 28 miles southwest of Saigon.

   On such missions, one helicopter beams its searchlights on the enemy while two flanking gunship helicopters open up with automatic weapons.

29 Jan 67   New York Times, Jonathan Randal
              SAIGON, SOUTH VIETNAM, Jan 28

   ...In the Mekong delta 28 miles southwest of Saigon, armed helicopters fitted with rocket launchers, machine guns and searchlights killed 44 Vietcong and destroyed 33 sampans.

   The night raids operate on the theory that any vessel moving on the thousands of miles of inland waterways after curfew is Vietcong.

30 Jan 67   The Sun (Baltimore), Robert A. Erlandson
              SAIGON, Jan 29

   American armed helicopters early today apparently killed 31 Vietnamese civilians and wounded 38 as they disobeyed the river curfew in an attempt to flee from the Viet Cong to a friendly outpost, according to American officials.

   The incident occurred on the Bassac River, 12 kilometers southeast of Can Tho, in the Mekong Delta, after the copters received automatic weapons fire from a fleet of sampans.

   ...The helicopters fired all their ammunition, returned to base to refuel and rearm, and returned to the area. They spotted a large group of sampans, apparently from the original flotilla, and were fired on again.

   ...Some time during the attacks, reports said, river patrol boats arrived and added supporting fire to the helicopters.

   ...Interrogation of the civilians, they said, indicated that they broke curfew when the helicopters flew over because there were numerous Viet Cong in the area. The villagers said they were trying to reach the safety of the Vietnamese outpost, spokesmen said.

30 Jan 67   St. Louis Post-Dispatch
              SAIGON, SOUTH VIETNAM, Jan 30

   ...The U. S. command continued an investigation of an attack by three U. S. helicopters on a fleet of 200 sampans in the Mekong delta in which a U. S. spokesman said 31 Vietnamese civilians were killed and 38 wounded.

The spokesman said the sampan fleet was attacked Saturday night and early Sunday after some of the sampans fired on the helicopters. He said the civilians told interrogators they were on the move in violation of the curfew because the Viet Cong were in the area and they anticipated Allied attacks.

...The helicopter incident occurred on the Bassac river 78 miles southwest of Saigon. The helicopters received automatic-weapons fire from two positions on the sampans and one on the river bank, a U. S. spokesman said.

The spokesman said the three helicopters were on a reconnaissance mission in an area where intelligence reports indicated that a Viet Cong main force unit was operating. They saw 200 sampans trying to cross the river in curfew hours in which river and canal movement is prohibited.

After expending all their ammunition, the helicopters returned to base rearmed and refueled, and went back to the fleet. The spokesman said they were fired on again and that they returned the fire, stopping when the sampans neared a friendly outpost.

30 Jan 67   New York Times, Tom Buckley
             SAIGON, SOUTH VIETNAM, Jan 30

Thirty-one Vietnamese civilians were killed and 38 wounded during an attack by American helicopters and patrol boats in the Mekong River delta, a military spokesman announced yesterday.

More than 40 American servicemen gave blood to the wounded after they were evacuated to a hospital in Cantho.

...Although details of the attack near the delta village were still fragmentary, it appeared that a "firefly" flight of three helicopters observed about 200 sampans crossing the Bassac River at 11:45 P.M. Friday in violation of a curfew that is in effect from 11 P.M. to 5 A.M.

A firefly flight, used for night operations, is composed of one helicopter equipped with a powerful searchlight and two gunships.

The spokesman reported that the circling helicopters were fired on from the sampans and the river bank. They returned the fire with their machine guns until their ammunition was exhausted, then sped off to get more.

...Questioning of the civilians indicated that they broke the curfew in an attempt to get away from the village when the helicopters appeared. They said they knew there were many Vietcong in the vicinity and feared being caught in the middle during an attack.

They were trying to reach the army outpost when the firing began, they said.

The American spokesman said the area in which the incident took place was regarded as under the control of the guerrillas. Allied forces came under fire there most recently on Jan. 4 and 6.

31 Jan 67   Baltimore Sun, Robert A. Erlandson
             CAN THO, VIETNAM, Jan 30

It was a mistake, an accident, but it was a relatively small mistake in a big war and everyone is sorry.

Nine-year-old Dang Thi Chinh is sorry.

She did not say so today, though. She was too busy writhing and moaning in pain on her hospital bed with bandages where her right arm and leg used to be.

Cao Ngoc Mai is sorry, but he did not say so either. He is only 2 and does not talk yet; he just whimpers in his mother's arms. He had been busy learning to toddle, but he will not toddle from now on; his left leg was shot off at the hip.

Ly Van Chieu, 12, and Vo Van Dang, 6, are sorry, too. Ly is sorry because his left leg was shot away. Vo lost his right hand.

The parents, at least those still alive, are sorry, because they broke curfew and tried to reach the safety of a popular forces outpost on the Bassac River. It was then that gunfire erupted nearby.

But, they said, the Vietnamese troops told them the curfew did not apply on the tributaries, only on the main river.

The American helicopter pilots who strafed the sampans with rockets and machine gun fire are sorry. They thought they were still firing on the Viet Cong who had tried to shoot them down earlier.

And they cleared the free fire order with sector headquarters and got the green light.

It was only when they realized that there was no return fire that they stopped shooting. But by then there were 31 dead and 36 wounded, 13 of them children under age 13, and 12 women. Two boys, aged 4 and 7, died by the time they reached the hospital here, as did another man and woman.

...There is no one in particular to blame for the incident. It simply illustrates what will undoubtedly become an increasing frustration as fighting intensifies with the American build-up in the heavy-populated Mekong Delta.

...The whole area is considered Viet Cong controlled, and the curfew is on from 7 P.M. to 5 A.M. The Americans understand that it applies to all waterways.

About an hour later, the fire team was headed back for the combat area, but while crossing a canal spotted some 40 motor sampans moving toward an allied outpost on the river at the canal mouth.

Captain Beauchamp, an earnest, articulate officer, said he radioed to the sector advisor's office at Soc Trang, expressing belief that it was part of the original flotilla and requesting instructions. After a short break, the team got the authorization and made two strafing passes over the boats, he said.

When there was no return fire, Beauchamp continued, the choppers ceased fire and waited to see what would happen next.

Shortly, the victims reached the friendly outpost where they were identified as civilians.

American and Vietnamese river patrol boats, coming to support the helicopters, rushed the people to Can Tho Hospital. More than 40 American servicemen donated blood.

Maj. Frank Camp, of Worcester, Mass., surgeon in charge of the United States Air Force medical team at the civilian hospital, and other volunteer surgeons worked all night, performing seven major and ten minor operations.

...Under normal operating conditions, they said, the copters do not fire unless fired upon. But since the engagement had been launched in the same area previously, they said they felt Captain Beauchamp had complied with the orders after checking with the Soc Trang base.

5 Feb 67   The Washington Post, Jesse W. Lewis, Jr.
            SAIGON

(The editors of The Washington Post have declined permission to give the verbatim text of a selection from the above cited article. The following describes the contribution of that selection.)

(Since everything that moves on the rivers after curfew is considered enemy by U.S. gunboats, it is difficult to avoid civilian casualties. An example is 4 year old Train Thi Cho whose family was wiped out in their sampan after curfew. Cho herself was not seriously wounded.)

27 Feb 67   New York Times, R. W. Apple, Jr.
                   SAIGON, SOUTH VIETNAM, Feb 27

The United States has begun dropping mines into rivers in North
Vietnam, the American command disclosed this morning.

A terse announcement said that "a limited number of air-delivered
non-floating" mines had been placed in rivers in the southern part of
North Vietnam. The mines, the announcement indicated, are designed
to stop the movement of sampans and junks.

...In explaining today's action, the American command said it had
been undertaken "to counter" increased North Vietnamese "use of waterborne logistic craft to infiltrate men and supplies into South Vietnam."

27 Apr 67   New York Times, R. W. Apple, Jr.
                   ABOARD U.S.S. COLLETT, OFF NORTH VIETNAM, April 26

...Operation Sea Dragon's primary goal, according to the Navy, is
to harass and destroy enemy coastal shipping, mostly barges and junks.

The word "junk" evokes a picture of defenselessness, so the Navy
prefers to call them "waterborne logistic craft," which sounds more
awesome but takes more time to say. Inevitably sailors shorten it to
WBLC.

B-52s

Pattern Bombing

18 June 65   Los Angeles Times
                   SAIGON

A fleet of twenty-seven eight-jet B52 heavy bombers from the U.S.
Strategic Air Command today raided a jungle hideout where the Viet Cong
was reported massing for a sneak attack. It marked the first time these
planes have been used in any combat.

...Using non-nuclear high explosives, the B52s, which roared in from
Guam, hit a target 25 miles north of Saigon, one by two miles in size,
near Ben Cat.

...After the heavy bombers swept over the area, a squadron of B57
twin jet fighter bombers made runs over the target pouring explosives
and firebombs, rockets and cannon shells into the dense foliage and along
streams and clearings.

...High altitude bombers had not been used in the Vietnamese war
before because U.S. Air Force planners felt in general that accidental
civilian casualties are too high in pattern bombing.

Raids over both North Viet Nam and Viet Cong concentrations in the
south have been made exclusively by low altitude dive bombers that can
pinpoint their targets with much greater accuracy. The objective today,
however, was area saturation rather than pinpoint accuracy. The spokesman said the attack had to be carried out as fast as possible over a wide
area to get the desired result.

...Air Force sources declined to evaluate the results of the rain of
bombs. Newsmen who flew over the area after the raid said there was no
sign of damage to huts in a jungle clearing but that no people or animals
were visible. Trees in the area are more than 100 feet tall, making an
accurate damage estimate from the air impossible.

Several sticks of bombs struck near the edge of jungle patches within
a few hundred feet of cultivated rice fields and clusters of houses. Newsmen said there seemed little doubt there were casualties and that many
must have been civilians.

The region around Ben Cat has long been a primary Viet Cong base area. Many large government offensives have failed to dislodge the Communist forces from the stronghold. The Viet Cong has built an enormous system of tunnels and bunkers in the region, which in the past has proved relatively impervious to bombing attacks.

...One report said some shocked women and children were found at the edge of the bomb zone.

U. S. Special Forces men have tried repeatedly but without success to penetrate the area, where a Viet Cong regiment is believed located.

Eyewitnesses said the bombs appeared to be spaced too widely apart to give saturation coverage...

18 Jun 65   The Evening Star (Washington)
              SAIGON, SOUTH VIETNAM

...After the B52s, a squadron of B57 twin-jet fighter-bombers plastered the area with explosives, fire bombs, rockets and cannon shells.

The Air Force declined to evaluate results of the raid until after a careful ground check. Three 60-man units of Vietnamese troops and about a dozen U. S. advisers were sent in to reconnoiter, and an estimated platoon of guerrillas opened fire on one of the units. Helicopter fire helped drive off the Red attackers.

The ground troops were pulled out of the area after several hours. They brought three women and four children with them but reportedly found no bodies.

Informants at Bien Hoa Air Base, 15 miles north of Saigon, said the B52s had missed part of the designated target area.

The Americans returning from the bombing zone refused to discuss their findings with newsmen. But informants said they found mostly foxholes and trenches. They said some craters left by the B52s were 250 yards apart and that the area had not been saturated.

Some of the jungle was burning, but apparently this was from the later strikes by the B57s and Skyraiders, the informants said.

...High altitude bombers had not been used in Viet Nam before because U. S. Air Force officials felt the danger of accidental civilian casualties was too great. Asst. Secretary of Defense Arthur Sylvester told newsmen in Washington that there were no villages within five miles of the target area in today's raid.

AP correspondent Malcolm W. Browne flew over the area and reported some bombs struck near the edge of open patches in the jungle, within a few hundred feet of rice fields and clusters of huts. He said while there was no sign of damage to the huts, no people or animals were visible.

15 Oct 65   New York Times, Charles Mohr
              SAIGON, SOUTH VIETNAM, Oct 14

...Soldiers who examined the scene of an American B52 air raid last Friday northwest of Saigon reported that some of the bombs had dug craters 50 feet across, and as much as 30 feet deep. The bombs collapsed some Vietcong tunnels as far as 200 yards from the impact point.

Another group of eight-engine B52s bombed a suspected enemy logistical and staging base in Binhduong Province, just northwest of Saigon, this morning. It was the fourth B52 raid in the province in one week.

2 Jul 65   (See Note Page 20)
              SAIGON, VIETNAM, July 21

Tactical squadrons stepped up the air war against the Viet Cong today, and 30 B52 jet bombers capped their efforts with a raid at dusk on a red-held jungle sector 30 miles north-northwest of Saigon.

A. U. S. Military spokesman announced the eight-engine B52s, striking from Guam for the fifth time in less than five weeks, loosed 500 tons of explosives "in a program of continuing harassment and disruption of known areas of Viet Cong activity."

10 Nov 65   New York Times, R. W. Apple, Jr.
             BIENHOA, SOUTH VIETNAM, Nov 9

...Suddenly, the platoon on the right, about 50 men, found itself in a circle of mud and thatch huts. The huts were invisible from the air because of the palmetto trees arching overhead and almost invisible from the ground because of the underbrush.

5 Jul 65   New York Times, Jack Langguth
            SAIGON, SOUTH VIETNAM, Monday, July 5

United States Air Force B52 heavy bombers from the Strategic Air Command based on Guam hit early today a suspected Vietcong communications and troop-staging area about 35 miles northeast of Saigon.
...The United States mission statement, noting that this second strike was made at the request of the Vietnamese Government, added: "This was a spoiling mission designed to harass the enemy and to disrupt his operations, facilities and morale."
...The statement on the raid from Guam said:
"The B52s were used because of their unique ability to place heavy concentrations of bombs over a wide area.
"They are especially useful in jungle areas where specific targets cannot be pinpointed for tactical bombing because of the heavy tree canopy."

13 Oct 65   (See Note Page 20)

...Troops of the 173rd Airborne Brigade supported by Australian soldiers ended another big search operation in the "Iron Triangle" 30 miles northwest of Saigon. An Australian spokesman said Viet Cong fortifications in the area had been smashed.
Previously 84 Viet Cong had been reported killed and 115 captured in the jungle area on the fringe of the Viet Cong's D Zone.
B52 bombers from Guam hammered the 40-square-mile area twice before the operation was launched last week. The U. S. spokesman said the bombers devastated much of the terrain and damaged or destroyed 15 huts used by the Viet Cong.

15 Nov 65   (See Note Page 20)
             SAIGON, VIET NAM, Nov 15

First the green valley floor began to tremble. Then smoke rose and orange flames bulged out of the forests. Finally you heard the tremendous explosions of the 750-pound bombs hitting 3,000 feet below.
Then everything fell silent and all the officers in the observation plane could see was the smoke rising and no movement at all on the ground.
...Into an area about two miles by one mile, a score of B52s dropped more than 350 tons of bombs. The U. S. troops on the ground had pulled back just before the bombers flew in at 20,000 feet.
A high-ranking Air Force officer tagged the target perishable and said it was the first time the eight-engine bombers had been used in an effort to knock out troops on the move. B52s have been used in the past in support of ground operations but only against fixed positions or areas where enemy troops were dug in. The planes also have been used many times to bomb suspected Viet Cong concentrations in Communist strongholds.

12 Dec 65   New York Times, R. W. Apple, Jr.
             QUESON, SOUTH VIETNAM, Dec 12

United States marines moved into the foothills of Quangtin Province today in pursuit of a Vietcong force of several thousand men.

On the fifth day of a combined United States — South Vietnamese operation called Harvest Moon, the Marines encountered only sporadic enemy fire. They they closed in on a valley where the guerrillas have maintained a base for years.

...An entire Vietcong regiment and three battalions are believed to be stationed in the area where the Marine Corps men have been operating.

...Earlier Strategic Air Force B52 bombers from Guam struck the valley to prepare for the movement of the marines. It was the first time B52s had provided tactical support for the marines, and General Walt said, "It was thrilling to see how accurate their strikes were."

Late in the afternoon, Brig. Gen. Jonas M. Platt, the over-all commander of marines in the operation, flew into the battalion command post, which is in a temple near the hamlet of Queson.

17 Jan 66   (See Note Page 20)

...Waves of B52s roared out of an early morning sun for saturation bombing runs on an area 10 miles northwest of Quang Ngai City on the central coast. South Vietnamese officials reported that perhaps two to three Viet Cong regiments were in the area 330 miles northeast of Saigon.

Government ground troops moved into the bombed area after the B52 strike and made light contact with the enemy.

No significant results were reported in Saigon.

The operation, planned for several days, was launched in retaliation for Viet Cong attacks on government outposts in the Quang Ngai City sector for weeks. The guerrillas have overrun several outposts in action apparently intended to let the inhabitants know that the Communists regard this as their territory. They have dominated Quang Ngai Province for years.

10 Apr 66   New York Times
             SAIGON, Apr 9

A fleet of United States B52 bombers battered a Vietcong communications center in War Zone D with a single-file attack today. It was a switch from their usual tactic, saturation bombing in formation.

Details announced by a United States Air Force spokesman indicated that at least 10 bombers, stationed on Guam, dropped perhaps 300 tons of explosives on the center, a combination of 10 buildings and various underground works in a jungle stronghold 35 miles north of Saigon.

...The spokesman said the planes on this flight had each been modified to carry 60,000 pounds of explosives; the previous capacity was 37,500 pounds. They went over the target in single file, zeroing in on the same target instead of blanketing acres simultaneously.

Vietnam in the Mud, James Pickerell, 1966, p. 64

...Every day hundreds of L-19s fly low-level patrols over South Vietnam looking for Viet Cong movement, and every day some of these planes are fired upon — sometimes by a large force and sometimes by just one or two guerrillas. If a flight of bombers or fighters is available at the time of the incident, the L-19 will direct them to the target where a raid will be made. Frequently, very little is known about the target area other than some fire was received for it, and quite often the target is a village. There are no statistics available on how many people — VC or innocent peasants — are hit by these bombing attacks. Calculations by anyone are pure conjecture.

The type of questionable bombing raids I have been discussing are made by the A-1E's, B-57's, F-100's and F-105's, but the most ridiculous use of air power to date in Vietnam are the strikes by the B-52 super-bombers. These operations are like trying to hit a fly with a baseball bat. The B-52 crews never even see their target. They drop their bombs on a pre-arranged target according to an electronic signal, and though the military planners know that all the bombs from one plane will land in a particular square mile of terrain, they cannot hope for much more accuracy than this.

9 Jan 67   Aviation Week
                Cecil Brownlow, "Airpower Gives U.S. Edge in Vietnam War"
                SAIGON

...High-altitude, pattern-bombing strikes against traditional Viet Cong strongholds and base camps by Boeing B-52B strategic bombers have proved so successful over the past year that a group of 18 aircraft is being established at Thailand's Sattahip base 60 mi. southeast of Bangkok to augment a unit on Guam. Even before this, B-52 sortie rates had been on the rise, from the one-a-day average of a year ago to three a day.

The new B-52 unit is being supplied at the request of Army Gen. William C. Westmoreland, who heads the U.S. Military Assistance Command Vietnam (MACV). Prime value of the B-52 is its harassing effect, forcing the Viet Cong and North Vietnamese army units to keep on the move, denying them any rest in their stronghold areas.

Harrassment

18 Jun 65   (See Note Page 20)
               WASHINGTON, June 18

...Defense officials told a reporter earlier that one of the big gains in the raid was to open a previously impregnable Communist stronghold to the troops of the Vietnamese Government who moved into the area quickly in several teams after the bombing.

...Sixty-seven minutes after the B52 bombing, the Pentagon sources said, 150 South Vietnamese troops entered the blasted area. Contact with the enemy was described as light, although fairly continuous.

Among other things, 2,500 (CQ) pounds of rice were destroyed and many documents taken.

One team of Vietnamese soldiers found several houses with small tunnels nearby and blew them up, it was said.

...The heavy jungle cover prevented pinpointing specific targets beneath it, the sources said, and thus the only way the area could be clobbered was with a carpet of bombs wreaking widespread destruction.

The sources also stressed what they called the psychological effects of the bombing which it is hoped will show the Viet Cong they will have to keep on the move without any assurance they can be safe anywhere.

7 Jul 65   (See Note Page 20)
              SAIGON, VIET NAM, Wednesday, July 7

U.S. Air Force B52 bombers today again blasted the dense, Communist-infiltrated jungle northeast of Saigon with heavy explosives.

It was the third such strike by the big strategic air command (SAC) bombers, which are based at Guam, 2,200 miles away. The B52s pounded the so-called "D-Zone," 35 miles northeast of Saigon, on June 18 and again on Monday.

A 2,500-man allied task force plodded through one section of the almost impenetrable Viet Cong lair yesterday, blowing up tunnels and the abandoned huts of guerrillas in one section of the D Zone. The soldiers were virtually unopposed, except for some hostile dogs. They shot every dog that barked.

A U.S. spokesman described the air attack as another "spoiling mission" designed to harass the Reds by hitting hard at their encampments and communications and destroying their morale.

8 Jul 65   (See Note Page 20)
           DANANG

...A few miles away, about 25 B52 jets of the Strategic Air Command had pounded a segment of the jungle with 500 tons of bombs in their third such strike from a base 2,200 miles away in Guam.

The spokesman said no ground assessment was made immediately. The B52 bombing runs are described as spoiling attacks, intended to churn up Red defenses and impair morale regardless of whether they hit any of the enemy.

5 Mar 66   Business Week, "Changing the Rules of Guerrilla War"

...From all indications the B-52 raids, which rain enormous tonnages of bombs down in pattern strikes on jungle redoubts day and night, deprive guerrillas of sanctuary and have severly damaged their morale. Each B-52 carries more than 50 750-lb. bombs.

15 Aug 65   Los Angeles Times (See Note Page 20)
           SAIGON

...There was no immediate report on results of the B52 strike. Even details as to the number of planes and bombs dropped were withheld. A briefing officer said a new directive has made this information classified.

Official announcements concerning previous B-52 strikes, the first of which was launched from Guam June 18, indicated from 25 to 30 took part and the bomb load was about 500 tons in each case.

In the absence of confirmed Viet Cong casualties, spokesmen have referred to the B-52 raids as harrassment operations to disrupt known centers of enemy activity.

1 May 67   Aviation Week, "B-52 Ranked Most Feared Viet Weapon"
           SAIGON

...Gen. Westmoreland on occasion has employed the B-52 in a "spoiler" role in much the same way he uses combined ground and tactical air "search and destroy" mission to break up Viet Cong concentrations and to keep the Communist forces from settling long in one area.

The B-52 also has given the U.S. the capability of striking deep into Communist territory with heavy bomb loads and often with near complete surprise. It is this latter factor that most impresses the Viet Cong and North Vietnamese army units in South Vietnam.

...A Rand Corp. study for the Defense Dept., drafted after the questioning of several hundred Viet Cong prisoners, says in part:

"Fear of B-52 attack seems to be widespread and not confined only to the areas that have experienced them. The B-52's were described as being the most devastating and frightening weapon used so far against the Viet Cong and were said to have great effect on Viet Cong morale."

...In addition, the heavy bomb loads of the B-52's have served on occasion to shatter morale through destruction of tunnels and bunkers 10 - 25 ft. underground, which the Viet Cong previously considered virtually invulnerable to air attack.

The sheer devastation and damage a single flight of B-52's can cause to the landscape also appears to have considerable impact upon the Communist troops as well as upon the civilian population living near the area under attack.

...For most of the strikes, prior permission must be obtained from the province chief of the region to assure that the South Vietnamese consider the proposed target a legitimate one and that there are no friendly troops or civilians in the area. Such requests and approvals invariably involve a number of people, adding to the risk of an advance warning leaking to the Communist infrastructure.

...While military targets in the northern portion of North Vietnam have been ruled off limits to the B-52's for political and military reasons, the aircraft have been used increasingly to strike Communist supply and infiltration routes above the Demilitarized Zone (DMZ), an area of growing concern to U. S. ground troops immediately to the south.

...From both Guam and Thailand, the aircraft currently are flying an average of three to five missions a day over Vietnam. Highest number registered for one day thus far is nine.

Numbers of aircraft per mission have ranged from a low of three to a high of 30, depending upon the target to be struck. Most flights, however, include 10 - 20 aircraft.

The converted D models of the B-52 can carry a total of 108 500-lb. bombs — 24 on external wing-mounted multiple ejection racks, and 84 in the bomb bay originally configured for nuclear weapons. This compares with the 51 capacity for either the 500 or 750-lb. bomb of the F versions available here when the aircraft first began operations in the summer of 1965. Total capacity of the D with 750-lb. bombs on board is 66 — 12 under each wing plus 42 internally.

The 750 and 500-lb. bombs continue to be the primary ordnance loads for the B-52's, although a variety of other ordnance currently is being employed. Other weapons now used include delayed-fuse bombs and mines as well as anti-personnel ordnance such as the CBU (clustered bomblet unit). The delayed-fuse weapons can either penetrate into the Viet Cong tunnel complexes or explode hours after their delivery to further add to the surprise, psychological and operational factors.

...Mission times of the Thai-based aircraft are averaging 2 - 4 hr. as opposed to the 12 hr. required for a roundtrip flight between Guam and Vietnam, which virtually eliminates the possibility of more than one sortie a day per aircraft.

Populated Target Areas

31 Aug 65   New York Times, Charles Mohr
              SAIGON, SOUTH VIETNAM, Aug. 30

Two new air strikes in South Vietnam by United States B-52 bombers were announced today and informants here said that attacks by the strategic bombers would soon be carried out at the rate of about one a day for an indefinite period.

The military command, which has been conscious of criticism of the B-52 raids, has apparently concluded that saturation bombing of suspected Vietcong "safe havens" is a profitable military operation.

...The B-52's operating in South Vietnam hit a Vietcong target in Quangtin Province, 325 miles north of Saigon, Saturday evening and a target in Zone D, a Vietcong stronghold 30 miles north of Saigon, before dawn yesterday.

...The controversy over the B-52 raids has centered on the question whether the big jets, which can carry 51 750-pound bombs, have actually done substantial damage to Vietcong areas and troop concentrations. The question has been difficult to answer because of the hazards and obstacles to making ground inspections after raids on the guerrilla strongholds.

...Military sources said one factor that had led to the request for B-52 raids was the experience of April 15, when saturation bombing was attempted with fighter-bombers against a Vietcong area in Tayninh Province.

It took 400 of the craft, virtually all that were available in South Vietnam, flying sorties for 12 hours to lay the bomb pattern.

...Fighter-bombers, which are capable of pinpoint accuracy against visible targets, are not suited to lay down a precise saturation pattern of bombs, the sources said. The B-52's, which bomb on instruments even in clear weather, can cover an area more evenly and destructively.

...Military officials are certain that the bombers have been hitting important targets consisting of heavily fortified and tunneled Vietcong regions....The officers said expert photo analysis showed that a number of the tunnels had been collapsed by the bombs.

The officers said there had been reports that the raids had forced the Vietcong leadership to consider moving their bases from wilderness regions to more populated areas, a move that could cause problems both to the American military command and to the Vietcong.

Surprisingly, the idea of saturation bombing in population areas, if this happens, is not completely ruled out — for instance, it is thought that leaflets could be dropped warning civilians to vacate the area.

...A qualified source said he had verified reports that civilians moved out of the area of a raid in Zone D last Thursday because they could not stand the smell of decomposing bodies, indicating that sizable casualties had been inflicted by the bombs.

13 Oct 65   (See Note Page 20)
           AN KHE, VIET NAM, Oct. 13

War blasted apart the normal life of a Vietnamese peasant family this week. When the stunned survivors collected their wits they found two dead children, one critically wounded, two others and the mother cut badly. The father and two more children escaped unhurt.

The family had the misfortune to live in a rice paddy on the fringe of an area where U.S. and Vietnamese forces launched their biggest operation of the war Sunday. They were the apparent victims of a U.S. B52 bomb strike, aimed at Viet Cong targets along a ridge line. A Vietnamese interpreter said the survivors told him they were wounded by "bombs that fell from the sky."

When troops from the 1st Cavalry Division moved in after the bombing and artillery bombardment, they found the battered family.

A medic, Pfc. Donnie Rutherford of Pound, Va., administered aid.

...A captain who is not a medic, Richard Sundt of Ft. Benning, Ga., helped while the Vietnamese interpreter learned two dead children and one critically wounded, lay in a field some distance away.

A patrol of volunteers went quickly into suspected Viet Cong territory and returned with a frightened boy about 5. His right leg was badly wounded, gashed deeply, the bone apparently broken.

12 Jan 66   (See Note Page 20)

Editor's Note: The U. S. Department of Defense this week for the first time permitted newsmen to accompany B52 bombing raids over South Viet Nam. An Associated Press newsman went on a B52 raid and describes the mission.

       ANDERSEN AIR FORCE BASE, GUAM, Jan 12

Miles high more than two dozen B52 Stratofortresses swept over Viet Cong strongholds in South Viet Nam Wednesday...

Targets were a Viet Cong stronghold near the Cambodian border and a Communist settlement southwest of Da Nang.

...In Operation Power Play they struck a Viet Cong stronghold used for staging operations against American troops.

Two hours later more than 14 bombers assembled under Col. William T. Comiskey dropped 500-pound and 750-pound bombs on a valley 23 miles southwest of Da Nang which intelligence officers said had been a Viet Cong stronghold for many years. Comiskey is Wing Commander of the 320th/454th Heavy Bombardment Wing of Mather and Columbus.

Dubbed Mink Stole, the mission target was a green valley nestled between a mountain ridge and the winding Song Thu Bon River. Dozens of tiny rice paddies, roads and trails could be seen between cloud banks from the air.

Lt. Col. Arthur J. Ulrich, the intelligence officer, gave the crewmen a briefing on the target site before they left Guam. Viet Cong, he said, control the population and surrounding villages and are forcing South Vietnamese to dig defensive positions tunnels and other facilities.

Enemy units reportedly in the area included a Viet Cong battalion and two separate regiments. Nearest friendly South Vietnamese area was said to be 13 miles away at Lanh Thuong.

...Meanwhile the other wave had struck a Viet Cong stronghold for staging operations. Ulrich said three Viet Cong had been captured and gave the location of the site. Two of the three were flown over the area and identified it. Ulrich said friendly forces were 13 miles away. All huts were Viet Cong occupied or abandoned, he said.

14 Jan 67   The Sun (Baltimore)
                SAIGON, Saturday, Jan 14

...The new American base site in the delta is at Dong Tan, 5 miles southwest of the town of My Tho, headquarters of the Vietnamese Army's 7th Division.

The idea of deploying United States combat troops in the delta, which is crisscrossed by 25,000 miles of rivers and canals, has been under consideration for months. It may be months more before the shift gets into high gear.

...The drive and firepower of American soldiers might break the delta stalemate that shadows allied gains farther north.

On the other hand they will have to move cautiously to avoid casualties among civilians, for more than a third of South Vietnam's 15,000,000 people live on the farms and in the settlements and sampan fleets of the delta, along with 22 hardcore Viet Cong battalions and scores of smaller guerrilla units.

18 Sep 65   St. Louis Post-Dispatch (See Note Page 20)
                SAIGON, SOUTH VIET NAM, Sept. 18

...U. S. Air Force B52s raided suspected Viet Cong targets in Xuyen Province at the southern tip of Viet Nam, about 185 miles southwest of Saigon, U. S. spokesmen said. No details were announced.

The Guam-based jet bombers first raided the Mekong Delta two days ago when they hit targets in Vinh Binh Province about 90 miles southwest of Saigon. All previous raids had been north of the capital.

4 Dec 65   Christian Science Monitor, Takashi Oka
               SAIGON

Six hundred thousand Vietnamese in the Mekong Delta have returned to government control since the beginning of 1965, informed sources here report.

Even so, only 35 percent to 40 percent of the delta's 6 million people are under effective government control.

...Air power has made a tremendous difference in the delta war. In the flat, paddy-covered delta, the Viet Cong cannot mass except in long-held sanctuaries such as the U Minh forest and the mangrove swamps along the coast.

...But increased air power, especially bombing raids by jet B-57s and giant B-52s, has inevitably caused increased civilian casualties in the populous delta. Many of the 600,000 persons who returned to government control this year came out of Viet Cong areas because they could no longer bear the continuous bombings. These refugees are supplied with material to build new homes, and cooking oil and bulgar wheat from American aid.

...The Viet Cong in the delta are natives fighting on their own ground. The only northerners captured so far are southerners who went north for training or education.

11 Jan 67   Denver Post, Robert Tuckman
                 SAIGON, SOUTH VIETNAM

...In an unusual raid in the Mekong Delta, B52 bombers hammered at dawn at a Viet Cong base camp in mangrove swamps in Vinh Binh Province 87 miles south-southwest of Saigon.

Forward air controllers, directing the rare delta raid, reported nine secondary explosions, indicating hits on munitions or fuel. There was no indication whether the strike by the Guam-based B52s was a forerunner of another U. S. invasion of the Communist-infested delta.

25 Oct 65   Newsweek

...Some critics of the President's decision objected that the high-flying B52s could not possibly know whether they were killing Viet Cong or innocent civilians.

...Last week, to watch the B52s in action, Newsweek's Francois Sully flew over the Iron Triangle in a small Army observation plane. His report:

"From our tiny L-19 aircraft, the Viet Cong territory below simply looked like a dense forest intermingled with green paddy fields and a few peasant huts."

...As soon as the radar reflection of the terrain matched the outline of the target area drawn on their radarscopes, each of the B52s dropped a string of 51 750-pound bombs. When the first wave passed, two more planes flew over, pounding parallel furrows in the jungle with their bombs. All told, ten B52s took part.

..."Two hours later, another wave of B52s hit another target in the Iron Triangle, 4 miles away, and then U. S. and Australian troops moved in.

...The raid on the Iron Triangle and its aftermatch made plain just how difficult it is to measure the immediate results of the B52 attacks. No one knows for certain, but most U. S. military men are convinced that the mammoth bombers kill very few Viet Cong. They are also inclined to believe that after an initial period of demoralization induced by the raids, the Viet Cong have now found it possible to cope with the bombings by reducing the size of their units and reverting to guerrilla fundamentals.

The B52 partisans, in turn, argue that this is precisely the point of the raids. In at least two instances, they claim, B52 attacks forced the guerrillas to disperse large forces which they had massed in preparation for major assaults. Beyond that, large caches of Viet Cong food and arms have been captured by ground units following up the attacks. "The bombings," a Pentagon spokesman says, "deny the Viet Cong sanctuary, even if for a short time, and eventually force them out of these hideouts."

11 Sep 65   New York Times
                 SAIGON, SOUTH VIETNAM, Saturday, Sept. 11

A wave of United States B52 bombers struck a suspected Vietcong concentration 325 miles northeast of Saigon yesterday in an area dominated for years by the Communists.

Their target was in Quangtin Province, whose mountainous western area is called Doxa — the stronghold — by the South Vietnamese. This

was the 21st B52 raid since the big planes from Guam began action
June 18.

After the strike, a team of United States and South Vietnamese
Special Forces moved into the area, sweeping through the village of
Phuongxatay. They reported that the bombers had hit their target, but
they found no guerrilla forces.

6 Aug 66   (See Note Page 20)
            SAIGON, Aug 6

Until a week ago, the demilitarized zone was the quietest place in
all Viet Nam.

...Last Saturday the zone's quiet was shattered by bombs blasting
the western part of the zone. They came from B52 high-flying bombers
coming in from Guam who were seeking out the North Vietnamese. The
B52s have been back since.

...The southern area of the zone is the Delta of the Ben Hai.
Several thousand people farm rice and grow vegetables in this small,
arable portion of the zone.

1 Aug 66   (See Note Page 20)
            SAIGON, Aug 1

...B52s roared in from Guam soon after dawn today and struck at
suspected Communist targets only 25 miles from Saigon. The eight-jet
bombers hit an area near Cu Chi, to the northwest of the capital, where
troops of the U. S. 25th Infantry Division have been engaging strong
enemy units in abandoned rubber plantations and farmland. Viet Cong
tunnel complexes undermine the area.

...The U. S. command said the second straight day of U. S. Air
Force B52 strikes on North Vietnamese hideouts in the demilitarized
zone loosed about 50 tons of bombs into an eight-mile strip running
below the Ben Hai River, the actual north-south border.

...The planes fly in waves dropping bombs in saturation patterns
miles long.

31 Oct 66   (See Note Page 20)
            SAIGON, Oct 31

It may take a carpet of bombs in the demilitarized zone to close
that Communist infiltration channel to South Viet Nam, some high-
ranking American military officers think.

Proponents of the measure envision massive flights of B52 bombers
— capable of near-pinpoint accuracy — blasting the theoretically neutral
zone into a wasteland where no North Vietnamese soldier could move
undetected.

It is uncertain how much such an effort would cost because calculations have not been completed on the number of bombs needed. But
such a project would involve destruction over an area of at least 100
square miles, and possibly as much as 300 square miles.*

---

*These population figures are estimates compiled by USAID (United
States Agency for International Development) in conjunction with the
government of South Viet Nam in 1958.

UNESCO, in a 1964 study, estimated the population of South Viet
Nam increases at a rate of 2.5% annually.

14 Oct 65   New York Times, Charles Mohr
            SAIGON, SOUTH VIETNAM, Oct 13

...Another group of eight-engine B52s bombed a suspected enemy
logistical and staging base in Binhduong Province, just northwest of

Saigon, this morning. It was the fourth B52 raid in the province in one week.

...A military spokesman said today that the paratroopers had swept through part of the area of two B52 raids in the Iron Triangle last Friday. He said that 750-pound bombs with instantaneous fuses made craters only about four feet deep but blew down the jungle 300 feet around the crater.

Delayed-fuse bombs, which go off after penetrating into the ground, left craters fifty feet wide, blew down trees to a distance of 75 feet from the crater rim and collapsed some tunnels 100 yards away.

One "complex" of about 25 farm huts was reported "75 per cent" destroyed by the B52s.

* Binh Duong province: population density – 402.4 people per sq. mile

6 Dec 65   New York Times, Charles Mohr
              SAIGON, SOUTH VIETNAM, Dec 6

In the morning, B52 heavy bombers blasted four suspected Vietcong targets in Tayninh Province, 45 to 50 miles north-west of Saigon.

* Tay Ninh Province: population density – 170.4 people per sq. mile

29 Jan 66   New York Times, Neil Sheehan
              SAIGON, Jan 28

...The air war in the South continued, with American and Vietnamese fighter-bombers raking suspected guerrilla troop concentrations and bases. B52s of the Strategic Air Command also struck suspected Communist positions three times today, twice in Phuoctuy Province, east of Saigon, and once in Longkhanh Province, north of the capital.

*Phuoc Tuy Province: population density – 154.6 people per sq. mile
*Long Khan Province: Population density – 53.8 people per sq. mile

13 Feb 66   New York Times, Charles Mohr
              SAIGON, Feb 12

...In Quangnam Province, 340 miles northeast of Saigon, B52 heavy bombers struck suspected Vietcong targets this morning.

*Quang Nam Province: population density – 214.0 people per sq. mile

8 Nov 65   New York Times
              SAIGON, SOUTH VIETNAM, Nov 7

...In air action over South Vietnam, B52 bombers of the Strategic Air Command staged their 60th raid of the war, striking a suspected Vietcong training and storage area in Kienhoa Province 65 miles south of Saigon.

*Kien Hoa Province: population density – 628.0 people per sq. mile

5 Sep 66   (See Note Page 20)

...Over South Viet Nam, giant, Guam-based B52 bombers plastered a suspected Viet Cong storage area and troop concentration in Binh Dinh province 15 miles north of coastal Qui Nhon Monday.

*Binh Dinh Province: population density – 318.4 people per sq. mile

30 Jun 66   (See Note Page 20)
             SAIGON, Jun 30

...Air Force B52 bombers struck two targets in South Viet Nam
this morning, a troop concentration 28 miles southwest of the coastal
city of Quang Ngai and a base camp 50 miles northwest of Saigon.

_____
*Quang Ngai Province: population density — 426.7 people per sq. mile

<u>Tunnel Destruction</u>

9 Oct 65   New Republic
            Bernard B. Fall, "Vietnam Blitz"

...Much has been said about the use of B-52s in a counterinsurgency
operation or, as it should properly be called, a revolutionary war. Joseph
Alsop, always willing to swallow uncritically every official handout on Vietnam, has again assured us in a recent column that the B-52s are necessary
to destroy "deeply dug-in" VC installations, thus making a few underground
bunkers covered with sandbags and bamboo look like the Siegfried Line.

His words had hardly appeared in print when the Air Force switched
targets on Alsop and flew three raids into the Mekong Delta, followed by
several raids along the Central Vietnam shore. The trouble with the Mekong
Delta is that it is so flat, and the water table so high that one cannot dig a pit
privy in the place without hitting water. It is well-nigh impossible to build
underground positions in it. And, as official population density maps of Vietnam clearly show, the Delta has (with the exception of one single district out of
perhaps thirty) an average population density of about 250 people per square
mile, with one belt of districts across the whole Delta reaching the fantastic
density of <u>one thousand people</u> per square mile! With an average bomb load of
500 tons per thirty-plane raid and a known bomb dispersion pattern of about
2,000 yards by 1,000 yards for such a raid, the effects of such a bombardment
on a heavily-populated area can be readily guessed.

...Even the old-fashioned military view that a given target must be
attained or destroyed before the operation can be called a success no longer
holds. The B-52 raids (or "in-country" raids by smaller aircraft) do one thing
regardless of whether they hit a VC installation or a totally innocent and even
pro-government village — they keep the Viet Cong on the move, day and night,
in constant fear of being hit. Gone are the days of large and even comfortable
jungle hospitals above ground; of the VC rest camp with warm food, clean
clothes and a good swimming hole; of the large ammunition depot and weapons
repair plant with electric generators chugging away peacefully. The heavy
bombers have changed all that. The VC is hunted down like an animal. His
wounded die unattended. A VC combat unit returns from an operation only to
find its camp area destroyed and its painfully-amassed rice and ammunition
reserve shattered.

...Indeed, as many an informed observer in Saigon will concede, what
changed the character of the Vietnam war was <u>not</u> the decision to bomb North
Vietnam; <u>not</u> the decision to use American ground troops in South Vietnam; but
the decision to wage unlimited aerial warfare inside the country at the price of
literally pounding the place to bits.

There are hundreds of perfectly well-substantiated stories to the effect that
this merciless bombing hurt thousands of innocent bystanders and that one of
the reasons why few weapons are found in many cases is that the heaps of dead
in the battle zone include many local villagers who didn't get away in time. And
every observer in Vietnam meets several American officers who will curse
loudly every time they hear a jet overhead, because it again means an invisible
objective hit blindly — for an F-105 travels far too fast to see what he hits and
must be guided on his target by a "FAC" — a Forward Air Controller in a
spotter plane. The same goes for the incredible wastage of artillery ammunition. "In my area," said an American provincial adviser to me, "we shot a
half-million dollars' worth of howitzer ammunition last month on unobserved

252

targets. Yet the whole provincial budget for information- and intelligence-gathering is $300."

...Here again, operations research comes to our rescue. Thus far, interrogations seem to show that there is no positively hostile association between the devastation wrought upon the countryside, and the United States or the Saigon government. In the words of one of the experts, the aerial attacks on the villages "of course cause unhappiness, no doubt on the part of the villagers, (but) do not cause them automatically to become VCs. In fact we have never met one who has become a VC as a result of this." But perhaps the answer should have read: "...who has been willing to admit that he has become a VC as a result of this."

6 Oct 66   New York Times, Charles Mohr
             ANMY, SOUTH VIETNAM, Oct 5

American troops swept through a heavily fortified group of hamlets near the South China Sea today and discovered the odd way of life of people who have been at war for many years.

The Anmy area consists of numerous hamlets about 300 miles northeast of Saigon in northern Binhdinh Province. It is a nightmarish world, most of it water. Small clusters of houses stand on islands and on long tongues of land surrounded by extensive and deep lagoons. Mud dikes, first built centuries ago, are the only footpaths.

The entire area is honeycombed with bomb shelters and fighting holes. The latter are evidence of the strong Viet Cong influence that has gripped northern Binhdinh for several years.

The shelters are evidence of the harshness of the long war. No sensible family in the area is without a sturdy cover against air strikes and artillery.

Every house has one or more bunkers built of gluey clay that is dredged from the bottoms of the lagoons and plastered over log frameworks. Many of the shelters are strong enough to withstand a direct hit from a 105-mm. artillery shell, and there was evidence to prove it. Other bunkers and foxholes are scattered along the dikes, sometimes only a few yards apart.

...Today, refugees clogged the trails as the troops of the Fifth Battalion, Seventh Regiment, of the United States First Cavalry Division (Airmobile) swept toward the sea.

27 Jan 67   New York Times, Tom Wicker
             PLEITOUNBRENG, SOUTH VEITNAM, Jan 26

This is a village of Djerai tribesmen just this side of the Stone Age.

...The Djerai, who are experienced in bombing and warfare, have learned to dig shelter holes throughout the village.

22 Jun 65   (See Note Page 20)
             SAIGON, June 22

A senior U.S. military spokesman has forecast a big role for B52 bombers in future operations against the Viet Cong.

...Many of the bombs the B52s used Friday had delayed fuses which exploded the weapons below the surface in an effort to get at the deep tunnel systems. As a consequence "The Blow Down" or lateral destruction was slight.

A spokesman said fuses that detonated the bombs on impact probably would have been better. Most of the Viet Cong presumably were in their huts or preparing breakfast when the bombers hit shortly after daybreak.

The spokesman said proximity fuses that detonate bombs in the air were considered too unsafe to be carried in large numbers. Air bursts would give the most effective anti-personnel pattern.

There was speculation that B52s on future raids would be followed by other aircraft with napalm fire bombs. To insure penetration of the jungle, napalm canisters might be dropped first without igniters to allow the jellied gasoline to penetrate to the ground, then "hot" napalm canisters dropped to ignite it.

Besides death by burning, napalm is capable of killing by using all the available oxygen in a given area while it is burning, thus causing death by oxygen starvation.

3 Jan 67   The Evening Star (Washington) (See Note Page 20)
               BOI LOI WOODS, VIETNAM

There is a deadly stillness in the Boi Loi Woods. No birds sing as the sun rises. Trees that once blanketed the forest with green are charred. The stick up black and stark.

"Everything in its right mind has gotten out of here... except the Viet Cong," a GI said.

... The Communists had stayed around despite more than a year of smash ing by jets and B52 Stratoforts with 1,000-pound bombs; by artillery shells; by fiery napalm and white phosphorous.

The U.S. 25th Infantry Division moved in last spring. To the Americans the Boi Loi Woods was not the terrible place the Vietnamese had come in (sic) think it was. The GIs pushed through, and the Viet Cong tried to stand and fight. The Communists took the worst of it. The Viet Cong resorted to hit-and-run swipes, antitank mines, pellet-spewing Claymore-type mines and boobytraps.

This was costly to foot soldiers. Armored units took over the attacks.

... The battalion rumbled into an expansive empty base camp with bunker deep tunnels, and fortifications. It was so large the vehicles pulled back, and a strike by B52s was ordered. The big bombs covered the camp. Next morn ing, the armor rolled back in. Wherever the men spotted a still-usable position, they called Skyraider fighter-bombers to zero in with special 1,000-pound bombs. To cap the process, they placed 55-gallon barrels of powdered riot-control gas in the large craters. Demolition men set time fuses on the barrels that exploded them after the carriers moved away.

Some of the GIs who had not put on their gas masks got a taste of the nauseating gas.

18 Jan 67   UPI, World Journal Tribune
               SAIGON, Jan 18

U.S. B-52 bombers turned a Viet Cong hideaway into a mass of raging flames today with a rare firebomb attack that engulfed 18-square miles of jungle northeast of Saigon.

U.S. military spokesmen said the strategic bombers dropped tons of the World War II incendiary bombs into the southeast corner of the Communist War Zone D — on the frings of the Iron Triangle.

A huge sea of flames spread through the foliage as the B-52s flying high above the clouds struck in wave after wave. A helicopter observer reported: "It looks like the Fourth of July."

An American spokesman said no villages were believed to be in the fire-bombed area.

... Spokesmen said officially, however, that the purpose was to "deny the area to the enemy." Firebombs have been used only rarely in the Viet Nam war, spokesmen said.

Lt. Cmdr. Lou Herzog who watched the attack from a hovering helicopte said the firebombs split into smaller magnesium bomblets at about 8,000 feet and then hit the jungle, setting off a thick blanket of fire and smoke "that look like the forest fires I've seen in California."

He said the bombers made 10 passes over the area in all, spreading the bombs over a four-mile sector in each pass.

"From a quick look," he said, "there will be few, if any, Viet Cong left there for a while."

Herzog said the raid was part of a "carefully laid" plan put into operation several months ago when defoliation chemicals were spread through the jungle.

19 Jan 67   Cleveland Plain Dealer
**   SAIGON**

U.S. B52 bombers dropped tons of incendiary bombs yesterday on War Zone D — a Viet Cong sanctuary — in an effort to burn off dense foliage hiding suspected enemy camps and infiltration routes.

The magnesium bombs were dropped in a 28-square-mile patch of heavily forested area 30 miles northeast of Saigon. Smoke billowed 15,000 feet in the air.

...In the incendiary raid, second of its kind in the war, 10 waves of B52s dropped their bombs along radar-controlled parallel patterns in a period of 50 minutes from an altitude of 30,000 feet.

Efforts had been made in the past to clear the jungles with chemical defoliants, but the dense undergrowth survived. The effects of the fire raid was not known.

28 Jan 67   UPI, The Evening Star (Washington)
**   SAIGON**

U.S. Air Force B52 Stratofortresses spread waves of fire across 18 square miles today in a scorched earth campaign against the War Zone C Communist jungle sanctuary reported to hold Viet Cong headquarters in South Vietnam.

...It marked the second time in this war the United States had unleashed the awesome fire-bombing power it used against German and Japanese cities in World War II. The Stratoforts January 18 burned out a similarly sized area in War Zone D, another former guerrilla hideout 32 miles northeast of Saigon.

The scorched earth raids spearheaded a U.S. campaign to root the Viet Cong out of the lairs they have occupied for years and to keep them on the run.

...The B52s roared in over the jungle radio broadcasters and began dropping strings of incendiary bombs neatly from one end of a four-miles plus long area to another. They came back again, gradually widening the area of fiery destruction until it was as wide as it was long.

The little bombs burst at about 8,000 feet into smaller bomblets of magnesium. Like hail from hell, they fired the dense jungles.

29 Jan 67   UPI, Boston Sunday Globe
**   SAIGON**

High flying B-52 Stratofortresses launched a scorched-earth offensive against the Communists "Zone C" stronghold northwest of Saigon, raining thousands of firebombs on an 18-square-mile jungle area believed to be headquarters for all Viet Cong operations in South Vietnam.

A military spokesman said the eight-engine bombers, in their second fiery strike against a Communist guerrilla sanctuary in 10 days, made 10 passes across a four-mile-long swath of jungle 60 miles from Saigon.

The B52s dropped World War II type incendiary bombs from an altitude of about 20,000 feet. The bombs burst at about 8,000 feet into smaller bomblets of magnesium and rained down to sear the jungle below.

...Military spokesmen said Saturday's firebomb raids scorched the northeastern section of War Zone C, just a few miles from the Cambodian border.

Officers hoped aerial reconnaissance today would show the flames spreading better than they had during the War Zone D raid on January 18. Results from that effort to open up the jungle canopy were spotty, the Associated Press said.

War Zone C is a staging area for Viet Cong operations and forms a main link in the supply chain through which men and war materials are smuggled into South Vietnam from Cambodia.

28 Feb 67   Reuters, Christian Science Monitor
                PHNOMPENH, CAMBODIA

Large-scale military operations and continuous bombings in the border areas have caused South Vietnamese civilians to seek temporary refuge several times in Cambodia, a Foreign Ministry communique was quoted here as saying.

1 Mar 67   The West Australian (Perth, Australia)

Even on the fringe of the Vietnam war its consequences were horrifying, Dr. M. A. Jaspan, head of the W. A. University's centre for Asian studies, said yesterday.

He has just returned with Mrs. Jaspan from a ten-week field trip to Cambodia to study the Cham tribe, near the South Vietnamese border.

Dr. and Mrs. Jaspan said that American aircraft intermittently raided Cambodian peasant villages near the border, making 50 to 60 attacks a year.

They had seen pregnant women and children hideously disfigured by third-degree burns from napalm.

22 Feb 66   (See Note Page 20)
                SAIGON, VIETNAM, Tuesday, Feb 22

...Other U.S. forces hit Communist positions Monday with tear gas, B-52 superbombers, navy guns, and ground fighters in twin operations to snare and destroy enemy regiments in a 50-mile stretch of South Vietnamese coastal plains.

...Monday's heaviest strike came in the combined U.S.-Vietnamese operation on the coastal plains about 12 miles south of Bong Song, after cavalry troops reported they might have come across a Communist regiment in fortified positions.

With precision timing, cavalry helicopters sprayed the positions with tear gas just ahead of the arrival of a flight of U.S. Air Force B-52s from Guam. The eight-engine superbombers saturated the target area with deep-penetration bombs.

When the smoke cleared, two battalions of the division's 5th Regiment flew into the target zone with orders to assess the damage of the B-52 strike and mop up enemy forces. The troopers made light contact with the enemy on landing, then night fell, and they held their positions.

...The gas and aerial attacks were aimed at an area the cavalrymen had nicknamed "Iron Triangle" because repeated attacks failed to dislodge the entrenched enemy fighters.

Artillery units of the 1st cavalry reported firing 6,061 shells into enemy positions in Monday's action. They said this was the greatest number of shells fired in a single day since the division landed in South Vietnam last September.

26 Nov 66   New York Times
                SAIGON, SOUTH VIETNAM, Nov 26

...Thursday morning a company of the 25th Infantry Division found 66 bodies in and around the entrance of a cave in the central highlands, 230 miles northeast of Saigon.

They also said there were about 90 collapsed bunkers in the area, which had been hit by several B-52 raids.

The Air Force bombers struck again in the highlands about a mile away Thursday afternoon. This morning, the bombers attacked a headquarters area of the 9th Vietcong Division, about 75 miles northwest of Saigon.

Creation of Refugees

Dec 65   Ramparts
                Bernard Fall, "This Isn't Munich, It's Spain"

...Mao's theory requires an effective political base in the country — but what is a political base against B-52s? The United States, by massive bombing, seeks to deprive the guerrilla of his population — the fish of his water. We want the population to flee to our side — after all, on our side you at least can get food, and get away from the bombing.

4 Mar 66   (See Note Page 20)
            SAIGON, Mar 4

...All the while, more and more peasants are caught in the crossfire of war, losing their homes, property and lives. Refugees continue to stream out of the countryside to escape B52 raids and ground fighting. There are now more than 800,000 of these refugees, most of them an economic drain on the government.

16 Sept 65   New York Times, R. W. Apple, Jr.
              BENCAT, SOUTH VIETNAM, Sept 15

American and South Vietnamese airborne troops continued a sweep of this Vietcong-controlled area north of Saigon today in one of the largest operations of the war begun yesterday.
    ...The operation, which involves thousands of men, began when B-52 Stratofortresses of the United States Strategic Air Command, based in Guam, bombed areas adjacent to the combat zone. Behind them came A-1E fighter-bombers.
    ...General Williamson said that even if he was unable to fight a set battle with the Vietcong — the kind the marines fought with such success near Chulai last month — this operation could be a productive one.
    "My first job is to destroy as many enemy forces as I can," he said. "If I could catch an enemy regiment I'd tear him to pieces; I've got the men and the firepower and the experience. But in this terrain you can't make a guerrilla fight if he wants to run." He went on:
    "There are still two things I can do, though. I can search for installations and supplies, and destroy them so he can't use them anymore. Every time we knock down something like that we reduce the VC's maneuverability, which is his main strength.
    'Then I can try to convince the people in this area that the Government side is the best side to be on. I want to try to get them to visualize us as something more than an element of destruction."

14 July 66   New York Times, Eric Pace
              SAIGON, SOUTH VIETNAM, July 13

...The amnesty offer, first formulated in 1963, is continually repeated through millions of leaflets scattered over the countryside and by low-flying planes with loudspeakers blaring tape recordings about the horrors of war.
    One widely broadcast message follows a bit of Buddhist funeral music with a woman's voice saying:
    "Each day that passes brings you closer to death. All men must die sometime, but if you stay with the Vietcong, you will die soon by bombs or bullets. It is much better to spend the rest of your life among your family and friends. Come home. Make your plans to leave the Vietcong now. Come home before you die. Come home."
    Other broadcasts follow a 30-page "Open Arms" Inducement Program manual prepared in April by the United States Mission here, which helps plan, finance and operate the program. Officials of the United States Agency for International Development are in charge of the American part of the program.
    The manual recommends that the message to potential defectors contain "fear output," exploiting, for example, "specific fear of the B-52 bomber, particularly the surprise element in B-52 raids, the sheer destructiveness of the bombs and the inadequacy of shelters once considered safe."

The giant B-52 stratofortress, originally designed to deliver atomic bombs, is used by the United States to devastate areas where Vietcong soldiers are thought to be.

The manual also recommends use of "the theme of enlightened self-interest to explain the presence of the U.S." in South Vietnam. It suggests that propagandists follow up air strikes immediately with warnings that there will be new strikes unless the Vietcong give themselves up.

12 Mar 66   New York Times, Felix Belair, Jr.
              WASHINGTON, May 11

...Quoting from an incomplete intelligence analysis just received from the fighting area, the Secretary said prisoners now expressed "considerable doubt" that the Communists can prevail even in a protracted war, and "some of them expect that the U.S. and government forces will win with their superior equipment and supplies."

The same report cited the "most serious impact" caused by the movement of some 900,000 Vietnamese who had left villages in areas dominated by the Vietcong and gone over to the government side. This, the report said, deprived the Vietcong of food supplies, intelligence sources and the use of the population as a shield and the villages as hiding places for guerrilla forces.

(Secretary of Defense Robert S. McNamara) did not say over what period of time the 900,000 villagers had moved.

25 Sep 67   UPI, The Evening Star (Washington)
              SAIGON

North Vietnamese peasants living near the demilitarized zone (DMZ) were warned to flee to South Vietnam if they want to save themselves and their children from a "rain of death and destruction" in massive B-52 bombing raids, a U.S. spokesman said today.

The warning came as the giant bombers continued to step up attacks against Communist artiller, mortar and rocket positions in the area which have killed or wounded more than 800 U.S. marines at the battered frontier fort of Con Thien since the first of the month.

The massive retaliation ... (sic) by the B-52s, 7th Fleet warships and American artillery has been called by American officials the heaviest concentration of conventional firepower in history. The warning hinted that it would grow even worse.

26 Sep 67   The Washington Post
              SAIGON, Sept 25

The United States has dropped leaflets on a North Vietnamese village urging the people to rally to the government of South Vietnam, a U.S. spokesman announced today.

...The U.S. spokesman said 240,000 of the two kinds of leaflets were dropped. The message on each kind was similar — a warning that B-52s will continue to be used and that the area is unsafe to live in. One kind has a picture of a B52 and the other has a picture of bomb blasts from a B-52 strike.

"This is the mighty B-52," the first leaflet said. "Now you have experienced the terrible rain of death and destruction its bombs have caused. These planes come swiftly, strongly, speaking as the voice of the government of Vietnam proclaiming its determination to eliminate the threat to peace.

"Your area will be struck again and again. But you will not know when or where. The planes fly too high to be seen or heard. They will rain death on you again without warning. Leave this place to save your lives."

26 Sep 67   St. Louis Post-Dispatch
               SAIGON, SOUTH VIETNAM, Sept 26

"A monumental foulup," an American source said today to describe the
dropping of a 250,000 out-of-date propaganda leaflets in the wrong place.
    ...When the drop was announced yesterday, questions were asked. Was
the United States for the first time encouraging defections from North Vietnam to South Vietnam? How would villagers get across the demilitarized
zone, which has been under almost continuous air and artillery bombardment
for several weeks?
    This morning there was an explanation. The leaflets have been used after
B-52 strikes for more than a year.
    In the past, though, this has meant use in insecure areas of South Vietnam,
a source said. With the bombers hitting in North Vietnam, he said, someone
forgot to concel the standing order for the leaflet drop.
    "They were emphatically not directed at the civilian population of North
Vietnam," the source said.

26 Sep 67   The Evening Star (Washington) (See Note Page 20)
               SAIGON

    ...U.S. officials, meanwhile, explained that a leaflet drop over a North
Vietnamese village last week was an attempt to draw troops into defecting to
the south. The announcement of the drop yesterday had left the impression
that the leaflets were aimed at North Vietnamese villagers.

TUNNELS

8 April 62   New York Times Magazine
               Jerry A. Rose, "The Peasant Is the Key to Vietnam"

    ...In Quangnam Province, Government artillery bombardment on hamlets
controlled by the Viet Cong has driven the people out — and into near-famine
poverty. On the Plain of Reeds, Vietnamese have dug foxholes into the dirt
floors of their homes.

15 Mar 65   (See Note Page 20)
               CAM LO, VIET NAM, Mar 15

    ...The troops jumped from the chopper and headed for the brush, firing
steadily. Fourteen helicopters came in, unloading 144 troops. The soldiers
disappeared into the brushy area and in a few minutes the whole site looked
deserted.
    ...Periodically the troops fired into pits and tunnels dug into the ground
around village houses. Near one hut there was an overturned plow and fresh
footprints leading into the woods.
    In another, a table was set for four persons. There was still warm soup
in the bowls, but no people.

Moving, Schwartz and his unit heard voices coming from one hut. Entering cautiously they found an old man with a dirty white beard holding the hands of two children who looked as if they were about 2.

A Vietnamese officer questioned the old man.

"No Viet Cong here," he said.

Troops spread out in flanking movements. The sound of small arms ripped through the air. A radio call said a Vietnamese soldier in a nearby company was hit. A medical evacuation helicopter swung down to pick him up.

Schwartz and his men moved on. They found a few women clutching half-dressed children and a few more old men.

30 Mar 65   (See Note Page 20)
             TRUNG LAP, VIET NAM, March 30

The tunnels spread like freeways under the forest floor. Apparently they were just as crowded.

"Throw smoke into that one," the battalion commander shouted as a camouflaged tunnel entrance was discovered.

A smoke grenade plopped in, and a few minutes later out came a woman and two children, spluttering and scared.

Elsewhere in the Viet Cong village northwest of Saigon, other families were dragging themselves from holes punched deep into the hard clay ground.

Heavy air strikes had blasted thatched houses and surrounding trees, but the tunnels were relatively unharmed.

...The guerrillas had ducked out of sight as the government advance on the fortified village began.

..."This is about the most frustrating terrain there is," a U.S. adviser complained wearily. "Just what do you do about these tunnels?"

...The forest was laced with trenches and tunnels, some 20 feet deep.

It was hard going. The armored vehicles crunched over the tunnel entrances without caving them in.

"We haven't got enough troops to secure this area and really blow up all these tunnels," a U.S. adviser said.

The snipers had a few tricks up their sleeves. One was to shoot at armed helicopters overhead. This would bring bursts of fire in return, sometimes right into friendly troops.

On these occasions the infantry dived into the tunnels and trenches the Viet Cong had built. Women and children dived in with them.

Viet Cong mines were hanging from trees, making progress hazardous for tanks. And there were large numbers of traps containing sharpened sticks for the feet of the unwary.

Many attempts have been made to clean out this tunnel region, which stretches for miles between Saigon and Tay Ninh. Aerial defoliating has been used, leaving the vegetation dead and blackened.

But the Viet Cong suited their camouflage to the new conditions and became just as difficult to spot.

As the infantry began moving out, the order was given to burn everything behind them. They departed followed by a wall of flame.

They were also followed by a sniper.

7 Jun 65   New York Times
            SAIGON, Jun 7

...Despite instances of rape by Vietcong troops, the leaders caution repeatedly against molesting village girls. American interviewers decribe the average Vietcong's life as "monkish".

...Some prisoners asserted that they had won the gratitude of villagers in newly captured areas by forcing them to build underground bomb shelters.

Later raids by American and Vietnamese planes confirmed their foresight in the eyes of the population, they said.

1 Jul 65   (See Note Page 20)
            SAIGON, VIET NAM, July 1

...Viet Cong positions were first prepared here years ago and with
each month the positions have been improved. The Viet Cong guerrilla
spends much of his day digging, even when there is no immediate need for
it.

The entrance to a tunnel might be under a heavy rock, it might be under
the hearth of a peasant's hut, it might be under water in the bank of a mountain stream. Only by sheer luck would a Government soldier find one, and
if he did, he probably would kill only a few Viet Cong. The rest would be
elsewhere.

In an air raid, some of the tunnels and bunkers would be crushed. A
jellied furnace of napalm would ooze down into some of the air holes. But
many of the bunkers would be deep enough to survive even direct hits by
heavy bombs, and their galleries of men and weapons would survive. At
nightfall, it would be safe to move around again.

...So far, the powerful weapons of the 20th century have had little
more effect on the Viet Cong guerrillas than did the British Redcoats, with
their superior musketry, on the American guerrillas of two centuries ago.

11 Jul 65   New York Times, Jack Langguth
             SAIGON, SOUTH VIETNAM, July 10

...Many American officers believe that the United States' mission and
the Saigon press corps attach too much importance to casualty figures and
not enough to putting the figures into some perspective.

That view was reinforced today when three American officers and an
enlisted man told of their performance for four days last week in Zone D,
a jungle area northeast of Saigon that has been dominated by the Vietcong.

Although the four had been involved in must of the heavy fighting during
a four-day American — Australian — South Vietnamese offensive, they could
claim first-hand knowledge of only seven Vietcong soldiers killed. They
were quite sure that 39 other Communist soldiers were killed or badly
wounded.

Their evaluation was far below an estimate of 350 Vietcong killed or
wounded issued by a spokesman in Saigon.

Many of the towns and hamlets were well fortified, the Americans said.
They said that the villagers had moved back to the same spots where airborne patrols had leveled houses and slaughtered livestock three weeks ago.

"But this time instead of building above ground they're building underground and the houses have metal roofs, sometimes made of beer cans,"
said Capt. Arthur C. Stang, a 28-year old airborne officer from Pennsylvania.

Capt. Stang, whose prisoners included eight women, said one had blasting caps and another was carrying morphine.

15 Jul 65   (See Note Page 20)
             SAIGON, VIET NAM, July 15

..."We have our flamethrowers primed for action, but some of the
entrances are so narrow and so deep the flames would blow back on us.

"We have vomit gas and tear gas available for use, but we are not permitted to use that."

A typical Viet Cong village tunnel system could have as many as 30
entrances, with tunnels linking with each other. Some tunnels have been
built at various levels, as deep as 30 feet.

Soldiers lob white phosphorous grenades into tunnels, but the Viet Cong
can use makeshift face masks for effective protection.

U.S. Forces are using heavy bombs and artillery to blast out Viet Cong
entrenchments. A direct hit is needed to do much by this method.

...Civilians have shown a remarkable capacity to survive battles by taking refuge in tunnels and holes. The Viet Cong is known to give intensive instruction in shelter construction.

The Government gives little or no instruction. High civilian casualties reported recently were in Government villages where no shelters had been built for civilians.

Aug 65   Argosy
              Milt Machlin, "Battlefront Report from Vietnam"

...The operation we were going on today was the first in the series of "while-the-sun-shines" campaigns attempting to disrupt the V.C. offensive plans for the rainy season before they could get a solid footing. The operation was called Hung Vuong 7 and was taking place in the Tay Ninh forest, seventy miles northwest of Saigon, in the area believed to be headquarters for the National Liberation Front of the Viet Cong.

The day before, the area had been blasted by 450 planes in what I believe is still the largest air-raid ever conducted in South Viet Nam. Plenty of evidence of supply facilities and training centers was uncovered as bombs stripped the foliage from the heavy jungle, but despite the concentrated bombing, even low-level choppers could not see into the forest to know who or what was there.

...About a kilometer later, we stumbled into the first V.C. camp.

...There were no V.C. bodies, though several sets of black pajama uniforms were found. From a network of tunnels, which had been collapsed by the bombing, came the nauseating odor of rotting flesh but nobody wanted to dig out the tunnels to get definite confirmation of V.C. dead. Besides, there was a theory advanced that it might just be a store of Nook Baum, the rotten fish sauce the Vietnamese use instead of ketchup.

4 Aug 65   New York Times (See Note Page 20)
              DANANG, SOUTH VIETNAM, Wednesday, Aug 4

...The United States Marine Corps commander in South Vietnam said today that he was deeply grieved by the death of four children and a woman during a marine attack Monday on a village controlled by the Vietcong.

...The marines were fired on from an area containing many caves and bunkers and they blasted back and attacked, killing nine Vietcong, the general said. His statement continued:

"Unfortunately in the same bunker area the marines found one woman and three children who had been killed, apparently by grenade fragments. Another child apparently had been killed by fire from an armed helicopter."

General Walt noted that a helicopter with a loudspeaker had flown over the area for about an hour warning all persons to go out into the open where they were promised safety. He said that about 400 to 500 had followed this advice.

9 Aug 65   New York Times, Charles Mohr
              DANANG, SOUTH VIETNAM, Aug 8

The attempts by public information officers to de-emphasize the importance of civilian deaths and the burning of village huts at the hands of United States marines have not been duplicated by senior Marine Corps officers here.

...The marines have also conceded that at least 51 huts were burned on another operation.

...Almost everyone agrees that the killing of civilians and the destruction of village property are a serious political mistake in a war in which political success is vital to military victory. But it is not so easy to solve the problem.

...The men of the unit have been whittled away by sniper fire, mines and booby traps. They are frustrated and some are bitter.

...Some observers assert that problems are caused not only by civilian deaths but also by the killing of Vietcong guerrillas based in their own villages.

Lieutenant Colonel David A. Clement, commander of the Second Battalion, Third Marines, which holds the right flank of the Marine force dug in around Danang, said:

"When you kill a local guerrilla, all you've done is kill somebody's husband or sweetheart or son — and not only that, he is probably related in some way to half the village. As soon as the military operation is done, you've got to start undoing the damage you've done."

...Some of them were appalled by what a few of their comrades did this week.

"They say they did it because the huts had fortifications," one marine said. "Don't they know that practically everybody in this country digs a hole near his house because of air strikes and artillery?"

16 Aug 65   Newsweek

...While Perry pursued the war in the jungle, Francois Sully participated in what some military theorists like to call "the sanitary war" by making a flight in an observation plane over the guerrilla-infested Boi Loi woods northwest of Saigon. Sully's report:

"...But Capt. Robert A. Norman, Bird Dog's pilot and a veteran of 300 missions of this sort, was completely cool. Pointing down to two small clearings ringed by bunkers and trenches, he said: "We're going to bush these bunkers and the three huts hidden under the trees."

...The bombing was amazingly accurate and the clearing soon became engulfed in a billowing cloud of smoke and flames from the napalm. If any guerrillas were in those bunkers and trenches, it was certain death for them.

16 Aug 65   Newsweek

...Added a Pentagon colonel, noting that the Viet Cong make frequent use of women and children in their operations: "The trouble is that in this kind of war you don't know the VC from the civilians...You've got to drop grenades into caves or tunnels and you can't always know there are some babies in them."

22 Aug 65   New York Times, James Reston
CHULAI, SOUTH VIETNAM, Aug 20

...General Walt explained in the helicopter what he had not known only 72 hours earlier, when he ordered the attack. He had been sending out patrols for weeks, and he knew that the Vietcong were just to the south, but he did not know until the battle was over how deeply they were entrenched.

The Vietcong were dug in not merely below the ground in trenches, but under the ground in tunnels, and not just under the surface, but 30 feet down.

From cunningly concealed entrances covered with branches in the piney woods, they had constructed channels deep enough for a man to walk upright, extending for more than a hundred yards in one direction and branching out from there to subsidiary channels, which concealed not only the Vietcong and their arsenal of weapons but also many of their wives and children.

In one section alone, the marines found more than 130 women and children.

5 Sep 65   New York Times (See Note Page 20)
QUINHON, SOUTH VIETNAM, Sept 5

...The trap was sprung by two companies of the Second Battalion of the Marine Corps Seventh Regiment. While one company crashed through barbed wire on the seaward edge of the hamlet of Vinhquang, another company was landing from helicopters in the north and west.

...F-101 jets pounded a thicket with napalm and high explosives.

...Guerrillas fired sporadically at the marines as they leaped from the troop carriers and rushed in small parties through a maze of ditches and small alleyways in Vinhquang.

...Marines, combing the village for inhabitants, peered into holes in the ground. Some terrified villagers were dragged out. Women wailed and clutched infants.

"It tears your insides out," said Sgt. Michael Zabrorowski, commander of the Third Platoon of one company. The sergeant, who is called "Sergeant Ski," has three children of his own in Santa Ana, California.

Old men and women knelt and begged for their lives.

Marines shouted for their Vietnamese Army interpreter to tell the villagers not to be afraid.

The Americans were less gentle on another score: all males between 16 and 60 were segregated and interrogated. Several were tagged with baggage labels as Vietcong or suspected Vietcong.

Three women were injured by a fragmentation grenade that a marine had dropped into a tunnel. A few seconds earlier, a Vietcong grenade had rolled out of a hole and exploded in the water. One woman lost an eye.

Marine medical corpsment treated injured and sick villagers. The women were sent to a hospital by helicopter.

The marines made a house search for rice hoards. There were plenty: even the altar of the hamlet's ramshackle Buddhist temple was filled with rice.

10 Sep 65 New York Times, Charles Mohr
     SAIGON, SOUTH VIETNAM, Sept 9

...In the ground action, United States marines have killed 87 Viet Cong guerrillas, including 66 men killed in a tunnel with a charge of TNT, in two days of fighting on the Batangan Peninsula, it was reported today.

...The 60 persons killed in a huge Viet Cong tunnel yesterday apparently died of concussion and blast after a Marine demolition team, covered by automatic-weapons fire, crept to the camouflaged entrance and placed a charge of explosives in it.

"I was so proud of my marines I could hardly talk," said Maj. Gen. Lewis W. Walt, commander of the Third Marine Amphibious Force. "The victory is encouraging, but we will not rest until we search out and destroy all the Viet Cong."

General Walt had been touring the battle area in his command helicopter. He landed in time to see the tunnel demolition.

...The tunnel fight began when two hand grenades were thrown at the marines from a so-called "spider trap" near the village of Chauthaun. A spider trap is a hole with a camouflaged cover that allows a sniper to pop up and then conceal himself again.

The marines advanced and threw grenades down the hole. Two wounded Viet Cong men and two uninjured women came out of the hold and surrendered, a military spokesman said.

The guerrillas still in the tunnel below refused to surrender, and the marines set off TNT charges in the hole.

Four marines then crawled into the opening, which was part of a 250-foot tunnel, 6 feet high from floor to ceiling.

In addition to the 66 guerrillas slain in the tunnel, the marines have killed and counted the bodies of 21 more Viet Cong in the last two days, captured 14 and detained 69 suspected guerrillas.

11 Sep 65 (See Note Page 20)
     CHU LAI, VIET NAM

The military doesn't want it to happen, but the innocent die daily in this cruel and puzzling war.

Phoen Thi Que was an innocent. She was born seven months ago in Loc Tu village, the fifth child of farmer Phan Qua and his brown-eyed wife. While

Phan Qua and his wife worked their rice paddy, bare feet and knees squishing in stinking gray mud, little Phoen Thi stayed in the village with her brothers and sisters.

...And then the Viet Cong came to Loc Tu. The village, part of the Binh Ky complex, became a company headquarters for the VC's elite 1st Regiment.

The village schoolteacher was bayoneted in both breasts, executed because she had taught. Two of her students had their legs riddled by bullets because they had listened and refused to join the Viet Cong.

For long weeks there were no more marble games for Phoen Thi to watch. Instead she was kept inside her parents' thatch and mud home while the Viet Cong left on their endless reconnaissance and combat patrols against U.S. marines stationed at Chu Lai, 15 miles north of the village.

But the marines received word of the 1st Regiment's location and began attacks of their own.

With the initial barrage, the first of many days of shelling to soften up the area for ground troops, Phan Qua and his wife were separated and sent to different shelters. Phoen Thi went with her father and two of her sisters. But there was no food or water in the sandy hole in the ground that was to be their home for six days.

For every hour of that time, Phan Qua held his daughter to his thin chest, trying all the while to quiet her baby whimpers at the noise of attack and the pains of an empty stomach. Finally, the earth no longer shook. There were no more rifle shots.

Phan Qua climed back into the daylight. U.S. marines were sweeping through the village and had routed the Viet Cong. The farmer begged a canteen from a marine's belt. He held it to little Phoen Thi's gray lips. The water just spilled. He tried again.

"Dammit, man," shouted a marine, trying desperately to appear tough. "Can't you see the kid's dead?"

Then Phan Qua saw it. While well-fed soldiers had been killing each other with bullets, Phoen Thi had starved to death. The marines wrapped the baby in rough green canvas and hacked out a tiny grave with their entrenching tools.

Jan 66   True
                Malcolm W. Browne, "Hell in the Highlands"

...Then the action shifted to the skies. "Look, it's the B-52's," someone yelled. "Hope they hit what they're supposed to and not us."

...And then the whole line of mountain peaks lifted up in billowing orange flame and gray smoke that soared thousands of feet in the air. The sticks of 750-pound bombs were landing right on the suspected Viet Cong mountain positions. Five or six second later that shock wave and sound blast of hundreds of mammoth explosions reached the valley floor, and soldiers who had just left helicopters stood gaping at the awesome fireworks display.

From the thatched huts of a little hamlet where C Company, 2nd Battalion, 7th Cav had landed, 50 women and children ran screaming. The shattering noise of the bombing had thrown the villagers into hysterics, and some clutched desperate at the GI's.

But there were no men in the outpouring. This was a Viet Cong hamlet, and the men had all gone off into the mountains, either to fight or to escape capture.

C Company began digging in and setting up mortars, preparing for a fight. The women and children were gathered up and told to wait along a rice paddy dike.

Next to the huts and under the scrubby trees, hundreds of Viet Cong spider holes pocked the hard ground. Each hole was dug to a depth of about five feet, angled inward, and was partly covered with palm leaf camouflage. The hard ground between the holes was studded with thousands of dagger-sharp bamboo stakes, imbedded so as to drive through the foot or ankle of a running man.

Five GI's already moaning, their ankles pierced by the devilish, fire-hardened stakes. Angry fellow soldiers charged through the hamlet firing bursts from their M-16s into each of the spider holes. The soldiers were worried about more than spikes. In the past 24 hours a dozen GI's had been shot by snipers concealed in holes just like these, and it wasn't the time to take chances.

But the Viet Cong were not there now. On trees and the sides of huts the words, <u>My Do Bo</u> ("The Americans are landing") had been chalked everywhere by fleeing guerrillas as a warning for others to leave.

All but one of the holes was empty. That hole contained a woman. She was alive and wailing when the GI's pulled her out of the hole. The blood pouring from the hole in her chest was all over the face of the baby she had been nursing when she was hit.

Jul 66   Atlas
              Kuno Knoebl, "A Visit to a Vietcong Village"

...We returned to the abandoned village. Nguyen Hoi picked up one of those broad, flat bamboo baskets used in Vietnam to dry meat, fish and fruit. He put the basket to one side and disappeared into the ground. I was told to follow him, and approaching the basket saw a narrow shaft that descended into the soft earth. I slowly forced my way into it and felt a hand touching my body — in order to guide me further. Through an opening in one of the tunnel walls I entered a cave. One of my companions followed me. Then I heard Nguyen Hoi's quiet voice beside me: "There are two women in here with their children." But it was too dark for me to see them and I could only hear their breathing. How many hours have these woman and children spent there in the last few years without knowing whether they would ever emerge alive?

Later, a helicopter flew over the village, but I did not hear it. I was alerted by the actions of a child about three years old and his mother. They had suddenly begun to run and when they saw that the plane was directly over the village and could not reach the defense tunnel in time, they threw themselves down against the clay steps of the nearest hut. They did not dare stand up or move until the village chief had calmed them and convinced them the danger was past. Nhuyen Hoi explained that their hut had been destroyed in a bombing attack. "Her mother was wounded and since then her husband has joined the guerrillas in the jungle."

5 Sep 66   The Sun (Baltimore) (See Note Page 20)
              AN BIEN, VIET NAM, Sept 4

It was a very small hamlet, only three huts and a handful of people scattered along a canal. But at this moment it portrayed the war's extremes of terror and tenderness.

...The soldiers entered the hamlet without resistance and began to search. Footprints led to bunkers and bombshelters.

Rangers pointed weapons into the dark holes and shouted: "If there is anyone in there, come out. If you don't, you will be killed!"

At one opening a soldier lobbed a grenade and followed in after the blast. The hole, a bomb shelter, was dug in a zig-zag and went many yards back. At the end, pressed deep into the mud were the mother and child, unhurt by the explosion.

The soldier led them out. Another soldier took the mud-coated child and walked with the mother to some clear water where they washed.

...Before he left, the soldier who had washed the child found some candy, brushed it off, and handed it to the mother and child who sat in the shade of a banana tree.

13/13 Vietnam: Search and Destroy, Gordon Baxter, 1967, pp. 88, 91

(The copyright owners of 13/13 Vietnam: Search and Destroy have declined permission to publish textual material in this documentation. The following describes the essential contribution made by a selection from this book.)

(The author describes scorched earth missions. Everything in an enemy village is ordered burned or destroyed. The troops find pigs and cows hidden in bomb shelters and shoot them.)

27 Feb 67   The Evening Star (Washington) (See Note Page 20)
             SAIGON

...In South Vietnam, the massive U.S. force pushing through War Zone C in Operation Junction City still met only sniper resistance during the sweep 70 miles northwest of Saigon.

...The operation, largest of the war, has been supported by 747 air strikes so far. U.S. troops have seized 178 tons of enemy rice and destroyed 192 underground fortifications and 103 enemy structures.

7 Apr 67   New York Times (See Note Page 20)
            LAITHIEU, SOUTH VIETNAM, April 6

Powerful air blowers that sweep Viet Cong guerrillas with 1,000-degree blasts are being used north of Saigon.

The blowers are used in tunnels long occupied by the Viet Cong in populated areas around Saigon.

Troops of the United States First Infantry division have been experimenting with the air blowers in the tangled Thuangiao Jungle near Laithieu, 10 miles north of Saigon. Heated air was blasted into a tunnel complex this week after a guerrilla had thrown grenades at two First Division soldiers. He did not come out, and apparently escaped through a hidden exit.

The hot-air technique uses the 30-pound Mighty Mite blowers that normally force tear gas into tunnels. The air is heated by a battery-powered power generator and forced into a tunnel entrance.

The device is being used by a force under Lieutenant Colonel Robert Schweitzer of Chicago.

Colonel Schweitzer said the hot-air technique was applied gradually to tunnels where Viet Cong were believed to be hiding. The habitants are warned by loudspeaker.

Then the blowers begin. While the loudspeakers continue calling on the Viet Cong to leave the tunnels, the temperature rises. Eventually, the blasts reach 1,000 degrees.

"Tunnel rats," or reconnaissance crews, can explore the tunnels soon afterwards because they cool quickly. If tear gas is used, the tunnels are contaminated for days.

"It is necessary for us to provide the utmost protection for our men, and this is one way of doing it," Colonel Schweitzer said.

26 Jan 67   Chicago Daily News (See Note Page 20)
             SAIGON

...American infantrymen trapped an estimated 100 Communist soldiers holding women and children hostages in a cave in the Bong Son area in the central highlands, United Press International reported.

An American officer who approached the mouth of the cave to try to win release of the hostages was shot and killed by the Reds.

The GIs, unable to flush the Communists and the hostages from the cave, sealed it off with explosives.

26 Jan 67   UPI, Denver Post
             SAIGON, SOUTH VIETNAM

U.S. Infantrymen Thursday trapped an estimated 100 North Vietnamese soldiers in a cave where the Reds held women and children hostage and shot to death an American officer when he tried to save the civilians.

It was not immediately known how many women and children were being held by the Reds in the massive granite cave fortress.

The cave-clearing operation took place in the Bong Son area in the Central Highlands.

A group of American paratroopers made one of the rare combat jumps of the war on a sandy peninsula along the coast to clear the way for a helicopter assault by 1st Air Cavalrymen driving inland toward the cave fortress complex.

UPI Correspondent Leon Daniel was with American infantrymen in the dangerous operation of clearing out the natural caves honeycombing a jungle-sloped mountain in the highlands about 280 miles northeast of Saigon.

When soldiers of the 25th Infantry Division, supporting the 1st Air Cav in Operation Thayer II, first ran onto the huge cave complex, they heard voices of women and children inside one of the dark, dank tunnel mouths.

The commander of one of the infantry companies went up to the mouth of the cave and tried to talk the civilians into coming out.

First Lt. Jerry Orenstein, 23, of New York City, said a North Vietnamese soldier pushed a woman and child out of the tunnel, using them as a shield. The company commander, a captain, lowered his gun — and the North Vietnamese shot him through the head, killing him instantly.

The cave was blown up with explosives, sealing in the Communists.

27 Jan 67   UPI, Boston Globe, Leon Daniel
             PHU CAT, VIETNAM

It was a dirty, dangerous job. High on the slopes of a jungle-covered hill there are a number of holes. They lead back into a maze of tunnels and underground rooms — a solid rock fortress.

The dank, damp passageways and rooms had been used as a hiding place and a headquarters and base for North Vietnamese troops before the Americans arrived. With them, as hostages, were a number of women and children.

Most of them are gone now. But some are still around. They are dead — at least 20 by body count and perhaps as many as 100 more entombed in the granite caves, sealed up in tunnels by high explosives that blasted entrances shut with tons of rock and debris.

Second Lt. Donald Nance of Rockford, Illinois, was one of the busiest men in the area when I arrived. His job was to blow up the complex of three large natural caves. He estimated it would take no less than 100,000 pounds of dynamite and TNT.

...Pfc. Charles M. Fink of West Liberty, West Virginia said it was tough. But he added:

"I'm a soldier. I just do what my job is."

6 Nov 67   New York Post (See Note Page 20)
            HO BO WOODS, VIETNAM

Artillery and air strikes have failed, so now American infantrymen are using water in efforts to flush Viet Cong guerrillas out of deep tunnels.

Ever since the 25th Infantry Division arrived in this area 30 miles northwest of Saigon in January, 1966, Viet Cong guerrillas have fought the Americans from underground.

...Water, the cheapest item in Vietnam, now is being pumped into the tunnels through six-inch steel pipes that run up to a mile from the Saigon River or the nearest of the many huge, water-filled bomb craters.

The water besides drowning anyone inside, has the effect of collapsing the tunnels and bringing down the soft soil, destroying the hiding places and burying ammunition and food caches.

CHAPTER X
WEAPONS

The following Articles from International Conventions relevant to this chapter are quoted in full:

Hague Convention No. IV, Annex
Regulations Respecting the Laws and Customs of War on Land
18 October 1907
(Short reference: Hague—Laws)

Article 23

In addition to the prohibitions provided by special Conventions, it is especially forbidden—

(a) To employ poison or poisoned weapons.

(b) To kill treacherously individuals belonging to the hostile nation or army.

(e) To employ arms, projectiles, or material calculated to cause unnecessary suffering.

NAPALM AND PHOSPHORUS

15 Feb 65   The Evening Star (Washington) (See Note Page 20)
             WASHINGTON, Feb 14

Policy set above the military level is banning the use of fire bombing in U. S. retaliatory air strikes at North Viet Nam.

Fire bombing with napalm weapons is a standard technique for producing substantial personnel casualties, customarily used in air attacks on both troops and buildings.

...McNamara obviously wanted the information about non-use of napalm to reach the free world and the Communist camp.

14 Feb 65   (See Note Page 20)
             WASHINGTON, Feb 14

...Napalm is one of the most rudimentary but most effective weapons. It is a concoction of gasoline and a jelly substance. It kills in two ways: by burning and asphyxiation.

15 Feb 65   The Evening Star (Washington) (See Note Page 20)
              WASHINGTON, Feb 14

Policy set above the military level is banning the use of fire bombing in U. S. retaliatory air strikes at North Viet Nam.

Fire bombing with napalm weapons is a standard technique for producing substantial personnel casualties, customarily used in air attacks on both troops and buildings.

...McNamara obviously wanted the information about non-use of napalm to reach the free world and the Communist camp.

14 Feb 65   (See Note Page 20)
              WASHINGTON, Feb 14

...Napalm is one of the most rudimentary but most effective weapons. It is a concoction of gasoline and a jelly substance. It kills in two ways: by burning and asphyxiation.

7 Mar 65   New York Times Magazine
              Jack Langguth, "Air Power Put to Test in Vietnam"
              SAIGON, SOUTH VIETNAM, Mar 6

...Although it is sometimes officially denied, the Sky-raiders have dropped napalm bombs throughout the South. No napalm has been used in either Laos or North Vietnam so far, however.

Restrictions on talk about the use of napalm came after the Vietcong gave particularly effective propaganda distribution to the photograph of a villager and his child after a raid. But the fire-bombs have been too valuable in penetrating caves and trenches to give up.

"The public seems to have this aversion to napalm," a senior American officer said, "because people think its kinder to blast a man's head off than to fry him to death."

12 Mar 65   New York Times, Jack Langguth
              SAIGON, SOUTH VIETNAM, Mar 11

A United States jet bomber crashed today during a raid in Binhdinh Province in Central Vietnam. A search was under way for two Air Force crewmen.

...The plane was flying at 500 feet, dropping napalm, or jellied gasoline. The exact nature of the mission was not disclosed, but United States military spokesmen in Saigon said the jets had probably been striking at a Vietcong concentration reported in the area.

20 Mar 65   New York Times, Jack Raymond
              WASHINGTON, Mar 19

The United States, apparently in a change of policy, is using napalm bombs in aerial strikes against North Vietnam.

Such bombs contain a sticky jelly substance that slows the rate of burning and increases the area of intense damage. They were used with devastating effect in World War II and the Korean War.

Emphasizing that napalm bombs are considered "conventional ordnance," officials said today that commanders had the authority to use or not to use them, depending on military requirements.

...Napalm has an awesome effect on personnel. When hurled into buildings, it not only burns them but consumes oxygen so rapidly that the people inside may be asphyxiated even when untouched by flame.

...Two Columbia Broadcasting System men, Correspondent Morley Safer and Cameraman Jerry Adams, were with the troops preparing to film the napalm strike when the canister fell.

Safer said in a dispatch to this headquarters in New York, it dropped no more than 50 yards from where the two were standing.

"We hit the dirt," he said. "I put my head up and the jungle in front of us was on fire. Running out of it were dozens of men, their clothes ablaze, some of them screaming, some rolling in the mud. In a moment it was all over.

"We reached them just as the medics were cutting away bits of skin and blackened uniforms. One boy of 19 kept asking: "Why are they doing it? Why are they doing it? Tell them to stop.'"

There was no immediate word of the effect of the fire raid within the enemy battalion, reputed to be the oldest Viet Cong unit of that size.

2 Jan 67   Journal of the American Medical Association
            "Wounding Power of the Missiles Used in the Republic
            of Vietnam"
            Maj. Norman M. Rich, MC, USA
            Maj. Egon V. Johnson, MC, USA
            Lt. Col. Francis C. Dimond, Jr., MC, USA

...There has been a variety of wounds, including those caused by the white phosphorus grenade, which adds the problem of continuing tissue destruction from the burning phosphorus until all the phosphorus is removed, and those caused by the latest type of fragmentation grenade. Extensive trauma from the blast as well as the fragments should be emphasized. Multiple wounds larger than the characteristic small fragments from the fragmentation grenade have been noted.

THE M-16

25 Mar 65   (See Note Page 20)
             SAIGON, VIET NAM, Mar 25

...Nonetheless a current of cynicism is apparent in various quarters here. One official who asked that his name not be used commented: "People on the outside just have no idea what this war is all about or how it is fought. It's a rough and brutal war. The Viet Cong has never heard of the Marquis of Queensbury or Geneva Conventions, and we can't afford to lose just because we have heard of them."

...Other weapons used by American and Vietnamese forces also have become controversial. One of these weapons is the .223-caliber Armalite rifle, introduced in combat for the first time in Viet Nam.

The rifle has a muzzle velocity so high that its metal-jacketed bullet virtually explodes when it hits a human being, causing a huge jagged wound. The effect is similar to the Dum-Dum expanding bullet outlawed by the Geneva Convention.

18 Mar 66   (See Note Page 20)
             WASHINGTON, March 18

Thousands of U.S. infantrymen and other troops in South Viet Nam will be relieved of heavier, long range rifles and given a lightweight weapon rated better for short range jungle fighting.

The Defense Department said today Gen. William C. Westmoreland, U.S. Commander in Viet Nam, had requested this action to improve "tactical effectiveness through increased use of firepower at short ranges."

As a result of Westmoreland's request, 100,000 more M16 rifles are being manufactured to replace M14 rifles in the hands of many U.S. fighting men in Viet Nam and to supply South Vietnamese and South Korean troops there as well.

18 Nov 66   Medical World News, "Medicine Battles the Odds in Vietnam"

...In actual combat weapons, the Vietnam war has seen the introduction of new high-velocity missiles that create wounds of a new kind. Says Dr. Harry H. Dinsmore of Punxsutawney, Pa., the surgeon at Danang who not long ago removed a live mortar shell from the side of a patient:

"The high-velocity missile creates a cone of damage which is not immediately apparent. Though it causes only a small opening at the point of entry, a modern bullet can create an internal cone of damage three to four inches in diameter. You have to open the patient up enough to evaluate the muscle and other tissue around the wound, and extensive debridement is necessary."

2 Jan 67   JAMA (Journal of the American Medical Association)
              "Wounding Power of Missiles Used in the Republic of
              Vietnam"
              Maj. Norman M. Rich, MC, USA
              Maj. Egon V. Johnson, MC, USA
              Lt. Col. Francis C. Dimond, Jr., MC, USA

...Wounds from the M-16 rifle (.223 caliber or 5.56 mm) are being seen frequently for the first time in Vietnam. It appears that this weapon has been very effective in the type of fighting being waged in Vietnam. The M-16 is standard for many units and some have fallen into enemy hands. We have seen 30 patients with wounds from the M-16, and, in general, these wounds have been extensive except wounds in the extremities at muzzle range. At muzzle range, entrance and exit wounds in the hands and feet have been noted to be 4 to 5 mm, with minimal tissue damage. The M-16 has a high velocity of 3,250 ft/sec, and the massive tissue destruction that we noted in the majority of our M-16 wounds emphasizes the importance of velocity in the wounding power of a missile. Another factor to be considered in the wounding power is attributed to what is termed the "tumbling effect" of the M-16 bullet. The marked difference in the wound entrance and exit size that is usually seen was demonstrated in one patient with an 0.5-cm entrance wound on the anterior area of the thigh and a 4 x 8-cm exit wound on the anterior of the leg. There is often a characteristic minute lead splatter from the soft core after the copper jacket fragments, and this is seen frequently on roentgenograms. Bone involvement, usually in the form of severe comminuted fractures, was seen in the majority of these wounds; trauma to nerves, arteries and veins was common. Included are injuries to the internal jugular vein, the superficial femoral artery, the external ilian vein, and the median and ulnar nerves.

27 May 67   New York Times, William Beecher
               WASHINGTON, May 26

The nation's No. 1 marine defended today the M-16 rifle, the principal American infantry weapon in Vietnam.

Gen. Wallace M. Greene, Jr., the Marine Corps Commandant, said at a Pentagon news conference that although the new rifle sometimes malfunctioned, charges that it had jammed in combat with disastrous results were isolated and misleading.

"The M-16 rifle has proved to be a reliable, hard-hitting lightweight weapon for our troops," he said. "It is a big improvement over anything we have had before."

General Greene spoke as a three-man House Armed Services subcommittee was laying plans to leave for the battle area late next week to investigate the performance of the weapons.

...The M-16 fires a .223-caliber bullet, compared with the M-14's .30-caliber cartridge. It travels at such a high velocity that it turns end-over-end on contact with the target, causing so much more damage. The fact that the new rifle and bullets are smaller and lighter permits each man to carry a larger load.

The Army introduced the M-16 to Vietnam about two years ago and has since made it the basic rifle for all its combat elements there.

Last August, General Greene said, the Marines asked for about 50 M-16's for each of its infantry and reconnaissance battalions in Vietnam to familiarize the men with the new weapon. Large quantities arrived in Vietnam in March to arm these units. About 20,000 of the 75,000 marines there have the M-16, Marine sources said, and the rest, who continue to use the M-14, will get them later.

Jun 67 Popular Mechanics
     Mort Schultz, "VC Firepower — Can We Match It?"

...But even the M14 is obsolete when compared to our newest rifle, the seven-pound M16, which is now being used by Army air assault outfits, special forces units and the Marines in Vietnam. It is pure murder.

The M16 makes a man a crowd, allowing him to lay down a fantastic 100 to 120 rounds per minutes, providing that he can change the 20 or 30-round magazine that fast. Accurate beyond description — a soldier 300 yards away can get endless groupings in a foot-square target — the M16 fires a .223 cartridge.

How effective can a bullet little heavier than a .22 be in combat? According to its manufacturer, the bullet is one of the most destructive made to date. It tumbles after it hits the target, and the massive wounds it inflicts have been compared to the old lead bullet.

...The M16 is quickly converted into a grenade launcher using the M148 adapter, giving each soldier both pinpoint and area firing capability. The M148, when placed on the M16, is as destructively effective as the M79 grenade launcher.

PUFF THE MAGIC DRAGON (THE C-47)

24 Nov 65 New York Times, Hanson W. Baldwin
     SAIGON, SOUTH VIET NAM, Nov 23

"Puff, the Magic Dragon" is among the many kinds of weapons, old and new, serving in the war aginst the Viet Cong.

...A war cannot be fought without a C-47, one flier says, and the old two-engine, propeller driven aircraft has proved useful in more than its original role as a transport. It has been fitted with machine guns in its door and in the port side of its fuselage.

The guns spew out 6,000 to 10,000 rounds a minute. When a ground unit needs air support, the C-47 circles one action and delivers a tremendous volume of fire.

24 Nov 65   St. Louis Post-Dispatch, John T. Wheeler
             SAIGON, VIET NAM, Nov 24

Puff, the Magic Dragon, wove its deadly spell so well against the
Viet Cong that 20 others have now joined her in belching flame and bullets.
    Newsmen were taken on a flight today.
    Puff is a pre-World War II C-47 that someone with imagination
outfitted with three Gatling-type Mini guns capable of delivering broad-
sides at 18,000 rounds a minute of 7.62mm bullets.
    ...Primarily an antipersonnel weapon, Puff circles a beleaguered
outpost while the pilot lines up the target in a gunsight pointed out of the
left window. Flying at 122 knots, he fires while he keeps the left wing low
and the pipper (illuminated sighting image) on the target.
    ...Capable of circling long hours over a beleaguered fort or outpost,
Puff can start the deadly circle quickly and in three seconds cover an
area the size of a football field with at least one bullet to every square
foot, says Lt. Col. Thomas E. Rickelman.

24 Nov 65   New York Times
             WASHINGTON, Nov 23

    ...In an age when the fastest fighter flies at more than 1,300 miles
an hour, the C-47's advantage in Vietnam is a lack of speed. It can
almost hang in the sky as a gun platform, pumping bullets at an incredibly high rate before enemy troops can scatter.

31 Jan 66   Aviation Week
             C. M. Plattner, "Limited-War Concepts Weighed in Battle"

    ...Early last year the Air Force modified five C-47s with different
types of machine guns — combinations of 30-cal. and 7.62 mm. Mini-
guns — on an experimental basis and evaluated them during night attack
missions in South Vietnam.
    ...Until the 4th Commando Sqdn. arrived Nov. 23, Air Force kept
the AC-47 under tight security, regarding it as a secret weapon against
the Viet Cong. Its high rate of fire and roar of the guns earned it the
nickname of "Puff, the Magic Dragon."
    Each of the Miniguns has a firing rate of about 6,000 rounds/mm.
for a total of 18,000 rounds. Up to 54,000 rounds have been fired on a
mission. The slow speed, large size and limited maneuverability of
the AC-47 make it more vulnerable to enemy ground fire than other
attack aircraft so it is used principally at night or against daytime targets which are not heavily defended.

13/13 Vietnam: Search & Destroy, Gordon Baxter, 1967, p. 34

    (The copyright owners of 13/13 Vietnam: Search and Destroy have
declined permission to publish textual material in this documentation.
The following describes the essential contribution made by a selection
from this book.)
    (Puff the Magic Dragon is described as a plane equipped with triple
gatling guns used on large groups of enemy troops or on a fortified hamlet
prior to assault.)

FRAGMENTATION WEAPONS

5 Mar 65   Time, "A Tale of Two Airports"

    ...It may not be enough just yet, but it was a considerable improvement.
In eight strikes last week, U.S. F-100 Super Sabres, B-57 Canberras and
prop-driven Skyraiders plastered Viet Cong concentrations, leaving scores

of guerrillas dead in their wakes. The planes dropped tons of newly developed anti-personnel bombs, including an aerial version of the artilleryman's cannister; a big bomb casing that opens after release to pour out a string of smaller bombs on a 100-ft. line.

3 May 65   New York Times, Jack Raymond
             WASHINGTON, May 2

Defense officials do not like the terminology, but they readily concede that Vietnam has given the United States armed forces a "laboratory for war."
Tactical theories are being tried, men trained and weapons tested.
Each military service — Air Force, Army, Navy and Marines — is involved.
...Among the gimmicks is the so-called Lazy Dog. This is a drum of steel pellets dropped from a plane that explodes at 6,000 feet. The pellets have a buckshot effect against men and equipment when they reach the ground.
A similar but more powerful weapon is the CBU, for Cluster Bomblet Unit. Small fragmentation bombs are released from a drum against guerrilla units in the jungle.

2 Aug 65   Newsweek

...New orders have been crackling out of the Pentagon, with requests sometimes going out by telephone and telegram — rather than mail — to speed up the process. American Machine & Foundry, for example, just got a $17 million order for Mark 82 bomb assemblies. Some of the work is still classified, such as Honeywell's $3.3 million order for BLU-3 cluster bombs. These are the high-explosive, anti-personnel bomblets being dropped on North Vietnam.

31 Jan 66   Aviation Week
             C. M. Plattner, "Limited-War Concepts Weighed in Battle"

...*Mk. 80 series of bombs.... These bombs, now in widespread use, have a low-drag profile which permits longer range for jet aircraft carrying them. When practical, the older "fat" bombs normally are assigned to the Douglas A-1s, where drag considerations are not as acute. In the case of the Republic F-105, carrying five Mk. 83 1,000 lb. bombs versus six M-117 750-lb. bombs, fuel flow is several hundred pounds per hour less. The Mk. 80 series of bombs was designed with the option of attaching a retarding fin for low-altitude delivery, but only occasional use has been made of this feature so far in the war due to heavy small arms and automatic weapons fire. The retarded bomb is known as Snakeye.

21 Mar 66   Aviation Week, "Vietnam Spurs Navy Weapons Advances"
             CHINA LAKE, CALIF

...Pinpoint delivery techniques are desirable for targets which can be located and identified. Thus, if the target acquisition problem can be overcome, then some accurate guidance technique is desirable. This includes television for Walleye and Condor, and possible backup systems for use in weather or in darkness. It also includes means to enhance the pilot's bombing accuracy, such as computers.
Shotgun technique is used when the target does not lend itself to pinpoint bombing either because it is spread out or because it is difficult to locate precisely. This approach has been taken in design of eye series weapons at Naval Ordnance Test Station, such as Rockeye, Gladeye, Wet Eye and Sadeye....

These are all area coverage weapons like bomblet dispensers, which are dropped visually by the pilot in the same manner that bombs or napalm are dropped, hence the reference to "eye". USAF is considering buying Rockeye and Sadeye this year ... as well as Walleye.

...One aspect of weaponry being studied at the Naval Ordnance Test Station is how to build a deterrent capability into conventional ordnance.

...An example of a deterrent factor in conventional ordnance is whistling bombs used by the Germans during World War 2 which had a separate and distinguishable psychological impact on allied forces apart from the actual destruction which they caused.

With the growing acceptance of the principle that conventional ordnance will continue to be the main type used in limited wars in the future years, there is increasing interest in finding ways to build a deterrent value into conventional weapons along the same lines as the strategic deterrent aspects of nuclear bombs.

1 May 66   New York Times
            Hanson Baldwin, Vietnam is a Proving Ground for New Weapons

...Many anti-personnel weapons of various types have also been tried with air dispensers — from bomblets and darts to a modern variety of cannister.

24 Oct 66   Aviation Week
             Cecil Brownlow, "New Viet Shortage Inquiries Seen"
             WASHINGTON

...In a subsequent appearance before the appropriations subcommittee, McDonald told Rep. Minshall he had received a direct report from Adm. U.S. Grant Sharpe, Jr., commander in chief, Pacific, "who stated that if the bomb load had perchance been limited in any particular instance, it was unquestionably due to distribution."

...Rep. Minshall asked, "What happens when our wings ask for the moderntype bombs, the delay-drag bombs? What do you do about it? You do not have enough to go around. What do you do?" McDonald replied.

"We tell them to use appropriate mix based on what they have."

In the letter published by AW & ST on Sept. 19, the Air Force pilot said, "Looking at three jet fighter bases in Vietnam containing a total of over 12 fighter squadrons, no 750-lb. GP (general purpose) bombs are to be found. The bombs used are 250-lb. Mk. 81 and 500-lb. MK. 82, the 'Snakeye' series, which can be dropped in either high-or-low-drag form.

"...The MK. 81 is, at best, a nuisance charge. Since all the 81s I have seen have been low-drag, they must be dropped by dive bombing from slant ranges of 4,000-8,000 feet, U.S. Air Force delivery qualifying criteria requires a CEA (circular error, average) of 140 ft. In our FAC (forward air controller) directed attacks, we are usually required to pin-point a small target such as a bunker or a thatched hut. Radio calls by the FAC are often heard such as '...nice bomb — put the next one about 10 meters at 12 o'clock...', 'i.e., a miss, but any pilot, fighter or bomber, can tell you that a 33-ft. bomb is damn fine shooting. A 750-lb. GP would have blast-damaged or destroyed the target at that proximity, a 250 digs a neat hole nearby."

He also said that USAF fighter squadrons in Vietnam have an authorized monthly expenditure of 80,000 rounds of 20-mm. high-explosive incendiary ammunition and noted that "there is nothing more demoralizing than the sight of an F-4 taxing out with nothing but a pair of (Mk.) 81s or 82s nestled among its ejector racks."

... Last week's Air Force reply to Rep. Minshall was presented in general terms. USAF said there are "sufficient quantities" of both 750-lb. bombs and 20-mm. ammunition in Southeast Asia but made no mention of 20-mm. high-explosive incendiary ammunition, which the pilot specified as being in short supply.

The Air Force reply pointed out that the Mk. 81 was not intended to be used against "bunkers," but did not deny they were being used against them, nor did it mention the pilot's contention that, with current accuracies, the detonation effect of a 250-lb. bomb often is insufficient.

... The Air Force rebuttal follows:

"Both the 750-lb. bomb and 20-mm. ammunition are stockpiled at our air bases in Southeast Asia in sufficient quantities to meet our tactical requirements. Our forces have been given and will continue to receive full support in obtaining any and all material and logistical assistance needed in connection with their activities.

"The Mk. 81 was designed as a fragmentation weapon. It was never intended that this bomb should be used against hard targets such as bunkers. Part of the military mission in South Vietnam is to harass the enemy, day and night, in order to prevent massing of large troop concentrations. The Mk. 81 has been extremely successful when employed for this purpose. Specifically designed heavier weapons are available for use against fortified positions.

"... In Southeast Asia, as in any other conflict, the sole objective in establishing sortie requirements is to achieve maximum combat effectiveness and destruction of the enemy capability. For example in South Vietnam where support of friendly ground forces, interdiction, and harassment of enemy forces has necessitated simultaneous coverage of large geographical areas to constantly keep the enemy off balance, the tasking of 40 or 50 sorties at full loads instead of 200 sorties at optimum loads would not do the job. By mixing the weapon loads to provide optimum destructive effect, and thereby increasing the number of sorties, the Air Force provides an around-the clock effort."

Nov 66   Flying
              Frank Harvey, "The Air War in Vietnam"

(The editors of Flying have declined permission to give the verbatim text of a selection from the above cited article. The following describes the contribution of that selection.)

(The contents of the CBU or Cluster Bomb Unit is described. Each of the 800 metal balls in the cannister has in itself a cluster of smaller balls called bomblets. Through a compression action the bomblets are scattered in all directions. Anyone within a given path about 200 feet wide will be killed or wounded both inside and outside huts.

Forward Air Controllers prefer CBU's as a weapon even over napalm.)

23 Nov 66   World Journal Tribune, Evans and Novak

...As soon as the first helicopter was hit, red smoke bombs went off in a signal to division commanders, watching the operation as we were from a helicopter, that this was indeed a hot LZ, thus, an instant after the first attack from the jungle, the Air Force F-100s were back, crossing and criss-crossing the narrow edge of jungle concealing the Viet Cong, dropping fire bombs, CBU's (a devilishly effective anti-personnel bomb) and high explosives.

1967   Aviation Week, Marketing Directory Issue
                "Munitions Test Group Mission Will Expand"
                EGLIN AFB, FLA

Munitions Test Directorate, a branch under the Air Proving Ground Center's Deputy for Test, conducts slightly more than 50% of the tests at Eglin annually and is a key member of the triumvirate established here by USAF to develop and test non-nuclear weapons.

...At present, the Munitions Test Directorate, commanded by Col. Frank L. Fisher, has 131 test projects under way (106 active and 25 suspended) and this figure is expected to grow to nearly 200 during 1967. Some idea of the impact which the Vietnam war has had on this center may be gained from the fact that this directorate had only 33 projects in 1961.

Col. Fisher said that his group covers the spectrum of conventional weapons: bombs, bomblets, guns, rockets, fuzes (sic), aerial mines, missiles, ammunition, dispensers and chemical-biological munitions. The directorate also is involved with aerial targets and scoring devices.

1967   Aviation Week, Marketing Directory Issue
                "Lab Stresses Non-Nuclear Weapons"
                EGLIN AFB, FLA

Air Force Armament Laboratory, an element of the Air Force Systems Command's Research and Technology Div., will spend approximately $80 million this fiscal year for non-nuclear munitions. About half that amount will be for initial stocks of production-line ordnance for U.S. Air Forces around the world and the other half for research and development on new bombs, guns and associated equipment.

...Col. Glover said the status of conventional munitions at the time the U.S. began playing a larger role in the Vietnam war "was terrible. In many cases, the stockpiled weapons were nor compatible with the high-speed aircraft and tactics (being used) there." Others, equally familiar with the situation at the time, add that many weapons also were not as effective as they were thought to be.

But the growth of the Southeast Asian war and the increasing U.S. involvement in it he said, has "caused a complete rejuvenation in this area." Starting with $3 million in 1961, USAF has aggressively pushed the development of non-nuclear munitions.

...More effective retardation devices for bombs of 250 lb. and larger. Devices now in use have not been consistently effective when released from a high-speed aircraft at low altitudes and the attacking aircraft has sometimes been subjected to ground reflections of the detonation pulse or ricochets from bomb fragments. Malfunctioning retardation devices also reduce accuracy.

Dispensers for all types of ordnance, from flares to rockets to bomblets. Col. Glover said that a large effort is being made and will continue to be made in this area. Emphasis is being placed on downward ejection techniques, safe and positive separation from supersonic aircraft, increased dispersion patterns for some types of weapons such as bomblets, and feasibility determination of rocket-assisted ejection.

6 Feb 67   Aviation Week
                Cecil Brownlow, "USAF Boosts North Viet ECM Jamming"
                SAIGON

...On the other hand, methods of destruction on North Vietnamese SAMs and anti-aircraft sites also have improved. Possibly the most effective weapons against the anti-aircraft sites are CBU anti-personnel clustered bomblet units. The CBUs are dropped at altitude, normally 10,000-15,000 ft., and the canisters containing the bomblets are destroyed by an explosive charge shortly after release, providing a wide pattern of coverage on the ground. Aside from the steel, razor-like pellets carried by the standard CBUs, other versions of the bomblets contain napalm and white phosphorous.

The success of the CBUs against North Vietnamese anti-aircraft sites has "probably saved more pilots' lives over the past six months than anything else," says one top official here.

Another prime flak-suppressent weapon is the 1,000-lb. low-drag bomb equipped with a "daisy-cutter" fuze timed to detonate just before impact in order to produce a good spread of shrapnel. Effectiveness of such bombs is described as "excellent."

...Use of the 2.75-in. rocket by strike aircraft in South Vietnam also is declining, although it still is a prime weapon for armed Army UH-1B helicopters. The drawback to its use in the south is the tendency to detonate as it strikes the tops of trees when fired into a jungle area. When this occurs, the shrapnel effect on the ground is negligible.

A similar problem is encountered in the south with napalm. Unfinned cannisters have difficulty in penetrating the jungle canopy before erupting. The relatively new finned canisters are more successful, although they tend to stick in the ground on impact, providing only a minimal spread of the jelled napalm payload.

The less-accurate unfinned canisters, hit the ground tumbling, with the napalm spreading over a wide area.

Despite these problems, napalm is used widely in the south. Drops sometimes are made within 150 ft. of friendly ground troops at the request of their commander.

Air Force officials, however, discourage such close-in napalm drops because of the unpredictability of the spread pattern.

21 Feb 67   New York Times, William Beecher
              WASHINGTON, Feb 20

...In a typical bombing mission against North Vietnam, some planes will carry Shrikes to try to silence the radar surface-to-air missiles and antiaircraft guns and some planes will carry antipersonnel cluster bombs and other weapons designed to kill those who man the air defense weapons.

23 Feb 67   New York Times, Dana Adams Schmidt
              LONDON, Feb 22

Laurence Daly, general secretary of the Scottish area of the National Union of Mineworkers, declared today on his return from North Vietnam that he was "deeply shocked" by evidence of "deliberate concentration by the United States Air Force on destruction of the civilian population."

..."We inspected towns, villages and the areas outside," Mr. Daly said, "and everywhere were struck by signs that the Americans were concentrating on a type of weapon which does not greatly damage concrete or steel but is deadly against people.

"This is what the Americans call the C.B.U. bomb, which, when it explodes, throws out 300 flanged iron balls which the Vietnamese call 'guavas' because they are shaped like the fruit.

"Each 'guava' contains 300 iron pellets which, along with the fragments of the balls, tear through the air with a speed I was told was greater than that of bullets."

Mr. Daly said that before he went to North Vietnam he believed that civilians had been bombed when bombs aimed at military targets fell wide of the mark.

"But now," he said, "I don't see any conclusion except that bombing the civilians is a deliberate policy of the Pentagon, presumably in hopes of inducing them to bring pressure on their Governemnt to surrender, in the sense of accepting negotiations without a promise of permanent cessation of bombing. But the effect is to redouble the support of the Government."

7 Apr 67   Life
              Lee Lockwood, "Recollections of four weeks with the enemy"

...Much of the outrage against U.S. bombing is directed at the use of
anti-personnel bombs — particularly the CBU's (cluster bomb units), canisters which burst in the air, each scattering 300 baseball-sized explosives
which detonate on impact, each spraying hundreds of pea-sized steel pellets
at high velocity over a wide area. The pellets are coated with napalm and
stick when they hit.

...The most convincing evidence of CBU's I saw was near Viet Tri,
northwest of Hanoi. Here, factory walls were scarred with characteristic
symmetrical patterns of pockmarks. Later, I visited the Viet Tri hospital,
which recently had been moved from the city to a rural village several miles
away. On Jan. 18, according to Dr. Le Hau Suu, even this village had been
bombed with CBU's. Pellet marks scarred the doctor's desk, chair, cabinet, sterilizer and other instruments. Outside, the crumpled half-shell of
a cannister lay across a narrow dike in a field stippled with cup-sized
craters. The doctor rounded up several patients he said had been wounded
by the pellets. One 18-year-old girl had taken a pellet through her left arm,
one in her intestine, one through her finger and lower lip, and one, which I
could feel with my fingers, embedded in the heel of her hand.

May 67   Ramparts
              Don Duncan, "And Blessed Be the Fruit"

...But what can be said of a bomb that cannot burn a bridge or a factory,
will not penetrate or blow up cement structures, does not penetrate roadways,
causes little damage to vehicles and less to trains? We have at least two
such types in common usage in Vietnam and possibly a third. They are
variously referred to as bomblets, cluster bombs, pineapple bombs or guava
bombs. The prototypes were called "Lazy Dogs" or LD's. When there is no
way to avoid the subject, our military refers to these weapons as "Ordnance,
Fragmentation." Everyone else calls them anti-personnel bombs.

...The pineapple, and guava, so dubbed by the Vietnamese, appear to be
refinements of the LD. The pineapples are carried in tubes under jet aircraft, with 25 bombs to the tube. Depending on the aircraft, each plane can
carry up to 20 tubes. When released, the pineapples sprout winglets which
either stabilize their descent or increase the dispersion pattern. The pineapple explodes on contact and spews 240 steel balls ten meters in all directions. The steel balls are 6.3 millimeters (approximately 1/4-inch) in diameter and hit with a velocity comparable to shotgun pellets fired at a distance
of three to four yards. The discharge from one aircraft creates an elliptical
killing zone five football fields long by two and one half football fields wide.

The steel balls have no effect on military structures. They cannot
pierce cement and can penetrate earthen or sandbag military revetments
only to a depth of two or three inches. The one thing they can penetrate
effectively is human flesh. Because of their shape and/or velocity, once
they tear into the body they move in a complex path, doing great damage
and complicating removal. There are cases where people have been hit
by as many as 30 pellets.

...Since the bombs have no ground penetration, and because they
explode on contact, people soon learned there was relative safety in the
nearest open ditch. A variation was then adapted involving mixed bomb
loads — HE or napalm was used to flush people into the open and then the
pineapples were dropped.

...The guava, although smaller than the pineapple, is far more effective. Each guava holds from 340-600 steel pellets, and because it is smaller,
more can be carried by each plane. From the standpoint of the pilots it is
much safer to use, since it can be dropped from much higher altitudes. But
that isn't the only refinement.

The guavas, or bomblets, are carried in a "mother" bomb. After release, the "mother" breaks open at an altitude of approximately 3200 feet to spew forth her "fruit."

...When the guavas are 30 feet from the ground they explode, hurling their steel "seed" not only outwards but also downwards.

Those bombs which do not explode in the air can still explode on contact, making them at least as effective as the pineapple. In addition to providing safety for the pilots, and having fewer duds, the guavas also have a longer killing zone — up to the length of ten football fields. The real advantage, however, is that because of the air bursts people in open ditches are no longer protected.

...Any kind of statistics for the South must remain speculative. That the bombs are used in the South was revealed on March 2, 1967, when a pair of Phantom jets using the bomb combination wiped out the village of Lang Vei, killing more than 100 people and wounding 175.

...The bombs are effective only against groupings of people in the open and are of as little use in the jungle as they are against military construction.

...Parts and pictures of the anti-personnel bombs have been circulated in Europe. The Japanese have made movies of them for television. Visitors to Hanoi have mentioned them, but the President and the Pentagon still insist we are not deliberately killing civilians. Both are reluctant to discuss either the guava or the pineapple, to the point of not even revealing their true nomenclature.

PERSONNEL DETECTION SYSTEMS

14 Mar 66   Aviation Week
             Cecil Brownlow, "Limited War Problems Challenge Industry"

...As a quick fix for Vietnam, USAF is studying the possibility of using an airborne magnetic field gradiometer to detect large quantities of metal on the ground. This might be used to detect hidden Viet Cong ordnance caches but not personnel. New proposals and solutions are needed urgently in the personnel-detection area. A major goal here is the detection of Viet Cong ambuscades before they can be sprung. One possibility is a sensing system that could detect the gases and odors emitted by a number of troops confined within a small area.

10 Nov 66   World Journal Tribune (See Note Page 20)
             SAIGON, Nov 10

Electronic devices that can spot cigarettes and belt buckles from an airplane several thousand feet high are being used nightly in Viet Nam to ferret out the Communists, an American military source said today.

..."The metal sensing gear is just as sensitive, but doesn't even need heat.

"They do the same thing on it. They fly over and make soundings under normal conditions and then later blast anything that is out of place. If there are half a dozen guys down there with belt buckles or knives or guns or anything made of metal, the plane will know it. In come the bombers and boom! No more belt buckles or people either. It's amazing."

28 May 67   New York Times (See Note Page 20)
             DIAN, SOUTH VIETNAM, May 25

The perils of body odor are normally associated with the social scene, but in the increasingly technological Vietnamese war a man can get killed if he sweats too much.

His nemesis could be an experimental American device nicknamed the "people sniffer." It picks up the odors of men digging foxholes under a thick jungle canopy, or camping beside a river, and shows the intensity of the smell on a meter.

A skilled operator, flying above in a helicopter, can see at a glance the area of a troop concentration and bring air and artillery fire to bear on invisible targets.

United States field commanders hope that the "people sniffer" may help to roll back the Vietcong's jungle cover.

The device is the latest in a line of technological gadgetry that has taken on bizarre overtones, even to the extent of attempting to use hungry bedbugs to detect a hidden enemy.

United States Army chemical war experts dealing with the smelling device have reported the experiments a success so far, and have made the once-secret project public.

"There is no question about it now, it works,"says Lieut. Col. Alvin Hylton, from Los Angeles, chemical officer of the First Infantry Division.

Another officer commented: "Everyone was laughing at first, including us. Now there is widespread interest."

The 20-pound device was designed at the Limited Warfare Laboratory at Aberdeen, Md., and the contractor is General Electric. It was originally designed to be carried and is officially known as an "E-63 manpack personnel detector."

The device could not specify how many of the enemy were underneath, whether they were men or women, or if they were friendly or unfriendly.

That degree of exactitude would be welcome, but it is not the way the war is fought today.

War Zone C and large areas of South Vietnam have been designated "free bombing zones." Anything that moves there is regarded as fair game. Previous high readings on the "people sniffer" have brought B-52 raids from Guam into the area.

The device cannot be used in polluted areas because of the high concentration of carbon and ammonia in the air. It is useless anywhere near where United States troops are operating.

American artillery and infantry units have already expressed keen interest in the device and dozens are being ordered.

CHAPTER XI
DEFOLIATION AND
CROP DESTRUCTION

The following Articles from International Conventions relevant to this chapter are quoted in full:

Hague Convention No. IV, Annex
Regulations Respecting the Laws and Customs of War on Land
18 October 1907
(Short reference: Hague—Laws)

Article 50

No general penalty, pecuniary or otherwise, shall be inflicted upon the population on account of the acts of individuals for which they cannot be regarded as jointly and severally responsible.

Geneva Convention
Relative to the Protection of Civilian Persons
in Time of War
12 August 1949
(Short reference: Geneva—Civilians)

Article 53.

Any destruction by the Occupying Power of real or personal property belonging individually or collectively to private persons, or to the State, or to other public authorities, or to social or cooperative organizations, is prohibited, except where such destruction is rendered absolutely necessary by military operations.

Article 147.

Grave breaches to which the preceding Article relates shall be those involving any of the following acts, if committed against persons or property protected by the present Convention: wilful killing, torture or inhuman treatment, including biological experiments, wilfully causing great suffering or serious injury to body or health, unlawful deportation or transfer or unlawful confinement of a protected person, compelling a protected person to serve in the forces of a hostile Power, or willfully depriving a protected person of the rights of fair and regular trial prescribed in the present Convention, taking of hostages and extensive destruction and appropriation of property, not justified by military necessity and carried out unlawfully and wantonly.

See also (pages 29-42) the following additional Articles relevant to this chapter: Hague—Laws: 23(a), (b), (c), (e), (g), 46; Geneva—Civilians 32, 33, 146, 147.

DEFOLIATION AND CROP DESTRUCTION IN SOUTH VIETNAM

15 Sep 64   New York Times, Jack Langguth
            VI THANH, SOUTH VIETNAM, Sept. p4

...Unlike the strategic-hamlet program, the pacification concept does not include surrounding the villages with fences of barbed wire that prevent departures as well as unwanted intrusions.

"These people want to live along the rivers and canals," one American active in the program explained. "We can't fence them in physically, so we are trying to do it psychologically."

Vietnam in the Mud, James Pickerell, 1966, p. 47

...The routes along which the Viet Cong will travel are the densely wooded strips that line the canals in the Mekong Delta. The land for fifty feet on either side of the canals is covered with heavy foliage under which the farmers build their villages. Movement of troops under the trees is very difficult to spot from the air unless the men are concentrated in large groups and as long as they remain dispersed they can move fairly freely.

10 Jun 64   New York Times, Peter Grose
            ASHAU CAMP, SOUTH VIETNAM, Jun 2

...Defoliation through burning has been tried and found almost useless since most of the tropical growth simply will not burn.

Chemical defoliants spread from low-flying planes have been somewhat more successful, though only against the growth they actually touch, perhaps the top 20 feet of jungle. The Americans say it would take a year of continued spraying to get through to the ground in many places.

25 Mar 65   St. Louis Post-Dispatch, Richard Dudman
            (from Congressional Record-Senate, Apr 1, 1965, p. 6556)

...The officers produced information on Operation Ranch Hand, the use of chemical defoliation sprays by four special U. S. Air Force planes. American authorities have de-emphasized this program because of world objection to destroying food, and because of Communist propaganda that the sprays harm human beings.

The reply was that there were 107 Ranch Hand missions flown in January and 58 in February. Officers said that they were unable to say how many were to destroy crops and how many were to kill jungle foliage at likely places of Vietcong concealment.

Crop destruction is understood to be the more important purpose, because food supplies are critically important to the guerrillas, but emphasis usually is given to the jungle defoliation in public mention of the program.

25 Mar 65   (See Note Page 20)
            SAIGON, VIET NAM, Mar 25

U. S. officials on the scene in Viet Nam have left it to Washington to answer international repercussions over the disclosure that nonlethal gases were used in the war against the Viet Cong.

Nonetheless a current of cynicism is apparent in various quarters here. One official who asked that his name not be used commented: "People on the outside just have no idea what this war is all about or how it is fought. It's a rough and brutal war. The Viet Cong has never heard of the Marquis of Queensbury or Geneva Conventions, and we can't afford to lose just because we have heard of them"

25 Mar 65   (See Note Page 20)
              SAIGON, VIET NAM, Mar 25

...In 1962, American planes began dumping chemical weed killer over stretches of jungle adjoining canals and roads, to destroy cover used by guerrillas for ambushes.

27 Mar 65   (See Note Page 20)
              WASHINGTON, Mar 27

...CBR, non-lethal or lethal, may be used against small groups of units of men, tactically, as it was in Viet Nam or as is done in ordinary riot control. Or it may be turned against whole armies or nations.

It can be delivered by a wide variety of methods, ranging from hand-thrown grenades or canisters up to warheads on missiles with ranges up to thousands of miles. Depending on the type, it can be used to put a man out of combat for a few minutes or to achieve a broad strategic objective of destroying crops and livestock, requiring months to take effect. This latter is biological warfare, which in addition to being intended for destruction of food supplies and contamination of water can be used for inducing disease in man — the so-called germ warfare.

Military men say CBR has an advantage existent in no other weapon. The army, in answering questions, has said that: "Chemical warfare can inflict personnel casualties without destroying physical facilities, such as factories, laboratories, bridges, ports, railroad yards...

"Further, the non-lethal incapacitating compounds offer the possibility of an aggressor temporarily incapacitating...troops without deaths or permanent injury.

"The incapacitation produced could be either physical or mental. The psycho-chemical compounds...produce mental disturbances such as confusion, apathy, inability to remember or to concentrate on the task at hand."

28 Mar 65   New York Times, Jack Raymond
              WASHINGTON, Mar 27

Weed killers are among the weapons being used against Communist guerrillas in what Secretary of State Dean Rusk has labeled the "mean, dirty struggle" in South Vietnam.

The weed killers, such as are used in many American gardens, are employed to strip jungle areas of foliage to expose Vietcong insurgents and to deprive them of possible ambush sites.

They are also used to damage farm crops in areas where Vietcong control has long been established.

United States military forces, while participating in most of the defoliating efforts, have not taken part in crop-damaging operations.

...The chemicals have been sprayed along roads and canals to destroy sheltering foliage that guerrillas might employ for ambushes. They are also used in the vicinity of headquarters buildings and around villages.

Until now, on the premise that the United States has not been engaged directly in the war against the Vietcong, United States planes have been kept out of crop-damage operations.

The South Vietnamese Air Force, however, has swooped on areas believed to be under cultivation by the Vietcong and has sprayed them with heavy defoliant concentrates.

Such operations have been a subject of controversy. Many officials believe that they have been only partly successful. They cite occasional errors, in which crops grown by loyal South Vietnamese civilians have been ruined.

3 May 65   New York Times, Jack Raymond
            WASHINGTON, May 2

...The defoliants have had erratic results. Defoliating large jungle areas to expose guerrillas and their camps has failed. But spreading defoliants on the perimeter of friendly military bases and along canals to eliminate hiding places has been quite successful.

3 Sep 65   (See Note Page 20)
            SAIGON, VIET NAM, Sep 3

Autumn came to South Bien Hoa one hot afternoon last week.

The residents were not expecting it. In South Vietnam's two-season climate there are only wet and dry, no in-between. Nevertheless, autumn came.

Autumn in this case came from nozzles attached to the wings of a U.S. Air Force C-123 defoliation plane.

Target for the day was a patch of jungled terrain which could have been a hideout for the Viet Cong.

Unfortunately, the hot air and the drift of the wind carried the airborne defoliant far from the target, over a French rubber plantation and plop onto a suburb.

Initially, those on the ground felt only a smarting of the nostrils and saw a bluish haze in the air.

The defoliant chemical used by the U. S. airforce in Viet Nam is said to be harmless to human life. In the days of President Ngo Dinh Diem, teams of psychological warfare personnel would tour the countryside, drinking the stuff to prove that it was harmless.

Within hours after the defoliant settled on the orchards and rubber trees and other evergreens around South Bien Hoa, leaves began falling, Vietnamese sources there at the time said. By next morning, they added, the French plantation owner was ready to seek indemnity for several acres of trees.

Some market garden crops keeled over in their beds, and all trees in the region were denuded.

3 Sep 65   (See Note Page 20)
            SAIGON, VIET NAM, Sep 3

...A controversial topic two years ago, defoliation is now taken as a matter of course.

The lower reaches of the Saigon river, miles and miles of highway, the mountains and the mangrove swamps of Camau have been defoliated. Special Planes flown by U.S. Air Force pilots are on constant call to defoliate regions. Vietnamese helicopters also defoliate, concentrating on Viet Cong crops areas.

The shower of defoliant over a populated part of Bien Hoa 20 miles east of Saigon is the first reported occasion when defoliant hit a friendly region.

26 Dec 65   New York Times, Charles Mohr
              SAIGON, SOUTH VIETNAM, Dec 19

...Four of these United States Air Force planes were hit again this
morning when they sprayed a chemical weed killer over a Mekong Delta
jungle occupied by Vietcong guerrillas.

...The spray unit, which is informally called Ranch Hand, is using
enough chemical to cover about 20,000 acres a month. Some of it is
used in crop destruction or herbicide missions, but pilots are not permitted to discuss the program.

Ordinary defoliation is used to thin out a jungle for several reasons.
One purpose is the prevention of ambushes along roads, canals and
rivers. For this purpose the foliage must be "burned" to a depth of
about 1,000 yards on either side of the road or canal.

...The Vietcong, and anyone else in the neighborhood, usually suffer when they do hit the spray planes. This morning three Super-saber
jets struck the village of Xomthu with 750-pound bombs, napalm and
20-mm. cannon fire when fire came from the village.

5 Mar 66   Business Week, "Changing the rules of guerrilla war"

...Defoliating agents are being used to kill vegetation and expose
jungle trails, and to destroy rice crops in enemy territory. But they
have been found to have only limited capability against the double-
canopied jungle growth common in Vietnam.

10 Mar 66   UPI, New York Times
              WASHINGTON, Mar 9

The State Department said today that about 20,000 acres of South
Vietnamese crops had been destroyed with herbicides to deny food to
the guerrillas.

...The figure does not include jungle and underbrush that has been
defoliated, or treated with chemicals so the leaves fall off, to deny
cover to the guerrilla forces. Officials said they could not estimate the
defoliated acreage.

..."Defoliation has been used to deprive Communist guerrillas
where possible of cover and concealment," the department said. "It
is used along roads, railroads and canals where the Vietcong have regularly taken advantage of thick foliage to set up ambushes against both
military and civilian traffic.

"It is used against remote Vietcong base areas, where the Communists have used thick natural cover to conceal their heavily fortified
training and regroupment centers."

...The State Department statement on crops said that "in some
cases herbicides have been used to destroy crops in remote areas long
occupied by the Vietcong."

"The areas affected are known to be used to produce food for Vietcong military units," it added. "In war, food is as essential to the
effectiveness of a military unit as weapons and ammunition."

The areas involved in the crop-destruction program are remote
and thinly populated, the department said.

"They are known from intelligence sources to be occupied by
Vietcong military units," the statement added.

"The herbicides used are nontoxic and not dangerous to man or
animal life. The land is not affected for future use."

...The State Department said all defoliation and crop-destruction
operations were initiated by the South Vietnamese themselves, usually
by a district or province chief.

14 Mar 66   Christian Science Monitor, David K. Willis
             WASHINGTON

...Further, officials describe the exact chemicals used: diluted
2,4,5T (tricholorophenoxyacetic acid) and 2,4D (dichlorophenoxyacetic acid).
More than 13,300 tons are sprayed annually. Exact figures are not given.

Nor are details on the amount of dilution, mixtures, and so on disclosed.

28 Mar 66   Christian Science Monitor, Takashi Oka
             SAIGON

The key to the defoliation question is discrimination. If the weapon
is used discriminately, it can be effective.

...Statistics show the number of defoliation sorties jumped from
60 during all of 1962 to 1,204 during the last six months of 1965.

The effect of the defoliation chemicals is to accelerate growth to
the point the plant dies. They are most effective when used during the
prime period of the growth cycle.

...To defoliate roads and railroads, a swath 1,000 meters wide on
each side is desirable; 300 meters on each side is the minimum. If
the swath is narrower, the Viet Cong, sitting in the undefoliated portion,
has a clear field of fire, with no compensating advantage for those using
the road.

...In mangrove swamps, which are in brackish water near the sea,
the effect of defoliation seems permanent; no vegetation has grown back.
In jungles with double or triple canopies, repeated applications are necessary; the effect may last up to a year, depending on conditions. In areas
sown to crops, since chemicals have no effect on soil, new crops may be
sown any time, according to officials here.

...When a friendly peasant's crops are accidentally damaged by
defoliation, the province chief has an indemnification fund from which
the peasant may claim damages. However, this action may be dilatory
unless some influential official urgently presses for indemnities.

One of the problems defoliation experts have to contend with is
whether a village that is considered Viet Cong today might be friendly
tomorrow, or vice versa.

And obviously, defoliation in populated cultivated areas is quite
different from defoliation of mountains and thick jungles.

28 Mar 66   Christian Science Monitor, John Hughes
             HONG KONG

...Sprayed from the air, these are used to defoliate areas adjoining roads, railways, canals, power transmission lines, and other sites
favorable for Viet Cong ambush as well as known Viet Cong staging and
headquarters areas. In addition, the State Department admitted earlier
this month that 20,000 acres of crops had been destroyed to deny food to
the Viet Cong.

...But though defoliation is supposed to be carefully controlled, and
indeed must be requested in an area by the South Vietnamese province
chief, there obviously are cases where non-Viet Cong lose their crops.

28 Mar 66   Christian Science Monitor, Takashi Oka
             SAIGON

...Defoliation is carefully controlled. It must be requested by the
province chief and his American advisers. Other hands through which
the request must pass include the Vietnamese Joint General Staff, the
American Embassy, and the United States Operation Mission, USOM as
the aid mission here is called. For instance, USOM might have a special
program going on in the area that spraying would render ineffective —
either materially or from a public-relations angle.

26 Mar 66   Chemical Week

...Stripping the Boondocks: Chemical agents are slated for new importance in the struggle to deny safe havens to the VC. Herbicides and riot-
control gases are helping to clear areas the VC and North Vietnamese have
long held and regarded as shelters — e.g., tunneled command posts, supply
depots and primitive hospitals.

C-123 spray planes on "ranch hand" patrols sweep clouds of herbicides
along access trails. Withered foliage reveals VC movement toward the
refuges. Stock piles and ambush points are bared. About 100,000 acres
of VC-controlled farmland have been sprayed with agents that kill standing
crops but do not damage the soil. The browned patches beside rivers,
roadways, trails, and crossroads are visible from the air.

Only the rain forests, with three and four layers of jungle growth, have
thwarted the herbicides. For this, Defense Secretary Robert NcNamara has
said he wants more-powerful and more-effective or longer-lasting herbicides
from commercial chemical researchers. Effectiveness of present herbicides
varies with weather and season. And in the rain forests, defoliating upper
tree levels may merely accelerate growth in secondary and tertiary layers
as the sunlight penetrates deeper.

Military men see the use of defoliants as one way to expand usuable
portions of the South Vietnam highway system. If the chemicals can keep
broad areas cleared beside the roads, armed helicopters can patrol stretches
that would otherwise require patrolling by hundreds of men on foot or in
armored cars.

26 Jul 66   New York Times, Eric Pace
             SAIGON, SOUTH VIETNAM, July 25

Chemicals lethal to plant life were sprayed over 59,000 acres of crops
in Viet-cong-controlled territory in the first six months of this year, American military officials reported today.

The officials said this year's spraying, carried out by American and
South Vietnamese planes, already had almost equaled all the crop killing of
previous years of the war. It is done to deny food to enemy soldiers and
their supporters.

The spraying, begun in 1962, has blighted about 130,000 acres of rice
and other food plants. The area is almost 10 times the size of Manhattan.

Analysts said the program, which is to be intensified, was a principal
cause of the food shortages plaguing Communist troops in parts of South
Vietnam.

26 Jul 66   New York Times, Eric Pace
             SAIGON, SOUTH VIETNAM, July 25

...The American military officials denied having used toxic gas and
called the chemicals "weed killer, the same as you buy in the hardware
store at home."

The chemicals used are known by the abbreviations "2,4-D" and
"2,4,5-T," which stand for "2,4-dichlorophenoxyacetic acid" and "2,4,5-
trichlorophenoxyacetic acid."

So potent are the chemicals, experts said, that if borne by a wind they
can kill plants 15 miles from where the chemicals are sprayed.

26 Aug 66   New York Times, Charles Mohr
             CUMONG PASS, SOUTH VIETNAM, Aug 23

Almost every day about 200 women from a Vietcong-controlled area
make their way along twisting Highway 1 to this mountain pass and, quite
unafraid, pass through a military checkpoint manned by South Korean troops.

...The women from the Vietcong area are badly in need of rice. They
elbow and shove and raise an ear-splitting noise as they crowd around the
women from Quinhon.

Each of the women from Quinhon is allowed to sell about five pounds of rice daily to the "enemy" women, but no more. The price is about double that prevailing in the Government-controlled towns.

...A Korean officer said the women from Longthanh village in Vietcong territory were short of rice because the Vietcong had confiscated or "taxed" so much of the crop.

A South Vietnamese soldier who serves as interpreter for the Koreans disagreed.

"It is because of the American spraying, which has killed all the crops in the district," he said.

10 Sep 66   New York Times, William Beecher
             SAIGON, SOUTH VIETNAM, Sept 9

...This year Operation Ranch Hand, using an average of six C-123 spray planes, has squirted 1,324,430 gallons of nontoxic herbicide over 530,872 acres of jungle hideouts, trails and crop-land in enemy-dominated areas of South Vietnam.

...Critics assert that crop destruction is a nondiscriminatory weapon that probably causes suffering among innocent peasants along with enemy troops. They fear, further, that once chemicals such as herbicide and tear gas are commonly used, it might not be a long step before more noxious chemical warfare agents are considered usable.

...The principal agent is a 50-50 combination of 2,4-D (dichlorophenoxy-acetic acid) and 2,4,5-T (trichlorophenoxyactic acid). It comes in an oil base and a water base. The other chemical used, primarily against high elephant grass and rice plants, is cacodylic acid. Neither defoliant is harmful to human life, officials insist, nor do the chemicals foul the earth to prevent new growth.

24 Sep 66   New York Times
             SAIGON, SOUTH VIETNAM, Sept 23

...A statement released by the military command here said:

"Defoliation operations are being conducted south of the demilitarized zone to deny cover and concealment to the 324B Division and any other North Vietnamese army units that might be using that area."

The military press office said that reports of spraying within the zone were erroneous.

Informed sources said privately, however, that they knew of no political or command decision that spraying within the buffer zone near the 17th Parallel would never be permitted. Aircraft have been bombing the zone in recent weeks.

Spraying south of the zone has been going on since late August, according to some sources.

Investigation indicated that at least one official source had told news agency reporters yesterday that spraying was under way in the southern half of the zone.

25 Sep 66   New York Times, Hanson W. Baldwin

...Chemical agents are used in Vietnam for three primary purposes: first, to defoliate certain areas — usually strips along both sides of roads — to destroy cover for enemy troops; second, to destroy Vietcong rice and other food crops; third, to flush Vietcong guerrillas out of tunnels, underground bunkers and huts with lachrymatory (tear-producing) and nauseating gases.

2 Oct 66   New York Times
            DANANG, South Vietnam, Sept 28

...On Monday, Gen. William C. Westmoreland, commander of United States forces in South Vietnam, asked Washington for permission to use herbicides to defoliate 50 square miles of the jungle-covered mountains of the demilitarized zone, which separates North and South Vietnam. The decision is up to President Johnson.

...One weary battalion staff officer said: "This terrain is tailormade for the North Vietnamese Army. We need some landscape engineering."

Some landscape engineering has already been done. B-52 bomber strikes have repeatedly scarred the demilitarized zone as well as the mountain areas just south of it. The B-52s and lighter bombers have blasted holes in the jungle growth, and where they have done so helicopters have found it relatively easy to land with supplies and take wounded out, even under mortar fire.

21 Sep 66   New York Times, Benjamin Welles
              WASHINGTON, Sept 20

...While conceding that the enemy effectively stirred up anti-American propaganda among Vietnamese civilians by labeling chemical agents "poisons," Pentagon sources stressed that these chemicals would be continued because they were deemed militarily useful.

"What's the difference between denying the Vietcong rice by destroying it from the air or by sending in large numbers of ground forces to prevent the enemy from getting it?" one source asked. "The end result's the same; only the first method takes far less men."

Similarly, Pentagon officials said, the defoliation program, in which aircraft spray chemicals that strip trees of all foliage along a path about 85 feet in width, helps expose enemy roads and supply trains. This increases the effectiveness of air strikes and helps foil possible enemy ambushes.

20 Oct 66   (See Note Page 20)
              WASHINGTON, Oct 20

Despite recent protests the United States continues to use defoliants and crop killers in Vietnam, a war tactic that so far has consumed around $10 million in chemicals.

A Pentagon spokesman acknowledged today that U.S. Air Force C-123's still periodically spray heavy jungle and rice-growing areas in an effort to deprive the Viet Cong of ambush cover and food.

...Over-all, more than 640,000 acres of jungle and cropland have been coated with what the Pentagon describes as nontoxic chemicals since January 1965.

The figure does not include the last three months, and a spokesman emphasized the 640,000 is cumulative — not representative of the actual land mass covered by the agents. Some thickly jungled regions are sprayed more than once and duplicated in the total.

Defoliating operations require about three gallons per acre at a cost of $5 a gallon.

Nov 66   Flying
              Frank Harvey, "The Air War in Vietnam"

(The editors of Flying have declined permission to give the verbatim text of a selection from the above cited article. The following describes the contribution of that selection.)

(Defoliation missions are flown in the Mekong Delta by C-123 Providers. A load of 11,000 pounds of defoliant chemicals can be spread in about 4 minutes and kills all green plants in an area of more than 300 acres. A normal load sprays 14 to 17 kilometers for a width of 80 meters.)

Victor Charlie, Kuno Knoebl, 1967, pp. 273, 274

...The war has afflicted the fields and soil just as much as it has the hamlets and villages, because the Americans are using sprays on a wider scale now to defoliate the jungle and destroy the food sources of the guer-

rillas. In many areas crops have declined by 50 to 70 per cent. At the
same time, the Viet-Cong keeps demanding greater tributes in produce and
money from the peasants.

...."We'll smoke Charlie out and then starve him to death. There's no
other way of getting at the little yellow devils," an American Air Force
colonel said to me. Until now, it is not "Charlie" whom the U.S. troops have
smoked out and starved, but mainly the peasants in the guerrilla zones.

20 Jan 67   Science
              "Chemical and Biological Warfare (II): The Weapons and the
              Policies"

...According to the latest information supplied by the Pentagon on request from Science, more than 500,000 acres of jungle and brush and more
than 150,000 acres of cropland have been, in DOD's language, "treated with
herbicides." While the Pentagon points out that this area is a negligible
fraction of Vietnam's arable land, the program is now tripling in capacity,
to 18 planes. (Correspondents in Vietnam report that, lettered above a
room in the headquarters of the men who fly the missions is a motto: Only
We Can Prevent Forests.) In other operations, the use of what the Pentagon
still terms "riot control agents," after a period of being closely monitored in
Washington, has passed to the initiative of local commanders. The Pentagon
told Science that it no longer knows how many times and for what purposes
they have been employed.

1 Feb 67   The Milwaukee Journal
              SAIGON, VIETNAM

Five Americans Tuesday died in a plane crash near the Laotian border
and another air accident sent United States bombs raining down on United
States marines.

The lost plane was a C-123 flying a defoliation mission along the fringes
of the demilitarized zone. It was shot down, possibly in Laos. It was one
of three planes trying to defoliate broad stretches of the demilitarized zone
with chemicals. A second C-123 was hit.

3 Feb 67   The Evening Star (Washington) (See B

Weed killer has rained down on more than 1 million acres of jungle in
South Vietnam, Air Force leaders say.

The purpose: To remove leaves from trees and vegetation which had
masked Communist supply lines.

"Spraying herbicides from UC123 Aircraft is a unique and highly successful special air warfare operation in Southeast Asia," Gen. John P.
O'Connell, Air Force chief of staff, told senators yesterday at a closed
hearing.

...By Dec. 31, "More than a million acres had been defoliaged," he
said.

7 Feb 67   St. Louis Post-Dispatch
              SAIGON, SOUTH VIETNAM, Feb 7

...The drive was coupled with a U.S. Air Force move to defoliate the
lower half of the demilitarized zone between North and South Vietnam to
uncover infiltration routes the Communists are expected to use during the
Tet cease-fire.

7 Feb 67   UPI, Chicago Sun-Times
              SAIGON

...U.S. spokesmen also confirmed that transport planes are pouring
tons of leaf-killing chemicals into the demilitarized zone separating North

from South Vietnam in an effort to hamper Communist troop and supply movements in that region.

The defoliation of the zone began Sunday, they said. There have been reports that some sections of the six-mile-wide buffer zone were hit with plant-killing chemicals as long as several months ago.

7 Feb 67   The Evening Star (Washington) (See Note Page 20)
            SAIGON

U.S. military planners are hopeful that defoliation of the demilitarized zone dividing the two Vietnams will release about 3,000 American and South Vietnamese troops from guard duty along the strip.

Official spokesmen disclosed in Saigon that twin-engine C123s equipped with special gear started flying over the zone Sunday spraying chemicals that kill vegetation.

...The planners also hope increased observation will make large-scale bombing in the zone unnecessary. If the Communists are subject to constant scrutiny, some officers feel they won't be likely to keep building the base camps and utilizing the troop staging areas that have been the targets of 41 raids by B52 bombers since last July 30 and many more attacks by smaller tactical jets.

There are problems in defoliation on such a mass scale. The most conservative estimates call for a minimum of 2,000 plane-loads of chemicals to do the job.

2 Mar 67   Reuters, Christian Science Monitor
            PERTH, AUSTRALIA

An Australian expert on Asian studies said Feb. 28 the American policy of defoliating parts of South Vietnam with chemicals was creating a refugee problem for Cambodia.

The expert, Dr. M.A. Jaspan, head of the West Australian University Center for Asian Studies, just returned from a 10-week field trip on the Cambodian border and was quoted here in a newspaper interview.

He said the chemicals often killed livestock and killed or maimed children. Nothing grew on destroyed land for several years, and many farmers would never again be able to work a farm, he added.

Dr. Jaspan said the war on the border common to Cambodia and South Vietnam had horrifying consequences, apart from creating a refugee problem with farmers and villagers heading for Saigon or Cambodia to find work.

He said he had also witnessed pregnant women and children disfigured by third-degree napalm burns.

Although there were cruelties from the North and South alike, Dr. Jaspan said it was the Viet Cong which was clearly winning the hearts and minds of the South Vietnamese peasants.

15 Mar 67   The Sun (Baltimore) (See Note Page 20)
             WASHINGTON, March 14

The U.S. effort to kill Vietnam's jungle and crops which hide and feed the Communists is escalating into a $100-million program.

In 1966 American planes spewed out an estimated $10 million in defoliants and herbicides over hundreds of thousands of acres of dense jungle as well as over Viet Cong-held riceland.

This year's Air Force budget provides $39.5 million for about five million gallons of vegetation-poisoning chemicals.

And in the nest fiscal year beginning July 1 the Air Force says it is asking Congress for $49.5 million more to expand the spraying program.

...In response to questions today the Pentagon said chemicals used in the spraying operations are neither harmful to human and animal life nor do they "sterilize" the soil against future vegetation.

Robert S. McNamara, (Secretary of Defense) told Congressional committees last month the decision on when and where to use chemicals has been turned over to commanders in the field. Such decisions are not made in Washingtion, McNamara said.

...The Pentagon said defoliation "routinely improves" visibility into jungle areas by up to 80 per cent.

The defoliation effort advanced from the experimental stage in early 1965 and the effects "are consistent and highly predictable," the Pentagon added.

25 Mar 67   Saturday Evening Post
             Richard Armstrong, "Believe me, he can kill you"

...But while Leslie Small tries to improve crops, another branch of the American war effort tries with at least equal know-how to destroy them. Many of its prime targets are only a few miles away from Can Tho. This is the Air Force operation known as "Ranch Hand." Their ready room is decorated with such sardonic slogans as THE SAIGON 4-H CLUB and ONLY YOU CAN PREVENT FORESTS. Just after dawn each day the Ranch Hands take off from Saigon airport in four C-123 transports, stripped bare so that the planes can get off the ground with a five-ton tank of commercial weed killer, which is sprayed from nozzles on the wing and tail. All the planes are pocked with bullet holes, since they are slow and defenseless, and the Viet Cong hate them.

...When their mission is a rice paddy adjudged to be Viet Cong, they do the same thing: dump tons of plant-killer to "deny" the Viet Cong the crop. The Pentagon has found this program so effective it plans to triple it this year.

25 Nov 67   The Christian Science Monitor, Elizabeth Pond
             KIEM TAN, VIETNAM

"We are people who live by farming alone and have fallen into a deficient, indigent situation because of the influence of defoliation .... American military performed this by planes spreading chemicals, and the effect ... has made various types of fruit trees lose their leaves, ruined fruit, and crops, such as green beans, white beans, peanuts, soybeans, and black beans lose their leaves, then die.... We sincerely request you suggest that the higher authorities send personnel to inspect the crops affected in order to compensate for our losses."

This is the petition that "six farmers" sent to the American adviser in Kiem Tan District, Long Khanh Province. And they are not alone in their complaint. Some 3,000 similar petitions, each presented by several farmers jointly, already have been filed with the Kiem Tan District chief. Many of them report crops down by two-thirds in this October-November harvest season.

The cause of this poor crop, the farmers say, is the American defoliation program.

...It appears unlikely that any of the affected farmers will receive cash compensation, despite legal provisions for such payments.

The United States maintains that this is strictly a Vietnamese affair. It gives the South Vietnamese Government funds for payment of war damages to civilians, but it has nothing to do with processing defoliation claims.

On the Vietnamese side, the province chief of Long Khanh has informed his district chiefs that anything over three kilometers from targeted defoliation sites cannot be compensated for, and most of the petitions are therefore automatically shelved as soon as they reach district headquarters.

The target for defoliation in the area is the Viet Cong stronghold of Song Dong Nai some 7 to 15 kilometers away from Kiem Tan's croplands.

In any case, for compensation to be paid, an on-the-spot inspection must verify that the damage really has been caused by defoliation.

Even if the experts were available to conduct such inspection — and they are not — the processing time of Vietnamese bureaucracy would prohibit definitive proof.

...And even if inspection were carried out immediately, it would be all but impossible to prove defoliants as a single or primary cause of crop damage in areas where there has not been deliberate, recorded spraying.

To amateurs the circumstantial evidence of damage by defoliation here appears convincing. An acknowledged forest defoliation operation was conducted nearby, and the defoliants generally used on forests are extremely harmful to crops, even in small amounts. Wind drift at the time of spraying and revolatilization — reevaporation of the fine particles of chemicals as the day gets hotter — do occur to an extent not yet established. The chemicals then travel in clouds over distances not yet established.

29 Nov 67   The Christian Science Monitor, Elizabeth Pond
             SAIGON

...The military function of defoliation is to improve visibility, especially from the air. Aerial reconnaissance pilots report 75 to 80 percent better visibility in defoliated areas. Tactical commanders report fewer ambushes in defoliated areas.

...Defoliation does not help in a tactical situation, as it takes three months after spraying for treated leaves to drop.

Deliberate crop destruction is a small part of the program — 8 percent. Military sources report that this is confined to isolated areas (1) that are significant sources of food that the Viet Cong would have difficulty replacing, (2) that the province chief reports he cannot control and could not send his own people in to harvest, and (3) that would divert manpower from shooting to toting rice.

These ground rules prohibit, for example, any targeting of crop destruction in the thickly populated Mekong Delta and in many places in III Corps area near Saigon.

The total amount of defoliation being carried on is classified. The amounts in I, II, and III Corps are about equal and outpace operations in IV Corps.

...Technically, the herbicides most in use on broad-leafed plants (trees) are 2, 4-D, and cacodylic acid. Dow Chemical's Tordon, or 4-amino-3, 5, 6, trichloropicolinic acid, is also used, in a blend with 2, 4-D.

Other chemicals are used on narrow-leaf plants such as elephant grass. 2, 4-D is a hormone stimulant that in the words of the military spokesman makes a tree "grow to death." Cacodylic acid is a desiccant.

These are defoliants, not sterilants. Their effect is said to last no longer than one growing season.

...There might be an exception to the single-growing-season limitation in Tordon, which in contrast to the other chemicals used does not become inactivated on contact with the soil. The commercial literature on this chemical cites its persistence in the soil, its susceptibility to leaching, and its solubility in water.

It warns that high-pressure sprays and aerial equipment should not be used in its application, that the chemical can move with water in irrigation or drainage ditches, and that treated areas should be removed from grazing and crop production until after the average three years needed for the chemical to become inactivated.

Tordon is sprayed from the air here, in strengths of three gallons per acre, or the strength equivalent to its use in the United States. Military chemists here were puzzled by the proposition that Tordon might remain active for three years and reported that nine months was the longest it could last.

When asked if there had been cases in Vietnam where the effect of defoliants lasted longer than a single season, one high-level American agricultural expert here said he preferred not to answer the question.

According to the commercial literature, available at military headquarters here, even "minute quantities" of Tordon and 2, 4-D can cause "severe injury" to fruit trees and to soybeans and other vegetables. The strictest controls thus need to be exercised to prevent injury to desirable plants.

...The initial request for defoliation may be made by either a district or province chief, with the concurrence of his American adviser. Among other things, the district or province chief must say that the targeted area is under Viet Cong or North Vietnamese control. He must pledge to reimburse any of his people in case of accidental damage to their crops. He must specify related plans for civil action and psychological warfare.

He also must promise to inform the people in the target area that it will be sprayed, tell them why it is going to be sprayed, and offer them the chance to come over to government-held territory if they wish to do so. He must have plans ready to handle any refugees expected to result from such an operation.

...The optimum time for spraying is early morning, when the necessary inversion conditions are most likely to prevail and pull the spray down rather than letting it float up and into clouds.

...How effective the controls are in practice in the various regions of the country is not clear. There have been incidents of accidental damage to "friendly" crops in all corps areas, but the hardest hit area at present, judging from the farmers' complaints, is III Corps just north of Saigon.

The problem is less serious in IV Corps, where there is less spraying because of the dense population, and in I and II Corps, where the highland jungle areas that are the prime targets are more clearly differentiated from the populated coastal strip.

IMPORTANCE OF RICE DESTRUCTION

1 Oct 65   Herald Tribune, Joseph Alsop
            SAIGON

...The last report in this space described the extremely positive results of a sweep through a Viet Cong fortress area near Ben Cat by the 173rd Airborne Brigade.

...In addition, 20-odd rice caches were found in the fortress area, one as large as 20 tons. Rice, unfortunately, is almost indestructible by ordinary means. It tamps explosives, to begin with, and even when blown all over the landscape, it still can be gathered up and washed and eaten. So the rice was not more than one-third destroyed.

The underground fortifications, the weapons factories and rice caches, moreover, are the main elements that make a fortress area into a fortress area. Hence means must be found to destroy all these things, if these areas, which have served the VC as their strong castles once served medieval robber barons, are to be put out of action. And right here, there may be image trouble.

Contaminants can of course be used to put the underground fortifications permanently out of action; but there is a question, unfortunately, whether the non-toxic gases will be sufficiently enduring contaminants. Chemicals to render the rice inedible can also be employed — the Pentagon research branch already has such a chemical, with a special injecting apparatus — but will the rice then be merely inedible or will it be poisonous if enough is stuffed down?

The image trouble can be perceived. But crippling the new strategy here strikes one as a rather more important sort of trouble, especially as the VC fortress areas are in the main only inhabited by the VC troops.

16 Dec 65   New York Times, James Reston

...Meanwhile a critical and largely unpublicized battle is going on here to reduce the Vietcong's supply of rice. Last year they managed to get more rice than they needed. In these last three months the U.S. has deployed large numbers of troops to enable friendly farmers to harvest rice and, in some areas where the Vietcong were in control, the South Vietnamese Government has approved U.S. chemical air strikes to destroy rice crops that would otherwise have been harvested by the Communists.

21 Dec 65   New York Times, Charles Mohr
             SAIGON, SOUTH VIETNAM, Dec 20

United States Air Force planes, spraying chemicals, have undertaken a drive to destroy rice crops in some areas under Vietcong control. The program uses the same chemicals as the "defoliation" program, which aims at destroying jungle canopy and undergrowth capable of sheltering guerrillas.

...The program which began last spring, has touched only a small fraction — 50,000 to 75,000 acres — of the more than eight million acres of cultivated land in South Vietnam. This is the intention of the policy-makers.

Although the Vietcong control or at least contest 70 per cent of the land area of the nation, crop-destruction missions are aimed only at relatively small areas of major military importance where the guerrillas grow their own food or where the population is willingly committed to their cause.

...Experience has shown that when the chemical is applied during the growing season, before rice and other food plants are ripe, it will destroy 60 to 90 per cent of the crop.

...The political control of the crop-destruction program begins with the South Vietnamese. A province chief must approve and, at least technically, must request any spray mission.

...In areas where such missions are likely to create refugees, plans must be made to receive and care for them.

Destruction operations are intended primarily for food fields in such Vietcong base areas as War Zone D, north of Saigon, and in areas where growers are considered willing Vietcong supporters.

Crop destruction is only one part of a large program of "food denial" to the Vietcong. The United States' 173d Airborne Brigade is conducting a "harvest protection" operation in Binhtuy Province, where troops are holding off Vietcong rice collectors while peasants are required to sell their surpluses to the Government or to the commercial market.

Until this operation materialized, a plan to destroy the rice by spraying had been in the making.

Even "harvest protection" programs are politically dangerous. In some cases, the peasants have been unable to sell their rice. It has therefore been confiscated in exchange for certificates redeemable later. But the peasants mistrust the certificates.

Both United States and South Vietnamese troops often try to destroy supplies of harvested rice that they find in areas under the political control of the Vietcong. All such supplies are described in press communiques as "VC rice caches," but officials concede that in some cases the troops have destroyed the property of civilian peasants, who may well remain resentful when attempts are made later to gain their political loyalty.

UPI, Milwaukee Journal, Michael Malloy
(from Congressional Record-Senate, February 16, 1966, p.3000
Article entered by Senator Proxmire without date)

...The contrast between the suffering farmers and the booming cities is partly intentional. Although officials do not like to talk about it publicly, American strategy is presently intended to force the peasants to take sides or suffer the consequences.

"They can come to the Governemnt or they can go join the Vietcong, but they can't remain neutral and indifferent," a high ranking American spokesman explained.

The Province of Long An, for instance, has 585 hamlets. American aid goes only to the 76 hamlets which are considered pacified and the rest of the countryside is written off as enemy territory. Police confiscate rice, salt, sugar, and medicine bound for these villages.

This kind of economic warfare is intended to keep food and supplies away from the Vietcong. But it also means that life is going from bad to worse for at least half of the population of South Vietnam.

The benefits of American aid go first to the city people, who have always been pro-government, and second to the secure villages, which have never been pro-Vietcong. The peasants in the insecure areas are untouched by the battle for their hearts and minds.

21 Feb 66   (See Note Page 20)

The first tentative effort at resources control did not come until October 1964 when the national police were ordered to stop the flow of strategic goods into Viet Cong hands.

At the time there were only about 20,000 police in the country. They were still suffering from bad morale and lost reputation from the days of ex-president Ngo Dinh Diem.

Today the police are 54,000 strong and their ranks are expected to swell to 72,000 by the end of the year. A major share of new men will be thrown into the resources control program. This type of program aided the British in crushing a Communist guerrilla uprising in Malaya.

...But knowledgeable sources say there is still a long way to go before anything approaching true control over strategic goods can be achieved.

Tens of thousands of tons of rice are gathered yearly by the Viet Cong in the lush Mekong Delta. This is shipped to Cambodia, moved northward along the border and then brought back into Viet Nam for Communist base camps.

...Once the Viet Cong shipped Penicillin by the truckload from Saigon. Now it is smuggled out inside bread loaves, in the bottom of vegetable baskets and the like. Police control has built up enough that 64,540 units of various medicines were seized last year. These included antimalaria drugs and vitamins as well as penicillin.

...Once rice is seized and put under government control it is doled out to the farmers. In areas where Viet Cong influence is high, such as Phu Yen, families theoretically are given small amounts at frequent and regular intervals. In some bad areas no one is permitted to carry more food out of the village than he needs for 24 hours.

14 Mar 66   Christian Science Monitor, David K. Willis
             WASHINGTON

...From universities and private citizens has come an outcry of moral indignation. In reply, Pentagon officials defensively but doggedly say:

In war, food is just as much a weapon as rifles. Standard procedure for American and South Vietnamese troops is to hold back as much food as possible from the Viet Cong.

If American troops find caches of rice hidden in sacks by Viet Cong outposts, they destroy them.

If troops invade a Viet Cong area and find the water buffalo that all Vietnamese depend upon, they round up as many as they can — the rest they kill.

Similarly, if it is felt that the Viet Cong need to be driven from an outpost, one way of making them move is spraying their crops with the crabgrass killer.

That, according to officials, is that. Unfortunate, unhappy, and to be avoided if possible. "But war is war," they say.

2 May 66   Congressional Record — 8977, Congressman Mize

(Mr. Mize asked and was given permission to address the House for 1 minute and to revise and extend his remarks.)

MR. MIZE. Mr. Speaker, I was amazed to read the following report in Friday's Wall Street Journal which would, if true, indicate a gross inconsistency on the part of somebody in our conduct of certain phases of the mess in Vietnam:

"Large caches of Vietcong supplies were turned up by U.S. troops seeking jungle terminals of the Ho Chi Minh trail near the Cambodian border. The Americans began destroying the hundreds of tons of rice, salt, cooking oil, and sheet tin — one of the richest such lodes ever unearthed in Vietnam."

How in heaven's name can we justify destroying food on the one hand, continue to acknowledge a shortage of it on the other, and do all we can to get more out there?

14 May 66   (See Note Page 20)
             WASHINGTON, May 14

...Food is rated here as a highly important item in the Viet Nam conflict. The United States sends food to South Viet Nam and helps farmers there boost production.

At the same time various efforts are under way to keep food from the Communist forces because, as an official put it, "in war food is as essential to the effectiveness of a military unit as its weapons and ammunition."

22 May 66   New York Times Magazine
             Herbert Mitgang, "Looking for a War"
             DIAN, SOUTH VIETNAM

..."You can be damn sure that this is V.C. rice," the battalion commander says. "The area in Zone D where it was captured doesn't have any villagers living anywhere near there. So we are not depriving any of the people, we are denying the V.C. their food supply.... What do we do once we capture it? We burn what we can't get out — I'm not going to risk my boys' lives that deep in the jungle. We also use chemicals to destroy rice, but chemicals wash off and they can still eat it. The best thing to do is slit the bags open and dump the rice in the river."

The operations colonel from headquarters adds, "The funny thing is that at the same time that we destroy the captured rice, we ship in rice for the villagers."

Nov 66   Flying
             Frank Harvey, "The Air War in Vietnam"

(The editors of Flying have declined permission to give the verbatim text of a selection from the above cited article. The following describes the contribution of that selection.)

(Crop-destruction missions are approved at the highest levels. Some of the money the peasants are supposed to get to make up losses from crop destruction is pocketed by corrupt Vietnamese officials.)

13 Dec 66   Look
             Laura Bergquist, "Never Before a War Like This"

(The editors of Look have declined permission to give the verbatim text of a selection from the above cited article. The following describes the contribution of that selection.)

(In this passage the author describes her meeting with an Air Force lieutenant who has flown many defoliation missions. He destroys crops in Binh Dinh province. When asked whether he approved of crop destruction as a tactic, he admitted that it was a controversial subject but maintained that the strategy was good since it forced the peasants to come over to the good side after realizing that the VC could not protect their crops. The success of defoliation has led to an increase in pilots from 28 to 45.)

A SELECTION OF RICE COUNTS

21 May 65   (See Note Page 20)
               SAIGON, VIETNAM, May 21

... Sniper fire met elements of the 173rd Airborne Brigade which moved by helicopter Wednesday to a guerrilla-infested zone 15 miles northeast of Bien Hoa, itself 12 miles northeast of Saigon. A spokesman said the paratroopers destroyed Viet Cong booby traps and a couple of tons of rice.

16 Jan 66   (See Note Page 20)
               SAIGON, Jan. 16

...The 1st Brigade of the U.S. 1st Infantry Division wound up its mission after four days around Phuoc Vinh, 35 miles northeast of Saigon. American troops seized more than 1,000 tons of rice stored by the Viet Cong. Half the stock was destroyed and the rest was being hauled out of the area. In addition, the infantrymen blew up five tunnel complexes, 32 bunkers and 59 houses.

6 Apr 66   (See Note Page 20)
               SAIGON, April 6

...A week-long operation by U.S. 1st Division infantrymen and allied Australian and New Zealand units has forced the Viet Cong from old stamping grounds 30 miles east of Saigon. The troops chased the Communists out of 28 base camps, killed 23, captured 15 and forced the rest to seek new hideouts in jungle or swamp. Seized supplies included 867 tons of rice.

21 May 66   (See Note Page 20)
               SAIGON, May 21

...Two brigades of the U.S. 25th Infantry Division, which trained in Hawaii for the jungle fighting, have destroyed dozens of enemy structures and trenches, killed 86 Viet Cong and captured two this week in a continuing sweep through rubber plantations and the Boi Loi woods 35 miles northwest of Saigon.

Carrying out a drive called Wahiawa, after an Oahu Island district, the infantrymen seized more than 23,000 rounds of small arms ammunition, 89 tons of rice, 334 tons of other grain, 1,700 pounds of peanuts and 3,600 yards of cloth.

13 Oct 66   (See Note Page 20)
               SAIGON, Thursday, Oct. 3

...The U.S. command announced that a unit of the 11th Armored Cavalry Regiment uncovered 200 tons of Viet Cong rice 11 miles southeast of Saigon.

A spokesman said the rice would be turned over to Vietnamese district officials for distribution to villagers.

31 Oct 66   New York Times
               SAIGON, VIETNAM, Oct 30

...Meanwhile, engineers of the 196th Light Infantry Brigade reported finding in the jungles northwest of Saigon enough rice to feed 10 Vietcong battalions of 500 men each for 137 days.

14 Nov 66   (See Note Page 20)
               SAIGON, Nov 14

...The U.S. spokesman said that in all Operation Attleboro has swept up 1,480 tons of rice badly needed by the Viet Cong. In addition, he said the Americans have seized huge quantities of cooking oil, fish, salt, weapons, ammunition, and explosives in storming through Viet Cong base areas. The spokesman said the number of weapons and explosives seized was staggering.

...On Operation Attleboro, the U.S. spokesman gave this breakdown of material captured from the communists:

108 individual weapons (rifles, etc.), 17 crew-served (machine guns, mortar), 4,361 rounds small arms ammunition, 200 rounds 50 caliber ammunition, 30 mortar rounds, 500 Claymore mines, 6 rockets, 12,281 hand grenades, 3,175 fragmentation grenades, 1,299 tear gas grenades, 5,681 rifle grenades, four anti-tank mines, 11 floating water mines, five anti-personnel mines, 1,000 pounds of explosives, 1,000 blasting caps, 3,000 booby-trap igniters, 752 Bangalore torpedoes, 500 Claymore fuses, 80 grenade launchers, 500 rifle grenades adapters, 759 tons of rice, 15 tons of beans, 15 tons of salt, 2,500 pounds of peanuts, 40 pounds of documents, 144 bicycles. In addition, equipment destroyed included 205 structures, 218 bunkers, 83 tunnels, six base camps, one Claymore factory, 10 sampans, 7,950 pounds of fish.

26 Jan 67   Denver Post (See Note Page 20)
             WASHINGTON

Defense Secretary Robert S. McNamara says the war in Vietnam is nearing a significant turning point: the Viet Cong apparently are running out of volunteers in South Vietnam and may be forced to rely more on the north for future fighting men.

...McNamara said tight sea surveillance by the U.S. Navy and Coast Guard has limited the amount of supplies coming into the south that way. Also significant, he said, is the fact that more effective search and destroy missions resulted in the capture of more than 19,000 tons of Viet Cong rice last year — enough to feed 78,000 men for a year.

STRATEGY OF FOOD DENIAL

8 Mar 65   Hearings before a subcommittee of the Committee on
             Appropriations, House of Representatives, eighty-ninth
             Congress, first session; part 3

...Mr. Andrews. Do they have any trouble living off the land?
General Wheeler. Some. In certain areas they find food hard to get, particularly where our people have been pursuing them and fighting.

In one respect it is unfortunate that South Vietnam is so productive. Rice is easy to grow. There is plenty of food, generally speaking. We have had instances of where the Vietcong have been very hard put for food, but then they turn around and steal from the villagers and take the food away from them.

11 Aug 66   New York Times, William Beecher
             SAIGON, SOUTH VIETNAM, Aug 10

American strategists are making detailed plans for placing a sizable United States military force into the Mekong River delta region of South Vietnam.

..."If we are going to defeat the enemy, we must destroy their morale," one top planner said. "One good way is to make them hungry."

"A North Vietnamese regiment requires about a ton of rice a day. They can't transport the necessary volume down the Ho Chi Minh Trail from North Vietnam or even in from nearby Cambodia. They must depend on local supply. Their main granary is the delta."

...Another source said the delta doesn't send much rice to Saigon any more. The Vietcong, he said, collect taxes from many of the delta villages and then buy up the rice for transshipment to their forces all over South Vietnam.

"We've got to disrupt the Vietcong control of the villages," he said. "For too long they have been free to collect taxes, food and fresh recruits."

14 Jan 67   New York Times, Hedrick Smith
              WASHINGTON, Jan 13

...General Wheeler said he did not know any targets had been removed from the authorized list of targets.

But he said that in the ground war in South Vietnam, the United States would expand military operations in the heavily populated Mekong Delta, where for months there had been a lull in major ground actions until very recently.

...In comments to reporters, General Wheeler said that the delta, the richest rice-growing region in South Vietnam, was a source of food and recruits for the Communists and would "have to be dealt with."

EFFECTS OF CROP DESTRUCTION

Feb 66   Federation of American Scientists Newsletter

The following statement was released over the signatures printed below; later it was endorsed by the Executive Council of the Federation of American Scientists meeting in New York on January 28-29, 1966.

"We emphatically condemn the use of chemical agents for the destruction of crops, by United States forces in Vietnam as recently reported in the New York Times of Tuesday, Dec. 21, 1965. Even if it can be shown that the chemicals are not toxic to man, such tactics are barbarous because they are indiscriminate; they represent an attack on the entire population of the region where the crops are destroyed, combatants and non-combatants alike.

...Signers:
            John Edsall et al.

Feb 66   Federation of American Scientists Newsletter
              Michael C. Latham, Harvard School of Public Health
              Jean Mayer, Harvard School of Public Health

...The latest U.S. move to destroy rice crops in South Vietnam by the spraying of chemicals from the air seems a peculiar tactic if the enemy is military, not civilian, personnel and if the object of U.S. policy is to win over and not destroy the local populace.

Certainly there are few surer ways of bringing misery to old people, pregnant and nursing women and particularly children than by destroying the staple food crops of any area. As nutritionists who have seen famine elsewhere, we know that throughout history whenever famine occurs it is the young children who suffer first and who succumb earliest. Bands of armed men are unlikely to starve. This present policy, therefore, is most unlikely to achieve its purpose of weakening the active Vietcong adults without at the same time seriously affecting the health and lives of women and children in the areas where spraying has been conducted.

29 Jun 66   The Christian Century
              Jean Mayer and Victor W. Sidel, "Crop Destruction in South
              Vietnam"

...The contention we are attempting to prove is that by every tenet of our traditional American pragmatic ethic the program of food destruction is wrong: it is wrong because it is likely to hurt a great many innocent people principally children, while accomplishing nothing toward decreasing the military capabilities of the Vietcong.

The program appears to have several components, the most widely publicized (and possibly the most important, on a quantitative basis) being the spraying of herbicides or defoliating agents. Among other phases of the program are the prevention of harvesting and the burning or scattering of the harvested rice.

...The Weed Control Handbook issued in 1965 by the British Weed Control Council describes the properties of these agents. They are categorized as nonselective herbicides; that is, they kill all vegetation present. They have relatively short persistence in the soil and are said to have a "very low level of toxicity to man and animals." The handbook points out, however, that "prolonged exposure, notably to oil solutions, may cause skin or eye irritation to some individuals..."

As a nutritionist who has seen famines on three continents, one of them Asia, and as a physician with a basic interest in preventive medicine, we can say flatly that there has never been a famine or a food shortage — whatever might have been its cause — which has not first and overwhelmingly affected the small children.

...The mortality picture is clear. Death from starvation occurs first and overwhelmingly in small children, then in older children and in the elderly. Adolescents are more likely to survive, though they are most susceptible to tuberculosis. Pregnant women not infrequently abort; lactating mothers invariably cease to produce milk and the babies die. Adult men are far less affected. Thus the bands of armed men who make up the Vietcong are not likely to starve; being unhampered by family ties with people in the communities where they rove, they feel entirely justified in seizing any available food in order to have the strength to continue to fight.

Destruction of food seems never to hamper enemy military operations but always to victimize large numbers of children.

In the United States in 1865 the Confederates had to be beaten militarily: Sherman did not starve them into submission. The Paris garrison held in 1870-71 and neither its operation nor that of the troops of the commune was ended by the food shortage, though children died by the thousands. The 1917-18 food blockade caused deficiency diseases and starvation among German and Austrian children but did not interfere with the operation of the armies of the Central Powers. Leningrad held in 1941-42 even though by January 1942 the deaths from starvation rose to as many as 9,000 per day — most of them deaths of children and the elderly.

A general consequence of famine is the state of social disruption (including panic) which often accompanies it. Starving people attempt to journey to other areas where they hope to find food and the chaos increases. Families are separated and children, particularly the very young ones, become lost — and in all likelihood most of them die.

...Finally, in an environment like that of Vietnam, where sanitary measures are often nonexistent and medical facilities are in short supply, the risk of epidemics which can grow like wild fire in a weakened, starving and migrating population is a great additional hazard.

...The experience of World War I shows that French and Belgian farmers whose land was exposed to constant artillery fire and who were much better informed and more easily reached than the Vietnamese peasants often refused to leave their homes and had to be moved forcibly. Many Vietnamese may also find it impossible to abandon their ancestral graves.

We base our case, therefore, on the undeviating pattern of past famines when we state that crop destruction constitutes a war measure primarily if not exclusively directed at children, the elderly and pregnant and lactating women. In other words, our point is not that innocent bystanders will be hurt by such measures but that only bystanders will be hurt. The primary U.S. aim — to disable the Vietcong — will not be achieved and our proclaimed secondary aim — to win over the civilian population — is made a hollow mockery.

13 Jan 67   Science
                    "Chemical and Biological Warfare (I): The Research Program"

...In recent years a good deal of attention has been focused on plant diseases also. Recently the Army's Distinguished Service Medal, the highest award the Army gives civilians, was awarded to a Detrick researcher for her contribution to development of a rice blast fungus, a disease that in its natural form has repeatedly damaged Asian rice crops.

13 Nov 67   New York Post, Thomas O'Toole
WASHINGTON

Two of the nation's foremost biologists have charged that the United States is waging chemical warfare in Vietnam that is not only a tactical failure but may also be poisoning Vietnamese plant and animal life for years to come.

Spraying chemicals on rice crops believed to be in Vietcong hands, charge the two men in the current issue of "Scientist and Citizen," has not caused suffering and starvation in Vietcong ranks. What it has done, the two men insist, is to trigger a shortage of food for innocent women, children, infirm and aged Vietnamese.

At the same time, writes Dr. Arthur Galston, president of the Botanical Society of America and Dr. Jean Mayer, professor of nutrition at Harvard University, the spraying of herbicides to defoliate the countryside has apparently failed to expose Vietcong trails and hideways. Instead, claim the two men, the spraying has resulted in widespread damage to fruit and rubber trees, spinach and bean crops.

The herbicides have also leaked into Vietnamese streams and rivers, Dr. Galston said, and "while they may not be directly toxic to fish they may prove toxic" by killing the microscopic animals fish feed on.

...Of particular concern to biologists, writes Dr. Galston, is the apparent escalation of the defoliation and crop spraying program. This year, Dr. Galston said, "plans were to spray 1,500,000 acres, with as much as 500,000 acres being crop land" — about 5 per cent of South Vietnam's 8 million acres under cultivation.

So huge is the spraying operation in Vietnam now, Dr. Galston said, that military demand for the herbicides used is four times what can be produced by U.S. chemical companies, one of the largest being Dow Chemical Co. Co.

CHAPTER XII
FORCED TRANSFER

The following Articles from International Conventions relevant to this chapter are quoted in full:

Geneva Convention
Relative to the Protection of Civilian Persons
in Time of War
12 August 1949

(Short reference: Geneva—Civilians)

Article 5.

Where in the territory of a Party to the conflict, the latter is satisfied than an individual protected person is definitely suspected of or engaged in activities hostile to the security of the State, such individual person shall not be entitled to claim such rights and privileges under the present Convention as would, if exercised in the favour of such individual person, be prejudicial to the security of such State.

Where in occupied territory an individual protected person is detained as a spy or saboteur, or as a person under definite suspicion of activity hostile to the security of the Occupying Power, such person, shall, in those cases where absolute military security so requires, be regarded as having forfeited rights of communication under the present Convention.

In each case, such persons shall nevertheless be treated with humanity, and in case of trial, shall not be deprived of the rights of fair and regular trial prescribed by the present Convention. They shall also be granted the full rights and privileges of a protected person under the present Convention at the earliest date consistent with the security of the State or Occupying Power, as the case may be.

Article 27.

Protected persons are entitled, in all circumstances, to respect for their persons, their honour, their family rights, their religious convictions and practices, and their manners and customs. They shall at all times be humanely treated, and shall be protected especially against all acts of violence or threats thereof and against insults and public curiosity.

Women shall be especially protected against any attack on their honour, in particular against rape, enforced prostitution, or any form of indecent assault.

Without prejudice to the provisions relating to their state of health, age and sex, all protected persons shall be treated with the same consideration by the Party to the conflict in whose power they are, without any adverse distinction based, in particular, on race, religion or political opinion.

However, the Parties to the conflict may take such measures of control and security in regard to protected persons as may be necessary as a result of the war.

Article 49.

Individual or mass forcible transfers, as well as deportations of protected persons from occupied territory to the territory of the Occupying Power or to that of any other country, occupied or not, are prohibited, regardless of their motive.

Nevertheless, the Occupying Power may undertake total or partial evacuation of a given area if the security of the population or imperative military reasons so demand. Such evacuations may not involve the displacement of protected persons outside the bounds of the occupied territory except when for material reasons it is impossible to avoid such displacement. Persons thus evacuated shall be transferred back to their homes as soon as hostilities in the area in question have ceased.

The Occupying Power undertaking such transfers or evacuations shall ensure, to the greatest practicable extent, that proper accommodation is provided to receive the protected persons, that the removals are effected in satisfactory conditions of hygiene, health, safety and nutrition, and that members of the same family are not separated.

The protecting Power shall be informed of any transfers and evacuations as soon as they have taken place.

The Occupying Power shall not detain protected persons in an area particularly exposed to the dangers of war unless the security of the population or imperative military reasons so demand.

The Occupying Power shall not deport or transfer parts of its own civilian population into the territory it occupies.

Article 56.

To the fullest extent of the means available to it, the Occupying Power has the duty of ensuring and maintaining, with the cooperation of national and local authorities, the medical and hospital establishments and services, public health and hygiene in the occupied territory, with particular reference to the adoption and application of the prophylactic and preventive measures necessary to combat the spread of contagious diseases and epidemics. Medical personnel of all categories shall be allowed to carry out their duties.

If new hospitals are set up in occupied territory and if the competent organs of the occupied State are not operating there, the occupying authorities shall, if necessary, grant them the recognition provided for in Article 18. In similar circumstances, the occupying authorities shall also grant recognition to hospital personnel and transport vehicles under the provisions of Articles 20 and 21.

See also (pages 29-42) the following additional Articles relevant to this chapter: Hague—Laws: 22, 23(g), 46, 50; Geneva—Civilians: 3, 29, 31, 32, 33, 53.

CEDAR FALLS: CHRONOLOGY

10 Jan 67   New York Post (See Note Page 20)
             SAIGON, Jan 10

A massive American force backed by planes, armor and artillery has launched the biggest offensive of the Vietnam War in an attempt to sweep the Viet Cong out of the jungled "Iron Triangle" 20-30 miles north of Saigon.
...The operation includes evacuation of up to 10,000 Vietnamese peasants living in the longtime Viet Cong bastion and their resettlement in other localities.

11 Jan 67   New York Post (See Note Page 20)
             SAIGON, Jan 11

...The four-day old campaign to neutralize the jungled triangular area 20 to 30 miles north of Saigon was supported by another raid at midday by B52 heavy bombers, the 11th since Operation Cedar Falls began.

U.S. Military spokesmen reported frequent contact with small enemy groups but no large-scale engagement so far. They said the 60-square mile area was pulverized by some 400 U.S. tactical air strikes in the last four days in addition to the heavy B52 raids.

11 Jan 67   Denver Post (See Note Page 20)
             SAIGON, SOUTH VIETNAM

...The meatgrinder combat operation is being accompanied by a mass evacuation of up to 10,000 peasants and their resettlement in other localities.

U.S. spokesmen said an estimated 3,000 villagers and farmers have responded to appeals from helicopter loudspeakers and 215,000 leaflets. Spokesmen said the Vietnamese brought their water buffalo, chickens, livestock and households goods to the collection point at Ben Suc, on the northwest point of the triangle.

"It's a regular Noah's Ark operation," one officer said.

11 Jan 67   New York Times
             SAIGON, SOUTH VIETNAM, Jan 10

...While conducting the operation, code-named Cedar Falls, the allies also hope to deprive the Viet Cong of one of their oldest and most utilized sanctuaries.

Military offices said they expected that during the operation up to 10,000 South Vietnamese peasants would be moved into refugee centers in Government-controlled areas.

...Their primary target areas are the Thandien Forest Reserve and what the Americans call the Iron Triangle, because of the difficulty in penetrating it. The southern tip of the Triangle is only 10 miles north-west of Saigon.

The spokesman reported tonight that 115 Viet Cong had been killed and 29 captured, with 230 suspects detained after the operation began. The total was higher than some officers had anticipated.

"There are probably no more than 100 there all the time," one American intelligence officer said last night of the Viet Cong in the Iron Triangle.

...In the first three days of the operation, 276 fighter-bombers flew attack missions and by today, B-52's had hammered the battle area 10 times.

12 Jan 67   New York World Journal Tribune (See Note Page 20)
             SAIGON, Jan 12

...On the ground, a task force led by the 11th Armored Cavalry Regiment pushed deeper into the jungle, U.S. spokesmen reported. These troops along with others in the surrounded triangle seized 508 tons of enemy rice yesterday and today to bring the haul so far to 1,306 tons.

13 Jan 67   Cleveland Plain Dealer (See Note Page 20)
              SAIGON

...The regimental camp will be destroyed, like the smaller bases previously unearthed, with explosives, fire and bulldozers.

Also being razed are the huts and hamlets of the area's 10,000 peasants and villagers who, willingly or otherwise, have been under Communist sway. They are being moved out — 3,250 so far — for resettlement elsewhere.

...The troops have seized 217 enemy weapons and 1,649 tons of rice.

13 Jan 67   New York Times
             SAIGON, SOUTH VIETNAM, Jan 12

...The forest and the Iron Triangle combine to form a single triangle of 60-square miles that is believed to be filled with enemy base camps, and supply dumps.

...In addition, perhaps 10,000 South Vietnamese peasants live in and around the operation area, and the allied commanders, suspecting that the peasants are at least passive Vietcong, have determined that they all must be resettled.

14 Jan 67   New York Times
             SOUTH VIETNAM, Jan 13

...A spokesman for the command also said that 8 American soldiers were killed and 34 wounded when artillery shells from a nearby unit landed among them this afternoon.

...At least three similar artillery accidents have occurred in the First Infantry Division. The division commander, Maj. Gen. William E. De Puy, uses far more artillery and air support than other commanders in Vietnam and the possibility of error in his unit has increased proportionately.

General De Puy has said that he operates on the theory that killing Viet Cong costs more dollars but saves American lives when heavy air and artillery bombardments are employed

Thirty artillery batteries with upward of 130 cannon have been hammering the Thanhdien forest and the Iron Triangle, long an enemy stronghold, since last Sunday, when Operation Cedar Falls began.

...In addition tactical fighter-bombers have hit the 60-square mile triangle, which includes both the forest and the Iron Triangle, with 478 strikes. Twelve other, most devastating raids have been flown by Air Force B-52's, the most recent coming just before dawn today.

...Enemy losses in the operation rose to 237 killed and 51 captured, but these figures were overshadowed by the vast amount of supplies and facilities taken by the allies committed to the operation, about 16,000 front-line combat troops and thousands of rear-echelon men.

...At the end of six days, the spokesman said, the troops had taken 21,000 tons of rice, or about 200 tons less than the record for an operation established in six-week-long Operation Attleboro.

...In addition, they have taken 3,100 pounds of peanuts, 1,000 pounds of salt, 7,600 black Vietcong uniforms, an assortment of outboard motors and two printing presses.

...Included in the haul also were 237 individual weapons and about 800 hand grenades.

...The troops have destroyed 192 buildings said to have belonged to the Vietcong, 416 bunkers, 87 tunnels and 101 sampans.

16 Jan 67   UPI, Chicago Tribune
             SAIGON, VIETNAM, Jan 15

...United States military headquarters reported today that the iron triangle drive–dubbed Cedar Falls-has billed 349 Communists and turned up 2,550 tons of Viet Cong rice. In addition, 72 Communists have been captured and 393 suspects detained.

21 Jan 67   New York Times (See Note Page 20)
              SAIGON, SOUTH VIETNAM, Jan

...The first 600 yards of the long-sought tunnel system explored through the day were marked by 18 graves, three dug recently. The American soldiers found and dismantled numerous booby traps.
Typewriters and medical equipment were also seized.

24 Jan 67   Los Angeles Times, John Randolph
              SAIGON

Operation Cedar Falls, the American military's biggest single effort in the Vietnam war, is setting new records almost every day in its drive to smash the huge Viet Cong base in the Iron Triangle north of Saigon.
...From the start of the Viet Cong uprising, the Triangle area, which begins near the town of Phu Cuong, 15 miles north of Saigon, has been a major and largely inviolable Viet Cong supply base and political and military headquarters.
"The most significant result of Cedar Falls so far is that we have denied to the enemy, for a long period of time, a vast logistical complex that the Viet Cong have enjoyed for the last 20 years," explained Lt. Gen. Jonathan O. Seaman, commanding general of the Second Field Force (Army Corps) that is directing the operation, using "two divisions plus" and some 30,000 men.
In a broad-scale review of Cedar Falls Monday, Gen. Seaman said that although the body count of Viet Cong killed since the start of fighting Jan. 8 is now 671, the operation is not, and was not expected to be, a major Viet Cong "killer" project.
Its main purpose was to destroy the base itself. In this, Cedar Falls has already set new records. Gen. Seaman listed part of the Iron Triangle "Bag" as follows:
A total so far of 369 Viet Cong defectors; 3,500 tons of rice — enough to feed 10,000 Viet Cong for one year; almost 59,000 rounds of small arms ammunition; 277,00 pages of enemy documents; vast quantities of critically important medicines, and hundreds of light and heavy weapons, tunnels, bunkers, and underground headquarters rooms — some with three subterranean levels.
"We even found a big box of tranquilizer pills," Seaman added with a smile. "They could probably use some of them right now."
...Critics contend that the Viet Cong just move back in and the whole job has to be done over again — with fresh allied casualties.
Seaman explained that in this case the civilian villagers in the area have been removed, some new roads opened up, and that allied troops will make periodic sweeps of the Iron Triangle to prevent any important Viet Cong reconstruction.
"If I were a Viet Cong, I would be pretty discouraged about that base right now," Gen. Seaman said. But he conceded that given enough time and determination the Viet Cong could restore at least a good part of their lost base.

28 Jan 67   Reuters, New York Times
              SAIGON, SOUTH VIETNAM

Some South Vietnamese peasants who refused to leave their homes may have been killed when villages in the Iron Triangle were razed, a United States official said today.
John Vann, who is in charge of all civilian aid programs in the Saigon area, said deaths of innocent villagers probably occurred because "even two days before the end of the operation people were still coming out of caves who must have been there throughout the operation."

He was referring to Operation Cedar Falls, in which the villagers and fortifications of an area 30 miles northwest of Saigon, long called a Vietcong stronghold, were bombed, buried and bulldozed.

The operation, involving 25,000 United States and South Vietnamese troops, ended last night.

More than 6,000 peasants were evacuated and will be relocated. About 720 Vietcong were killed and 725 captured as the district was systematically laid waste during the sweep, officials said.

28 Jan 67   New York Times (See Note Page 20)
             SAIGON, SOUTH VIETNAM, Jan 27

...The end of the broadest sweep of the war, Operation Cedar Falls, left American and South Vietnamese authorities with a tremendous resettlement problem: about 6,100 peasants moved from their homes in the scorched-earth campaign by about 30,000 American and South Vietnamese troops in the so-called Iron Triangle.

Fertile land is to be cleared and homes are to be built for the peasants near Laithieu, 10 miles north of Saigon. United States officials hope they can be moved from their tent camp by April 15.

CEDAR FALLS: EYEWITNESS STORIES AND AFTERMATH

10 Jan 67   (See Note Page 20)
             (Operation Cedar Falls)...The biggest operation of the
             Vietnam War is under way in the Iron Triangle area north
             of Saigon. To get it started allied troops undertook a major
             shift of population. Here is how it went, as reported by an
             AP man who accompanied troops at the start of the mission.
             BEN SUC, VIETNAM, Jan 10

The 50 village elders sat tensely in the old, burned-out schoolhouse as the Vietnamese province official told them: "You and your people must leave this town, abandon it.

"You cannot take your houses, but we will arrange transport for your cattle, your chickens and your children. You will be safely taken to a refugee center."

This was the first time a whole town had been moved. The village elders did not like it.

"We don't want to give up our fields and our homes," their leader told the Vietnamese official. "We have worked here all our lives, we have had nothing from the Government in years.

"We don't want to live under the tyranny of the Viet Cong, but we don't want to abandon our birthplace either."

But there was no reprieve.

Ben Suc, a Saigon river town 26 miles northwest of Saigon, had become a showcase of Viet Cong organization.

A Government battalion once was based there but military reverses in the area led Saigon to abandon the town.

The Viet Cong quickly moved in, organizing the 6,000 inhabitants.

According to Vietnamese officials, almost everyone in Ben Suc was committed in one way or another to the Viet Cong movement.

The area Lasvar (sic) became a major supply point and organizational center for Communist guerrillas and troops.

U.S. authorities decided upon drastic measures, in secrecy, the Vietnamese being informed only on the eve of the operation. Relocating the people in Ben Suc and surrounding villages, possibly 10,000 people was one objective.

Another was to try and capture a Viet Cong headquarters group that controls political organizations and terrorist groups in the Saigon and Gia Dinh regions.

...As the helicopters landed, people in the village ran in all directions, diving into the holes and houses. Several men tried to escape. Three were gunned down, including one who attempted to bicycle away down a trench-sliced road.

The American troops did not enter Ben Suc. That was the job of Vietnamese infantrymen brought in an hour after the U.S. troops landed. The American mission was to seal off the village.

Vietnamese helicopters began swooping over the village, broadcasting in Vietnamese, and in English for the benefit of the American troops, this message: "You are surrounded now, there is no hope of resistance. Stay on the streets and move in to the center of town, assemble in front of the old school building. If you try to escape to the river you will be shot."

By late Sunday, 3,800 men, women and children were gathered in the center of town.

At this point the Vietnamese province official led the elders aside and told them that the village was no longer safe, that they had to move to the province capital of Phu Cuong, and enter a refuge (sic) camp.

Vietnamese soldiers started hunting through the houses of Ben Suc, loading their packs with chickens, and cooking rice they were discovering.

A group of Vietnamese-speaking American intelligence officers arrived to interrogate prisoners. One young man who confessed to being with a unit that attacked American troops last year was bashed in the face by Vietnamese soldiers.

Ben Suc is scheduled to be wiped off the map when the residents leave.

11 Jan 67   New York Times
             BENSUC, SOUTH VIETNAM, Jan 8

For years this quiet, ill-kept village hugging an elbow of the Saigon River 30 miles northwest of the capital has been a haven for the Vietcong.

One pacification program after another has failed here and, since a Government military post was abandoned more than a year ago, Bensuc has been considered a "hostile" village. It has been an embarrassing problem for Saigon.

This morning, 600 allied soldiers — mostly Americans — descended on the village and began "solving" the problem.

Within two weeks, the more than 3,800 residents of Bensuc will be living in a new refugee settlement 20 miles to the southeast, and it is likely that the tattered huts and small shops here will be flattened by bulldozers.

The village of Bensuc, which for so long served as a meeting place for Vietcong political cadres and as a supply point for insurgent troops in two provinces, will be swept from the face of the earth.

"This is probably the only military or political solution for this place," said an American colonel.

Allied officers in Bensuc acknowledged that the residents might be reluctant to leave their property and the revered graves of their ancestors, but they said that new land would be given to them along with frame, tin-roofed homes that will be "a lot better than what they have now."

Vietcong villages are typically found in disrepair, but Bensuc is an extreme example. There is no evidence that any new buildings have been put up in months. The old ones are crumbling and chronic illness is widespread.

Firmly supporting the resettlement, the colonel said: "I imagine there will be a lot of wailing and gnashing of teeth, but they'll do what they're told."

Sixty helicopters landed the troops in seven clearings within the village walls this morning so a human net could be quickly drawn around the residents and the soldiers could avoid the maze of booby traps around Bensuc.

Shortly afterward, a helicopter equipped with loudspeakers began broadcasting this message:

"Attention, people of Bensuc! You are surrounded by Republic of South Vietnam and allied forces. Do not run away or you will be shot as V.C. Stay in your homes and wait for further instructions from the air and on the ground. You will not be hurt if you follow instructions."

Then came a second message telling men, women, and children: "Go immediately to the schoolhouse. Anyone who does not go to the schoolhouse will be considered a V.C. and treated accordingly."

Most of the residents, considered to be passive Vietcong, followed the instructions. Forty-one did not, and during the day they were tracked down and killed. There was little question that the men fleeing on bicycles, crawling through rice paddies and thrashing in the murky river were Vietcong. Some carried rifles, others wore packs. Three were discovered at the mouth of a cave with an assortment of surgical instruments and commercially produced drugs.

At the schoolhouse, the people were separated into groups according to age and sex, interrogated, given a warm meal and were seen by an army doctor. One hundred males, 15 to 45 years old, unable to prove their identity, were taken away as Vietcong suspects. Eleven men were judged on the spot to be Vietcong.

The villagers were allowed to file home this evening, but to-morrow they will be ordered back to the school, their homes will be searched, and in a day or so more, the troops will begin loading them into barges for the trip downstream. Part of their houses, their furniture and their livestock, will go with them.

...More than 15,000 soldiers are being deployed in what the military describes as the most thorough search ever of the 60 square miles of the Thandien Forest and the thick jungle that the Americans call the Iron Triangle.

Intelligence officers believe there may be no more than 100 enemy soldiers in the 60 square miles. But they hope to find a tunnel the length of the seven-mile-long Triangle and to disrupt operations at the head-quarters of Vietcong Military Region 4. The headquarters, which controls Vietcong operations in and around Saigon, has been traced to the Triangle.

The allied goal at Bensuc was to deny the Vietcong a strategic base, and to capture important political figures. At least three of the 11 taken today appear to be prime suspects. The allies also believe that they will be able to win the allegiance of the people once they have been removed from the Vietcong sphere.

13 Jan 67   The Sun (Baltimore), Robert A. Erlandson
BEN SUC, VIETNAM, Jan. 12

The largest military offensive of the Vietnam war is being accompanied by the largest planned civilian evacuation. Hundreds of Viet Cong families are involved.

A major part of it is under way at this village of some 250 families which soon will be razed into just another jungle bare spot.

Typical was the wizened, crippled woman who squatted silently in the shade of a banana tree, staring ahead dully while one hand clutched the rope that leashed her white pig who was rooting nearby.

...The woman offered no protest when Vietnamese soldiers grabbed her squealing pig and bound it. Nor did she protest when an American private half-carried, half-walked her into the huge waiting helicopter.

Perhaps she did not know, or care, that within a few days, in the village where she had undoubtedly spent her life, bulldozers would level the grey-mud walled, palm-thatched huts, called "hootches" by the troops, and explosives would blast the Viet Cong escape tunnels beneath them.

...All day, as the villagers awaited evacuation, the artillery batteries a few hundred meters away thundered steadily.

Brass shell casings piled up around the sweating, powder-stained gunners. Jets streaked overhead, their passage marked by the crump of bombs, towers of black napalm smoke and the rattle of mini-guns.

No able-bodied men or youths were around today to help soldiers load the oxen, ox-carts, water buffalo, rice and household possessions aboard the personnel boats drawn up on the Saigon River shore, or to clamber aboard the twin-rotor Chinook helicopters for the resettlement camp at Phu Cuong.

This was because Ben Suc is a Viet Cong village and has been for many years.

The menfolk were either hiding in the tunnel networks, from which periodic sniper fire spat, or were in the jungle trying to evade the encircling American and Vietnamese troops.

The villagers are being displaced because the allied forces mission is to clear Viet Cong out of the "Iron Triangle" and adjacent Than Dien Forest "once and for all," and they do not want to leave the Reds with the human shield they have used so many times before.

"We now have enough combat power on the scene to crush the Viet Cong, and the "Iron Triangle," which they call Nam Bo (liberated area) will no longer be the great V.C. redoubt it has been for so long," said Maj. Robert Schweitzer, of Chicago, the Vietnamese-speaking 1st Infantry Division officer in charge of the evacuation.

The decision to evacuate was difficult, he said, but "It was the right one." This way, Schweitzer said, the villages will be discommoded, but none will be killed.

Nearly 4,000 had been evacuated by land, river, and air by tonight. The area is about 50 miles northwest of Saigon in Binh Duong Province.

"Your heart goes out to them," Schweitzer said, "and you can't under-estimate the hardship ... but these are not innocent civilians, these are 100 percent Viet Cong families, an enemy population, and we've been under fire from inside the hamlet ever since we've been here."

In Ben Suc alone since the operation began, troops have killed 53 Viet Cong, captured 52 confirmed Viet Cong and detained many persons as suspects.

15 Jan 67   The Denver Post (See Note Page 20)
              Peter Arnett
              (Editor's Note: U.S. troops north of Saigon are conducting
              the largest American military operation of the Vietnam war.
              The operation also has important sociological and engineering
              aspects.)
              THE IRON TRIANGLE, VIETNAM

Acres of tall rubber trees were devastated, and the trunks lay tangled across the ground as though flattened by a typhoon.

Along the rutted clay roads, thatched-roof homes burst into flames as troops methodically threw in fiery rags. Bulldozers were poised to tear down concrete structures.

Gathered at crossroads and at an assembly point on the winding Saigon River were crowds of Vietnamese huddled together, their pots and pans, bedding, family pictures and keepsakes packed into baskets and bags.

A small Buddhist shrine, its candles broken in transit to the river continued to exhale clouds of incense across lowing cattle and sweating American officials and Vietnamese soldiery attempting to get yet another convoy moving south down the river.

The methodical thud of bursting artillery shells and the nearer cracks of sniper bullets added to these scenes of war.

The locale was 60 square miles of jungle and fields, stretching from the base of the Iron Triangle, long used as a secret Communist meeting place, to the rubber plantations above the town of Ben Suc.

Burning homes, crying children, frightened women, devastated fields, long lines of slowly moving refugees, brought back memories of the resettlement of millions of peasants during the era of the late Ngo Dinh Diem and of the scorched-earth policies of other wars.

American commanders handling the current operation, named Cedar Falls, say the circumstances are entirely different, that the devastation this time is the final move in a struggle that has lasted five years, and that there has been an absolute minimum of civilian casualties.

They add that more Viet Cong have been killed, captured and surrendered for fewer allied casualties than in most other actions.

Many Americans were surprised to discover that as many as 10,000 continued to live in Ben Suc and areas in the northern portion of the Iron Triangle.

The war has ebbed and flowed through the region ever since Ngo Dinh Diem moved most of Ben Suc's population to refugee centers in the South in 1961 and replaced them with politically reliable refugees from North Vietnam.

These people left Ben Suc under Viet Cong pressure. The original inhabitants moved back, and as the years went by the Viet Cong built up a formidable political, military and social apparatus in the town that defied government attempts to dig it out.

Ben Suc and the six villages around it were doomed to failure from early 1965 when it became clear that the only way to break down diehard Communist resistance was to resettle an entire population, a policy put into effect by the U.S. Army's 25th Division. From the division base at Cu Chi to the north, and across the Saigon River, the Viet Cong main force units were pushed farther and farther north. The people who assisted them, and the villages they preyed upon, disappeared, with the population moving to resettlement areas and the villages destroyed.

With the U.S. Army's 1st Infantry Division permanently based to the east and northeast, the U.S. 25th Division to the south and southwest, and a brigade of the U.S. 4th Division to the northwest, it was just a matter of time before the Iron Triangle, Ben Suc, and the villages around it, would be completely evacuated for resettlement, then devastated in a move to drive the Viet Cong main force units north.

This region at one time had been a fertile area of French-run rubber plantations, orchards and paddy fields surrounding clumps of jungle. The war had taken a frightening toll, driving the French from the plantations and destroying paddy dikes. The people who stayed there eked out a precarious living.

This week, the hammer fell with a suddenness that seemed to catch the people of Ben Suc completely off guard. The town was surrounded as U.S. armored and infantry columns swept into the Iron Triangle and the northern jungles.

There were unexpected side effects. Each day in Ben Suc Viet Cong officials popped out of tunnels and surrendered because the air was going bad and food supplies were running out.

Prior intelligence about the positions of base camps and supply caches turned out to be fairly correct. As expected, also, there was little contact with the enemy.

"If we were out looking for the Viet Cong main force we wouldn't have gone here," a 1st Infantry Division officer explained. "The object of this is not to kill Cong; it is to remove the population from the enemy's control."

The population was not happy to leave, and the temporary refugee camp they were moved to near the Binh Duong province capital, Phu Chong, hardly inspired their confidence.

Province officials had laid no groundwork in the camp, people were initially living under parachute tents. Latrines took days to build, and little water was available. As the week went by the tangle began to sort itself out.

Meanwhile, scores of bulldozers set about remodeling the countryside, grinding down troublesome patches of jungle, cutting swaths through the

Iron Triangle to facilitate future military operations, and carving out helicopter landing zones in the middle of the northern jungles.

Experience has shown that landing zones will be necessary in the future. The Viet Cong keep returning to "scorched earth" zones in small numbers. In the current operation, the heaviest contact with the Viet Cong was made by the 25th Division in the Ho Bo Woods, an area blasted all of 1965 by B-52s and artillery.

The western edges of Hau Nghia Province west of Saigon underwent the scorched earth treatment in January 1965; yet Viet Cong guerrillas still abound there. However, main force units stay out of the way.

The commander of the 1st Infantry Division, Maj. Gen. William F. Depuy, explained:

"The best way to get the enemy to stop fighting and to give himself up is to hit him with the heaviest amount of artillery fire and aerial bombardment that is possible. We can drive him out that way."

With the population moved out of the Iron Triangle and the Ben Suc region, the heavy guns and the bombers can now get to work, U.S. military men say.

19 Jan 67   (See Note Page 20)
BEN CAT, VIETNAM, Jan 12

At first only a couple of women stepped forward. Then a handful came. Finally dozens swarmed over to the Vietnamese soldiers. Clamoring for the little leaflets that offered forgiveness for Viet Cong who give up.

It was on a hot, dusty road near Ben Cat, skirting the northern fringe of the Iron Triangle.

These women had been removed two days earlier from their homes in a string of villages a few miles northwest of Ben Cat. American troops had swept in on Operation Cedar Falls — the largest offensive of the war.

The men in the villages, with few exceptions, fled into the jungles or hid in tunnels.

Vietnamese and American authorities said there was no doubt the men were guerrillas — or worked with the Viet Cong.

The area in and around the Iron Triangle — 60 square miles starting 20 miles north of Saigon — had for years been used by the Communists for training and supply bases, for growing food and as a sanctuary for planning and troop recuperation.

Now, once the civilians had been cleared out, the area would come under devastating attack by ground troops, planes and artillery. The object was to deny the triangle to the Viet Cong once and for all.

Someone had the idea that this would be an ideal time to try to woo the men to the Government through their women.

So it was that the women were gathered on the dusty road. They were in a convoy — led by tanks and other armored vehicles of the U.S. 1st Infantry Division and 173rd airborne brigade — taking them back to their village one last time.

The return had a double purpose: to allow the refugees to pick up belongings they had left behind, and to retrieve their men.

A Vietnamese officer explained over a loudspeaker that the men should be given safe conduct leaflets saying the bearers were to be treated not as prisoners of war, but as returnees, welcomed with open arms into the Government fold. After some hesitation, the women closed in for the leaflets.

Four trucks were destined for Rach Kien, on a gentle slope next to rich green rice paddies.

As the trucks neared the village, the refugees could see smoke curling up from many places.

Before the trucks could stop, the villagers were leaping off and running toward their homes.

"We're too late!" a woman cried. "Everything is burning!"

An American officer who had helped organize the return said bitterly: "Somebody didn't get the word."

The people, some weeping, tugged at smoldering debris to get at their household goods and stores of buried rice.

Maj. Jim Ipsen, 36, of Honolulu, the Senior American Adviser in Ben Cat district, muttered: "Damn it, I'm afraid this destruction may have scared off some of the men that were hanging around."

An American sergeant from the 1st Infantry Division strode up. "What's going on here?" he said, "Who are these people — VC or what? I was with my squad about 150 yards down the line when we heard people coming. We set up an ambush. Damned good thing I saw they were women and children before we opened up."

The imaginative plan to woo the men had gotten snarled in the machinery of the offensive.

Still, some women did bring in their men.

One young wife, Dang Thi Phan, 23, went into a trench in a thicket and came out with her husband, 25, her brother, 21, and two other young men.

"We never would have found them," said Lt. Samuel Boozer of San Pablo, Calif., assigned to the 246th Psychological Warfare Company.

29 Jan 67   St. Louis Post-Dispatch, Sunday Magazine

To the Americans, Operation Cedar Falls was another move to weaken the grip of the Viet Cong on South Vietnam; to 10,000 South Vietnamese civilians, it was goodbye to home. As they lined up with their possessions to wait for a ride or armed escort to an unknown destination, they watched U.S. troops burn the wooden huts they had lived in, and raze masonry buildings with bulldozers.

Operation Cedar Falls was part of an intense American attack on the "Iron Triangle," a zone northwest of Saigon where the Viet Cong have had strong influence since the time of Ngo Dinh Diem, the assassinated dictator. Diem himself transplanted thousands of Iron Triangle dwellers to refugee camps, but they drifted back over the years. This time the Americans had the Triangle's chief town, Ben Suc, almost surrounded and wanted to evacuate the civilians again so that they would not be hurt in the coming military sweep. The eventual aim is to drive the Viet Cong north and secure a big part of South Vietnam for Saigon's control. As the Iron Triangle drive began, the Americans had their worst week for casualties so far in the war: 144 killed, 1044 wounded, six missing.

The 10,000 evacuees were deposited in a camp near Phu Chuong, the capital of Binh Duong province, where there were parachute tents to live under and latrines to dig. If things go according to plan it will become a new town, and the scorched earth of the Iron Triangle will finally be too inhospitable even for the Viet Cong.

28 Jan 67   Christian Science Monitor, John Dillin
             LAI KHE, SOUTH VIETNAM

Following the largest battle of the Vietnam war, American commanders are satisfied that the Viet Cong's once-impregnable "Iron Triangle" has been hammered into a more acceptable shape.

...Most American troops now are withdrawing from the area, while a few are left behind to continue probing the labyrinth of underground tunnel hideouts.

Military officials indicate they are highly pleased with the operation, code-named Cedar Falls. Crushing the "Iron Triangle" fits into the allies' 1967 plans to eliminate Viet Cong base areas.

An estimated 711 Viet Cong were killed and 722 prisoners detained in the whole operation, which ended on Jan. 27. Nearly 6,000 Vietnamese peasants were forced from their homes into refugee camps as part of the operation during which whole villages were deliberately bombed, burned and bulldozed into the ground, Reuters reported.

A spokesman said that a record 3,709 tons of Viet Cong rice supplies were captured and 573 weapons seized. Nearly 500 guerrillas defected to the allies while the sweep was under way.

...One intelligence officer noted:

"We've progressed to this type of operation over a number of months. This is the highest point of our operations so far....It seems to me that all of our skills that we developed paid off.

"Most important was knowing what we would find, where we would find it, and then coming in with tremendous firepower."

The "Iron Triangle" has long been a threat to the capital region. A heavily jungled area, it lies like a giant arrowhead pointed almost directly at the capital city. From it, attacks were launched against Saigon and nearby provinces. And it also served as a funnel for supplies.

Troops searching the area found vast amounts of documents, including a complete plan for last month's attack on Saigon's Tan Son Nhut Airfield. There were also detailed maps of the United States First Division's base here at Lai Khe.

In addition, it was learned that nearby Ben Suc served as the central source for medical supplies for VC forces all over the Third Corps area as well as part of the Second Corps. The triangle also channeled rice supplies to large Communist forces in War Zones C and D.

...Within 36 hours, some 25,000 American and South Vietnamese troops swooped down upon the jungle.

Their attack was preceded by wave after wave of B-52 bombers which had pounded the area for days.

Simultaneously with the larger attack, forces moved against the village of Ben Suc a few miles away. Later it was learned that the villagers had been warned by the Vietcong that the Americans were planning some action. They had warned the villagers to remain in their huts or face retaliation.

But the allied thrust came so swiftly and so powerfully that the villagers were caught by surprise. Within 90 seconds, an entire battalion of American troops descended on the village. Moments later a battalion of Vietnamese troops followed the Americans in.

Then, in one of the most thorough operations of its kind in the war, the villagers were picked up — livestock and all — and carried by truck, river barge, and helicopter to a resettlement area 30 miles away. Bulldozers soon arrived to flatten the village. The villagers will not be permitted to return.

The military vigorously defends this forced resettlement. The geographic position of Ben Suc, they say, had made it a vital link in the Viet Cong logistical system. The population, especially at night, was moving supplies, aiding Viet Cong travelers, and digging tunnels.

Ben Suc has long been a problem. Once before, in the early 1960's, the population was moved out and Roman Catholic settlers, loyal to the government, were moved in. But Viet Cong harassment eventually drove many of them away, the government troops were pulled out, and Ben Suc reverted to the Viet Cong.

...Of the Viet Cong killed, most were members of signal units, rice-supply teams, ordnance workers, medical technicians, and other support units who were thrown into a last-minute defense of their base.

They had scarcely a chance. The Americans raced over the area and sustained only light casualties, mostly from booby traps.

5 Feb 67   The Washington Post, Jesse W. Lewis, Jr.
            SAIGON

(The editors of The Washington Post have declined permission to give the verbatim text of a selection from the above cited article. The following describes the contribution of that selection.)

(It is noted by Americans in Vietnam that Americans at home are shocked by civilian casualties because of their lack of experience of war on American soil.)

It is expected that the rate of civilian casualties will increase as American troops come into the Mekong Delta. A senior officer explains American reluctance to move into the Delta for this reason. He maintains that there is still reason to worry even though there are plans for massive resettlement of civilians.)

25 Apr 67   Christian Science Monitor (See Note Page 20)
             SAIGON

...The United States high command, preoccupied for two years with hunting down North Vietnamese regulars, now is looking more toward the populated valleys and lowlands where the enemy wields potent political influence and gets his sustenance.

Quick gains are hoped for by forced resettlement of chronically Communist areas, followed up with scorched-earth operations that deny enemy troops all food, shelter, and material support. Central-highland valleys are being denuded of all living things; people ringing the Communist war zones in the South have been moved.

Some American observers recently in the Mekong Delta say that the Vietnamese Army, long hated and feared, now is regarded as less of a threat to the countryside than the Americans.

16 Jan 67   New York Times, Tom Buckley
             PHUCUONG, SOUTH VIETNAM, Jan 19

In canvas-topped sheds thrown up on a wasteland, 6,000 Vietnamese, all but a handful of them women, children and old people, were trying today to put together the pieces of suddenly shattered lives.

Under threats of relentless bombing, they fled last week from four villages at one corner of the bastion of Vietcong strength that has come to be known as the Iron Triangle.

The fertile, 60-square-mile area of paddy fields, orchards and rubber plantations about 30 miles north of Saigon is being devastated as part of operation Cedar Falls.

About 16,000 combat troops are taking part in the operation. Its objective is to deny this sanctuary to the guerrillas permanently. American commanders are convinced that to succeed they must render its population centers uninhabitable.

The four villages — Bensuc, Rachhap, Bungcong and Rachkien — have in fact already ceased to exist. As they left, weeping, many of the women saw their homes put to the torch, or bulldozed flat.

...The arrival of the 6,000 villagers apparently caught by surprise the Vietnamese officials who had been given primary responsibility for arranging their housing and other necessities. As a result, an emergency call for assistance went out to the First Infantry Division, which has headquarters at Dian nearby. It rushed in water, food and bamboo for sleeping platforms and tent frames.

Despite these efforts, and the hope that the villagers will be resettled soon on a tract of land not far away, there is much bitterness behind the barbed wire that fences off the camp.

"I was very poor in my village, but I didn't mind that," said Mrs. Le Thi Tau, 24, who is pregnant with her second child. "I wanted to stay. Last week the fish-shaped planes (gunship helicopters, apparently) flew over our fields. My husband didn't know what they were. He stood up and they shot him down and killed him."

"I wish I had stayed and got killed too," she said, crying. "But I was afraid I would only be wounded and that there would be no one to take care of me."

Some American officials at the camp indicate privately that they regard relocation as a dubious strategy at best.

318

28 Jan 67   (See Note Page 20)
             SAIGON, Saturday, Jan 28

...The windup Thursday midnight of the biggest offensive of the War,
Operation Cedar Falls, left American and Vietnamese authorities with the
War's biggest resettlement problem.

This is the disposition of 6,100 peasants moved from their homes in
the scorched earth campaign waged since Jan. 8 by about 30,000 American
and Vietnamese troops in the Viet Cong's Iron Triangle.

Fertile land is to be cleared and homes built for them near Lai Thieu,
10 miles north of Saigon. U.S. officials hope they can be moved in by
April 15. At present the peasants, whose farms and tax money helped
support the guerrillas, are housed in a tent camp near Phu Cuong, at the
tip of the triangle 20 miles north of Saigon.

11 May 67   Christian Science Monitor (See Note Page 20)
             PHU LOI, VIETNAM

What happens to Vietnamese peasants when military action forces them
out of their home areas?

Here at Phu Loi, the immediate answer is not encouraging, but the
future holds some hope.

A hot, dusty tent city has been home for 3,200 refugees for three
months.

For 20 years, the "Iron Triangle" north of Saigon was undisputed
Communist territory, providing easy access into Saigon and between War
Zone C to the west and D to the northeast.

Last January, during Operation Cedar Falls, 11 hamlets in the triangle
were evacuated, the homes were burned, and bulldozers moved in to finish
the job.

About 5,900 refugees, with what livestock and household possessions
they could salvage, were brought to the tent city to await movement to a
permanent government-built settlement.

The tent city is still a dirty, congested place. Women, carrying
rusted buckets, crowd about concrete water cisterns. Scraggly ducks,
chickens, turkeys, and pigs wander about the roads between makeshift
tents. Mud wallows for the animals are scattered through the area,
attracting flies.

The tents are patchwork structures, made of canvas, cardboard,
burlap, and corrugated tin.

The new hamlet under construction, named Ap Binh Noa and filled
with bright rows of aluminum-roofed houses, is starting to receive its
first families. The rest are to be moved in at the rate of 50 families each
week. It is hoped the move will be complete by the end of May when the
rainy season sets in.

The United States is spending several hundred thousand dollars on this
single resettlement program, but United States officials consider it a
Vietnamese government program.

One hundred persons identified as Viet Cong have been arrested in
the camp itself.

Viet Cong propaganda aimed at the tent-city residents has been heavy —
and there has been much to make propaganda about.

There were times when no water was available for more than a day.
Food distribution at times was insufficient. The tents are stifling hot during
the day and cold at night.

Of the 5,900 men, women, and children moved here, only 3,200 remained
as the move to Ap Binh Hoa began.

Some of the original number went back to their farm areas, which are
now in an area open to firing at will. During the Vietnamese new year
festival, the Binh Duong Province chief allowed about 1,800 persons to
leave. Several hundred others were relocated.

There were times, United States aid officials admit, when this re-settlement program could have turned into a disaster.

Fewer than 500 men were among the original 5,900 Ben Suc refugees. It was estimated more than 800 men from the hamlets stayed behind with the Viet Cong in the bush.

However, a school has been started for 585 children. Most of the teachers are Vietnamese government soldiers who were teachers before they were drafted. Milk and vitamins are distributed to the children. Vietnamese, Philippine, and Korean medical teams make periodic visits.

Most families have had to sell much of their household possessions to buy meat and vegetables to supplement the quart of rice given each person daily. Some canned fish and vegetables have been distributed, but most of the refugees do not know how to prepare canned vegetables — least of all sauerkraut, which was among the distributed food.

A lot has to be learned. The Vietnamese Government's Special Commissariat for Refugees estimates there were 1.8 million refugees in Vietnam as of last March. This includes refugees resettled without government assistance. There are 297 temporary refugee camps in the country.

The refugees here, from a place called Ben Suc, were the first group forcefully removed en masse from an area.

The permanent resettlement hamlet under construction has long rows of aluminum-roofed houses being built on land cleared from the Co Mi jungle, another former Viet Cong redoubt.

The homes are built with pressed concrete and mud bricks made by refugees.

The same materials will be used to construct a school, a warehouse, a Buddhist pagoda, a community house, and a chapel.

The clearing of part of the Co Mi jungle will provide land for the refugees and deny the jungle's cover to the Viet Cong. The land was cultivated as recently as 15 years ago. But it became overgrown when the government was unable to provide protection.

Security for the new hamlet will be provided by a nearby detachment of the 5th Vietnamese Infantry Division.

FORCED TRANSFER

Dateline: Viet Nam, 1966, p. 92
Jim G. Lucas

(The editors of Dateline: Viet Nam have declined permission to give the verbatim text of a selection from the above cited article. The following describes the contribution of that selection.)

(On June 3, 1964, it is decided to destroy all homes in the district of Long Toon in Vinh Binh province. Long Toon has been dominated by the Viet Cong for 8 years. The population of a series of villages are uprooted and the villages destroyed.

The area around the village of Ap Long Binh has been a free-fire zone for a long time. After the population is removed the village will be completely destroyed. Lt. Col. Crain of Alexandria, Virginia says that destruction of VC villages is a way to destroy the guerilla's economic base.)

14 Feb 65   New York Herald Tribune, Beverly Deepe
             HOALONG, SOUTH VIET-NAM

...We stopped at the edge of the village to talk with Nguyen Linh, who was riding his toffee-colored bull in a small grassy area near sawed-off trees, foundations of destroyed houses and a modest-sized Buddhist pagoda. Mr. Linh, who voiced Viet Cong arguments, said he was actually 43 years old, but when he was born it took so long to get his birth registered that he is officially only 40 years old.

"Several days ago government troops went to a village six kilometers from here and told the people they would have to move. The people were allowed to take nothing except what they had on their backs. They all wanted to take something, because everyone must have something new to put on the first days of Tet, but the soldiers wouldn't let them. Then yesterday at noon the people came back to their homes — but their homes had been looted — everything worthwhile was gone. I don't know who did it — both the government troops and the Viet Cong are capable of doing something like that."

...When we asked about the troops looting the houses in the neighboring village, an American marine adviser tugged at his sweaty T-shirt and yelped:

"They should have burned those houses. That's a Viet Cong village — they have trenches 13 feet deep all along the village perimeter. The Viet Cong have tunnels leading from the houses out 50 yards into the forest.

"The Special Forces moved the people out so they could wait for the Viet Cong to return. What do the people have to complain about? We lost one of the best Vietnamese troopers there just a couple of days ago?"

6 Mar 65   New York Times, Seth S. King
            DANANG, SOUTH VIETNAM, March 4

Almost 7,000 South Vietnamese crowded around the large American-manned air base on the outskirts of Danang will soon be uprooted from their homes and moved to another sector of city.

As part of an effort to provide greater security for the airfield, a zone 500 yards wide is being cleared around the base. When the operation is completed within the next two months, this will become a no man's land in which only authorized persons will be permitted to move during the daytime and no one at night.

2 Jun 65   (See Note Page 20)
            VEN VINH, VIET NAM, June 2

...The nearly 200 men from Bravo company were to get water and food a short time later but after a five-mile trek through the dense jungle to secure three positions they had learned the hard way what fighting a war in Viet Nam was like.

"Tarzan wouldn't go through this," complained Pvt. Craig Marcus of Fort Lauderdale, Fla.

"At least we have a cool breeze blowing in Georgia," chimed in Sgt. Willie Tanksley of Savannah.

The same day some of the men visited a nearby Viet Cong village with an interpreter. They found tunnels filled with tons of rice under each of 30 huts in the village.

The district chief gathered the few remaining women and children in a square and told them to go. He said the village would be bombed. There was no rain. Only the sound of friendly artillery fired across a river into a known Viet Cong area. The paratroopers slept well and broke camp early Tuesday morning.

10 Jun 65   (See Note Page 20)
            KHE TRE, VIET NAM, June 10

U.S. Marine helicopters snatched 2,600 villagers out of the hands of the Viet Cong this week and dropped them into comparative safety among the tombs of Viet Nam's ancient emperors.

...Helicopters were used because the road to the coast had been cut by a landslide.

Later they were trucked to a nearby area where they had lived until just over three years ago, when the regime of the President Ngo Dinh Diem forced them to move.

The village was counted as solidly progovernment. If there were any pangs of regret among the oldsters over returning to the coast and giving up farms they had hacked out of the jungle, few showed it.

The marines ran the show on the order of a combat assualt with troops. Time was of the essence since it was considered imperative to move the entire population in one day.

...The rule was that each family must carry whatever it wanted saved. Furniture and heavy objects were left behind. One exception to the rule were several bags of seed rice.

Household belongings generally were carried in two ways — in huge back packs or swung from baskets at the end of shoulder poles. One woman carried her smallest child in one such basket. Odds and ends were carried in hand baskets and wire cages were used for small dogs, chickens, ducks and pigs. Large livestock was left behind.

The villagers new homes will be not far away from a U.S. Marine Infantry Battalion guarding the Phu Bai Airstrip south of Hue. The Marine chopper crews felt their charges couldn't be going into a better or safer area.

21 Jun 65   New York Times
           SAIGON, SOUTH VIETNAM, June 20

...In a related development, it was announced today that United States Marines had moved more than 400 Vietnamese villagers to safety after completing a two-day search-and-clear operation 15 miles northwest of Danang.

1 Jul 65   (See Note Page 20)
           CHEO REO, VIET NAM, July 1

...The Government force was hit on its way to Thuan Man, eight miles from Cheo Reo. Its mission was to evacuate Thuan Man's 2,000 people, who have lived on the verge of starvation since floods ruined their crops last fall, and raze the town to prevent the Viet Cong from getting a foothold there.

25 Jul 65   The Evening Star (Washington) (See Note Page 20)
           PHUNG HIEP, VIET NAM, July 24

Driving rains and blankets of clouds hang over the Mekong Delta in late July. But Vietnamese troops and their U.S. advisers are carrying the war to the Viet Cong in highly mobile operations linked with close air support.

Bomb hits tear huge craters in the soggy land of the Delta, throwing up piles of mud and at times changing the course of the canals. Soldiers leap from helicopters and sink waist deep in water and mud, but charge ahead. Helicopters circle overhead and dart down to quickly unload or pick up troops.

One of these operations was carried out Friday in this delta area 100 miles south of Saigon. The basic idea is to act on the basis of intelligence reports and to move against major Viet Cong units by lifting troops around them in small groups, boxing them in and hitting them hard from the ground and the air.

The operation began after intelligence reported 600 to 800 Viet Cong were moving in an area near this delta town. Troops of a crack Vietnamese Ranger Battalion were moved to two points to begin the action. Weather during the morning was so bad that it was impossible to confirm the intelligence reports from the air...

Helicopters carrying psychological warfare teams and medics and equipped with loudspeakers swooped over the attack area. They told the people to move out, identify themselves in their sampans and go to nearby government posts.

When the people reach the posts, the psychological warfare teams talk with them, distribute leaflets and explain the purpose of the presence of American troops and bomb strikes. The medics treat the sick or injured.

Many people were seen from the air, moving out along the waterways of the delta.

30 Aug 65   New York Times, Charles Mohr
             SAIGON, SOUTH VIETNAM, Aug 30

United States Marines won a sharp engagement yesterday in a swamp near Da Nang Air Base and reported killing or wounding 23 Communist guerrillas in return for "light" marine casualties.

...Helicopters equipped with powerful loudspeakers flew over the populated area before the marine attack began to warn civilians to leave the area. The spokesman said that 700 civilians had done so and were being given food and shelter by the marines.

15 Dec 65   New York Times, Hanson W. Baldwin
             BIENHOA, South Vietnam, Dec 14

...United States officers say the Iron Triangle no longer exists; it has been bombed and the 173d has swept through it. The Vietcong, they say, cannot safely use the area as a base for large forces and their movement through it is circumscribed. The congested and important airfield at Bienhoa is far more secure than it was.

29 Dec 65   (See Note Page 20)
             AP LOI NGUYEN, VIET NAM, Dec 29

In the Mekong Delta, you're a million miles from nowhere when you're 26 miles from home.

Up until six weeks ago, this thatched hamlet was 22 miles north of Can Tho, a thriving market city. Now it's four miles below Can Tho.

The entire hamlet with its population of 528, most of them rice farmers, was moved by the Vietnamese government when the area surrounding their old location was declared a free-strike zone for bombing raids against Viet Cong troop concentrations. At first the people of Ap Loi Nguyen were lonely and frightened in their new hamlet, even though the government with the help of USOM (U.S. Operations Mission) funds provided clean new bamboo houses fronting on a wide new road.

They hesitated to go to market in the nearby town of Cai Rang, because they wouldn't be dealing at the shops and stalls their ancestors had been dealing with for generations. They couldn't get their children into school because the local schools were already crowded. They had no general merchandise store in their new hamlet, no church, no barbershop, no corner coffee shop for the heady dark French coffee and the beer redolent of formaldehyde that the Vietnamese love.

There was a graveyard, weather-beaten headstones barely visible in the tall tropical weed growth, but it was a Buddhist graveyard and the people of Ap Loi Nguyen are all Catholics.

Because land is scarce in the overpopulated Mekong Delta and because no one seemed to have lived here in a long, long time, the citizens of Ap Loi Nguyen planted their first crops in the old cemetery.

...Nights were the worst of all. Ap Loi Nguyen, being new, had no perimeter guard, no barbed wire fortifications, no popular force company to sit in little sheet metal watch towers and wait for the Viet Cong. Whenever small arms fire crackled in the darkness, the hamlet dwellers never knew if they were about to be overrun.

Then one day the advisory team arrived from Cai Rang, led by Capt. Ken Johnson of St. Louis, Mo. It brought a doctor to examine the sick and innoculate the babies, and an agricultural specialist to show them how to grow lettuce and beans and other vegetables to woo them away from a one crop economy, and a guerrilla expert to show them how to defend their new hamlet.

Finally and most important of all, they brought Maj. Alvin Campbell, Catholic chaplain at Can Tho. Father Campbell, a big bubbling man with a grin as broad as the Mekong, brought them the gift of friendship that took them out of their strangeness and loneliness.

He helped them build a church, encouraged them to start their own school rather than wait for available desks in the village and, by visits several times a week, showed them that someone cared.

Soon there were a little store at the head of the long rows of huts, and a new barbershop out under the banana trees, and row on row of budding new crops, already growing taller than the headstones.

The old folks of Ap Loi Nguyen still pine for the old hamlet, but the children would never think of going back to a place that didn't have a Father Campbell.

28 Feb 66   (See Note Page 20)
             CU CHI, VIETNAM, Feb 28

Two armed Viet Cong marched into the Government's Trung Lap Ranger School and threw down their weapons and packs.

"Too much American artillery," one said later, explaining his surrender.

"Eight men in our platoon were killed last night," the second added.

...Around Cu Chi, whole villages have been resettled and movement is prohibited on roads at night. Wide areas are free fire zones where any movement is assumed to be that of the enemy. Firing on targets just north of the base has resulted in numerous secondary explosions indicating that ammunition or fuel was hit.

13 May 66   New York Times, Charles Mohr
             BUPRANG, SOUTH VIETNAM, May 22

...Since last October, thousands of North Vietnamese soldiers have slipped and stumbled on the paths of mountainous Quangduc. According to reports from South Vietnamese intelligence agents, at least 12 battalions of North Vietnamese have entered or passed through the province since then.

...One of the main reasons why the United States paratroops were in Quangduc was to interdict the little red lines on the map — to kill enemy soldiers and, more important, to deny them the almost complete freedom of movement they have had for so many months. However, the long-range prospects of interdicting the Ho Chi Minh Trail are not bright.

...The men of the First Brigade cannot stay here long. Although there are now about 250,000 United States troops in South Vietnam, this total is not enough to allow a strong, permanent force of trail watchers.

The South Vietnamese Government cannot control the land area of Quangduc, so it has decided not to try. The 35,000 inhabitants of the province are being moved from scattered villages and concentrated around Gianghia, Quangduc's little capital.

Thousands of mountain tribesmen have already been relocated, 1,900 in April alone. Soon all but 2,000 tribesmen who refuse to move will be concentrated in a circle within artillery range of Gianghia and a few nearby district towns.

...There is no practical alternative to this policy. Quangduc's provincial chief, Lieut. Col. Nguyen Hju Man, has only eight companies of regional force troops at his command.

Of these, all but one are tied down on static-defense missions and cannot undertake mobile operations. All of the companies are greviously understrength, mustering only 45 per cent of their authorized men or little more than 500 in all.

...Colonel Man hopes that he will at least deny the enemy food and help from the mountain tribesmen by resettling them around the provincial capital.

But he knows that, by doing so, he is surrendering the countryside to the Vietcong and North Vietnamese and that Quangduc may become even more of an enemy staging area than it has been.

18 May 66   The Christian Science Monitor, Charlotte Saikowski
                  HUE, VIETNAM

United States marines are not usually in the hog business. But it is a different kind of war in Vietnam — and it is often fought with different kinds of weapons.

In this case, it is hogs.

It all began last year when the First Marine Division moved into the Chu Lai area, about 100 miles down the coast from here, in order to build an airstrip. During clearing operations, numbers of farmers had to be evacuated and, as a result, the Chu Lai New Life Village was formed — combining four hamlets and 3,600 people.

In an effort to get the displaced villagers on their feet, several marine units got together, built a pig farm, and organized 55 families into a hog cooperative.

...But the point to this story is more than the raising of a few hogs. It illustrates that this is basically a political war and that it is not enough to search and clear a hamlet of Viet Cong and then leave the impoverished and terrorized peasants to salvage their former meager lives.

...Whatever its future, Chu Lai New Life Village won't be the same when the marines leave. And the population will have grown — by quite a few hogs, ducks, and carp.

17 Oct 66   (See Note Page 20)
                  QUI NHON, VIET NAM, Oct 17

"This is harsh, but this is war," said the spokesman for a division of the 4,500 Korean troops in Viet Nam.

"We recognize that this is a pity for the civilians who are not Viet Cong — that they must suffer."

In six days the soldiers of Korea's Capital (Tiger) Division had brought 3,500 refugees out of the rugged, cave-dotted Phu Cat mountains 270 miles northeast of Saigon.

It was part of a pacification program that goes farther than various plans used by American commanders.

The refugees from war — old men, women carrying babies, frightened children — marched down winding trails toward the valley floor.

Guarded by troops, the civilians picked their way between the boulders and thorns, clinging to small bundles of belongings.

There were few tears now. Some had wept when they were ordered to leave their homes, or the caves in which they lived, but now they seemed resigned.

The refugees were taken to collection points on the coast and in the "Death Valley" area. There they received food and blankets.

The Phu Cat mountains have been held by the Viet Cong for more than 20 years, and are believed to harbor a main force, the E2B Battalion.

"The French never went into the mountains and the American G.I.'s called the main valley 'Death Valley'," the spokesman said. "We must consider the people of the area as hostile."

Maj. Gen. Lew Byong Hion, commander of the Tiger Division, describing the over-all plan, said:

"We call it our sit-on tactic. It is a matter of patience for us and for them (the Viet Cong).

"I don't like to leave any remnants of the enemy in there. One time is enough. We'll stay until we can't find any more guerrillas."

The Koreans send two-or three-man teams into every cave and bunker they come across.

In the first week of the operation they killed nearly 30 Viet Cong, captured about 200, and detailed more than 250 suspects. They also collected some 120 rifles plus machine guns, mortars and hand grenades.

"We have many patrols and when we are confident we have eliminated the Viet Cong the people can return," the Division spokesman said. "Through our civic action program our soldiers will help them repair their homes and bridges and build irrigation dams. Then the Vietnamese popular forces (militia) will provide security and we will move to another place."

The Koreans say that their program, although it disrupts the civilian population in the battle zone, saves lives. They explain:

The refugees are moved from the collection points by foot, truck, helicopter or boat to the rear to await shipment to resettlement camps established by the Vietnamese government. The refugees from the mountain area of 60 square miles exceed the facilities available. It probably will be weeks before many of them will be placed in camps to await the conclusion of Phu Cat mountain fighting between the Koreans and the Viet Cong.

Then, those who have been classified as loyal to the government will be permitted to return to their homes.

The forced resettlement of all civilians in such a large area is the Tiger Division's solution to the problem of separating civilian noncombatants from guerrillas.

The Division spokesman said:

"If we do not do it this way, the war will not end, ever.

"We want all of the people to be evacuated from the area under VC control. If the population remains, the Viet Cong will return and set up their organization again."

The Division used similar tactics when it was assigned to pacifying about 900 square miles of Binh Dinh Province around Qui Nhon when it arrived in Viet Nam a year ago.

"We are proud to say our area is now the most secure in Viet Nam," the spokesman said. "You can travel on Highways 1 or 19 day or night without any Viet Cong sniper or ambush."

"Our soldiers go into battle to kill or capture the enemy. We must remove the civilians to do our job."

Two divisions of U.S. Marines operating in the northern provinces have rarely removed hostile villagers while extending their perimeters around Hue, Da Nang and Chu Lai.

The U.S. 1st Air Cavalry Division and other American units operating in Central South Viet Nam have concentrated on finding and fighting large enemy units and then pulling out of the battle area.

The U.S. 1st and 25th Infantry Divisions, working north of Saigon, generally have confined their pacification projects to areas near unit headquarters, quarters, with limited resettlement of villagers.

3 Dec 66   (See Note Page 20)
            AN HOA, Dec 3

Hundreds of South Vietnamese peasants — some claiming to have been under the control of the Viet Cong for three years — began a march today from their homes to a protected town near the big U.S. base of Da Nang.

The pilgrimage was planned Thursday after some 200 residents of an area about 40 miles south of Da Nang sought help from units of the 5th U.S. Marine Regiment which was conducting a search-and-destroy operation in the area.

After the Marines agreed to help the peasants leave their village and move to the protected town of An Hoa, 30 miles south of Da Nang, more asked to come along. Estimates of the number of refugees involved now range from 800 to 1,500.

Marine officers said today that the Vietnamese told them the Viet Cong had held them virtual prisoners for up to three years. The peasants said Communist guerrillas came into the villages and demanded that working parties be supplied.

The villagers said the Viet Cong also took rice from them and forced the young men of the area to serve as soldiers.

...They will be moved to An Hoa, where a Marine spokesman said they will build new homes and be "protected from Viet Cong harassment and terrorism."

Local militiamen are helping Marines provide protection for the refugees during their journey.

The Marine search-and-destroy operation in the area has killed 10 Viet Cong and another 10 are listed as probably killed, a U.S. spokesman said.

10 Dec 66   Philadelphia Bulletin (See Note Page 20)
           RACH GIA, VIET NAM, Dec 10

About 2,300 Vietnamese, heeding Government pleas, fled a Viet Cong stronghold this week in southwest Viet Nam.

Allied authorities credit a combination of propaganda and bombs. A Kansas major said it resulted from a "finger of fate" pointed at the home of a guerrilla chieftan.

Guerrillas moved two years ago into three prosperous hamlets which lie in a mountain mass rising abruptly from the Mekong Delta's flatness 125 miles southwest of Saigon.

...The "finger of fate" incident was described by Maj. Richard E. White, 38, of Salina, Kansas, adviser to the district leader, Maj. Dao Vinh Thi.

American planes made their first raid on the mountain redoubt Oct. 16.

One of the bombs missed its target by 1,000 feet and plunged through the roof of the Viet Cong village chieftan's house while he was entertaining some staff officers of the 512th Battalion.

The casualties were carried away. Then Viet Cong leaders, trying to support their previous claims that the hamlets would not be bombed, executed four villagers who they claimed were spies responsible for the attack.

The guerrillas' boast of invulnerability was cracked, however, so Lt. Col. Sam Tan Phuoc, province chieftain, and Maj. Thi decided to follow up with a molasses-and-lightning approach.

First, the villagers were told by leaflets of the benefits the government offered if they would leave the Viet Cong area and accept government protection. The, they were warned, the planes would renew their attacks.

After the leaflet drops, fighter-bomber raids became almost a nightly event. The pilots aimed at guerrilla mountain forts rather than directly at the hamlets. Phuoc said.

Last Saturday, 27 guerrillas surrendered under the government's Chieu Hoi (open arms) program. Then civilians streamed out of the mountains.

14 Dec 66   Philadelphia Bulletin (See Note Page 20)
           SAIGON, Dec 14

An elaborate allied program that removed 2,466 peasants from their village to refugee centers appeared doomed today because South Vietnamese troops have failed to move in to secure the area.

The cleared area is in the Hon Chong Mountains, near the Gulf of Siam, 125 miles west of Saigon.

A U.S. Air Force spokesman, Maj. Theodore D. King, 38, of New Windsor, New York, said the refugees have told American officials their rice will be ripe within two weeks, and they are going home to harvest it — with or without military protection.

...Pinpoint bombing of Viet Cong encampments by Vietnamese Air Force planes was one phase of the allied campaign, launched last month. This was linked with a massive psychological warfare program that enticed the farming families away from their homes.

...King a forward air controller, called in air strikes on the top of the mountains and then had these followed up by leaflet drops telling the villagers that there would be more strikes. The leaflets told the villagers to go to one of the three refugee centers.

The bombing raids disposed of Viet Cong claims that they could protect the villages. Soon artillery and naval gunfire joined the attack, and the exodus began.

..."We started Nov. 16 with the strikes, we used psychological warfare. The people would be warned away from an area before it was hit. They learned that the psywar speakers and pamphlets told the truth, and that each air strike hit announced targets a little lower (down the mountains) than the last.

"We kept the pattern of strikes creeping down the mountain side and the people in the houses could see the explosions at night above them.

"These are great family people, and they had to be increasingly concerned about the security of their families. When the psywar people told them an area was dangerous, they believed.

"It got so, during, the exodus phase, that a forward air controller could just fly over and fire a smoke jobby (target-spotting rocket), and there would be an immediate increase in the number of boats leaving the seaward side of the mountain."

25 Jan 67   The Washington Post
              SAIGON, Jan 24

Four thousand South Korean troops have captured a large area of Phuyen Province from the Vietcong and cleared out 16,000 South Vietnamese villagers in an attempt to hold the region, a South Korean spokesman announced today.

Maj. Gen. Chung Yuk Jin reported that the Tiger Division, beginning Jan. 3, swept in by air and land to gain control of a 344-square-mile-area 260 miles north of here. He said 153 Viet Cong were killed and 375 guerrillas and 653 suspects were captured, Reuters reported.

Turning Mao Tse-tung's dictum against the Communists, Chung said the 16,000 villagers were evacuated from the 20-year guerrillas stronghold because "the Vietcong are the fish and the people are the water — if we remove the people, the Vietcong, like the fish, are left high and dry."

The resettlement of the civilians, most of them from Vietcong families, was believed to be one of the largest population movements of the war. By comparison, 6,000 people have been relocated in the Iron Triangle, where U.S. troops are currently engaged in their largest operation of the war.

...Chung said the drive began when troops surprised about 150 villagers returning from a market and held them so they could not give an alarm. As the Koreans moved along Highway 1 and dropped down from helicopters, he said, the Vietcong fled before them.

1 Feb 67   (See Note Page 20)
             LANDING ZONE HAMMOND, VIETNAM, Feb 1

There are 11, 14, 19 or 22 enemy dead each day in the Battle of Binh Dinh province, a prolonged campaign of attrition characterizing the war these days in Vietnam.

...At the same time, the military and Vietnamese government have been emptying the misty green mountain draws and portions of the coastal plain of Binh Dinh of peasants thought to be under control or aiding the enemy.

...Civil affairs officers say about 20,100 civilians have left their homes, in many cases voluntarily, for refugee camps and eventual resettlement in Government controlled areas.

26 Feb 67   (See Note Page 20)
             DA NANG, VIETNAM, Feb 26

...The fiercely independent Central Vietnamese distrust and dislike the Northerners even when they are battling for a common cause.

There are no pencil and form-carrying pollsters roaming Vietnam to measure such things as popularity, but Gen. Walt sees the rising number of refugees flowing into Government areas as a solid indicator of sentiment in the countryside.

"For instance, we had 2,400 refugees come out of the valley where Operation Mississippi was conducted. They'd had enough of the North Vietnamese trying to take their food, their money and their young people and forcing them to do so much labor.

"After Operation Independence, 3,400 people came out of that area for Government protection," said Gen. Walt.

There is an added inducement, he added, for the South Vietnamese peasants to leave Communist dominated areas:

"They know that as long as the Viet Cong and the North Vietnamese troops are in there, we're coming after them. They (the local residents) know they will be subjected to air strikes and artillery barrages once in a while.

"But the primary reason they are leaving these areas is that they no longer believe that the Viet Cong way is the best way and they believe the Government can and will protect them."

13 Apr 67   World Journal Tribune, John Randolph
            SAIGON, April 13

The Vietnamese government is reported to be debating a sweeping plan to evacuate the entire civilian population from all or part of its embattled northern border province of Quang Tri.

The object would be to turn this Viet Cong-infested frontier area into a "free-killing zone" where anyone not wearing an Allied uniform could be shot on sight as a Communist guerrilla or North Vietnamese Army invader.

Proponents of the evacuation say it would expose the Communist fighters to swift attack — or compel timely retreat back across the border into North Viet Nam or neighboring Laos.

American military men are believed to favor the plan — and some of them may even have inspired it.

As reported — so far without official confirmation — the Vietnamese government would proclaim Quang Tri Province, or some norther portion of it, a "special war zone" from which all civilians would be barred.

Communist sympathizers would be offered unmolested freedom to move to North Viet Nam if they choose. All others who chose to remain in South Vietnam would be evacuated to the South and given government assistance in resettling.

Once cleared of civilians, the zone would be for soldiers only — like the 10-to-30-mile zone behind the front in the Korean War. Civilians would be subject to immediate arrest and removal — and when suspicious could be shot on sight.

With coastal fishermen out of the way, a similar zone probably would be extended three miles offshore as a "sink on sight" area for trespassing civilian watercraft — often suspected to be Communist gunrunners.

17 Apr 67   Christian Science Monitor, Joseph C. Harsch
            WASHINGTON

...In the upper battle area, just below the demilitarized zone which separates North from South Vietnam, the initiative has passed to the hands of the enemy. They have blown the bridges between Da Nang and Quangtri, thus cutting the front-line outposts of the first United States Marine division from their main base. They have attacked Quangtri with heavy mortars.

...One suggested remedy is the removal of the 350,000 native civilians from the battle zone south of the demilitarized zone. This would give the marines freedom to fire at anything moving. It would also impose a sudden and major burden on housing and food agencies of the South Vietnam Government. There is some doubt that there is still time for such a movement of people.

18 Apr 67   Christian Science Monitor, John Dillin
            SAIGON

... (Reuters reported, from informed sources, that a decision has been made to evacuate all villages in an area immediately below the zone stretching from the coast 18 miles inland. About 19,000 people would be involved.

The Vietnamese Government is further debating a plan to evacuate the whole civilian population — 273,000 people — from Quangtri. Some American military men are said to favor the plan.)

...The fortified barrier, which will include a depopulated strip three to five miles wide, will make the job of allied troops in First Corps only slightly easier.

The barrier at present will extend only from the coast to the mountains. But since most infiltration comes through the mountains and through Laos, its effect will be limited.

15 Apr 67   UPI, Eugene V. Risher
              SAIGON

Premier Nhuyen Cao Ky sent paratroop and engineer battalions to South Vietnam's northern frontiers Saturday to build a "little Maginot line" to halt Communist infiltration.

Ky announced that 20,000 Vietnamese villagers are being evacuated from the frontier area to permit building of the "fortified barrier" that will stretch 14 miles from the mountains to the South China Sea.

The strip, extending about three miles below the southern fringe of the Demilitarized Zone will be stripped of vegetation. Anything that moves will be fair game for planes prowling overhead and Allied artillery covering every inch of the area.

...Even as the Premier was announcing the barrier project, Vietnamese troops with huge bulldozers and other earth-moving equipment moved northward from the Da Nang area.

One American official said the huge equipment will be used to remove trees and bushes from the border strip.

"They're going to dig 'em out by the roots," he said.

Ky disclosed the barrier project during a visit to the Bien Hoa air base Saturday afternoon before he returned to Saigon to talk with former Vice President Richard Nixon. It was not known whether he discussed the matter with Nixon.

Under the plan, the southern half of the six-mile-wide Demilitarized Zone will, in effect, be doubled in depth. The new three-mile-deep no man's land will serve as a "free fire" zone, and the fortified barrier will be erected on the southern fringe of the strip.

Ky did not disclose just what type of fortifications will be used. But sources said that at least part of the area will be sown with land mines and other anti-personnel devices in addition to various types of warning systems.

The Premier said he already had given the order to begin evacuating 20,000 villagers from the border strip. He said the resettlement is necessary so that "innocent people will not be killed."

Ky said his war cabinet decided to set up the barrier because of last week's raids across the "freedom bridge" by North Vietnamese troops. The thrust was repulsed by American artillery.

The Premier, speaking at the Bien Hoa air base 14 miles northeast of Saigon, mentioned the possibility of sending American troops into the Demilitarized Zone.

25 Apr 67   Christian Science Monitor (See Note Page 20)
              DONG HA, VIETNAM

The United States and South Vietnams officials are planning the most ambitious resettlement project of the war.

This is the evacuation of about 20,000 persons from the southern area of the demilitarized zone and adjacent South Vietnamese territory.

The resettlement plan is part of a new military approach to the theoretically neutral buffer territory which has served as a virtual highway for the infiltration of fresh troops and supplies from North Vietnam to the south.

Coordinated with it is the clearing of a 12-mile-long strip, 220 yards wide, across the coastal lowland between Con Thien and the sea. This is being bulldozed two miles below the six-mile-wide zone.

The resettlement plan applies to hamlets in the path of the strip and in the southern portion of the DMZ, below the Ben Hain River, which divides the buffer zone equally between north and south.

The result will be a fortified strip underlining an expanse of rice paddies and scrubland depopulated of civilian support and sympathy for infiltrating North Vietnamese soldiers. The actual movement of families should take about one month, South Vietnamese sources estimate.

18 May 67   New York Times (See Note Page 20)
             SAIGON, SOUTH VIETNAM, May 17

The South Vietnamese Government began moving the first of about 11,000 peasants today from the area south of Giolinh, near the demilitarized zone where burned-out homes, shell craters and fresh burial mounds bear witness to the fighting.

They will be resettled farther south, at Camlo. Some left reluctantly. A woman kicked and screamed as her household belongings were loaded on a truck.

The vacated area is expected to become a "free-fire zone" — an area in which allied troops will consider any remaining person an enemy. Anything that moves will become a target.

The enemy has conducted an intensive drive against the resettlement program. On Tuesday Vietcong terrorists killed eight pacification workers and wounded five in an attack on a village.

29 Apr 67   UPI, Thomas Corpora
             CAM LO, VIETNAM

... Father Co packed his church treasures again this month, this time for a move 13 miles farther south to a refugee camp near the town of Cam Lo, a district headquarters about eight miles south of the DMZ and one-third of the distance from the South China Sea to the border with Laos.

Father Co and his 1300 parishioners are the first of 23,000 South Vietnamese who are leaving their homes in northern Quang Tri province for refugee camps at Cam Lo.

The exodus, which hasn't really started yet, is part of an over-all plan to turn northern Quang Tri into a no-man's land which U.S. and Vietnamese forces can fire into at will without fear of hurting civilians.

The move hasn't been easy. Farther Co said some of his people were "crazy" with grief.

"They had everything they needed there," said the slight, bespectacled French-trained priest. "They had to leave the pepper unharvested, and the tapioca and the fruit trees.

"But is better to leave because they would get hit by mortars," he said.

Father Co has tried to explain the necessity of the move to his people and to soften it as much as possible by going direct to the Americans — both military and civilian — for help.

The Government has promised help, too, but so far "We've got very little from the Government, mostly from the Americans."

Other refugees from the area of Gio Linh haven't had the luck of a dedicated Catholic priest to help them and Vietnamese officials concerned with the move seem to have frightened the people more than anything else.

The families now trickling down highway 1 with their belongings — including roofs and walls of their homes when it is possible to move them — say they were told in no uncertain terms to get out and that if they didn't the Americans would destroy their villages with artillery.

One elderly Vietnamese man said he and his family had lived in the same hamlet for more than 100 years, that his ancestors were buried there and that he just wouldn't know what to do anywhere else.

American identification with the unpleasant business of moving the people is being held to a minimum. The people move themselves or Vietnamese army trucks move them. U.S. aid officials supply food, building materials, seeds and other necessities, and marine bulldozers will help construct building sites and paddies.

But U.S. military and aid officials are confident the problems can be solved.

"We've got the land for 'em," said Capt. Irving Smith of Margaretsville, New York, a U.S. Army advisor at Cam Lo. "There's plenty of land. Hell, we've got more land than we know what to do with."

The land is barren of crops and housing now and has no water. It's good land, though, and once wells are built crops can be planted. Until then, aid through the Vietnamese government will have to feed the people.

2 May 67   New York Post (See Note Page 20)
           BONG SON, VIETNAM

Hundreds of peasants fought among themselves and tried to storm through tear gas in a scramble to board six U.S. Army trucks — not to flee from anything but to re-enter a valley threatened by the Viet Cong.

Their rice was there and they were determined to harvest it.

The peasants were refugees from the fertile An Lao valley, 300 miles north of Saigon. For the second time it has become a major battle field between the Viet Cong and the U.S. 1st Air Cavalry Division.

An estimated 9,000 inhabitants moved out when U.S. troops tried to destroy the guerrillas in February, 1966. When the Americans had to pull out to check infiltration of North Vietnamese troops across the Cambodian border, at least 7,000 valley residents went home.

The Viet Cong came right back, too, continuing to tax the families of their money, rice and young men.

The Americans returned early last month, warning that anyone not in government-controlled areas would be considered an enemy. Some 6,000 men, women and children moved from the valley into refugee camps and resettlement villages in Bong Son.

Food was scarce in the refugee villages, while rice planted by the valley residents was ripening under the noses of the Viet Cong. So the Americans began Operation Chop Suey.

U.S. trucks began carrying refugees to the valley each morning. They harvested rice until nearly dusk, under the protection of Vietnamese militiamen.

By the third day, the size of the harvesting group was too large and the militiamen and U.S. military police had to drag many persons off the trucks.

On the fourth day, soldiers used tear gas and fired warning shots in efforts to keep back refugees for whom the trucks had no room.

About 1,200 persons gathered on the fifth day and ended up walking seven miles to the fields when no trucks were available.

The Viet Cong picked that day to ambush a convoy carrying 90 militiamen out to stand guard at the fields. This reporter was on a jeep at the rear of that convoy when a grenade sailed over and exploded 20 yards away.

...Four helicopter gunships arrived, the militiamen joined the battle and two armored vehicles hurried down the road. The guerrillas slipped back into the jungle.

Trucks came out that evening and returned to Bong Son carrying refugees laden with sacks, baskets and cans of rice, stems of bananas, clusters of coconuts, bundles of firewood, old bed frames, pots and pans.

22 May 67   New York Times
           CAOXA, DEMILITARIZED ZONE, SOUTH VIETNAM, May 21

The Vietnamese woman lifted her weatherbeaten face for a long last look at the rich rice fields.

As the truck began to move, she buried her head in her arms and wept with body shaking sobs.

Mrs. Ngo Ngoc Chung was being evacuated from this farming hamlet inside the demilitarized zone, which has now become a battlefield.

Fourteen United States Marine trucks rumbled out of the village to Highway 1 for the long ride south to the resettlement camp at Camlo, where almost all the 10,000 villagers inside the zone had already been settled.

Mrs. Chung was more fortunate than most of the villagers, who are classified as refugees. Her husband, a 45-year-old rice farmer, was with her along with her five children, ranging in age from an infant in arms to a robust daughter in her late teens.

Most of the others being moved were old women and young children. There were few able-bodies men.

Second Lieutenant Paul J. Cashman, 24, of Berkeley, California, the marines' convoy commander, stood stripped to the waist in the dusty country lane, his lean body heavily tanned.

"We moved 600 to 700 yesterday," he said, "we're trying to move the same today with all their gear. They are taking everything they own, including cattle and pigs. Yesterday it looked like a rodeo here with our marines trying to catch and load the cattle."

The Chung family, Mr. Chung said through an interpreter, lived a "long, long time" in the same simple thatch-roofed farmhouse. They brought with them everything they could carry, including the beams and timbers from the house, which they had dismantled for the move.

Pigs, chickens, and ducks were loaded onto the trucks along with two wooden beds, two tables, a number of woven reed mats, trays of various household goods, and odds and ends, including sheets of tin roofing taken from a shed.

Lieutenant Cashman said everyone was being evacuated from the center of the demilitarized zone to well below Giolinh, a mile south of the zone, where a United States outpost has been subjected to almost daily shelling from North Vietnam and the demilitarized zone.

He said 32 Marine trucks and 32 South Vietnamese trucks were moving the civilians as soon as they could be accommodated at a resettlement camp.

Capt. J. C. James, 26, of Niagara Falls, New York, the assistant civil affairs officer for the Third Marine Division, said a plan to move all civilians out of the zone had been formulated after March 19, when Premier Ky announced that he wanted the area evacuated.

The captain said the plan called for a phased six-month movement, scheduled to begin March 24, after the resettlement camp at Camlo had been prepared.

When the farmers were asked to give up their homes and move to the camp on May 16, they all refused, he said. This year has the best harvest of rice in 14 years, and none of the farmers wanted to give it up, he said. "But on the 18th when the Marine operation kicked off to clear the zone, the people came willingly," he said.

As a result, he said, a rush started that changed the planned movement of 55 families a day to 1,200 a day, with bombs and shells falling throughout the eastern half of the zone.

United States military commanders have instructions to remove all civilians they find in the southern half of the zone.

The Chung family took stoically the two-hour truck ride to Camlo, a tent city with numbers of families living under the canvas, crowded in with all their possessions.

The United States aid mission in Saigon is helping by donating roofing materials, cement and nails for new housing as well as food, blankets, clothing and fertilizer to heop the relocated people begin new lives.

One of the many problems, a local official said, is that most of the new refugees were rice farmers and the land they have been given is suitable only for vegetable farming.

12 Jun 67   Nation
             Desmond Smith, "There Must Have Been Easier Wars"

...The First Cav love their war. Basically it is Indians and Cavalry
spread over an AO (area of operations) of some 3,000 square kilometers
(called "clicks" by the briefing officer).
...From a briefing on how the First Cav "softened up" the Bong-Son
plain preparatory to moving in:
"Three hundred and sixty-five air strikes."
"Yes."
"More than thirty ARCLIGHTS — that's code for B-52 strikes."
"Yes."
"And that was the start. Then we lobbed in better than a million shells."
"Yes."
"In between the air strikes, we dumped more than a million psywar leaf-
lets on the plain."
"Yes."
"Well, do you correspondents have any questions?"
"Well, only one. According to your handout, all you have captured so far
in OPERATION PERSHING is thirty hand grenades, four rounds of large cali-
ber ammunition, 3 tons of rice, and 3 tons of salt."
"Sir?"
"It appears that you've leveled virtually every village and hamlet, killed
or driven more than 50,000 peasants off the land with your firepower. My
question is, how do you intend to go about winning the hearts and minds of
these people?"
"I'm afraid you'll have to take that up with the S.5, sir, but jeeze, it's
a real good question."

15 Jul 67   The New Yorker
             Jonathan Schell, "The Village of Ben Suc"

...The term "hostile civilians" was a new one, invented during Operation
Cedar Falls for the people in the villages that had been marked for destruction
The question of what to call these villagers was one of many semantic problems
that the Army had to solve. At the scene of an evacuation, they usually used th
phrase "hostile civilians," which hinted that all the villagers at least supported
the enemy and thus all deserved to be "relocated." But later, at Phu Loi, the
officials in charge reverted to the more familiar term "refugees," which suggested that the villagers were not themselves the enemy but were "the people,"
fleeing the enemy.

STRATEGIC HAMLETS

29 Mar 62   New York Times, Homer Bigart
             BENCAT, VIETNAM, March 28

Deep in a rubber plantation four miles north of here, South Vietnamese
and Americans are engaged in an important test in isolating the rural population from the Viet Cong Communist Guerrillas.
This experiment is crucial to the success of Operation Sunrise, the first
comprehensive plan to pacify South Vietnam. Operation Sunrise was begun
modestly in this area a week ago. The operation is subsidized directly with
United States money, military planning and technical aid.
In this region, 1,200 families are to be moved voluntarily or forcibly
from the forest controlled by the Viet Cong and resettled in new strategic
villages. The abandoned villages will be burned to deprive the Viet Cong of
shelter and food.
The Communist guerrillas have been blackmailing and threatening
villagers to force them to provide supplies.

The first step in Operation Sunrise involved encirclement of a half dozen settlements. Government forces failed to make the maneuver a complete surprise; a hundred men were able to flee to the forest before the ring closed.

...The Government was able to persuade only seventy families to volunteer for resettlement. The 135 other families in the half dozen settlements were herded forcibly from their homes.

This harsh, desperate measure was approved by the Americans because it worked so well for the British in Malaya. There, the forced resettlement of a half-million people was the turning point in the British defeat of the Communists.

The vital features of the Malayan plan are discernible in Operation Sunrise. An important difference is noted, however, in matter of compensation.

In Malaya, the British paid compensation on the spot for anything the farmers left behind. Here, the money is withheld until the resettled families indicate they will not bolt to the woods.

So far, little of the $300,000 in local currency provided by the United States Operation Mission has reached the farmers. Some volunteers have received the first part of the 1,500 piasters, or $21, promised by the Government.

By way of further compensation, the Government has promised land, building materials, agricultural tools and emergency food and clothing. Until homes are built, the families are housed in long communal barracks without walls.

...Some families had been allowed to carry away beds, tables and benches before their homes were burned. Others had almost nothing but the clothes on their backs. A young woman stood expressionless as she recounted how the troops had burned the familiar two tons of rice. She was overheard by a man in black peasant garb who had identified himself as an army psychological warfare lieutenant. He cautioned the woman's listeners that she was "very bad" and that the burned rice was probably Viet Cong stores.

Only a few old men were visible among the uprooted families. The Vietnamese officers were what was being done to get the husbands to emerge from the forest and rejoin their families.

They replied that planes had dropped 24,000 leaflets promising amnesty. Also, the women are allowed to make one trip back to the deserted settlements that have not yet been burned to retrieve household effects. It is almost certain, officials said, that during this journey the wives will seek out their husbands and give them safe-conduct passes to the temporary camp.

The families were being subjected to a barrage of Government propaganda. Loudspeakers told them why they had been uprooted; first, the old settlements had no doctor and no schools; second, the Viet Cong conscripted their rice and made them sabotage roads; third, when forced to work for the Viet Cong, they were often victims of Government bombs and bullets.

The trees were plastered with cartoons: banners suspended between the trees promised, "we will root out all the Viet Cong who destroy our villages."

The camp seemed well-organized. Civic Action officials distributed food and clothes. Nurses instructed mothers in infant care.

"It's no happy hollow," Maj. Marvin L. Price of New Kensington, Pa. conceded. "But at last we've got a framework for getting people in the mood for helping themselves." The Major had helped plan Operation Sunrise.

Observers said it certainly was better than former operations wherein families were roughly ordered out of their homes, often with no time to gather their possessions, and marched off to a stockade with no provisions for food or water.

Last week, for example, Miss Eliza M. Corbin of University Park, Pa., a United States Mission adviser on rural home-improvement, found 630 tired, dirty women and children living in a stockade in adjacent Phouc Thanh

Province. They were getting insufficient rice and the children were ill from impure water. Miss Corbin quickly collected three tons of relief supplies from the Mennonite Central Committee and Roman Catholic relief agencies.

1 Apr 62   New York Times, Homer Bigart
            SAIGON, VIETNAM, March 31

Strategic villages are springing up all over Vietnam. Thousands of Vietnamese farmers are moving into settlements protected from Communist guerrillas by mud walls, moats, barbed wire and bamboo hedges.

Today the most elaborate of the strategic villages and one that has already become a showpiece for visitors was opened officially by Ngo Dinh Nhu, brother and chief adviser of President Ngo Dinh Diem. The village, Cu Chi, consists of four hamlets with a total population of 6,270.

...The village shows disheartening signs of over-regimentation. Almost everyone who greeted Ngo Dinh Nhu was in uniform. Most of his audience consisted of blue-uniformed young troops. There was little spontaneous enthusiasm. Security measures were tight and grim soldiers with submachine guns were seen everywhere along the route of inspection.

Americans who know Cu Chi said they had heard complaints from farmers. These farmers said they had had to work six to eight weeks without pay on fortification of the hamlets and had not even been supplied with food. They also said they had to contribute bamboo, a crop they usually sell only when they have a bad year. They were further annoyed by having been ordered to buy flags and then having to buy more flags because the first set was not the proper size.

Ngo Dinh Nhu arrived, with a large group of diplomats. They inspected several elementary schools and a Buddhist temple. The officials said Cu Chi was 85 percent Buddhist.

William Z. Gardiner, director of the United States Operations Mission, was delighted to find at one school a notice acknowledging that the United States had contributed most of the required funds.

From the flag-draped stand along the main highway Ngo Dinh Nhu said that the Communists had boasted of dominance over the Cu Chi district. He said that the people here had been considered pro-Communist. But that all they really wanted was peace and freedom.

Once security was assured, Ngo Dinh Nhu said, the village would have the opportunity to elect local leaders. There would be no more arbitrary arrests, he said, and laws would be applied justly.

Cu Chi's opening was not connected with Operation Sunrise, launched in another part of Binh Duong Province last week. That operation involves the transfer of rural families out of isolated areas vulnerable to Communist control.

A Vietnamese official estimated that 500,000 rural families would be moved by Operation Sunrise and subsequent operations.

4 Apr 62   New York Times, Homer Bigart
            SAIGON, VIETNAM, April 3

The United States, besides subsidizing compensation for the Vietnamese peasants uprooted by Operation Sunrise, will give them a free weekly newspaper telling why they were forced to move. It also will include new briefs and the latest soccer results.

Produced by the United States Information Service, the paper, named Toward the Good Life, is being distributed to families in the Bencat district of Binh Duong Province north of Saigon. About 200 families have been escorted there from isolated hamlets.

In regrouping centers these families now await resettlement in areas more secure from Communist guerrilla control. Thousands more face compulsory relocation in ten provinces surrounding Saigon.

Douglas E. Pike, a special projects officer for the Information Service, has run off 35,000 copies of Toward the Good Life. The service will continue putting out the paper for 12 weeks. After that, Mr. Pike hopes the Vietnamese will take over the publication.

...The first issue was given over almost entirely to explaining Operation Sunrise, which aims to isolate the rural population from the Communists. Few of the first batch of uprooted families left their homes voluntarily.

Whenever possible, they were allowed to bring their pigs, chickens and water buffalo. But all things left behind were to be destroyed to prevent their use by the Communists who are called Viet Cong.

The United States has set aside $300,000 in local currency so that each family can be paid 1,500 piasters, or about $21 for the property destroyed.

The leading article in the paper told the uprooted farmers why the drastic step was necessary. "The Government of the Republic of Vietnam has opened a great military and social improvement campaign in Binh Duong Province. It is called Operation Sunrise."

"The purpose of the operation, officials explain, is to destroy the power of the Viet Cong and to improve living conditions in rural areas of the Province," the paper added.

"People of the Bencat vicinity of Binh Duong Province are being urged by officials to gather at regrouping centers. In some cases they are being required to move.

"The people will live in these regrouping centers for a few weeks while new homes are being constructed. They will be given money and tools and other help in construction of their new homes. They will also be given one hectare (2.47 acres) of land on which to build each house."

Le Viet Nam Entre Deux Paix, Jean Lacouture, 1965, p. 103
(Translated from the French)

The great idea of the family reign, of Mr. Nhu especially, was the creation of strategic hamlets in 1961. The idea is familiar to French observers for it is the same that led to the construction of regroupment camps in Algeria two years earlier. It involved the bringing together of the rural population into fortified or protected enclosures in order to withdraw the source of popular support from the rebellion, to take away from the renowned "revolutionary fish" the water in which it lives and flourishes. The same causes produced the same effects: a growing hostility of the peasant masses towards those regrouping them...

By tampering with the village, Mr. Nhu and his supporters attacked the very foundations of Vietnamese peasant civilization where the community, pressed within its bamboo enclosure, remained the fundamental unity, the prime matter of public life and the very root of private life. The village, more than man himself, was a unity. It was this unity that was taxed and carried on the dialogue with the central power. Everything went out from this unity, and returned to it. It expressed that "harmony under heaven" that each member of a society impregnated with Confucianism considers essential.

In attacking this unity, Mr. Nhu was, from the mechanical point of view, more revolutionary than the Vietminh who never dared to tamper with the basic cellular unit. But this so-called revolution, although it turned a society upside down, brought no solutions for the problems it had created. It was an end in itself, and only claimed to play a strategic role in the light of a purely circumstantial mission, namely the struggle against guerrillas who appeared to the poor people of the Vietnamese countryside as dangerous brothers rather than enemies.

29 Sep 63   Saturday Evening Post
            Stanley Karnow, "The Edge of Chaos"

...In too many places, local officials have thrown up bamboo fences and barbed wire, forced people to move in, and announced that their hamlets are ready. Of the 4,000 settlements officially claimed to exist in the strategic Mekong Delta, only about 1,000 are regarded as "viable" by U.S. experts. "There's a basic difference between ourselves and Vietnamese officialdom," says an American who works in the field. "We see security in terms of people; they see it in terms of territory. I don't think they've yet grasped the political aspect of this war."

23 Dec 63   New York Times, David Halberstam

...The hamlet program, which in the delta region did not suit the population as it did in the central coastal region, was often forced on the people. Hamlets were built too quickly as province chiefs competed with one another to please the powerful Ngo Dinh Nhu, who strongly backed the program, and the hamlets were often poorly administered.

"We were taking people from areas they liked, where they had plenty of land, and moving them to where they didn't want to go to protect them from someone they didn't necessarily think was an enemy — and all they got was the Cong An," one American said. "No wonder that when the Vietcong came into hamlets and killed some of the local officials, they began to look like Robin Hoods."

12 Jan 64   New York Times, Hendrick Smith
             TAN AN, SOUTH VIETNAM, Jan 9

...From an American helicopter over Long An's rice paddies, one can see ample evidence of the mistakes that have been made. Entire villages lie in ruins, roofs of houses torn off, walls knocked in, inhabitants gone.

...Because the peasants' homes in the delta are scattered over their farmland, the Government had to move thousands from their traditional homes to establish the hamlets. In Long An 80,000 people were relocated. Their resentment at having been moved was exploited by the Communists, and more than half have left the hamlets.

Ten thousand more — originally permitted to remain in their family homes — are reported to have quit the hamlets because living in them brought the guerrilla war to their doorsteps. A trickle of dissatisfied villagers can be seen trudging away from hamlets, beds and personal belongings strapped to their backs.

...Often the militia provided little protection for the villagers and even abused those they were supposed to guard. In one hamlet peasants said corpsmen had shot at them when they tried to protect their crops from being eaten by militiamen's ducks.

...The hamlets were considered complete, an official explained, once the villagers were inside and when fences and moats had been built, even if the militiamen were untrained and defenses weak and even if "there was no sense of community."

Many relocated families were not paid Government relocation allowances. Peasants were sometimes forced to buy construction materials that were supposed to be furnished by the Government and by United States aid programs.

Rich settlers bought their way out of serving in the militia, and officials sometimes drew the hamlet boundaries to protect their holdings. Hamlet council elections were not infrequently rigged in favor of friends and relatives of the hamlet chief.

338

22 Feb 64   New Republic
              Bernard Fall, "How Much Time Do We Have In Vietnam?"

...The regrouping of the civilian population into fortified hamlets to protect it from Viet-Cong pressure was the cornerstone of the whole counterinsurgency program. It involved displacing close to nine million people, most of whom did not want to be moved. Many were moved before harvesting time, thus losing a crop; others were forced to destroy their own houses, for which the Diem regime paid them $10. It costs, according to official American estimates, at least $56 to build a Vietnamese peasant house. Many villages were created in areas where the people could not make a living; others were indefensible. The strategic hamlet program is in bad trouble in many key areas. Yet last summer the official mythology was that the hamlet program had changed for the better the "security, and even more important the psychology of huge areas of South Vietnam." Has it?

22 Jun 64   UPI, New York Times
              LONG HOI, SOUTH VIETNAM, June 27

...Colonel Loc identified the enemy as the 519th and 517th Companies of the hard-core Vietcong Cuu Long Battalion which has kept the area around Long Hoi subdued for many months. The colonel has been trying to destroy the battalion's base by forcibly moving out civilians and applying a scorched-earth policy to the villages and rice fields.

So far, he has moved out 1,448 civilians, and the Cuu Long Battalion has begun fighting back against his clearing parties. Today's trap was baited by moving in the one militia company in the hope of convincing the Communists it was just another small clearing force.

22 Aug 64   Saturday Evening Post
              Stanley Karnow, "This Is Our Enemy"

...Traditionally attached to their ancestral lands, peasants were uprooted and forcibly shunted to the new settlements. An average family house costs $200 to build, but the government allocation was only $20. And surveying 1,500 families in Long An Province, a U.S. Information Service team found nobody who had received more than $10 and many who got nothing. At tiny Ap Moi, with a population of 62 families, the bamboo walls were down, the hamlet council had fled, and the Viet Cong passed through at will. The USIS team noted: "Evidence of overwhelming neglect."

28 Dec 64   New York Herald Tribune, Stanley Karnow
              SAIGON

...Under the late President Ngo Dinh Diem's government, overthrown last year, such ambitious schemes as the "strategic hamlet" program uprooted peasant families and forced them into new stockades without sufficient funds to build new houses.

Profiting from the upheaval, corrupt officials commandeered people to work without pay, bilked them of money or stole their livestock.

Similar practices still continue. Last August, in a drive to enforce conscription, government troops fanned across the rice fields in Mekong Delta provinces, rounding up youths of service age. Altogether, some 4,000 young men were taken. Many were still in their black working shorts when put into government camps, and most were sent to other parts of the country without seeing their families.

In several cases, authorities now admit, entire Viet Cong guerrilla bands were probably incorporated into the government army without screening. As a cabinet member told me: "It was sheer idiocy."

The Making of a Quagmire, David Halberstam, 1964, p. 185, 187, 188, 189

...The Delta was quite a different story; yet the difference was never recognized in high American councils. It took only the most superficial knowledge to realize that the programs which worked farther north were unsuitable in the Delta. For one thing, the Delta guerrilla found it easy to live off the land. Even more important was the fact that the population of the Delta was not clustered into convenient little groups; it was spread out aimlessly and endlessly over this rich soil. Therefore, all too often this meant relocating people from an area which they loved and had held for many generations, to a region for which they cared not at all — in order to fight an enemy they did not really consider their enemy. By and large the population of the Delta had been on the fence, but the very act of relocation turned thousands of peasants against the Government.

...The dream envisaged remained only on paper, for Mr. Nhu saw it as a means of population control instead and put his people in charge of the program. Province chiefs competed with one another over the number of hamlets they could build.

...Inside the villages — which could not protect themselves from atatck in any case — the people were either passive about having been shoved around or actively angry about the broken promises of medical and educational services. "Sometimes all you found representing the Government inside these hamlets were the Cong An — the local police officials working for Nhu — usually ill trained, men who were there because they were related to someone in Saigon, who were ignorant and tough, and who abused the population. No wonder the Vietcong looked like Robin Hoods when they began to hit the hamlets," one high civilian in the Delta told me.

...The Americans and the Government had hoped that the hamlet concept would force the Vietcong to attack the people; this would enrage the population and encourage them to defend themselves against the guerrillas; at the very least it was thought that it would turn the peasants against the enemy and put them on the side of the Government.

But it did not work out that way. The Vietcong were not hungry, and they did not need to prey off the villagers. Since they were usually local Southerners, often from the region in which they were bivouacked, they knew the area well — and they had infiltrated the hamlets. When they attacked, they attacked only the symbols of the Government: the armory or command post of the hamlet, the hamlet chief or the youth leaders (who were particularly hated because they were Nhu's men). They rarely harmed the population, and so the people of a village, who saw that the Government had not kept its promises and could not protect them, often sided with the Vietcong after a raid.

Victor Charlie, Kuno Knoebl, 1967, pp. 255—260

...But the Americans were caught in a dilemna. They could not satisfactorily explain to the peasants the reasons for the resettlement program, not even to those who were pro-government. And without the agreement of the villagers, the operation was doomed. The peasants did not want to abandon their villages or to endure the hardships of relocation.

...However, the success of the Staley Plan demanded that the peasants abandon their villages. The depopulated settlements were burned down, and the crops destroyed to deprive the guerrillas of hiding places and food. Frequently the peasants had nothing but their personal belongings when they moved into the strategic hamlets.

When peasants resisted resettlement — this happened often — they were driven out of their villages by force. The Vietnamese Army did not always use humane methods. The ambitious American program was a disaster before it really got started. Other unfortunate measures, too, damaged the reputations of the Saigon government and the United States. In some cases, villages were burned down when their inhabitants put up determined resistance to resettlement. Peasants or village elders who opposed resettlement were often executed by government troops to serve as examples. Both unoccupied and occupied areas were poisoned. Rice fields, plantations, and jungles were sprayed with chemicals to destroy plant life — a measure that has done the United States tremendous harm throughout the nonwhite world. The chemicals were not injurious to man and beast in most cases — but this is hard to explain to a peasant who sees his meager crop wither after it has been poisoned.

...Nonlethal gases — such as tear gas — were also used. I have seen unconscious women and children dragged out of tunnels and bunkers into which tear-gas bombs had been thrown. The effect on the peasants was frightful. Several times peasants who had been brought under control this way tried to flee, screaming. They believed that the troops wanted to gas them to death.

...I once asked a U.S. Operations Mission official in Saigon why Americans believed they could win over the peasant at the same time they were ravaging his crops and razing his village. His reply was: "The United States pays compensation for all damages — down to the last dollar and beyond." I believe the idea that payment of money can solve political and social problems reveals a profound misunderstanding of the issues that today agitate the nonwhite world.

...Government representatives started a program of political purges. Those whose families lived in guerrilla areas were officially ordered to join relatives in strategic hamlets within three months. If they did not comply, the people in the hamlets were punished. The hamlets were combed for Communists; anyone suspected of having collaborated or maintained contact with the Viet-Cong was arrested, jailed, and often executed.

Life in the hamlets was strictly controlled. The people were provided with identity papers. Some were required for moving about inside the hamlet, others for moving about outside. A guard was kept on entrance and exit gates. They were open from 6:00 A.M. to 7:00 P.M. No one was allowed to leave or enter the village during the night.

...Peasant housing was either shoddy or not built at all. The promised compensation money was not paid out; unjustified deductions and taxes were imposed. Food supplies and other aid were partly or totally kept back. "A few people were driven together, a roll of barbed wire was thrown over their heads and the strategic hamlet was finished," a New York Times article said in 1963, accurately describing what was wrong with the program.

CHAPTER XIII
REFUGEES

The following Articles from International Conventions relevant to this chapter are quoted in full:

Geneva Convention
Relative to the Protection of Civilian Persons
in Time of War
12 August 1949
(Short reference: Geneva—Civilians)

Article 24.

The Parties to the conflict shall take the necessary measures to ensure that children under fifteen, who are orphaned or are separated from their families as a result of the war, are not left to their own resources, and that their maintenance, the exercise of their religion and their education are facilitated in all circumstances. Their education shall, as far as possible, be entrusted to persons of a similar cultural tradition.

The Parties to the conflict shall facilitate the reception of such children in a neutral country for the duration of the conflict with the consent of the Protecting Power, if any, and under due safeguards for the observance of the principles stated in the first paragraph.

They shall, furthermore, endeavour, to arrange for all children under twelve to be identified by the wearing of identity discs, or by some other means.

Article 50.

The Occupying Power shall, with the cooperation of the national and local authorities, facilitate the proper working of all institutions devoted to the care and education of children.

The Occupying Power shall take all necessary steps to facilitate the identification of children and the registration of their parentage. It may not, in any case, change their personal status, nor enlist them in formations or organizations subordinate to it.

Article 59.

If the whole or part of the population of an occupied territory is inadequately supplied, the Occupying Power shall agree to relief schemes on behalf of the said population, and shall facilitate them by all the means at its disposal.

Such schemes, which may be undertaken either by States or by impartial humanitarian organizations such as the International Committee of the Red Cross, shall consist, in particular, of the provision of consignments of foodstuffs, medical supplies and clothing.

All the Contracting Parties shall permit the free passage of these consignments and shall guarantee their protection.

A Power granting free passage to consignments on their way to territory occupied by an adverse Party to the conflict shall, however, have the right to search the consignments, to regulate their passage according to prescribed times and routes, and to be reasonably satisfied through the Protecting Power that these consignments are to be used for the relief of the needy population and are not to be used for the benefit of the Occupying Power.

See also (pages 29-42) the following additional Articles relevant to this chapter: Hague—Laws: 22, 23(g), 46, 50; Geneva—Civilians: 3, 5, 7, 27, 29, 31, 32, 33, 49, 53, 56, 146, 147, 148.

CAUSE OF REFUGEES

13 Aug 65   New York Times, Jack Raymond
              WASHINGTON, Aug 12

...It is expected that as the war engages increasingly larger units of both the Communists and defenders of the Saigon Government, many hamlets and villages will be severely damaged, and the flow of refugees will increase.

...Inevitably, officials note here, the physical damage to South Vietnamese hamlets and villages will mount. The experience of marines near Da Nang who felt compelled last week to burn down the houses of a hamlet as a precaution against sniper fire, may have their counterpart in the destruction by artillery fire and aerial bombardment of other villages believed to be harboring the enemy.

And, inevitably, there will be refugees. Already, it has been reported, more than half a million refugees from flood and war have crowded Government centers. Plans are being made to cope with as many as 1,500,000 refugees by the end of the year — the sure sign that war in Vietnam is becoming "conventional."

12 Sep 65   New York Times Magazine
              James Reston, "We May Win the War but Lose the People"

...Officials here are constantly coming up against the question: Will the Viet Cong crack under the steady American bombardment and the power of the helicopters, or will the social and political structure of South Vietnam crack first?

The war has already produced more than half a million refugees. Feeding and housing them alone is an immense problem that is not being done with any sense of pity, or even decency, and the air war is just beginning.

By the end of this year, American air power will have doubled at the very least — a fact that raises two prospects, neither of them very pleasant. The first is that in order to attack the Viet Cong, who terrorize and hide in the villages, the bombers will have to hurt the civil population in the villages even more.

...On the one hand, there is almost no disagreement in Saigon, even among the French, that without the introduction of American bombers this war would probably have been lost already. But with the introduction of American air power, especially as used indiscriminately by the South Vietnamese forces, the danger of losing the people in the long run, even while winning the military war in the short run, is very real.

24 Sep 65   The Times (London)
              SAIGON

...In this respect the absence of plans is pathetic. Before anyone could take seriously the tiny "oil spots" of pacification, the fury of military operations has brought not the government to the people, but the people fleeing to the government enclaves where, at least, they are safe from bombing. Hundreds of thousands, 500,000 or 700,000 — no one really knows — have now sought asylum, as it were.

9 Dec 65   New York Times, Seymour Topping
              SAIGON, Dec 9

...In the countryside, the traditional structure of village life is also crumbling. Hundreds of thousands of peasants are fleeing to urban areas to escape expanded ground operations and United States air strikes against the Vietcong, who mingle with the population.

The long-term implication of abandonment of the countryside has not yet been fully assessed by either the South Vietnamese Government or United States officials, nor has an adequate refugee program been set up.

26 Feb 66   New York Times, Neil Sheehan
              SAIGON, Feb 25

Economists predict that South Vietnam, which three years ago exported 300,000 tons of rice, may have to import 400,000 tons from the United States this year.

...In the past there has been a tendency to blame the Vietcong for these rice shortages on the assumption that they intercepted shipments to Saigon.

Closer examination, however, discloses that although the guerrillas are hindering the collection of rice from the farmers and are inflating the price by taxing the merchants who collect and transport it, they do not appear to be stopping shipments to the capital.

...Now, however, substantial amounts of rice land have been abandoned by peasants fleeing the guerrillas or fleeing the constant bombing and shelling by the Vietnamese and American forces.

Vietnamese officials in some delta provinces estimate that as much as 20 per cent of the rice land in their areas has been abandoned.

...A final significant factor in the rice shortages appears to be the gradual disintegration of the mercantile structure that supported the rice trade.

Aug 66   International Review of the Red Cross
              "The International Committee and the Vietnam Conflict"

...a) Categories of displaced persons. — A large section of the South Vietnam rural population has been compelled by air raids and military operations against the NLF to evacuate their homes. According to government statistics, approximately 484,000 Vietnamese have had to be sheltered in temporary reception centres since the end of 1964. Some 60 to 70% of these people are living in camps. The remainder have been taken in by the inhabitants of the towns where they sought refuge. In addition, the number of civilians who have been able to return to their villages is estimated at 123,000 while those who have been re-settled in new villages are estimated at 325,000. These figures, reflecting the situation at the end of April 1966, vary constantly as a result of military operations. They do not include a large number of persons evacuated but not registered as "refugees."

Most of the displaced persons are in the coastal provinces of the north and centre of the country, particularly in Quang-Ngai, Phu-Yen and Binh-Dinh. They belong to all sections of the population, including, no doubt, Vietnam families known for their sympathy for the rebel forces.

6 Oct 66   (See Note Page 20)
            SAIGON, Oct 6

...An increasing number of rich acres in the Mekong Delta are not being cultivated. The Delta is Viet Nam's rice bowl and, with 6.5 million of this nation's 15 million people, the population center.

Elaborate irrigation systems built by the French in colonial days have fallen into disrepair. Other rice acreage is lost as farmers flee their plots. Many refuse to work in the paddies in fear of being caught between the Viet Cong and government forces.

25 Jan 66   The Evening Star (Washington), Richard Critchfield
            (from Congressional Record — Senate, February 17, 1966, 3223)
            TANAN, SOUTH VIETNAM

...During a conversation marked by long silences, distant gongs, and burning incense, the bonze, a shaven-haired intelligent-looking man in his midthirties, had no opinion on land or any other concrete reform to help the peasantry.

"The Buddhist doctrine is tolerance, not violence," he said. "People move to town because they are afraid of bombing and artillery. I hope it is possible you can cease the bombing and shelling. Even where there is no engagement made with the Communist forces, the Americans still bomb, causing much harm to the people."

The New Face of War, Malcolm W. Browne, 1965, pp. 150, 151

...An American propaganda expert summed up the essential difference between red and white propaganda in Viet Nam this way:...

..."Within these limitations, our propaganda program has to be divided according to three basic groups — the Vietnamese who have had virtually no contact with Saigon authority in thirty-five years or more, the Vietnamese who have had little or no contact with Saigon since Vietnamese independence in 1954, and the others.

"For the first group, most of whom live in Viet Cong base areas, the only kind of propaganda with which we can reach them is threatening. We drop leaflets saying, in effect surrender or die. We mention that this year, 20 per cent of the men in this or that village were killed by government troops, and say that next year another 20 per cent will die unless resistance ends.

10 Oct 67   New York Post, Warren Hoge
            WASHINGTON

The U.S. is turning great parts of Vietnam into squalid refugee, ghettoes, a Senate subcommittee was told today.

Donald Luce, the former director of the Vietnam mission of International Voluntary Services, told members of Sen. Edward Kennedy's subcommittee on refugees and escapees that the U.S. was to blame for the burgeoning numbers of neglected Vietnamese who have been driven from their homes and deposited in teeming refugee centers.

Luce, who with three other volunteers quit his job last month in protest over American actions in Vietnam, testified that when he first arrived in the war-torn nation five years ago it was "Communist terrorists" who forced people to flee their homes. "In such a situation I fully supported American policy of assisting the Vietnamese government in resettling the refugees," he told the Senators.

"Today, however," he continued, "rural Vietnamese generally become refugees out of fear of American bombing or are forced to leave their farms during a search and destroy mission. As a volunteer worker in Vietnam I could fully cooperate with resetting the refugees but I could not and cannot support U.S. Policy in the creation of refugees," Luce said.

The 33-year old argronomist described for the subcommittee the filthy and overcrowded conditions of centers he had seen, marking the second day in which the hearings had dwelt on charges of U.S. neglect of wounded and displaced Vietnamese civilians.

POLICY TO CREATE REFUGEES

31 Mar 65   (See Note Page 20)
           SAIGON, VIET NAM, Thursday, March 31

U.S. and Vietnamese warplanes launched massive scorched earth raids against the Viet Cong yesterday and attacked a half dozen targets in North Viet Nam.

...The war's tempo had sped up in the wake of the terrorist bombing of the U.S. Embassy in Saigon, although no direct connection was evident between that and the expanded strikes.

...Nearly 200 planes and 25 helicopters were aloft. Planes poured tons of napalm, phosphorous bombs and fuel oil on the Communist-infested Boi Loi forest 25 miles northeast of Saigon with the aim of burning all its 19,000 acres.

Maj. Gen. Joseph H. Moore, commander of U.S. Air Force units in Viet Nam, said the fire was burning briskly when he flew over the area late in the day and he hoped it "will keep burning for some time."

However, several infantry officers, recalling vain efforts in the past to root the Red guerrillas from that area, were skeptical about the operation's strategic value.

Moore said the fire attack culminated a three-month Air Force project begun with saturation bombing of the Viet Cong base camp in the area in January.

This was followed by what the general described as the biggest defoliation mission ever attempted in Viet Nam. Planes daily spread tons of kerosene-based plant-killing chemicals over the forest.

Broadcast leaflets warned civilians to get out. About 2,000 left the woods for resettlement camps.

The fuel oil, napalm and phosphorous bombs were aimed at two primary points in the forest, which is filled with Viet Cong caves, tunnels and fortifications. Each of the target areas was about a half mile square. Much of the forest, laced with trees 100 feet tall, is tinder dry as a result of both the chemical defoliation and the current rainless hot season.

1 Apr 65   New York Times, Seth S. King
           SAIGON, SOUTH VIETNAM, March 31

More than 70 United States Air Force planes unleased the greatest incendiary attack of the war on a Vietcong concentration 25 miles northwest of Saigon.

...Maj. Gen. Joseph H. Moore, commander of the Second United States Air Division, said that large fires were burning when he flew over the area that was the target of the incendiary attack. It is in Boiloi Forest and is known as Zone D, an assembly, training and storage area of the Vietcong.

General Moore said preparations for the fire raid got under way in January when Air Force C-123's began spraying trees to defoliate them.

Recently more than three million leaflets were dropped on the area warning the population to leave. For 40 hours American loudspeaker planes flew over the forest repeating the warning. Before today's raid 2,000 Vietnamese left the target area, General Moore said.

The planes dropped incendiary bombs and bombs filled with incendijel, which General Moore described as "a successor to napalm." They were followed by C-123's dropping drums of fuel oil.

27 Apr 65   Le Figaro
              Max Clos, "The Machine against the Guerrilla"
              (translated from the French)

...First of all, half the province has passed physically under the control of the Vietcong. It is easy to see on the sector map. Thirty kilometers north of Tayninh begins a zone marked off in red. South of this zone one can see around ten spots similarly marked off. The general was embarrassed in trying to explain these spots. In reality, they concern areas where the pacification has been abandoned, areas which are considered entirely under the control of the Vietcong.

These spots are called free zones, meaning that the army and especially the air force treat them as enemy territory. Everything that moves and lives, animals included, is considered as the enemy and is killed. Before declaring an area a free zone the population is warned for about a month. Leaflets are dropped. Planes fly at low altitudes and through loudspeakers inform the civilian population that they ought to evacuate the sector and present themselves at control points where they will be taken in charge and then installed in model villages, or hamlets of the new life, known under the Diem regime as strategic hamlets.

On the 31st of March, the sector 30 kilometers north of Tayninh became a free zone. Two thousand peasants out of an estimated total of eight thousand presented themselves at the control posts. On the same day, the American air force unleashed an immense operation in this region. First twenty planes dropped incendiary bombs. Then around one hundred cargo planes dropped tons of napalm. An immense fire broke out. The last week in the same area th Americans had dropped 1000 tons of bombs in 18 square kilometers of forest where they suspected Vietcong troop concentrations.

16 Oct 65   Christian Science Monitor
              Takashi Oka, "Friendly Guerrilla"
              NUI TUONG, VIETNAM

Some of South Vietnam's most effective fighters against the Viet Cong are soldiers who were guerrillas themselves for many years.

...Bay Dom rallied to the government side in June, 1964, eight months after the military revolution that toppled President Diem. Since then he has commanded an independent regional battalion in the province of Chau Doc, composed of three companies of 132 men each.

...Bay Dom, who had received us in pajamas, changed into green army fatigues to show us around Ba Chuc. As we did so, he explained why he had committed most of his forces to the defense of one village.

"There is really no point in liberating a village unless one intends to stay there," he said.

Some days ago he had participated in an Army operation against the village of Luong Phi, which was at the foot of a mountain still held by the Viet Cong.

American planes bombed the village. Then the Army rounded up the inhabitants and burned down their surviving huts. They told the villagers to take refuge in Lac Quoi village by the Vinh Te Canal, because as long as they stayed in Luong Phi the government would be unable to protect them.

The government's reason for doing this was that Luong Phi village supplied the Viet Cong with rice and food. Unless the villagers were forcibly evacuated, they would continue to do so.

But, said Bay Dom, it was not because the villagers were Viet Cong that they did this. It was because they had no choice. Government troops never came to Luong Phi. The Viet Cong were there all the time.

The government's action might make some sense if it could provide Luong Phi villagers with other rice fields, other sources of income. So far, it had failed to do so.

"The Americans consider Luong Phi a free bombing zone. The villagers know that if they return, they may be bombed any time. But what can they do? Their livelihood is there. And so, by twos and threes, they have filtered back to their village."

16 Nov 66   (See Note Page 20)
               SAIGON, Nov 16

...The count of enemy dead in Operation Attleboro rose to 965 with the discovery of 15, reported killed by air strikes, in a Viet Cong camp that a 1st Division unit destroyed. Uncovering of two enemy rice caches totalling 490 tons raised to a near record 2,000 tons, the supply of that food grain seized since the Operation was launched Oct. 15.

Official sources said the hostilities have made refugees of more than 15,000 Vietnamese in the zone, a jungle territory adjoining the Cambodian frontier where the Viet Cong have built up supply bases and fortifications for years. Newsmen in the field said many were made homeless by U.S. artillery and air strikes supporting the infantry advances.

10 Dec 66   New York Times
               RACHGIA, SOUTH VIETNAM, Dec. 8

The exodus of 2,300 people from a Vietcong-dominated village 36 miles northwest of here to havens protected by the South Vietnamese Government means different things to different people.

Saigon and the United States military and civilian officials view the recent action by the people of Binhtri as a victory in the war for "the hearts and and minds" of the populace.

One official said today that the people were "happy as clams" to be away from the Vietcong, and some officials talked of soon adding the people of Binhtri to the villagers-in-Government-control column.

Some villagers, no doubt, were happy, but not all.

To the people who felt that the Vietcong were taxing them too much in cash crops and labor and conscripting too many of their young men, leaving Binhtri was a blessing. To those who found life under the Vietcong tolerable — and some said they did — the move was an intrusion.

Whether their sympathies lay with the Vietcong or with the Saigon Government, it was clear that only one thing moved the people of Binhtri: allied bombs.

Thousands of leaflets addressed to the "compatriots" of Binhtri and others addressed to the Vietcong began raining on the village overlooking the Gulf of Siam on Nov. 26.

"The powerful forces of free Vietnam will continue to shell, bomb and conduct operations in this area until all Vietcong are forced to surrender or are killed," the message said. "To protect the lives of your family and yourself, you must leave this area at once."

The language of the leaflet aimed at the Vietcong was even stronger.

To illustrate the point, a few days later allied planes bombed the 600-foot limestone plateau that shields Binhtri from the sea.

On Dec. 3 the people started moving, with 93 families leaving the village and 27 Vietcong defecting.

"They came out of there because they were told to," said Maj. Richard E. White, a 38-year-old United States Army adviser from Salina, Kan. "We dropped bombs along that ridge line after the leaflets went in, and by God those people came out — just about like you and I would have done."

Major White said allied military forces focused on the village after intelligence reports indicated that a Vietcong company had massed there in mid-October for co-ordinated attacks on three outposts and a government cement factory.

By the time the leaflet campaign and the ensuing air raids began, the Vietcong company had slipped away, allied officers believe, leaving behind a platoon of 30 to 40 men and perhaps 40 more part-time guerrillas.

By this afternoon, 67 of these had defected.

Huynh Van Hai, a 44-year-old defector, said a number of villagers who had become disenchanted with the Vietcong organized the exodus while Communist cadres were fleeing for cover during the air strikes. Other peasants, however, said they had left Binhtri simply because they felt their lives were in jeopardy.

One of them, 69-year-old Chau Op, a farmer and caretaker of the Binhtri Roman Catholic Church, said:

"I did not want to leave my property, but I saw some people killed by the bombs and I read the leaflets and I thought I had to go or be killed myself. I did not have time to harvest my rice crop."

American sources said two civilians were killed and five were wounded in the air raids, which continued through Tuesday.

But Mr. Op said he saw 15 to 25 people killed when a bomb smashed the vehicle in which they were riding. He said three other persons, including his father-in-law, died from napalm burns.

Saigon officials, staring sternly at the old man and attempting to supply answers for him during an interview, said he had been indoctrinated by the Vietcong and was replying as he had been taught.

28 Oct 67   New York Times, Tom Buckley
           SAIGON, SOUTH VIETNAM, Oct 27

In the last three and a half years the war has swept millions of rural Vietnamese from their hamlets into the anonymity of refugee camps and shanty towns.

Official figures state that more than two million people have passed through camps, but American sources believe that the figure may be considerably higher.

...George Goss, the head of the United States mission's refugee division, Dr. Nguyen Phuc Que, the South Vietnamese refugee commissioner, agree that most of the peasants who voluntarily leave their homes do so to escape battles bombardments.

More and more, though, the people called refugees have been forced into the camps by allied troops to deny to the Vietcong workers or soldiers. Their villages have been razed and declared "free fire zones," where anything that moves can be shot.

United States commanders have denied that any policy of "generating refugees" exists, but one civilian official said: "Policy or not, they're sure doing it."

There are indications that the policy is being reviewed. Since August, when the South Vietnamese Refugee Administration virtually collapsed, the number of people entering the camps is said to have dropped.

In any case, the policy, if such it was, appears to have been only partly successful. When allied sweeps have taken place in hostile territory, only a few able-bodied men have accompanied their wives, children and parents into the camps.

MALE REFUGEES TREATED AS RALLIERS

12 Apr 65   New York Times, Seymour Topping
           SAIGON, SOUTH VIETNAM, April 11

...In the IV Corps area, which embraces the Mekong River delta, the number of men entering the Open Arms rehabilitation camps is averaging 100 to 150 a month.

United States sources on the scene pointed out that some of the men surrendering could not be properly termed military defectors but were peasants simply abandoning Vietcong-controlled areas for personal reasons.

16 Dec 66   (See Note Page 20)
             RACH GIA, VIETNAM, Dec. 16

The ex-guerrillas, in their cheap black uniforms, sat erectly behind the rows of desks in a school-room atmosphere. They were Hoi Chanhs — ralliers — who had switched their allegiance from the Communist Viet Cong to the Vietnamese government. Now, they were undergoing a three-week indoctrination course at the Chieu Hoi (open arms) compound in this Mekong Delta town.

...Among the ralliers at Rach Gia were 64 youths and men who surrendered two weeks ago after the guerrilla structure collapsed in the Binh Tri Mountains.

The Allies first dropped leaflets in the Mountains, warning the villagers to leave the Viet Cong-controlled area or be killed. Then fighter-bombers raced in, strafing and bombing guerrilla positions. The civilians rebelled against the red rule by packing their belongings on their back and striking out for the valley below, driving chickens, cattle, and water buffaloes ahead of them. The guerrillas, many of whom had been recruited from the youths of the hamlets, didn't particularly want to fight, either, and they followed the civilians out, surrendering to Vietnamese militiamen.

Of the 64 Viet Cong admitted to this camp from the Binh Tri mountains, most said they had been in the Cong's information, medical or political services.

4 Jan 67   New York Times
            SAIGON, SOUTH VIETNAM, Jan. 3

A United States spokesman announced tonight that 20,242 Vietcong had defected during 1966. He said this was an increase of 82 percent over the previous year.

...But critics assert that the figures are misleading. They charge that hundreds of people counted as "returnees" support neither the Vietcong nor the Saigon Government, but file into refugee centers merely to escape the horrors of the war.

9 Feb 67   New York Review of Books
            Bernard B. Fall, "The View from Vietnam"
            DANANG, South Vietnam

...Yet, in Vietnam during 1966 a total of 20,242 Chieu-Hoi ("Open Arms" defectors) came out of the jungle, bringing with them a total of only 1,963 weapons — i.e. most of these defectors were unarmed civilians, a fact which is not denied here. Meanwhile the South Vietnamese Army lost, that same year, at least 110,000 men, who simply walked off and out of the war. Apparently, fourteen years of American organization here have yet to match the effectiveness of the Viet Cong's organizational efforts.

REFUGEES FROM FREE-BOMB ZONES

Vietnam in the Mud, James Pickerell, 1966, p. 64

..."Free strike zones" are areas in which everyone is supposed to be a Viet Cong soldier or a VC sympathizer. Unfortunately, many of the people thought to be sympathizers stay in the Viet Cong areas for the same reason as the woman above — because they cannot afford to leave what little land they own. Sometimes the government drops leaflets in these areas telling the people to leave and they will be cared for and given money for relocation, but most of the people who do leave the areas find that it often takes the government a long time to distribute the promised funds and word of this filters back to those who remained.

9 Jul 66   (See Note Page 20)
             SAIGON

The sound of bombing reached into Saigon today as other U.S. Air Force planes joined by Vietnamese craft struck the free bombardment zone alongside Nha Be, site of mammoth oil storage installation about 10 miles from the South Vietnamese capital. The attack apparently was aimed at Red guerrillas in the canal-laced area surrounding the oil installation.

The Saigon government recently declared the area free for aerial attack and asked all persons to evacuate. (The Vietnamese press indicated the declaration of a free zone was taken on the possibility that the Viet Cong would hit oil storage depots in reprisal for American attacks on fuel installations in the Hanoi and Haiphong area.) Parentheses added.

1 Jun 65   New York Times, Jack Langguth
           POLEI KRONG, SOUTH VIETNAM, May 28

When United States bombs began to fall this week in Kontum Province, mountain tribesmen left their homes and began walking to safety.

More than 300 men, women and children of the Rangao tribe have arrived at a refugee center on the outskirts of Polei Drong, the provincial capital.

"They come willingly," said Michael Benge, the American aid representative for the province. "They see the air strikes coming in, and they don't want to be in combat."

The strikes were part of a week-long Government attempt to find and kill 600 to 800 Vietcong guerrillas believed to be in the area between the Laotian border and the town of Kontum. But the Communist troops were evading the Government soldiers.

Along the border, a broad strip of land has been designated a "free-strike zone." This means that American and Vietnamese pilots may bomb there without specific permission from the province chief. Such zones have been set up in areas considered totally controlled by the Vietcong.

About 16,000 Montagnards, or mountain tribesmen, live in the Kontum zone. They are considered, while not necessarily sympathetic to the Communists, lost by the Government.

...On most issues, few outsiders know what the many small tribes of central Vietnam prefer, expect or think. A Montagnard official sent by the Government was haranguing the new arrivals about the atrocities of the Vietcong.

But Americans and Vietnamese on the scene could not be sure that the dark, impassive people did not blame the United States planes for their uprooting. The officials hoped that the number of Rangao youths wearing silver crosses around their necks meant that they, as Roman Catholics, would support the Government's position.

What few social services are available around Kontum are run by the Catholic Relief Services Organization with assistance from the South Vietnamese and United States Governments. French nuns operate an orphanage, a school for girls and a leprosorium, and American Catholic women staff the province's best hospital.

...The Vietcong exploit what antipathy remains, however, and many of the 1,500 part-time Communist guerrillas in the province are known as "VMC," or Viet Montagnard Cong.

As Colonel Be left the center, the Montagnard leader asked for a round of applause. The refugees responded dutifully before lining up for their food and blankets.

Aug 66   International Review of the Red Cross
           "The International Committee and the Vietnam Conflict"

...The ICRC has given special study to the plight of tribes living in mountainous regions who have been compelled to flee their villages to seek refuge elsewhere. It is estimated that there are some 100,000 refugees from the mountains now spread throughout the provinces of the high central plateau and enquiries have revealed that the state of health of a large proportion of these people is alarming. For a number of reasons many of them are not registered with the Vietnamese Refugee Commission or are in regions too difficult of access to enable them to be given assistance similar to that received by the Vietnam refugees in organized camps. The local organizations looking after them have but limited means. The most urgent needs are rice, milk, malted-milk, blankets, clothing, mosquito-nets, dressings and medical supplies (anti-malaria drugs, anti-biotics, anti-tuberculosis drugs, anti-dysenterics, tonics and vitamins).

REFUGEE CONDITIONS

6 Aug 65   New York Times, Seymour Topping
             SAIGON, SOUTH VIETNAM, Aug. 5

More than half a million refugees from war and floods have crowded into Vietnamese Government resettlement camps, causing extensive security problems.

...Well-informed sources estimate that 100,000 of the refugees are not receiving adequate food, shelter and medical attention.

Little has been done to inculcate in the refugees a feeling of loyalty to the Government. In the absence of a good information program, many of the refugees have become susceptible to Vietcong propaganda. Vietcong agents have been identified among them.

United States officials say that there is some evidence that the Vietcong have driven refugees deliberately into Government areas to burden local officials and that these tactics may be used more often in the future.

The most critical refugee problems are in Quangnam, where there are big United States Marine Corps and Air Force bases near Danang, and Quangngai. In Quangnam there are an estimated total of 53,000 refugees and about 77,000 in Quangngai.

Most of the refugees in the Government areas live in shacks or straw hovels clustered around district towns and provincial capitals occupied by Government forces. Most of the countryside is held by the Vietcong.

In the provinces of Quangnam, Quangtin, and Quangngai, about a third of the people under Government control are refugees.

The bulk of the refugees fled from their homes after floods last year and during heavy fighting in February and March. The influx has continued since then on a reduced scale.

Many of the refugees are leaving their villages because they have become battlefields. The inhabitants alternately are subjected to Vietcong harrassment or attacks by Government artillery and United States aircraft. Some of the refugees have opted for the Government side to escape Vietcong political structures, military draft and heavy taxation.

In Government-held areas the refugees only infrequently are made to feel that they are welcome and have a stake in victory by the anti-Communist forces.

Conditions vary from province to province. One observer who visited a number of camps praised the work being done by Vietnamese authorities in Danang, where there are about 13,000 refugees. But this is the way he described a typical scene in a camp at Pleiku, in the Central Highlands:

"In a filthy hovel a child was sitting on the slats of a bed that did not have a mat. He was covered with filth, his own excrement, and there were flies all over him. There was no water to wash him."

Pleiku, which has 5,000 refugees, is ranked as one of the five most critical provinces because of inadequate facilities. Two other refugees, (sic)

353

and Binh-dinh, with 80,000 refugees, are also considered among the most critical.

...The refugee problem encompasses not only those in camps or re-settlement areas but also thousands who have swarmed into the over-crowded towns and cities. The problem in Saigon is manifest in the form of ragged children sleeping on sidewalks or held in the arms of their beggar parents.

31 Aug 65   New York Times, Richard Eder
              WASHINGTON, Aug. 30

The United States, reversing a previous policy, is setting up a full-scale program to assist the 400,000 refugees made homeless by the Vietnam fighting.

Eight hearings held by a Senate subcommittee on refugees of which Mr. Kennedy is chairman brought out, as one high official of the Agency for International Development said, that "in effect we have had no refugee program as such."

...The first thorough studies on the refugees are now being made. These will include how many there are, where they are and how they are living, and in just what ways they are being helped now.

The United States Government does not now know how many refugees there are. South Vietnamese Government figures, which are not considered accurate, give rise to tentative estimates that there are 200,000 in camps, and an equal number crowded into urban slums.

...Aid administered by private agencies, which was to run at $8.5 million this year, is expected to rise considerably.

...In Vietnam, the United States has had the Government send teams around to provincial governments to spur their programs. Some $12 million is available to the provincial authorities, but little has been spent.

...Since many details are still being worked out, officials here are unable to give a close estimate of how much the program will cost. One rough estimate was $20 million. Any calculations are complicated, however, by the fact that much of the aid will be a rechanneling of existing programs.

For example, the major part of the United States health, education, and possibly housing programs in Vietnam will now be specifically aimed at the refugees.

...Former Ambassador Maxwell D. Taylor and his aid chief, James S. Killen, believed that refugee assistance should be an initiative of the Saigon authorities with the United States providing help as requested.

Partly because of a lack of interest and competence and partly because of the massive increase of refugees, this formula was not working.

According to A.I.D. officials, this was brought home by a series of "alarming reports" from the interior. Henry Cabot Lodge, the new Ambassador, told the Senate subcommittee earlier this month that the situation was gravely unsatisfactory.

12 Sep 65   New York Times, Neil Sheehan
              SAIGON, Sept. 11

As casualties mounted in South Vietnam's war this week, so did the number of refugees fleeing from bombs, bullets, artillery barrages and life under the Viet Cong guerrillas.

...According to Vietnamese Government statistics, there were 620,708 refugees in the country by the end of August. About one-third of the refugees are in temporary camps of wooden, tin-roofed huts and bamboo shacks in the four central coastal provinces of Quangnam, Quangngai, Binhdinh and Phuyen. The others are crowded into urban slums.

...U.S. and Vietnamese Air Force planes and Navy and Marine aircraft flew approximately 11,000 combat sorties in South Vietnam last month, unleashing thousands of tons of napalm, bombs, rockets and 20-millimeter cannon fire. Such air strikes result in destruction of large numbers of peasant huts and considerable civilian casualties. As the number of air strikes increases in coming months, the lines of refugees seeking to avoid death can be expected to grow longer.

...Central Vietnam has traditionally been a food-deficit area and as a result of the disruption of transportation, food shortages have arisen in some rural areas controlled by the Communists. Officials believe that at least some of the refugees crowded into the camps in the coastal provinces are families of guerrillas and have come over to the Government side because of their empty stomachs.

There have been reports that the Viet Cong were deliberately driving peasants into the refugee camps in order to put a further strain on the Government, but officials dismiss these reports as largely unfounded.

12 Sep 65   New York Times, Neil Sheehan
             SAIGON, Sept. 11

...U.S. officials contend that despite these difficulties the Vietnamese have, with American help, managed to provide most of the refugees in the 194 camps throughout the country with a bare subsistence level of food and shelter and enough medical attention to prevent epidemics.

Since the beginning of 1965, the Vietnamese Government has spent more than $220,000 on refugee relief, and American agencies have added at least $1 million in food, housing materials, medical supplies and transportation costs.

Each refugee receives seven piastres a day (about six cents at the black market rate of exchange) as well as some kind of shelter and a daily rice ration. When he finds a job and resettles, he receives 3,500 piastres (about $127) to finance a new start in life, along with a rice ration for another six months.

12 Nov 65   (See Note Page 20)
             WASHINGTON, Nov. 12

South Vietnamese torn from their homes by war may increase to a million over the next year, reports tonight indicated. This would be about one in 14 of all the troubled country's inhabitants.

This would mean further demands on U.S. relief funds and personnel. Officials of the Agency for International Development reported that there now are 720,000 displaced persons in South Viet Nam although 250,000 of these have been resettled in temporary shelters.

...Sen. Edward Kennedy, D-Mass., who recently completed a quick on-the-scene study of the refugee problem, estimated the original aid forecast of 100,000 refugees may be exceeded by 900,000.

...The report of the voluntary aid agencies to President Johnson said that the cause of the exodus traces to terrorism and increasing pressure from the Viet Cong and the steadily increasing scale of military action.

U.S. officials acknowledged intensification of the war effort, including increased bombing and ground action against the Viet Cong, unquestionably will magnify the refugee problem. At the same time, they feel an increase in the secure areas will facilitate the resettlement program.

The costs of the expanded refugee program have not been made known but at the rate of ten cents a day for each of the displaced women, children and elderly persons, the bare subsistence costs could quickly mount to more than $30 million dollars in ten months. The costs of medicines, schooling, rehabilitation, refugee centers would be in addition to that.

19 Dec 65   New York Times
             QUANGNGAI, SOUTH VIETNAM

...Captain Arrington and his deputy, a first lieutenant, advise and assist Quangngai's province chief, Dr. Bui Hoanh, and the four-man United States aid mission here on a multitude of problems involving in housing, feeding and resettling approximately 51,000 war refugees and rebuilding shattered hamlets.

Quangngai Province desperately needs the services of the team. Since last spring the province of about 700,000 people on the central coast 325 miles northeast of Saigon has been ferociously contested by Government troops and guerrillas.

The province has succeeded over the last three months in resettling 49,000 refugees in villages it is attempting to pacify, but 51,000 still remain and each military operation produces an average of 2,000 more refugees from the fighting.

On a typical day recently Captain Arrington inspected a camp of about 5,000 refugees on a beach southeast of the town of Quangngai, the provincial capital. Most of the refugees were fisher folk who had fled their hamlets farther down the coast about three weeks earlier to escape fighting. The hamlet was still in guerrilla hands and they could not return.

...None of the refugees appeared to be suffering from malnutrition, but the huts were small and cramped. Flies and mosquitoes swarmed and sanitary facilities were practically nonexistent. Although the team's doctor and preventive-medicine sergeant have done what they can to treat the refugees, about a dozen have died from malaria and intestinal diseases.

...''We don't want to give them too much,'' he said. ''If we did they would become professional refugees and stay here and take handouts. They wouldn't return to their hamlet when we clear the Vietcong out of it and the whole point of this business is to get them back home earning a living as fast as we can.''

...While Dr. Schiffer treats the sick and wounded, a first lieutenant who is the team's engineering officer has been showing resettled refugees how to rebuild their destroyed and damaged homes with tin roofing and concrete provided by the American aid mission and local building materials.

...Hearings in July and August, in which United States officials testified, indicated that despite the gravity of the refugee problem — an estimated total of one million South Vietnamese, or one-fifteenth of the population, will be in the refugee category by the end of this year — there was no coherent program to deal with it.

27 Dec 65   New York Times, Hanson W. Baldwin
           SAIGON, SOUTH VIETNAM

...There are, however, a record number of refugees from Vietcong-dominated areas — about 730,000 — many of them half starving.

10 May 66   Christian Science Monitor, Charlotte Saikowski
           SAIGON

...American refugee officials are encouraged by the government reorganization of refugee affairs and they believe Dr. Que is ''his own man.''

...As of March 31, AID officials report, some 470,000 were living either in camps or in improvised shelters in secure towns and hamlets. The bulk of the refugees are in the northern provinces where the fighting has been heaviest.

...About $21 million in refugee aid will have been spent by the United States in the 1965-1966 fiscal year.

Behind the extensive aid is a recognition here that if there is to be overall progress in Vietnam, the government must be identified with an improvement in the daily life of the people. Therefore, say American refugee officials, the South Vietnamese must carry the burden of caring for the refugees.

As United States aid refugee coordinator Edward B. Marks told me, ''My philosophy is to give the Vietnamese aid and encouragement so they can do the job themselves.''

22 Aug 1966 Congressional Record, Senate, 19354-56
        Senator Morse and "Statement of William T. Pepper..."

Mr. Morse. Mr. President, Mr. Pepper is from New Rochelle, N.Y.
He recently spent 5 weeks in Vietnam studying refugee problems. As Mr.
Pepper's statement makes clear, by far the majority of present refugees
in South Vietnam have been rendered homeless by American military action,
and by far the majority of hospital patients, especially children, are there
due to injuries suffered from American military activities. The plight of
these children, and the huge burden they impose upon physical facilities, has
been almost totally ignored by the American people.

Yet Mr. Pepper's statistics make it evident that the population of South
Vietnam is nearly half under age 16, and that the breakdown of family life
which the war has caused will bring adverse repercussions for decades
to come.

...Exhibit 2

Statement of William T. Pepper to the Subcommittee to Investigate
Problems Connected with Refugees and Escapees of the Committee on the
Judiciary, U.S. Senate Session, Summer and Autumn, 1966, Hon. Edward
M. Kennedy, Chairman

...The cumulative figure of "tactical refugees," or persons displaced
from their normal habitations by the conflict, and unable to return, some
while ago passed the one million mark. Only a small percentage of them
have been classified as "permanently resettled."

My observations indicate that a great number of these "tactical
refugees" are children and that there are others who have not been
counted — also mostly children — who reside in institutions, makeshift
shelters, hospitals, with friends and relations or on their own, in the
cities, and provincial towns.

5 Sep 66   New York Times, Charles Mohr
            SAIGON, SOUTH VIETNAM, Sept. 4

...Perhaps the worst case of all is that of payment to more than a
million war refugees. When the program began, a refugee got 7 cents a day
subsistence for 30 days and then about $35 to "resettle."

After more than a year, the only improvement is that the refugee gets
10 cents instead of 7 cents for the first 30 days.

One informed source said: "Everybody knows that refugee payments
are too low, but nothing is done about it because the Vietnamese Government doesn't want to raise them and we don't want to make an issue out of
it. We turn our head."

A New Kind of War, Martha Gellhorn, 1966, pp. 24, 26, 27

... we stopped at the first miserable shack because I could not bear to
walk farther. It was about eight by ten feet in size, nearly filled by two beds,
reeking of poverty, with dingy rags of clothing hung on nails, and the battered
household goods on a narrow shelf. A woman, who looked 55 and was perhaps
35, drained, exhausted, gaunt, lived here with seven children and her husband.
By trade, he repaired clocks and watches, but was ill and, besides, could
find no work.

Three young children lay on the bare boards of the beds, silently; yes,
they were sick. She didn't know what their sickness was, but she could not
give them enough to eat. Only her teenage daughter had a job, miles away.
"Maybe two hours to go there, two hours to come home," Tri said. The
girl earned 80 piastres a day, 48 US cents, 3 shillings and threepence, the
entire income for the family.

...In every camp, the children hem you in, shouting gaily: "Okay!
Okay!" It is the one American word they know and the least fitting. These
children were meant to be beautiful and happy; their beauty is spoiled
because they are ill fed and dirty. It is not the refugees' fault that they

are overcrowded in wretched shacks or sheds, too poor to buy soap, deprived of an adequate water supply. Many of the children are made repellent by contagious skin diseases, some have cataracts, some are crippled by war wounds, some deformed from birth due to the undernourishment of the mother.

...The camp leader said, casually, that they had had cholera and plague in this camp but were now vaccinated. Plague is beyond my imagination, but I will never forget one close sight of cholera in China: a peasant woman staggering towards us like a drunk, then vomiting a torrent of blood, and falling in it, unconscious or dead. It is amazing that the refugees stay sane. First the bombs, perhaps the "battle" around them, their casualties, their naked helplessness; then the flight, leaving behind everything they have worked for all their lives; then the semi-starvation and ugly hardship of the camps or the slums; and, as a final cruelty, the killing diseases which only strike at them.

Jan 67   Ramparts
             William F. Pepper, "The Children of Vietnam"

...With misery comes despair, and one of its most shocking forms was called to my attention by Lawson Mooney, the competent and dedicated director of the Catholic Relief Services program in Vietnam. Mooney said he has noticed, between the autumn of 1965 and the spring of 1966, a fantastic increase in the rate of adolescent suicide.

I began to check the newspapers every day — and indeed, there was usually one, frequently more than one suicide reported among the city's children. In several cases, group suicides were reported: a band of young people, unable to face the bleakness and misery of their existence, will congregate by agreement with a supply of the rat poison readily available in Vietnam, divide it, take it, and die.

Jan 67   Ramparts
             William F. Pepper, "The Children of Vietnam"

...About eight percent of Vietnam's population live in refugee shelters or camps; about three quarters of the shelter population, or over 750,000 persons, are children under 16. In shelters like that of Qui Nhon, which I visited, there is unimaginable squalor and close confinement. There were 23,000 in that camp when I was there, and I have been told that the figure has since tripled.

Father So, unquestioned leader of these thousands of refugees in Qui Nhon and in the rest of Binh Dinh Province, works for 20 hours a day to provide what relief he can, particularly for the orphaned children. These usually live in a hovel-like appendage to the main camp, frequently without beds. Food and clothing are scarce.

...The shelter child receives little if any education. Crossed strands of barbed wire form the perimeter of his living world. There are no sanitary facilities — those in camps near a river are lucky. Even shelters with cement floors have no privies for as many as 160 families. Plague and cholera increasingly threaten the health of the children (and of course the adults, though to a lesser degree), and I noticed an amazing amount of body infection on the youngsters, ranging from minor to extremely serious in nature.

18 Feb 67   Boston Globe, Herbert Black

Dorchester's Dr. Tom Durant is physician for 5000 persons who live in a cemetery.

The graveyard is in Saigon where Dr. Durant is Public Health Officer for the Agency for International Development (AID). The patients are refugees from the Viet Cong who have found living space among the dead in the graveyard of the Church of the Holy Rosary.

...He says some refugees have built small houses among the gravestones and told his wife that some even have taken refuge in burial vaults.

Dr. Durant takes a mobile clinic into the cemetery once a week to treat the sick on the front porch of the gatekeeper's house. "The most important thing we need here is soap and water," he reported to the AID. "I can't treat skin infections without it."

One of the goals of Dr. Durant and Dr. Mao, the chief health officer for Saigon, is to develop an immunization program among the refugees. The poeple living in the graveyard lack water, sewerage and sanitation facilities.

5 Feb 65   World Journal Tribune, Tom Tiede
             SAIGON, Feb. 4

...A quarter of them die in infancy. Half fail before five years. As for the ones who survive the first 10 years, at least 10 percent are certain of contracting pulmonary tuberculosis.

But that's only the first decade. The remaining 27 years of life expectancy are often worse. Poverty, war, cruelty, slum living ... a kid learns the brutal way here and the only law that endures in all the human decay is to eat or be eaten.

...They are easily identified. In the downtown streets they stand near the pub doors in small, ragged clusters — and pick the pockets of the American soldiers.

In the side districts they sit on garbage cans at the front of dark houses and yell out lewd propositions to the streetwalkers.

In the alleys they gather in bands to plot savage acts in the name of revenge, reward or kicks.

And in Saigon police stations, they sit unsmiling on benches, suspected of robbery, rape, murder or collaboration with the enemy.

Statistically, the outlaws do not represent the majority of young people in Viet Nam. But they may one day. In the capital alone, the guess is that 200,000 children are jail bait.

...Life is too short here as it is. A kid can expect only 37 years.

15 Feb 65   Los Angeles Times (See Note Page 20)
              PHY MY, SOUTH VIETNAM

...Two other children stood among rifles and packs on the back of a truck, cracking jokes with soldiers and making faces at a photographer. They, too, had lost their fathers. Their mothers had died, also.

They still hadn't realized they were orphans.

These children had survived a concentrated Viet Cong mortar attack on this town headquarters. But their parents hadn't. Now, the morning after, the children were being gathered up, packed into a truck, and taken to an orphanage in Saigon.

Their lot was a hard one, and all too frequent in South Viet Nam, where an average of about 800 Government soldiers are being killed every month. In many villages and outposts such as this one, mothers are dying also.

It is estimated that 20,000 children running around Saigon streets lack parents.

Many foreigners believe the Vietnamese government has paid too little attention to the orphans of war. Government officials answer that these children should be taken care of by relatives.

Many of the orphans do make their way back to relatives, some of them living deep inside Communist zones.

Other children are left to wander the streets of the cities.

The situation is worsened by the Vietnamese habit of having families living with soldiers in remote outposts.

When the Viet Cong strike, civilian casualties are often higher than those of the soldiers. At Cai Be, south of Saigon, 12 women were killed and

25 women and children wounded when Communist fire smashed into the shacks they lived in beside a military outpost.

23 Jun 65   New York Times

Leo Cherne, chairman of the International Rescue Committee, announced yesterday a program to aid war orphans in South Vietnam.

...Mr. Cherne said the committee had set the highest emergency fund goal — $2.5 million — in its 33-year history. He added that even if it were attained, "it would not adequately meet the needs of the refugees." The bulk of the program will deal with the more than 100,000 war orphans.

Most of these are concentrated in the central lowland provinces. Almost half are huddled near the coastal cities. In addition, "pockets" of refugees may be found in every province in Vietnam.

Senator McGovern, on a separate trip to Vietnam, during which he visited some of the camps, was "shocked" at the lack of effort toward instruction of children.

...Both Senators Kennedy and Tydings felt they were being shown only "the best refugee camps."

It was obvious, they concluded, that the people had been coached in preparation for the visit.

"The children stood in line by the gate, waving Vietnamese and American flags and cheering," Senator Tydings recalled.

..."A camp may be a public building, a warehouse, a school. I have seen refugees living in tents, almost completely in the open," he said in an interview.

"Some include regular sanitary facilities. Some have outside privies. Some don't even have those.

"And in some places, conditions are so bad the people have gone back to the Viet Cong."

28 Oct 67   New York Times, Tom Buckley
              SAIGON, SOUTH VIETNAM, Oct 27

...The removal of familiar village rituals, the lack of meaningful work and the absence, in many cases, of their fathers are believed to be having a harmful effect on the children, who make up perhaps two-thirds of the nearly 800,000 persons who are officially stated to be in camps and other temporary habitations.

During visits last week to five camps in the five northern provinces that form the I Corps area, which has nearly half of the refugees in the country, this correspondent spoke with scores of children and adults through an interpreter.

Although many of the children appeared pale, and probably undernourished, they said they found the life in the camps more exciting than in their hamlets.

Some camps, in fact, have schools. None is belived to have playgrounds or recreational equipment. For the most part, the children run wild.

Dr. Que, while arguing that the camps are humanitarian, notes that as the children approach their teens the "excitement" become a growing familiarity with racketeering, petty theft and in the case of girls, prostitution.

...Meanwhile of scores of adults with whom this correspondent spoke at the five camps, none reported having received his authorized Government allowance of 10 piasters (about 8 cents) a day for months.

In the camps near cities such as Danang and Saigon where the vast American military presence creates thousands of civilian jobs, such administrative failures are not usually crucial.

For Vietnamese who have sought refuge in isolated areas, however, the result can be disastrous. Only last week, Dr. Que was forced to make a public appeal for air transportation to bring food to thousands of refugees at Camlo, near the North Vietnamese border.

He said they were threatened by starvation after floods had halted road traffi

...The plans for resettling refugees in secure areas, assisting them in building homes and in starting farms and small businesses and learning marketable skills are hardly off the ground.

Land in secure areas suitable for growing rice, the staple of the Vietnamese diet, is at a premium. None is available for generally penniless refugees.

As a result, the relatively few who have been resettled by the Government — the official figure of more than 600,000 is generally thought to be inflated — have been assigned to villages built on wasteland that requires in some cases uneconomically large amounts of labor, fertilizer and equipment to produce enough to permit a family to support itself.

16 Oct 67   Statement of the Honorable William S. Gaud, Administrator
             Agency for International Development
             Before the Senate Judiciary Subcommittee to Investigate Problems
             Connected with Refugees and Escapees

...Deficiencies in the handling of the refugee program have led some to raise the question of whether the U.S. should take over the refugee program and operate it directly. The proposition, as I understand it, is this: if the Vietnamese are incapable of doing the job, or are unwilling to do it, let us move in and do it ourselves.

I strongly disagree with this proposal. To date A.I.D. has limited its role to advising, assisting and supporting the Vietnamese Government in carrying out its refugee program. I believe we should stick to that role — the U.S. should not take over operational control from the Vietnamese.

Direct interference in the affairs of another nation, no matter how well intentioned, is contrary to our traditions. It is also self-defeating in that it not only reduces the ability of the government and people of the developing nation to work out their own solutions to their problems, but makes them more rather than less dependent on American aid.

Something much more fundamental is at issue here than Vietnamese pride and the Vietnamese desire to maintain their own traditions, customs and attitudes. The ultimate objectives of the "other war" in Vietnam are to strengthen the bonds between the Vietnamese people and their government, help them build viable institutions which will enable them to live their lives as they wish to live them, and help them acquire the ability to solve their own problems. But this "other war" can be won only by the Vietnamese. We cannot win it for them. I feel strongly, Mr. Chairman, that while a takeover by the U.S. of the refugee program in Vietnam might result in a better job in the short run, and might salve our own consciences, it would go a long way towards making it impossible for either us or the Vietnamese to realize our basic objectives.

18 Dec 67   CDN, New York Post
             SAIGON

More than 450 little Vietnamese Oliver Twists live in the Chi Hoa prison in Saigon, sent there for the "crimes" of sleeping on the street or stealing something to eat.

...Many of them are refugees or sons of refugees from the bitter war that has scourged their country for 20 years. Most do not have parents.

...Sister Nicolle, a charming French-educated Vietnamese nun who runs the Caritas Catholic orphanage, stopped on one of her weekly visits to teach the children and put her hand under the chin of a sad-eyed little boy of 13.

..."He came from a refugee family but he doesn't know where his parents are now. He's been here five months. He doesn't know how long it will take for the tribunal to hear his case. Sometimes it's up to a year. Then he'll get a sentance of two or three years.

"He lived in the market because he was very poor and had nothing to eat," she explained. "He doesn't know what village he's from and he doesn't remember when he came or whether he had parents."

...The jail is not a bad place, as jails go. It is a large yellow circular building with a lot of air and light in the big rooms. The boys sleep 61 to a room on mats on the floor and the only decoration the walls are signs reading "discipline" and "order." Most go to school once a week for four hours in nicely decorated rooms or in the hallways. They all work in the jail and at 6 p.m. the doors are closed.

10 Dec 67   UPI, New York Times
            DANANG, SOUTH VIETNAM, Dec 9

United States experts in psychological warfare today reported details of a new program offering rewards to South Vietnamese children who furnish military information about the Vietcong and turn in guerrilla weapons.

A related plan involves giving to children thousands of little toy balls bearing a message urging guerrillas to surrender under the Chieu Hoi program for defectors.

Both plans were put into effect yesterday, and American commanders said that they were sure of some success. The Marine officer in charge of the program, Maj. R.L. Payne of Charlotte, N.C., explained:

"U.S. troops in all wars have been successful in proselytizing children to our way."

10 Oct 67   Congressional Record — Senate, S14531
            Statement of James R. Dumpson, Dean, Fordham University School
            of Social Service, and Chairman, AID Social Welfare Task Force
            to Vietnam, before the U.S. Senate Subcommittee to Investigate
            Problems Connected with Refugees and Escapees.

...Since January, 1964, there have been one million nine hundred thousand known refugees 950,000 of whom are still considered to be in a "temporary" category. By "temporary" is meant that they are receiving the barest require-ments of food and shelter, a few piasters a day and 400 grams of rice while they await resettlement or return to their homes. Living in large congregate camp establishments, many are without adequate medical care, adequate sanitation facilities. Families, made up of a mother, an aged relative, and four or five children live in one room with dirt floors, bamboo sides, and aluminum roofing. For the great majority of the children ranging from infancy to 16 years of age, there are none of the basic, minimum facilities and services required for child care.

Responsibility for the care and protection of refugees is assigned to the Commissariat for Refugees in the Central Government. After a three month period, the meager assistance of the SCR terminates irrespective of the needs of the refugees. Technically, the refugees then become responsibility of the Ministry of Social Welfare which has neither the funds nor personnel to carry out this responsibility. Aside from the efforts of voluntary agencies which cannot possible meet the needs of 5 or 6 hundred thousand refugees, these people are left on their own.

16 Oct 67   UPI, Providence Evening Bulletin
            SAIGON

South Vietnam's refugee chief said today that thousands of refugees in the country's northern quarter are threatened by starvation because no helicopters are available to bring rice to their remote camps.

Some of the refugees are kept alive on food donated by U.S. troops stationed near their camps, according to Dr. Nguyen Phuc Que, the govern-ment's commissioner for refugees.

He said 12 remote refugee camps holding perhaps 10,000 refugees were accessible only by helicopter because roads leading to them were insecure and that at some of them the food shortage is so severe starvation is a threat.

A month ago, he declared he wrote "a high American official pleading for one helicopter for refugee relief in each of the five northern provinces, but so far he has not received a reply.

...Dr. Que, a French-trained physician highly praised by his American counterparts for his dedication, complained that he frequently gets only a day's advance warning when U.S. military operations suddenly create thousands of refugees.

He did not question the military decision to move people from their villages for tactical purposes, but said he can make no arrangements for receiving the refugees — sometimes in groups of 10,000 at a time — when he is not told beforehand.

He said 14 military operations so far this year have generated about 300,000 refugees.

12 Oct 67   New York Times, Neil Sheehan
             WASHINGTON, Oct 11

The General Accounting Office said today that the United States refugee and medical aid programs in South Vietnam had suffered seriously from low priorities and shoddy implementation.

In separate reports on the two programs presented to the Senate Subcommittee on Refugees and Escapees, the Congressional investigative agency cited a number of significant shortcomings in both operations. The reports were prepared at the request of the subcommittee.

Senator Edward M. Kennedy, Democrat of Massachusetts, the subcommittee chairman, said the findings "show that the refugee program and the medical program in South Vietnam are a scandal."

...The agency cited as one example of shoddy implementation the fact that nearly half the 573,546 so-called temporary refugees carried on the rolls as of last August were not receiving their daily subsistence allowances of 400 grams of rice and three Vietnamese piastres (about 2-1/2 cents at the official rate of exchange).

Temporary refugees are the more recent arrivals who are entitled to this subsistence allowance for two months. They are then supposed to be resettled and given an allowance of 5,000 piastres (about $42) and a six-month supply of rice.

Officials of the Agency for International Development said 2,008,098 refugees were listed as of last August when the latest report was available.

In the country's five northernmost provinces, where the refugee problem has been greatest this year because of the intense fighting, only 25 per cent of the eligible refugees have received this larger resettlement allowance, the agency said.

...The number of refugees in South Vietnam has grown by nearly 750,000 a year since the fall of 1965, however, and shows no sigh of decreasing.

Only 15 to 20 per cent of refugee children attend school in contrast to an estimated 60 to 70 per cent of other Vietnamese children. So far, 838 refugees have been given short courses in masonry, carpentry and other subjects.

The G.A.O. said much of the available data on refugees "must be discounted for management planning and decision purposes" because it is "conflicting and inconsistent."

As an example, the report noted that the Vietnamese Government reported only 25,028 new refugees in the five northernmost provinces between April 1 and July 31 of this year, but the American refugee officer for the area reported an increase of 150,000 refugees over nearly the same period of time.

The report on the civilian medical program in Vietnam cited similar low priority and shortcomings in implementation.

The G.A.O. quoted from a briefing paper presented at the Guam conference last March, that said the United States and South Vietnam "do not consider the present overcrowding of hospitals or limited access to medical treatment in remote areas critical to our success in the political-psychological side of the war effort."

American officials estimate that civilian casualties are occurring at the rate of about 100,000 a year, about half of whom require hospitalization.

The report said $17-million in Defense Department funds had still not been committed to build three new hospitals with a capacity of 1,100 beds for civilian casualties.

U.S. POLICY: LOOKS FAVORABLY ON CONTINUING FLOW OF REFUGEES

4 Feb 67   (See Note Page 20)

...By bleeding guerrilla units in 1966 to stock up the main-force battalions the Viet Cong risked losing control of the third of Vietnam's population they are credited with controlling. As it was, fleeing refugees and the forcible resettlement of population from the Iron Triangle, Zone C, and the mountain valleys of Binh Duong province drained the Communists of one million possible supporters in 1966.

Some military campaigns, such as Thayer along the Central Coast, Prairie at the demilitarized zone, and Paul Revere in the Central Plateau, have been proceeding for months. The more vigorously the Allied units push, the fewer people the Communists will have to recruit as guerrillas.

Depuy claims that the Communists planned to recruit 6,000 guerrillas in his operational region in 1966 and got only 600. A similar situation exists in other areas where U.S. forces are deployed.

3 Sep 65   Time

...Through miring monsoon rains and along dusty sun-seared roads they file, the wretched refugees from Viet Nam's awful war. Behind them lie their hamlets, shattered by recent battle or terrorized by the Viet Cong. Ahead are crowded refugee camps in their district and provincial capitals. Since May, when the pace of the fighting suddenly increased, the population of the camps has doubled and the total number of refugees has swelled to 600,000. By the end of the year, the figure is expected to rise to 1,000,000 — the greatest uprooting of people since the country was cut in two in 1954.

...Driven from their homes by everything from full-scale battles to the threat of government bombardment or V.C. reprisal, new waves of refugees are liable to turn up in any province at any time. Indeed, so confused is the situation that the USOM last week dispatched three teams of American specialists on a tour of the camps to count noses.

So far, the heaviest exodus has come from the central highlands, where most of the year's major battles have been fought. More than 100,000 homeless peasants and villagers have flooded Binh Dinh Province alone, transforming Qui Nhon, the provincial capital, into the refugee capital of the country. There are now 95 reception centers and camps in Binh Dinh, but only ten trained Vietnamese social service workers to run them. In Danang, when the camps filled to capacity, the authorities had to put up roadblocks to prevent thousands more from streaming in.

The Viet Cong take advantage of the confusion to infiltrate their own agents into the centers. To head them off, each incoming villager is required to fill out detailed entrance papers and is then interviewed by a panel of refugees from his home (sic) before being granted final admittance. Once inside, he is given rudimentary housing and a mere 10¢ a day to buy food and clothing from local merchants. "It's the best we can do at present (sic) just enough for living," says a Vietnamese official.

...To some Saigon officials, the refugees are little more than a massive nuisance that is siphoning off energy and funds from the war effort. To others, however, they could play a vital role in the outcome of the war. "This war is about people more than about real estate," says one American diplomat. "The side that has the loyalty of the people ought to win it. This is a good opportunity to add a few thousand friends to our side." The U.S. has already allocated $1,000,000 to the refugee camps in stopgap relief, is now considering a major aid program. Most of the work, however, must be done by the

Saigon government. "It's no use if we do it," says a USOM officer. "The Vietnamese have to help their own people."

28 Dec 65   The Christian Science Monitor, Josephine Ripley
              WASHINGTON

The welfare of nearly a million Vietnamese war refugees has become a major policy concern in American councils.

...That, with education and training, these refugees can form the basis of the new nation that will rise after the war "has been resolved in an honorable settlement," as Sen. Edward M. Kennedy (D) of Massachusetts put it.

That, therefore these refugees should be considered as an asset rather than a burden.

..."We have a unique opportunity with these refugees, now that they are under the supervision of the Vietnamese Government, to help provide training and education," he will tell Congress.

"Then, when they go back to their villages after the war, they will form the nucleus of a new society — a society prepared to carry one," the Senator says.

...The latest official refugee count indicates there are more than 800,000 in camps. Increased military action is expected to boost this to more than a million before the new year.

25 Jan 66   The Evening Star (Washington), Richard Critchfield
              (from Congressional Record — Senate, February 17, 1966, 3224)
              TANAN, SOUTH VIETNAM

...A 25-year-old Vietcong defector, who used to lead a 37-man guerrilla platoon, explained why peasants like Mua were turning against the Vietcong.

In his area, he said, the Vietcong initially redistributed land. But now they have raised taxes 300 percent.

"The more air strikes, the more people moved away and the heavier taxes became," he said. "The National Liberation Front (the Vietcong's political arm) failed to solve anything. There was no security to work in your field. An F-105 jet got there too fast, there was no time to run for cover. Those and 250-pound bombs were most feared."

He said if he were directing the war in Saigon he would intensify air and artillery attacks on the Vietcong villages, and then would offer the peasants amnesty and safe harbor elsewhere.

25 Feb 66   New York Herald Tribune, Seymour Freidin
              PHAN THIET, SOUTH VIET NAM

...The defections are real, carry momentum and cause profound disturbance among the VC and in the North.

Bombing, by the Americans and to a lesser extent by the government forces, has been in large measure responsible for creating the crack. So have artillery strikes. These may come as a shock to critics who hold that pounding from the air impairs neither guerrilla will nor movement.

...Villagers, among whom the VC boast they can swim safely, are also becoming somewhat turbulent and upset. Guerrillas take cover in their hamlets. Bombing strikes blast the areas. Peasants, increasingly, blame the presence of the VC for their plight.

12 May 66   New York Times, Felix Belair, Jr.
              WASHINGTON, May 11

...Quoting from an incomplete intelligence analysis just received from the fighting area, the Secretary said prisoners now expressed "considerable doubt" that the Communists can prevail even in a protracted war, and "some of them expect that the U.S. and government forces will win with their superior equipment and supplies."

The same report cited the "most serious impact" caused by the movement of some 900,000 Vietnamese who had left villages in areas dominated by the Vietcong and gone over to the government side. This, the report said, deprived the Vietcong of food supplies, intelligence sources and the use of the population as a shield and the villages as hiding places for guerrilla forces.

(Secretary of Defense Robert S. McNamara) did not say over what period of time the 900,000 villagers had moved.

16 Jun 66   (See Note Page 20)
             WASHINGTON, June 16

President Johnson was told today the Civilian Pacification Program in South Viet Nam "is really beginning to roll" and that about 20,000 refugees are leaving Viet Cong-infested areas each month.

"Large numbers of people are leaving the Viet Cong area to live in areas that have government protection," Porter said. He reported this has greatly hampered Viet Cong military operations.

The envoy said, too, that "it's having a snowballing effect" and that the hope is to add 14 per cent of South Viet Nam's population to government-controlled areas by the end of the year. He said that would boost the total proportion to about 60 per cent.

"The effort on the civilian side is really beginning to roll," he said.

Porter said "A great outflow of persons from Viet Cong areas began late last year" following the American military successes.

While reporting "substantial progress" in the program to pacify and secure outlying villages, Porter said there have been "some setbacks" because of political troubles in the northern provinces.

...Under an expanded effort inaugurated this year, trained pacification teams are being sent into villages deemed secure from the Viet Cong to offer help in the areas of agriculture, health, and education.

...Robert Komer, special assistant to Johnson, said that as these teams do their jobs, more people feel they can receive better security, support, and livelihood in the government-controlled sections.

In response to a question, Komer conceded that some of those who leave Viet Cong areas also do so because their villages are in the center of military operations.

Porter said Americans in Viet Nam no longer designate areas as Viet Cong-controlled, but rather as being "infested" with the Communist Guerillas.

"There is now no place — no place — where they are secure," he said.

Asked if many South Vietnamese were leaving government territory, he said, "We find very little evidence of that."

26 Jul 66   Christian Science Monitor, John Dillin
             SAIGON

...While the Viet Cong seem to be holding their fighting forces together, they are apparently losing some of their influence over village and hamlet peasants who more and more care only about having the war end.

The best indicator of this shift is the flow of refugees. Since the allied forces boosted their war effort here in the first part of 1965, between 1 million and 2 million refugees have poured into areas controlled by the Saigon government, it is estimated.

Two reasons are given for this:

First, the war simply has become too hot. Increased American and South Vietnamese attacks have made many villages and hamlets unsafe. The war is being carried to areas formerly thought to be secure for Viet Cong.

...Says one analyst:

The increase in airplanes was something the villagers and the Viet Cong could see. They'd never known the government of Vietnam was that strong.

For many peasants, airpower made the presence of Viet Cong guerrillas a hazardous experience as they found their villages suddenly the target of air raids. Some of them have moved out into their fields for safety, despite efforts of the guerrillas to make them return to their homes.

1 Feb 67   New York Times, Tom Buckley
             SAIGON, Jan 31

A million people may have slipped from Vietcong control since early 1965. This possibility was based on American intelligence appraisal of an enemy document captured earlier this month.

...''A comparison with the early part of 1965,'' the notebook says, ''shows a decrease of one million people in the rural areas because of the presence of U.S. troops. The people who frequently go in and out of the rural areas are not under our control nor under the enemy's.''

It is on this passage that the analysts base their finding of the loss of Vietcong strength in rural areas. On the other hand, it could be read to mean that, because of resettlement plans and the crowding of refugees into the cities, there had been a loss of a million from the total rural population rather than just from Vietcong areas.

8 Apr 67   Business Week

...Only a few years ago, South Vietnam was still an overwhelmingly rural country, with a quiet, shady French colonial town as its capital. Since 1965, a flood of refugees from the countryside has turned Saigon and its sprawling suburbs into a crowded noisy urban complex with a population of 2.5-million. Most of them will never go home again.

...Through no design or plan at all, the labor shortage is liquidating, if not remedying, one of the great tragedies of the war — the flight of 1.5-million villagers from the savage fighting that sweeps back and forth through the Central Highlands of Vietnam.

...Short-term, all these shifts of population help bring more of South Vietnam's people under the Saigon government's control. Out of a total population estimated at 16-million, about 7-million now live in government-controlled areas — up 1.5-million from a year ago.

Long-term, if the Saigon government follows reasonably enlightened policies, the agonizing upheaval could greatly speed Vietnam's transition from a rural, feudal society to a modern mixed farming and industrial economy.

CHAPTER XIV
CIVILIAN WAR VICTIMS
IN SOUTH VIETNAM

See (pages 29-42) the following articles relevant to this chapter: Hague—
Laws: 22, 23(a), (b), (e); Geneva—Civilians: 3, 33, 146, 147, 148.

---

3 May 65   New York Times, Emerson Chapin
             QUINHON, SOUTH VIETNAM, May 2

A solemn-faced Vietnamese girl of about 8 walked slowly, stiffly out
of the operating room.

...The little girl was one of the hundreds of civilians victims of the
Vietnam war to be treated in the Binhdinh Province hospital here. Wounded
by rifle fire, artillery, grenades, sometimes burned in napalm attacks,
they make their way arduously into Quinhon for treatment by the six-
member New Zealand surgical team.

"They come on foot, by bicycle, by bus, sometimes carried — on
shoulders," explained Dr. Patrick F. Howden of Auckland, head of the
team.

The hospital, a group of five-year-old, two-story concrete buildings,
has 150 beds. Often there are about 250 patients, most of them casualties
of the fighting, two or three to a bed.

At times most of those crowding the hospital have been victims of
American or South Vietnamese actions. There now are six patients
burned by napalm. In this central lowlands area of heavy Vietcong activity
there is bitterness against American and South Vietnamese military operations
that make victims indiscriminately.

But recently many patients bear wounds from grenades tossed by Vietcong forces seeking to clear an area of all residents to be free from interference or spying.

The greatest problem for the New Zealanders — two surgeons, an
anesthetist and three nurses — is the blood supply for transfusions.

"Among the bad cases we lose about one out of three or four because of
a lack of blood," Dr. Howden said. "These people are averse to giving
blood, and if a severe case comes in without a relative who can give blood
for him, it is very difficult."

...The patients are stoic with the weight of 20 years of war. The family
unit is all-important and even among the hospital staff there is what appears
to Westerners to be a lack of concern. Seriously wounded patients without
relatives to tend them have been known to die of thirst.

27 May 65   (See Note Page 20)
           WASHINGTON, May 27

Thousands of South Vietnamese are so badly disfigured by gunshot and burn wounds they'll never be able to lead useful lives, says an American plastic surgeon who recently returned from the stricken land.

Only four Vietnamese plastic surgeons are available in that country of 14 million people, a severe shortage that represents a national tragedy, said Dr. Richard B. Stark, Chief of Plastic Surgery at St. Luke's Hospital, New York.

Stark returned recently from Saigon after spending a month training and assisting the four Vietnamese plastic surgeons who face, he said, a staggering task of treating casualty cases that includes civilians and soldiers. Stark was an emissary of Medico, a nongovernmental medical group that provides aid in underprivileged areas of the world.

"Many of them (the victims) need 40 to 50 operations in order to be salvaged," said the doctor in a report to Medico. The report was made available to a reporter by Care Inc., which is holding a world conference here. Medico is a service of Care.

"Based on U.S. experiences in World War II and the Korean war," the report said, "it would take 15 years to perform the amount of reconstructive surgery needed to restore these people."

"Medico has made an important first step in tackling the problem," he said, adding that he and seven other American plastic surgeons lectured and operated under a program "calculated to upgrade the Vietnamese surgeons."

But plastic surgery is not the only medical deficiency in the area, he said.

"South Viet Nam," Stark said, "is a medical jungle. Statistics tell just part of the story.

"There are only 700 physicians in the entire country. However, 400 of these are serving up to 10 years in the armed forces. That leaves 300 physicians who must care for the civilian population of 14 million.

"The casualties pouring into Saigon's crowded hospitals today from the country's battlefields are double what they were on my first visit in February 1964. More than 400 weekly are sped by helicopter to the Cong Hoa and Cho Ray hospitals. These casualties include civilians as well as military .... I did some 38 operations (in February) as my Vietnamese colleagues looked on."

...The doctor said a new phase of the plastic surgery and other surgery training program is under way with the cooperation of St. Luke's Hospital.

"It is designed," he said, "to pave the way for Vietnamese surgeons to train in U.S. hospitals under approved internship and residency programs."

2 Jul 65   (See Note Page 20)
           DA NANG, SOUTH VIET NAM, July 2

...Covered with massive, red napalm burns, the boy whimpered in pain as the nurse removed the bandages from his skinny, scorched body. He would die.

A pretty girl dozed in a twilight state of semi-consciousness with a bullet wound in her chest. She had also been shot in the thigh eight months earlier.

Another boy, suffering deep shock, looked into space with an expressionless stare. He had seen his mother, father, and two sisters killed in their peasant village.

These are victims of the Vietnamese war. They are Vietnamese children with no future and a past filled with horror. They were brought to Da Nang's only civilian hospital where a skilled team of American doctors and nurses try to practice 20th century medicine under 19th century conditions.

...Perhaps 60 per cent of the 180 patients at the Vietnamese-operated hospital are war casualties. Most are women and children. Perhaps a third of the casualties are suspected Viet Cong, many hit during U.S. air strikes.

"You don't ask a man near death whether he's with the Government or the Viet Cong," explained Fitchett.

Half the war victims suffer from gunshot wounds, some of them superficial. Others, however, have been hit by mortars, grenades or napalm. The doctors guess that probably half the wounded die in the field, without treatment.

The city of Da Nang, with a population of about 160,000, has only four Vietnamese doctors, a ratio of one doctor for 40,000 persons. The only hospital of its kind in Central Viet Nam, it attracts patients from 50 miles away.

5 Mar 66   Le Monde, Alain Raymond (Translated from the French)

The young girl says nothing. Some sort of paper leaves hindered the flies from coming to suck up the ointment abundantly spread over the burns which extend over all the right side of her face. With a wan smile, almost imperceptible, or with a shake of the head, she answers the questions that a doctor puts to her in Vietnamese.

She is one of the civilian victims of the Vietnam war. "She has been burnt by napalm. Her village has been entirely destroyed. We received her several days ago. Her wounds are going to make her suffer terribly from now on. She will remain scarred not only in her skin, but especially in her spirit, all her life. She has only a dozen or so years," the doctor adds, impassive — or almost impassive.

This spectacle, reinforcing the atmosphere of a court of miracles which reigns in the ward of the civilian hospital of Cantho, stirs up a man's heart. From time to time, amid the hubub of visitor's voices, there is a groan. We are in the pavilion of civilian victims of the war. Every day, the hospital receives twenty or thirty of them. Some are wounded by the explosions of shells from Vietcong mortars, as is this weakened militia member; or as is this woman, stretched on the matting of her bed beside her infant, by the explosions of bombs from airplanes.

The visit to this regional hospital establishment, where the sick and wounded are at times put up two to a bed, in a fetid gloom, and where chickens peck up the rice grains from plates or drink out of greenish gutters, constitutes in some way a gripping condensation of all Vietnamese humanity in war. Babies at the breast hang from their mothers near their wounded fathers. In another place, a poor woman, come in a few minutes earlier from an attacked village, walks out, held up by two nurses, towards the operating room, a rubber drain hanging out of her back.

...Other victims of the war are the inhabitants who live under the terror of bombardment. I have learned, for example, that in Vietcong villages the women become hysterical after they hear the whine of a plane or whizzing of a helicopter.

So they throw themselves over their dearest belongings, pack them up, and wait for the danger to become clear. If the noise comes closer, each person must jump into the holes by the entrances of the houses. It is always necessary to clean out these narrow, vertical trenches in advance and chase out with a stick the water snakes who find refuge there. In the holes, someone told me, one sometimes has water up to the shoulders.

12 Mar 66   Le Monde, Robert Guillain (Translated from the French)
              HUE, March

...The civilian hospital in Hue has some wards full of peasants who are wounded or burned by napalm.

...In another city of Central Vietnam — I will not specify the place, but I am certain that it is hardly different at Hue — I visited the civilian hospital. In 1964, the number of civilian patients wounded in war action

had already reached, for some months, about fifty. Last year during the
first American build-up, it had reached almost a hundred. For some months
now, the number is between about sixty and eighty a month.

The wards reserved for them are full. They lie sometimes two in a
bed, sometimes three. They are all peasants of both sexes and of all ages,
and they are all in very bad condition. Abdominal wounds are numerous,
caused by bullets, explosions of shells or of bombs, grenades, mines,
whatever one can think of.

"Half from Vietcong action, half from that of the Vietnamese and the
Americans," a Vietnamese doctor of the hospital tells me. "Those you see
here, they are the ones who have been able to come. For every one who
reaches town, there are ten who do not arrive and who die in the village or
in the field where they have been hit. Especially the gravely burned, the
victims of napalm or of phosphorus shells...."

The "napalmed ones" — there are some of them here. An old man,
whose torso and arms have disappeared under a bulky outfit of dressings.
A young girl, her face fearfully inflated and all bespattered with burns. A
little fellow, twelve years old perhaps, who is recovering in a wheel chair:
at the end of his legs, he has nothing more than some kind of horrible reddish
stumps, the remains of his poor feet destroyed by napalm.

Nov 66   Flying
              Frank Harvey, "The Air War in Vietnam"

(The editors of Flying have declined permission to give the verbatim text
of a selection from the above cited article. The following describes the contribution of that selection.)

(The author examines the effect of napalm and white phosphorus on its
victims. At the end of his trip to the Delta he spent a lot of time in the Con-
Tho civilian hospital where he saw civilian victims of the war. He reports
seeing a man with some white phosphorus still burning in his flesh. The
hospital was overcrowded and the American doctor in charge reported that
they treated more civilian casualties than the military hospital treated
military casualties.

A large number of the civilian casualties seen are women and children.)

10 Dec 66   William Pepper
              Telephone Interview with Dr. Bernard Casselman of Los Angeles

He was an A.M.A. doctor assigned to the Provincial hospital at Qui
Nhon during January and February of 1966. He said that they had no water,
no electricity, no laboratory facilities, and no working toilets. In fact, they
had to get permission to blow up toilet facilities that were there, because
they were contagious.

During one plague epidemic he said that they ran out of drugs and he
personally had to go to Saigon and argue with USAID personnel in order to
acquire the necessary medicines. He then personally carried the drugs back
to the hospital.

Dr. Casselman stated that there were over 1,000 TB patients, who
were under treatment at the hospital; 10,000 known others in the area; and
an estimated 100,000 others. They had to stop all treatment of TB because
they ran out of drugs. At one point he and the New Zealand staff members
who also worked at the hospital threatened to close it, and he personally
called Major General Humphreys to complain.

Dr. Casselman stated that 50% of the medicine earmarked for their program went into the black markets or to the Viet-Cong. This explains part of the
reason for them being so terribly short of supplies. He said the Qui Nhon
Provincial hospital was the only one in Binh Dinh Province. It had between 250
and 300 beds and always between 500 and 750 patients, many of whom have a
relative or relatives living with them in the hospital, thus greatly improving th
overcrowded situation. They treated 150 out patients a day.

It was impossible to make changes in the situation because the hospital was controlled by local politicians, etc. The hospital staff had no control at all.

He reported that one of the New Zealand nurses died of a diarrhea attack. He said that while this was hushed up, her death was caused by neglect. When she had an initial attack, they didn't realize it was serious and the tremendous burdens upon their time caused them not to give her careful attention. The attack was escalated quickly and she died very rapidly before anything could be done.

He spoke of the great extent of American village bombing and the effects of the bombing. He recalled one instance where an Army ambulance brought in the survivors from a village on which phosphorous bombs were dropped. The only survivors they saw were children between the ages of 6 and 9, 9 being the oldest.

He said that the youngsters upon entering the hospital, "were still smoking"..."it was as though you put a piece of flesh in a toaster. They were actually on fire and still burning." Shortly afterward they all died. He maintained that about 40-50% of the patients were 15 and under, but they usually died quickly and there was a rapid change over. He said that this figure may be deceiving because the children were frequently less able to get to the hospital than most others, and he cannot tell how many never made it.

He agrees with my projected figure of 1,000,000 injured and killed children from 1961-66. In his words, "I would agree with that, easily."

Dr. Casselman said he signed more death certificates than he will ever again sign in his life, even if he were to work in a terminal Cancer hospital. He states that the terminal "kids" were always taken home to die. That this was a constant pattern. He saw Napalm victims in great frequency and phosphorous casualties less often. He stressed the fact that most burn victims die and that little if any reconstructive surgery is done there. He also said that a significant percentage of the children have no one to care for them in the hospital, but that usually others attempt to help them.

He observed many Amer-asian kids. He feels there is a place for such a program as the one we propose. He told a story of another youngster whom he observed, whose arm and leg were completely fused to his abdomen skin. This resulted from the burning of the arm, abdomen, and thigh, and when the 9-year-old child assumed a fetal position, as the burn healed in secondary fashion, he grafted himself so that he was only able to crawl. In passing, Dr. Casselman noted that there was no help at all for kidney disorders, and that the suicide rate was very high in Qui Nhon. He particularly recalls suicide incidents involving 17-18-year-old girls. He stated that the New Zealanders particularly noted that 80% of the casualties resulted from "friendly forces" military activity.

23 Mar 66   Medical Tribune and Medical News,
                Medical Tribune Staff Report, "Medicine in Vietnam": Part II
                SAIGON

...The number of civilians wounded in the war and the number who die of their wounds are impossible to determine, but except when major engagements are occurring they are commonly thought to be twice as great as the numbers of military wounded and killed. Most civilian casualties are the result of minor skirmishes that go unreported in the foreign press, but such incidents take a heavy toll. Province hospitals report that half or more of their case loads are casualty patients, and at some of these hospitals between 80 and 90 per cent of all surgery performed is on civilian war casualties.

20 Dec 66   William Pepper, Telephone interview with Dr. Robert Brittain,
                Surgeon, of Denver, Colorado

Dr. Brittain said that he was in Viet Nam as a participant in the AMA's Project Viet Nam. He was there for three months between February and May in 1966 and stationed at the civilian surgical hospital in Danang. He described the hospital facilities as antiquated at best, with the primary need being for trained personnel. He said that 85% of the patients were war injured victims. Speaking about the burned cases he said that, "really severe burn cases died." They never got there. He commented that they had "...no time for reconstructive surgery on serious burns."

15 May 66   Saginaw News, John D. Tucker
                (from Congressional Record, House, May 18, 1966, 10429)

   ...At Can Tho, where Dr. Sulfridge is stationed, about 80 percent of the patients have had traumatic incidents, such as gunshots wounds, mine fragments, napalm and phosphorus burns. The small hospital averages 15 major operations and many more minor operations each day, Dr. Sulfridge reported.
    "The death rate," he added, "from every conceivable disease is high."
   ...Three in a bed. Surgeon Sulfridge, who often has to make do without electric power or running water, has three Vietnamese nurses (two women, one man) to assist him. He makes rounds with an interpreter and is lucky to have one — many project doctors have to elicit symptoms and give instructions by sign language. Like all newly arrived Americans, he was appalled at first by the filth and overcrowding in the wards, with two or three patients in a single dirty bed. Within 48 hours he was performing as many as seven major operations a day, was so immersed in work that he hardly noticed the conditions.

           Congressional Record — Senate, July 22, 1966, 16014.
           (A letter inserted into the Record by Congressman Byrd)

"I just felt like writing a letter thanking God for Christianity and Christian ministers. The only spark of love and compassion I have seen in Viet Nam so far has been from Christians. All day long I am operating on women and children with severe injuries — arms and legs blown off by mortars, abdomen and severe chest injuries. Many lay out in the woods and rice paddies several days before being brought to the hospital. The Vietnamese without Christianity are without pity or compassion even for their own people. Even the native doctors and nurses are indifferent and compassionless. A few Catholic Vietnamese exhibit pity for the injured....

               "Sincerely, Bob Neilson, M.D."

Vietnam in the Mud, James Pickerell, 1966, p. 63

   ...Recently, I paid a visit to a provincial hospital in the Mekong Delta where I ran across two rather interesting stories concerning the bombing. One lady in the hospital had received a nasty napalm burn on her arm, and when she arrived at the hospital, the doctor, a young American, tried to find out when and where she had received the burn. At this the woman was indignant, as she reasoned that being an American, the doctor should know where the bombs were being dropped. This doctor gets many patients with napalm burns or wounds from bombing, as this is a province where the VC are very active, and all the people who come in with burns or wounds know that the Americans are dropping the bombs. The Viet Cong have made sure of that.

22 Aug 66   Congressional Record, Senate, 19354-56
             Senator Morse and "Statement of William T. Pepper..."

   ...Exhibit 2
    Statement of William T. Pepper to the Subcommittee to Investigate Problems Connected with Refugees and Escapees of the Committee on the Judiciary, U.S. Senate Session, Summer and Autumn, 1966, Hon. Edward M. Kennedy, Chairman
   ...My introduction to the extent of actual war injury was provided by Mr. Le Tuan-Anh, the chief nurse at Cho-Ray Hospital in Saigon. The

Cho-Ray children's ward consists of 40 beds and usually, not less than 70 to 85 children. In many instances one can encounter beds with two or even three children in them. The injuries vary. Some are the victims of grenade explosions, some are contacted by mortar fire and shrapnel and others by bomb explosions. A large number are the victims of napalm and the more horrible white phosphorous bomb explosions. (White phosphorous is more terrifying because it does not extinguish as readily as napalm. So long as the surface receives air it will burn.)

...Without question, however, the greatest physical damage to children, indeed to the rural civilians, generally, who reside in the 2600 odd villages, is caused by the bombing. This is the permanent physical effect that will live for the lifetimes of the scarred bodies and then some.

It cannot be denied, Mr. Chairman, it is happening, daily, there, and for every child that is visible in a hospital bed, there must be scores that never make it that far. It is a direct result of this conflict and I submit that we as a nation have as real a responsibility for its alleviation, as we do for its perpetration.

A New Kind of War, Martha Gellhorn, 1966, pp. 5-6

...The tiny children do not cry out in pain; if they make any sound it is a soft moaning; they twist their wounded bodies in silence. The cot by the door is a child burned by napalm. He is seven years old, the size of a four-year-old of ours. His face and back and bottom and one hand were burned. A piece of something like cheesecloth covers his body; it seems that any weight would be intolerable but so is air. His hand is burned, stretched out like a starfish; the napalmed skin on the little body looks like bloody hardened meat in a butcher's shop. ("We always get napalm cases in batches," the doctor had said. And there's white phosphorous too and it's worse because it goes on gnawing at flesh like rat's teeth, gnawing to the bone.) An old man, nearly blind with cataract, was tending this burned child, his grandson. The napalm bombs fell a week ago on their hamlet, he carried the child to the nearest town, and they were flown here by helicopter. The child cried with pain all that week, but today he is better, he is not crying, only shifting his body to try to find some way to lie that does not hurt him.

In theory, the peasants are warned of an air attack on their hamlet, by loudspeaker or leaflets 48 hours in advance, but as the military say, this is not always possible. Obviously I did not canvass the country, but I found no case in the hospitals I visited where this timetable was kept. In the areas call Free Air Strike Zones, or some such jargon, there is no warning and the people can be bombed at will day or night because the area is considered entirely held by Vietcong, and too bad for the peasants who cling to their land which is all they have ever known for generations. In this child's hamlet, the people were warned to leave by loudspeaker from the air in the night; but no one in Vietnam moves readily by night and besides, in the dark and the haste and the fear, how could they take with them their possessions which they value fiercely just because they have so few.

That night, the boy and his grandfather, his mother and older brother got away from the hamlet with two of their four buffaloes. The buffaloes were their only capital, their fortune, without the buffaloes they could not cultivate their fields. At the first light, many of the peasants crept back to the hamlet to rescue more of their livestock and household goods. The old man, too blind to go alone, took the child with him to try to find their remaining two buffaloes. But the jet fighter-bombers came at once. The two buffaloes were killed by the napalm, the old man said, and so were many of the people, and many were burned. No damages for lost property, death or wounds will be paid to these people, though the whole business of damages to civilians looks like another of the many dreams on mimeographed paper which characterize this war. But damages, if ever paid, are only paid for accidents; these people were warned, their hamlet was destroyed as an act of war.

20 Dec 66   William Pepper
              Telephone interview with Dr. Wade R. Eckert of
              Mammoth Lakes, California

Dr. Wade Eckert was in Viet Nam as a Project Viet Nam member during September and October, 1966 and stationed at Cantho Hospital in the Mekong Delta. Dr. Eckert is an orthopedic surgeon. He said that 80% of the patients at Cantho were war injured persons. In his specialty — 95% were war casualties. In the Delta, he estimated that for every military person killed, there are five to ten civilian casualties. He pointed out that this is so because until recently most of the firing in that area had been carried on by "popular forces" units. These combatants bring their families with them.

He said, "In the Delta it is undeniable that the family and the civilians are hit much harder than the fellow with the gun." With respect to the total figure of civilian injured which I have offered i.e., 1,600,000 he said, "that would be pretty difficult to dispute. It would not be very far off. If just Cantho and the Delta area were considered these figures would be an absolute minimum."

Oct 66   McGill News
              Duncan McLeod, "A Doctor's View of Viet Nam"

...In this and other letters Dr. Vennema, who since 1964 has been helping thousands of sick and wounded peasants in a hospital at the town of Quang Ngai, 365 miles north of Saigon, presents a doctor's view of what he says is "The Tragedy of Viet Nam." Primarily these letters describe the lack of medical facilities and personnel which he says is South Viet Nam's most pressing problem. But they also detail other contributory factors which have heightened this problem to horrifying proportions, such as the war, malnutrition, ignorance, primitive sanitation, and a small governing caste which he says "leeches off" the peasantry.

...Surgically there is a predominance of two classes: war wounds and obstetrical problems. The war injured usually come from anywhere, near as well as afar, sometimes from two or three to twenty or thirty a day, mostly with artillery wounds, napalm, and gunshot wounds, in that sequence. In serious battles, as many as 100 civilians have reached the hospital; these are the ones that reach the town when their injury is at least 24 hours old, and they are in the minority. The majority of the seriously wounded civilians do not reach the district dispensary, let alone the provincial hospital. They die at home! For a civilian to leave a battle area within 24-48 hours is virtually impossible. Not even the soldiers have this privilege in the province. It takes at least 16 hours, and most of the time 24 hours, to get a Vietnamese military man evacuated by helicopter. The Vietnamese Air Force simply refuses to fly the missions. Hence the great majority of the more seriously injured soldiers die. What thought does this evoke about civilians who are injured as the result of battle?"

20 Dec 66   William Pepper
              Telephone interview with Dr. W. Wyan Washburn,
              Administrator of Royster Memorial Hospital in Boiling
              Springs, North Carolina

Dr. Washburn said, "that there were a lot of children among the 500 to 600 daily patients in the Danang hospital." He continued, "We have a lot of burns that come in from outside villages. Burns and broken bones were among the most common injuries."

He remembered one family bringing in a young boy in a bamboo bed. He said they walked for 14 miles. They were described as women.

He stated that there were 200 to 300 burns that came under his observation during the two month period that he was in the hospital. "Children seemed to get burned worse than older people. Lots of times they would be left in the huts while the adults would be out somewhere, down in the paddies or working on the fringe of the hamlet. When the firing began, the adult would run or be unable to get back to the child, being cut off by the surprise attack. This was very common."

He noted that the number of children in the rural population was indeed very high. He said that older ones were killed off or eliminated by disease, etc. With respect to my figure of 1,000,000 children wounded or killed out of a total population of 1,600,000 killed or wounded, he said specifically, "I doubt if that's exaggerated. I doubt if it's excessive, and God knows how many more will get it until this is over."

"Of the 200-300 burn patients who made it to the hospital, close to 90% lived and left with their scars for they had neither time nor space to do reconstructive surgery."

With respect to the removal of the children for adequate treatment in the U.S., Dr. Washburn said, "It would be fine if permission could be obtained. It would be excellent. It would even be better for their rehabilitation and after care. General Humphreys spoke of the possibility of taking seriously injured children who need rehabilitative care to the Philippines, Okinawa, and Formosa. In one two-hour question and answer period he even raised the possibility of treatment in the U.S."

Oct 1966   David McLanahan, "Notes on a Summer in Vietnam"

The following is an account of some of my experiences in Vietnam in the two months I spent there this summer. I was one of five American medical students sponsored by the State Department's Agency for International Development. We each worked in a different civilian hospital at which AID had an American Advisory Team. I was in Danang.

My purpose in going to Vietnam was to provide medical care for innocent civilian war casualties and learn as much about the general situation as I could while fulfilling the first function.

...Ninety percent of our patients had directly war-related traumatic injuries. Another five percent were pedestrians or bicyclists struck by fast moving military vehicles. Most of the patients were peasants brought in from the countryside by military trucks. It was rare that we got these patients less than sixteen hours after injury. All transportation ceases after dark. A small percentage of war casualties are lucky enough to make it to the hospital. I believe the figure is one in eight.

...Saigon told us that one-third of our patients were Vietcong. I take this to mean that one-third came from areas under the control of the Vietcong and consider one-third a modest estimate. I would say that about 80% of our patients received injuries as a result of American or government forces action. Probably most of these were included in the casualty ratios of which the military is so fond.

...Many times patients would tell the Vietnamese students that they were injured by Americans but would tell me that they didn't know. One would only say that he was shot by a "big" soldier.

25 Oct 66   The Sun (Baltimore) (See Note Page 20)
NEW YORK, Oct. 24

Vietnamese civilians are suffering far more casualties in Viet Nam than U.S. and South Vietnamese military forces, an American doctor back from a study there said today.

Dr. Wayne W. Hall, of Ridgewood, N.J., said both declining health conditions and war violence are taking their toll among the native population.

"Many more civilians are injured by bombs than army personnel," he said.

At a hospital in Saigon serving both military personnel and civilians, he said the war-injured ratio was 10 civilians to one soldier. Noting that more than 5,000 Americans have died in Viet Nam since 1960, he said:

"The probabilities are that there are 5,000 civilian deaths from the war every six months." Many, he added, die from wound infections which are not adequately treated.

Hall, who spent six weeks in Viet Nam to survey medical needs there for Church World Service, an interdenominational Protestant and Orthodox relief agency, said health care for civilians has gradually shrunk.

"The war is consuming the medical care and the beds," he said. "This leaves the average sick person who would get well, if he were properly treated, without that treatment. The time and care goes to the war-injured."

Hall, 59, who retired last year as chief surgeon of the general hospital in Paterson, N.J., where he served for 40 years, said anti-biotic drugs and doctors are sorely needed for Vietnamese civilians.

10 Oct 66   JAMA (Journal of The American Medical Association)
             Joseph F. Fazekas, MD, "Medicine in Saigon"

...Saigon is a city which normally is populated by about 1-1/2 to 2 million people. It is estimated (although reliable vital statistics are no longer available) that the population is now about 3 million. The large number of civilians forced to leave their provincial homes magnify and complicate already existing medical problems, overwhelming the relatively primitive sanitation and preventive public health facilities. These people must seek help in already overcrowded, understaffed and poorly equipped hospitals. The large number of civilian casualties requiring emergency care so tax the limited hospital resources that relatively little attention can be given to those dying of preventable and reversible diseases. They commonly lie on the bare hospital floors because each dirty, sheetless bed cannot accommodate three patients. The hospital provides an effective milieu for the further transmission of diseases acquired outside its doors.

...I was assigned to supervise two medical wards (male and female) at the Cho Ray Hospital. Each ward had a nominal capacity of 20 beds, but patient occupancy varied between 50 and 60 patients.

...About 50% of the patients presented with febrile disturbances based on seldom-identified enteric infections, but there were typical cases of typhoid fever, tuberculosis, and malaria. One could never be absolutely certain of the diagnosis since sputum, blood, stool and urine cultures, and smears could not be obtained, and we had no recourse but to resort to gunshot anti-biotic therapy; at least effective dosages were prescribed.

...Good symptomatic and supportive care was difficult, if not impossible, there being no way to measure fluid-balance intake and output, and even the polluted water at times was at a premium.

...There was no way to test urine for sugar and no insulin for the diabetic patients, nor were there drugs for the treatment of hyper-thyroidism. There were about 20 of the latter patients, and I was told they had for some time been awaiting a supply of radioactive iodine.

...This situation prompted me to visit the Third Field Military Hospital to see if I could beg or borrow some drugs for my acutely ill patients. Believe me, it was a good feeling to see again a well-equipped hospital staffed with such capable and dedicated physicians. I was saddened by the sight of our wounded young men brought in by helicopter for emergency care, but was reassured by personally observing that they were receiving the best possible medical attention. Many of the physicians, including the commander of the hospital, had received their training in the Washington area, and this made me doubly proud. They gave me the medicine I needed, and the new antimalarial agents worked miraculously.

...In conclusion, there can be no doubt that medical problems in Vietnam significantly influence the war effort. I don't see how there could be further deterioration of the medical situation in Saigon except for the outbreak of disease in epidemic proportions. The morale of the people is low, for corruption, inflation, disease and poverty have caused an almost complete disruption of their social struction.

13 Dec 66   Look
                Laura Bergquist, "Never Before a War Like This"

(The editors of Look have declined permission to give the verbatim text of a selection from the above cited article. The following describes the contribution of that selection.)

(The author describes the crowded scenes of civilian war wounded in the Danang Surgical Hospital. She is stirred by one child badly burned by napalm.)

19 Dec 66   William Pepper
                Telephone Interview with Mrs. Pauline Maas of
                Mountain Lakes, New Jersey

Mrs. Maas described seeing burned children in Nhi Dong hospital and also at Cho Ray hospital in the children's ward.

She stated that the burned children were "...really like monsters... They were a mass of raw and melting flesh." She said that an American doctor whispered to her at one point, "We can't say anything because we are the cause of all this."

She wanted to take two burned children from Cho Ray hospital and was told by the International Red Cross Representative, Dr. Lothar W. Kempter, that "There are just thousands and thousands of war injured children — burned, amputees and the like, who need more medical attention than they can ever get in Vietnam." She said he almost "begged her" to wait and try to take some out.

Mrs. Maas further stated that many of the amputees are burn victims. She said that Dr. Kempter and Dr. Raymond P. Schaffler, a Special Assistant to the Executive Vice President of the American Red Cross, both told her that they did not have facilities there to properly treat burned children, and consequently, they often amputated quite readily. Dr. Kempter, who in his capacity was allowed to travel all over South Vietnam with immunity, told her that if they did not die of their wounds, children in the bombed out villages often died of starvation when women and other adults were wounded and killed. There is absolutely no means of transportation in such circumstances. No care and no way of getting food.

She further mentioned the fact that Dr. Kempter delivered in his official capacity with the IRC a number of protests to the U.S. Embassy on July 26, 1966 against the American policy of destroying VC hospitals wherever they found them.

Jan 67   Ramparts
                William F. Pepper, "The Children of Vietnam"

...Napalm, and its more horrible companion, white phosphorus, liquidize young flesh and carve it into grotesque forms. The little figures are afterward often scarcely human in appearance, and one cannot be confronted with the monstrous effects of the burning without being totally shaken. Perhaps it was due to a previous lack of direct contact with war, but I never left the tiny victims without losing composure. The initial urge to reach out and soothe the hurt was restrained by the fear that the ash-like skin would crumble in my fingers.

In Qui Nhon, two little children — introduced to me quietly by the interpreter as being probably "children of the Viet Cong" — told of how their hamlet was scorched by the "fire bombs." Their words were soft and sadly hesitant in coming, but their badly burned and scarred bodies screamed the message. I was told later that they evinced no interest in returning to their home and to whatever might be left of their family.

Jan 67   Redbook
               Richard E. Perry, M.D., "Where the Innocent Die"

...Men, women and children with missing arms and legs are a common sight in Vietnam, and most remain invalided for lack of artificial limbs. In South Vietnam in October, 1965, only one plant made artificial limbs, and its output for the year did not exceed 300. More than 300 people need such devices every week.

...The number of civilian casualties, then and now, is enormous. By way of comparison, from 1962 until January 1966, our American forces in South Vietnam had lost 1,500 men. But there have been times when the Vietnamese civilian population sustained this many casualties in a single week. Moreover, when a soldier is wounded he can expect prompt medical care and will probably survive. A wounded civilian is unlikely to get prompt medical care and will probably die.

Civilian casualties reached such proportions that in several areas the Vietnamese people, long fed up with the war, demonstrated against the American forces. The demonstrations were particularly strong and hostile in Danang in May, 1965, and they embarrassed our government, since our troops are in Vietnam nominally at the request of the Vietnamese people.

...I think for example of an experience at a hospital at Danang. While I was there a truck arrived with 23 Vietnamese women, who represented almost the entire female population of a nearby village. These women had been aboard an old bus with a wooden bottom, on their way to a wedding. The bus ran over a road mine. The explosion ripped the bus apart, driving splinters like nails deep into the women's bodies, shattering their heels, their lower shin bones and their buttocks. Dust and dirt from the road contaminated the wounds. I saw the women being unloaded from the truck as if they were hindquarters of beef. One woman was already dead.

...Who had placed that land mine on the road — the Vietcong? South Vietnamese soldiers? We Americans? It could have been an American mine; the Vietcong did not have any that powerful. But as happens so often, the Vietcong may have stolen it from American military supplies. Does it matter who put the mine there? It was on the road because of the cursed war in which we too are fighting, and 23 innocent women had had their bodies torn.

...Hundreds of such cases came before me, but I recall one in particular. A village had been strafed by fighter planes. I do not know whether the pilots were American or South Vietnamese. Among those wounded was a little girl; her parents both had been killed in the attack. I advised Dr. James Beeby, a member of the Navy's surgical team at Rach Gia, to amputate her right hand. I worked on the left hand and was fortunate in being able to save it. A few days later Richard Nixon, the former Vice-President, visited the child in the hospital. A picture of the two together was given a good deal of publicity. Mr. Nixon, I later learned, sent the little girl a doll and his best wishes.

...The Vietcong do not use napalm; we do. This highly incendiary, jelly-like substance is dropped in bombs. When the bombs explode, the napalm spews out in all directions like a molten geyser. It sticks to whatever it hits, including human flesh, and burns it black. I have been an orthopedic surgeon for a good number of years, with a rather wide range of medical experience. But nothing could have prepared me for my encounters with Vietnamese women and children burned by napalm. It was shocking and sickening, even for a physician, to see and smell the blackened flesh. One continues for days afterward getting sick when he looks at a piece of meat on his plate because the odor of burned flesh lingers so long in memory. And one never forgets the bewildered eyes of the silent, suffering, napalm-burned child.

22 Jan 67   The Cleveland Plain Dealer, Alton Blakeslee
               SAIGON

...Cho Ray Hospital is Vietnam's largest civilian hospital. It has more than 30 buildings, accommodating some 1,200 patients.

...At a children's ward, Dr. Durant talks cheerfully with two boys whose faces are masks of pink and white scar tissue, their eyes torn slits — victims of U.S. napalm.

27 Jan 67   Life
               Robert Sherrod "Notes on A Monstrous War"

(The editors of Life have declined permission to give the verbatim text of a selection from the above cited article. The following describes the contribution of that selection.)

(A British Commonwealth doctor in a Provincial hospital tells the author that his hospital usually has 600 patients for 400 beds. He also says that American and South Vietnamese firepower account for 90% of the injuries to civilians. The peasants are not warned prior to bombing as often as they are supposed to be. They are reluctant to leave their villages, even under threat of bombing, because of poor conditions stemming from corruption in the refugee camps.)

6 Jun 66   New York Times, Neil Sheehan
               CANTHO, SOUTH VIETNAM, Jun 5

In a civilian hospital in this country are to be found the unreported casualties of this war — the Vietnamese men, women and children who get in the way of bombs, mines, and bullets unleashed by both sides.

Here at Cantho in the Mekong Delta, 80 miles south of Saigon, is one of these hospitals. Its overcrowded wards mirror the agony of the Vietnamese masses who live in a countryside where war in an intimate part of life.

About 500 civilians, most of them ordinary peasants, enter this hospital each month with wounds of every conceivable variety. They are not listed in the battle statistics published in Hanoi, Saigon or Washington as evidence of alleged military successes.

...The hospital has only two ambulances and no helicopters. Most of the wounded must make their way to Cantho as best they can.

...The result of this lack of transportation, according to the Vietnamese and American surgeons at the hospital, is that almost all of the wounds are at least 12 hours old. Many cases arrive 24, 48 or even 72 hours after the accident. Because of this, almost all of the wounds are infected and many of the patients are in deep shock.

...About 300 of the 500 casualties each month require major surgery. The gravely wounded, who might be saved by rapid evacuation, apparently never reach the hospital but die along the way.

Just as the patients reflect the punishment that the war is inflicting on the Vietnamese peasants, so the hospital is an example of the grimly inadequate means available to alleviate this suffering.

The Cantho hospital was built in 1895 by the French colonial administration. It was the first civilian hospital in the Mekong Delta. Except for the surgical suite, which has been renovated with United States aid funds, little appears to have been done since 1895 to the physical plant.

Most of the wards are dilapidated two-story, stucco and red-tile-roofed structures. The buildings are dirty and infested with rats.

...The hospital cannot care for severe burn cases and grave head wounds — there are about two patients with serious napalm burns each week — and these must be evacuated to Saigon by ambulance. The surgeons suspect that some of the severe head cases die from the long, bumpy trip, but the United States and Vietnamese military have refused to carry these civilians in their aircraft.

There are other problems, such as a chronic shortage of whole blood, which has caused some deaths on the operating table.

"Just make up a list of what a hospital has and we need it," said Dr. Frank A. Camp, 36 years old, of Rochester, N. Y. Doctor Camp is an Air Force surgeon. He heads the team of seven American doctors and eight nurses and technicians who work with the regular hospital staff of five Vietnamese doctors.

...Despite its inadequancies, the 456-bed hospital is the only one available to the estimated total of 420,000 inhabitants of Cantho and the province of Phongdinh, of which Cantho is the capital. Because of its sizable American staff, the hospital also serves as a regional surgical center for the lower Mekong Delta.

24 Oct 66   New York Times, Jonathan Randal
             CANTHO, SOUTH VIETNAM, Oct 23

Civilian casualties of the war still make up 70 per cent of the patients in the civilian hospital in this provincial capital in the Mekong Delta, 80 miles southwest of Saigon.

But in five months, Maj. Frank A. Camp, who heads a 12-man Air Force surgical team, has seen hospital conditions "improve 1,000 per cent."

...In May, the 34-year-old surgeon from Rochester said: "Just make a list of what a hospital needs and we need it." He said he had received an official reprimand for his candor.

...Today, the 450-bed hospital is well-stocked. "You can get almost anything you want in Vietnam," Dr. Camp said. "It's just a question of finding someone or something. I've found the key."

...Five American nurses have helped improve the level of cleanliness and nursing care in the overcrowded wards, where as many as three patients often share a single bed.

Dr. Camp has persuaded a nearby Vietnamese air force base to use its helicopters to evacuate civilian casualties when the helicopters are not tied up with military operations.

He hopes to organize a regular helicopter service to Saigon twice or three times a week for civilians suffering from burns or severe head injuries.

...Most of the wounded Vietnamese who enter the hospital have been carried or have traveled on foot, some as far as 100 miles. By the time they arrive, their wounds are anywhere from half a day to three days old.

21 Apr 67   New York Times, Jonathan Randal
             SAIGON, SOUTH VIETNAM, Apr 20

United States officials have disclosed that the number of civilian casualties in South Vietnam is rising as the tempo of the war increases.

About 50,000 civilians may be treated for war-related injuries in Government hospitals this year, according to an estimate by Maj. Gen. James W. Humphreys, director of the United States aid mission's Office of Public Health.

In an interview, the Air Force general disclosed the first major American statistical effort to keep track of civilian casualties in South Vietnam.

Before the survey, no reliable statistics were kept by either South Vietnamese or United States authorities. Civilian casualties were not distinguished from other hospital cases. The change is generally attributed to criticism from opponents of the Johnson Administration's position in Vietnam.

...Another high-ranking American official said:

"We've been taking a licking on civilian casualties. It has been a major cause of criticism of our effort in Vietnam. But no one is happy about civilian casualties. The figures in Ramparts will not stand up under examination."

But the American statistics, based on tabulations made in 150 military and civilian hospitals and dispensaries in all 45 South Vietnamese provinces are also considered open to question.

There is no way to gauge the numbers of civilians killed or wounded within Vietcong-controlled territory; they are never brought to hospitals and dispensaries in Government-held towns.

In addition, overworked American and allied medical staffs are described as too busy to record the cause of injury among hospital patients in all cases.

... "If you want absolutely honest, valid statistics and reliable information on civilian casualties," General Humphreys said, "you would need something on the order of 300 full-time medical statisticians to cover every civilian hospital around the clock."

"Frankly," he added, "we need medical workers more than we need record keepers." The general noted that his medical staff was short 188 of its authorized 390-man contingent.

8 May 67   New York Times, Neil Sheehan
             WASHINGTON, May 7

Senator Edward M. Kennedy asserted today that war casualties among South Vietnamese civilians were occurring at a rate of more than 100,000 a year.

In response to inquiries by the New York Times, the Massachusetts Democrat said in a statement that his conclusion was based on an investigation conducted in February and March by him and the staff of his Senate subcommittee on refugees and escapees.

Senator Kennedy and the subcommittee staff interviewed about 70 physicians and surgeons who had served in Vietnam, and they read nearly 200 written reports submitted by physicians on their experience in Vietnam.

Last month, in the first official report on civilian casualties, the United States mission in Saigon estimated that 50,000 civilians would be treated for war-related injuries in Government hospitals this year.

Mr. Kennedy said his 100,000 figure was "derived from the fairly hard statistics of an average of at least 4,000 civilian casualties currently reaching medical centers each month and the virtually unanimous view of the medical personnel, both here and in Vietnam, that only one out of two or perhaps even one out of three civilian casualties actually reached these medical facilities."

According to Senator Kennedy's report, it takes a civilian an average of 36 hours to reach a medical center after being injured. He blamed a "lack of transportation or inability to move to medical facilties due to continued military activity of the areas."

In practice, physicians interviewed have pointed out, this means that many critically injured civilians die because they cannot reach hospitals in time.

The Senator said his estimate included "all casualties, whether inflicted by the Viet Cong, as is often the case, or the result of United States or South Vietnamese military activity."

The monthly statistics to which Mr. Kennedy referred were obtained by the Saigon mission of the Agency for International Development through surveys at civilian and military hospitals in South Vietnam. The surveys showed 2,500 civilians hospitalized for war wounds in December, 4,150 in January, and 3,920 in February. Figures for March and April are not yet available.

Members of the subcommittee staff said they had reason to believe, as a result of their investigation, that the statistics were still incomplete because some hospitals were not included, and the number of civilian casualties admitted to others was understated.

Maj. Gen. James W. Humphreys, director of the aid mission's Office of Public Health in Saigon, has estimated that 50 per cent of the civilian casualties are caused by allied military action and 50 per cent by the enemy. Other experienced officials suggest that a majority are victims of allied military activity.

"There is also widespread agreement," Senator Kennedy said, "that the rate of civilian casualties in Vietnam is on the increase, particularly as military activity grows in the heavily populated Mekong Delta region."

The Mekong Delta, the rich rice-growing area south of Saigon, houses 40 per cent of South Vietnam's 16 million inhabitants.

...Administration officials said in April that a helicopter airlift would be provided to evacuate wounded civilians to hospitals, but it is reported that permanent assignment of helicopters to this task had not yet been approved.

General Humphreys has tried unsuccessfully for 18 months to obtain two twin-engine Caribou aircraft to carry civilians with critical injuries, such as head wounds.

18 Apr 67   Look, Chandler Brossard

(The editors of Look have declined permission to give the verbatim text of a selection from the above cited article. The following describes the contribution of that selection.)

(The author reports the estimate that a million children have been wounded in the Viet Nam war and more than 250,000 killed.)

CHAPTER XV
CARE OF CIVILIAN WAR VICTIMS

The following Article from an International Convention relevant to this chapter is quoted in full:

Geneva Convention
Relative to the Protection of Civilian Persons in Time of War
12 August 1949

Article 55.

To the fullest extent of the means available to it, the Occupying Power has the duty of ensuring the food and medical supplies of the populations; it should, in particular, bring in the necessary foodstuffs, medical stores and other articles if the resources of the occupied territory are inadequate.

The Occupying Power may not requisition foodstuffs, articles or medical supplies available in the occupied territory, except for use by the occupation forces and administration personnel, and then only if the requirements of the civilian population have been taken into account. Subject to the provisions of other international Conventions, the Occupying Power shall make arrangements to ensure that fair value is paid for any requisitioned goods.

The Protecting Power shall, at any time, be at liberty to verify the state of the food and medical supplies in occupied territories, except where temporary restrictions are made necessary by imperative military requirements.

See also (pages 29-42) the following additional Articles relevant to this chapter: Geneva—Civilians: 3, 24, 29, 32, 50, 56, 59, 146, 147, 148.

HOSPITAL CONDITIONS

28 Mar 66   Medical Tribune and Medical News
              Medical Tribune Staff Report, "Medicine in Vietnam"; Part III
              SAIGON

...The number of scientifically trained physicians now practicing in South Vietnam is around 900, according to the best estimates; the exact number is unknown.

...As of the first of this year, 650 of the country's physicians were in uniform serving the 565,000 members of the South Vietnamese armed forces and their approximately 1,975,000 dependents, however, so that in the armed forces the ratio was one to 3,900, while in the remaining civilian population it was one to 51,800. Since almost all armed-forces doctors spend two-fifths of their time treating civilians, a truer ratio for the civilian population would be one to 25,400. Further attempts to refine the national ratio would be complicated by the facts that little is known about medical care in the one-third or more of the population controlled by the Vietcong.

...''And the whole thing is thrown completely out of kilter by the fact that at least half of the civilian physicians practice in Saigon,'' noted an American doctor who was helping to work out the above ratios on a tablecloth in a local restaurant.

Thus, while there may be one physician for every 500 wealthy Vietnamese in the capital, the ratio in some of the remoter parts of the countryside may be one to 250,000. The safest generalization to make about South Vietnam's medicine, then, is that it is atrociously distributed.

2 Jul 65   (See Note Page 20)
             DA NANG, SOUTH VIET NAM, July 2

...''Our main purpose is to pay our bills and to save as many people from dying as possible,'' said Louis M. Wahrmund of Fredericksburg, Tex., a regional director.

The medical experiment started off with four civilian teams but dwindled to half this number because of lack of recruits from the United States. The American doctors, who volunteer their services, wind up frustrated and embittered, victims of what they call cultural shock.

Dr. Vernon Fitchett, 37, of Newell, Iowa, the chief medical officer, describes the condition this way:

"You come here thinking you're going to change things. Then you find out the hospital has no hot water, no sewage system and often no electricity.

"The flies in our wards wouldn't be tolerated in a pig sty. Hospitals in the states have semiprivate rooms, but we have semiprivate cots, two or three patients to a cot.

"You perform a five-hour operation, but the patient dies because no blood is available or there's a lack of trained nurses."

26 Aug 65   New York Times, James Reston
             SAIGON, Aug 25

...A day in the country here is equally illuminating about the Vietnamese attitudes toward the war. Haunghia Province lies 30 miles northwest of Saigon. It has a population of 228,000 and not a single doctor. Most of it is under the control of the Vietcong.

13 Jun 66   Medical Economics
             Paul W. Kellam, "Vacation in Vietnam?"

...Another doctor, who had wanted more experience with trauma, got a concentrated dose when his 400-bed hospital received 100 civilian wounded within a few hours.

...Hospital bed capacity, not surprisingly, is woefully inadequate. Dr. Stephens sometimes finds beds tight in Columbus, Ohio, where there are 3,259 beds for 550,000 people. At Danang he had only 100 beds for a provincial population of 1,000,000. Patients convalesced two, three and even four to a bed. Sometimes the patient's family slept under the bed or on the porch. It's the relatives, rather than nurses, who perform most of the nonmedical hospital tasks.

21 Mar 66   Medical Tribune and Medical News
              Medical Tribune Staff Report, "Medicine in Vietnam" (Part I)
              SAIGON

Conditions in the ward were very bad. Hanging from the cracked ceiling at regular intervals down its length were five naked light bulbs, two of them burning. At irregular intervals along the bottom of the stained, peeling walls, there were green, 3-inch lizards, waiting motionlessly. ("Our insecticide," the physician said.) The grayish brown sheets covering the mattresses on the iron-frame beds were streaked with dried blood and pus. Refuse emitting a pungent odor littered the floor.

...Most of the 40-odd patients were sharing beds. One patient whose right leg was in a cast and another whose left leg was, were in traction together. Three teen-age patients lay in one bed. The cholera patient was dying, but the ward's one attendant, who had served a three-month apprenticeship, was away taking his siesta.

...Could not some effort be made to sweep the floors and wash the bed linen? "We have to have relatives in the wards to feed and bathe the patients because we haven't enough attendants, and they would continue to litter. They are simple people and don't know any better. We have no laundry ... sometimes washerwomen do the sheets in the stream."

What was surgery like in the hospital? "I am not a surgeon, but I try. I do a lot of amputations."

Did he have enough drugs? "No."

Elsewhere in the country the same correspondent visited a U.S. Army hospital in a former school. The contrast was complete.

The commanding officer, whose comfortable office was the former principal's, said his large, highly trained staff included eight surgeons as well as specialists — unknown in most province hospitals — in radiology and psychiatry. "Our greatest number of admissions in one day was 65, including 40 surgical patients, but we could cut it," he commented.

The hospital's wards were immaculate, and when during a tour the commanding officer noticed some dirt outside the ward area, he quietly but urgently started talking about decapitating the section head responsible. Two registered nurses were in the intensive-care ward, once the school's library, one briskly doing routine work and the other comforting a badly wounded soldier.

Apr 66   Clara Maass Hospital News, Bellville, N.J.
              S. William Kalb, M.D.
              (from Congressional Record — Appendix, July 20, 1966, A3837)

...I was sent to a small town about 80 miles south of Saigon in the Mekong Delta. There I was to do general practice. I was the only medical man in a 400-bed hospital consisting of thirteen one-story buildings. Sanitation was something you talked about, but was not a reality.

Forty iron beds in every ward with boards for mattresses. Two or three patients in every bed. One would find a diabetic, a typhoid, and a cholera patient all in one bed. If a mother had an amputation or some other wound or sickness, the husband and all the children moved in. Some of the family sleeping with the patient and the rest of them under the bed. The hospital fed the whole family. A forty-bed ward might easily have a hundred people living there. Lizards crawling all over the cracked walls and ceilings. These helped to reduce the census of flies, mosquitoes, and ants.

Jul 66   International Review of the Red Cross, p. 362

Hospital needs. — A member of the delegation of the International Committee of the Red Cross in Saigon, Mr. Jacques Moreillon, has just completed a tour of Central Vietnam to examine various hospitals and their needs. The chief places he visited were Kontum, Da Nang, Hue and Nha Trang.

The ICRC representative first visited the hospital at Kontum on the high plateau where the Swiss Red Cross medical team is working. In this area, the state of health of the population is deplorable, 90 per cent of patients treated at the hospital suffering from tuberculosis. Malaria is also very frequent, especially amongst the children. The other most common diseases are bacterial and amoebic dysentery, typhus, thphoid and many forms of infection. In addition the entire population appears to suffer from malnutrition.

Sep 66   International Review of the Red Cross, p. 485

At Ben Tre, Kien Hoa Province, a twenty-member Iranian medical team is bringing the benefits of modern surgery to thousands of Vietnamese peasant farmers who would otherwise go unattended in this Mekong Delta city, 84 kilometers south of Saigon.

Staffed by two surgeons, Doctors Siamak Shakibi and Reze Soleymani, two technicians and fifteen nurses, the team is headed by Colonel Esmahail Gilanpour. The team is sponsored by the Iranian Red Lion and Sun Society. The provincial hospital at Ben Tre is the only medical facility for the 600,000 inhabitants of the province.

...Recalling her early impression of Viet Nam, Chief Nurse Omolbanin Hahanzadeh said: "The first night, we couldn't sleep because of the artillery firing around the city. Now, we go to sleep without trouble. The noise is nothing."

...On several occasions, during military operations in the province, the team has worked at the hospital continuously for 48 hours treating the wounded. Unfortunately, non-combatants caught in the middle of the war zone are sometimes hurt ....

Today the people in Ben Tre, and those throughout Kein Hoa Province come to the hospital more freely. When they need medical attention, the villagers know that they will receive it.

Jan 67   Redbook
            Richard E. Perry, M. D., "Where the Innocent Die"

...It is hard to exaggerate the grim state of medicine in South Vietnam in 1966. I offer a single, simple comparison with the United States. In our country, many a parent has had a child suffer a compound fracture — that is, one in which the bone penetrates the skin. With modern surgical techniques, such injuries need not be particularly alarming. Apart from a scar, the child is not likely to suffer any permanent harm. In Vietnam, however, because of the lack of medical facilities, a child who has a compound fracture of an arm or leg will almost certainly have the arm or leg cut off. Not since the Civil War have we in this country treated compound fractures with amputation.

...On August 16, 1965, I arrived in Saigon as part of Project Vietnam. I met with AID representatives and officials of South Vietnam's Health Department, who briefed me on existing problems. My interest centered on American surgical teams in the cities of Danang, Nha Trang, Can Tho and Rach Gia. Approximately 16 physicians were serving, most of them military men working in a civilian capacity.

...I flew down to Can Tho. formerly the center of Vietnam's rice market. Its hospital was built by the French in the 1890s and now has two additional Quonset huts. I had arrived during the monsoon period and everything seemed mildewed; to go from one place to another meant tramping in ankle-deep mud. Around the buildings were open-trench sewers smelling of human waste. Some windows had screens that were torn; others had no screens at all; flies and mosquitoes filled the hospital. The doors were badly warped, leaving gaps at the bottom for insects and vermin. At night, when it was quiet, rats could always be heard pattering through the wards.

The female surgical ward had approximately 60 beds. Here, as in almost all hospitals that take care of Vietnamese civilians, there were two patients in every bed. There were no sheets or rubber mats on the beds.

There were no privacy screens. There was no running water; the patients were never bathed. The windows admitted insufficient light, and few electric fixtures were working.

The male wards, in the Quonset huts, were terrifying. They were enveloped in such perpetual darkness that it was difficult to dress wounds and almost impossible to determine their condition. When it rained, water leaked through the roof. When the sun shone, the sheet-metal huts became unbearably hot; on occasion I literally burned my skin by accidentally brushing against the walls.

Everywhere the smells were vile enough to weaken even a physician. The stench of human waste, burned flesh, pus-soaked bandages and open, draining wounds trapped in hot, stale air would eventually overpower me. I could work for an hour or two and then dizzy with nausea, I would have to go outside and get far enough away to breathe fresh air before returning. And in those hellholes people — some men, a great many women and a few children — lived for months on end, never having a breath of fresh air, never feeling sunlight, never having a bath.

Outside the buildings women and children squatted, either cooking meals for ill or wounded members of their families who were patients or waiting to tend their most primitive needs. This was the only care a patient could count on; if there were no one outside to look after him, he would almost certainly die.

5 Feb 67   The Washington Post, Jesse W. Lewis, Jr.
           SAIGON

(The editors of Washington Post have declined permission to give the verbatim text of a selection from the above cited article. The following describes the contribution of that selection.)

(The author describes the civilian hospital at Bien Hoa as overcrowded and unsanitary, especially the children's ward.)

7 Apr 67   New York Times, Hedrick Smith
           WASHINGTON, April 6

The United States announced plans today to set up three field hospitals in South Vietnam as an emergency measure to treat the most critical cases of civilian casualties of the war.

The move apparently was taken, at least in part, in response to rising Congressional and private American concern about the problem of civilian casualties and their treatment.

Congressional sources said that Senator Edward M. Kennedy urged the Administration about six weeks ago to take steps to ease overcrowding of Vietnamese civilian hospitals by war casualties. The Massachusetts Democrat warned the administration he planned to hold public hearings if effective action was not taken.

Officials in the Agency for International Development announced that the Government would provide 600 to 1,000 surgical beds at three military field hospitals in central Vietnam.

They said it would cost $15-million to $20-million to set up the three hospitals and operate them for a year. The first is expected to be in operation in about six months, officials said.

The Administration is planning to provide a helicopter airlift to bring civilian patients from combat zones to the three new hospitals, which are to be at Danang, Quangngai and Quinhon, three cities in Central Vietnam. ...military personnel.

Officials said that the new hospitals would double the number of civilian surgical cases that can be handled in the area. ...Public concern over civilian war casualties in Vietnam has been mounting recently in the wake of disputed reports that American napalm was responsible for numerous cases of burns suffered by Vietnamese children.

May 67   Commentary
              Joseph J. Weiss, "Vietnam — A Doctor's Journal"

...An Xuyen is the size of the state of Rhode Island, and holds about 250,000 people. At present no accurate census is possible since the Vietcong control over 90% of the area and approximately 40 percent of the population. The South Vietnamese believe Vietcong strength in the province is 1,200 men.

...The Camau Hospital, with its one hundred beds, is the only one to serve the 250,000 people living in An Xuyen province. Until July 1966, the hospital staff consisted of only one doctor, nine nurses, seven midwives, three operating room assistants, a pharmacist, a laboratory technician, and three janitors. Then the MILPHAP (U.S. Military Public Health Assistance Program) team arrived.

There are twenty MILPHAP teams in Vietnam. Their purpose is to render medical care for the civilians in the country and by doing so, to illustrate the extent of America's intent to assist South Vietnam. The Camau group included three U.S. military doctors, thirteen corpsmen, and, with my arrival, one volunteer physician.

Electricity for the hospital is available only eight hours a day and is sufficient to run a few overhead fans and the hospital sterilizer. There is no running water in the wards or clinic. The Vietnamese staff works from 8:00 A.M. until 5:00 P.M. with a two hour break from noon until 2:00 P.M. There is no one for night duty, not only because of the shortage of staff, but for the reason that the hospital lies at the edge of town and is within the night boundaries of Vietcong control.

The only medicines regularly on hand are aspirin, vitamins, cough syrup (though no small bottles in which to dispense it), penicillin, and soap. At times there is a shortage of medicine like digitalis and supplies like plaster-of-Paris splints. Blood for transfusions is never available since stored blood requires constant refrigeration.

...Why is there such a problem with supplies? First the hospital budget is only $30,000 a year. Besides taking care of hospital needs for drugs and supplies, this money must pay wages for the Vietnamese staff and provide upkeep on the hospital. Upkeep expenses are considerable since the hospital lies a quarter of a mile behind the American compound. In September, the V.C. mortared the installation, and one shell blew a hole in the roof of the hospital's medical ward.

Second, the hospital budget for 1966 was made on the basis of the needs of one Vietnamese doctor. The effect of increasing the hospital staff by four (U.S.) doctors and thirteen corpsmen was to use up, in less than three months months, supplies intended for a year.

Oct 66   David McLanahan, "Notes on a Summer in Vietnam"

...The facilities in Danang's Surgical hospital (separated by a few blocks from the older Medical hospital which is not U.S. supported) has approximately 350 beds and at least two patients/bed. The pediatrics room often has four children/bed. There are always at least three times as many non-patients as patients. They sleep almost everywhere.

...Our situation was much better than the Medical hospital which often ran out of antibiotics, digitalis, etc. One of the other U.S. medical students who was in charge of a pediatrics ward in Quang Ngai, sixty miles to the south, occasionally had to use cocoanut IV's — which is a common practice in outlying areas and of the Vietcong. We received ample outdated blood from the military hospitals and had good luck with it. Most of the other hospitals are chronically short of blood.

11 Jul 65   New York Times, Howard A. Rusk, M.D.

...There are an estimated 10,000 civilians in South Vietnam who have suffered amputations as a result of the war. Despite several surveys by

United States official and voluntary agencies, nothing has been done to assist these men. Most are below-knee amputees who could be fitted with modern plastic limbs with a minimum of personnel, equipment, and money, and become productive workers rather than discouraged invalids.

There is a 100-bed rehabilitation center for handicapped children in Saigon. The center is within a large compound where the Roman Catholic order of the Sisters of Vincent St. Paul, has a boarding school, a kindergarten and other activities. Funds for the center were raised through Catholic Relief Services.

...Mr. Cherne has reported that in Vietnam today there are about 100,000 orphans as a result of the war. Many of them are severely disabled. The children's hospitals in Saigon and Chalon are jammed with youngsters, two or three to a bed. Most of them have yet to learn the worst news of all — that their parents are dead.

What is desparately needed in Vietnam is a large-scale expansion of assistance both from United States official and voluntary agencies. The situation there is similar to that of war-torn Korea in 1953.

29 Jan 67   Chicago Tribune, (See Note Page 20)
             SAIGON, VIET NAM, Jan 28

On most Sunday mornings, John Wells gathers up a group of eager, happy children and adults and flies with them aboard United States air force planes to little air fields in the hinterlands of Viet Nam.

...Only 10 to 14 days before, they had come to Saigon lacking an arm or leg, or both arms or both legs — victims of land mines, shell fire, bombs, and grenades from 20 years or more of war.

They go home with new plastic arms and legs, individually fitted, from a remarkable assembly line producing 500 artificial limbs and braces per month at the National Rehabilitation institute.

Just a year ago, a small shop here was producing only 40 or so wooden limbs and braces a month.

...Wells returns to their country homes each month up to 100 persons who had come to the institute with hope for a new productive life.

The institute, started 10 years ago, began making artificial limbs, mainly from wood, for amputee war veterans from World War II and later the Vietnamese war with the French.

In September, 1965, Dr. Howard Rusk of New York, a world-renowned specialist in rehabilitation, came over at President Johnson's request to survey needs and to make recommendations.

...Now, 70 to 100 people show up at open clinic days held three times a week. The great majority are amputees, and 75 percent are civilians, from children as young as 3 to men and women over 65.

...The institute is expanding with a new building for retraining broken bodies and for fitting artificial limbs, and a 20-bed ward for paraplegic soldiers, paralyzed from the waist down.

MEDCAP PROGRAM

30 Mar 66   Medical Tribune and Medical News
             Medical Tribune Staff Report
             "Medicine in Vietnam" : Part IV
             SAIGON, VIET NAM

...The American armed forces in South Vietnam are trying to improve the health of Vietnamese civilians through their own Medical Civil Action Program (MEDCAP), which is related to USOM only in that the drugs used in it are bought with USOM's funds.

...The program, which is closely linked with phychological warfare efforts to solidify peasant support for the Saigon Government, is actually a three-fold one — MEDCAP I, MEDCAP II, and MEDCAP III. MEDCAP I was started three years ago and is now widespread and well-organized, MEDCAP II is only three or four months old and is still limited in scope, and MEDCAP III is still in the planning stage.

For the most part, the first MEDCAP is run by the 308 U. S. Army medical sergeants assigned to American military advisory teams counseling South Vietnamese provincial and district militias. Its purpose is to enhance the image of the South Vietnamese Government by having militia medics give basic medical treatment to civilians with drugs supplied by the United States and advice given by the American sergeants.

...Since MEDCAP I is designed to give basic medical treatment to peasants who never before have had it, rather than definitive treatment (neither the South Vietnamese Government nor the American armed forces here have the personnel or facilities to definitively treat all the country's inhabitants), the drugs dispensed in the program are essential ones.

MEDCAP II is operated by the medical personnel of American tactical units, rather than those of advisory teams, and is designed to enhance the image of the United States rather than that of the South Vietnamese Government among the peasantry. Like MEDCAP I, it consists of basic medical treatment only.

...In 1963, MEDCAP I medics treated 619,118 Vietnamese, and the following year they aided 2,705,898. Last year the two active MEDCAP's treated somewhat more than 4,500,000 civilians.

17 Feb 66   (See Note Page 20)
            MC VILLE, N.D., Feb 17.

An American doctor in the embattled jungles of Viet Nam finds a variety of challenges he never dreamed of back home on the plains of North Dakota.

"In this province there are 105,000 people. They have two civilian Vietnamese doctors. During our one and a half days in the field, we gave some 490 treatments. In every place visited, we had to cut off sick call before finishing, leaving long lines, because of security or lack of supplies or simply time."

Those are excerpts from a letter to friends here, written by Maj. Raymond Coultrip, a general practitioner in McVille. While his wife and four children wait for him at home, he is now in Phouc Tuy Province, South Viet Nam, where he commands the 345th Medical Detachment.

Of course Coultrip has his military servicemen to treat, but the natives are eager to line up to see the "American Bac Si," as they call him.

Coultrip writes about a shortage of medicine and doctors, but never a lack of patients. He said: "Upon entering a village or hamlet, a loud-speaker blared the happy tidings, and soon throngs of patients appeared. Capsules would have to be divided into halves, tablets into quarters, and dissolved in water in many cases, with the resulting nauseating taste, to accommodate the needs of the children.

"One little girl in Dat Do had an eye disease virtually unknown in the United States. We took the little girl back with us (to a hospital) for possible surgery. I won't forget her. Another little girl, about seven years old, had an old shrapnel wound. Her left leg was shortened and deformed. She also came back with us."

He also stressed the need for teaching people fundamentals about disease, how to use soap and keep clean, adding: "I believe quite firmly that medicine is one of the most effective, direct weapons to combat this insurrection and gain our objective."

Bumping up against sickness in a foreign land has its challenges too: "In several cases I suspected tuberculosis," writes Maj. Coultrip, "but had no laboratory means to verify it. One simply had to use one's own best judgment. May God bless me!"

Jan 67   Redbook
             Richard E. Perry, M.D., "Where the Innocent Die"

...One memory is especially vivid. In April of 1963, four months before Betty and the children and I were to return home, I was asked to come to Kontum by an American woman physician, Pat Smith. Pat, who is in her late 30s, has been in Vietnam for six or seven years under the sponsorship of the Catholic Relief Services. She lives as the Vietnamese in that region do, in a crude house with walls and floor of packed earth, a Coleman lamp for light at night, and eats rice and nuoc man — a rather obnoxious liquid obtained from putrefied fish that happens to be quite nutritious.

Pat Smith runs a hospital built with money supplied by the German Bishops' Fund. She serves the montagnard people, primitive nomadic tribesmen who live in the mountains, farming poor land until the soil is depleted and then moving on to another strip. They are always on the verge of starvation; for several months of every year, having exhausted their meager food supply, they eat roots and insects and rats. They suffer from chronic malnutrition and illness.

...I went there and performed some orthopedic surgery. During my stay, I had an opportunity to go out on a Medical Civic Action Project, which is run by our American military. The basic purpose of MEDCAP, as it is called, is to provide a semblance of medical care in the rural areas in the hope that this will help win the confidence of the people. The American medical unit in this case consisted of two sergeants with a jeep pulling a cart loaded with candy and medicine. We were accompanied by a handful of Vietnamese troops and the chief of the province, who wore leather boots and dark glasses, carried a swagger stick and smoked a pipe.

When we arrived at the first village we found about 150 mountain people lined up in front of a cluster of huts. The provincial chief gave them a political harangue, but since he spoke Vietnamese and they had their own dialect, they understood almost nothing of what he said. At the end of his political talk he gave a gift of candy to the village chief.

Then the villagers flocked to the cart and through an interpreter began describing their illnesses. No examinations were given. If someone complained of diarrhea, he received medicine for diarrhea; if he complained of a cough, he received cough medicine; if he complained about headaches, he received medicine for malaria — a three-day supply of medication was given, with instructions to take one dose four times a day. Within 15 minutes or so the medicine show was shut down, and we packed up and drove off to the next village, where the same act was repeated. As we left each village one sergeant would yell to the other: "How many did you see?" And the second GI would answer, "Sixty or seventy."

We visited a total of seven villages and were back in Kontum by 4 P.M.; we had left shortly before 10 A.M. and had taken an hour-and-a-half siesta at lunchtime. During that time we had, in theory, seen and treated 500 patients. I did not feel that anyone had been significantly helped by the venture; but it hadn't occurred to me that anyone could have been harmed.

Later, however, I went back to one of the villages with Pat Smith, who speaks excellent montagnard dialect, and I learned about the aftermath of our visit. In the ignorant, primitive minds of the hill people, it seemed logical that if one pill four times a day for three days was good, all 12 at once would be better, so some villagers swallowed all 12 and got sick and vomited.

19 Mar 67   New York Times, Arnold H. Lubasch

"It's a strange war in a strange country. From the Stateside papers it seems that nobody cares very much either. We don't feel that way over here — we care a lot."

This passage is from a series of letters by Capt. Barbara Anne Smith of Huntington, L. I., an Air Force Nurse serving in South Vietnam. She wrote to Sister Charles Maureen, her former classmate at Mary Immaculate Hospital in Jamaica, Queens.

...''We have a little project here at the hospital called MEDCAP — you know how the government loves abbreviations,'' Captain Smith wrote in one letter. ''I can't remember exactly what it all stands for, but in essence it boils down to a medical team which goes out into the villages dispensing medical aid.

''Most of the villages consist of shacks or grass-roofed huts with a population of roughly 100 to 300. These people have nothing. The incidence of disease is unbelievable.

''We usually set up shop in the largest hut or building and see about 200 patients — they come in from the entire surrounding area. We feel that many are Vietcong sympathizers, if not outright Vietcong, but in a situation like this it is immaterial.

''We wash and redress sores and wounds, pull teeth, give out iron pills, antibiotics, worm pills and soap,'' she wrote.

''Sometimes the patients trade pills if they don't like the ones they got, but since anything we give them would probably help them, we don't get too upset...''

MEDICAL AID TO SOUTH VIETNAM

30 Mar 66   Medical Tribune and Medical News
                  Medical Tribune Staff Report, ''Medicine in Vietnam'': Part IV
                  SAIGON

...The impact that foreign medical aid is making on South Vietnam's health is hard to determine. If the country were at peace, the American Government's strategic concern about it would probably lessen and so, consequently, would its efforts to bring in medical aid. As it is, the United States' public health activities in the country are considerable, but the war itself constantly undermines them.

While USOM's health program seems sizable, the money spent on it is but a minute fraction of what the U. S. Government spends on other projects in South Vietnam. The health program's current budget is about $8,000,000; the military budget to replace aircraft damaged or destroyed in combat operations is $1,800,000,000.

...Before USOM took an interest in them, the province hospitals varied in quality from bad to mediocre. Most of them had — and many still have — only one physician, who might at the same time have one or more medical jobs outside his hospital. Nurses and orderlies were in short supply, wards were overcrowded, sanitation was quixotic, and mortality was high.

In 1962, USOM started financing the construction of surgical suites in 26 province hospitals. The suites — square masonry buildings containing two operating rooms, a five-bed recovery ward, a central supply room, a small toilet, and dressing rooms — were completed in 1964, but several of them have never been used for lack of trained Vietnamese surgeons.

1 Feb 67   New York Times, Neil Sheehan
                  WASHINGTON, Jan 31

A statistical survey in hospitals in South Vietnam during December indicates that the war caused more civilian than military casualties among the South Vietnamese.

To meet this and other critical medical problems in South Vietnam, the United States has doubled its medical aid program there from $21-million in the 1966 fiscal year to $49.6-million for the current fiscal year, which ends next June 30.

The survey, conducted by the United States civilian mission in South Vietnam, informed sources said, showed that of 33,475 civilian patients admitted to all Government hospitals there during December, 7.5 per cent, or 2,510, were wounded as a result of the war.

...Because of administrative chaos and the control of large areas of the country by the Vietcong, no statistics are available on the number of civilians killed by the fighting during the month. But if the same military ratio of two wounded to one dead is applied, a minimum figure of 1,250 civilian dead for the month is reached.

The civilian patients covered by the survey did not encompass all civilian victims for the month since the survey included only those who reached hospitals.

Conditions in South Vietnam make it clear that many others never reach a hospital because of primitive transportation and disruptions of the war. These victims either die without treatment or obtain help at South Vietnamese military outposts or Vietcong field hospitals and dispensaries.

The survey made no attempt to determine who was responsible for wounding the civilians. The wounded included victims of mines and bullets and South Vietnamese and American air attacks. But the majority, it is likely, were wounded by South Vietnamese artillery and air bombardments.

...There are only 1,000 South Vietnamese doctors for a population of 16.5 million. Of these 700 have been drafted.

18 Apr 67   Look, Chandler Brossard

(The editors of Look have declined permission to give the verbatim text of a selection from the above cited article. The following describes the contribution of that selection.)

(Several U.S. officials in Viet Nam admit that the refugee aid program is tokenism. More than 800,000 children are refugees.)

20 Dec 66   William Pepper
             Telephone interview with Hugh Campbell, former Squadron
             Leader and Canadian Delegate to the International Control
             Commission between New York and British Columbia

Mr. Campbell stated that he was in Viet Nam between 1961 and 1963 as a member of the Canadian contingent of the ICC. His duties as a team member caused him to travel in both North and South Viet Nam and to conduct site inspections in both sectors. In the South he inspected the following sites: D.M.Z. (two sites); Nha Trang; Vung Tao; Qui Nhon; and two in Saigon. In his official capacity he had access to official figures with respect to civilian casualties. He estimated that there indeed were some 160,000 civilians killed between 1961 and 1963. Subsequent to his return he has spoken with others who followed him and they have given him the strong impression that the number of civilian casualties has been "increasing greatly" since 1963. With escalation it is inevitable. "I believe that this must be so." When questioned about the ratio of civilian to military casualties, he said that he would speculate that the 10 to 1 civilian to military ratio is more realistic than smaller figures. "I would begin to look around from that figure."

Jan 67   Redbook
          Richard E. Perry, M.D., "Where the Innocent Die"

...Civilian casualties reached such proporations that in several areas the Vietnamese people, long fed up with the war, demonstrated against the American forces. The demonstrations were particularly strong and hostile in Danang in May, 1965, and they embarrassed our government, since our troops are in Vietnam nominally at the request of the Vietnamese people.

As part of an effort to stop the demonstrations, President Johnson in June, 1965, promised massive medical assistance to the Vietnamese civilian casualties. He expected these emergency services to be provided by our military forces. As a result of the rapid increase in American troops at that time, only minimal medical personnel could be spared. The State Department's Agency for International Development could not be of help, either. For several years AID had attempted to provide medical care for the Vietnam population without much success, and now it was in no position to back up the President's promise.

Recognizing the crisis and wanting to do everything possible to relieve the suffering of wounded Vietnamese, project HOPE agreed to undertake a program of recruiting physicians and coordinating medical treatment for civilian casualties. With the cooperation of the American Medical Association and a number of private organizations, and with funds supplied by the State Department, the People-to-People Health Foundation launched Project VIETNAM. An appeal was sent out to American physicians to volunteer for two-month tours of duty, for which they would be paid $10 a day.

...Although legitimate criticism can be made of our announced objectives in Vietnam and of the methods being used to obtain those goals, I as a physician believe it is a moral obligation to assist our government in taking care of Vietnamese civilian casualties.

9 Aug 67   New York Times

A new international medical relief organization will build a 40-bed children's hospital in South Vietnam, under a project to be sponsored by the United States Agency for International Development, South Vietnam and private sources. The hospital, which will provide plastic and rehabilitive surgery, will welcome any child patient in South Vietnam needing such surgery.

22 Sep 67   New York Times, Hedrick Smith
              WASHINGTON, Sept 21

A team of prominent American physicians recommended to President Johnson today that the United States expand its support for South Vietnam's health programs and facilities to provide better care for civilian patients.

..."There simply must be more money spent on the health problem of that country," he asserted. "They spend less than 1 per cent of their budget on health services, less than any country — with or without a war."

In provincial hospitals, which handle the bulk of civilian patients, "you need potable water, better sanitation, reliable power supply, and diagnostic facilities," Dr. Knowles said.

The team's 100-page report and other members individually spoke of similar shortcomings.

Only brief excerpts of the team's report were made public by the Agency for International Development, which financed the team's trip. Some members indicated privately that they were unhappy about the omissions in the Government statement.

...Dr. Knowles estimated that 30 per cent of theVietnamese people had tuberculosis, 80 per cent suffered from "worms of one sort or another" and that 30,000 to 50,000 were amputee cases, some of whom would have to wait five to 15 years for artificial limbs.

10 Oct 67   New York Times, Neil Sheehan
              WASHINGTON, Oct 9

The Agency for International Development intends to reduce its budget for medical aid to South Vietnam this year despite recommendations to the contrary from a team of prominent American physicians who recently surveyed South Vietnamese medical needs.

Dr. John H. Knowles, general director of the Massachusetts General Hospital and a member of the survey team, said in Congressional testimony today that he was disturbed to learn that the agency's medical budget for Vietnam would be reduced.

...Well-informed sources later confirmed the planned reduction in the agency's medical budget for South Vietnam for the current fiscal year.

They said that officials concerned with the program had originally requested $40-million for the 1968 fiscal year, which began July 1. However, these officials were informed by higher authority that the best they could hope for was $27-million and that they might have to settle for $20-million, the sources said.

During the fiscal year of 1967, the agency's medical budget for Vietnam was $31-million. About $21.7-million of this amount was actually spent during the fiscal year because the mission in Vietnam was unable to make arrangements soon enough for the planned construction of additional hospital facilities there.

Officials of the agency believed that they would be able to spend the $40-million originally requested for this year, however, and that the money was needed.

In addition to the agency's program, the Defense Department spent about $15-million on civilian medical work in South Vietnam during the 1967 fiscal year. It plans to spend at least that amount this fiscal year to construct three hospitals with a total capacity of 1,100 beds to care for civilian war casualties.

ATTITUDES TOWARD CIVILIAN VICTIMS OF WAR

5 Feb 67   World Journal Tribune, Jesse W. Lewis, Jr.
             SAIGON, Feb 4

...The medical teams, which work in 41 of the 43 provincial hospitals, reported that 34,000 civilians received treatment for war-connected injuries from September, 1965, through November, 1966.

About 9,000 of them required major surgery for wounds from "small projectiles, bullets or fragments from bombs, shells and grenades." Some required extensive treatment for napalm burns.

"Many injured do not go to hospitals," the AID official said, "and we don't know who cause the injuries — the VC or Americans."

...Some commanders feel "shackled by the elaborate precautions to keep civilian deaths to a minimum."

"What does a commander do when his troops are endangered by fire from a village?" an officer asked.

5 Feb 67   Cleveland Plain Dealer, Jon Bixler

"These people (Vietnamese) are a sorry sight. You wouldn't believe how these people really live and work. Their houses are worse than the worst slum you've ever seen. These people are undernourished and hideous looking. I can see now why they need our help."

These words were written by an American GI six days after he arrived in Vietnam.

...Pfc. Clark Eckenrode wrote to his mother, Mrs. Michael Feranchak, 3550 Raymont Boulevard, University Heights: "I can see why guys go a little crazy over here. The heat, the jungle, all the disease, filth and the people not caring what happens to them...Maybe one of these days people will realize that war doesn't solve problems, just creates more problems...

"Looking at these people, unhealthy, the suffering going on, all the evils of it grows to a guy. Even though these people wouldn't have a slight feeling of kindness for what we're doing we still try to help them. I don't know, maybe what we're doing over here is wrong. I hope we're doing right. Seems the people don't think so."

11 Oct 67   Congressional Record — Senate, S14691
             (U.S. General Accounting Office, Oct 1967)
             Inquiry Concerning the Civilian Health and Casualty Program for
             Vietnam

...An indication of AID's position relative to casualties and health is shown in this excerpt from a Guam Conference briefing paper in March 1967:

"Neither the U.S. Mission in Saigon nor the GVN advocate a radical acceleration in the presently planned steady expansion of the civilian medical assistance effort. They do not consider the present overcrowding of hospitals or limited access to medical treatment in remote areas critical to our success in the political-psychological side of the war effort. They assign much higher priority to improving Vietnamese capacity to respond to popular needs for local security and other aspects of the revolutionary development effort. They have not sought to give hospital construction and airlift priority over certain military requirements which have generally preempted military capacity to meet these civil needs.

MEDICAL CARE FOR U.S. MILITARY

15 Nov 65   New York Times, Seymour Toppings
             CLARK FIELD, THE PHILLIPINES, Nov 14

...The voice crackled in on the hand radios of doctors who stood beside a fleet of ambulances on the concrete runway below. The 173rd Airborne Brigade had suffered heavy casualties in a Vietcong ambush in Zone D north of Saigon and now the wounded were beginning to come in.

Another transport plane from Danang with casualties from the fighting around Pleime was also landing.

This was a typical day for Clark Field Hospital, which receives all the casualties from Vietnam, treats the critical cases and moves the others as quickly as possible by air to military hospitals in Okinawa, Japan, Guam, Hawaii and the United States.

Some of the critically wounded have been on operating tables at Clark Field Hospital six hours after they were hit in combat in Vietnam.

31 Dec 65   Time

...First copter stop may be either a MASH (mobile army surgical hospital) or the division unit. These are fairly close to the scene of action, and are used mainly for grave emergencies in which a ten-minute delay in starting treatment might mean death. Division hospitals average only about ten beds each, with four doctors. Each MASH has 60 beds, along with 80 medical personnel, including ten doctors. Behind these, in turn, are field hospitals and evacuation hospitals — all misnamed, judged by their current functions. In South Viet Nam, there are now two U.S. MASH units and one Korean, three field and two evacuation hospitals, and the Navy's 3rd Medical Battalion.

One recent patient at the 85th Evacuation Hospital in Qui Nhon in the Central Highlands was a first lieutenant whose family does not yet know he has been wounded.

...The lieutenant needed all kinds of doctors, and the 85th had them all. Besides a platoon of general practitioners, it has six general surgeons, two neurosurgeons, two orthopedists, one thoracic and one urologic surgeon, two anesthesiologists, two internal-medicine specialists, two dentists and one psychiatrist; also 39 U.S. Army women nurses and 16 male nurses.

31 Dec 65   Time

...The triage officer looks over the wounded and makes the vital, split-second decisions as to which require immediate surgery, which can wait a few hours, and which need only more first aid.

There was no triage problem in the case of Marine Colonel Michael R. Yunck, 47. As operations officer of the First Marine Air Wing, Yunck had helped to Plan Operation Harvest Moon; later he went out in a four-man armed "Huey" helicopter, directing fighter-bomber attacks south of Danang. He was about to call in a strike on a tiny, nameless hamlet when he looked down. His chopper was low enough for him to see women and children. It was also low enough for a Viet Cong machine gunner to sight in on the Huey. "I knew I couldn't call in a strike," said Yunck soon afterward. "And that was when I got the fifty caliber." Commented a surgeon: "He's going to lose his leg because he was too compassionate."

The slug tore through the Huey's door, smashed both bones in Yunck's left leg, and severed the main artery. A crewman tied a tourniquet below the knee, and the copilot sped the little chopper at 100 m.p.h. to a medical sorting and clearing unit only minutes away. There Yunck received morphine, blood and other intravenous fluids. Then he was flown immediately to Charlie Med. Elapsed time: 35 minutes — five minutes to the clearing station, ten minutes there, 20 minutes to Danang.

16 Aug 66   Armed Forces News Bureau, New York Times
             WASHINGTON

The Army Medical Service has increased available hospital beds in Vietnam from 200 to more than 3,100 within a medical complex there that equals or surpasses that of the war in Korea.

8 Nov 66   New York Times
            CASTLE POINT, NEW YORK, Nov 7

...The 28-year-old veteran is one of 56 South Vietnamese flown here in November, a year ago at President Johnson's request. Their spinal cords had been severed by enemy fire and they were near death from lack of proper medical attention in Vietnam.

...When the men were brought into the Veterans Administration Hospital here on the banks of the Hudson River, each was what medical corpsmen often describe as "last-stop litter cases." But intensive care by specialists has enabled all of the men either to use crutches or move around in a wheelchair.

U.S. OPPOSITION TO MEDICAL RELIEF FOR NORTH VIETNAM

18 Jun 66   (See Note Page 20)
             SAN FRANCISCO, June 18

The U.S. Treasury Department reprimanded the Wells Fargo Bank yesterday for an unlicensed transfer of money to Communist North Viet Nam.

H. Stephen Chase, Wells Fargo President, said it was the result of an unwitting mistake by a clerk.

Early this year the Medical Aid Committee in nearby Berkeley took $1,500 to a bank branch and ordered it sent to the Liberation Red Cross, Chase said. Wells Fargo sent the money to a Swiss bank which deposited it to the Liberation Red Cross account in the Obchodni Bank of Prague, Czechoslovakia.

Chase said, "It was a routine transaction and the clerk checked the prohibitive list furnished by the Treasury and didn't find the Liberation Red Cross on it. As far as we know, it still isn't on the list."

The Treasury says the organization distributes medical aid in North Viet Nam and to the Viet Cong.

In reprimanding the bank, the Treasury said it had blocked the $1,500 in an Obchodni bank account in New York and expected that the Czech bank would deduct the money from the Liberation Red Cross account.

22 Aug 66   Letter from Leo Stern, New York Yearly Meeting of the
             Religious Society of Friends to the President of the United
             States. (from Congressional Record-Appendix, August 30,
             1966, A4587)

...In recent months individual Friends, Friends Meetings and Agencies have undertaken to open channels for the transmission of relief material to war victims in all parts of Vietnam. Friends have now succeeded in establishing such relief operations in South Viet Nam, through the good auspices of the American Friends Service Committee.

However, similar efforts to extend humanitarian relief to the suffering peoples of North Vietnam have encountered considerable difficulty. Friends seeking to mail GIFT parcels of humanitarian relief to the Red Cross Societies of North Vietnam, South Vietnam and the National Liberation Front have experienced a wide variety of responses from local postal clerks ranging from irate rejection to routine acceptance. A visit and interview with Commerce Departmental officials in Washington, D.C., revealed that those parcels addressed to the Red Cross Society of North Vietnam had in all probability been confiscated by Postal or Customs Authorities without notification to the senders.

21 Jan 67　　Toronto Star
　　　　　　　OTTAWA

Trade Minister Robert Winters said in the Commons yesterday the federal government will continue to impress on U.S. authorities the view that Canadian subsidiaries of American firms must obey Canadian laws and not those of a foreign country.

But the minister indicated that no specific action would be taken on the case of American-owned drug firms who are prohibited by American law from selling medical supplies for shipment to North Vietnam.

...Winters was reporting on his investigation into material contained in a Washington dispatch in The Toronto Star Thursday.

The article quoted the chief counsel of the foreign assets control branch of the U.S. treasury department as citing regulations which prohibit American-owned subsidiaries in Canada from supplying material for North Vietnam.

...Winters made his statements during the question period as the government appeared heading for a confrontation with U.S. authorities over several aspects of alleged American control of Canadian business.

A few minutes later, Prime Minister Pearson said the government was not concerned with possible retaliation by the U.S. in the field of banking legislation.

21 Jan 67　　Toronto Star, Robert Reguly
　　　　　　　WASHINGTON

The U.S. government has signalled a harder crackdown on all Quaker medical aid through Canada to North Vietnam.

The normally reticent state department last night issued a statement threatening to stop the aid that sympathetic Americans had sent legally to North Vietnam.

The statement denounced as illegal the money being sent by American Quakers to Toronto Quakers without first obtaining a government license. Now, the state department is threatening to have such licenses abolished.

The Toronto group buys medical supplies with the money and says it divides it equally among South Vietnam, North Vietnam, and the Viet Cong.

U.S. Quakers say they are forced to sidestep the law because the state department has been sitting for months on applications to send money legally to Toronto. They say it is immoral to wait while the war's victims suffer.

...The 6,800 member New York Yearly Meeting of Friends defied the government — and risks arrest of its courier — after vainly waiting three months for government approval of the money transfer.

The foreign affairs department statement lamented that "certain Americans have attempted to violate these regulations by sending money to the Canadian Friends' Service Committee for North Vietnam without the necessary license."

...The state department is reported by the Quakers to be holding up applications covering $40,000.

The last license authorizing U.S. Quakers to send money to Toronto was issued Oct. 12, 1966. On that license, $1,000 was sent.

Since then, the treasury has sat on applications for licenses, not only from Quakers but from other religious and humanitarian organizations. None has been issued to any group.

...The diplomatic statement also mildly criticized the Royal Bank of Canada for cashing American cheques payable to Toronto Quakers.

Reviewing communications with the bank's New York agency, the department said it asked Royal to "refrain from handling unlicensed remittances. The bank declined to do so."

It said the bank offered to handle the cheques on a "collection basis" — that is, refusing to pay money until the cheque had gone back to the American issuing bank and had been cleared.

The U.S. Treasury agreed, provided the cheques were accompanied by a note warning the U.S. bank that cashing them might be illegal under U.S. law.

"The Royal Bank refused to follow this procedure," the statement said. "The Treasury therefore has instructed all American banks not to pay any collection item of this nature without a Treasury license."

22 Jan 67   New York Times, John M. Lee
            TORONTO, Jan 21

Reports of United States efforts to prevent Toronto Quakers from shipping drugs to North Vietnam have touched off a political uproar in Canada.

...Government leaders were peppered with questions in Parliament yesterday concerning United States restrictions on Canadian subsidiaries of American drug companies, and concerning a United States request that the Royal Bank of Canada refrain from handling illegal remittances from United States residents to the Toronto group.

...The criticism in Ottawa was precipitated by comments made earlier in the week to Canadian reporters in Washington by Stanley Sommerfield, chief counsel of the Treasury's Office of Foreign Assets Control.

...Mr. Sommerfield said the Royal Bank, Canada's largest and the depository for the Toronto Quakers, had agreed to accept United States checks made out to the Quaker group on a "collection basis" — that is, it would return the check directly to the issuing bank and not credit it for payment until the check had been cleared.

He said the bank had refused to attach a note saying the remittances were illegal and suggesting that the United States banks determine whether they could be liable to prosecution. The Treasury then instructed some 14,000 United States banks not to honor the checks. This occurred last autumn.

28 Feb 67   New York Times
            WASHINGTON, Feb 27

The Treasury announced today that it would deny all applications to send dollars to such organizations as the Canadian Friends Service Committee for the purchase of medical supplies to be shipped to North Vietnam.

The reason it gave was that Hanoi had refused permission to foreign relief agencies to make the customary supervision of the distribution of the supplies to be sure they went to civilians.

4 Mar 67   New York Times, Farnsworth Fowle

Quaker groups are continuing to send medical aid to North Vietnam through the Canadian Friends Service Committee despite the Treasury Department's ban this week on all applications to send money abroad for this purpose.

...Mr. Stern said the reason given by the Treasury for deciding to deny all future applications for this purpose — that Hanoi had refused permission for foreign relief agencies to make sure the supplies went to civilians — seemed "rather unfounded".

According to Mr. Stern, the Canadian organization turns over medical supplies to the local Red Cross in both North and South Vietnam and both are members of the International Red Cross.

...One Quaker relief group that has already had its bank accounts frozen because of aid to North Vietnam, the Vietnam Relief Program of the Quaker Action Group of Philadelphia, is considering a test of the right of the United States Government to take such action.

THE "TERRE DES HOMMES" AFFAIR

14 Sep 66   The Christian Century
              Marjorie Hope, "Vietnam's Wounded Waifs"

...Terre des Hommes is an international nonpolitical, nondenominational organization founded in 1960 for immediate help to child victims of war. Between 1961 and 1965, it placed 1,159 children (most of whom had been wounded in the Algerian war) in clinical institutions and foster homes. It has never criticized U.S. military policy in Vietnam but has limited itself to humanitarian aid. The organization needs funds to support the work of a nurse who is seeking out seriously wounded or burned children, for a clinic it expects to open in Saigon, for an intensive care center at the Nhi-Dong hospital, and for pharmaceutical products now being sent to two of its doctors in Kontum. At the moment, however, the most pressing need is for planes to transport drugs, doctors, and children.

31 Jan 66   Letter from Terre des Hommes to the White House

Mr. Chester L. Cooper
THE WHITE HOUSE
WASHINGTON, D.C. (U.S.A.)

Dear Sir:

I have the honor to acknowledge receipt of your letter of the 17th inst., the text of which constitutes the reply of the United States government to the requests we have made on behalf of Vietnamese children who have been cruelly stricken by the war. This reply calls for the following comments:
...(The United States Government letter states:)
3. "The most effective way of extending assistance is on the scene in South Vietnam where children and others can be treated near their families and in familiar surroundings."
Our viewpoint differs from yours:
a) To help "on the scene" may appear the most logical plan of action, but it is not therefore, the most "effective." For the "effective" way of extending assistance is actually to save victims through supplying treatment truly suited to the nature of the malady, under the safest technical conditions, with the aid of a sufficient number of highly specialized medical and paramedical personnel (in plastic surgery, for example). They must have modern equipment which is is indispensable, and sanitary conditions that have nothing in common with the horrors of the Vietnamese hospitals we have visited (only one in four is an exception).
The "most effective" manner of saving burned or wounded children who have been insufficiently treated, not treated, or who are untreatable on the scene is obviously then to save them elsewhere, with medical and surgical procedures which are suitable and which modern science makes available.
We would further note that, according to information received from the most trustworthy authorized sources, a very great number of these wounded and burned children are not in hospitals, but are suffering (or dying) "at private homes," either because they cannot be transported to hospitals, or because overcrowded hospitals cannot receive them, or because the hospitals have no facilities for giving them proper care; care that would be dangerous in any event because of a total lack of sanitation facilities. This lack of sanitation is often accompanied by an absence of the most elementary equipment: fans, air-conditioners, protection against flies, etc.

b) The families of these children are frequently absent, far away, wounded themselves, dead or missing.

c) As for their "familiar surroundings," these may be only a straw hut or a village where one suffers or dies without assistance, or else those hospitals whose indescribable destitution makes them veritable charnel-houses for the living.

Two Dutch doctors whom we did not know made a trip to Vietnam shortly after we did, made the same observations as we did, and drew the same conclusions: there is no possibility, on the scene and in the immediate circumstances, of being able really to cope with all the problems. This explains the favorable response with which General J. and his colleagues have received our movement's program.

... (The United States Government letter states:)

<u>5</u>. "U.S. Military aircraft cannot be provided for airlift to Europe of Vietnamese children who may need medical treatment, and no United States funds are available to support your activities in Europe."

The members of our movement — and the world will share our feelings — experience some difficulty in picturing the United States unable to furnish aircraft which might be used to transport our children, or without the financial means to support our activities in Europe, that is, to finance the chartering of an airplane. We have never asked for funds from the United States, but simply for the loan of one or several military hospital planes, or the offer of unoccupied places in American planes.

(The United States Government letter states:)

<u>6</u>. "We were somewhat surprised to learn that at a press conference on January 12 in Geneva you were reported as having stated that the U.S. Government response to your request for U.S. military aircraft to airlift needy Vietnamese children to Europe is not to be considered finally negative."

At the time of that conference, I declared: "I cannot bring myself to consider as absolutely negative the reply which a member of the Department of State gave us, in the name of the U.S. government."

Here are the reasons for that declaration, whose optimism will be either justified or disappointed by the future:

a) I was not able (and I am not able) to keep myself from hoping, indeed from being certain, that the American people are prepared to furnish aircraft or funds for the rescue from Vietnam of burned or wounded children who at this moment cannot be saved in their own land.

b) I have good reason not to forget that part of the world owes its liberation from Hitlerian executioners to the American people. Thus, for reasons of discretion, and so to speak, in the name of the American people, I did not dare to admit publicly to the press of the world that the U.S. government has answered "NO" to the request of Terre des Homes.

(The United States Government letter states:)

<u>7</u>. "U.S. aircraft are definitely not available for this purpose."

The American military air force includes hospital planes. And even if we admit that they are not available for the transportation of burned and wounded children, it would be in keeping with the humanitarian obligation towards these children of the American government and people to make these planes available.

(The United States Government letter states:)

<u>8</u>. "Since neither U.S. aircraft nor U.S. funds are available in support of the activities which you plan to undertake in Europe, your plan is a matter to be decided upon by your organization and the Government of South Vietnam."

Even if American aircraft and American funds cannot be used in the rescue work which has been undertaken, and taking account of the reception given by the Government of the Republic of Vietnam to the program of Terre des Hommes, we deem it useful to emphasize that our plans are far from being limited to the concerns of that government and our organization.

Indeed, without making any judgment at all on the direction of this war, we feel that the armed forces of the United States, involved in acts which have mutilated our little ones, can in no way shed that involvement when it is an urgent question of saving the lives of those children. At the very moment when it is both possible and necessary to lend support, the U.S. armed forces cannot content themselves with falling back on an organization without aircraft and without large financial support or on the government of an unfortunate people.

In conclusion, in order that you may have the opportunity to express publicly the surprise occasioned by my declaration at our press conference, I am releasing to the international press copies of the correspondence between the U.S. Government and Terre des Hommes, together with a memorandum on our activity. All items are reproduced in full, without additions, deletions or commentary; only the names of the American General and Officers favorable to our plans are replaced by initials.

With the conviction that the people and government of the United States will want to assist Terre des Hommes to rescue a large number of wounded and burned Vietnamese children, may I assure, you, Sir, of my most respectful and cordial sentiments.

TERRE DES HOMMES
(Signed: spokesman for Terre des Hommes)

Jun 66   Terre des Hommes, Lausanne, Switzerland
            "Vietnamese Children in Fire and Blood"

Introduction

A letter from the International Red Cross Committee (IRCC) to Terre des Hommes (9 - 2 - 1965) mentioned the Vietnamese provincial hospitals "crowded with wounded, particularly people suffering from extremely severe burns. There are among these many civilians and therefore many children." Burns and wounds resulted from bombs, bullets, grenades, napalm, phosphorous, flares.

2) Terres des Hommes simultaneously and in identical terms established contact with the government of the Vietnamese Republic (South), with the representative of the NLF (Vietcong) in Algiers, and with the government of the Democratic Republic of Vietnam (North). It offered to each its immediate and direct help to Vietnamese children who were burnt or wounded and cannot be cared for properly in their present location.

3) The government of the Democratic Republic of Vietnam (North) did not answer this offer. The representative of the NLF's response (received after three month's delay) expressed only the desire that Terre des Hommes should make a protest with a political character. Only the government of South Vietnam gave enthusiastic support to our proposal.

4) A representative of Terre des Hommes met twice with Mr. Maunoir and Mr. Durand, delagetes of the IRCC, who expressed approval of the projects of Terre des Hommes (treatment in Europe or elsewhere of children seriously hurt but not treated, or not treatable locally). At the same time they asked their colleagues in Saigon to open the doors of the public health and social action ministries as well as of the Vietnamese Red Cross to Terre des Hommes.

5) Terre des Hommes then contacted (10-15-66) a representative of the State Department (Washington) at the United States Mission in Geneva, who was relatively open to our plans and asked to see us again upon our return from Vietnam. He recommended strongly that we contact Dr. J. who is an American General there.

6) Terre des Hommes reserved hospital beds in different countries (Switzerland, Austria, Germany, Belgium, Luxembourg, Holland, Denmark) and the delegates, upon their departure to Vietnam already had "in their pocket" about 400 beds. The expense of hospitalization was assumed by Terre des Hommes.

...b) Visit in Vietnam

1) In the course of numerous encounters and official interviews (minister of public health, highly placed health officials, Vietnamese heads of medical

departments and hospitals, American military doctors) our projects were unanimously well received. The reason for this unanimity is the obvious impossibility in a large number of cases of practicing locally any type of really efficient medicine or serious surgery (especially orthopedic surgery) because of lack of facilities and personnel.

2) Besides orphanages and baby centers, which take in innumerable children, who are starving, very seriously ill or abandoned, we visited four provincial hospitals. Only one of these (Rach-Gia) which benefits from the presence of an American medical team, seems to operate normally. The three other hospitals (Hue, Cantho, Mytho — but particularly Hue) show the frightening spectacle of an immense distress: To the extent that one finds children burned from head to foot who are treated only with vaseline, because of lack of a) ointment for burns, b) cotton, c) gauze, d) personnel. In places, with the atmosphere of slaughter houses for people, where flies circulate freely on children who have been skinned alive, there are no facilities for hygiene, no fans, and no air conditioning. We know, from reliable sources, that this extreme lack of facilities is repeated in many Vietnamese hospitals. This latter information was given to us by competent specialists or official people. One of them, the head doctor of a large hospital, told us: "I have received many representatives from diverse institutions, but, before you, none even asked to see a single child."

3) It is important to be very conscious of the fact that most of the children who are wounded, burned or sick are not in hospitals (treated in hospitals). This is because they are never found, because there is no means of transportation, or because of non-existent medical or para-medical personnel and the lack of specialized equipment or sanitary facilities. There children suffer and die without care, "at home," in villages, in straw huts, etc.

4) Out of a total of 500 (800 or 1000) Vietnamese doctors only 200 minister to the needs of the civilian population (14 million) which amounts to only a little more than one doctor per 100,000 people (end of October, 1965). The other doctors are used for military needs.

5) About the same time, a little bit later, and independently of Terre des Hommes, two Dutch doctors visited Vietnam. One of them was a specialist in plastic surgery, and the other an internist. Here are extracts from texts that were published upon their return in the Dutch press: "It is indescribable. Thousands of people suffering from untended burns arrive from the interior of the country. Nobody takes care of these unfortunate people because no one seems to know what could be done. In Vietnam, one encounters all the forms of infectious diseases and their complications. Every tenth South Vietnamese suffers from tuberculosis. Numerous types of sickness are not treated. There is an unimaginable number of people suffering from war wounds. The few existing hospitals are overflowing with pateints. It is not rare that three people share the same bed. There are practically no nurses. Most people are tended by members of their own family, who usually sleep in the hospital itself, under the bed or next to it, anywhere where they can find room. No efficient treatment of burns is used."

...8) Conclusion

a) Efficient medical and serious surgical procedures in local areas are impossible in the present circumstances, depending upon cases and location;

b) Not only in the hospitals, but everywhere, it is urgent to detect sick, wounded or burnt children who are unattended or insufficiently cared for;

c) Relevance of the Terre des Hommes projects: transportation to Europe, Thailand, and other countries of children who have been found to need care. The existing national and international help will remain for a long time incapable of coping with all cases;

d) It is illusory to imagine that external initiatives, even powerful ones, could create from nothing, a sufficient number of hospitals perfectly provided with rigging (beds, nursing and medical personnel, supplies, and equipment). The present Terre des Hommes project is not new for this organization.

Several years of experience have proven that it is just, humane, and efficient to treat elsewhere those who because they are not attended to, where they are, suffer, wither or die. It is another illusion to wait hopefully but helplessly until "others" (governments, institutions) should "do something." Even if this "something" is presently beginning to show signs of life, although for the time being the immense and intense need cannot be met.

e) For financial reasons, it is necessary to have at our disposal free airplanes or free places in airplanes with unoccupied seats.

f) One or several competent and permanent representatives of Terre des Hommes should be sent to Vietnam.

Present Conditions

...5) Because it was impossible to contact the delegate of the State Department who, according to General J., is the only "competent" official Terre des Hommes wrote to President Johnson in order to obtain his personal intervention; transmission of this request was confirmed by the chief of the U.S. Mission in Geneva, following which, the much-desired encounter between the representative of Terre des Hommes and the representative of the State Department finally took place. But he is opposed to any cooperation with Terre des Hommes under the desired conditions. American help could eventually be obtained if the Terre des Hommes organization limited its efforts to local work, Therefore, in spite of the competent support of General J for the Terre des Hommes project, we shall not have the assistance of military medical planes to aid the wounded, burned or sick Vietnamese children whom we wish to help.

Notes

...2) We are all in agreement with respect to the principle that local work is most desirable, but who has done it efficiently and sufficiently since the beginning of the war? Was there any action from those who could do something, continue to be able to do something or preach action? To organize local hospitals would be the logical and wise thing to do. But who would make the plans, draw the blueprints, supervise the construction? When? Where? And how much time would it take? Where are the funds, the supplies, the equipment, and the personnel? Where can one find large numbers of available and highly trained specialists? How many are there? Where are the necessary army of male and female nurses? If it is so easy to save locally by modern means thousands of burned, wounded, and sick people, children as well as adults, why has this not already been done? Now as in the past centuries, whenever horrors beyond measure are encountered, it is affirmed that "someone is going to do something about it, somewhere." Terre des Hommes has chosen to save immediately, by available means, those little ones that can be saved. There exists an irremediable difference between the notion of working "on the scene" and the need for saving people right now.

6 Jun 66   Letter from Malcolm E. Phelps, M.D., A.M.A. Field Director, Project Viet Nam, to Mrs. Janet Neuman, Women's Strike for Peace; Washington, D.C.

Dear Mrs. Neuman:

I have just received your letter and appeal and have noted your plan to fly injured Vietnamese children to Europe for treatment. This plan is so impractical that it would be ludicrous if it was not such a serious situation.

Have you ever been to Viet Nam? Do you have any idea of the family ties that exist in the oriental people and how they would resent being separated from their children?

Recently the American Medical Association has assumed the duties of operating "Project Viet Nam". In this project American doctors are volunteering their services and going to Viet Nam so that the civilians will have medical care. These American doctors donate their time and their talents and accept the hardships in this humane effort. Since September more than one hundred doctors have donated at least two months of their time in this endeavor. At the present time more than five hundred are on the waiting list and many will soon be in Viet Nam.

On July 1, I am leaving for Viet Nam and plan to stay there six months in an attempt to implement the program.

The moral and financial support of organizations, such as yours could really make a contribution if they would assist in "Project Viet Nam". If you have any constructive suggestions we will be glad to hear from you and I do solicit your support.

Yours very truly,
Malcolm E. Phelps, M.D.

12 July 66   York, Pa. Gazette and Daily, Jane Armstrong (from the Toronto
              Daily Star)
              LONDON

Two little faceless children from Vietnam, sent here for free plastic surgery at the famous McIndoe Burns Center, have aroused all Britain to the horrors of a war in which the innocent and young seem to be the chief victims of napalm, grenades and saturation bombing.

...Yet politics in South Vietnam almost prevented the first group of injured children leaving there too. When Swiss philanthropist Edmund Kaiser, founder of Terre des Hommes, asked for help by U.S. military transport, American generals in the area at first backed the idea as good propaganda. But the final decision, like the others in the Vietnam war, was made in the White House by the president. The answer was "No." Although the Americans airlift wounded Vietnamese soldiers, their policy is that civilian casualties should depend for treatment on foreign medical teams sent in.

...Within two weeks both children had a first successful operation to restore their upper eyelids. Luan had extra surgery to free his chin which had "melted" into his neck so that he could not close his mouth. Now he can. A Vietnamese girl student flew from Geneva for a few days so that the youngsters would not be frightened on awakening to find their eyes blindfolded.

...There is, inevitable, some mystery as to who these children are and how they were chosen from thousands of other needy cases. There is only one children's hospital in South Vietnam where patients lie two in a bed and the death rate is depressingly high.

The Vietnam embassy, also in the dark, is sending reports on all the children to Saigon where it is hoped the ministry of social welfare finds it possible to inform relatives. No one can say what will happen to Luan, the orphan. There are at least 30,000 known children like him without anyone to care if they live or die. Lady Sainsbury hopes to bring over orphans for adoption here.

Letter from Rutherford M. Poats, Assistant Administrator, Far East - Department of State, Agency for International Development, Washington, D.C. to the Honorable Daniel K. Inouye, United States Senate, Washington, D.C.

September 3, 1966

Dear Senator Inouye:

Your letter of August 5 to President Johnson expressing concern for the suffering of the civilian population of Vietnam has been referred to this office for further study and comment.

As you are aware, the United States Government, through its AID program, is supporting an extensive program of medical assistance to Vietnam, designed both to upgrade the standard of medical practice and to alleviate the sufferings of civilian victims of war and disease. At present, we are supporting over 700 medical and paramedical personnel engaged primarily in the care and treatment of Vietnamese civilians. Included in this number are forty-two medical assistance teams, seventeen of which are from other Free World nations, deployed throughout the country.... Also included in this number are thirty-two volunteer American doctors who serve two-month tours in Vietnam under the Volunteer Physicians Program. In the course of the past year, extensive renovations have been carried out at ten provincial hospitals, and we have launched a program to improve the facilities of several more. Our expenditure for medical supplies alone will amount to almost $40 million this fiscal year. In addition, we are supporting a number of other activities of a longer term nature such as medical education, malaria control, urban sanitation and immunization....

Your concern over the inadequate care for child victims is especially understandable. This is a problem of great concern to us. One important step which has been taken in this area is the recent assignment to the Childrens Hospital in Saigon of a British team of pediatric specialists which is committed to serve there for five years. It is hoped that they will be able to improve the care available to children throughout the country by their example and the influence which they can exert through teaching.

We are especially glad that you agree with the Administration as to the desirability of treating sick and injured children in their own environment. From experience gained in Korea, and more recently from the observations of our doctors in Vietnam, we have concluded that by removing a sick child from his family and placing him in a strange environment, his powers of recuperation may be seriously impaired, quite apart from any psychological trauma he may sustain. This is particularly important in view of the strong family ties which prevail in the Vietnamese culture. Another reason for treating as many cases as possible in country is that we are trying to upgrade the standard of medical practice in Vietnam. We believe that by performing medical procedures there, we can teach the Vietnamese doctors and nurses what it is possible to do and thereby encourage them to do it for themselves. Moreover, because it is infinitely more expensive to bring patients to the United States for treatment than to treat them in their country, we feel that we can accomplish a great deal more with the combined public and private resources which may be available if we concentrate our efforts in Vietnam.

...In summary, we believe that the deplorable lack of medical care which has been brought to your attention is rapidly being corrected. Foreign medical teams and doctors whom we are in varying degree supporting are treating nearly 2 million needy patients in Vietnam each month, four or five times the scale of direct medical service available only a few months ago. Further improvements are being made every day.

Sincerely yours,
Rutherford M. Poats
Assistant Administrator, Far East

9 Jan 67   Boston Sunday Globe (Editorial)

It is exciting and heart-warming news that a nationwide "Committee of Responsibility" is being formed to bring war-wounded South Vietnamese children to this country for medical treatment. This organization, which includes some of Boston's most distinguished medical men, will be formally unveiled Wednesday in Washington.

Thousands of burned and mutilated children — many of them the unintended victims of American war-making — roam the South Vietnamese countryside and cannot be properly cared for where they are, doctors say.

The project, of course, cannot get off the ground without the help of the U.S. Government, which would have to provide transportation and authorize visas.

One doctor says skeptically, "There is obviously a reluctance on the part of our government to have these hideously burned children before the public in this country."

But it is inconceivable that our government would turn down this great humanitarian project for propaganda reasons! Besides, nothing could do more to improve the standing of the United States in the eyes of the world that for it to welcome these unfortunates to our shores. President Johnson should give this project his enthusiastic and unqualified approval.

24 Nov 67   Reuters, New York Post
             GENEVA

Thirty South Vietnamese children suffering from heart conditions, polio or wounds and burns in the war arrived here today for treatment.

The children, between 4 and 16, were brought from Saigon by the Swiss charitable organization Terre des Hommes.

...The organization has taken care of 170 South Vietnamese children and has found treatment for them in Britain, Italy, The Netherlands and West Germany.

15 Aug 67   New York Times

Dr. Herbert Needleman, chairman of a national committee that has sought to bring injured Vietnamese children to the United States for medical treatment, said yesterday that he and a colleague returned from Saigon last Wednesday after having been thwarted in their efforts by South Vietnamese governmental red tape.

...In a telephone interview, Dr. Needlemen, reporting on the civilian hospitals he and Dr. Ervin visited in the northernmost combat zone, said that flies were crawling in patients' open wounds of patients.

"Typhoid cases and other cases of other communicable diseases were placed in beds next to patients who had been operated on." he declared.

CHAPTER XVI
THE SEIZURE AND DESTRUCTION
OF MEDICAL RESOURCES

The following Articles from International Conventions relevant to this chapter are quoted in full:

Geneva Convention
for the Amelioration of the Condition
of the Wounded and Sick in Armed Forces in the Field
12 August 1949
Article 19.

Fixed establishments and mobile medical units of the Medical Service may in no circumstances be attacked, but shall at all times be respected and protected by the Parties to the conflict. Should they fall into the hands of the adverse Party, their personnel shall be free to pursue their duties, as long as the capturing Power has not itself ensured the necessary care of the wounded and sick found in such establishments and units.

The responsible authorities shall ensure that the said medical establishments and units are, as far as possible, situated in such a manner that attacks against military objectives cannot imperil their safety.

Article 21.

The protection to which establishments and mobile medical units of the Medical Service are entitled shall not cease unless they are used to commit, outside their humanitarian duties, acts harmful to the enemy. Protection may, however, cease only after a due warning has been given, naming, in all appropriate cases, a reasonable time limit, and after such warning has remained unheeded.

Article 22.

The following conditions shall not be considered as depriving a medical unit or establishment of the protection guaranteed by Article 19:

(1) That the personnel of the unit or establishment are armed, and that they use the arms in their own defense, or in that of the wounded and sick in their charge.

(2) That in the absence of armed orderlies, the unit or establishment is protected by a picket or by sentries or by an escort.

(3) That small arms and ammunition taken from the wounded and sick and not yet handed to the proper service, are found in the unit or establishment.

(4) That personnel and material of the veterinary service are found in the unit or establishment, without forming an integral part thereof.

(5) That the humanitarian activities of medical units and establishments or of their personnel extend to the care of civilian wounded or sick.

Article 33.

The material of mobile medical units of the armed forces which fall into the hands of the enemy, shall be reserved for the care of wounded and sick.

The buildings material and stores of fixed medical establishments of the armed forces shall remain subject to the laws of war, but may not be diverted from their purpose as long as they are required for the care of wounded and sick. Nevertheless, the commanders of forces in the field may make use of them, in case of urgent military necessity, provided that they make previous arrangements for the welfare of the wounded and sick who are nursed in them.

The material and stores defined in the present Article shall not be intentionally destroyed.

---

30 Mar 65   New York Times, Jack Langguth
                SAIGON, SOUTH VIETNAM, March 29

...In the war in South Vietnam meanwhile, Government troops discovered a major Vietcong camp 60 miles northwest of Saigon, in Tayninh Province. It included 72 huts, 4 training schools, 5 dispensaries and 12 kitchens.

Supplies and rations that were confiscated included 440 pounds of dried fish, 200 rounds of .45-caliber ammunition, 1,000 grenades, 150 large antitank mines and 440 pounds of medical supplies.

14 May 65   (See Note Page 20)
                SAIGON, May 14

...An air strike was called in Thursday night on suspected Viet Cong concentrations in a region near the town of Song Be.

...By 4:30 A.M. the spokesman said, government forces had taken their objective, leaving 39 Viet Cong dead and 48 captured, with no friendly losses.

Six individual Viet Cong weapons were seized there along with a quantity of medical supplies.

30 Jun 65   The Evening Star (Washington) (See Note Page 20)
                SAIGON, June 30

It is a hard fact of war in South Viet Nam that hospitals become a target for both sides.

Vietnamese troops rate the destruction of a Viet Cong hospital probably higher than anything short of killing Viet Cong troops.

The Viet Cong shoot at medical helicopters with big red crosses on their sides, or mortar public hospitals.

Government forces destroyed a Viet Cong hospital near Tan Hiep about 45 miles south of Saigon Sunday, and took 12 patients as prisoners.

They burned the thatched roof structures, after destroying cases of penicillin, bandages and other medical equipment.

This complex of hospital buildings lay near the Plain of Reeds, a vast expanse of waterlogged terrain that is used extensively by the Viet Cong.

With U.S. air support, Government forces pounced on a meeting of top Communist officials being held there, killing seven of them, U.S. military sources said.

The hospital was a complex of 12 thatch buildings, serving as regular hospital wards, a surgery and an outpatient clinic.

The buildings were hidden under coconut trees. It appeared to be essentially a military hospital, but some civilian patients were reported being treated there.

The building complex looked like a rear hospital for Viet Cong troops wounded in heavy military engagements in the 7th Division area, which stretches around the town of My Tho.

"This installation is as important to the Viet Cong as weapons," one U.S. advisor said, while discussing the destruction of a similar type of hospital in Tay Ninh Province earlier this year.

"Here is where they return to get treated. From here they go back to the battlefield. By destroying this complex, we can help demoralize all the Viet Cong forces."

Many Viet Cong troops wounded in action are left in friendly villages for treatment, and only the most serious cases reach hospitals.

25 Jul 65   New York Times (See Note Page 20)
SAIGON, SOUTH VIETNAM, July 24

...When the Vietcong guerrillas fight, they face a conventional force armed with heavy artillery, fighter-bombers and other weapons with enormous destructive power. Such weapons tend to kill more than they wound.

The Vietcong wounded-to-killed ratio is also reduced by the fact that many injured Vietcong guerrillas die for lack of medical facilities. While the Vietcong have a few field surgeons and some nurses and corpsmen, conditions in the jungle are primitive.

Vietcong surgeons must operate in thatched huts, where even the routine of sterilizing instruments becomes a major problem. The Vietcong are critically short of drugs, particularly antibiotics. Some drugs reach the guerrillas from North Vietnam and others are smuggled from pharmacies in Saigon.

But a badly wounded Vietcong guerrilla stands little chance of surviving.

24 Aug 65   (See Note Page 20)
GENEVA, Aug. 24

The Viet Cong guerrillas in Viet Nam are trying to replenish their dwindling medical supplies through the International Red Cross.

Red Cross headquarters here sent out appeals to branches throughout the world for shipments of antibiotics, blood plasma, transfusion and surgical equipment and bandages for the guerrilla units in embattled Viet Nam.

The appeal went out after the request for aid was received from the Viet Cong through the British Red Cross. The request apparently followed months of indirect negotiations for help.

The Red Cross said in a statement that so far Communist North Viet Nam has not requested any help for war victims or refugees.

Yesterday the Red Cross announced it has earmarked equal sums of 50,000 Swiss francs ($11,600) each for aid to war victims in North and South Viet Nam.

The decision was taken "in view of the extension of the conflict and the undoubtedly growing number of victims," a Red Cross announcement said. At the same time, the organization offered to channel all gifts and contributions to war victims in both Viet Nams.

22 Sep 65   UPI, Philadelphia Inquirer
                 SAIGON, Sept. 22

Allied forces sweeping a Viet Cong hideout 40 miles northwest of Saigon uncovered an abandoned 200-bed Communist hospital and an ammunition factory in addition to bagging a dozen guerrillas and 44 suspects, a military spokesman said Wednesday.

...In the giant Allied sweep 40 miles northwest of the city, units of the 173rd Airborne Brigade uncovered a hospital capable of handling about 200 patients, the military spokesman said. The heavily camouflaged complex of 25 buildings, underground tunnels and a firing range, was unoccupied when located.

Huge quantities of medical supplies and some Vietcong documents were seized and carried out by helicopter. Paratroopers destroyed the installation.

14 Oct 65   New York Times, Neil Sheehan
                SAIGON, Oct. 13

Vietcong guerrillas, after fighting an all-night delaying action, disappeared today after having prevented United States troops from overrunning a first aid station until it had been evacuated.

Military sources said a battalion of guerrillas had, for 12 hours, kept a battalion of the First Cavalry Division (Airmobile) out of the ravine where the station was situated. Shortly after dawn, the Vietcong force vanished into the seemingly impenetrable hills. All the wounded guerrillas who were being treated at the station were evacuated (sic).

When the Americans finally pushed into the ravine they found nothing but pools of blood and trenches so well concealed they were invisible from the air.

Dec 65   Ramparts
              Bernard Fall, "This Isn't Munich, It's Spain"

...In this war, there is no respect for hospitals, either. I saw a South Vietnamese civilian ambulance which had been raked with machine gun fire by the Viet Cong. All four patients and the driver were killed inside. This sort of brutality has become normal on both sides: Joseph Alsop reported recently, unblinkingly, that there had been three Viet Cong hospitals destroyed in Zone D along with "vast stocks of medicine." This followed on complaints from the North, now verified by non-Communist outside observers, that at least one hospital had been completely destroyed by bombers. Canadian officials who recently returned from North Vietnam also told me that the city of Vinh was "flattened." It used to have a population of 60,000. I can't believe that the whole city was a "military objective."

22 Jan 66   (See Note Page 20)
                PLEIKU, Jan. 22

"Where's Charlie?"

This question has been nagging thousands of sweating, dust-stained American soldiers for weeks as they scoured the jungles along the frontiers of neighboring Cambodia.

They found plenty of signs that Charlie — nickname for the Communist enemy — had been there, sometimes only hours before. Supplies of rice, salt, ammunition and medicines were captured or destroyed.

22 Feb 66   New York Times, Neil Sheehan

...Vietcong regulars have been fighting troops of the First Cavalry Division (Airmobile) in the area for four days, military sources said.

...The small patch of jungle, surrounded by steep slopes, is located on the edge of the so-called Crow's Foot region in Bindinh Province.

...The military sources said that five miles farther north today the division's first brigade discovered a 70-bed Vietcong jungle hospital and captured 400 pounds of medical supplies. The Americans also killed six guerrillas found nearby.

28 Feb 66   (See Note Page 20)
            BONG SON, VIETNAM, Feb. 28

There was only one way for Alpha Company to capture hospital hill: A frontal assault. And that's the way Alpha Company took it this afternoon.

The way up led through dense thicket, thorns, and creepers. Every few yards was a Viet Cong bunker or a fresh grave. In the bunkers were wounded Communists left behind to fight to the death.

Men of Alpha Company of the 2nd Battalion 8th Cavalry Regiment counted 17 Viet Cong bodies on the hill where the 18th North Vietnamese regiment had set up its hospital to nurse men wounded by the U.S. 1st Air Cavalry Division during a month-long onslaught around Bong Son, about 280 miles northeast of Saigon.

The hill's defenders hit Alpha Company with automatic fire Sunday afternoon as it moved into the hospital's kitchen and operating theater set up in bamboo and thatched huts. One cavalryman was slightly wounded before Alpha Company withdrew a short distance to let artillery do some work.

Helicopters smothered the hill with tear gas. After dark, a flare ship lit up the hill for strike bombers with napalm. After a final, intensive artillery barrage, Capt. Thomas Forman from Twenty Nine Palms, Calif., ordered his men forward this morning. American automatic rifle fire punctuated their advance. But then a long burst sounded a different note. "Machine gun," shouted one soldier as the company vanished into the jungle floor.

More shooting, then an order. "Let's get moving," Forman yelled.

Soldiers clambered upward cautiously to the hidden bunkers, firing as they climbed. Many Viet Cong defenders didn't get a chance to use their weapons.

Halfway up the 200-foot-high hill there was a shout, "Grenades." Men flattened themselves behind trees. The grenades rolled out and blew up. Nobody was hurt. Chinese-made potato masher grenades followed.

A group of Americans rushed forward. One leveled a rocket launcher and fired. There was a tremendous boom as the missile exploded inside the bunker, less than a yard away. The result wasn't pretty. Half buried in the dirt lay the remains of a soldier.

A soldier's foot slipped and there was a fluttering pop. White smoke billowed from a grenade. "It's gas." Men retched and tears streamed down from burning eyes. The stumbling soldier had set off one of dozens of gas grenades that littered the hillside.

While the cavalrymen crested the ridge, mopping up began. The lead man, Spec. 4 Leonard Lawrence from Charleston, W. Va., claimed he killed five Viet Cong.

Lawrence also helped capture two of the three wounded Communists who were brought alive to the hilltop.

Spec. 4 Robert Elkinson from Seaside, Calif., spoon-fed one prisoner with ham and lima beans from a C ration can. There was little Elkinson, a paratrooper medic, could do, but he comforted the wounded man until a helicopter took him to a hospital.

Another medic, Spec. 4 Gary Owens Bowles from Augusta, Me., went through stacks of medicine and surgical equipment.

There were vials of Bulgarian and Chinese Communist penicillin, East German surgical catgut, anti-tetanus serum, Russian bandages, and Japanese blood plasma.

While mopping up was still going on, Spec. 4 George Hansen from Oshkosh, Wis., jumped into a bunker where two bodies lay. Suddenly he felt a Viet Cong soldier grasp his leg. Hansen scrambled out of the bunker, twirled and emptied his automatic rifle into the bodies. A minute later one corpse still twitched and an arm flopped aimlessly.

"He's still alive."

"No, he's deader than hell. I cut him to pieces with my M16." Hansen said.

"This is all part of an education," said 2nd Lt. Gill Cochran from Baltimore, Md., commander of Alpha Company's 2nd platoon. He plans to go to law school as soon as he gets out of the army.

24 Mar 66   (See Note Page 20)
               SAIGON, Mar. 24

America's giant B52 bombers in 191 massive raids on South Viet Nam have ripped old Viet Cong jungle hideouts apart and sharply reduced the Communist will and ability to fight.

This conclusion was reached today in official quarters after a detailed study of the raids which started last June and now are almost daily occurrences.

The assaults average 10 eight-engine stratoforts from Guam to a mission. Each carries 50 750-pound bombs, a total of 37,500 pounds of steel and explosives for each flight.

When the raids started, about 1,000 Viet Cong were defecting each month to the Saigon government forces. The number now is double that. Many told interrogators the big bombers were making life intolerable for the guerrillas, wrecking their rest havens and hospitals, their hitherto safe tunnels and caves, and destroying precious food caches. Some ground sweeps by troops have substantiated these reports.

26 Mar 66   Chemical Week

...Chemical agents are slated for new importance in the struggle to deny safe havens to the VC. Herbicides and riot-control gases are helping to clear areas the VC and North Vietnamese have long held and regarded as shelters — e.g., tunneled command posts, supply depots and primitive hospitals.

7 Apr 66   New York Times (See Note Page 20)
             SAIGON, April 6

United States marines have destroyed a complex of Vietcong camps, hospitals, and storage areas 18 miles southeast of Saigon, a spokesman announced today.

...The allied troops chased the Vietcong out of 28 base camps, killed 23 guerrillas, captured 15 and forced the rest to seek new hideouts in jungle or swamp. Seized supplies included 867 tons of rice.

18 May 66   New York Times
             SAIGON, Wednesday, May 18

...Operation Birmingham began April 24 in the dense jungles north of Saigon. All the B-52 strikes and much of the infantry maneuvering was carried out about 75 miles northwest of the capital, an area known as War Zone C, which for years has been considered a Vietcong stronghold.

In their three-week sweep through the area the infantrymen also located and destroyed 66 base camps, four factories, six aid stations, three hospitals, 68 supply caches and six fuel dumps.

They captured 2,103 tons of rice, 323 tons of salt, 30 tons of wheat, 1,240 gallons of cooking oil, thousands of uniforms and several tons of ammunition. The soldiers carried away as much of the supplies as they could, the spokesman said, and destroyed the rest to keep it from falling into Vietcong hands.

14 Jul 66   (See Note Page 20)
             WASHINGTON, July 14

The South Vietnamese government and U.S. agencies have moved to block the Communist Viet Cong from getting antibiotics or other medicines from the black market or across drug store counters in Viet Nam.

This was disclosed by the Defense Department today when it was questioned about reports that the Communists had been obtaining drugs for their military needs from these sources.

...The Pentagon said it is assumed the Communists are interested primarily in such antibiotic-type drugs as tetracycline and penicillin.

To deal with the problem, the Pentagon said, the South Vietnamese government has imposed regulations controlling the sale of pharmaceuticals.

All sales must be registered and customers identified, and limits have been placed on the amounts that can be bought.

...U.S. military medical supplies are guarded and their usage is monitored.

"When enemy caches are captured," the Department said, "they are immediately checked for points of origin."

Aug 66   International Review of the Red Cross
            "The International Committee and the Vietnam Conflict"

...b) <u>Destruction of field infirmaries</u>. — In addition, the ICRC has intervened with the responsible authorities on the subject of the destruction of NLF field infirmaries and stocks of medical supplies uncovered in the course of military operations.

31 Aug 66   (See Note Page 20)

...In another South Vietnamese action, government forces reported today they destroyed an enemy training camp, arms manufacturing facilities and two small medical stations Tuesday about 50 miles southwest of Saigon.

3 Sep 66   (See Note Page 20)
             SAIGON, Sept 3

...On the ground, South Vietnamese reported killing 57 of the enemy, when more than 1,000 government troops fought a quick, savage battle in a mangrove swamp in the Mekong Delta about 120 miles southwest of Saigon yesterday.

The troops reported seizing a large supply of ammunition and weapons and destroying enemy communications material, other equipment and a small medical station. Government casualties were unreported.

18 Sep 66   New York Times
             SAIGON, SOUTH VIETNAM, Sept. 17

...Less than a month after it landed, the Airmobile Division plunged into the battle of the Iadrang valley.

...In late January, the division swept into the coastal lowlands just north of Quinhon and nearly equaled its Iadrang Valley success by killing 1,342 North Vietnamese and Vietcong soldiers in the 41-day Bonbson campaign, named for a village near the field headquarters.

Earlier, in the first 17 days of 1966, the division conducted its first operation in which more Americans than enemy soldiers died. Officers said they had learned that the enemy was using Cambodia as a sanctuary. The division captured an elaborate field hospital.

10 Oct 66   (See Note Page 20)
             SAIGON, Monday, Oct. 10

...On the ground, a unit of the U.S. 1st Air Cavalry Division chased a group of Viet Cong into a cave about 25 miles north of Qui Nhon on the central sea coast Sunday and reported capturing 46 of them, including a nurse.

This brought to 438 the number of Communists taken prisoner by U.S. Air Cavalrymen since they launched Operation Irving Oct. 2 in a coordinated drive with South Korean and South Vietnamese troops.

The overall prisoner bag for the combined allied force reached 658, making it the largest roundup of captives of the war.

14 Oct 66   New York Times
             SAIGON, SOUTH VIETNAM, Oct. 13

...In the ground war, only light and scattered action was reported. Soldiers in the airmobile division's continuing Operation Irving said they had killed three Vietcong and added two more to their record of 506 captured when they attacked a house pointed out by a prisoner. Other elements of the division seized an enemy field hospital and a cache of ammunition.

Oct 66   David McLanahan, "Notes on a Summer in Vietnam"

...I also saw some evidence of the US's cynical detachment from, but condoning of, the mistreatment of prisoners of war. Several times I talked with an Army intelligence officer whose job is to interrogate Vietcong suspects and investigate various other matters around the Danang area. Once he came to the hospital to talk to a "Vietcong nurse." She had been spotted by a Marine patrol moving towards an area of suspected Vietcong concentration (from which an American position had been mortared). She and two men with her were ordered to stop but tried to run away. Both the men were killed and she was wounded three times. The patrol reported the three were carrying medical supplies. In the hospital she denied this. I asked what would happen to her if she recovered. The intelligence officer said she would be turned over to the Vietnamese Army interrogation center. That would probably be the last of her. He said that sometimes they have tried to find out what happened to people they sent there and the usual reply was that there was no record and no one knew anything about the person. He said they could usually see mounds of fresh earth behind the center. I asked if that's what he thought would happen to her and he said "That depends on how much they get out of her." He also told me that much of his job was "covering up atrocities" — that one shot from a village would cause it to be leveled. He said he couldn't blame soldiers who saw their buddies killed by snipers. He also described a Vietcong atrocity where all 12 members of a family had been murdered because a member had given some evidence which led to a Vietcong being killed.

16 Nov 66   (See Note Page 20)
             NORMAN, OKLA., Nov. 16

A young Oklahoma marine says blood plasma and medical supplies from America are helping the Communists to keep their fighting forces in the field in Viet Nam.

"Why are Americans helping to kill us?" demanded 20-year-old Corp. Donnie R. Fountain of Norman in a letter to his parents, Mr. and Mrs. Tommie Dee Fountain. "This makes us all want to sit down and cry."

Fountain said four members of his patrol were cut down by Viet Cong fire in a village earlier this month. He said a marine company returned to the village the next day and "besides finding the dead they found 15 tons of rice, 6,000 rounds of Red ammunition.

"They also found boxes of blood plasma and medical supplies stamped 'Berkeley, Calif.'"

8 Jan 67   UPI, Chicago Sun-Times
            SAIGON

Viet Cong forces vanished Saturday in the path of U.S. Marines driving up a swampland peninsula in the first American assault against the Communist-dominated Mekong Delta.

...The Marines were methodically scouring the 60-square-mile peninsula where about 12,000 of the delta's nearly 8,000,000 population live. They had reports the Viet Cong maintained hospitals, educational facilities, arms factories, engineering shops and rest and recreation areas for their troops in the vicinity.

24 Jan 67   The Sun (Baltimore), Robert A. Erlandson
            SAIGON, Jan. 23

The Viet Cong are apparently well supplied with modern American medicines.

Lt. Gen. Jonathan O. Seaman, commander of the 2d Field Force which is sweeping the Communists' "Iron Triangle" bastion northwest of Saigon, today released a long list of captured hospital supplies.

He said they were a mixture of American, French and East German goods.

Unofficial sources said several days ago, however, that the largest quantities were newly packed American drugs, particularly 625,000 vials of penicillin and 100,000 ampules of antibiotics, mostly streptomycin.

...The "Iron Triangle" trove is believed to be the largest Viet Cong medical cache discovered so far in the war. An element of the 1st Infantry Division located it shortly after Operation Cedar Falls began January 8. Most of the goods were reported concealed in small metal drums.

One officer said American doctors did not have some of the items in their own kits and helped themselves to the Communist supplies.

Another officer said the cache contained enough medicine to stock a good-sized military dispensary "for a month."

The detailed breakdown of the drugs and supplies had not been made public before. The military command in Saigon simply reported "medical supplies, 15 pounds, medicines, 4 lots, surgical and medical equipment, quantity unknown."

...Seaman said the captured supplies have been turned over to Vietnamese authorities for distribution and use.

Among other items tallied were surgical rubber gloves, blood pressure gauges, 500 intravenous feeding needles and tubes, a case of orthopedic surgical equipment and six bolts of bandage material, as well as morphine, glucose, dextrose, vitamins and saline solution.

25 Mar 67   Saturday Evening Post
            Richard Armstrong, "Believe me, he can kill you"

..."We are hurting them," he said. "This area used to be so secure that they had a post-office address, just like our A.P.O. numbers, for every man stationed in War Zone D. Now we have been sitting on top of their major supply routes. We have captured their salt, which in this climate you cannot do without. We have destroyed their motor pools of trucks and bicycles, and their hospitals — including one three-hundred bed affair that we found underground."

1 Mar 67   (See Note Page 20)
            PHUOC THANH, SOUTH VIETNAM, March 1

...Truong's special job was guarding provincial officials of the Viet Cong shadow government operating in the tactical area being swept by Korean troops. He was badly scalded in January while trying to boil water in an ammunition box and was taken to a Viet Cong dispensary deep in the mountains. The hospital once had consisted of four buildings, but because of air strikes had been reduced to a single hut staffed by one doctor, two medics and a nurse.

...He said VC malaria sufferers used to recuperate at farmhouses in friendly villages "but now the people are afraid to house sick soldiers. They know the Koreans will come to seek them out."

5 Apr 67   New York Times, Felix Belair Jr.
             WASHINGTON, April 14

...Under the A.I.D.-financed public safety program, the civil police forces had been expanded from 33,500 at the close of 1964 to more than 63,000 on Jan. 1, 1967, Mr. Poats said.

The civil police, who now have responsibility for the security of South Vietnamese cities, will gradually take responsibility for the security of the villages as well. The same and equipment for the national public safety program, for which $38 million has been programmed for the new fiscal year, also provides advisory services, policy and a police field force.

One function of the national police was to carry out the "resources control" program and reduce Vietcong access to critical goods. Last February about 700 checkpoints throughout the country were manned by the national police.

"Since late 1964," Mr. Poats said, "this resources control program has resulted in the arrest of 15,000 known or suspected Vietcong and in the confiscation of more than 8,500 tons of food, medicine, firearms and other equipment and supplies."

18 May 67   The New York Review of Books
              Mary McCarthy, "Report from Vietnam III: Intellectuals"

...The Chieu Hoi program, of course, is not dependent for its success on its absurd leaflets and broadcasts but on military pressure, especially bombing, defoliation, crop-spraying, destruction of rice-supplies, and what is known as "Resources Control." The stated object is to deprive the Viet Cong of food and other resources, including medical supplies and nurses: a native nurse suspected of treating the Viet Cong is liable to be executed, while an American nurse or an RVN nurse, if kidnapped or killed by a Viet Cong terror group, is, naturally, a civilian. What is not stated, though, is that the punitive measures taken to starve and weaken the Viet Cong punish more cruelly the non-combatants in VC territory, who, being non-combatants, cannot even interest the CIA as defectors. It has been estimated by a former Chieu Hoi who has made his way to Europe that a quarter of the population — peasants — will be killed or die of malnutrition or from lack of medical care.

OFFICE OF THE ASSISTANT SECRETARY OF DEFENSE
WASHINGTON, D. C. 20301

PUBLIC AFFAIRS

26 August 1966

ATTRIBUTABLE - ON THE RECORD STATEMENT BY GENERAL WESTMORELAND

I'd like to say that let one fact be clear. As far as the United States Military Assistance Command in Vietnam is concerned, one mishap - one innocent civilian killed, one civilian wounded or one dwelling needlessly destroyed, is too many. By its very nature, war is destructive, and historically civilians have suffered. But the war in Vietnam is different. It is designed by the insurgents and the aggressors to be fought among the people, many of whom are not participants in, or even closely identified with the struggle. People, more than terrain, are the objectives in this war, and we will not and cannot be callous about those people. We are sensitive to these incidents and want no more of them. If one does occur, mistake or accident, we intend to search it carefully for any lesson that will help us improve our procedures and our controls. We realize we have a great problem, and I can assure you we are attacking it aggressively.